AUTOCOURSE™

The World's Leading Grand Prix Annual

HAZLETON PUBLISHING

BAT OUT OF HEAVEN. For all the demonic power of the XKR's supercharged V8 powerplant, the car's adaptive cruise control, satellite navigation and computer active technology suspension (CATS) make it absolute heaven to drive.*

XKR

For information visit www.jaguar.com

*Satellite navigation and adaptive cruise control available at extra cost.

contents

AUTOCOURSE 2000-2001

is published by
Hazleton Publishing Ltd,
3 Richmond Hill,
Richmond, Surrey
TW10 6RE.

Colour reproduction by
Barrett Berkeley Ltd, London.

Printed in England by
Butler and Tanner Ltd,
Frome, Somerset.

© Hazleton Publishing Ltd 2000.
No part of this publication may be
reproduced, stored in a retrieval
system or transmitted, in any form or
by any means, electronic, mechanical,
photocopying, recording or otherwise,
without prior permission in writing
from Hazleton Publishing Ltd.

ISBN: 1-874557-79-9

DISTRIBUTORS
UNITED KINGDOM
Haynes Publishing plc
Sparkford
Near Yeovil
Somerset BA22 7JJ
Telephone: 01963 442030
Fax: 01963 440001

NORTH AMERICA
Motorbooks International
PO Box 1
729 Prospect Ave.
Osceola
Wisconsin 54020, USA
Telephone: (1) 715 294 3345
Fax: (1) 715 294 4448

REST OF THE WORLD
Menoshire Ltd
Unit 13
Wadsworth Road
Perivale
Middlesex UB6 7LQ
Telephone: 020 8566 7344
Fax: 020 8991 2439

Dust-jacket photograph:
World Champion
Michael Schumacher
Photograph by Bryn Williams

Title page photograph:
Schumacher wins in Japan
Photograph by Paul-Henri Cahier

acknowledgements

The Editor of AUTOCOURSE wishes to thank the following for their assistance in compiling the 2000–2001 edition: France: ACO, Federation Francaise du Sport Automobile, FIA (Bernie Ecclestone, Max Mosley, Francesco Longanesi-Cattani, Agnes Kaiser, Anne–Marie Guichon, Charlie Whiting, Herbie Blash and Pat Behar), Peugeot Sport (Jean–Claude Lefèbvre), Prost Grand Prix (Alain Prost, Dany Hindenoch, Sophie Sicot and Virginie Papin), Supertec; Germany: Formul 3 Vereinigung, BMW Motorsport (Gerhard Berger, Mario Theissen and Guido Stalman), Mercedes-Benz (Norbert Haug, Wolfgang Schatting and Xander Heijnen); Great Britain: Arrows (Tom Walkinshaw, Daniele Audetto, Ann Bradshaw, Fiona Cole and Mike Coughlan), Autocar, John Barnard, British American Racing (Craig Pollock, Adrian Reynard, Rick Gorne, Malcolm Oastler and Graham Jones), Martin Brundle, Colin Burr, Timothy Collings, Bob Constanduros, Cosworth Engineering, Steve Cropley, Peter Foubister, Mike Greasley, Maurice Hamilton, Nick Henry, Ian Hutchinson, Ilmor Engineering (Mario Illien), Jaguar Racing (Jackie Stewart, Paul Stewart, Neil Ressler, Gary Anderson, Andy Miller, Colin Cook, Cameron Kelleher, Lindsay Morle and Emma Owen), Jordan Grand Prix (Eddie Jordan, Ian Phillips, Trevor Foster, Giselle Davies, Christine Gorcham, Mike Gascoyne and Lindsay Haylett), McLaren International (Ron Dennis, Adrian Newey, Martin Whitmarsh, Olivier Panis, Justine Blake, Beverley Keynes, Ellen Kolby, Anna Guerrier, Jo Ramirez, Bob McMurray, Simon Points, Neil Oatley, Steve Hallam, Peter Stayner, Stuart Wingham and Nancy Edwards), Stan Piecha, Williams Grand Prix Engineering (Patrick Head, James Robinson, Dickie Stanford, Nav Sidhu, Silvia Frangipane and Sir Frank Williams); Italy: Benetton Formula (Rocco Benetton, Flavio Briatore, Pat Symonds, Nick Wirth, David Warren, Andrea Ficarelli and Julia Horden), Commissione Sportiva Automobilistica Italiana, Scuderia Ferrari (Ross Brawn, Claudio Berro, Antonio Ghini, Stefania Bocci, Jean Todt and Tim Watson), Minardi Team (Giancarlo Minardi and Stefania Torelli), Giorgio Piola; Japan: Bridgestone (Hirode Hamashima, Yoshihiko Ichikawa and Melanie Holmes); Switzerland: Peter Sauber and Agnes Cartier; USA: CART, Daytona International Speedway, FOSA (Pamela Lauesen & George Good), Indianapolis Motor Speedway, Indy Lights, NASCAR, Roger Penske, SportsCar.

With special thanks to Simon Taylor for his invaluable help and enthusiasm in 1975, and since — Richard Poulter

photographs published in AUTOCOURSE 2000–2001 have been contributed by:
Allsport UK/Clive Mason, Mark Thompson, Mike Hewitt, Ker Robertson, Graham Chadwick, Allsport US/Robert Laberge, Jon Ferrey, Al Bello, Jamie Squire, Darrell Ingham, Craig Jones, Diana Burnett, Bernard Cahier, Paul-Henri Cahier, Steve Etherington/EPI, Graphic Images (UK) Ltd/Dave Cundy, LAT Photographic/Lorenzo Bellanca, Jeff Bloxham, Jeff Bloxham, John Overton, Matthias Schneider, Nigel Snowdon, Words & Pictures/Bryn Williams, Michael C. Brown, Peter J. Fox.

publisher
RICHARD POULTER

editor
ALAN HENRY

managing editor
ROBERT YARHAM

art editor
STEVE SMALL

production manager
STEVEN PALMER

business development manager
SIMON SANDERSON

sales promotion
ANNALISA ZANELLA

marketing and new media manager
NICK POULTER

results and statistics
DAVID HAYHOE
NICK HENRY

f1 illustrations
IAN HUTCHINSON
NICOLA CURTIS
MARK STEWARD

chief photographer
PAUL-HENRI CAHIER

chief contributing photographers
ALLSPORT U.K.
BRYN WILLIAMS
MATTHIAS SCHNEIDER

AUTOCOURSE
www.autocourse.com

Paul-Henri Cahier

foreword

by michael schumacher

AFTER my second stop in Suzuka, Ross Brawn talked me down the pit lane. 'It's looking good, it's looking good,' he said, but I thought in a few seconds he would say '...but not good enough.' Then he said 'it's looking bloody good!' and my heart began to jump.

So finally after 21 years we have brought the F1 World Championship title back to Maranello. I have been asked many times how it feels to finally have done it, but I still did not manage to find the right words, as they need to be appropriate to something so special and enormously important to so many people.

Winning the championship with and for Ferrari is incomparable to everything I did before – and I don't want to narrow what we have achieved with Benetton. It's special. It's impossible not to be touched by the myth and warmth that are around and inside our team. And I can only try to understand what this title means to the *tifosi* who waited for 21 years when also for me waiting only five years was so hard.

We have been trying so long, we have been so close several times, we have been so disappointed after losing. That's why now we are so absolutely happy. Also winning the constructors' title was the crowning moment to what has been an unforgettable season and the passionate work of passionate people in Maranello.

I want to thank them all.

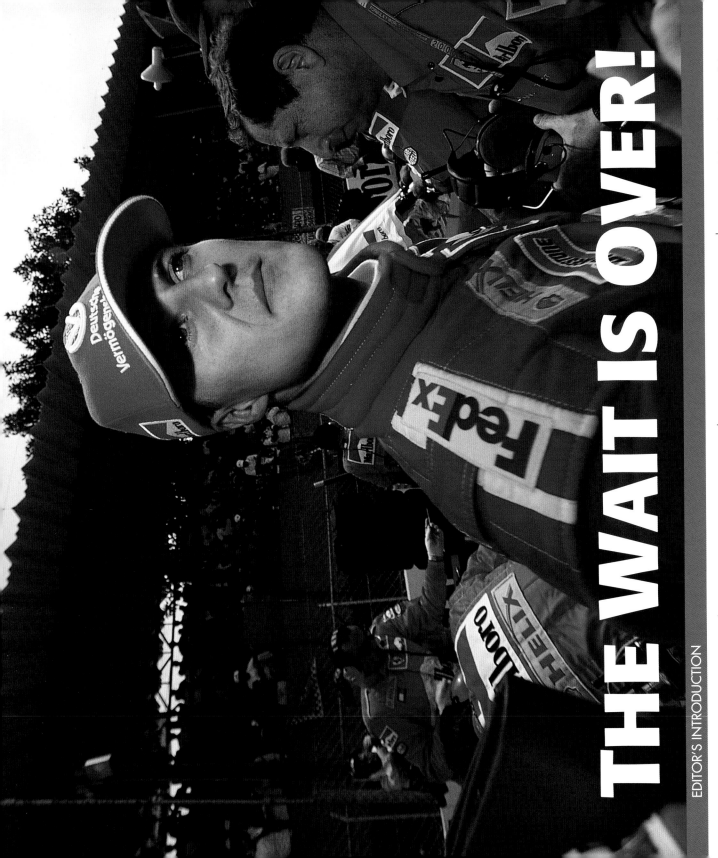

THE WAIT IS OVER!

COMETH the hour, cometh the man. For the first time since 1979 AUTOCOURSE this year carries the portrait of a scarlet Ferrari on its front cover, a testimony to 'mission accomplished' by Michael Schumacher and the legendary Italian team whose Prancing Horse logo is now one of the most highly visible, and indeed bankable, of trademarks anywhere in the world.

Thanks to the efforts of the dynamic Michael Schumacher, Ferrari started the year with a win and finished on the same note. Nine of the 17 races were won by the motivated and driven 31-year-old whose consistency and commitment over the past five years represented the rock on which Ferrari's resurgence had been founded back in 1996.

True, sporting director Jean Todt played a key role in shaping, planning and cajoling the team, progressively re-inventing Ferrari as an F1 force over a gruelling seven-year period. Ross Brawn and Rory Byrne have built a formidable technical armoury, but it's unlikely they could have done it without Michael. Whatever one thinks about Ferrari's stance on the political

stage, Schumacher again showed himself uniquely capable of turning situations to his advantage.

Ferrari's F1-2000 was a formidable contender from the outset, its promise matched – perhaps exceeded – only by the McLaren-Mercedes MP4/15 handled with such success by Mika Häkkinen and David Coulthard. Not since 1988 – when McLaren won 15 of the season's 16 races and Ferrari the one remaining – have two teams shared out the race victories between them.

Ultimately McLaren was thwarted in its efforts to carry Mika Häkkinen to his third straight Championship. Yet despite this Häkkinen emerged stronger than ever, the one man who Schumacher clearly respected, and the one man he knew would definitely give as good as he got. Coulthard did well enough, but somehow never quite emerged as the potential title threat we'd perhaps anticipated in the middle of the year. Truth be told, it was a case of Häkkinen's form momentarily dipping, not Coulthard raising his game.

Frankly, amongst the also-rans, there was much gloom and precious

little promise. The most spectacularly impressive members of the supporting cast were BMW Williams who showed both a promising new Munich-built V10 engine and a dramatic young British talent in the form of Jenson Button.

Yet Williams set high standards. Being 'best of the rest' was no consolation to highly motivated individuals like Sir Frank and his technical director Patrick Head. They may not have won a grand prix since 1997 and seem firmly lodged in Division Two. Yet their mind set is unquestionably that of a Division One player. They will be back.

British American Racing also emerged as a credible F1 operation, a new partnership with Honda helping Jacques Villeneuve and the Brackley-based team go up a gear. In doing so they successfully buried dire memories of their awful 1999 season with Supertec power.

There were three key disappointments on the F1 scene, each failing to make a mark for very different reasons. Jordan should have been challenging Williams, but their level of mechanical unreliability was desperate.

Jaguar struggled to make sense of the F1 business with a deficient car, initially unreliable engines and a management structure which was trying to learn the intricacies of the grand prix game while at the same time fighting fires on every front.

Finally, Prost was simply at sea, wrestling to make sense of their political battles with unsympathetic engine partners Peugeot who were intent on quitting at the end of the year. 'The trouble with Peugeot is that they are just not racers,' said one McLaren insider, recalling that team's ill-starred 1994 partnership with the French car maker. Prost may have concluded much the same, but he didn't have the established reputation as a proven F1 team operator to call the shots in quite the same way as McLaren. It was a disaster for both parties.

In many ways the biggest single development in 2000 was the return of F1 to the U.S.A. for the first time in nine years. This time, however, it was not a case of point-and-squirt through the concrete barriers lining the streets of Phoenix, but a spectacularly adapted road circuit incorporating a banked corner of the famous Indianapolis Motor Speedway. The inaugural race was a huge success, thanks to Bernie Ecclestone cutting a deal with Speedway boss Tony George which will probably ensure F1's continued presence in Indiana on an open-ended basis. How long it will take to educate U.S. spectators, accustomed to all-action sports with plenty of scoring every few seconds, to appreciate the strategic 'chess-board' philosophy behind contemporary F1 pit-stop racing is another issue on which the jury is still out.

Ironically, F1's reappearance in the States may leave the CART series at something of a commercial disadvantage. Once again, CART offered a strange motor racing paradox. It offers consistently great racing and a diversity of venue ranging from street circuit to super-speedway to regular road tracks.

Yet Mercedes dropped out of the business after an uncompetitive final year and both Ford and Honda are watching developments carefully. With more races than ever, the car companies are concerned over the 'bang for the buck' it really offers.

Left: Under pressure. Schumacher on the grid before the start of the Brazilian Grand Prix. Michael duly delivered a victory in an early-season burst of wins which underpinned his ultimate championship success.

Paul-Henri Cahier

Below: Schumacher and Ferrari were the centre of attention throughout the season which finally saw their championship dreams realised.

Bottom: Mika Häkkinen and McLaren-Mercedes provided the only serious opposition to the Prancing Horse.

Both photographs: Paul-Henri Cahier

At the end of the day the CART title deservedly went to Brazilian driver Gil de Ferran at the wheel of the re-invigorated Penske team's Reynard-Honda.

DaimlerChrysler board director Jurgen Hubbert made it clear that Mercedes was getting out of champ cars because they could get better value from a combination of F1 – returning to the U.S., remember – and the resurgent DTM 2000 series which attracted huge crowds to German domestic meetings where eight Mercedes CLKs were pitched against a similar number of Opel V8 coupés and a quartet of Audi TTs.

Sports car racing continued to plough its idiosyncratic furrow and retain a loyal, and not inconsiderable, fan base. Audi harnessed success at Le Mans to great promotional advantage while future Toyota F1 test driver Allan McNish emerged as front runner in the increasingly popular American Le Mans (ALMS) series.

As good as it gets. Michael Andretti and Juan Montoya battle side by side at well over 200 mph on the Michigan Speedway. CART offers close racing and thrills and spills galore, but finds it hard to gain the wider audience it deserves.
Craig Jones/Allsport USA

Overwhelmingly, of course, the FIA Formula 1 World Championship had continued to consolidate its position as a giant amongst international sports. Between them, Bernie Ecclestone and Max Mosley had seemingly tapped into the D.N.A. of everlasting commercial success by following one basic rule. That is, the more exclusive and difficult to obtain something becomes, the more the world is ready to do anything to grasp even a fleeting taste of it.

Take F1 testing as an example. Most teams want dramatic restrictions on the amount that can take place in the future. Yet the fact remains that official F1 tests are invaluable when it comes to schmoozing the sponsors, investors and their guests. There simply isn't sufficient 'entertainment capacity' at the 17 races which make up the World Championship.

Not that everything ran smoothly. FIA president Max Mosley – the subject of a detailed interview within these pages – found himself both on the offensive and defensive at various points during the course of the season. Rejecting allegations of partiality towards Ferrari in particular, Mosley takes a hard line over the FIA's defined role in the sport. Not putting too fine a point on it, he is almost Thatcherite in his firm belief that the governing body is there to govern. And that, in his view, is the bottom line.

That relentless unwillingness to compromise could be gauged by the way he leaked two key letters to the media during the course of the season. One was to Sir Frank Williams admonishing him over his joint approach with McLaren chairman Ron Dennis to the European Court in a bid to revise the FIA appeal court procedure.

The second was to Dennis himself, suggesting that he was out of order

implying that an Italian FIA steward, Roberto Causo, presiding at the Japanese Grand Prix, might be less than totally impartial. Both Mosley's missives were eloquent, impeccably phrased and, more worryingly perhaps, reflected the obvious pleasure which this qualified barrister had clearly derived from framing them.

These exchanges caused concern at a time when the major car makers are in negotiation to take a financial stake in the F1 business via a stake in Bernie Ecclestone's SLEC empire which controls his F1 Administration business. Unquestionably, the car companies see F1 as good business, but their interest in making a substantial investment is in no way prompted by altruism.

In F1, they see a sound business with a lucrative bottom line. Yet there are strings attached to their investment. In exchange, they want a say in how the business works and how the rules are framed and implemented. It will be a matter of absorbing influence to see whether Ecclestone and Mosley have the flexibility to accommodate those ambitions. And the willingness to do so.

Alan Henry
Tillingham, Essex
November 2000

Publisher's preface to the 50th Anniversary Edition

WHEN the first edition of AUTOCOURSE appeared in 1951, it set itself high standards and ambitions:

'to provide the most complete data obtainable with interesting and authentic information, settle arguments and provide countless hours of interesting study and amusement.'

50 years on, I hope AUTOCOURSE has fulfilled those promises.

If it has, it would not be possible without dedication. The fact that AUTOCOURSE has reached its 50th birthday is true testimony to everyone at Hazleton and our editors, photographers and contributors whose talents, hard work and integrity have achieved this.

The motor sports industry, the governing bodies and sponsors have played their part. AUTOCOURSE has grown with their support but the most important element of our success is you, our readership. If we fail in what we provide, our future will be thus governed.

In 1963, Jim Clark started a great tradition of the newly-crowned F1 World Champion writing the Foreword to AUTOCOURSE each year:

The publication of AUTOCOURSE is something I eagerly await each year. It is certainly the best record of the year's racing, with race reports as informative and accurate as it is possible to find anywhere, combined with the most comprehensive set of results available. AUTOCOURSE remains truly international and unbiased in its treatment of the sport. It makes excellent reading now; but even more impressive is the immense value this book will have in years to come, when those fortunate enough to own all the editions will have a unique encyclopaedia of motor racing.

Hazleton has published many titles under the AUTOCOURSE name and you will find details of these on our new web site. We are proud to have achieved a Queen's Award for Export

(1985) and we will strive to continue our efforts to provide a worldwide audience with an ultimate record of international motor racing.

In conclusion, the words of Ferrari President, Luca di Montezemolo, in his Foreword to our recently published 50 Years of World Championship Grand Prix Motor Racing, eloquently express this sense of history and reflect our enthusiasm:

'Like us, AUTOCOURSE has followed the difficult path of Grand Prix motor racing for 50 years, reporting and photographing every facet of the fascinating struggles that have developed during a season over the years. AUTOCOURSE has earned a reputation for presenting the world of Formula 1 in an individual and unique way. I sincerely hope that in 50 years' time, AUTOCOURSE will still be there following our progress and, of course, our successes.'

I hope so too – here's to the next 50 years.

Richard Poulter
Richmond, Surrey
November 2000

THE British Racing Drivers' Club, which owns Silverstone Circuit, grew from an informal dining club organised by Dr J.D. Benjafield, one of the Bentley Boys, and himself a Le Mans 24 Hours winner in 1927. The Club actually commenced to function in April 1928, with 25 members and a clear set of objectives, which were:

1. to promote the interests of motor sport generally,
2. to celebrate any specific performance in motor sport,
3. to extend hospitality to racing drivers from overseas, and
4. to further the interests of British drivers competing abroad.

MEMBERSHIP was restricted to racing drivers of proven success and experience. By the time of the first AGM, in December 1928, the membership had grown to 69, and as part of the Club's expansion it was decided to move into race organisation. The first BRDC race was the '500 Miles' at Brooklands on October 12th 1929. By the end of 1930 the Club had continued to grow and it became necessary to turn it into a company limited by guarantee, and so it was on July 23rd 1931, that the BRDC became the British Racing Drivers' Club Limited. In later years modern business practice dictated that the Committee became a 12-strong Board of Directors, all current and ex-racing drivers, which today controls the BRDC.

IN 1952 the BRDC took over the lease on Silverstone from the RAC, and has remained in occupation ever since, finally being able to purchase the freehold from the Ministry of Defence in 1971. The Club, through its wholly owned subsidiary company Silverstone Circuits Limited, formed in 1966 to develop the commercial aspects of the property, then set in motion a major redevelopment of what had been a wartime bomber training base. That development programme continues to this day and has produced one of the foremost motor racing facilities in the world, the only Grand Prix track owned and operated by a racing drivers' club.

ALTHOUGH the BRDC, through its trading subsidiaries, always seeks to maximise the commercial opportunities available on the 800-acre site, all profits are ploughed back into the maintenance and improvement of the circuits and the development of UK motor sport. Considerable sums are also donated to charity and in excess of £1 million per annum is raised from goods or services given to various charities. The Club is a major contributor to the Motor Trade Benevolent Fund (BEN) with a particular interest in the new day centre at Coventry. Considerable assistance has also been given to the Brooklands Trust and the new BRDC Benevolent Fund.

THE very active BRDC race department organises almost all of the 40 race meetings held annually at Silverstone, including four World Championship events (Formula 1, Formula 3000, GT and World Sports Cars) as well as several race meetings at other circuits. The BRDC now promotes 11 Championships including the British Formula 3, National Saloon, Historic Sports Cars, and what is now one of the most prestigious, the Privilege Insurance British GT Championship for Le Mans-style GT cars.

THE Club is proud that every aspect of motor sport is within the circuit boundary. The adjoining industrial estate controlled by another wholly owned subsidiary, Silverstone Estates Limited, encourages motor sport-related tenants, and the units are leased to a wide variety of teams, designers, fabricators, parts suppliers and many other associated businesses. The new Advanced Technology Park for motor sport and related industries is under construction.

IN keeping with one of the Club's original aims, very substantial funds are provided to the young British stars of tomorrow to help with the furtherance of their driving careers, the most visible part of this being the involvement in the BRDC McLaren Autosport annual award.

THE entry criteria remain very strict with full membership offered only to those ladies and gentlemen who have attained international racing success over a number of seasons. Associate membership is offered to those persons who have made a significant contribution to the sport other than being drivers, and Honorary Membership is bestowed upon a very special few, including FI World Champions who by dint of nationality do not otherwise qualify. Every British or Commonwealth World Champion is, or has been in their lifetime, a full member of the Club and over the 70 years of its existence the BRDC has grown to become the most prestigious motor racing club in the world.

THE Silverstone Drive now operates in excess of 100 vehicles, providing a complete range of activities starting with driving experience days in everything from karts, through skid cars, off-road 4 x 4 cars, rally cars, sports cars, and single seaters, all the way to serious race tuition skills. As well as using the three circuits, National, Southern, and the purpose-built Stowe track, SDC now has operations at Croft and Donington. SDC also gives help to young, promising drivers.

THERE is rarely a free day in the circuit diary, as the tracks and hospitality suites are in constant demand for testing, photographic sessions, driver tuition, filming, exhibitions or events. Future plans include the building of a new FI Pit Complex, and a 120-room hotel overlooking the GP circuit.

THE entire estate functions to encourage and supply motor sport, giving Silverstone its deserved title as The Home of British Motor Racing and perhaps, most importantly, the Home of the British Racing Drivers' Club.

HONDA
200 Grands Prix
1964-2000

At Monza in 2000 Honda reached the milestone of 200 Grands Prix. Only Ferrari (637), Ford (501), Renault (286) and Alfa Romeo (212) have contested more Formula One races than the famous Honda Marque. Yet none can match an astounding record of success that has seen Honda power claim the top step of the podium on 71 occasions, a win ratio of more than one-in-three.

Honda has now completed 203 Grands Prix, yet its third period of participation at the highest level of motorsport has only just begun. The New Millennium heralded a new era as Honda joined forces with the British American Racing Formula One Team.

The relationship, focusing not only on engine supply but also on developing a greater understanding of chassis technology, represents a fresh challenge for the company as it considers the 'whole-car' approach to engineering solutions. There is confidence that the lessons of the past and the technologies of the future can be combined to take Honda to even greater heights in the years to come.

6
World Constructors' Championships

74
Pole Positions

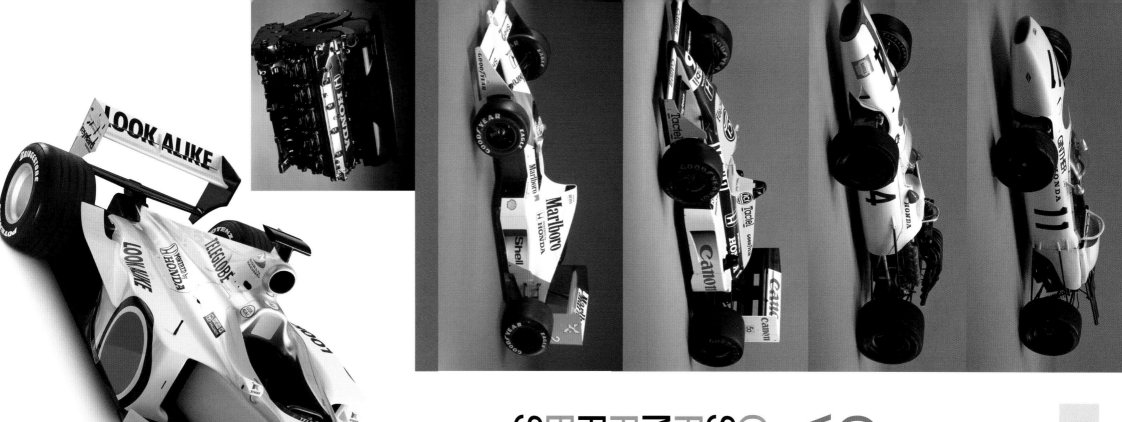

HONDA

LOOK ALIKE

Grands Prix Victories

Ginther
Surtees
Rosberg
Mansell
Piquet
Prost
Berger
Senna

THE ASTON MARTIN DB7 VANTAGE

power & poetry

A mighty V12 within seductive curves.

420 brake horsepower in the lap of luxury.

Five seconds to sixty with grace and poise.

Intense muscularity honed by craftsmen.

A study of contrasts, power and poetry.

Unmistakably English, uniquely Aston Martin.

The DB7 Vantage.

ASTON MARTIN

An English Passion

Stratstone
Wilmslow
Tel: 01625 548802

Paramount Derby
Derby
Tel: 01332 385222

Grange of Exeter
Exeter
Tel: 01392 202202

Grange Aston Martin
Brentwood
Tel: 01277 216161

Grange of Welwyn
Welwyn Garden City
Tel: 01707 266255

Lancaster Sevenoaks
Sevenoaks
Tel: 01732 456300

Aston Martin Sales of Mayfair
Park Lane, London
Tel: 020 7235 8888

Stratton Motor Company (Norfolk) Limited
Norwich
Tel: 01508 530491

HWM Limited
Walton-on-Thames
Tel: 01932 220404

Reg Vardy Plc
Houghton-Le-Spring
Tel: 0191 512 0101

P. J. Evans
Birmingham
Tel: 0121 666 6550

Porfield Sports and Classics Limited
Chichester
Tel: 01243 528500

JCT 600 Leodis Court
Leeds
Tel: 0113 244 0600

Murray Motor Company
Edinburgh
Tel: 0131 442 2800

Paramount Cardiff
Cardiff
Tel: 029 2075 5766

Charles Hurst Limited
Belfast
Tel: 028 9038 1721

Five Oaks Garage
Jersey
Tel: 01534 482341

Lancaster Reading
Reading
Tel: 0118 965 8500

www.astonmartin.com

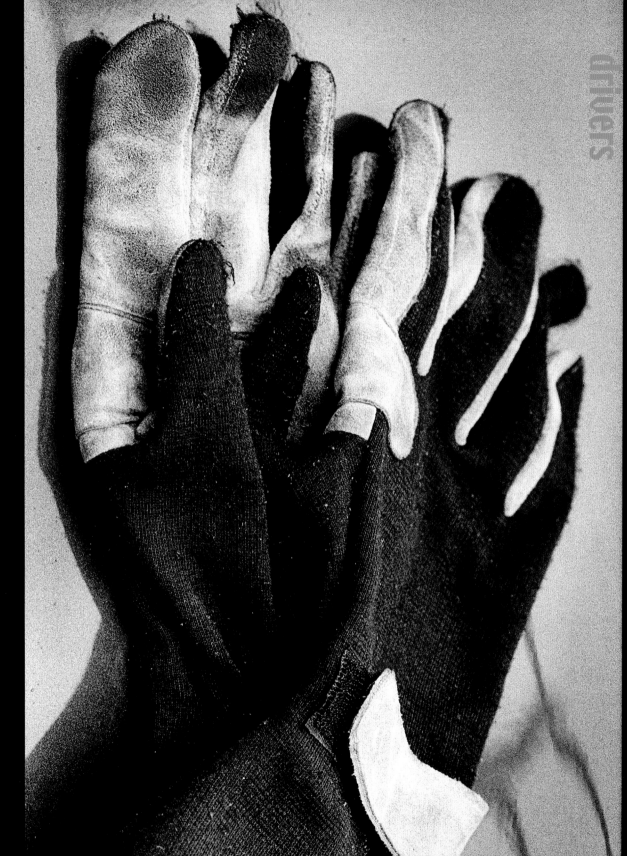

top ten

drivers

Chosen by the Editor, taking into account their racing performances and the equipment at their disposal

FIA FORMULA ONE
WORLD CHAMPIONSHIP 2000

photography by
Matthias Schneider

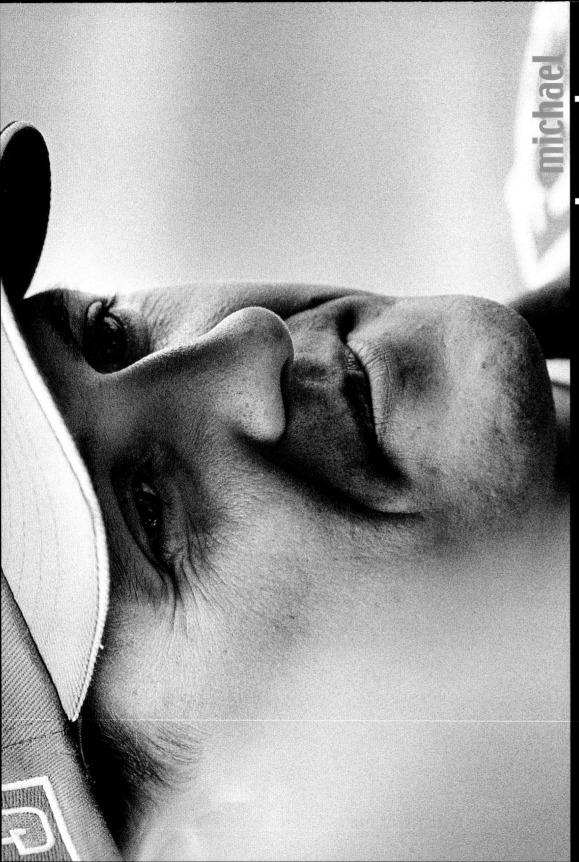

michael
schumacher

MICHAEL'S utterly unwavering and relentless focus in his ninth full season of grand prix racing has been awesome. Apart from the obvious factors such as his magical car control and incredible attention to operational detail when strapped behind the wheel, the German ace also has a remarkable ability to turn any hint of an opportunity into a massive performance advantage.

More to the point, there has been precious little indication that his genius is peaking. Those looking for chinks in his psychological armour would be unwise to divine too much from that emotional interlude when he wept under the dispassionate gaze of the media after posting his 41st career victory at Monza. Even for the 'ice man', it was a totally understandable outpouring of elation at having apparently stemmed McLaren's advance after being taken to the cleaners by Mika Häkkinen both at Budapest and Spa-Francorchamps.

This was Michael's fifth season with Ferrari, the fourth in which the Italian squad could seriously be regarded as a front-line threat. Yet somehow this year's campaign had the heady tang of success about it from the outset. Rather than grappling with early-season problems and then playing catch-up in the second half of the year, Michael won four of the first six races in commanding style. It seemed from the outset that surely this would be his year.

Yet critics would argue that Schumacher and the Ferrari system threw away a crucial 20 points with first-corner accidents in the Austrian and German Grands Prix. At the A1-Ring, the tensions surrounding Ferrari's contention that Michael must be allowed the fast track to success so unsettled team-mate Rubens Barrichello that the Brazilian tried a bit too hard to allow him through at the first corner while maintaining some pretence that they were really allowed to race each other. At Hockenheim it was simply a touch of over-exuberance.

By the same token, the manner in which he kept his nerve to deliver those psychologically draining victories at both Monza and Indianapolis were formidably impressive.

Like Ayrton Senna, Michael shares the same capacity for rationalising his lurid and potentially hazardous driving tactics which have attracted censure from some quarters. Like

Date of birth: 3 January 1969

Team: Scuderia Ferrari Marlboro

Grand Prix starts in 2000: 17

World Championship placing: 1st

Wins: 9; Poles: 9; Points: 108

mika häkkinen

2

...racing folklore seemed to apply anyway, coming to terms with the fact that Mika Häkkinen was stressed out in the middle of the season and needed a mid-summer holiday also seemed slightly bizarre at first glance.

Perhaps it was simply a reflection of the fact that he was in his tenth year of F1 competition, possibly a reminder of just what huge reserves of nervous effort had been expended in clinching back-to-back World Championships, both apparently against the odds, both at the final race. The final straws must have come at the Australian and Brazilian Grands Prix. Mika was on course to win both races, only for Mercedes engine failures to let him down. Then he was beaten by Schumacher at Imola, and by team-mate David Coulthard at Silverstone.

By the end of the year, paddock humourists were suggesting that it would give McLaren a big boost if test driver Olivier Panis was allowed to drive free practice for Häkkinen, set up the car and then hand it over to the Finn for qualifying. Team insiders grinned knowingly, expressing indulgent amusement at such a tongue-in-cheek suggestion.

Increasingly Häkkinen spent Friday free practice struggling for balance, making too many set-up changes and generally confusing himself. Yet once he had a properly balanced car, his uncanny ability to get on the throttle exiting corners a millisecond ahead of team-mate Coulthard usually paid dividends.

Even so, circumstances conspired to delay his first win of the season to the fifth round of the title chase in Spain. Then Häkkinen seemed to fade marginally, being out-paced by Coulthard at Monaco, Canada and France. For a fleeting moment it looked as though the onset of impending fatherhood might have taken the edge off his competitive appetite. Then came his restoration in Austria, from which point he never looked back, wins in Hungary and Belgium indicating that he was as good as ever.

His bold overtaking manoeuvre at Spa as he and Schumacher lapped Ricardo Zonta's BAR was the talk of the season. It also sent a signal to remind Michael that Mika was another man unlikely to be intimidated by his tactics.

Date of birth: 28 September 1968
Team: West McLaren Mercedes
Grand Prix starts in 2000: 17
World Championship placing: 2nd
Wins: 4; Poles: 5; Points: 89

Jacques Villeneuve

THE Canadian driver marches to a different beat than most of his rivals. He remains absolutely, uncompromisingly his own man. Things are done his way or not at all.

Just as McLaren kept Coulthard this season rather than opt for Eddie Irvine, so they have retained the talented Scot again for 2001 rather than take a gamble on Villeneuve. It is quite understandable. Jacques' free spirit as the F1 paddock's back-packer is not everybody's cup of tea. He demands contracts which stipulate the absolute minimum in terms of public appearances, much in the manner of triple World Champion Nelson Piquet. He also demands top dollar for his services.

In return for all this, British American Racing's hopes have been kept alive throughout the 2000 season by Jacques' indomitable fighting spirit. He has not won a grand prix in over three years, yet he is still a potential winner. And on the strength of what we have seen this season, few would bet against Jacques winning with the BAR-Honda sooner rather than later.

After a bruising maiden season with BAR during which he failed to score a single championship point, Villeneuve launched the team's new Honda partnership on a very promising note by posting fourth place in the Australian Grand Prix. He was fifth at Imola — best of the rest after the two Ferraris and McLarens — and then bagged strong fourth places in France and Austria.

One of his most impressive races came on his home turf at Montreal where he ran a strong third ahead of Häkkinen for many laps before scrambled tyre-change strategy dropped him from contention. After ramming Ralf Schumacher off the road later in the race, he quipped: 'I always said I'd find my way back into the cockpit of a Williams.' It was a rare lapse in a season characterised by honest effort and raw, undiminished speed.

Villeneuve's efforts in qualifying fourth at Monza were also extremely praiseworthy and his refusal to be in any way depressed by the BAR 02's performance shortcomings in certain circumstances generated a huge motivational force to power the team's efforts. At the end of the season he received a big money offer to switch to the Benetton-Renault squad for 2001, but preferred to stick with what he knew and continue to put his effort behind BAR. With ever-increasing collaboration from Honda, who knows what Jacques

3

Date of birth: 9 April 1971

Team: British American Racing

Grand Prix starts in 2000: 17

World Championship placing: 7th

Wins: 0; Poles: 0; Points: 17

david
coulthard

...rilliant victory in this year's French Grand Prix is likely to slip into historical perspective as the 'high noon' of David Coulthard's F1 achievement. That is in no way to suggest there are no more good times ahead for the pleasant Scottish driver, but for two glorious months this past summer, he looked like a genuine World Championship contender and radiated the confidence which goes with such status.

David hit the headlines unexpectedly after he, his fiancée Heidi Wichlinski and his trainer Andy Matthews escaped virtually unhurt from a crash landing at Lyon airport which cost the lives of the two pilots in their chartered Learjet. Five days later, a bruised and battered Coulthard drove to a brilliant second place in the Spanish Grand Prix behind team-mate Mika Häkkinen. In many ways it was the most impressive single drive of the 2000 season.

It is absolutely characteristic of David's ingrained Caledonian resilience that he should not have made a fuss about his discomfort. By this stage in the year he had already scored a well-judged victory in the British Grand Prix at Silverstone and would be perfectly placed at Monaco to bag a second win after Michael Schumacher's dominant Ferrari wilted with overheated rear suspension.

After his third win of the season in France it really began to look as though he had the momentum to take over as Schumacher's number one challenger. Yet if Coulthard had the cards falling in his favour during the first half of the season, after France it all went wrong. In Austria he had to play second fiddle to Häkkinen, and at Hockenheim a misunderstanding over the timing of his first refuelling stop dropped him from contention. He was third in Hungary, fourth in Spa and then his title challenge came crashing to a literal halt on the opening lap of the Italian Grand Prix.

Stalling prior to the parade lap at Montreal and jumping the start at Indianapolis were minor blemishes on an otherwise pretty satisfactory canvass. Yet for me Coulthard deserves the greatest credit for his behaviour in the immediate aftermath of his French Grand Prix victory. The dignified manner in which he admonished Michael Schumacher for what he saw as his unacceptable driving tactics carried all the more weight for its measured maturity. For those few moments David was eloquently expressing the feelings of many in a manner that made him a credit to his sport.

Born: 27 March 1971

Team: West McLaren Mercedes

Grand Prix starts in 2000: 17

World Championship placing: 3rd

Wins: 3; Poles: 2; Points: 73

4

rubens
barrichello

THE job of number two to Michael Schumacher in the Ferrari squad is at the same time enviable and something approximating to a poisoned chalice. There is the heady blend of fame and prestige which goes hand-in-hand with driving for the most famous team in the F1 pit lane, yet it is a task which brings with it unique pressures and problems. By any standards, Rubens Barrichello has handled his new situation with considerable aplomb.

There were those in the F1 pit lane who believed that Barrichello had bitten rather more than he could chew signing up with the Maranello brigade. He was branded too gentle and sensitive a creature to handle a situation which even proved wearing to his immediate predecessor, the laid-back Eddie Irvine.

As it turned out, Barrichello proved ideally suited to what initially proved a somewhat ambiguous position. At the start of the season Ferrari proudly proclaimed that both their drivers would receive equal treatment and whoever was fastest would be accorded number one status.

These amusing devices amounted to a sideshow which fooled nobody. Michael Schumacher was, is and will be Ferrari's team leader, a state of affairs unlikely to change in the forseeable future. Yet the popular and pleasant Brazilian driver never underestimated the magnitude of the task before him. Starting the year with a strong second place to Schumacher in Melbourne, there were times when Barrichello seemed to be struggling with the set-up of his car, but other occasions when he looked positively inspired.

He drove superbly to qualify on pole position at Silverstone, leading the race in disciplined style until gearbox problems intervened. In Canada, where Schumacher was troubled by braking problems, he had to be slowed up quite blatantly in order to preserve his team leader's advantage. He also performed well to take third place with a damaged car in Austria and saved the day for Ferrari at Hockenheim where, thanks to a helping of good fortune and some brilliantly precise overtaking manoeuvres, Rubens finally joined the exclusive grand prix winner's club. Few successes in recent years have been more universally applauded.

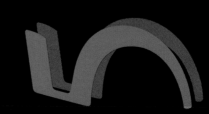

Date of birth: 23 May 1972

Team: Scuderia Ferrari Marlboro

Grand Prix starts in 2000: 17

World Championship placing: 4th

Wins: 1; Poles: 1; Points: 62

jarno trulli

A line-up and hire somebody more capable of consistently pressuring Heinz-Harald Frentzen. The decision to opt for Jarno Trulli proved absolutely correct under the circumstances, and although his tally of championship points accrued this season is undeniably modest, the Italian definitely consolidated the promise which had seen him confidently leading the Austrian GP for Prost back in 1997.

Trulli injected a sense of upbeat optimism to the Jordan squad which admirably complemented Heinz-Harald Frentzen's more laid-back, surgical manner. Trulli was quick off the mark from the start of each practice session and comfortably out-paced Frentzen when it came to qualifying sessions, although he was less fortunate when it came to translating that promise into hard results.

Electronic problems sidelined Jarno on his debut outing for the team in Melbourne, but he followed that up with fourth place behind Frentzen at Interlagos after a dogged climb from a lowly grid position, but failed to finish at Imola and then squeezed a sixth at Silverstone.

Canada and France both yielded sixth places which was a poor reward considering Trulli qualified in fine style alongside Schumacher's Ferrari on the front row at Monaco and held a strong second place, refusing to be ruffled by the presence of eventual winner David Coulthard in his mirrors until his gearbox packed up.

At Spa-Francorchamps he again performed brilliantly to qualify second alongside Mika Häkkinen's McLaren MP4/15, but was bundled off the road early in the race by an over-anxious Jenson Button. When that scenario was repeated in the early stages at Indianapolis, Trulli did not seek to moderate his temper.

If there is any downside to Trulli's enthusiasm and willingness it may be a slightly tentative approach in damp conditions, as witness the fact that he dropped back immediately it started to rain in Canada and was perhaps a little more cautious in the opening stages at Spa than even his heavy fuel load might have led one to expect. He also has a charmingly Italian hair-trigger response to major disappointments, but I understand the Jordan team is currently working on smoothing out those emotional ripples as Trulli strides towards his F1 maturity.

Born on 13 July 1974

Team: Benson & Hedges Jordan

Grand Prix starts in 2000: 17

World Championship placing: 10th =

Wins: 0; Poles: 0; Points: 6

JENSON Button was never going to stay in the Williams line up beyond the end of the season, this time round with Sir Frank's team, at least. The team owner knew that, so did the 19-year-old novice who acquitted himself with such composure and maturity for much of the season. It was therefore curious that the team — and, indeed, Button's advisors — sought to maintain the charade that he might conceivably stay with Williams in 2001 for a large part of the year. Frank Williams had quite clearly forgotten that he told the British media the previous winter that the onus was on the former karting champion to keep CART star Juan Pablo Montoya out of the vacant seat for 2001.

Before being leased to Benetton for next season, Button did enough to prove that he is an outstanding talent. He didn't set the world alight in the manner of Ayrton Senna or Michael Schumacher, but his was a pretty impressive debut. Much was made of his maiden F1 performance at Melbourne, but his climb up the field from his lowly grid position on the opening lap was more due to alarms and excursions by his immediate rivals than any great genius on his part.

In truth, it would take longer for Button's talent to stabilise and it was well into the season before tangible evidence emerged that he had outstanding judgement and skill. Granted, he ran very well at Silverstone to take fifth place on a day when the BMW V10s were close to technical collapse by the chequered flag, but it was fourth place at Hockenheim on a wet track which really laid the foundations of his reputation.

His qualifying efforts at Spa and Indianapolis were also absolutely outstanding, so it was unfortunate that both these races were blighted by early collisions with Jarno Trulli. Most impressive of all have been Button's confidence and charm out of the cockpit. At an age when most youngsters tend to be gauche and uneasy, Jenson is exceptionally mature and assured. These qualities, perhaps even more than his undoubted driving ability, could offer the most crucial index as to what this young Englishman might achieve in the future.

Date of birth: 19 January 1980

Team: BMW WilliamsF1 Team

Grand Prix starts in 2000: 17

World Championship placing: 8th

Wins: 0; Poles: 0; Points: 12

jenson
button

JEAN Alesi's career total reached the 180-race mark at Spa-Francorchamps so it was perhaps appropriate that the veteran French ace should produce one of the most impressive performances of his personal season on this, one of the most challenging circuits on the F1 schedule.

Generally speaking, Alesi and the Prost-Peugeot team had a pretty dismal year, but on this occasion they read the unfolding race with impressive accuracy. Jean ducked into the pits to change from wet to dry rubber a lap ahead of the majority and was rewarded by running strongly in the top six before his Peugeot V10 wilted and he retired. It was the closest he got to scoring a World Championship point and, indeed, was the first season since his F1 debut in 1989 in which he failed to appear on the title scoreboard.

Few would dispute that Alesi remains one of the best and most committed drivers in the business. Sure enough, he can make silly mistakes and often errs on the side of over-exuberance, but the whole point about the Frenchman is that Formula 1 is his life. He is extremely wealthy and, at 36 years old, need never work again should that be his choice, but he nurtures a genuine passion about his chosen profession which is almost touching in its lack of complexity.

Signing with Prost was always going to be something of a risk. Alain and Jean have been close personal friends ever since they were team-mates at Ferrari in 1991 and, perhaps surprisingly, their mutual affection has survived the transition to an employer/employee relationship. Despite the occasional tensions, the partnership has flourished and strengthened. As an indication of Jean's loyalty, when there was speculation that the team might only survive if Alain relinquished control, his number one driver made it clear that he would only be staying if his old friend remained in charge of the operation.

Alesi qualified an impressive seventh at Monaco, a whisker behind Rubens Barrichello's Ferrari and held that position in the opening stages of this demanding and competitive race. He eclipsed his highly touted and promising young team-mate Nick Heidfeld who, like Jean, was a former Formula 3000 champion. It is difficult to imagine that Alesi will ever increase his total of grand prix victories beyond that sole success at Montreal in 1995, but he remains a worthy and consistently underrated member of the Formula 1 community.

jean alesi

Date of birth: 11 June 1964

Team: Gauloises Prost Peugeot

Grand Prix starts in 2000: 17

World Championship placing: unplaced

Wins: 0; Poles: 0; Points: 0

ralf
schumacher

I N the BMW Williams camp Jenson Button may have claimed the lion's share of the headlines, but it was the experienced and seasoned Ralf Schumacher who came away with the hard results, frequently assuming the role of best of the rest in a season monopolised by McLaren and Ferrari success.

Patrick Head once described the younger Schumacher as 'the sort of driver who qualifies sixth and then comes round fourth at the end of the opening lap. Very much a motivating force within the team. Yet there were occasional signs during the course of the season of Ralf's frustration that his first career victory had not yet arrived. In his fourth season of F1 he clearly felt that this was overdue, yet fully appreciated that the new technical alliance between Williams and BMW gave him the best chance of being in on the ground floor of the partnership most likely to challenge Ferrari and McLaren-Mercedes in the longer term.

Ralf boosted the team's confidence by recording a podium finish in the first race of the season, finishing third in Melbourne behind the two Ferraris. It was a performance which owed much to the remarkable mechanical reliability of the new car/chassis combination and Schumacher's ability to keep out of trouble. He finished fifth in Brazil, retired at Imola and then produced extremely convincing fourth places at both Silverstone and Barcelona.

At Monaco he looked set for another possible podium finish, but slid into the barrier at Ste. Dévote and suffered an unpleasant cut to his left leg which threatened to leave him sidelined for the Canadian Grand Prix at Montreal. Williams put test driver Bruno Junquiera on standby, but Ralf recovered sufficiently to drive at the Circuit Gilles Villeneuve only to be pushed out of the race by the son of the man after whom the track was named.

In France he finished fifth, losing out in a close battle with Villeneuve, then failed to finish in Austria and Germany. He was fifth – again 'best of the rest' – in Hungary and an excellent third at both Spa and Monza. At Indianapolis he was running a strong second behind his brother's winning Ferrari when the BMW engine's pneumatic valvegear lost pressure.

At the end of the day fifth in the drivers' World Championship was as good as it was going to get for anybody not fortunate to be driving for McLaren or Ferrari. Yet Williams have the pedigree to become the third force in Formula 1 in 2001, ironically a season in which Ralf Schumacher may find his strongest opposition coming in the form of his new team-mate Juan Pablo Montoya.

Date of birth: 30 June 1975

Team: BMW WilliamsF1 Team

Grand Prix starts in 2000: 17

World Championship placing: 5th

Wins: 0; Poles: 0; Points: 24

heinz-harald
frentzen

THE AUTOCOURSE number one in 1999, Heinz-Harald Frentzen had a bitterly disappointing season this year which effectively mirrored the Jordan squad's high level of technical misfortune. Having won two races last year it seemed that the equable German driver was poised to help propel the Silverstone-based team into F1's first division. But it did not happen.

Frentzen managed to get on the podium on just two occasions thanks to third places at Interlagos and Indianapolis. Beyond that, it was all pretty barren. He did well to make the front row alongside Rubens Barrichello at Silverstone, but a two-stop strategy did not look as though it would work out prior to his eventual retirement. There were also sixth places in Spain, Hungary and Belgium but precious little else for a driver who had so successfully reinvented himself during his first season with Jordan in 1999.

Frentzen also drove strongly at Monaco where he held fourth place ahead of Häkkinen for many laps and again looked set for a top-three placing before becoming one of the many victims of the Ste. Dévote corner late in the race. At Monza he was extremely unfortunate to be involved with team-mate Jarno Trulli in the first-lap accident, flying debris from which caused the death of trackside fire marshal Paolo Ghislimberti. In the aftermath of this most unfortunate multiple collision, Heinz-Harald found himself on the receiving end of an intemperate barrage of criticism from Ferrari driver Rubens Barrichello who, in the shell-shock immediate aftermath of the tragedy, called for the Jordan driver to be banned for ten races.

The mature and reasoned manner in which Frentzen handled and responded to this outburst said much for his intelligence and sensitivity. That he was able to settle his mind after this episode and produce such a storming run at Indianapolis perhaps accurately reflected just how much of Frentzen's talent was wasted on the tides of unpredictable circumstance throughout the 2000 season.

Date of birth: 18 May 1967

Team: Benson & Hedges Jordan

Grand Prix starts in 2000: 17

World Championship placing: 9th

Wins: 0; Poles: 0; Points: 11

MICHAEL'S HOLY GRAIL

by Mark Hughes

Opposite: Keeping tabs on the opposition. Michael Schumacher checks the practice times of his fellow competitors.

Below: Master at work, Michael in the cockpit of his Ferrari.

WHERE can he go from here? As the man who delivered the Holy Grail, who will recall what happened to him after the delivered it? Oh, there are a couple of targets left for Michael Schumacher to aim for: Juan-Manuel Fangio's five world titles and Alain Prost's 51 grand prix wins. But even if he achieves them, he will still be remembered primarily as the man who brought a world drivers' title to Ferrari after a 21-year drought.

For the rest of eternity Schumacher will bestride the pages of motor sport history as a giant because of this single momentous achievement. Prost tried but failed to do it 10 years ago, Ayrton Senna dreamed of doing it one day, but only Schumacher has done it.

Is he really as pre-eminent as those history books will suggest? Over his peers, the evidence stacks up overwhelmingly in his favour.

In a pit-stop era of F1 that is more completely sprint-oriented than ever before, his speed is breathtaking. With that same format placing enormous emphasis on the ability to nail a lap time on cold tyres, his out laps are invariably fantastic, fuelled by competitive desire, controlled by a delicacy of feel unrivalled by any of his generation. With the outcome of races so often precariously balanced on the pivot of tenths of a second won or lost, he never does a bad lap, never once allows himself the luxury of a comfortable one before the battle has been won. In an era where permutations of strategy are so complex, he never loses the plot, is always aware of what is needed.

His nearest rival Mika Häkkinen can arguably be said to be at least as quick over a qualifying lap. He also handles the pressure of a race or championship situation more serenely. But he is not in the same league in changeable conditions — for a snap-shot, refer to lap 11 of the European Grand Prix at the Nürburgring this year as the Ferrari slices unwavering down the inside of a tentative McLaren the instant rain begins to fall. See also Häkkinen's out lap in Japan — the moment that turned that race and secured Schumacher's title. Sure, Mika was unlucky the rain started falling heavily just as he was doing his first lap on cold tyres; but you can be sure that in the same situation Michael would not have lost as much time.

But his virtuosity in compromise conditions is just the most obvious of the many facets of Schumacher's superiority. Where Häkkinen needs the frequent guidance from his crew *re* where he is relative to the chosen strategy — the analysis of the race history chart in Brazil, for example, shows quite clearly the lap on which he fell asleep and received a wake-up call — Schumacher is invariably ahead of the game. In Ross Brawn he has the pitlane's best tactician, but Michael magnifies the advantage of that. It's the product of a racing mind that is always furiously active, and of how much time his talent allows that mind to be used.

Even by the standards of a World Champion, he is completely immersed in his profession, enabling his approach to be multi-tentacled. On his way to the loo pre-race, he'll be the only driver to look to the sky, checking the clouds, searching always for information he may be able to use. When he makes his first out lap in testing or practice, it will be full-on, not a cruise up to speed; that way his feel for how the car is in low-grip situations can be noted, logged and used at the crucial moment. He is always the first to give the pit lane entrance a maximum attack run. He's the only guy who never seems to find traffic on his qualifying runs. He's the only front-runner who makes a point of talking to tail-enders to discuss the best way of him lapping them.

Given that mentality it's easy to see why and how he has moulded his team around him: he's involved at every level in a way that makes him much more than just a driver. There is, in fact, no visible delineation between team and driver. If the car is below par, he never seeks to separate the overall performance from his own. In five years at Ferrari — four of them with the team underachieving — when has he ever directed a raised eyebrow of criticism their way?

For all these reasons he is the best driver in the world. The correlation between this fact and hard results could have been made earlier and stronger had he taken the easy route a few years ago and signed for McLaren. The record books would long-ago have been rewritten. But what he has done stands as a greater achievement.

Which leads on to the altogether more difficult and subjective matter of his true place in the historical pantheon of great drivers. He's flawed, but so too were some other greats.

He has featured in three final-round title showdowns. In every one of them — Adelaide '94, Jerez '97 and Suzuka '98 — he made crucial pressure errors, at his cynical worst. In the split second of desperation when all that he'd worked for threatened to get away from him, he resorted to unsubtle professional foul.

While Michael did nothing as blatant this year, he twice made moves that were downright dangerous. At Barcelona against Coulthard and at Spa against Häkkinen he hovered in the middle of the track, waited for the other guy to commit to a line, then cut him off. An aircraft-scale accident was just millimetres away in the latter case. He definitely smudges the line between a champion's ruthlessness and operating outside agreed terms of combat.

Ayrton Senna admitted to the same offence — Suzuka 1990 — but his move was pre-meditated. Which morally perhaps makes it even less excusable, but professionally doesn't expose the same weakness of panic.

Then again, Schumacher's speed seems to come easier than Senna's did, appears to take less out of him. This effortlessness begs comparison to Clark or Moss.

But Clark, like Fangio or Prost, was happy to be forever in the best machinery. Schumacher has wilfully steered away from that course. Is that a flaw in itself or just a further underlining of his greatness?

A psychologist may be able to explain why he needs to take the difficult route and make it work, why he loved creating a world-beater out of Benetton then moved on to magnify that at Ferrari. Now that's achieved, we're back where we came in. Where to from here? After all, for him, it's how the victories are won rather than their quantity.

Is he greater than Fangio, or Clark or Nuvolari? These are questions to which there can be no answer. But that they can legitimately be posed suggests that, yes, Schumacher's destined place as a giant in the sport's history can be justified beyond just the statistics.

Perhaps it's best not to ponder the questions too much right now. Let's wait until he's stopped. In the meantime we can just enjoy and feel privileged to witness the boy from his dad's kart track just doing his stuff. That's still the essence of him. The races have got bigger, the crowds more massive, the money off the scale, but he's still there trying to pull off the impossible, with style and drama.

WRESTLING WITH THE TOP TEN

by Alan Henry

Inset centre left: The remains of Senna's Mclaren after he had rammed Prost off the track at Suzuka 1990.
Bernard Cahier

Inset left: The irrepressible James Hunt lived life in the fast lane.
Bernard Cahier

Far left: Ayrton Senna, a flawed genius.
Paul-Henri Cahier

Inset bottom left: The great Juan Manuel Fangio won the championship five times between 1951 and 1957.
LAT Photographic

IF there is one element of the AUTO-COURSE editorial equation which I never ceases to attract comment – be it approval or sniggering derision – it is the Editor's assessment of the Top Ten drivers of the season. It's some years since Keke Rosberg, the 1982 World Champion, frankly admitted that the drivers pretend they don't care where they are placed, but in fact lots of them really do.

Speaking from my occupancy of the Editor's chair for what I hope has been a lucky 13 editions, it's my view that Rosberg is probably correct in 50 per cent of the cases. There are several celebrated instances which back up this belief.

Back in 1976, publisher Richard Poulter was telephoned by the late James Hunt and asked discreetly if he could be told where he'd been rated in our list.

Richard replied that he'd rather keep it to himself for the moment but, when pressed, admitted that he had been placed number two behind Niki Lauda. James, who'd clinched the championship by a single point from the Austrian driver after Niki had missed three races in the aftermath of that terrible fire at Nürburgring, said 'I absolutely agree'.

Hunt, of course, came from a different age. He could be quite a handful at times, but he was basically an extremely intelligent and mature individual who knew where his place was in the overall F1 order. I was always impressed with that.

In 1982, Maurice Hamilton, my predecessor as Editor, took the bold and imaginative step of leaving the number one slot unfilled as a tribute to the remarkable talent of Gilles Villeneuve. The famous Canadian ace had been killed practising for that year's Belgian Grand Prix at Zolder, so the rest of the likely lads – Rosberg, Alain Prost, Nelson Piquet and Niki Lauda – all lined up from second place down.

I've often been tempted – and indeed urged – to follow Hamilton's example on this, but somehow I felt it would undermine Villeneuve senior's memory. I was also never quite brave enough.

However, I am happy to say that one man who very definitely *did* care where he was placed in our Top Ten was late, great Ayrton Senna. In 1990 I'd made up my mind that he should be number one only to watch in disbelief as he rammed Alain Prost's Ferrari off the track at Suzuka on the first corner of the Japanese Grand Prix.

I have always regarded this as one of the most outrageous pieces of driving I've witnessed in almost 30 years on the F1 trail and, irrespective of the 're-visionists' who have since sought to

excuse it, feel as strongly about it as I did on the day it occurred. As a direct result, I moved Senna down to second place behind Prost. And explained why I'd done so.

Ayrton, so I'm told, regarded me – and indeed, one or two journalistic colleagues – as 'dangerous'. Putting aside my underlying amazement over just why any professional sportsman should care what a journalist says or thinks, I have to confess that Senna duly settled that particular account.

Even as he surged towards the 1991 World Championship I was getting messages back from the Senna camp effectively telling me not to bother to ask for another introduction. Knowing that this was a battle which could not be won, we gratefully accepted a foreword from Honda President Nobuhiko Kawamoto, a great Formula 1 enthusiast, and chalked it down to experience.

In recent years, the one driver who has taken me to task most regularly is David Coulthard; something which genuinely pains me because I just wish he was good enough to win a World Championship as he would be the best ambassador for Formula 1 imaginable. Sadly, I suspect he is not destined to scale such heights. Still, this year he's up two places from sixth to fourth in the Top Ten, so I am hoping that he will still talk to AUTOCOURSE in the future.

The inevitable snag with the Top Ten is that the great drivers of the 1950s are not included in our overall calculations. The AUTOCOURSE ratings have been a feature of the book only since the mid-1960s which meant that the likes of Alberto Ascari, Juan Manuel Fangio and Stirling Moss get no mention and the legendary Jim Clark only squeezes in briefly towards the end of his illustrious career.

Some may say that our driver rankings state the obvious, but I think they go further than that. They endorse what might not always be absolutely obvious. For example, just as in 1970 it is arguable that Stewart did a better job than either Jochen Rindt or Jacky Ickx, because he didn't have the best car at his disposal, so Mansell and Prost deserved similar accolades in 1989 and '90 because their Ferrari was not consistently as good as the McLaren-Honda opposition.

That is the fundamental point. We have always attempted to identify who did the best job taking into account the machinery at their disposal. Unlike most other sports, the reliance of a Formula 1 driver on a complex piece of machinery in order to display his talents means it is often necessary to look

past the results on the page. Analysis is more important than the capacity for straightforward observation.

Taking a straightforward historical context, it would be a brave man indeed who placed Jackie Stewart as the number one driver of the past 50 years. Yet I would contend that he was certainly the most *significant* Formula 1 driver of the past 50 years. Put aside his sheer natural ability behind the wheel, and Stewart is a pivotal character on two crucial counts.

Firstly, he was a tireless campaigner for safety at a time when such a stance was unfashionable, single-handedly manufacturing a bandwagon which others have since climbed aboard and attempted to hijack. Secondly, he was the first superstar millionaire F1 sportsman, laying the foundations for the current era in which the top drivers call the financial shots.

During this 50-year period, F1 racing was transformed from a sport which killed up to half a dozen participants every season to one in which a competitor had to be really unlucky to die in a racing car. Stewart reckoned that, when he raced, the batting average was a three-in-five chance of dying in a racing car if you survived for more than five years.

More than anybody else, he was responsible for the great strides in circuit safety during the mid-1960s, reasoning that he was paid to demonstrate his skill, not to risk his life unreasonably. This put him on a collision course with the traditionalists who reckoned he was

a softy, but the passing of time has shown such people to be eccentrics and Stewart was bang on the nail.

Those six years during which Stewart dominated the ratings also represented a period of remarkable accelerated development in terms of F1 technology. In 1950, Giuseppe Farina won the first official World Championship with an essentially pre-war car, the Alfa Romeo 158.

19 years later Stewart won his first World Championship in a high-technology Matra chassis, the first grand prix car built to contemporary aerospace standards. During that period the front-engined layout had been abandoned in favour of the more efficient mid-engined configuration and tubular spaceframes had given way to monocoque chassis.

Yet this was just the start. These were followed by anti-impact structures (1973), ground-effect aerodynamics (1977) and, finally, by far the biggest single leap forward in terms of driver safety, the carbon-fibre composite chassis (1981).

Meanwhile, the calendar was evolving at a similar pace. The so-called World Championship effectively started out as a European-based series on traditional tracks. In 1953 it first went out of Europe with the introduction of an Argentine GP, then a Moroccan GP in 1957 and the US race in 1959.

Since then it has expanded to include places which I dare say the likes of Farina and Moss hardly knew existed at the height of their own F1 careers. Indeed, in the case of Malaysia, the

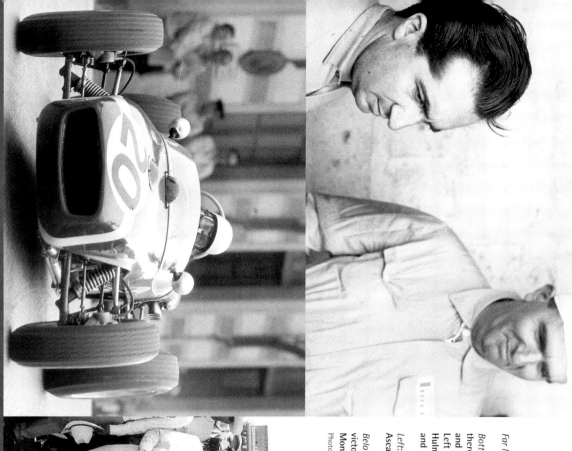

Far left: Fangio in the Maserati 250F.

Bottom far left: Nürburgring, 1967, when there were four cars on the front row – and they were all different makes! Left to right are: Jim Clark (Lotus), Denny Hulme (Brabham), Jackie Stewart (BRM) and Dan Gurney (Eagle).

Photographs: Bernard Cahier

left: Giants of the early 1950s, Alberto Ascari and Giuseppe Farina.

Below left: Moss the maestro drives to victory in the Rob Walker Lotus 18 at Monaco, 1960.

Paul-Henri Cahier

Below centre left: Jackie Stewart appears exhausted but satisfied after winning the 1971 Monaco Grand Prix.

Bernard Cahier

Below: Dangerous game, Mexico, 1966, and the drivers attend a pre-race briefing. From left to right are: Clark, Surtees, Hulme, Bondurant, Rindt, Stewart, Hill and local hero Solana.

Bernard Cahier

Bottom left: Jochen Rindt and Lotus 49c in full flow during his epic drive to a last-corner win in the 1970 Monaco Grand Prix.

Bernard Cahier

Far left: As it was. Grand prix cars buzz through the dunes at Zandvoort in 1953. Bernard Cahier

Bottom far left: The face of grand prix racing in 2000. The Sepang circuit boasts state-of-the-art facilities and even the occasional overtaking move as Johnny Herbert passes Mika Salo. Paul-Henri Cahier

Left: Colin Chapman was one of Formula 1 racing's great visionaries. LAT Photographic

Below centre left: Paddock facilities were primitive even in the late 1960s. Denny Hulme, Bruce McLaren and his boys make do at Watkins Glen in 1968. Bernard Cahier

Bottom: Everything concerning F1's business interests comes under Bernie Ecclestone's umbrella. Bernard Cahier

Below left: Mobile advertising. Graham Hill drifts his Gold Leaf-liveried Lotus 49B through the daunting Woodcote corner at the 1969 British Grand Prix. LAT Photographic

country didn't even exist in its current form at the time Moss's career ended with that terrible accident at Goodwood on Easter Monday, 1962.

The British GP has enjoyed a nomadic existence, wandering between Aintree, Brands Hatch and Silverstone for many years, and regional rivalries saw the French GP take place variously at Reims, Rouen, Dijon-Prenois, Paul Ricard, Clermont Ferrand, Le Mans and Magny-Cours. At the time of writing we have at least one more British GP at Silverstone to look forward to in 2001 and, I suspect, many more besides once the wrangling with Brands Hatch – who hold the rights, but have no circuit – is finally resolved.

At the start of the story, motor racing was bankrolled by car manufacturers eager to gain promotional success from their achievements. Incidental backing was derived from tyre, fuel and accessory manufacturers, but when Lotus boss Colin Chapman introduced Gold Leaf cigarettes as his team's major sponsor in 1968, he triggered a shift of emphasis which has dictated the entire commercial development of the sport through to the present day.

In the early 1970s, the F1 Constructors Association would develop a strong power base under the vigorous direction of Bernie Ecclestone, a former car dealer and part-time racer who had managed both Vanwall driver Stuart Lewis-Evans (in the late 1950s) and 1970 World Champion Jochen Rindt.

Ecclestone was the visionary who could see the commercial possibilities of grand prix racing and its position today as the most successful televised sport taking place on a regular annual basis (only eclipsed by the Olympic Games and, possibly, the football World Cup) leads us to the edge of the new millennium.

Ecclestone, who we last interviewed for AUTOCOURSE back in 1984, once coined the memorable phrase 'first you get on, then you get rich, then you get honest'. With a crystal clarity of thought and foresight he has surged towards achieving those ambitions with a single-mindedness which is almost frightening.

With his old confederate Max Mosley now occupying the position as FIA president, we F1 old hands regard this pair of poachers turned gamekeepers. A prime example, if you like, of yesterday's renegades becoming today's establishment.

20 years ago Ecclestone and Mosley were in the forefront of a major battle with the FIA, pitching the teams into direct confrontation with its then president Jean-Marie Balestre over what was

basically who controlled the commercial rights. Taking an historical perspective, the FIA was something of a pushover at that time because Bernie and Max correctly judged the power of the commercial flood tide on which they were riding.

Whoever said 'money makes the world go around' must have been thinking of Formula 1. In 1985 Niki Lauda earned $3.3 million from McLaren as reigning World Champion, a figure which literally rocked the F1 paddock on its collective heels. Nowadays you'd be lucky to get a top-class technical director in a front-line team for that money and McLaren spend far more on its corporate entertaining in a single season.

Early in 2000, Bernie, in his role as F1's Commercial Rights Holder, sold 50 per cent of his SLEC empire – the umbrella corporation which controls all his F1-related business interests – to the German EMTV network. At a time when the world's major motor manufacturers are clamouring for a stake in Bernie's empire, not least because they hope it will give them more influence over the rule-making process, the wheel is showing signs of coming full circle.

Tobacco sponsorship is gradually being phased out and the car makers are seeking to increase their influence. F1 has also become the automotive equivalent of Henley or Wimbledon, where rock stars and dodgy entrepreneurs rub shoulders with the Schumacher and Häkkinen generation of throttle jockeys.

In that respect, grand prix racing has a remarkable capacity for throwing together unlikely bedfellows. In 1950, the snobs in the paddock may have tittered when Her Majesty the Queen was presented to bluff Derby garage owner Reg Parnell, then Britain's top F1 star.

Yet in retrospect this seems no more unlikely than the sight of FIA president Max Mosley escorting Deputy Prime Minister John Prescott through the paddock at Silverstone, the deputy, one might remember, of the man who accepted a one million dollar cheque on behalf of the Labour Party from Bernie Ecclestone.

In a way, it is all very encouraging. Formula 1 is at the same time highly political and totally apolitical. Behind the scenes, it may be a world of multi-million dollar deals on wheels, but when the lights go off on a Sunday afternoon and the pack sprints for the first corner, for about 90 minutes the business reverts to something which all instinctively recognise.

In other words, absolutely as it should be.

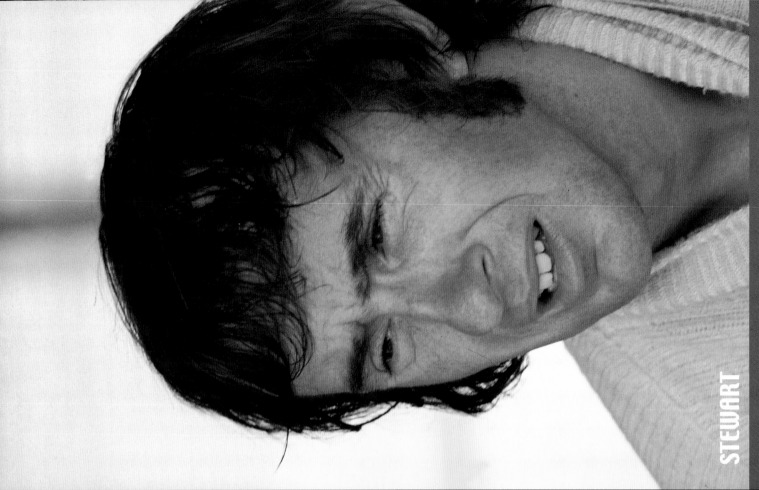

STEWART

PROST

BEST OF THE BEST
Top Ten AUTOCOURSE Chart Toppers

1
JACKIE STEWART
6 consecutive number ones 1968–'73

2
ALAIN PROST
5 number ones 1984, '85, '86, '87 and '90

3 = *
MICHAEL SCHUMACHER
4 number ones 1995, '96, '98 and 2000

3 = *
NIKI LAUDA
4 consecutive number ones 1975–'78

5
AYRTON SENNA
3 number ones 1988, '91 and '93

6
ALAN JONES
3 consecutive number ones 1979–'81

7
JIM CLARK
2 number ones in 1966 –'67

8
NIGEL MANSELL
2 number ones in 1989 and '92

9
NELSON PIQUET
1 number one in 1983

10
EMERSON FITTIPALDI
1 number one in 1974

Other Number Ones
Jacques Villeneuve (1997),
Damon Hill (1994) and
Heinz–Harald Frentzen (1999)
have also claimed the
AUTOCOURSE number one slot.

* Joint ranking as they both won three
World Championships.

JONES

LAUDA

SCHUMACHER

PIQUET

CLARK

SENNA

FITTIPALDI

MANSELL

BEST OF THE BEST

SUCCESS ON ALL FRONTS!

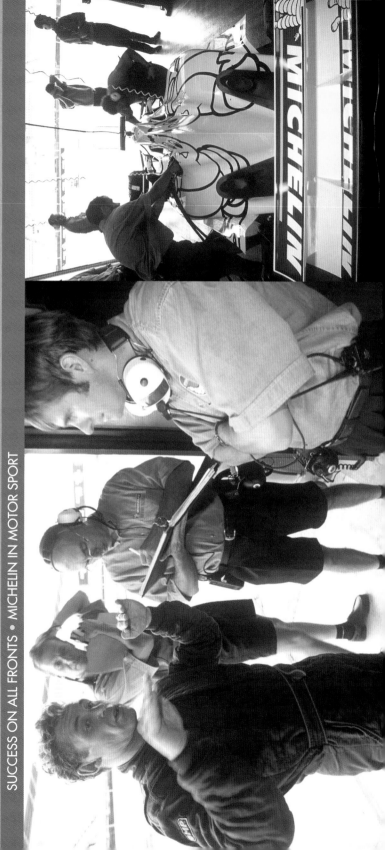

FORMULA 1:
A RECORD
TO LIVE UP TO

A LITTLE over 12 months after the official confirmation of its return, Michelin tyres will race in anger again in Formula 1 for the first time since 1984 at the Australian Grand Prix in March.

The French firm is as conscious as anyone of the high-class act it will be following on from (3 drivers' titles, 2 constructors' titles and 59 wins from 112 grands prix between 1977 and 1984), yet given the references of its throughout 2000...

And white commitment to all these activities will continue unabated in 2001, Michelin has spent the past year carefully preparing for its imminent return to the Formula 1 arena.

Over the months ahead, the battle at the sharp end in each of these premier competitions promises to be as fierce as ever, and tyres are poised to play the same decisive role they did throughout 2000...

NO other tyre manufacturer is as actively involved in so many forms of world class motor sport as Michelin. That's no hollow claim, for the French firm has long been at the peak of the competition pyramid – on both four wheels and two.

In 2000, from the Le Mans 24 Hours and World Championship rallying to Grand Prix 500 motorcycling and the Superbike world series, not to mention the world of off-road biking and countless key national championships, Michelin tyres have once again harvested an impressive list of titles and individual race and rally wins.

future rivals nobody is expecting it to resume at once its presence in motor racing's blue riband formula in all-conquering, steamroller fashion.

At the time of going to press, Michelin's announced partners for this new adventure are BMW-Williams and Jaguar (plus Toyota from 2002) and both teams participated actively in the crucial preparation and build-up phase that has marked the past 12 months or so.

Respectively driving a Stewart and a 1999 Williams, test drivers Tom Kristensen and Jörg Müller completed more than 10,000 kilometres round some of Europe's finest venues developing and fine-tuning a catalogue of products in readiness for the season to come.

Circuits like Monza, Jerez, Barcelona, Silverstone, Magny-Cours and Estoril, not to mention BMW's own testing ground at Miramas in the south of France, all made their own specific demands on the prototype tyres, enabling Michelin's engineers to investigate and evaluate a vast variety of solutions.

After an initial period geared notably to out-and-out performance work, the emphasis progressively shifted to the notion of durability, with technicians continuously feeding the database that will allow them to correlate the information collected over the year for use at other circuits or in different track conditions.

This process will carry on right up to the moment the cars are crated for shipment to Melbourne. And will even continue well beyond. For winning at this level is a long-term game – although the experience accumulated by Michelin on its way to five previous F1 world titles surely cannot hurt!

Main picture: **The Audi R8 of Frank Biela/Tom Kristensen/Emanuele Pirro led an Audi clean sweep in the Le Mans 24 Hours race where track temperatures reached 42°C.**

The summer of 2000 has seen Michelin continuously testing in preparation for a return to Formula 1 in 2001.

Far left: **Test driver Tom Kristensen provides feedback to Michelin technicians.**

Centre left: **The test car is prepared for action.**

Left: **Kristensen takes the re-liveried 1999 Stewart through its paces on Michelin rubber.**

SUCCESS ON ALL FRONTS • MICHELIN IN MOTOR SPORT

Michelin's multi-faceted involvement in motor sport has seen manufacturers gain success in all disciplines. From the gruelling Le Mans 24 Hours race, to the gravel and ice and the high-speed thrills of the Moto Grand Prix and World Superbike championships.

Motor sport giants such as Audi, Peugeot, Ford, Suzuki and Honda all choose Michelin.

LE MANS 24 HOURS: NINE OUT OF NINE!

THE 2000 Le Mans 24 Hours saw Michelin runners fill the top nine positions at the finish to make this the Clermont Ferrand firm's most emphatic success ever in the French endurance classic.

This year's hat-trick triumph with Audi was also Michelin's third-consecutive win in La Sarthe with three different manufacturer-partners after its BMW-led one-two-three-four result last year and its one-two with Porsche-Michelin in 1998. The win by Frank Biela/Tom Kristensen/Emanuele Pirro last June was Michelin's ninth since the creation of the race in 1923 and its seventh in the last 12 races.

In the blazing sunshine that marked this year's event, and which saw ground temperatures peak at a searing 42°C, Michelin's race team was delighted with the performance of its products throughout the race. And more particularly with the capacity of its 'hot-weather' tyres to deal with triple stints at the hottest moments of the race. Indeed, the performance and durability of these products no doubt figure amongst the cornerstones of the firm's success.

Meanwhile, lapping on tyres more suited to the relative coolness of night, as ground temperatures fell to a refreshing 20°C, all Michelin's 'prototype' partners were able to put in triple stints during the hours of darkness which of course enabled them to gain further time during pit stops by not having to change rubber.

Not only did Michelin's partners top the overall timesheets throughout the race, they also led from flag to flag in the GTS category with the Oreca-run Chrysler Vipers. Beretta/Wendlinger/Dupuy went on to head the company's class one-two, a repeat of its one-two-three-four success in the 1999 race.

MOTORCYCLING: WORLD CLASS SUCCESS ON TWO WHEELS

THE 2000 500 cc motorcycle World Championship proved rich in ground-breaking achievements for Michelin who not only celebrated a record 250th 500 GP win thanks to Alex Criville (Honda-Michelin) in May but also collected its 20th 500 GP Riders' title with Suzuki-Michelin's Kenny Roberts.

Meanwhile, Honda-Michelin's Colin Edwards collected Michelin's seventh-consecutive crown in the Superbike World Championship, putting the make of the fastest tyres on two wheels beyond any possible doubt.

The battle for the 500 Grand Prix title provided motorcycle fans with one of the most spectacular and fiercely fought championships in years, with no fewer than eight different riders claiming at least one win from the season's 16 rounds.

Up-coming Australian star Garry McCoy (Yamaha-Michelin) set the ball rolling with the first of his three victories on the year's curtain-raiser in South Africa. Shortly afterwards, Kenny Roberts (Suzuki-Michelin), son of the American racing legend, made his championship intentions clear with success in Malaysia, the first of his three wins that helped him clinch the series three rounds from home.

Other race winners were Alex Barros (2), Valentino Rossi (2), defending champion Alex Criville (3) and Loris Capirossi (all Honda-Michelin), plus Yamaha-Michelin's Max Biaggi (2) and Norick Abe.

To appreciate the amazing skills and commitment it takes to triumph at this level, and also to grasp the huge demands placed on 500 GP tyres, two simple statistics put the whole discipline into crystal clear perspective: today's bikes boast a power-to-weight ratio comparable to that of a Formula 1 car but with a rubber-to-asphalt contact patch that is not only 13 times smaller but also continuously shifting under cornering, acceleration and braking.

Thanks to its experience of these constraints, Michelin's 2000 season was notably marked by the success of its new 16.5" rear slick (an alternative to the traditional 17" tyre), while the firm's famed dual-compound rears continued to give riders the edge on the tracks that make contrasting demands on different sides of the tyre.

Finally, Texan Colin Edwards won eight of the season's 26 races for Honda-Michelin in the increasingly popular World Superbike Championship, the manufacturers' crown going to the Ducati-Michelin team led by Australia's Troy Bayliss and American rider Ben Bostrom.

WORLD RALLYING: HIGH PERFORMANCE ON ALL SURFACES

WHEN this year's AUTOCOURSE 'went to bed', as they say in publishing, two rounds of the 2000 World Rally Championship (Australia and Great Britain) remained.

As teams left their European bases for Perth, the situation at the top of both the manufacturers' and drivers' championships points tables was at something of a cliff-hanger stage, with three teams (Peugeot-Michelin, Ford-Michelin and Subaru) still in the running for the former and no fewer than four drivers (Marcus Gronholm, Richard Burns, Colin McRae and Carlos Sainz) split by a mere six points in the latter!

And in both, Michelin's partners were in pole position to take the French firm's score from 28 to 30 WRC titles since the creation of the championship in 1973.

Rally fans will of course now know the names that figure on each of this year's trophies, but perhaps one of the most significant lessons to be drawn from the season that has just come to a close is the stage-winning performance of Michelin's WRC range over the full spectrum of surfaces that make up the series.

For not only did Michelin tyres claim yet another grand slam in 2000 on asphalt (with wins on the wintry Monte Carlo, as well as the predominantly dry Catalonia, Corsica and Sanremo Rallies), they also triumphed on both smooth and rough gravel, including 1-2 successes on the two most punishing European-style loose surface events: Greece and Cyprus.

The only setback of the year came on Kenya's uniquely challenging Safari Rally where the firm failed to build on its record of seven wins since 1991, although competitions chief Pierre Dupasquier has stressed Michelin's determination to return to its winning ways in Africa at the first possible opportunity.

Even so, with a score of nine wins from twelve outings with two rounds to go, he can be justifiably proud of his company's record in the sport this year, a record that lends significant clout to Michelin's claim of competition success on all fronts — on and off track — on four wheels and two!

THE SEVEN AGES OF MAX

Main photo: The steely gaze of FIA President Max Mosley, the man who guides Formula 1 in such a persuasive manner today.
Matthias Schneider

Inset: Young hopeful. Max in his carefree days as racing driver.
LAT Photographic

MAX Mosley keeps a 32-year-old copy of the Italian sports newspaper *Il Giorno* tucked away in the modest London office he occupies in his role as FIA President. Motor racing's most powerful and influential administrator admits that he uses it from time to time as a stark reminder of what motor racing was like in the 'stone age'.

Dominating its front page is a photograph of a multiple pile-up in the 1968 Formula 2 Monza Lottery race. The grass on the exit of Parabolica is strewn with abandoned cars while, in the middle of the track, Jean-Pierre Jaussaud's upturned Tecno burns ferociously as its injured driver is carted away on a stretcher by two medical attendants.

In the foreground, a Brabham BT23C is passing the scene, its driver wearing the open-face helmet and goggles which were *de rigueur* at the time. It is 28-year-old Max Mosley, heading for an eventual eighth place.

In many ways, this was a defining moment in the career of this youngest son of the controversial pre-war politician Sir Oswald Mosley who was already well qualified as a barrister, being called to the bar in 1964 after which he specialised in patent and trademark law.

He raced on an amateur basis, retiring after he crashed his F2 Lotus 59B during practice for the 1969 Eifelrennen at the Nürburgring. That – and the episode at Monza – gave him first-hand experience of the sport's potential hazards.

'Each time I went past it, I could feel the heat from Jaussaud's burning Tecno,' he said. 'I remember resolving when I was racing in F2 that if I ever got into any position of authority within the sport, I would try to reverse the attitude "if you don't like it, you don't have to do it" and "if you think a corner is dangerous, just slow down" which is all nonsense.

'Funnily enough, my mother recently sent me a letter I'd written to her in 1968 recounting a dinner when I was exchanging funny stories with Jochen Rindt and Piers Courage, mainly about a third driver who will be nameless.

'I mentioned to my mother in this letter that it was slightly depressing and they were all younger than me. I was 28 at the time and all three of them – Rindt, Courage and the other driver – were dead before the time they were 30. That's how it was, absolutely horrific.

'So sometimes drivers come in here to talk about safety and sometimes I say to them "that's not dangerous, this

is dangerous" and show them that page from the newspaper. That was motor racing in 1968.'

Later Mosley would have first-hand experience of a fatality when Roger Williamson was killed driving a works March 731 in the 1973 Dutch Grand Prix. 'I had to tell his father, who doted on him,' he reflected. 'It was awful.

'Competing in F1 during the 1960s and early '70s was like being in a front-line regiment during a major war. You just lost contemporary after contemporary. But of course while it's difficult to imagine a war taking place without people getting killed, it's perfectly possible to have motor sport where people don't get killed.

'Moreover, motor sport generally is much more popular amongst the wider, non-enthusiast public than ever it was when it was so dangerous.'

Paradoxically, Mosley agrees that the deaths of Ayrton Senna and Roland Ratzenberger at Imola in 1994 gave a boost to television viewing figures. Yet he also believes that this tragic weekend also reinforced the reality that, criticisms notwithstanding, motor racing is primarily a sport.

'Before Senna was killed there was – and still is – the underlying accusation that motor racing is just a money-making circus,' he said. 'But when you get two people killed in the same weekend it served as a serious reminder that this was a sport. Albeit a deadly serious one.'

Mosley is clearly extremely gratified over the progress which has been made in the area of F1 safety even in the relatively short time since the Imola tragedy. He also believes that it is clearly the FIA's responsibility not only to implement the most demanding safety standards achievable in racing, but to ensure that safety lessons learned from the track are applied to the road car environment.

'There is no doubt that carbon composite materials have made a huge contribution to safety,' he said, 'although the FIA cannot claim credit for that. It was introduced by the teams in the interests of performance, but also had the side effect of offering a safety benefit.

'Yet there were many other aspects. Safety fuel cells, self-sealing fuel couplings, rigorous crash testing and all sorts of padding and impact resistance materials to absorb shock and minimise the effect on the drivers.

'Meanwhile, as far as circuit safety is concerned, the FIA continues to take a great deal of trouble to research methods of dissipating the energy of the accident at a rate consistent with keeping the driver unhurt.

'We have the advantage over road

Knock three times. Max Mosley pays a visit to Bernie Ecclestone's inner sanctum in the F1 paddock.

cars in the sense that we can spend much more per car on safety in F1 – and we have complete control over the circuits. On the roads, of course, it makes a great deal of sense to try and introduce similar levels of safety and impact resistance.

'We've done that to a large extent with the Euro NCAP test programme which has led to dramatic improvements in car design above and beyond what legislation alone has achieved. With the 20 'superminis' we tested during 2000, seven of them have achieved our four-star rating with the best one, the Toyota Yaris, being the third-highest scoring car we've ever tested in all categories.

'Now these tests would never have happened had not NCAP called together all the diverse people who were carrying out this sort of car testing. And the whole mind-set behind this has come from the F1 business.' Mosley finds this technology transfer enormously satisfying and radiates a degree of understandable pride over its success.

Interestingly, despite this commitment to safety, Mosley sees no irony in the controversy which has embroiled Ferrari team leader Michael Schumacher throughout the past season. The 'one move' rule, he insists, is perfectly permissible.

'Schumacher has got the role in many people's minds as the man they love to hate,' he said. 'But there is no hard and fast rule. The first corner at a grand prix is like Hyde Park Corner in the rush hour – cubed.

'It's all a psychological thing with the other driver. Drivers today learn in karting that if you give an inch, your rivals will walk all over you. By the time they get to F1 they become very hard.

'The "one move" rule was introduced to prevent repeated weaving. Schumacher does it to other people, and they complain. People do it to Schumacher and he doesn't complain. It is part of the rough and tumble of the business.

'It is very difficult where you draw the line. For my part, I have never seen Schumacher do anything illegitimate other than his move on Villeneuve at Jerez in 1997, which in the end he admitted. You see the World Championship slipping away, you might be tempted to do something in a split-second which in another split-second you will regret.'

With this in mind, I asked Mosley to reflect back ten years to the moment when Alain Prost's Ferrari was rammed off the circuit by Ayrton Senna's McLaren on the first corner of the 1990

Japanese GP. Would he have penalised Senna for that transgression?

'Absolutely,' he insisted, 'but by the same token, if I'd been the stewards and the Court of Appeal, I would not have disqualified him from the 1989 race which was taken away from him completely unfairly and wrongly.

'Had that injustice not been done to him in 1989, he wouldn't have done what he did in 1990. But what he did was crazy, because a Formula 3000 driver was killed accidentally doing what Senna did deliberately at the same corner less than a year later.'

Of course, as FIA President, Mosley also knows that handling criticism and dissatisfaction from members of the F1

community goes with the badge. This most costly and lavish of international sports relies for its success on a complex inter-dependency between the competitors, the governing body and its commercial rights holder Bernie Ecclestone for its success and, by definition, its cashflow.

In particular, the teams expressed the view that the technical regulations which govern Formula 1 are not clear. Too frequently, they claim, the FIA uses the medium of a 'rule clarification' as a device effectively to alter the rules concerned.

Some hint darkly, but anonymously, that such devices have been used to favour the Ferrari team who Bernie Ec-

clestone, the F1 commercial rights holder, would like to win the World Championship in the belief that it would be good for business.

They are also concerned about the way in which Mosley has negotiated the leasing of F1 commercial rights for Ecclestone's F1 Administration empire for 100 years starting in 2011.

Yet Mosley is resolutely unapologetic. He feels that today's F1 team owners could usefully adopt a more realistic perspective on the FIA F1 World Championship.

'They go into the paddock where everybody is talking about F1, every journalist is writing about F1 and wants to get into their motorhome to

talk to them, and they start to think that this is the whole world,' he said.

'When the original FIA World Championship was started in 1950, not only was there not a McLaren team, Bruce McLaren himself was still in short trousers and hadn't driven a racing car for the first time,' he said.

'So when the F1 entrants say that they have some interest in Formula 1, certainly they have an interest in their teams. They complain about the FIA disposing of the commercial rights, but they certainly don't have any rights in the championship.

'They entered it because it suits them. As I pointed out to the team principals, they don't have to tell the FIA when they sell their team to a car manufacturer. And we don't have to ask the teams if we sell our rights to Bernie or anybody else.'

Mosley firmly believes that the teams have a very good deal as things stand. 'They share 47 per cent of the gross income from the commercial rights,' he said. 'If, say, it costs Bernie £200 million to organise digital television coverage and he only gets £100 million income, the teams share £47 million of that and Bernie takes the loss.'

Back in the 1960s, the economics of F1 were all very different. 'Race organisers would have said to Ferrari and McLaren "we know you've got to come because you need World Championship points" so we won't pay you much,' he said.

'Once an organiser had been granted World Championship status from the FIA, they could go off and negotiate from a wholly unfair position of strength with the teams. That was counter-acted when the teams started to negotiate collectively in 1969–70 – and they took me along, although the March team was very new, because I was a lawyer and they thought I might be helpful.

'Out of these negotiations eventually emerged the Concorde agreement which, I think, is a very fair compromise. The next major evolution – which is happening at the moment – will be when the FIA divests itself of its commercial interests on a long-term basis, becomes simply a regulator and, in the case of F1 at least, should get a large capital sum with which it will start a foundation from which it can underwrite a lot of its public interest activities.'

Mosley clearly plans to oversee this transition as he intends to stand again for re-election to the FIA Presidency in 2001. Beyond that? 'I really don't know,' he shrugs unconvincingly. 'Opportunities tend to present themselves from the most unexpected directions. Fundamentally, you know, I'm really quite lazy.' I doubt anybody in contemporary F1 would agree with that statement.

Paul-Henri Cahier

41

The New Maserati 3200 GT

'Unbelievable'

Spectacular performance from the 370bhp V8 twin-turbo engine.

0-60 in 4.9 unforgettable seconds.

The most elegant luxury car in a long line of legends.

Handling to match the breathtaking pace.

'Believable'

3 year/44,000 mile fixed price servicing.

From £60,755 on the road with finance from Maranello financial services.

3 year/60,000 mile warranty.

Two real seats in the back.

Unsurpassed relationship with your dealer.

Available in manual or automatic option.

MASERATI

MARANELLO SALES LTD

01784 436431

WWW.MARANELLOSALES.COM

INFO@MARANELLOSALES.COM

50 YEARS OF F1 CAR DESIGN

TO celebrate the 50th anniversary of AUTOCOURSE we are delighted to have Gordon Murray pen this anecdotal, very personal technical trip down memory lane through the past half-century of grand prix racing. Gordon gained a deserved reputation as one of F1 racing's most imaginative and innovative motor racing engineers, occupying the position of Chief Designer (1972–'73) and Technical Director (1974–'86) at the Brabham team followed by a spell as Technical Director of the McLaren–Honda squad through until the end of 1989. Thereafter he became Technical Director of McLaren Cars where he masterminded the concept, design and manufacture of the BMW V12-engined McLaren F1 super-performance road car which, in racing guise, won the 1995 Le Mans 24-hour race. He later oversaw the design of the unique McLaren–Mercedes MP4-98T grand prix two-seater and is currently working on the Mercedes McLaren SLR coupé which will be produced by the British company from 2003.

GORDON MURRAY

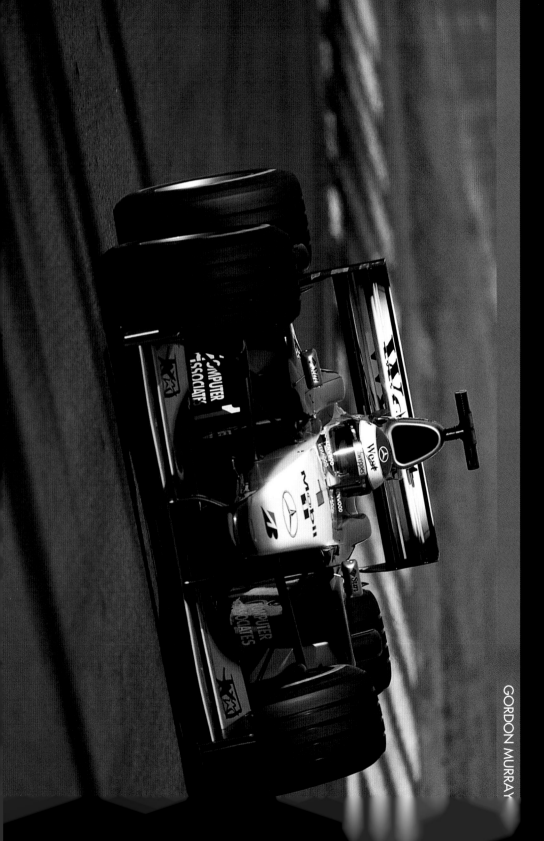

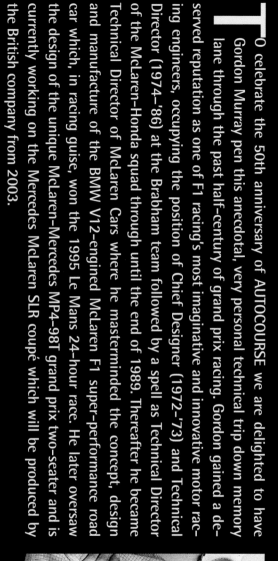

Left: Giuseppe Farina wins the 1950 British Grand Prix at Silverstone in the all-conquering Alfa Romeo 158/50.
LAT Photographic

Bottom: 50 years on, and Mika Häkkinen's McLaren MP4/15-Mercedes V10 represents the state of the art in F1 car design.
Paul-Henri Cahier

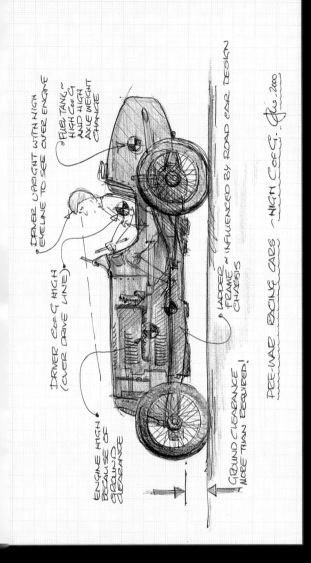

ENGINE HIGH BECAUSE OF GROUND CLEARANCE

DRIVER UPRIGHT WITH HIGH EYELINE TO SEE OVER ENGINE

DRIVER C of G HIGH (OVER DRIVE LINE)

FUEL TANK — HIGH C of G AND HIGH AXLE WEIGHT CHANGE

LADDER FRAME ~ INFLUENCED BY ROAD CAR DESIGN

LADDER FRAME CHASSIS

GROUND CLEARANCE MORE THAN REQUIRED!

PRE-WAR RACING CARS — HIGH C of G. GV 2000

UNQUESTIONABLY, my great passion for cars and motor racing was fired even before I was a teenager back in South Africa during the mid-1950s. I used to get *Autosport* and *Motor* magazines sent out from Britain — by sea mail in those days, of course, so it was about three weeks later by the time I set my eyes on them — and there wasn't a single detail about the cars of that time which didn't completely absorb me.

I was always interested in the cars from a technical viewpoint, whether we're talking about the

Maserati 250F, the Lancia D50 — my personal favourite from that era — or the Mercedes W196. But when it comes to assessing whether the designers and engineers of the time were doing a particularly good or bad job with the knowledge and technology they had at their disposal, I believe there are two key aspects to consider.

If you consider the immediate post-war period of grand prix racing, leading into the early years of the World Championship, the first element which always amazed me was the fact that people were apparently not paying attention to the basic laws of physics.

Consider an ERA, for example. Granted, this was a pre-war design, but its general configuration was pretty well copied in most cars of the immediate post-war generation. You think well, people obviously didn't have 16-inch-wide tyres a their disposal because the technology wasn't available, bu you could surely have made the track wider and the centre o gravity lower.

By then we were living in ar era when jet fighters were being made which could fly a

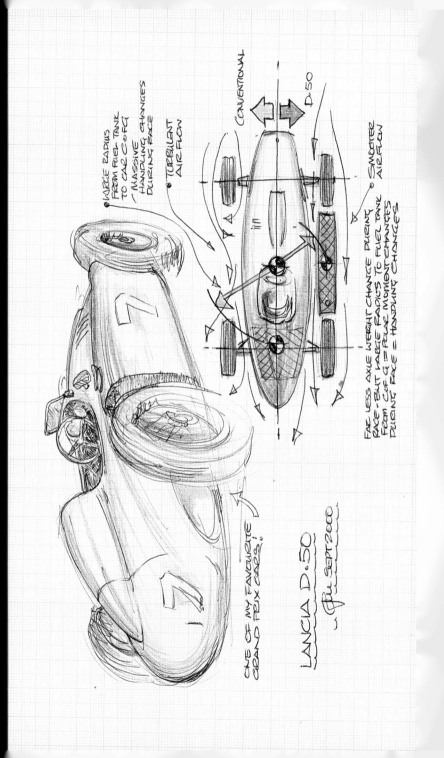

LARGE RADIUS FROM FUEL TANK TO CAR C of G

MASSIVE HANDLING CHANGES DURING RACE

TURBULENT AIR FLOW

FAR LESS AXLE WEIGHT CHANGE DURING RACE — BUT LARGE RADIUS TO FUEL TANK FROM C of G (= POLAR MOMENT CHANGES DURING RACE = HANDLING CHANGES)

CONVENTIONAL

D-50

LANCIA D.50

ONE OF MY FAVOURITE GRAND PRIX CARS!

GV SEPT 2000

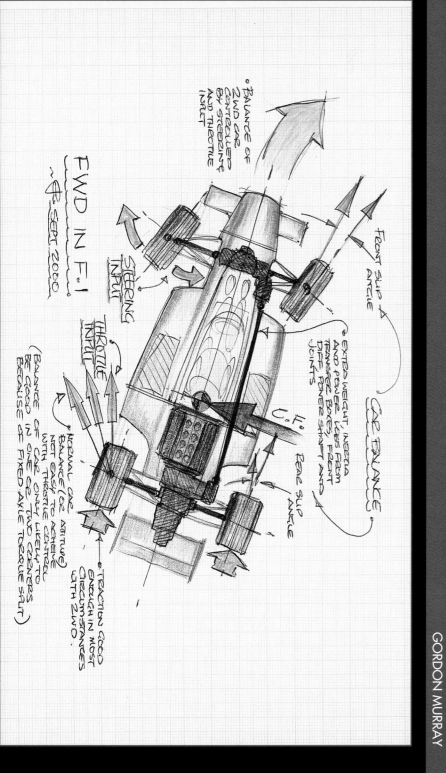

• BALANCE OF CONTROLLED 2WD CAR BY STEERING INPUT

FWD IN F.1

– GM SEPT. 2000

FRONT SLIP ANGLE

STEERING INPUT

THROTTLE INPUT

(BALANCE OF CAR ONLY LIKELY TO BE GOOD IN ONE OR TWO CORNERS BECAUSE OF FIXED AXLE TORQUE SPLIT)

• EXTRA WEIGHT, INERTIA AND POWER LOSS FROM TRANSFER BOXES, DIFF, POWER SHAFT AND JOINTS

CAR BALANCE

U.F°

REAR SLIP ANGLE

• NORMAL CAR BALANCE (OR ATTITUDE) WITH THROTTLE (OR CAR) ONLY CONTROL TO ACHIEVE BALANCE OF CAR IN 2WD.

– TRACTION GOOD ENOUGH IN MOST CIRCUMSTANCES WITH 2WD.

450 mph, handle well and fly at night. Yet they were still making racing cars which looked like they were lateral tipper trucks.

Why? Why didn't they just lower the whole thing six inches? Why didn't they try moving the propellor shafts sideways in order to lower the whole driving position? But if you take that thinking towards its logical conclusion, the most recent missed opportunity of that sort must surely be the introduction of wings in 1968.

Think about it — and that includes my generation, because although I was not yet designing F1 cars, I was at college studying engineering. Here were all these aeroplanes flying around lifting hundreds of tons into the air, harnessing basic laws of physics which had been around forever. So why the hell did it take until 1968 for anybody to think that if you turned a wing upside-down it would generate downforce?

The evolution of wings in 1969 was, in my view, well over-due, particularly as Michael May's hill-climb Porsche in the 1950s experimented with an aerofoil to generate downforce. Wings were not debatable or optional, such as a discussion about whether to have a five- or six-speed gearbox. It was a case of you are going

to go quicker. Low increase in lateral mass and lots of vertical downforce equal higher cornering speed. Somebody studying first level mathematics could tell you that. You just had to have it.

By contrast, four-wheel-drive was one of those panic attacks which periodically afflict F1 designers. We fell into a similar trap at Brabham in 1976 when Bernie and I decided we had to have a 12-cylinder engine rather than a V8. It wasn't the case — and the four-wheel-drives fell into that category.

The Ferguson P99, which Stirling Moss used to win the 1961 Oulton Park Gold Cup in the rain, looked promising enough. But four-wheel-drive with those skinny little tyres was probably not such a bad thing, particularly at a time when most F1 cars were heavier than they needed to be and designers were hardly battling for tenths of a second a lap.

But four-wheel-drive with late-'60s F1 technology — and without sophisticated mechanisms such as computer-controlled differentials which are used by today's top rally cars — was an absolute non-starter. Forget the extra weight and the horsepower the systems were absorbing, with the technology available at the time it was never going to work.

The cars were only ever going to be properly balanced, with a fixed torque split, on one corner each lap. The rest of the time the car was not going to be any-where near properly balanced.

Under-car ground-effect aerodynamics were a bit different, of course. That phenomenon was there, but nobody really understood it properly. But generally the failure of people getting to grips with the basic laws of physics really struck me as remarkable, even when I was a kid growing up.

Of course, there is a second point to consider. If you look at cars like the HWM, Cooper-Bristol or the Gordini in the early 1950s, all you are seeing, in effect, is a slightly lower ERA, if you like. They had no sophisticated thinking or tech-nology behind them. All pretty basic stuff.

To some extent I think the 1950s suffered from the eco-nomic after-effects of the war in that there was, understand-ably, a shortage of materials and people had to make do with what they'd got. Even so, the lack of sophistication in terms of suspension geometry and the torsional rigidity of the chassis seems to have evaded a remark-able number of people. Chassis, in particular, seemed to be re-garded as little more than

lumps of tube in which to in-stall the engines.

The flip side of this were cars like the Mercedes-Benz W196, very sophisticated from the en-gine viewpoint with desmod-romic valvegear and its chassis was a very early, almost pure ex-ample of the spaceframe. It also had inboard brakes and arguably the only mistake was the choice of geometry for the rear axle, even though it was a low pivot-point swing-axle set-up it must have been quite a handful for the drivers in some conditions.

On a personal note, I have al-ways regarded the 1955 Lancia D50 as one of the prettiest grand prix cars of all time. It was also quite clever in its layout and, in a sense, probably embod-ies all three elements of my feel-ings about cars of that era.

The basic car was still quite crudely made, although it had quite a sophisticated engine and its designers certainly dis-played a sense of innovation with the fuel tanks positioned in streamlined pods between the wheels, but it totally ig-nored the laws of physics, the polar moment of inertia.

They took the fuel out of the tail, eliminating the axle weight change from full to empty tanks, but replaced it with a ra-dial polar moment of inertia monstrously as wide as you can

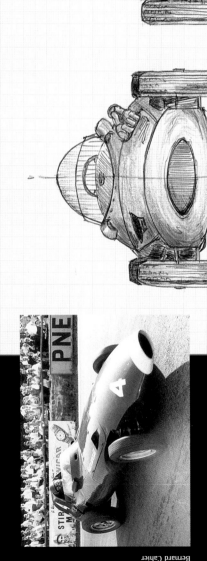

Above: Tony Brooks takes the Vanwall to victory at the 1958 Belgian Grand Prix.

VANWALL VERSUS LOTUS 16 ~ FRONTAL AREA & CDA!
— Sep 2000

50 YEARS OF F1 CAR DESIGN

get it. This also ensured that the handling and responsiveness of the car would change quite dramatically as the fuel load was used up.

Another key car from that era which caught my attention was the aerodynamic, Frank Costin-designed Vanwall which first appeared in 1956. I was ten years old at the time and, as I say, already paying very strong attention to racing cars. When I first saw a photograph of the Vanwall I remember being impressed with how fantastic it looked and that somebody had obviously paid a lot of attention to its aerodynamics.

But I also found myself thinking – strangely, you might think – that the driver's head was too small! It was only when I saw another photograph of the Vanwall standing alongside another car that I realised it was 120 per cent scale.

That car should have been significantly smaller, in my view. I thought that then and I still think that now. But the truth is that the aerodynamics of most of the other cars at the time were probably so bad, that even though the Vanwall had a bigger frontal area, its total aerodynamic efficiency was much better than that of other cars.

Nevertheless, the Vanwall was one of the first really serious attempts to make an aerodynamically efficient grand prix car. But one of my favourite cars of all time also came from that period, the Lotus 16 – which is pre-cisely what the Vanwall *ought* to have been.

The Lotus 16 is a mini-Vanwall, incorporating exactly the same aerodynamic principles, but with the driver positioned much lower with the propellor shaft positioned to one side and the 'legs splayed' driving position.

Of course, the advent of the mid-engined cars in my view changed the whole emphasis of post-war grand prix engineering. Up to that point there was a distinct shortage of lateral thinking and most of the really bright engineers were channelled into the area of engine development rather than thinking about how to make really innovative progress on the chassis side. The driver and fuel were almost inconveniences in the design process.

Of course, once the mid-engined era started and you had brains like Cooper and Chapman tackling F1, then things changed very rapidly.

Getting an accurate perspective on the mid-engined revolution is perhaps a little more complicated. From one viewpoint, you're bound to ask why it took as long as it did since, once again, we're back to the basic laws of physics.

With the skinny tyres they had in the late 1950s, it's easy to say in retrospect that, given the height of the car and the weight transfer under acceleration, you would need more than 50 per cent of its weight on the rear wheels. If the car is in a steady-state corner, the moment you have more power than the tyre's contact patch can handle you need aggressively more weight on the back axle.

I think people did consider it again after the hugely powerful pre-war Auto Unions, but there was still an 'old wives' tale' doing the rounds which worried me even as late as 1973 when I was designing the Brabham BT42. This ran to the effect that if you put the driver too close to the front axle, he will never feel the rear end of the car breaking away and he will never be able to react quickly enough to drive the car as close to the limit as he needs to.

It was such a prevalent story, that the first time I shifted the driver forward and loaded a lot of fuel between him and the engine, when I looked at a side view of the car I was really worried. Of course, now we know it is absolute bullshit, but it was certainly worrying at the time.

There was another major commercial challenge to be surmounted by the relatively small teams who were competing in F1 at the time. This was the issue of obtaining, or developing, a transaxle which was a huge outlay for a smaller team. The only surprise to me was the fact that Ferrari was not the first to produce a mid-engined car. They were making their own powertrains, had total control over their programmes and were making things quite quickly and efficiently. By contrast, Cooper was a tiny concern.

Cooper dominated the 1959 and '60 World Championships, after which the technical baton was taken up to a large extent by Colin Chapman and Lotus. John and Charles Cooper, and Chapman, were all innovators, but they were innovators in different ways.

Chapman was an original thinker, but if he didn't have a new idea, he had the capacity to take existing ideas to fresh levels of achievement. In the early 1960s that was the case with mid-engined technology and the philosophy remains the same in F1 to this day. There are some teams which copy an existing idea, others which take an idea and make it one hell of a lot better.

Frank Williams's team in the late 1970s provided a very good example of this. Previously, Williams had perhaps not been so commercially stable with the result that their philosophy was rather 'let's see what's fast and copy it.' Then they evolved to the point where they could say 'well, that's a good idea, but we'll put a lot more thought into it and make it better.' And that is what they did with the FW07 in 1979, developing the ground-effect technology pioneered by the Lotus 79 and making it a whole lot better.

It's also worth mentioning that the 1970s saw the commercial tempo of grand pri-

racing pick up pace quite dramatically. As that decade progressed there would be more
finance available and this would
release more funds for technical
development.

From the standpoint of my
personal career, I was fortunate
that I took over as Chief Designer at Brabham when Bernie
Ecclestone bought the company
in 1972. To be honest, Bernie
made the right decision, he really did, with his approach to
our new cars.

I inherited a real scrappy
hotch-potch of cars, a bit like
leftovers from the war. We were
still trying to run the Brabham
BT33, 34 and 37 throughout
1972, on virtually no money for
development and with virtually
no spares. It was chaos.

Bernie then said 'O.K., you
can design a totally new car,
but I don't want to use a single
component from any of these
cars. I want something completely new.' And we produced
the BT42.

It was the turning point for
my career, a major decision to
start with a clean-sheet approach and put all those leftovers in the bin. And in those
days, of course, I literally did
all the work, as did the Chief
Designers at many of the F1
teams.

This leads me to another area
of major change. Today, there is
no such thing as a racing car
designer in F1 any longer, there
are Technical Directors. Up until
1978 at Brabham, when I recruited David North, I knew I
was a racing car designer because there was nobody else in
the office – even if you turned
round very quickly!

So from 1973 to '78 I worked
totally on my own. I drew the
entire cars, made copies of the
drawings, took them down to

Below centre: Carlos Reutemann in the Brabham BT44B winning the 1975 German Grand Prix.
LAT Photographic

the workshops and gave them to
the guys to make the bits.

I drew everything: gearboxes,
engine installations, wings,
monocoques, suspensions,
brakes, whatever. And at Brabham we tended to make much
more of our own stuff, modify-
ing components such as off-
the-shelf Hewland gearboxes to
include dry-sump systems, for
example.

Today I look back and think
'how on earth did I do all that?'
because I was also running the
company from a technical
standpoint.

I did every test, every gran
prix, and I was probably the las
designer – stupidly, in retro
spect – to engineer both car
because I didn't trust anothe
engineer to talk to the drivers.

Nowadays, if you asked
Technical Director to draw
complete car there would be n

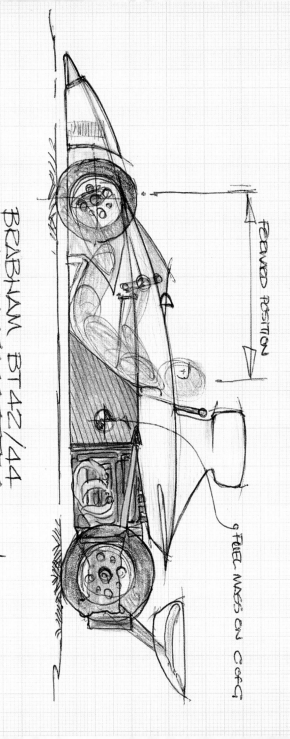

BRABHAM BT 42/44
FORWARD DRIVER POSITION

FORWARD POSITION

FUEL MASSES ON C of G

GORDON MURRAY

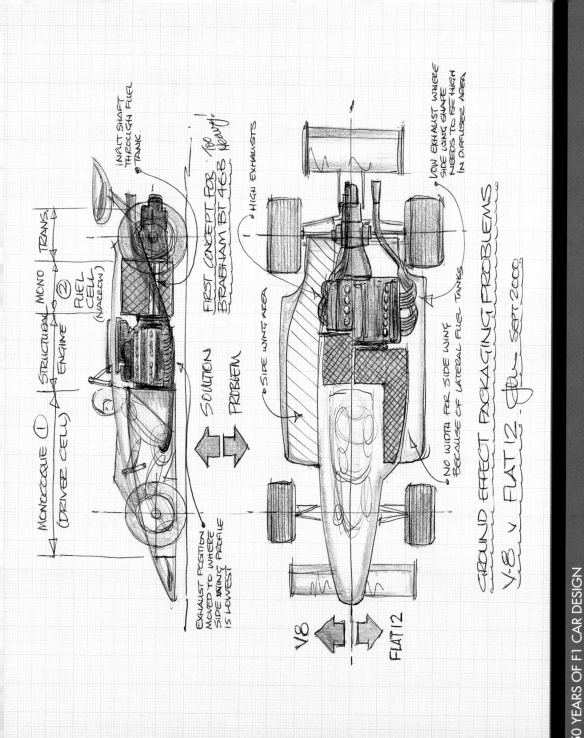

...ay they could do it. They just ...on't have the knowledge, just ...s I would not have the knowl-edge to write a software pro-gram to control an electronic gearbox, because I didn't grow up with it. But apart from that, if you locked me in a room, I would be able to design a complete car.

Interestingly, these design horizons are also getting wider and wider in contemporary F1 to the point where the role of a Technical Director will eventu-ally die out. Eventually, when the Adrian Neweys and Patrick Heads die out — as the Gordon Murrays and Mauro Forghieris already have — where will you find an F1 Technical Director who knows every aspect of how a grand prix car goes together? The teams will have to find an-other system.

Returning to the Brabham theme brings me to the ques-tion of engine development which, in many ways, was my first love. From 1972 to '75 all the Brabhams I designed were powered by Cosworth DFV V8s and I think it is important to record that the arrival of the DFV back in 1967 was every bit as significant as the move to central-engined chassis.

It was the first time that any-body had thought about a properly integrated F1 engine. Its obvious benefits went way beyond simply being a compact engine which could be used as a stressed member. The DFV changed the face of grand prix racing because suddenly here was a power unit available to a designer which worked reliably, they knew how to mount it and which fuel and electrical sys-tem could be used and — to-gether with the Hewland gearbox — offered an instantly installable package.

Suddenly the chassis design-ers found themselves in a posi-tion where they could focus maximum innovation on the rest of the car. The DFV period was unkindly called the 'kit car' period in F1 history, because almost everybody used the same engine, but I regard it as the complete opposite.

This made the cars far more di-verse and far more interesting, because people were now able to concentrate their time, effort and money on chassis development. So it was a massive — and very positive — turning point in F1 history. All the brain power sud-denly switched from the engines to the chassis.

Of course, by 1976 we got to the point where the DFV was reaching a performance ceiling, so we switched to the Alfa Romeo flat-12 engine. As I said, a bit of a panic attack!

Once we'd got over the chal-lenge of switching engines, the next challenge was to accom-modate ground-effect aerody-namics. By 1976 we were just latching onto it, but when we had a bloody great 12-cylinder engine taking up all the poten-tial venturi area at the side of the car, we were stuffed.

To get round this I did actually draw a car with two monocoqu... — the Brabham BT46B. The fir... monocoque contained the drive... and front suspension, with th... engine attached to the back o... that, then a second monocoqu... carrying the fuel tank with... tube carrying the input shaf... through to the centre of th... tank to the gearbox bolted t... the back of it. I didn't really g... very far with it, because it soo... emerged that it was going to b... 35 kg overweight. But it wa... something I considered.

Ultimately we did the Brab... ham BT46B 'fan car' as an in... terim programme, which Nik... Lauda used to win the 197... Swedish Grand Prix, but I tol... Bernie the only long-term wa... of getting around the ground-... effect question was letting Alf... Romeo loose on a V12. The... duly did that for 1979, bu... eventually the unreliability wa... so bad that it was a relief to ge... back to Cosworth DFV power... which we did towards the end...

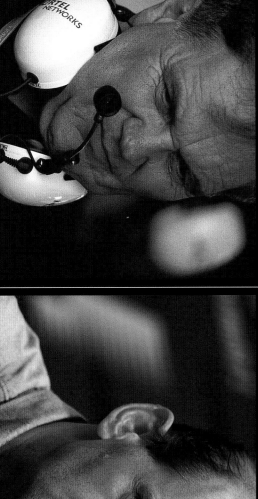

I am sure that Brabham would have won another couple of World Championships in the 1970s if we hadn't switched to the Alfa Romeo flat-12s in 1976. That said, I'm glad we went through the partnership with Alfa Romeo because it was character-building for me as a designer and for Brabham as a team.

Today, of course, the F1 engine rules are very specific. But in the early 1970s there were several options you could take, never mind just cylinder configurations. I got quite a long way down the road towards doing a gas turbine-engined car powered by a helicopter engine.

I flew to Van Doorn transmissions in Holland to look at a steel-belted, infinitely variable transmission, but since the most powerful road car using their transmissions at the time was the DAF road car with 45 bhp — and I was considering an engine with a shaft horsepower of 650 bhp when the DFV was giving 450 bhp — I went back and scrapped the idea.

In reality, of course, this diversity of engine choice in those days — four-stroke, two-stroke, gas turbine, supercharged, turbocharged — sounds romantic from a designer's viewpoint, but it's actually misplaced. The engineering and financial resources required to build an F1 engine are simply enormous when compared with the chassis.

So if some outsider came along with a competitive two-stroke, you'd effectively be consigning several million dollars of investment and dump it in the bin. That said, I think the FIA's decision to ban V12 configurations and only permit V10s is certainly going a step too far.

One of the elements which made F1 engine technology so fascinating in the late 1970s and early 1980s was the harnessing of turbocharged engine technology. When the equivalency rules were introduced at 2:1 they were written with supercharging in mind, with all its downside in terms of mechanical efficiency and heat dissipation problems.

When Renault came up with exhaust-driven turbochargers in 1977 it was painfully obvious that the equivalency was way out of bed. The only problems were throttle lag and a slight weight handicap, so in my view the equivalency should have been 3:1. Had it been, then I doubt anybody would have pursued that route. The rule makers should have spotted turbochargers coming.

Although the turbo era was pretty silly in some ways, it was pretty bloody entertaining. Being a designer in the days of the Brabham-BMW turbo was a bit like being in a war. You just had to find more power, more boost, more traction by the next race meeting to keep competitive.

The four-cylinder BMW turbo, which powered Nelson Piquet to the 1983 World Championship was a terrific little engine. BMW was a fantastically innovative partner and I had a great three-way relationship with Nelson and their Chief Engineer Paul Rosche. It was a case of 'well, what can we try next?' and we would just get on and do it.

Unlike Renault, for example, BMW was small, agile and responsive. If we agreed we wanted a new tweak, Paul would just go off and make it.

There was also the matter of refuelling stops, which we re-introduced to F1 in 1982. Throughout the 1960s and '70s nobody had given any consideration to the possibility of refuelling stops being used as a tactical weapon and it's perhaps a little difficult to believe that our strategy started almost as a bit of a joke.

We'd been bandying the idea about — 'why don't we start light and

Right: Gordon, Paul Rosche *(centre)* and Nelson Piquet.

Below right: Gordon at the front of the Brabham as the team practise a pit stop in 1984.

Both photographs: Paul–Henri Cahier

make a pit stop?' – round the office for some months. It was a fairly easy sum to do, working out whether the idea was worthwhile, because we knew how long a fresh set of tyres would be effective and, indeed, how much you would lose in the three laps involved – that's to say one lap slowing down, the time in the pits and the speeding up again.

So in the middle of the season we equipped one of the Brabham BT50s with all the necessary gear, including the air jacking system, and went to test at Donington Park in secret. We came to the conclusion that we had to do the whole slowing-down, speeding-up process – including the stop itself – in under 40 seconds. The first time we practised it, with Nelson coming into the pits very slowly indeed, we lost only 26 seconds. So we knew we were O.K.

We used refuelling to great effect through to the end of 1983, when Nelson won his second championship in a Brabham–BMW turbo, and then it was banned. Not until 1994 was refuelling reintroduced, but this time round I think it has been used simply as a marketing strategy intended to inject a few more possibilities into the races which would otherwise potentially be processions. But I think that the television viewers have now got used to refuelling stops and I think F1 needs them until it develops some other means of being livened up.

Yet if I have a criticism about F1 today, then I would have to say that there is too much control over the chassis regulations. The regulations effectively take the 'major mass' decision, let's call it, for you. Building a racing car is all about placing major masses – and if you want to encourage lateral thinking, and build a different car, you have to package the car differently. If you don't, then you produce a car like the guy's next door.

The F1 rules at the moment dictate the major masses in a specific place by a matter of centimetres. The aerodynamics and bodywork rules also pretty well design the outer bodywork. Being competitive in the first decade of the new millennium is now mainly down to being a lot more organised as a team, being able to do things quickly and accurately and operate the car reliably and efficiently.

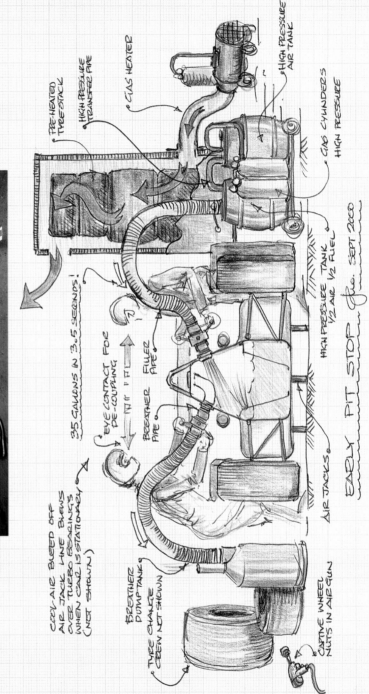

CROWN JEWEL

Clutch shown actual size

Every leading F1 contender races with an

AP Racing clutch. Competitors come and go

but every champion for the last 33 years has

relied on one. Our latest F1 Carbon/Carbon

clutch pictured here is less than 4 inches in

diameter yet can handle the energy of an

F1 start. Our brakes have also

had their share of successes, winning

8 of the last 10 World

championships. The level of

technology and service that makes this

possible is available for all forms of

motorsport and high performance road cars.

AP Racing, Wheler Road, Coventry, CV3 4LB, England   Tel +44 (0)24 7663 9595 Fax +44 (0)24 7663 9559   email: sales@apracing.co.uk

website: www.apracing.com

SLICK AND GROOVY

TYRES • 50 YEARS OF DEVELOPMENT

Above: Tyre testing at Silverstone 50 years ago. Dunlop's H.R. Fletcher and D.W. Badger, replete with trilby hats and leather gloves, inspect an R1 diamond-treaded tyre. Driver Reg Parnell *(left)* busies himself with his Maserati.
LAT Photographic

Right: Dunlop were the sole tyre suppliers for much of the 1.5-litre era between 1961–1965. Here a competition tyre is tested on a rig.
LAT Photographic

by Alan Henry

Far left: Grooves were introduced to modern F1 tyres in 1998 in an attempt to reduce speeds.

Left: Michelin brought radial construction techniques into grand prix racing in 1977 and their tyres were highly successful until the company's withdrawal in 1984. In 2001 the French giant returns to F1.

Below left: The Goodyear slick tyre which held sway in Formula 1 for the best part of two decades.

Photographs: Paul-Henri Cahier

TYRE development has been one of the key cornerstones of the F1 technical story throughout the past 50 years. The business which centres round that tiny contact patch between rolling rubber and abrasive tarmac is undoubtedly the crucial area in which the biggest single performance advantage can be achieved. Yet at the same time the involvement of the major tyre companies also brought with it a distinct political dimension which endures to this very day.

Whereas unfettered technological development was permitted for much of the history of the FIA Formula 1 World Championship, more recently tyres have come to be regarded as an area where a major brake can be applied to car performance. It is a far cry from the halcyon days of the mid-1960s when tyre widths expanded almost by the race and the early 1970s when Goodyear introduced slicks to F1 for the first time.

Pirelli dominated F1 from the start of 1950, although Firestone was technically in on the World Championship ground floor thanks to the anomalous situation whereby the Indy 500 was included as a round of the title chase up until 1960. There was never any serious cross-fertilisation between the two categories, but Firestone reigned supreme during this period at this most famous of all U.S. oval races.

Until the start of 1952 Pirelli held sway, after which Ferrari hedged its bets and also began sampling Englebert products, Ascari winning the '52 Belgian GP on those tyres to start a run of ten victories on the Belgian rubber which would end with Peter Collins's British GP win in 1958.

Meanwhile Continental arrived on the scene in 1954 with the works Mercedes-Benz team and the Silver Arrows scored all their F1 victories on its products through to the company's withdrawal from the World Championship at the end of 1955. Continental would score their tenth, and last grand prix win courtesy of Stirling Moss's historic efforts in Rob Walker's tiny Cooper-Climax in the 1958 Argentine Grand Prix.

The mid-1950s saw two tyre developments which would have profound effects on the F1 business. In 1957 Tony Vandervell's Vanwall team switched from Pirelli to Dunlop rubber and, in the U.S.A., Goodyear appeared in the stock car racing arena and quickly established itself as a competitive force. It would be a trailer for the American company to make a serious F1 challenge during the following decade.

By the end of the 1958 Dunlop would take over as F1's sole tyre supplier. They were loyal and popular supporters of grand prix racing through to the mid-1960s when the pressure really began to intensify with the arrival on the scene of two brash American newcomers.

Prior to this, Goodyear also made a preliminary foray, almost unnoticed, onto the grand prix scene. In 1960, Lance Reventlow, the millionaire son of Woolworth heiress Barbara Hutton, used Akron's rubber for his lavishly over-ambitious F1 foray to Europe. Disappointingly, his front-engined Scarabs were a year or so behind the times. The rear-engined F1 revolution was in full swing and the cars proved to be a failure.

In 1964, Goodyear established its international racing division in Wolverhampton, Great Britain, from where an intensive programme of F1 competition would be sustained for the next two decades. In 1965, Goodyear struck up a partnership with both the Brabham and Honda F1 teams, Richie Ginther posting Akron's maiden grand prix victory at Mexico City in what was the final race of the 1.5-litre Formula 1.

In 1966, Goodyear's F1 contracts were signed with Gurney's new Eagle team, in addition to Brabham, but it was Jack Brabham who dominated the season, winning the French, British, Dutch and German Grands Prix to give Goodyear its first F1 World Championship. It was a success repeated the following year by Brabham's team-mate Denny Hulme, a new range of massive, square-shouldered tyres now providing the vital interface between car and track surface.

By the end of the 1966 season the tyre scoreboard was Dunlop two wins, Firestone three and Goodyear four. The run of the tide by now was firmly against Dunlop whose small racing department was rapidly being overtaken by the massive financial and technical resources that the American giants were prepared to deploy in F1.

Moreover, the sudden arrival of three tyre companies where previously there had only been one had far-reaching consequences, not only for the tyre technicians but also for the team managers. Commercial clout was now so unyielding in those days, for although the tyre companies' commercial managers could be seen going grey as their carefully prepared contracts were ignored, nobody intervened to prevent comparative testing on rivals' products.

This was demonstrated at the 1969 Dutch Grand Prix, where the Ferrari

Below: When do grooves become slicks?
The partial wear on these Bridgestones
highlight the problems in waiting for the
scrutineers in 2001.

team tested both Goodyear and Firestone rubber against Dunlop and eventually raced on Firestone tyres even though they had a contract with Dunlop. It is a scenario which would be impossible to imagine in the first season of the new millennium.

Ironically, the 1969 season would be Dunlop's best with Jackie Stewart romping to his first World Championship title on the British tyre maker's products at the wheel of Ken Tyrrell's Matra-Ford. Unfortunately by the end of 1970 Dunlop concluded it could no longer afford the huge investment involved in F1 and withdrew from the sport.

As a direct result, for the 1971 season, Goodyear's international sporting image went up a gear when it entered into a partnership with Jackie Stewart and the Tyrrell team. Stewart's relationship with Goodyear, from both a promotional and technical development standpoint, lasted for more than two decades after his retirement from racing at the end of the 1973 season.

It set the tone for the company's future partnerships with front-line F1 drivers and teams over the years that followed, underpinning a level of support for the FIA Formula 1 World Championship in general which displayed an unwavering consistency of commitment.

Goodyear was also the first company to introduce slick-treaded tyres into F1, these new covers making their debut in the 1971 French Grand Prix at Paul Ricard, a race won by Jackie Stewart's Tyrrell on his way to his first World Championship title achieved on Goodyear rubber. He would repeat this title success in 1973 before retiring from the cockpit.

Despite a brief hiatus in 1981 caused by the political problems between the FIA and Formula One Constructors' Association, Goodyear became the sport's most loyal and consistent tyre supplier. By the time they withdrew from F1 at the end of 1998, they had scored 368 grand prix victories.

This was more than the combined total of every other tyre company who'd ever competed in F1 during the course of the official World Championship. Dunlop was next on 83 wins followed by Michelin (59), Firestone (49), Bridgestone and Pirelli (42) and Continental and Engelbert (10).

Michelin brought radial construction techniques into the arena in 1977 and there was vigorous rivalry between the French company and Goodyear, who only adopted radial F1 tyres across the board as late as 1984, which lasted through until Michelin's withdrawal at the end of 1984. In 2001

Michelin is set to resume its F1 involvement, going head-to-head with Bridgestone which has been the category's sole supplier since the withdrawal of Goodyear at the end of the 1998 season.

Commercial pressures were the main reason behind Goodyear's decision to quit, although it had disagreed with the FIA's decision to introduce grooved dry-weather tyres in an effort to reduce lap speeds. For that season the front tyres had three grooves and the rears four, while for 1999 the front tyres also had four grooves.

'Controlling speed by reducing downforce was the method which had been used for 30 years up to last year,' insisted FIA President Max Mosley, 'and it has been completely unsuccessful. Putting grooves in the tyres has contained speeds for the first time ever.

'I believe that the way forward is to reduce grip without reducing engine power so the cars will become more difficult to drive and that will enhance the difference between the best drivers and the less good.'

Three seasons into the grooved tyre regulations it remains debatable whether the grooved tyres have achieved their purpose. Certainly there are potential problems in terms of interpreting just how much the tread

pattern is permitted to wear away during the course of a race, transforming what had started out as a grooved tyre into what amounts to a slick – although opinions vary as to how much additional grip this offers.

Michelin has already indicated that it is seriously considering lodging official protests at any Bridgestone-shod car which finishes a race in 2001 with its tyre worn so badly that the tread pattern has effectively vanished.

For its part, Bridgestone seems satisfied that the rules will remain the same next year. 'We are pleased with this decision as it will help to maintain costs at the same level, although due to competition, our research and development costs will increase,' said Hiroshi Yasukawa, Bridgestone's Motorsport Director.

'This holds true, not only for us and our logistical and new tyre development costs, but also for our teams. We can see that the performance gap between the front and back rows has closed up considerably in 2000, which contributes to more exciting racing.

'With any rule change, it is always the bigger teams who get the benefit, as they have the means to adapt quickly to any changes. The status quo is good for the teams, the sport and for us.'

BAR: A COMING OF AGE

BEARING in mind British American Racing's season-ending position at the bottom of the 1999 World Constructors' Championship standings, there was really nowhere for the Brackley-based organisation to go but up in 2000. That, it transpired, was exactly what the team did, moving into fifth place in the championship at the penultimate grand prix of the year and having a very real chance of stealing fourth at the final race, in Malaysia. In the end, it wasn't to be, but in the space of a season, BAR had made its point: it was a team to be taken seriously.

After the disappointment of its first season in the sport, BAR's likely performance in its sophomore year was very much an unknown quantity. The biggest problem for BAR in 1999 had been a lack of mechanical reliability, the team's star driver, former World Champion, Jacques Villeneuve, not even finishing a grand prix until the 12th race of the 17-event schedule. When it was running, though, the BAR 01 had shown real flashes of speed on occasion, clearly indicating there was potential present.

British American Racing effectively 'went to ground' after the end of its first season, and when the team re-emerged in early January, at the official launch in London, it was visually a very different-looking organisation that appeared. Gone was the previous year's controversial 'split livery' that had appeared on the team's cars and uniforms, to be replaced by an altogether more corporate white and silver paint scheme featuring the distinctive Lucky Strike bull's-eye logo.

Also missing were the over-confident predictions about race performance that had set the team up as a prime target for media criticism when it failed to deliver. The language at the unveiling of the BAR-Honda 002 was notably circumspect and statements to the media decidedly low-key. The clear impression conveyed to the assembled motor sport media was that the cocky new boys in the Formula 1 'class' the previous year had taken their licks, learned their lesson, and were going to let any talking be done on the track in 2000.

Without doubt, the most significant development for British American Racing in 2000 was the arrival of Honda as official engine supplier and exclusive technical partner. The Japanese company has a proud and highly successful history in the sport — it celebrated its 200th Formula 1 start at this year's Italian Grand Prix — and the surprise decision, announced in May of the previous year, to tie up with BAR was a major boost for the young team.

The arrangement would see Honda supply its new RA000E V10 engine to BAR and also become involved in a joint test and development programme with the team, extending to such aspects of Formula 1 technology as suspension design, aerodynamics and advanced chassis control systems.

An important new weapon in the team's technical armoury arrived with the opening of the new wind tunnel. The commissioning process for the open-jet, moving-ground tunnel was completed on February 7, the facility providing a significant resource for the team in its continuing drive to be as self-sufficient as possible in terms of technological development and manufacturing.

To the great relief of all concerned, BAR emphatically laid the ghost of 1999 to rest at the very first grand prix of the new season, in Australia, when Jacques Villeneuve flashed across the finish line in fourth place. Adding to the team's collective joy, Ricardo Zonta was promoted to sixth place, and the final points-scoring position, after Mika Salo's Sauber was excluded from the results for a technical infringement.

But had the result been just a flash in the pan? Any chance of the team getting carried away on a wave of ill-founded optimism was snuffed out only two weeks later, in Brazil, when Villeneuve failed to finish and Zonta could only manage tenth, both BAR002s suffering gearbox maladies.

There was another points finish for the hard-charging Villeneuve at the first European round of the season, the San Marino Grand Prix, the F1 paddock's most dedicated non-conformist celebrating his 29th birthday in fine style by taking the chequered flag in fifth place. Zonta also ran well, climbing as high as sixth before a broken exhaust affected his car's performance. He eventually finished 12th. The team then experienced a distinct fallow spell, which effectively lasted through until the Monaco Grand Prix.

The next race — Canadian-born Villeneuve's 'home' event in Montreal — yielded only an eighth-place finish for Zonta. In terms of on-track performance, however, the situation looked to have improved significantly, Villeneuve qualifying sixth and Zonta eighth, with both men then running in top-six positions for much of the race.

With the benefit of hindsight, it seems clear that Canada did mark a watershed for the BAR team, its drivers rattling off seven points-scoring finishes between them in the remaining nine races and generally performing well in qualifying. But 'We knew that the basics of the

HONDA RETURNS TO THE FORMULA 1 FRAY — BUT WHY?

W HEN Honda announced in May of 1999 that it was to return to Formula 1 as official engine supplier and exclusive technical partner to British American Racing, there were more than a few raised eyebrows to be seen in the grand prix paddock. This was partly down to the fact that the Japanese motor manufacturing giant's choice of partner — BAR was the youngest and least experienced team on the grid, and was also having a nightmare first season in the sport — but also because Honda had enjoyed two previous successful spells in the sport. In the most recent, between 1983 and 1992, the company's engines effectively dominated Formula 1.

Why, then, having proven their technical capabilities beyond a shadow of a doubt in the world's toughest motor racing arena, would Honda want to return to the fray?

Realistically, it had nothing to prove and everything to lose.

The answer to that one came in a surprisingly non-corporate reply to a media question posed to Honda's F1 Project Leader, Takefumi Hosaka, during the BAR 2000 team launch in London, last January. His response, 'Just because Honda loves racing,' was delivered with obvious feeling and elicited a spontaneous round of applause from the normally blasé Formula 1 media. Honda marketing chiefs obviously quite liked it as well, since the phrase 'We love racing' began to feature on much of the company's motor sport press material later in the year.

In fact, there were a couple of other, more tangible benefits for Honda as far as a return to Formula 1 was concerned. Firstly, with the global motor manufacturing industry in as competitive a state as it has ever been, the exposure and prestige attached to competing — and winning — at the top level of motor sport yet again would do the company's international image no harm at all.

Secondly, Hosaka, who also heads up Honda's all-important R&D division, was determined that the advanced work carried out on race engine design would complement the company's future production car technology. Such developments as hybrid and advanced diesel engines look increasingly like the way forward for the road car power units of the future, and although current Formula 1 engines are not directly related, exposure to such 'leading-edge' engineering could provide useful technological cross-over.

In addition, the concept of attracting and 'case-hardening' the best young engineers by immersing them in Formula 1 for a limited time has long been a Honda 'Holy Grail', dating back to the company's original involvement in the sport, in 1963. 'It was always the intention to use the Formula 1 programme to attract the best engineers,' explained Hosaka prior to the start of the 2000 season. 'We had a huge amount of interest, both within Honda and externally, when we announced the programme. The unique challenges of Formula 1 will be extremely important in developing the minds of our young engineers.'

But there was another important dimension to Honda's standpoint was that the young, ambitious team was prepared to 'throw open' its doors so there could be a free flow of technical information between the companies' respective engineering staffs.

'We know there is a great deal more to recognise than just [engine] horsepower output,' observed Hosaka. 'Racing chassis technologies, the total management system and a thorough knowledge of the whole picture are areas in which Honda is keen to develop, and these represent a fresh challenge for our third generation in Formula 1. When we looked for a partner in F1, it was important that we could form a relationship that allowed us to accumulate this technology. We felt that British American Racing would provide us with the best opportunity and facilities to do so.'

One of the great attractions of BAR from Honda's standpoint was that the young, ambitious team was prepared to 'throw open' its doors so there could be a free flow of technical information between the companies' respective engineering staffs.

Honda engineers had been based at the BAR Operations Centre at Brackley from the beginning of the year, but the first tangible evidence of the technical co-operation between the two organisations came with the appearance of the Honda 'Athena' car at a Nogaro test in late May. As the season progressed, the chassis, a joint development between BAR and Honda, frequently ran alongside the team's two normal test chassis and provided a 'platform' for Honda engineers to put their latest ideas on Formula 1 hardware and software to the test.

Outwardly, the company's senior managers had appeared reasonably satisfied with the progress BAR was making during only its second season in the sport, but then, not for the first time, they surprised the F1 paddock. For 2001, they revealed Honda would supply the latest version of its RA000E engine to two teams: BAR and Jordan. The company, however, would retain its exclusive technology link with BAR, and that, the Brackley-based team hopes, will continue to be one of the 'aces' in its hand.

Far left: Jacques Villeneuve got BAR's 2000 campaign off to a great start with fourth place in the season's opener in Australia.

Far left, centre: Jacques and Jock Clear enjoy a joke during qualifying at Spa.

Bottom far left: Ricardo Zonta put in a number of gutsy race performances. Here he leads Ralf Schumacher and Alex Wurz in Germany.

Below left: Seventh place and no reward after a hard weekend's work at Monaco for Villeneuve.

1999 car were not too far off the mark,' explains BAR Technical Director, Malcolm Oastler. 'Our big problem was obviously reliability. We therefore concentrated on evolving the car technically for 2000, and re-designing those areas where necessary to improve reliability. In the early races this season, our car wasn't particularly quick, but we did benefit from our new-found reliability while other teams were having problems. We then had a spell of poor results, partly through bad luck and partly the result of some technical issues. We worked hard on developing the car, though, particularly in terms of the aero package, and by mid-season, you could start to see the results.

'The car was definitely a much more competitive package in the second half of the season, and our improved pace meant results were achieved on merit rather than through luck or the misfortune of others. The team definitely made good technical progress in 2000, and the lessons learned will be incorporated in next year's car.'

Motor racing is about more than just machinery, however; it is also about the human element. In the case of BAR, its driver line-up of Villeneuve and Zonta carried over from the previous season and the improved reliability of the car/engine package meant they were able to show their abilities to much greater effect. Villeneuve, as ever, demonstrated total commitment every time he was on the track. He out-qualified his less-experienced team-mate on all but two occasions and generally outraced him.

He also frequently made the best starts of any driver, rocketing away from the grid in truly electrifying fashion and thrusting himself into the thick of the action among the race leaders. Once there, he could be relied on to mount the strongest possible defence of his position, but in the early-season performances didn't have quite enough performance available to retain his place in the running order. As the BAR-Honda 002 package improved, however, Villeneuve took full advantage and was a genuine top-six contender at most circuits in the second half of the season.

High points for the feisty Canadian this year included scoring BAR's first-ever World Championship points in Australia, being a genuine podium contender at Monza, and a

potential third-place contender in the U.S. Grand Prix. He also listed his rain drives — there were quite a few of those in what was a particularly soggy F1 season — and jack-rabbit starts as aspects of the year with which he was particularly pleased. 'We had some good fights toward the end of this season and the team has done a fantastic job,' he commented after the conclusion of the Malaysian Grand Prix. 'It has been a positive year.'

Inevitably, there were also low points, notably Monaco, where the team struggled for pace, and Villeneuve, to his considerable irritation, took the chequered flag seventh, one place out of the points, as was also the case in Belgium. 'It is no consolation to finish seventh,' he observed after the Monaco Grand Prix. 'In fact, it is very frustrating to miss out on a point after the huge amount of work that goes into a race weekend.' In a way, the same could also be said of the Italian Grand Prix, for although Villeneuve ran strongly in what appeared to be a secure third place up to quarter distance, an electrical problem forced him to retire from the race.

He also missed out on a points-scoring opportunity at the Canadian Grand Prix, the result of unpredictable weather and a pit stop mix-up. Making matters even less palatable, he ended the wet race covered in embarrassment after making a hopelessly optimistic lunge at Ralf Schumacher's Williams under braking. The resulting collision eliminated Villeneuve and the hapless German from the race with only three laps remaining.

In mitigation, it was one of very few mistakes of any note that Villeneuve made all year. 'It is annoying not to be in a position to win races at the moment,' he observed late in the season, 'but I'm driving the hardest I've ever driven in the last two years, even harder than for winning the championship. I believe my skills have improved in the last two years and once we get a winning car, then that is going to be very useful.

'If you're still hungry for winning, then you'll work as hard as you can to get there. I'm still very hungry, so I haven't given up.' Villeneuve's full-on notice that Villeneuve's full-on

57

Far left: Real progress. Jacques sits in the cockpit of his car during practice at Monza with the satisfaction of a third-place grid position.

Bottom far left, centre: In a soggy season the innate speed of both drivers often shone in adverse conditions. Ricardo Zonta cuts through the spray in the European Grand Prix.

Left: The BAR002 chassis was notably more successful than its predecessor.

Below left: Jacques and Craig Pollock share a mutual trust.

JACQUES VILLENEUVE: WILL HE GO OR WILL HE STAY?

A S far as the Formula 1 media were concerned, the longest-running saga this year was undoubtedly the future of BAR's star driver, Jacques Villeneuve. Almost as soon as the season was under way, stories began to circulate to the effect that, having shocked the Formula 1 world with the news that he was moving to BAR in 1999, Villeneuve was going to depart the team at the end of the current season, frustrated by a lack of results. At various times, possible destinations included the McLaren, Ferrari, Benetton (recently purchased by Renault), Williams and Jaguar teams.

The speculation reached fever pitch around the time of the Monaco and Canadian Grands Prix, but although Villeneuve and BAR Managing Director, Craig Pollock, admitted the driver was 'considering all his options,' his final destination for 2001, and beyond, ultimately remained a mystery.

As the weeks passed, however, it gradually became clear that Villeneuve's options had come down to two choices: BAR or Benetton/Renault. The majority of the media seemed to feel the 'big-buck' blandishments of Renault Sport, with whose engines the Canadian won the world drivers' crown in 1997, would be sufficient to lure him away.

On July 24, Villeneuve once again stunned the Formula 1 world by announcing that he would be re-committing himself to BAR Honda – for a further three years! It was a bold decision, predictably criticised in some F1 circles, but reached with Jacques' usual brand of clear-headed logic.

'It was a difficult decision,' he explained, 'but I am happy to stay with the team after two years of hard work. It is rewarding to see progress and I would like to continue with the team and with that progress. It would be a shame to give up on this dream.'

Pollock, for his part, was understandably elated at the news that his star driver, and close personal friend, had decided to remain with the team. 'We are absolutely delighted with Jacques' decision and the fact that he has registered a significant vote of confidence in British American Racing,' he said. 'Jacques has been an integral part of the team since its formation two years ago, and his commitment to stay indicates that he can win races, and ultimately the World Championship, in the future.'

commitment behind the wheel is as strong as ever.

Villeneuve, then, was unquestion-ably fast, but that was not to say Zonta was slow. On the contrary, the 1997 Formula 3000 champion and 1998 FIA GT champion displayed very strong race pace at times, but often made the job more difficult for himself, and missed out on potential points-scoring opportunities, with poor qualifying performances. In fact, he didn't crack the top ten in qualifying until the Canadian Grand Prix, and only managed it on a fur-ther two occasions thereafter. Even so, the young Brazilian scored points three times and frequently turned in race lap times that were at least the equal of his team-mate.

Undoubtedly, one of Zonta's best races of the season came at Monza and, in many ways, his performance there encapsulated his two years with British American Racing: weak qualifier, strong racer, and often desperately unlucky.

He qualified a lowly 17th – Villeneuve started from the second row of the grid, in fourth place – after encountering electrical problems during qualifying and being forced to switch to the team's spare car. Zonta and the BAR Honda 002, however, were clearly a much quicker package than a number of the cars in front of them. The team therefore decided that the best approach would be to put Zonta on a two-stop strategy and start his car with a very light fuel load to give him the best possible chance of overtaking his rivals at the beginning of the race.

The strategy could have worked well, but the tragic, multi-car, opening lap crash that claimed the life of Italian fire marshal, Paolo Ghislimberti, understandably caused the Safety Car to be deployed and effectively foiled the BAR plan. Complicating matters for Zonta was the fact that he had to make an un-scheduled pit stop to replace a tyre, punctured in the first-lap mêlée. When racing eventually resumed, the Brazilian staged a charge that stunned spectators. At one stage, he scythed past 11 cars in 10 laps, in the process making a mockery of the ongoing complaints about the 'lack of overtaking' in Formula 1.

He made his two scheduled stops for fuel and tyres, both beautifully executed, and then pounded home to the chequered flag to claim sixth place and his second points finish of the season. 'I started the

race with a light fuel load in the hope that I would be able to over-take a number of cars in the open-ing laps of the race,' he explained, 'but when the Safety Car came out, we lost the opportunity. When my car was hit on the first lap and punctured a tyre, I had no choice but to come in for an extra stop. If it hadn't been for that, I would have finished right in front of Ver-stappen in the race. That would have seen Zonta claim fourth and his best-ever Formula 1 finish.

Unfortunately, motor racing is not about 'could', 'if' and 'maybe', and along with highly competitive performances from Zonta, there were also some that were less than impressive. Undoubtedly, the low point for the personable Brazilian occurred in the German Grand Prix, at Hockenheim, when what had the potential to be another double helping of World Championship points for the team came to noth-ing. This was the result of an inci-dent on lap 34, which saw Zonta's challenge for track position on his team-mate cause Villeneuve to spin out of seventh place. The Canadian recovered to finish eighth, but the incident had clearly left Zonta rat-tled and he crashed out of the race four laps later.

The post-race comments from team boss, Craig Pollock, indicated he was less than impressed by his young driver's on-track behaviour. 'The result today does not indicate the true potential of the team,' he observed icily. 'Given the conditions and our race strategy, potentially we had fifth and sixth places in sight. Unfortunately, it's never nice when there's an incident between team-mates on the track.'

Whether the incident was the cat-alyst or not, a little over two weeks later, the team announced it had signed the experienced French dri-ver, and Monaco Grand Prix win-ner, Olivier Panis, to replace Zonta in 2001. Happily, the future is not as bleak for the Brazilian as it probably appeared to be late on that Sunday afternoon in July at Hockenheim. After considering his options, which included the possibility of a move to champ car racing in the U.S. Zonta and his management team elected to sign up for a Formula 1 package with Jordan that will see him testing for the team in 2001, and racing again in 2002.

Zonta's baptism into the world of grand prix racing has undoubtedly

WANNA HAVE FUN

THE Formula 1 paddock can be a pretty intense place on race weekends, and once drivers take to the track to do battle, the tension rises to pressure-cooker levels. The members of a team like British American Racing obviously have a life outside the sport, although it is a major challenge to live that life when trying to reconcile it with the sort of non-stop, race schedule the sport has thrown at them for the last two seasons. Even so, when the opportunity for a bit of fun arises, the boys from BAR are never backward in coming forward.

Immediately before Formula 1's blue riband event, the Monaco Grand Prix, the team's title sponsor, Lucky Strike, made a pair of high-performance racing powerboats available to drivers Jacques Villeneuve *(bottom)* and Ricardo Zonta for a pre-GP blow-the-cobwebs-away blast in the waters just outside the harbour of the famous principality.

It didn't require much imagination to guess that the two dedicated 'speed junkies' who are also residents of Monaco, would jump at the offer, particularly since there was also the opportunity of some expert tuition from three-time Class One World Offshore Powerboat Champion, Steve Curtis, to help them hone their waterborne driving skills.

The Honda-powered, 21-foot hulls fairly skipped and danced over the waves, Villeneuve and Zonta quickly getting to grips with their machines. The two even performed an impromptu ballet at one point, their boats just meters apart as they moved in unison while a low-flying helicopter carrying a film crew and photographers tracked their every move.

'We were trying to have fun, jumping a few waves,' Villeneuve explained with a broad smile once back on dry land. 'It's not too difficult to drive. You just step on it and go straight, the boat flies off the waves and lands. It just depends on how scared you get, I guess. If you turn the boat over, you just swim up. No problem!' Water sports aficionado, Zonta, was in his element and explained that his experience of powerboats comes from his long-time love of water skiing. 'I have a boat in Brazil, a little like this one,' he said. 'It's nice for water-skiing, but I never really go outside the harbour. Here, you have big waves, the sea is rough, and that makes the boat quite hard to drive, but it's a good challenge.'

Both men impressed Curtis with the way they mastered the less-than-perfect sea conditions — there was a four-foot swell with a two-foot 'break on top at the time — in the relatively short spells they had at the wheel. 'I think they could both make good boat racers,' he observed. 'Most people who are involved in motor sport have a synergy with machinery — and they certainly did.

And might some time spent powerboat racing improve their skills on dry land? Well, I think it would make them better drivers in the wet... maybe,' responded Curtis, his tongue apparently caught in his cheek.

The next such diversion occurred in June, the week before the Canadian Grand Prix in Montreal, and once again had a decidedly aquatic flavour to it. Billed as a 'team-building' exercise, the plan was that Zonta and his hard-working pit crew *(above)* would shoot the raging rapids of the Ottawa River in inflatable rafts.

At the end of a sun-drenched day of almost non-stop excitement and hard physical effort, there were smiles and sunburns in equal measure, but everyone agreed that it had been the perfect tonic to set them up for the approaching race weekend.

The rush was mega,' said lead race mechanic, Darren Beacroft. The longer we spent on the river, the better we got. It's so exciting, heading into a drop with just a sheer wall of water ahead of you.'

For Mark Willis, the man who has the critical responsibility for controlling the refuelling hose during BAR pit stops, the experience had racing connotations. 'The intensity of some of the sections was just like doing a pit stop for five minutes straight,' he explained.

The team's larger-than-life Chief Mechanic, Alastair Gibson, felt the real benefit of the day spent on the water was in building team spirit. 'When you see videos of whitewater rafting, it looks awesome,' observed the lanky South African, 'but it's not half as scary as when you're in the raft. But it's also excellent for team-building. The events of today will be talked about for the rest of the year, and when we're having a tough time, working all night at a race weekend, someone will crack a joke about the whitewater rafting, and it will help get the guys through. For me, that's what today was all about.'

It was the teamwork element that had also impressed whitewater rafting expert, Luke Procher, who coached the BAR team members before they took to the rapids. 'There's certainly a lot of camaraderie and friendship involved,' he said. 'It only took the Lucky Strike guys 10 minutes to work together as a true team and watch out for each other, whereas a normal group would take half a day to get to that level. It's obvious they respect one another and are just really comfortable with each other, which is the main thing.'

Zonta, too, had clearly revelled in the experience and thoroughly enjoyed being with his mechanics outside of the normal environment of the F1 paddock. 'It's pretty physical,' he explained, 'which I enjoyed, and there's a lot to learn, too, but above all, it was good fun, especially being away from the circuit with my mechanics, yet still working as a team. They are a great bunch of guys.' And judging by the trademark toothy grin, the young Brazilian very obviously meant what he said.

been a difficult one, but he remains a popular figure with many in the paddock and will always have a special place within BAR as one of the team's two original drivers. Craig Pollock summed up the situation well after the conclusion of the final grand prix of the year, in Malaysia, when he commented, 'I'm so proud of everyone, both here and back at the factory. I would also like to thank Ricardo for his efforts today and over the last two years. We sincerely wish him all the best for a successful career with his new team.'

A modern Formula 1 team, though, is about far more than just the people who go racing every two weeks. Among the unsung heroes are the members of the test team. BAR has enjoyed the input of a permanent test team virtually from its inception and this year its schedule was at least as gruelling as the race team's. The services of Frenchman, Patrick Lemarie, were retained for 2000, while rising young British star, Darren Manning, joined the test team for his first real taste of Formula 1 life.

Both men found themselves very busy at times, particularly when the Honda Athena systems chassis became operational in May (see separate story). On occasion, the team even found itself running three cars with Villeneuve and Zonta undertaking the driving chores as well. The workload was enormous, particularly for people

like BAR Chief Engineer, Steve Farrell, who as part of his responsibilities, had to attend every race weekend and all test sessions.

'It was a mammoth undertaking, both technically and logistically, to prepare and run three cars,' he explained immediately after the conclusion of a particularly ambitious programme at Nogaro in France. 'It allowed us to conduct several different programmes concurrently, but it required a really big effort from everyone here at Nogaro and back at Brackley. We had nearly 80 people on site, such was the amount of work we wanted to get through. At the end of two hectic days, it's fair to say that we met nearly all objectives and are very happy with the overall results.'

It was also a baptism of fire for newly appointed Test Team Manager, Andrew Alsworth. Something of a veteran of the F1 paddock, 'Oz' assumed his new-found responsibilities with aplomb, and his efforts, along with those of the rest of the test group, undoubtedly contributed to the genuine strides in overall performance made by BAR during the 2000 season.

It's a fact of Formula 1 life that no team can run without the backing, financial and technical, of its sponsors and partners. It is also generally true that the more successful a team is on the track, the easier it becomes to secure new commercial backing. BAR's new-found competitiveness,

combined with Villeneuve's decision to commit to the team for a further three years, undoubtedly helped to convince new sponsors, Sonax, K-Way/Multimoda Network, World Online, Bee-Trade.com and ART (Advanced Research Technologies) to come on board in the course of 2000. Sadly, the team also lost a valued backer, the Canadian-headquartered Teleglobe organisation deciding to pull out of Formula 1 sponsorship following its acquisition by telecommunications giant, BCE.

No discussion of British American Racing's fortunes can ever ignore the ongoing political situation surrounding the organisation. This has been a high-profile team attracting considerable media attention from its inception, and the stories continued to swirl around the BAR Operations Centre and its inhabitants in 2000.

It started with the announcement in January of a re-alignment of management responsibilities within the team, followed by the appointment of Ron Meadows, formerly Factory Team Manager, to the position of Team Manager, replacing Robert Synge. Later, there were heavy testing crashes at Silverstone and Monza involving Ricardo Zonta, both of which were traced to technical problems with the car. In fairness, the team held its hand up to these immediately, but the spectacular nature of the accidents ensured they received heavy media coverage.

The longest-running story of the year, of course, involved the future plans of Jacques Villeneuve (see separate story). At various times, the 1997 World Champion was linked with at least five of the Formula 1 grid's 11 teams. As the will-he, won't-he drama was discussed and debated at length in the specialist press and on the F1 websites, though, Villeneuve, true to form, did the one thing the majority of the media hadn't anticipated: he committed to BAR... for a further three years!

Anyone lucky enough to observe the BAR team at close quarters this past season will have witnessed a skilled, confident group of people going about their business in a highly professional manner. The cars and the garage were always immaculately presented, the pit stops consistently among the fastest all year, and any problems dealt with calmly and methodically. Ignoring the 'slings and arrows' flying around them, the people who make up British American Racing came together as a team in 2000, functioning as a cohesive, well-oiled machine.

The foundations have now been put in place for the future, and although the chest-beating rhetoric of the first season may have subsided, it is clear that British American Racing collectively remains a team with burning ambition and a great hunger for success.

Photographs: Paul-Henri Cahier

FORMULA 1 REVIEW

CONTRIBUTORS

Bob Constanduros

Maurice Hamilton

Alan Henry

F1 ILLUSTRATIONS

Ian Hutchinson

Nicola Curtis

Mark Steward

1 McLAREN 2

MIKA HÄKKINEN   **DAVID COULTHARD**

THE McLaren-Mercedes team had a year to kill for, judged by the standards of most of its rivals. Yet its latest MP4/15 only won seven of the season's 17 races in the hands of Mika Häkkinen (four wins) and David Coulthard (three) so by McLaren's own high standards this represented something of a disappointment, particularly as so much effort had been expended in a quest for improved mechanical reliability over the previous winter.

Testing became more of a priority than ever at McLaren and, to this end, the team became the first in recent times to have three F1 winners on its driving strength. Supplementing regular men Mika Häkkinen and David Coulthard, who were starting their fifth-successive season paired together, the team also signed 1996 Monaco Grand Prix winner Olivier Panis as third driver.

Unquestionably, Panis's contribution to the sustained development of the evolutionary McLaren MP4/15 was one of the key factors behind the car's consistent level of competitiveness. 'It was a great benefit,' confessed Coulthard later in the season. 'We had somebody fulfilling this role whose judgement we could absolutely depend on and who was quick enough not to raise any doubts. It certainly helped us to get through a lot more work.'

That said, the new MP4/15 underwent its preliminary trials in the hands of Häkkinen while Coulthard initially continued his pre-season test work with the interim MP4/14 development chassis, both machines fitted with the latest Mercedes FO110J V10 engines.

TAG McLaren M.D. Ron Dennis said that the new car represented a logical evolution of what had gone before and that the team was more than ever committed to winning the World Championship again in 2000.

The distinctive exhaust system – with a central exit and other refinements which the team was unwilling to discuss – had been developed over the winter with all due consultation with the FIA.

'We don't anticipate any problems over legality,' said McLaren International M.D. Martin Whitmarsh at the car's launch, 'but we will obviously be interested in the view the race stewards take towards it, particularly if they are wound up by any of our rivals.' As it turned out, there was no problem.

Whitmarsh also made it clear that this was a crucial season for David Coulthard. 'It is very important for him,' he said. 'He is intelligent enough to realise that we considered other drivers for this season.

'When he is strong and performing, he is very good. What he now has to do is to take those peaks and turn them into a plateau. There is no sentimentality here, we have to have the best drivers. David has earned his position in the team and knows that this is the year to prove his capability.'

The launch of the MP4/15 also coincided with confirmation that Daimler-Chrysler had exercised its option to purchase 40 per cent of the TAG McLaren Group, an investment variously speculated as valuing the group in the region of £700 million. Simultaneously, it was also confirmed that the McLaren F1 team would continue to benefit from its Mercedes engine supply deal at least until the end of the 2004 season.

Häkkinen and Coulthard went into the first race of the season confident they had a car quick enough to do the job. That was demonstrated pretty convincingly, but the MP4/15 didn't have the initial reliability. Running first and second in the Australian GP, Häkkinen and Coulthard both succumbed to pneumatic valve seal problems on their Mercedes engines.

It was a bitter blow, for these failures handed Ferrari an easy 1-2 victory. Ilmor Engineering worked hard to ensure there was no repetition of these failures in Brazil, but again Häkkinen's car wilted with the same problem while the Finn seemed right on course for a strategically astute win on a one-stop strategy. As it was, Schumacher won again and took a third straight win at Imola where Häkkinen at last got his Championship points score off the deck with second place.

Interlagos also produced a bitter blow for Coulthard who had battled

McLAREN MP4/15-MERCEDES

Sponsors: West, Boss, Mobil 1, Loctite, Computer Associates, Schweppes, Schuco, Warsteiner, TAG Heuer, Sun, Bridgestone

Team principal: Ron Dennis **Technical director:** Adrian Newey **Team manager:** Dave Ryan **Chief mechanic:** Mike Negline

ENGINE **Type:** Mercedes-Benz FO110J **No. of cylinders (vee angle):** V10 (72°) **Sparking plugs:** NGK **Electronics:** TAG Electronic Systems **Fuel:** Mobil **Oil:** Mobil

TRANSMISSION **Gearbox:** McLaren seven-speed longitudinal semi-automatic **Driveshafts:** McLaren **Clutch:** AP Racing (hand-operated)

CHASSIS: **Front suspension:** double wishbones, pushrod **Rear suspension:** double wishbones, pushrod **Suspension dampers:** McLaren/Penske **Wheel diameter:** front: 13in.
rear: 13in. **Wheels:** Enkei **Tyres:** Bridgestone **Brake discs:** Hitco **Brake pads:** not given **Brake calipers:** AP Racing **Steering:** McLaren (power-assisted)

Radiators: not given **Fuel tanks:** ATL **Battery:** GS **Instruments:** TAG Electronic Systems

DIMENSIONS **Wheelbase:** not given **Track:** front: not given rear: not given **Formula weight:** 1322.8 lb/600 kg including driver **Fuel capacity:** not given

Mika Häkkinen just failed in his bid to clinch a third-consecutive world title.
Paul-Henri Cahier

Our Formula

David's car

Mika's car

Doctor's car

Medical car

Our Sunday drivers at a glance.

1 line-up.

FIA car

VIP car

Safety car

Driver's parade car

Mercedes-Benz
The Future of the Automobile.

S&J 001.034 MS

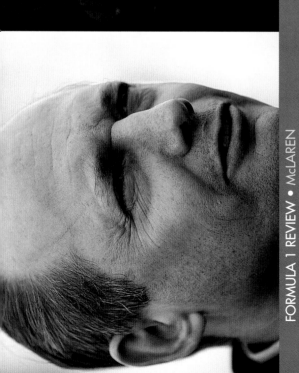

Far left: Ron Dennis was in combative mood during 2000, crossing swords with the FIA as well as taking the fight to Ferrari.

Left: Adrian Newey and his team again produced the fastest car of the field in the MP4/15.

Below: Work of art. Engine cover detail of the beautiful MP4/15.

All photographs: Paul-Henri Cahier

gearbox problems to cross the finishing line second. Unfortunately after a lengthy period of scrutineering after the race, during which Coulthard's car was examined and re-examined exhaustively by officials, the FIA technical delegate Jo Bauer concluded that the front wing of the second-place McLaren-Mercedes was 7 mm too low according to the regulations.

That left the threat of disqualification staring McLaren in the face as once Bauer's report was submitted to the stewards they could be expected to exclude the car as a matter of course. The whole episode revived memories of the exclusion of the Ferraris of Schumacher and Eddie Irvine from 1999's Malaysian Grand Prix when their aerodynamic bargeboards were found to infringe the dimensional rules.

On that occasion, Ferrari won the appeal when it was established that a 5 mm tolerance was allowed on such components in the horizontal plane, even though most F1 engineers in the pit lane believed this was an interpretation which nobody had ever previously anticipated or believed was valid. At Interlagos, however, there would be no benefit of the doubt directed towards McLaren and David was disqualified.

Yet even at this early stage of the season there was no doubt that MP4/15 was a better car than its predecessor. 'It was better in responding to [set-up] changes and more comfortable to drive on the limit,' explained Whitmarsh.

'Development was structured and routine, although there were no hugely radical technical developments during the course of the year. Routine development of the aerodynamic package, including a variety of diffusers, was part of the programme and eventually we returned to using a power steering system, not least because the drivers were saying "well, everyone else has them" even though this involved slight issues of complexity and additional weight.'

Coulthard finally gave McLaren-Mercedes its first win of the season in the British Grand Prix at Silverstone, round four of the title chase. Häkkinen then took the initiative, posting a strong second to Schumacher's Ferrari at the Nürburgring and then winning the Spanish GP ahead of Coulthard only four days after David survived the crash-landing of a chartered Learjet at Lyon Satolas airport in which both the pilots died.

David's determined run to second place in Spain heralded a golden month of achievement for the Scottish driver who, from the touchlines, seemed to have gone up a gear in terms of confidence and all-round accomplishment. He kept out of trouble to score a well-judged and precise win through the streets of Monaco and while Canada saw him picking up an unfortunate 10s stop-go penalty after his mechanics stayed on the dummy grid too long prior to the formation lap, his victory in the French GP at Magny-Cours was an absolutely top drawer performance.

Having removed the gurney flap from his rear aerofoil on the starting grid to balance out a touch of last-minute understeer, Coulthard found his McLaren-Mercedes perfectly balanced through the fast Estoril right-hander beyond the pits and was able to press home a successful onslaught on Schumacher's Ferrari. He boldly overtook the German ace and was pulling away when the Ferrari's engine failed.

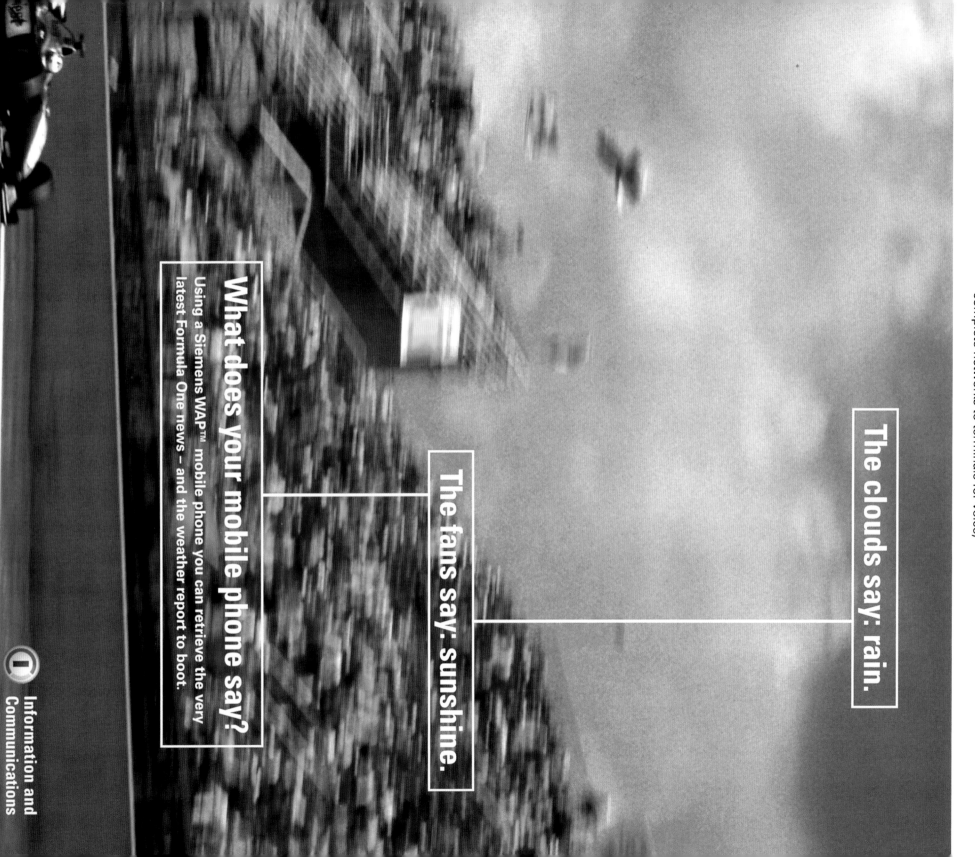

SIEMENS

www.siemens.com/f1

Our leading-edge information and
communications technology makes us
the ideal partner for everyone who sees
mobility as the key to the future. From
complete networks to terminals for voice,

data and video communication, we
are the only provider worldwide to offer
the full spectrum of mobile business
solutions from a single source.

The clouds say: rain.

The fans say: sunshine.

What does your mobile phone say?

Using a Siemens WAP™ mobile phone you can retrieve the very
latest Formula One news – and the weather report to boot.

**Information and
Communications**

Above: David Coulthard launched his championship bid by winning the British GP, and also won at Monaco and Magny-Cours before losing momentum.

Right: Big Brother is watching. McLaren jealously guards its hard-earned secrets.
Both photographs: Paul-Henri Cahier

Far right: Häkkinen and Coulthard were greatly aided during the year by test driver Olivier Panis (*centre*).
Bryn Williams/Words & Pictures

Throughout this period Häkkinen was feeling rather stressed-out, the cumulative result of the two years' endeavour involved in winning and successfully defending his 1998 World Championship. Ron Dennis would later admit that he blamed himself for not having recognised the problem and duly despatched Häkkinen on a well-deserved mid-season holiday.

On his return in Austria, Mika won commandingly and then went on to finish second at Hockenheim – where an eccentric spectator wandered onto the circuit, triggering the emergence of the safety car, something which badly disadvantaged the McLaren drivers in terms of their overall race strategies.

Häkkinen then continued to dominate the Hungarian Grand Prix and wrested the lead of the Belgian race at Spa-Francorchamps in a daringly bold display of overtaking, squeezing ahead of Michael Schumacher with

three laps to go as they both lapped Ricardo Zonta's BAR-Honda. Thereafter Ferrari took the initiative at Monza and Indianapolis, where Häkkinen was closing on Schumacher when his engine failed, and the Finn led the lion's share of the crucial Japanese Grand Prix until a rain shower tipped the outcome of the title battle in the Ferrari driver's favour.

In total McLaren won seven races, with Coulthard squandering the opportunity to make it four each after running off the road while leading in Malaysia, the resultant debris picked up in his radiator ducts overheating his engine to the point where the team had to make damaging amendments to his race strategy.

Statistically, it seemed that Coulthard was getting closer to Häkkinen with 73 World Championship points scored compared with the 89 accrued by the Finn. In reality, Häkkinen invariably showed himself to be the more

effective racer, as he has done so every year since 1996.

The McLarens also fell under the scrutiny of FIA officials again during the course of the season with Häkkinen initially excluded from his Austrian GP victory after an official paper seal was found missing from his car's electronic control box. It did not matter that it was probably the FIA who'd omitted to fit it in the first place, for it was McLaren's responsibility to ensure it was present.

The net result was a $50,000 fine and loss of the ten constructors' championship points which went with the win, but Häkkinen was permitted to retain his own points in the drivers' championship.

There was another mildly concerning issue which rumbled away behind the scenes involving a radical transmission programme which had been under joint McLaren/Mercedes development for the previous three years.

Intended for the 2001 season, its details had been shared with the FIA during its development in order to satisfy the rule makers that it complied with the regulations. After a positive initial response it appeared that the FIA had decided that this was money down the drain.

The bottom line for the McLaren-Mercedes team was that they had absolutely sustained their performance with a car/engine package which was arguably the best of the season. They did not win the World Championship, perhaps because of their firm policy of giving both drivers an absolutely equal chance until the mathematical possibilities are exhausted. But most F1 insiders continue to believe that theirs is the most fair and equitable policy. And Ron Dennis has made it clear that it won't be changing.

Alan Henry

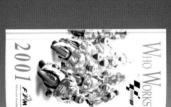

MICHAEL SCHUMACHER

RUBENS BARRICHELLO

3 FERRARI 4

FINALLY, finally. After 21 seasons and more than 340 races, Ferrari managed to win the drivers' World Championship. It was not an easy ride, made more agonising than usual by the fact that, mid-season, Michael Schumacher had a lead of 22 points. By three-quarter distance, he was several points behind. It seemed Ferrari was destined never to be free of a statistical millstone which was growing bigger and more unmanageable each year.

In the end, Schumacher wrapped up the title at the penultimate round. That epic weekend in Japan would sum up Ferrari better than any of the drama which had taken place in the previous 15 races. At Suzuka, Ferrari and McLaren were incredibly closely matched. That was the truth of a season in which, for the first time, Ferrari produced a car which had the measure of the silver-grey machine. The F1-2000 was a totally new package, using a revised V10 engine with a V-angle increased from 80° to 90°, allowing the technical team, led for the fourth

year by Ross Brawn, to lower the car's centre of gravity and substantially improve its aerodynamics.

'I think we've probably had the best car we have ever had at the beginning of the season since the present group has been working together here at Ferrari,' says Brawn. 'It was the strongest start we have ever made because, in the past, we were still catching up after the first race. I remember 1999 when, even though Eddie [Irvine] won in Melbourne, we were all a bit glum because of the performance deficit we seemed to have on McLaren. But this year, that wasn't the case. I wouldn't say we had an advantage, and I don't think they had an advantage, but for once we were starting off very close on performance.'

It's true that Schumacher won the Australian Grand Prix – and the next race in Brazil – but, on each occasion, McLaren-Mercedes shot themselves in the foot thanks to engine failures. But, come the third round at Imola, it was 'game on' as both teams ran faultlessly to the flag. Significantly, Ferrari

didn't just win, they beat McLaren all roads.

'Michael's driving at crucial moments has been the key this season,' says Brawn. 'When we won at Imola, it was because he responded exactly when we needed it. That was a very tough race and I think McLaren had a performance advantage. I know they had a small problem in the race, but I think they misjudged the pit stops.

'When we saw their first stop was shorter than ours, we thought we were in with a chance. Just like we were to do at Suzuka, we took on extra fuel to give us a long middle stint. And Michael paced himself beautifully so as not to alert Häkkinen too much. Then, as soon as Häkkinen was in the pits for the second time – bang! – Michael did the business. It was a race we won which they should have won thanks in part to that longer middle stint and in part to Michael putting in the fast lap times at exactly the right moment.'

Schumacher did it again in the British GP, salvaging a hard-won third

through strong tactical driving after spending the first half stuck in eighth place behind Villeneuve's BAR. Thanks to a yellow flag and changing track conditions at Silverstone, Schumacher had qualified fifth, his lowest starting position of the season.

He made up for that by being fastest in every session and leading the opening sector of the next race in Spain. Then it all went wrong with a tyre problem and a chaotic pit stop which saw Schumacher break the ankle of his fueller and chief mechanic, Nigel Stepney. Schumacher finished fifth to retain his lead of the championship. He increased it two weeks later with a brilliant victory thanks to destroying Häkkinen in the wet at the Nürburgring.

So far, so good. That made it four wins for Ferrari. Then their campaign began to unravel, slowly at first, starting at Monaco. Schumacher had this race in the bag, so much so that he was able to get in and out of the pits without losing his advantage. Unbeknown to the driver and his team,

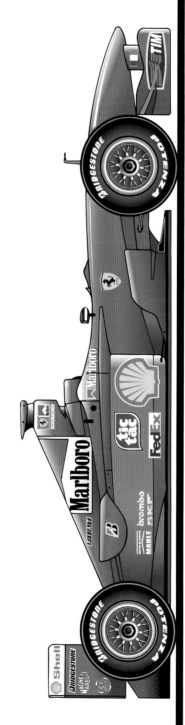

FERRARI F1–2000

Sponsors: Marlboro, Shell, Fiat, Bridgestone, Tictac, TIM, FedEx, Magneti Marelli, Tommy Hilfiger, GE, Arexons, Brembo, Mahle, SKF

Team principal: Jean Todt **Technical director:** Ross Brawn **Team manager:** Stefano Domenicali **Chief mechanic:** Nigel Stepney

ENGINE Type: Ferrari 049 **No. of cylinders (vee angle):** V10 (90°) **Sparking Plugs:** Champion **Electronics:** Magneti Marelli **Fuel:** Shell **Oil:** Shell

TRANSMISSION Gearbox: Ferrari seven-speed longitudinal semi-automatic sequential **Driveshafts:** Ferrari **Clutch:** AP Racing (hand-operated)

CHASSIS Front suspension: double wishbones, pushrod **Rear suspension:** double wishbones, pushrod **Suspension dampers:** Sachs **Wheel diameter:** front: 13 in. rear: 13in.

Wheels: BBS **Tyres:** Bridgestone **Brake pads:** Brembo **Brake discs:** Brembo **Brake calipers:** Brembo **Steering:** Ferrari **Radiators:** Secan **Fuel tanks:** ATL

Battery: Magneti Marelli **Instruments:** Magneti Marelli

DIMENSIONS Wheelbase: not given **Track:** front: not given rear: not given **Formula weight:** 1322.8 lb/600 kg including driver **Fuel capacity:** not given

however, the left exhaust was over-heating to the point of failure, the subsequent flame-outs torching the rear suspension. Ten easy points collapsed in a heap after 55 laps.

'It was totally unexpected and, in retrospect, we understand what happened', says Brawn. 'Whatever people may say, F1 is a fuel-economy formula in that you have to start the race with the minimum amount of fuel possible because fuel is weight and weight is performance. People may not think of Monaco as a fuel economy circuit but the whole system is developed to run the engine as lean and as economic as possible. We have been doing a lot of work in that area.

'So, you run it leaner and things get hotter. That does not usually present a problem but, because of the engine duty cycle at Monaco, the exhaust just wasn't strong enough over the period of the race. We didn't have that problem the previous year because we were not running the engine so aggressively on the fuel consumption.

'It's such a weird duty cycle at Monaco because, from Casino through to the tunnel, you are in first or second gear a lot; on and off the throttle all the time. There are no long periods of full throttle which would allow the exhaust to cool. The temperature gradually built up and stressed the exhaust too much.'

Schumacher made up for that disappointment by winning from pole in Canada, his job made easier when Coulthard's attack was blunted by a ten-second stop-go and the fast-starting Villeneuve kindly delaying the rest of the field. With the season having reached the half-way point and Häkkinen apparently off his personal pace, there was talk of Schumacher securing the championship by Hungary in August. After all, he was 22 points in front. What could stop him now? Quite a lot, as it would turn out.

France began well enough with another pole position but Schumacher had to first deal with a pumped-up Coulthard, then rear tyres which had gone off and, finally, a broken engine.

Above: The Red Baron. Michael Schumacher finally brought the drivers' World Championship back to Maranello after a wait of 21 years.
Paul-Henri Cahier

Top: Luca di Montezemolo *(left)* and Ross Brawn had every reason to smile.
Photographs: Bryn Williams *(left)* and Paul-Henri Cahier

FORMULA 1 REVIEW • FERRARI

Top left: Schumacher and Ross Brawn in conversation on the grid.

Paul-Henri Cahier

Top right: Jean Todt scratches his head whilst Michael muses. For the most part they had the answers when the questions were asked.

Bryn Williams/Words & Pictures

Above: Rubens Barrichello provided excellent support to Schumacher and scored enough points to ensure that Ferrari retained the constructors' title.

Paul-Henri Cahier

'It was a bearing failure and we still don't know what caused it,' says Brawn. 'All the other bearings in the engine were perfect and this one gave up. Michael felt the engine tighten, and that was it. Before that, Magny-Cours was the first race where the rear tyres really suffered. In all the other races we may have been a bit worse than McLaren but it hadn't shown because it wasn't critical. So, after France, we made a concerted effort in the way we used the tyres and I think we saw some benefit from that, certainly at Monza where the durability was very good.'

Meanwhile, Schumacher had been having his own problems with first-corner collisions taking him out at the A1-Ring and Hockenheim. There was consolation for the team at the latter when Rubens Barrichello, Irvine's replacement, took a gamble and ran on grooved slicks when everyone else switched to wets in the closing stages. It was a truly superb drive and worthy of the Brazilian's first victory.

'We've got the best reference point you could have,' says Brawn. 'You can see what Michael can do and it's very easy to dismiss his team-mates, even though they may be very, very good. Rubens has done an excellent job. There have been slight inconsistencies which will disappear. He has been

learning to work with the team and we have been discovering what he needs. Once or twice we have made wrong moves; once or twice he has not been able to get it together with the team. Monaco wasn't great, for example. And he struggled a bit at Imola. But we are starting to understand why. Rubens is a good guy to work with and he has settled in well; he's very open and relaxed in the debriefs with Michael in all the discussions we have about what the car is doing – which is essential for the good working of the team.'

Barrichello was not quite on Schumacher's pace in Hungary and Belgium, where Michael managed to

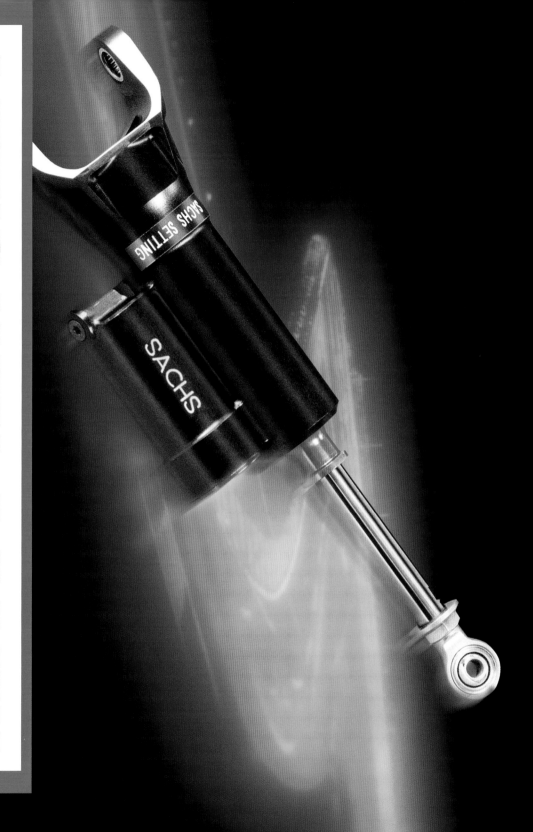

LET'S WIN AGAIN!

SACHS RACE ENGINEERING

From Streetsport to Formula 1, advanced shock technology from SRE sets the place. Superior design and materials deliver state-of-the-art performance to the best racing partners in the world. Developed with enthusiasm for motorsport in Schweinfurt, Germany, the SRE engineers constantly redefine the competitive advantage, as proven by Michael Schumacher in Formula 1. Congratulation to the world champions at team Ferrari, as we meet the challenge again in the opening season. Race to race – victory to victory – engineered to race.

Sachs Race Engineering GmbH
Ernst-Sachs-Strasse 62
97424 Schweinfurt
++ 49 97 21 98 43 00
katja.deutscher@sachs.de
www.sachs-race-engineering.de

SACHS
automotive future

SACHS
RACE ENGINEERING

Top: The Ferrari pit crew were often a crucial factor in Schumacher's ability to win races after changing tactics.

Above right: The Ferrari flag overwhelms the *tifosi* at Imola.

Both photographs: Paul-Henri Cahier

Above: Another take on letting your hair down. Rubens Barrichello and Michael Schumacher don red wigs as they join Jean Todt, test driver Luca Badoer and the Ferrari mechanics in championship celebrations.

Steve Etherington/EPI

finish second twice. But the point was, he had been well and truly beaten by Häkkinen on each occasion. In the space of four races, Schumacher had scored just 12 points; Häkkinen, back to his old self, had claimed 42 and the lead of the championship. With Monza next on the schedule, Ferrari was in mild crisis.

'Everyone was getting a bit tense,' admits Brawn. 'Hungary had been a mystery because we had been in pretty good shape up until the race. Michael was on pole. In all the sessions he had been quick while, on the contrary, Häkkinen had struggled. Then, that amazing turnaround by Häkkinen on Sunday; he just disappeared and we didn't really have an explanation. So that was a bit of a blow.

'I was actually quite pleased with

Belgium. Although we lost it in the last few laps, I expected Spa to be one of our toughest races compared to McLaren. I think the qualities of their car and our car perhaps differ a bit and it was one of those circuits where, if you look in detail, Ferrari has not been strong in the past. We have won some races there – but not because we have disappeared into the distance. So in some ways I was quite happy – although that view wasn't shared by many people! I was trying to give everyone a lot of encouragement because, in my own mind, we had been so close to winning it. In slightly different circumstances, we would have done in what should have been one of the strongest races for McLaren. But there was no doubt that the pressure was beginning to tell as we went to Monza.'

In a test of fortitude as well as speed, Schumacher began to turn the tide, first with a hugely emotional win at Monza and then a skilful result in difficult conditions at Indianapolis, helped by Häkkinen suffering his third engine failure.

Back at the head of the championship once more, victory at Suzuka would seal it with one race to go. Appropriately enough, Schumacher scored his eighth win of the season through an all-too-familiar combination of pace, tactical brilliance and brilliant team work. Finally, finally, the job had been done. But it had been close.

Maurice Hamilton

76

40 YEARS OF MARANELLO CONCESSIONAIRES LTD.

1960–2000

by Keith Bluemel

IN the austerity of post-war Great Britain that seemed to take well into the Fifties to shake off, the chances of seeing a Ferrari on the race tracks was extremely rare, and of seeing one on the street virtually nil. This was in part due to a slow economic recovery, but there were also import restrictions and taxes on foreign goods making them extremely difficult to import, even if you had the money. These restrictions were equally applicable to European-produced goods; remember there was no EEC in those days. Those British racing drivers wealthy enough to purchase a Ferrari usually did so under the auspices of a foreign team, thus avoiding the problem of trying to import the car and paying punitive taxes on it.

Although Brooklands of Bond Street had a Ferrari concession in the early Fifties, and subsequently so did Mike Hawthorn's TT Garage, very few cars were actually imported and sold on the British market. Mike Hawthorn displayed two 250 GT Pinin Farina coupés at the 1958 London Motor Show, one of which he sold to an Irish client, whilst a trio of friends were interested in the second example. These were Gawaine Baillie, Colonel Ronnie Hoare, and Tommy Sopwith. Mike Hawthorn suggested that they all had a test drive, and although Colonel Hoare fell in love with it, Tommy Sopwith was the one who bought it.

Colonel Hoare was running a Mercedes 300 SL Roadster which he had bought from Tommy Sopwith's Mercedes dealership. However, he had qualms about its roadholding, and took it back to query whether these were due to a mechanical problem, or due to something inherent in the design. Tommy Sopwith suggested that he try his similar car to see whether that displayed similar traits. It did, and he decided that, as he was not confident and comfortable with it, that the car would have to go. Rather

ironically Tommy Sopwith was experiencing problems with his recently acquired Ferrari, as it would rarely run cleanly on all 12 cylinders, and the honeymoon period was over! They agreed on an exchange deal, which provided Colonel Hoare with his first Ferrari.

It wasn't long before the Colonel started experiencing the same problem, and he quickly became an expert at plug-changing. Driving home one dark evening the misfiring occurred again and he stopped to investigate, leaving the engine running whilst he did so. Upon opening the bonnet the reason literally flashed before his eyes, as the HT leads arced to their metal guide tubes. The following day all the leads were replaced with aviation quality ones, and there was never a recurrence during the 25,000 miles that the subsequently covered in the car.

When Mike Hawthorn died in a road accident in January 1959, the

trading relationship between his TT Garage and Ferrari lapsed. Meanwhile, Colonel Hoare was very impressed with his car now that it was running consistently on all 12 cylinders, and he thought that there must be others like him in Great Britain who would appreciate and enjoy the Ferrari experience. He had his F. English Ltd Ford dealership in Bournemouth, and thought that if he was successful in securing a Ferrari, with the proviso that they would be an agent if he was successful in securing a deal. Colonel Hoare then sent a proposal to Enzo Ferrari, explaining how he foresaw the business operating from within his established Ford dealership.

The proposal interested Ferrari, as Colonel Hoare received an invitation

to meet the commercial manager, Girolamo Gardini, at the 1960 Brussels Salon. Subsequent to this meeting, Colonel Hoare then received an invitation to meet Enzo Ferrari in Modena. Colonel Hoare recalled that Enzo Ferrari asked him how many Ferraris he thought that he could sell in a year. He thought quickly, and said 'four', reasoning that he would run two, one as a personal car with another as a demonstrator, also that he could probably sell one to Gawaine Baillie, and that surely he must be able to sell at least one more car. This greatly pleased Enzo Ferrari, as they had only sold that number in the previous decade! Great Britain granted the concession and Ferrari granted the concession into being on 1 April 1960, although it was July before it became operational. For the first six years of its life it operated out of two bays at the F. English premises in Bournemouth, whilst a London service centre was

opened in Wellesley Road, Chiswick in 1964.

The first Ferrari ordered was a 250 GT SWB Berlinetta, chassis number 1993GT, in February 1960, which was delivered in July. The Colonel used this as his personal car before selling it to David Clarke, founder of Graypaul Motors Ltd. The Colonel's original sales estimate to Ferrari proved conservative, as during 1960 Maranello Concessionaires sold a total of six cars, five 250 GT Berlinettas and a 250 GT 2+2 coupé.

Colonel Hoare reasoned that the best way to promote the Ferrari name in Great Britain was by exposure. To this end he determined that a presence at the then annual London Motor Show was essential, and that the best way to project the image of the marque to the masses was to go motor racing, as he had been an active competitor both before and after World War Two, and on the organisational side had co-run the United Racing Stable Formula 2 team in 1957. At the time the Colonel was thinking about setting up the GT racing operation, his friend Tommy Sopwith was doing the same thing with saloon cars, planning to run a pair of Jaguar 3.8 models. The national calendar for the GT and saloon car races followed a similar pattern, so they decided on a joint venture to run a 250 GT SWB. The car would race under the banner of the Equipe Endeavour banner of the Sopwith team, with Mike Parkes as the main driver for the 1961 season.

During 1960 the Colonel sold two alloy-bodied 250 GT SWB competition cars in Great Britain whose racing careers preceded those of his own team. The first of these was to Graham Whitehead, a silver left-hand drive car, chassis number 2009GT, and the second to Rob Walker, this being the dark blue example, chassis number 2119GT, in which (Sir) Stirling Moss won the

1960 Tourist Trophy at Goodwood. It was this latter car that would form the basis for Maranello Concessionaires' competition debut the following season, having been taken back in part exchange for the second Rob Walker/Stirling Moss 250 GT SWB, chassis number 2735GT, in which he took his second-consecutive Tourist Trophy victory.

The debut race for the Equipe Endeavour/Maranello Concessionaires team was in a GT race at Snetterton on 25 March 1961, where Mike Parkes provided the team with a win and equal fastest lap on their debut. He won again at Goodwood a week later, whilst Jack Sears took 2119GT to a fourth place at Oulton Park in mid-April, with 2119GT's final outing for the team resulting in another victory for Mike Parkes at Brands Hatch in June. For the final two races of their season a second-hand GT SWB, chassis number 2417GT, was purchased from the factory. Mike Parkes scored a victory at Snetterton, and a second place in the Tourist Trophy at Goodwood, behind Stirling Moss. Thus the first season yielded four wins, a second, a colourful account of this trip in one of his columns for *Road & Track* some years ago.

fourth and a single retirement. The 1962 was the year that Ferrari produced their answer to the 'E' Type in aesthetic terms, this was of course the sensational 250 GTO, that has gone on to become one of the most revered Ferraris of all time. Before Maranello Concessionaires took delivery of their first 250 GTO, the 250 GT SWB 2417GT had a final outing with the team in a race at Oulton Park in early April, where Mike Parkes gave them their first victory of the 1962 season, and the last with the 250 GT SWB model. Their first 250 GTO was chassis number 3589GT, finished in dark blue, which Colonel Hoare drove back from Modena in convoy with Innes Ireland in the pale green UDT-Laystall example, chassis number 3505GT. Innes Ireland gave a colourful account of this trip in one of his columns for *Road & Track* some years ago.

At the Goodwood Easter Meeting Mike Parkes took 3589GT to a GT class victory and second overall behind Innes Ireland in a Lotus 19. The Lotus was to have been driven by Stirling Moss, but he suffered his career-ending accident that fateful weekend, even if most of reer-ending accident that fateful weekend, even if most of the spectators were supporting the svelte new 'E' Types.

1962 was the year that Ferrari produced their answer to the 'E' Type in aesthetic terms, this was of course the sensational 250 GTO, that has gone on to become one of the most revered Ferraris of all time. Before Maranello Concessionaires took delivery of their first 250 GTO, the 250 GT SWB 2417GT had a final outing with the team in a race at Oulton Park in early April, where Mike Parkes gave them their first victory of the 1962 season, and the last with the 250 GT SWB model. Their first 250 GTO was chassis number 3589GT, finished in dark blue, which Colonel Hoare drove back from Modena in convoy with Innes Ireland in the pale green UDT-Laystall example, chassis number 3505GT. Innes Ireland gave a colourful account of this trip in one of his columns for *Road & Track* some years ago.

At the Goodwood Easter Meeting Mike Parkes took 3589GT to a GT class victory and second overall behind Innes Ireland in a Lotus 19. The Lotus was to have been driven by Stirling Moss, but he suffered his career-ending accident that fateful weekend that Innes Ireland took the car over, leaving the pale green GTO sitting in the paddock. An interesting aside to this is, that both Stirling Moss and Innes Ireland practised in the GTO, the only time that Stirling Moss drove the definitive 250 GTO in its heyday.

A second 250 GTO, chassis number 3647GT, joined the Maranello Concessionaires racing stable in June 1962, to be driven by John Surtees. During the season these two cars recorded a number of victories and podium finishes for the team. In 1962 the team also made its international debut in the Paris 1000 km race at Montlhéry. Here they proved that they could compete beyond national level, with Mike Parkes and John Surtees sharing 3647GT to take second overall.

In 1963 the 250 GTO was again the prime weapon in their racing programme. Their first GTO, 3589GT,

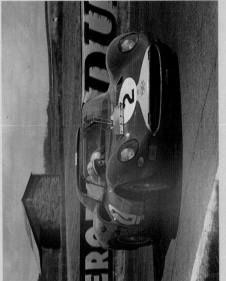

40 YEARS OF MARANELLO CONCESSIONAIRES LTD. 1960–2000

was sold at the end of 1962, and a new red example chassis number 4399GT acquired, whilst the white-painted John Coombs example 3729GT was also used after 3647GT was sold early in 1963. The Colonel also bought a 4-litre 330 LM berlinetta, chassis number 4725SA, specifically for the Le Mans 24 Hours race, and was rewarded by being the only one of the three examples entered to finish the race. Mike Salmon and Jack Sears drove it to fifth overall and third in their category. At the Tourist Trophy at Goodwood in September 250 GTO 4399GT, now sporting a Cambridge blue band around the nose, was driven to victory by Graham Hill. Apart from Le Mans, only one other continental trip was made, to Monza in September for the Coppa Inter Europa, where Mike Parkes finished a close second in 4399GT (now plain red again), after a race-long duel with Roy Salvadori in the Aston Martin Project 214. Its final race of the season was the Snetterton Three Hours where, again in plain red, Mike Parkes' car took class victory and second overall. Although the red and Cambridge blue colour scheme didn't appear until nearly three years into their racing programme, it has come to be regarded as Maranello Concessionaires team colours. The team also had their first experience of a 12-cylinder sports prototype Ferrari in 1963, at the British Grand Prix meeting. Mike Parkes drove a 330 P, chassis number 0814, loaned by the factory in the GT and sports car support race. This car had started life as a 250 P, but the 3-litre engine was replaced with a 4-litre unit by the factory prior to this race.

Due to their success in establishing the Ferrari marque in the British market, and their performances on the race track, Maranello Concessionaires were offered the loan of a works prepared and maintained sports prototype at a fixed rate for the 1964 season, with the option to purchase at

the season end. This was initially loaned as a 275 P for the Nürburgring 1000 km race, before receiving a 4 litre engine to become a 330P, chassis number 0818, for Le Mans and subsequent races. The car was driven mainly by Graham Hill, backed up by Jo Bonnier in long distance races, their best international results being a win in the Paris 1000 km race, and a second place in the Le Mans 24 Hours race. Graham Hill took it to victory in the Tourist Trophy at Goodwood, and Ludovico Scarfiotti drove it to win the Coppa Inter Europa at Monza. The team's 250 GTO chassis number 4399GT was re-bodied to the 1964 style over the winter of 1963–'64, and continued to perform well in the GT category. A 250 LM was also purchased, and Graham Hill and Jo Bonnier took it to what Colonel Hoare regarded as one of his team's greatest victories. This was the 12 Hours of Reims, where they triumphed after a race long duel with Surtees/Bandini in the similar NART entered car, with their re-bodied 250 GTO, 4399GT, finishing third driven by Parkes/Scarfiotti.

For 1965 they focused on the major international races, although it turned out to be a disappointing season with a number of retirements, the best results were second places at Reims and Zeltweg. In 1966 they decided to concentrate on the 2-litre category with a Dino 206S, although this proved to be fast it was also rather fragile, with a class win and sixth overall in the Spa 1000 km being their best result. The only exception to the 2-litre category was at Le Mans, where a 275 GTB/C was entered in the GT class, and a 365 P2/3 in the sports prototype class, along with the Dino in the up to 2-litre class. The only survivor of the trio was the Pike/Courage driven 275 GTB/C, chassis number 9035, which won the GT class and finished eighth overall.

For the 1967 season the racing activity was mainly British-based,

apart from the Spa 1000 km and Le Mans. The team used a 250 LM, chassis number 6167, and a 412 P, chassis number 0854, during the year. After two years of disappointing results they fared better in their final full season of competition. Richard Attwood partnered by Lucien Bianchi finished third at Spa in the 412 P, although it retired at Le Mans, and was seventh at Brands Hatch, in its only other outing. The 250 LM recorded three third places, and a win driven by Richard Attwood, plus a second place driven by Mike Parkes. Colonel Hoare decided that his racing programme over a six year period had achieved its objective, and called it a day. It had firmly established the Ferrari name in the United Kingdom, and spread the name of Maranello Concessionaires globally.

The team was resurrected in 1972 for one final outing at Le Mans. The factory's Assistenza Clienti had built a small series of competition-prepared 365 GTB/4C 'Daytonas', and the Colonel felt that it could be competitive in the GT category. Maranello Concessionaires purchased chassis number 15681 to race in the GT category, but it turned out to be a disappointing finale to the team's racing career, with retirement at one third distance with reported piston failure.

Returning to 1967, a new face came onto the scene in the person of Shaun Bealey, who had become a friend of the Colonel over the years. He purchased 40% of the shares, and remained a partner until the business was sold in 1988. The business had also outgrown its space at the Ford dealership in Bournemouth and the small premises in Chiswick. A 21-year lease was taken from Shell on Tower Garage on the Egham bypass, and the Ferrari operation moved under a single roof. Since that date the town of Egham and its environs have become synonymous with Ferrari in the United Kingdom. Tower

Garage is a listed building and still remains a focal point of Ferrari interest, as today it houses the showrooms and workshops of Maranello Sales Ltd.

The introduction of the Dino 246 model to the British market in 1970 saw a rapid expansion in business, with a national dealer network being formed in 1972. A new headquarters building incorporating a workshop and stores was opened at nearby Thorpe in January 1974, which today is almost solely occupied by the greatly expanded spare parts department. Further expansion came in 1975 when Maranello Concessionaires were appointed concessionaires for Australia, and later for the Far East through wholly owned subsidiary companies.

During the latter years of the eighties the Colonel's health was unfortunately failing and he decided to sell the business to the TKM Group. Under their ownership a new technical centre and headquarters building was constructed close to the existing one at Thorpe. This was officially opened in September 1991, with the original Egham premises at Tower Garage being totally refurbished at the same time. Unfortunately the Colonel didn't live to see this next phase in the evolution of the business that he had created and built, as he died at his home in Monaco in 1989.

The next phase in the development of the business came in early 1992, when the TKM Group was acquired by the Inchcape Group. Under them the trading title became Ferrari UK in 1994 to align with other world markets, although the registered name remains that initiated in 1960, Maranello Concessionaires Ltd. The business continued to flourish with a continuous increase in new car registrations during the nineties. This has led to the UK Ferrari market becoming the third largest in the world, headed only by

The Roy Pike/Piers Courage 275 GTB/C–
9035 at Le Mans in 1966 on its way to
class victory and eighth overall.
LAT Photographic

40 YEARS OF MARANELLO CONCESSIONAIRES LTD. · 1960–2000

the USA and Germany, with around 450 cars sold in 1999. In 1996 they were awarded the concession for the Middle East. Further international expansion occurred in May 1998, with the purchase of one of their old adversaries on the race track during the Sixties, the famed Garage Francorchamps in Belgium.

When Ferrari purchased 50% of the Maserati shares from the parent Fiat Group in 1997 (with the option to purchase the remaining 50% taken up in 1999), it was logical that the sales of the two marques should be channelled through common outlets, although they would be aimed at different market sectors, and retain separate identities. Maranello Concessionaires Ltd were one of the first importers to take up the option of the Maserati franchise in June 1998. Now a large number of the dealer network have dedicated Maserati sales areas in their showrooms. Naturally wholly owned Maranello Sales Ltd were one of these, and the Tower Garage premises were completely refurbished and upgraded during 1999 to incorporate Maserati.

One aspect of the company's philosophy throughout its existence has

been the importance of service and the availability of spare parts. The continuous upgrading and increase in capacity of the latter has resulted in a total of 35,000 different Ferrari lines being carried, with a value of around £5 million at any one time. Although the period of the Maserati connection is relatively short, this marque's spare parts inventory already runs to nearly 3,500 items with

a total value of £350,000. Maranello Concessionaires are the appointed world distributor for Ferrari production car parts that are no longer supplied by the factory, for cars greater than ten years old. In addition to this there is an ongoing programme for remanufacturing obsolete parts under their Marpart label, to do everything possible to service the needs of the owners of the earlier models.

In recent years there has been a return to the racing roots, with support of drivers in the 348, F355 and now 360 Modena Challenge series, both in the United Kingdom and Belgium, where separate national teams are run. In addition to this, support has been provided for a number of years to the Ferrari Owners' Club organised and run Maranello Challenge series. In 1998 a special organisation for Ferrari owners was formed under the title Club Fiorano, which is headed by former grand prix driver Peter Gethin, to provide owners with exclusive use of current models and/or their own cars on the finest tracks in Europe with expert tuition and guidance. Within the Ferrari dealer network purchasers have the exclusive offer of Maranello Financial Services to fund their acquisition, together with the Ferrari Formula warranty that is available on all approved used cars.

The past 40 years have been an interesting story, celebrated by Ferrari winning the F1 Drivers' and Constructors' Championships, it will be interesting to see what has been added by the time that they reach their Golden Jubilee.

F1 2000 - V10 - 40 VALVES - 770BHP - 7 SPEEDS - 600KG

Campioni del Mondo 2000

Ferrari

SALES   SERVICE   PARTS   BODY REPAIRS   FINANCE

An Inchcape
Company

Maranello Sales Ltd. Tower Garage, The By Pass (A30), Egham, Surrey TW20 0AX   Telephone 01784 436431
Web Site:- www.maranellosales.com   email:owen@maranellosales.com

5 JORDAN 6

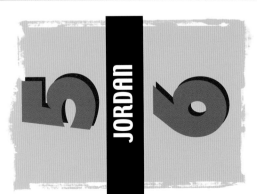

HEINZ-HARALD FRENTZEN

JARNO TRULLI

Both photographs: Paul-Henri Cahier

JORDAN Grand Prix could hardly believe what was happening to them. They had finished third in the constructors' championship at the end of the previous year and it was perhaps stretching optimism – even Eddie Jordan's infectious version – to presume that the team from Silverstone would challenge Ferrari and McLaren in 2000. At the very least, however, Jordan expected to maintain the status quo.

Yet, by the end of the season, the Benson and Hedges team was in sixth place. Worse than that, Jordan was behind British American Racing, the butt of paddock humour in 1999 and, more important from a political standpoint, the team which had been given the works Honda engine for the first time. Jordan were entering their third year with Mugen Honda but a decision, announced mid-season, that works V10s would come their way in 2001 merely added to the discomfort created by the continuing struggle to beat BAR, never mind achieve anything like the desired results this season.

The final tally showed just two third places from 34 starts. And this from a team which had gone into the season knowing they not only had their best ever financial package but that it had been in place good and early. Jordan was about to prove the old adage that money isn't everything. Before even thinking about making the final step into the Ferrari and McLaren league, you need a strong infrastructure, full manufacturer support, a consistent car – and a decent helping of luck. Jordan's average of one point per race was not merely inadequate, it was a huge embarrassment.

Matters were not helped by Mike Gascoyne announcing mid-season that he would become technical director for the revamped Benetton team as Renault made an official return in 2001. Gascoyne, who had acted with his usual correctness in this matter, was put on 'gardening leave' in September but, by then, it was already clear that one or two of the bold technical steps thought necessary to move Jordan into the front line were not paying off. Rather than follow the logical sequence and refer to the new car as '100', the chassis designation was changed from a pure numeric system (which had started with 191 in 1991) to EJ10 in recognition of Jordan's leader and the fact that this was their tenth season in F1. But, no matter what the car was called, you couldn't doubt its potential: Jordan was the only team to twice break the McLaren/Ferrari monopoly of the front row of the grid. The trouble was, that promise was either destroyed by unreliability or, as happened more than once, it could not be unlocked in the first place. Generally speaking, if the EJ10 was not on the required pace within the first hour of practice, then it never would be. In the end, though, it was the reliability issues – and the time and resources spent chasing them down – which did for one of the most popular teams in the paddock.

Some of those technical problems were caused indirectly by Mugen Honda. Such a bald statement may seem grossly unfair in the light of the usual diligence from the Japanese company but there can be no denying that the V10, essentially a customer engine, was getting long in the tooth. Attention had, perhaps understandably, been switched to the new works Honda engine for BAR, to the point where winter development on the Mugen Honda had been virtually zero. It was up to Jordan to make up for that shortfall in performance.

'We pushed very hard to build a car capable of winning,' said Trevor Foster, managing director, Jordan Grand Prix. 'We wanted to make it as light as possible, with a lower centre of gravity, as much aerodynamic performance improvement as we could; all the usual things. We did find more downforce but, the problem was, it wasn't enough. And in other areas such as the gearbox, we probably pushed too far regarding its weight. We could have gone the conservative route and decided to take only ten percent out of the weight rather than the 20 per cent we actually achieved.

JORDAN EJ10-MUGEN HONDA

Sponsors: Benson & Hedges, Deutsche Post, MasterCard International, Pearl, Lucent, Brother, PlayStation, Intercond, EMC^2, Imation, Hewlett Packard

Team principal: Eddie Jordan **Chief engineer:** Tim Holloway **Team manager:** Jim Vale **Chief mechanic:** Tim Edwards

ENGINE **Type:** Mugen Honda MF301HE **No. of cylinders (vee angle):** V10 (72°) **Sparking plugs:** not given **Electronics:** TAG 300 **Fuel:** Elf **Oil:** Elf

TRANSMISSION **Gearbox:** Jordan six-speed longitudinal semi-automatic **Driveshafts:** Jordan **Clutch:** Sachs (hand-operated)

CHASSIS **Front suspension:** double wishbones, pushrod-operated dampers/torsion bars **Rear suspension:** double wishbones, pushrod-operated rockers/torsion bars
Suspension dampers: Penske **Wheel diameter:** front: 13 in. rear: 13 in. **Wheels:** OZ **Tyres:** Bridgestone **Brake pads:** Brembo/Hitco
Brake discs: Brembo/Hitco **Brake calipers:** Brembo **Steering:** Jordan (power-assisted) **Radiators:** Secan **Fuel tanks:** ATL
Battery: Jordan **Instruments:** Jordan

DIMENSIONS **Wheelbase:** 3050 mm **Track:** front: 1500 mm rear: 1418 mm **Formula weight:** 1322.8 lb/600 kg including driver **Fuel capacity:** not given

"Leader of the Pack"

by Scania

Scania. Europe's leading truck maker, Jordan's choice for transportation.

SCANIA

Tel.01908 210210 www.scania.co.uk

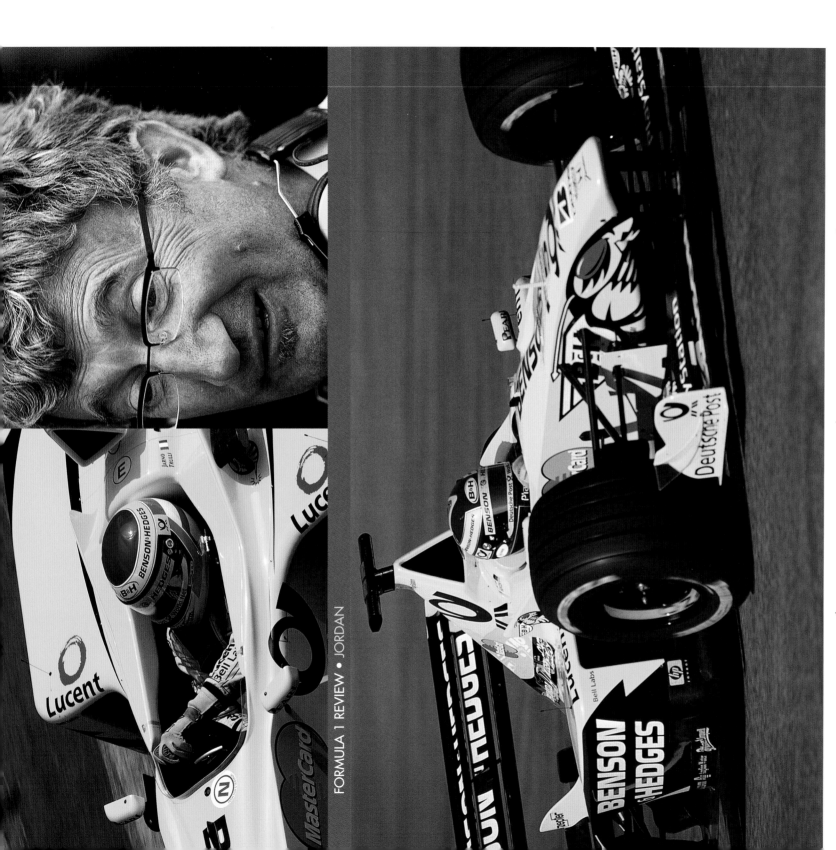

Top left: Jarno Trulli impressed with his speed in qualifying, but was often unlucky in race situations.

Top right: Eddie Jordan endured a disappointing 2000 season, and will be looking for much improvement when the team takes delivery of works Honda engines.

Above: After two wins in 1999, Heinz-Harald Frentzen had to make do with a couple of third-place podium positions for a season's work.

All photographs: Paul-Henri Cahier

gearbox potentiometer. Then we would change the engine and the same potentiometer would fail after 50 km. When that sensor failed, it actually confused the gearbox control unit and therefore damaged mechanically all the gears and the selector mechanism. So we thought we had only one problem, which was the electronic sensor.

'We did eventually get on top of that, which was just after the British Grand Prix. But, once we were able to run the car for longer, we discovered that the gearbox was too weak. So we had to set about modifications to the mechanical side of the gearbox and that took some time. Then, when we did manage to get some reliability and had the car running in reasonably competitive situations, we weren't actually getting to it the finish.' The mounting frustration

'We could have found more reliability, but we wouldn't have had the speed. We had to go for the 20 per cent because we knew we were going to struggle to keep up with the works engines. The Mugen Honda was about 20 kg heavier than most of its competitors. So it's a tall order knowing before you start that you need to design 20 kg out of the car.' Problems surfaced immediately. During pre-season testing, gearbox sensors failed – but at irregular intervals.

'That made it quite difficult to pinpoint,' says Foster. 'We eventually found that it was related to engine vibration. This was not the fault of Honda. It was so marginal that it would happen with one engine, but not another. We would get a sensor to run the whole engine mileage in the

was being felt by the drivers, particularly Jarno Trulli, who had been recruited from Prost as Damon Hill's replacement. The young Italian, who saw this as his big chance, never finished in the top three and scored points just four times. If it wasn't gearbox problems (particularly at Monaco, where he had put his yellow car on the front row after one of the most sensational qualifying performances of the season), then he was usually the innocent victim of collisions.

'I think Jarno has come on amazingly well,' said Foster. 'It took him a while to settle into the Jordan way of doing things; I think it was different to what he was used to at Prost. But, once he gained confidence in the team and the fact that we treat both drivers equally and we share everything regardless of

Goldline – the Race Leaders – Bearing up to the millennium!

Goldline F1 drop-link bearing

Ceramic/Cronidur 30®

Goldline have been producing high quality bearings for motor sport, aerospace and high precision industrial applications for 27 years.

Goldline F1 suspension bearings

AMPEP XL/AISI440C/AMS5643

Goldline produce different ranges of bearings to meet different requirements across the whole spectrum of the motor sport, automotive, aerospace and transport industries. If you have a bearing need we can fulfil it. Goldline will prove that Formula 1 know-how and real cost-effectiveness are not mutually exclusive!

Goldline F1 push-clutch bearings
Ceramic/Cronidur 30®

All of our products are manufactured to a standard, but with cost-effectiveness still strongly borne in mind, which is why so many teams and drivers have won on Goldline bearings over the years, and why this number continues to grow.

Goldline F1 wheel bearings

Ceramic/Cronidur 30®

Nowadays, Goldline is not so much a supplier to top line motor sport, but more a technical partner – in the truest sense – working with teams and manufacturers to solve motor sport bearing problems to satisfy specific needs.

We will work with you to fulfil your specific requirements.

This is why we are the Race Leaders.

Goldline F1 pull-clutch bearing
Ceramic/Cronidur 30®

whether one driver has been with the team longer than the other, then he got better and better as the season went on.

'As much as we had some good luck last year – and although I am a person who believes you make your own good luck – we have also had some bad luck. Four times Jarno has been in the top six and been taken out by another driver in a racing incident. Then, at Hockenheim, he had that stop–go for allegedly passing Barrichello. I think everyone realises now that the penalty was a mistake, but the damage was done because Jarno was running second at the time. Your luck doesn't get much worse than that.'

Heinz-Harald Frentzen, in his second season with the team, might disagree. A broken alternator (only the second such failure experienced by Jordan in two and a half years of racing and testing) robbed him of second place four laps from the end of the German Grand Prix, other possible podiums having gone the way of the gearbox in the early races. It's true that Frentzen was a little disappointed in the car from the moment he first drove it but, that said, the German made arguably one of the most disastrous mistakes of the season when he crashed out of second place eight laps from the end of the Monaco Grand Prix.

'It's been so competitive this year that we just couldn't afford the smallest mistake, either from the team or the drivers,' said Foster. 'Because of the stability of the regulations, the grid closed up. We were actually closer to McLaren than we were last year – but, then, so was everyone else!

'We openly accepted that the 10 per cent extra downforce we had found was not enough. That meant we had to keep working through the early part of the season and, although the team has grown during the last year or two, we still only have so many resources when compared to the teams we were trying to beat. When you have got to get the car to finish, suddenly all the energies of a large percentage of the work force have to focus on reliability. Once that's done, then you can start to look at performance. Hence, we came up with the revised side pods and radiator layout, which was a reasonable step. But, by then, we were already behind, so you never catch up.

'We had to go to the edge with this year's car but, in doing so, we probably went over the edge in certain areas – not as regards safety, but reliability. But you've got to do it if you want to win. And that basic philosophy has not changed within Jordan despite the season being a huge disappointment.'

Maurice Hamilton

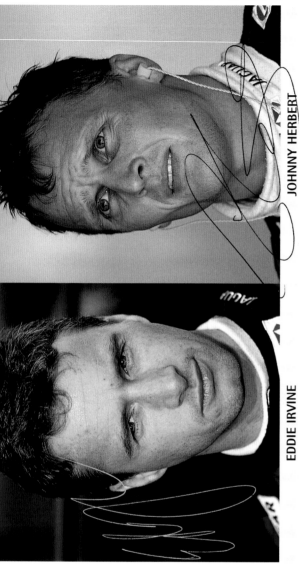

JAGUAR 7 8

EDDIE IRVINE

JOHNNY HERBERT

THE biggest challenge facing Jaguar Racing was expanding and restructuring from its previous incarnation as Stewart Grand Prix into the size of team necessary to be able to lay the long-term challenge for the future.

In the summer of 1999 the Stewart family had sold its F1 operation to Ford for a reputed £100 million and, not long afterwards, the giant Detroit car maker decided it would re-brand the team under the Jaguar banner for the 2000 season. It was a strategy which drew a mixed response from members of the F1 community.

Putting aside the technical issues, the Jaguar management initially seemed to struggle to appreciate just what was involved in the F1 business. Not the racing team's management, of course, which remained pretty well unchanged since the Stewart-Ford days. But Jaguar Cars seemed seduced by the novelty value of having a grand prix team to play with. For the first few races, the paddock seemed swamped by a sea of green shirts to the point where the Jaguar enclosure looked less an F1 operation, more the Third Milton Keynes Wolf Cub Pack at their annual jamboree.

From a track performance standpoint, the weakest link of the Jaguar R1, and one admitted to by technical director Gary Anderson, was its aerodynamics. High-speed rear-end stability was a problem, particularly pitch sensitivity under harsh braking. It was also short on mechanical grip. Aero development was further compromised by the fact that the team used the Swift wind tunnel for its development, 6,000 miles away from its Milton Keynes base in California. This did not make for smooth running and the loss of talented aerodynamicist Eghbal Hamidy was another setback which outsiders believed Jaguar could have well done without.

The Cosworth V10 engine powering the R1 developed around 810 bhp at 17,600 rpm and is also one of the smallest and most compact engines in the F1 business. Yet its promise was compromised early in the year by a joint lubrication system shared with the gearbox which threw up all manner of technical problems and caused a huge amount of unreliability during pre-season testing.

There was also a shortage of engines at the start of the season. Additionally, there was such a serious internal oil circulation problem with the new CR2 that it prompted Cosworth to fit a camera inside the engine precisely to establish what the oil was doing. The dual lubrication system was clearly causing some of the problems, not all of them.

Pre-season testing was also hobbled by this unreliability. Whenever the team attempted to run really high revs, a slight oil pressure fluctuation would prompt the automatic shutdown systems to cut them out. This aggravated the problem in pinning down the aerodynamic and mechanical shortcomings on the chassis. Cosworth may now have been an integral component of the Ford empire, but there were still some traditional barriers which needed to be broken down to improve communication with the team.

The team's management structure was also in a state of flux for much of the year. At the launch of the car Jackie Stewart announced that he would be standing down as chairman and his role would be taken by Ford senior executive Neil Ressler, an immensely shrewd man who concealed a perceptive mind beneath a relaxed and civilised exterior. Shortly after the San Marino Grand Prix it was announced that Paul Stewart, Jackie's elder son and the driving force behind the family's involvement as motor racing team owners, was undergoing treatment for cancer of the colon. He stepped down from his position as chief executive officer; happily, it seems as though his medical programme was a success. Yet the bottom line was that the Jaguar R1 was difficult and unpredictable to drive, a factor which contributed to Johnny Herbert leaving the team at the end of the season. The veteran 36-year-old could see that his F1 career was busy going nowhere and was happy to take the opportunity to look elsewhere for a change of scene.

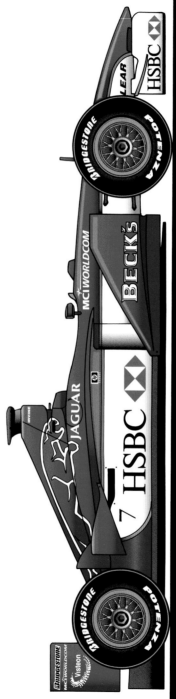

JAGUAR R1-COSWORTH

Sponsors: HSBC, MCI Worldcom, Beck's, hp invent, DHL, Lear

Team principals: Neil Ressler (Chairman), Bobby Rahal (C.E.O. from December 2000) **Technical director:** Gary Anderson **Operation director:** Andy Miller **Chief mechanic:** Dave Boys

ENGINE Type: Ford Cosworth CR2 **No. of cylinders (vee angle):** V10 (angle not given) **Sparking plugs:** Champion **Electronics:** not given **Fuel:** Texaco **Oil:** Havoline

TRANSMISSION Gearbox: Jaguar magnesium-cased six-speed longitudinal semi-automatic **Driveshafts:** not given **Clutch:** AP Racing (hand-operated)

CHASSIS Front suspension: double wishbones, pushrod **Rear suspension:** double wishbones, pushrod **Suspension dampers:** Jaguar/Penske

Wheel diameter: front: 13 in. rear: 13 in. **Wheels:** BBS **Tyres:** Bridgestone **Brake pads:** Carbone Industrie **Brake discs:** Carbone Industrie **Brake calipers:** AP Racing

Steering: JRL **Radiators:** Secan/IMI **Fuel tanks:** ATL **Battery:** JRL **Instruments:** not given

DIMENSIONS Wheelbase: not given **Track:** front: 1469 mm rear: 1408 mm **Formula weight:** 1322.8 lb/600 kg including driver **Fuel capacity:** not given

WE APOLOGISE FOR
THE LACK OF EXCITEMENT
IN THIS ADVERT.
WE PREFER TO SAVE
IT FOR THE TRACK.

COSWORTH

It's in the blood

www.cosworthracing.com

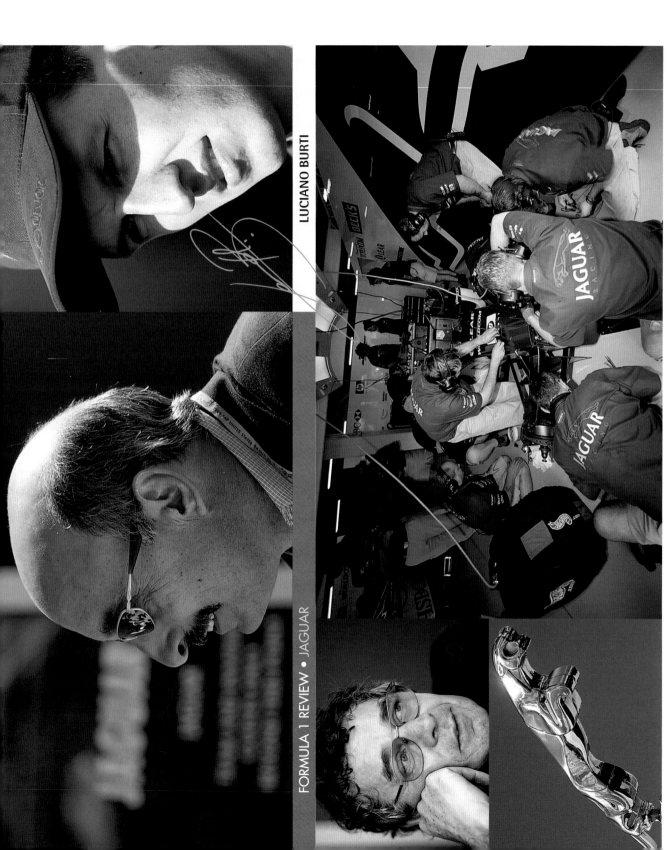

FORMULA 1 REVIEW • JAGUAR

Top left: The respected and immensely popular Bobby Rahal brings his vast experience to bear on the next stage in Jaguar's evolution from the end of 2000.
Paul-Henri Cahier

Top right: Luciano Burti has been promoted from his role of test driver to back Eddie Irvine in 2001.
Bryn Williams/Words & Pictures

Above centre left: Gary Anderson and his team struggled to get the best from a difficult car.
Paul-Henri Cahier

Above right: The mechanics hard at work on the recalcitrant R1 chassis.
Paul-Henri Cahier

Above: The Big Cat made a bigger impression in the paddock than on the track. While it lasted...
Mark Thompson/Allsport

In reality, the technical problems faced by Jaguar made the issue of selecting a second driver for the 2001 season almost a secondary one. By the end of the season it was, in truth, a little difficult to see just why the team was replacing Herbert. He'd run well at Indianapolis, Suzuka and at Sepang, where a possible points finish was first frustrated by a botched refuelling stop and then ended by a massive rear suspension failure which pitched him into a 150 mph accident.

'I was carried to my car for my first F1 race,' he quipped in reference to his Benetton debut in 1989 when his smashed feet had yet to fully heal, 'and I was carried away from my car on my last race.' Jaguar should have felt grateful that Herbert was able to see the ironic side of such a worrying technical failure.

The Jaguar R1 was not initially fitted with power steering which made life a struggle, particularly for Eddie Irvine, the new team leader, who'd been used to such accessories at Ferrari.

'I knew it was going to be difficult,' said Irvine two thirds of the way through the season. 'We have aerodynamic problems, there's no doubt about that. Even last year's Stewart-Ford was aerodynamically lacking in a couple of areas, which I put my finger on immediately I arrived here, but it's

taken a long time for these guys to find the problem.'

Irvine has not been without his critics throughout the year. Yet the Ulsterman likes to project an analytical and sympathetic level of appreciation as to precisely the challenge he is up against. Seemingly undeterred by a maiden season with the team in which he scored a mere four Championship points, he is absolutely certain that Jaguar will improve significantly in 2001.

'I think we will get better,' said Irvine. 'We have areas to work on, but we know them now so that makes it a little bit easier. I think we will see big changes for next year. We have gone through all the points where we need to improve and I think if we get it right we will be O.K. next season.'

Of course, the Jaguar Racing administration is set to be shaken up by the arrival of former CART chief executive officer Bobby Rahal, the U.S. team owner who is charged with the task of turning Ford's blue riband F1 operation into a credible force.

Irvine is upbeat about the prospects under this new management regime, being sufficiently shrewd to appreciate what Rahal may be able to offer. 'I believe that we have enough experience here and we have some new people here, so my feelings and thoughts are that you are going to see

some improvements,' said Irvine. 'We are going to be stronger and there is going to be better fight in the Jaguar team next year.

'I think we have to wait and see what Bobby does. Some good people have already joined us and we will get more, but we have good guys already. For all that, Irvine is aware of the role he must play if Jaguar is to go up a gear in 2001.

He believes that his knowledge of the recent process of evolution at Ferrari means that he is ideally equipped to judge precisely how much progress his new team is making. Equally, he feels that those who fire off generalised criticism towards Jaguar are dramatically wide of the mark, simply because they have no conception of the magnitude of the task which faces the team. 'I have to raise my game, everybody has,' he said. 'The whole thing will start to snowball and we will get better. The potential is there. Maybe I can't drive faster, but we can be more careful and work harder. It was only possible to work on a certain level last season, as we couldn't get any better. But if we don't get better from December we are in big trouble.'

Alan Henry

WorldCom is an ordinary phone company.

Like this is an ordinary car.

T he most modern and efficient vehicle for transporting your voice, data, and Internet traffic is WorldCom.

In the U.S. alone, we own and operate 45,000 route miles of long distance fiber, with dedicated Internet facilities in more than 70 cities. Outside the U.S., our 60-Gbps transatlantic (joint-venture) cable system connects to our wholly owned pan-European telecommunications network—and more than 5,000 buildings throughout Europe. And the WorldCom/UUNET Internet network is the world's premier IP-only backbone.

On land and under sea, the WorldCom network continues to expand worldwide—in Latin America, Asia, and the Pacific Rim—so your voice, data, and Internet traffic will have fewer detours to other networks.

Get in the fast lane with WorldCom's superior portfolio of integrated products.

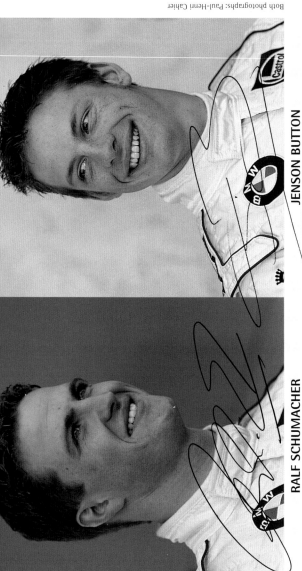

RALF SCHUMACHER

JENSON BUTTON

WILLIAMS 9 10

FOR the third-successive season Williams stayed away from the winner's rostrum, but the famous British team was no longer marking time. This year a new engine supply partnership with BMW saw Williams striding out with a purpose along the road to sustained recovery and a position as regular contenders close to the front of the field.

For BMW, this marked a return to motor racing's senior international category for the first time in more than a decade. Back in the early 1980s the Munich company forged a spectacular reputation for prodigious 1000 bhp-plus power outputs from its remarkable production-block 1.5-litre turbocharged four-cylinder engine.

That engine was produced by a small engineering group headed by the respected engineer Paul Rosche, but the demands of F1 in the first season of the new millennium were dramatically different. BMW established a totally new engine development team at its Munich headquarters and developed its all-new type E41

72-degree V10 in time to have its first run.

'In September 1999 we produced an FW21B development car for the new engine' said Williams technical director Patrick Head. 'This basically had the FW21 suspension geometry and the Step 3 version of the engine which was installed in the chassis with the oil tank ahead of the engine rather than in with the gearbox.

'This produced an oil system problem which, in fact, had a relatively simple solution but took a bit of time to sort out because the problem only arose when the engine was installed in the car rather than on the dynamometer. The FW22 chassis was again developed by the engineering team including chief designer Gavin Fisher and aerodynamicist Geoff Willis, overseen by Patrick Head. 'It has some similarities to last year's FW21,' said Head. 'We worked to build on the strong points of that car and to eliminate its low points, in particular its poor aerodynamic performance on high-downforce circuits. We made

some worthwhile progress on the aero package, but while our form was certainly improved in Hungary, for example, there were still some circuits where we struggled for set-up. We also pared off some weight, which was useful, because the BMW was a bit heavier than the Renault [Supertec] engine we'd previously used, so that reduction really balanced out that added weight.'

In order to maximise the potential of the new BMW V10, the new Williams was fitted with a seven-speed longitudinal gearbox rather than the six-speed transmission employed on the 1999 Supertec-engined car.

During the course of the season the BMW progressively increased its power output from 740 to around 800 bhp. It was enough to keep the team in play with all but Ferrari and McLaren-Mercedes.

'The BMW engine always had reasonable power,' said Head, 'but the main concern was concentrating on achieving reliability. Early problems with quality control were overcome and once BMW felt confident with

that the power improvements were quick to follow.'

Williams had quite a dilemma on the driver front, however. Former CART Champion Alex Zanardi had failed demonstrably to come to grips with the challenge of F1 during 1999 with the result that Frank Williams and Head wanted to dispense with his services. Unfortunately this was complicated by the fact they'd signed a three-year deal with the pleasant Italian and it took some months to reach a financially acceptable means of disentangling themselves from the contract.

That wasn't all. Seeking out a replacement was not the work of a moment because Williams had given an undertaking that he would give Colombian driver Juan Pablo Montoya a drive in 2001. That meant anybody coming into the team as Ralf Schumacher's running-mate faced the prospect of being dismissed after only a season. In the event, Williams resolved the matter outstandingly well.

After holding comparative tests between the F3000 front-runner Bruno

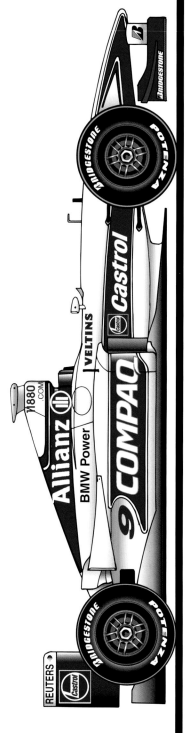

REUTERS **Castrol**

WILLIAMS FW22-BMW

Sponsors: Compaq, Allianz, Andersen Consulting, Castrol, Intel Inside, Nortel, Reuters, Veltins, 11880.COM

Team principal: Sir Frank Williams **Technical director:** Patrick Head **Team manager:** Dickie Stanford **Chief mechanic:** Carl Gaden

ENGINE Type: BMW E41 **No. of cylinders (vee angle):** V10 (72°) **Sparking plugs:** not given **Electronics:** not given **Fuel:** Petrobras **Oil:** Castrol

TRANSMISSION Gearbox: Williams seven-speed longitudinal semi-automatic **Driveshafts:** Williams **Clutch:** AP Racing (hand-operated)

CHASSIS Front suspension: double wishbones, pushrod/torsion bar **Rear suspension:** double wishbones, pushrod/coil spring, damper

Suspension dampers: Williams/Penske **Wheel diameter:** front: 13 in. rear: 13 in. **Wheels:** OZ **Tyres:** Bridgestone **Brake pads:** not given

Brake discs: Carbone Industrie **Brake calipers:** Hitco **Steering:** Williams (power-assisted) **Radiators:** Secan/IMI **Fuel tanks:** ATL **Battery:** not given

Instruments: Williams

DIMENSIONS Wheelbase: not given **Track:** front: not given rear: not given **Formula weight:** 1322.8 lb/600 kg including driver **Fuel capacity:** not given

Up Front in Formula One

BMW Recommends **Castrol**

The partnership between BMW and Castrol includes R&D, manufacturing and after sales care. Up front in F1, Castrol provide technical assistance both at the race track and in testing for the BMW WilliamsF1 Team.

Y2K was a hugely impressive debut season for the Castrol lubricated BMW V10 engine and we congratulate the Team on an outstanding year. We now look forward to being 'Up front in 2001'.

Research and Development

Manufacturing

After Sales Care

Motorsport

Lubrication solutions since 1899

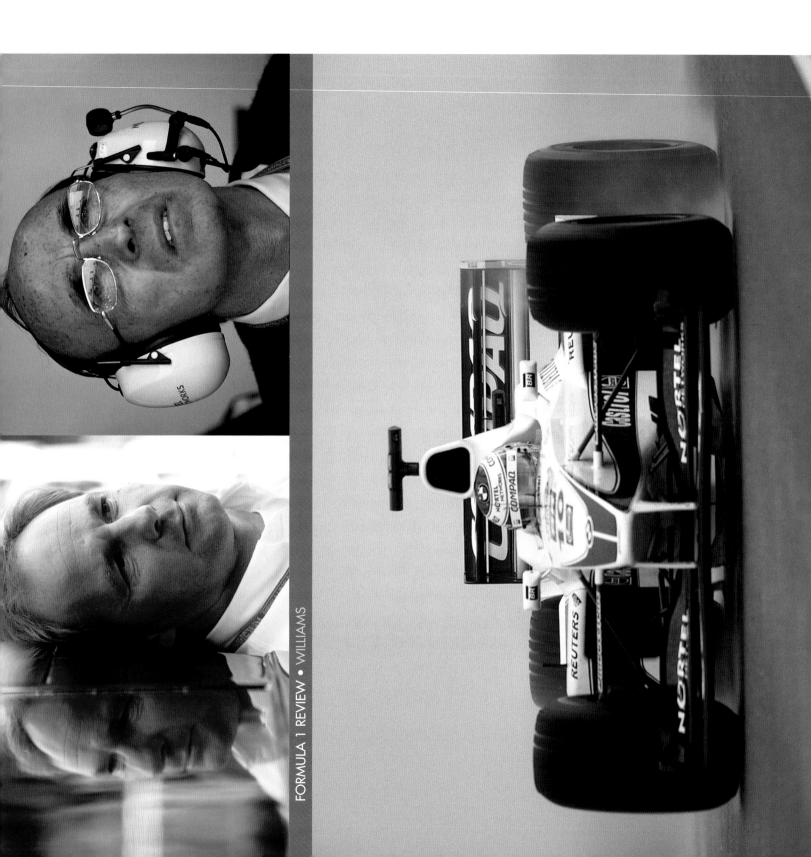

FORMULA 1 REVIEW • WILLIAMS

Top left: A reflective Gerhard Berger can be quietly satisfied with BMW's burgeoning partnership with Williams.
Steve Etherington/EPI

Top right: Sir Frank Williams's shrewd choice of Jenson Button leaves him with strong driver options over the forthcoming seasons.
Paul-Henri Cahier

Above: Jenson Button silenced all doubters with his tremendous speed on the track and maturity off it.
Bryn Williams/Words & Pictures

Junqueira and 19-year-old Jenson Button, who'd finished third in the 1999 British F3 Championship, Williams opted for Button. They signed the youngster on a five-year contract, but Williams laid down very firm guidelines even before the start of the season when he said 'Jenson has got to perform in a manner to keep Juan Pablo out of the team.'

By the end of the season, one could have been forgiven for thinking that Button had done just that. However, by the time he really hit top form in the second half of the season, the decision had already been taken that Montoya should definitely switch to F1 with the team in 2001. Button was 'leased' to Benetton for two years with the apparent intention that he should return to the Williams fold in 2003.

For Button's part, he admitted he could hardly believe what he was hearing when the offer came through from Williams.

'I was having a drink with a few friends just before Christmas when my mobile rang and the voice at the end said it was Frank Williams,' he remembered.

'I had suspected that it was somebody playing a joke, but it was Frank who said he just wanted to touch base with me and he later phoned back with the offer of a test drive.'

Williams was hugely impressed with Button's personality, but decided to check his impressions with BMW's newly appointed Competitions Manager Gerhard Berger. The Austrian former F1 racer had taken to his new post like a duck to water, confounding all those critics who suggested he had too much of a free-wheeling, playboy personality. In fact, Berger's level of commitment in this new position was one of the most impressive elements of the entire 2000 F1 season.

Berger admits he thought Button was an interesting character and was keen to give him a test run. What happened next at Jerez left Gerhard simply stunned.

'What you've got to remember is that I knew Jerez extremely well, having driven my last grand prix there in 1997,' said Berger, 'so I knew instantly what I was looking for when I went up to the top of the control tower and watched Jenson lapping the circuit.

'You know, it was quite incredible. He'd not driven an F1 car before, but he was instantly on the line, never

Thanks Jenson.
Thanks Ralf.

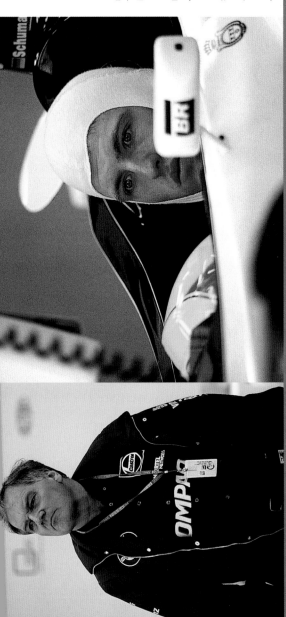

For left: Patrick Head oversaw Williams's return to the sharp end of the grid, with the team finishing best of the rest behind Ferrari and McLaren.

Left: Ralf Schumacher appeared to have been startled by the speed of team-mate Jenson Button towards the end of 2000.

Ralf nevertheless delivered the lion's share of the team's points with some impressive drives including podium finishes in Australia, Belgium and Italy *(below).*

All photographs: Paul-Henri Cahier

ran wide, and the only indication that he was pushing hard came from the occasional locked brake as he probed the limit.

'For me, this was just incredible. And he has followed that up throughout the year. I can't think of a new driver in F1 who has made so few mistakes in his first season.'

Yet it is not Button's sheer ability behind the wheel which won respect from the touchlines, for he had a few indifferent races. Even the enormously impressive manner in which he mastered Hockenheim in the wet, Spa and Suzuka almost take second place to his remarkable maturity and even temperament. These are qualities which will turn out to be unimaginable advantages to him as his career unfolds over the next few years, helping him to take a philosophical and resilient view of the ups and downs which he will inevitably experience.

'Jenson was excellent,' said Head. 'He had probably a few more engine problems early in the season as compared with Ralf, but he was a quick learner and adapted well to the challenge of circuits which were unfamiliar to him. In short, he was almost perfect.'

Scanning the championship points table, it may seem extremely unfair to mention Ralf Schumacher almost as an afterthought. After all, the German produced all the BMW Williams team's podium finishes – in Melbourne, Spa and Monza. He was driving superbly at Indianapolis, keeping pace with brother Michael's leading Ferrari, and fought back manfully from a painfully cut leg sustained at Monaco to race again a fortnight later in Canada. Yet he was worryingly inconsistent at times and struggled to shake off several colds during the course of the year.

'Jenson rattled his cage and he didn't like it one bit,' said one Williams insider wryly, 'and he was out to lunch certainly in the last two races of the season.' Unquestionably, there is huge talent still lurking in Schumacher junior, yet he needs to realise it on a more consistent basis. Certainly well before contract renewal time at the end of 2002.

As far as the future is concerned, both Williams and BMW are intent on building on the promising first year of their partnership. Next season they switch to a Michelin tyre contract which is a good long-term move, even should it prove a handicap in the short-term. 'But generally I would say we are in a position at the present time when we take things as they come,' said Head. 'We had a few strong races this year, but 36 Championship points when you look at the other two [Ferrari and McLaren] look pretty feeble.

'There is obviously a challenge ahead – it's not an aspiration of ours to be third – but everyone seems a bit lacklustre if you're not McLaren or Ferrari.

'Nobody else has anything to shout about.'

Alan Henry

ALEXANDER WURZ

GIANCARLO FISICHELLA

11 12 BENETTON

HALFWAY through the season, Benetton were taking a serious look at third place in the championship, a result which would be as good as it could get for anyone other than Ferrari and McLaren. In the end, the team from Oxfordshire managed to hold on to fourth place by the skin of its teeth but, even so, that was a marked improvement on sixth place and a dismal season in 1999. It looks even better when you consider that all bar two of the points were scored by just one car, Alexander Wurz struggling his way towards the end during a second-successive year of disappointment for the Austrian and his team.

That said, Giancarlo Fisichella was hardly the model of consistency, his early-season enterprise and enthusiasm disappearing into mediocrity as Jacques Villeneuve and BAR-Honda closed in on that fourth place. Indeed, had it not been for Fisichella's six points in Brazil in March, Benetton would have lost out. But that should not cloud a year of improvement for the former champions as they set in motion a recovery from the technical disasters of 1999.

'I do believe we have moved forward quite a lot with the B200 but, to be honest, that wasn't difficult because we were at our lowest ebb in 1999,' says Pat Symonds, Benetton's technical director. 'Last year's car was far too close to the weight limit because we had invested in technologies that, had they worked, would have been worth the weight disadvantage. But they didn't work. More serious than that had been an aerodynamic inconsistency that we couldn't identify until we were about three quarters of the way through the season.

'All of this meant a fundamental change – to the philosophy, almost – which had to be incorporated in the B200. I think we lost out a little because we were aiming mainly at getting rid of this aerodynamic inconsistency rather than trying to improve performance. Nevertheless we now had a car that aerodynamically behaved as it should, so we were very happy with that side of things. At the same time, we made chassis improvements. The car was an unbelievable amount lighter than the B199, and stiffer in areas where we had identified problems the previous year.'

While all of this had been going on, Symonds had been keeping his eye on the broader picture as he sought to return the team to the glory days of 1994 and 1995. To do that, the team would need to secure manufacturer support rather than continue with Supertec and the customer version of the Renault/Mecachrome V10. At which point, exit the Benetton family after more than 10 years and enter – or, re-enter, to be more precise – Flavio Briatore to head up the team and prepare for a return by new owners, Renault. Not surprisingly, perhaps, the engine performance improved immeasurably during 2000.

'We started the season with an engine that was already a big improvement on 1999,' says Symonds. 'Then the commitment by Renault to come back into F1 meant that the work they were doing with Supertec/Mecachrome became much more aggressive. We were seeing much more of the old Renault. So, everything came together much better in 2000 and therefore bodes well for the future.'

With extra power from the engine and a more consistent chassis, Benetton should have been challenging Williams all the way for third place rather than simply during the first half of the season. So, where did it go wrong? 'Just as last year, there has been a first and a second division,' says Symonds. 'The reliability of F1 cars is astonishing these days. It's something we have prided ourselves in for many years, but now everyone else is just as reliable. More often than not you had two McLarens and two Ferraris finishing, which meant the second division was a race for two or three points. Occasionally the first division guys didn't finish and suddenly you could make a big jump in your points.

'But it was unfortunate that nearly all our points were scored with one car and, in the second half of the season, that car either didn't finish or was out

BENETTON B200-PLAYLIFE

Sponsors: Mild Seven, United Colors of Benetton, Playlife, Marconi, Agip, D2 Mannesmann, Korean Air

Managing Director: Flavio Briatore **Technical director:** Mike Gascoyne **Engineering director:** Pat Symonds **Team manager:** Carlos Nunes **Chief mechanic:** Michael Ainsley-Cowlishaw

ENGINE Type: Playlife **No. of cylinders (vee angle):** V10 (not given) **Sparking plugs:** Champion **Electronics:** Benetton/Magneti Marelli **Fuel:** Agip **Oil:** Agip

TRANSMISSION Gearbox: Benetton six-speed longitudinal semi-automatic **Driveshafts:** Tri-lobe **Clutch:** AP Racing (hand-operated)

CHASSIS Front suspension: double wishbones, pushrod/torsion bar **Rear suspension:** double wishbones, pushrod/coil spring **Suspension dampers:** Koni

Wheel diameter: front: 13 in. rear: 13 in. **Wheel rim widths:** front: 12 in. rear: 12 in. **Wheels:** BBS **Tyres:** Bridgestone **Brake pads:** Brembo

Brake discs: Brembo **Brake calipers:** AP Racing **Steering:** Benetton (power-assisted) **Radiators:** Marston **Fuel tanks:** ATL

Battery: Benetton **Instruments:** Benetton

DIMENSIONS Wheelbase: not given **Track:** front: 57 in./1450 mm rear: 56 in./1425 mm **Gearbox weight:** 121 lb/55 kg **Chassis weight:** 110 lb/50 kg

Formula weight: 1322.8 lb/600 kg including driver **Fuel capacity:** 33 gallons/150 litres

of the points completely. That hurt us badly. Having said that, we were still gratified that we were competitive in Austria, on a track where we had struggled the previous year. We were competitive on two very different circuits in Germany and in Hungary, and we were also on the pace in Belgium.'

The same could not be said for Imola and Barcelona, where Fisichella qualified 19th and 13th respectively. Symonds admits that the San Marino GP was a low point but says it was one of the rare occasions – a late-season surge notwithstanding – when Wurz was quicker than his team-mate. Rather than indicate a return to form by the Austrian, it was evidence that Fisichella finds just as much difficulty with Imola as do the team's technicians. Overall, Wurz's performances remained something of a mystery. 'This has been an immense disappointment for me,' says Symonds. 'I fought hard to keep Alex in the team for 2000 because I really did believe that it was something we were doing wrong. Last year we had a dreadful car and it seemed that Giancarlo had been able to use some of his, let's say, more natural skill to make a better job of a deficient car. I felt we had seen in Alex, way back in '98, that the guy had an above-average ability. So, because he wasn't demonstrating that ability in 1999, I felt that it was our fault.

'Alex tried very hard and I will never criticise him for that. But for reasons which I could simply no longer understand, we were not getting there. It's a great shame. He's a lovely guy. He's had full commitment to the team but it just got to a point where it wasn't working. I do hope McLaren can maybe find out where we went wrong and get him back to where he was, because that looked like an exceptional young talent a few years ago. The return of Briatore (replacing the comparatively ineffective Rocco Benetton) marked a renewal of the familiar no-nonsense summaries when things were not going according to plan. Wurz felt the sharp end of the Italian's scathing remarks, as did Fisichella when the number one driver seemed to lose interest during the last three races. Symonds had seen it all before and was neither surprised nor unduly upset by Briatore's brutal tactics.

'We've worked together since 1988 and we get on very well,' said Symonds. 'Flavio is a master at the big deal. He sees the big picture and acts on it. That means people either love him or hate him. I'm in the former category. I love the way he works. But he's different this time round because he's got a massive responsibility – as we all have – to get this team back to the top. But I believe he is one of the people who can do it.'

The value of Briatore's return has also been recognised by loyal personnel who remember the good times. Having survived a terrible season in 1999, the Benetton team remained intact and a model of optimism and professionalism.

'Spa was a classic example of that,' says Symonds. 'From Saturday lunchtime onwards, we could not have had a worse weekend. It started with an engine failure on Alex's car on his first timed run, which required us to put him in the spare car which was prepared for Giancarlo. While all this was going on, we sent Giancarlo out for his first run – and experienced another engine problem during his timed lap. This required us to limit Alex to one flying lap before getting the T-car back for Giancarlo. The mechanics then managed to get Giancarlo out for what would be his only timed lap. The discipline of the team when handling that situation was stupefying. No one had to really say anything; it was clockwork.

'And then to have Giancarlo roll his car in the warm-up. As soon as I saw the T.V. pictures, I thought it would be a write-off. These days you are so lucky if you haven't punched a wishbone through the monocoque. The damage was extensive but we had that car ready for the race. I was really proud of the team that weekend.

'Looking at the season as a whole, we may have improved from a very low point, but we improved in a very positive way. I'm not going to look back on the year 2000 and say, "yes, that was a great season." But I can look back on it and be proud that we identified our problems in total and went a long way towards fixing them. We started building up a very solid foundation for further improvements, which is exactly what we need now that Renault is coming back.'

Maurice Hamilton

Top left: Giancarlo Fisichella ran strongly at the start of the season with fine second-place finishes in Brazil and Monaco (pictured). But his performances seemed to slip alarmingly as the season drew to a close.
Bryn Williams/Words & Pictures

Top right: Flavio Briatore was back to take overall control of the team in preparation for a welcome return of Renault power.
Paul-Henri Cahier

Above: Alex Wurz once again struggled with his car throughout the year, and will be replaced in 2001 by Jenson Button. The Austrian, however, has landed himself a testing role with McLaren which could reinvigorate his career.
Bryn Williams/Words & Pictures

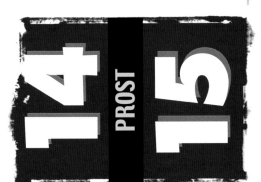

JEAN ALESI

NICK HEIDFELD

'LET'S say that it has been a very difficult season. There have been two things: the lack of reliability throughout the year, and aerodynamically we have been handicapped. The handling has suffered consequently. The reliability has been catastrophic. And the engine hasn't been good. Then there have been small problems which have been equally disastrous. Quality control has been bad as well.'

Jean Alesi, Prost's number one driver, never hid his feelings about the team and Peugeot throughout the 2000 season. Not surprisingly. The disastrous year dragged him and the team to the bottom. The boss almost lost his team altogether; Peugeot pulled out. So did primary sponsors Gauloises. Technical director Alan Jenkins found his position untenable and his place was taken by Jean-Paul Gusset. It didn't change anything; Prost were still at the bottom of the table.

The year started with a new technical team and a new engine. Jenkins had joined in June of the previous year, but almost immediately he had to ease up on the design of the AP03 as Peugeot's commitment was in question. Two months later, he could re-start.

With the help of a staff of around 40, he would design most of the rear end of the car and former technical director Loïc Bigois would do the aerodynamics at Magny-Cours. John Barnard's 20-strong team at B3 in Godalming, Surrey, would do the front end of the car – front suspension, steering, pedals, master cylinders – and the rear suspension, which was derived from the AP02 anyway.

The previous car had been long and big. Now, with a new, shorter engine – not derived from the 3.5-litre block as the previous two had been – and a new small seven-speed gearbox at the request of Peugeot but not carbonfibre due to the engine delay, there was a lower centre of gravity and the car was the right size. Bigois claimed the aerodynamic numbers were O.K.

With a lower centre of gravity, a more compact and stiffer car, the potential gain was 1.5s per lap. The risks were a new gearbox, a common gearbox/engine oil system and a vital new in-house hydraulic system to replace the antique ex-Benetton/Ligier version, operating gearbox control, differential, clutch and engine parts.

Peugeot's A20 engine was 53.5 mm shorter than the A18, 15 mm narrower and 20 mm lower. At 109 kg, it was also 13.5 kg lighter. But like Peugeot's previous engines, the new A20 was also less powerful than the final development of its predecessor. Peugeot had also contracted to use TAG's 2000 electronic system, with no input from Prost.

The AP03 was launched on February 1, but within minutes of its first test, it was on its way home again. A rear suspension flexture had broken up and the team thought it better to be safe than sorry and to investigate the cause.

It was a one-off problem but the suspension was slightly changed and it never ran with the rear suspension designed for it. The team had so many electrical problems at the next test that they ran out of ideas and went home early from that too. They had done less than 2,000 km when they went to the first race, a third of what was needed. It was a knock-on effect from the summer's delay.

Once the season began, unreliability came thick and fast. Software problems in the electrics masked an unsuitable installation because the system was being affected by temperature and vibration. When a car stopped with a scrambled gearbox, the chain of problems to be investigated would include the common oil system, the electronics and the hydraulics. With no contact between TAG and Prost, it took time to solve. Jordan had the same electrical problems, but enjoyed a closer relationship with TAG.

Then there was the engine. Firstly, Peugeot hadn't delivered the spec they promised at the start of the season. There were no variable trumpets, for instance. The power curve wasn't good. But then the bore linings began breaking up from the block. After being used once, the blocks would crack. Peugeot began to run out of

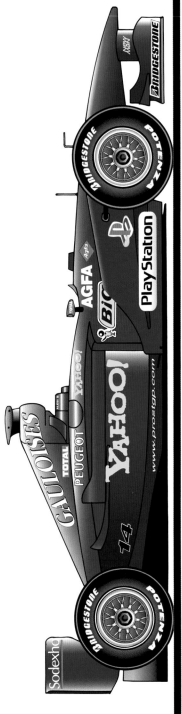

PROST AP03–PEUGEOT

Sponsors: Gauloises, Peugeot, Yahoo, Bridgestone, PlayStation, Bic, Agfa, Sodexho, Total, Altran, Newman, Cegetel, 3M

Team principal: Alain Prost **Technical director:** Jean-Paul Gusset **Team manager:** Jean-Pierre Chatenet **Chief engineer:** Vincent Gaillardot

ENGINE Type: Peugeot A20 **No. of cylinders (vee angle):** V10 (72°) **Sparking plugs:** NGK **Electronics:** TAG Electronic Systems **Fuel:** Total **Oil:** Total

TRANSMISSION Gearbox: Prost/Xtrac seven-speed longitudinal semi-automatic **Driveshafts:** Prost **Clutch:** AP (hand-operated)

CHASSIS Front suspension: double wishbones, pushrod **Rear suspension:** double wishbones, pushrod **Suspension dampers:** Penske/Prost

     Wheel diameter: front: not given rear: not given **Wheels:** BBS **Tyres:** Bridgestone **Brake discs:** Carbone Industrie

     Brake calipers: Brembo **Steering:** Prost **Radiators:** not given **Fuel tanks:** ATL **Battery:** Fiamm **Instruments:** Prost

DIMENSIONS Wheelbase: 3020 mm **Track:** front: 58.1 in./1475 mm rear: 55.5 in./1410 mm **Formula weight:** 1322.8 lb/600 kg including driver

engines, so that cars would arrive at the circuit without any at all. The engines were flexing as well and some four different specifications of block were produced. It became very public too. Alesi said his Formula 3 car had more power. Prost and Peugeot's Corrado Provera weren't even speaking.

At the same time, the power curve was curious, in that it would happily reach 785 bhp at 15,860 rpm in long-trumpet spec. It would then rev higher, but the power dropped off after another 50 rpm rather than flat-ten. So the car's performance would quickly be compromised by wind or another car. It was also best in cool conditions, in spite of being designed to run at 110 degrees. Best straightline speeds were usually posted early on Saturday morning, or in the Sunday warm-up.

It didn't get much worse than the

European Grand Prix at the Nürburgring, the circuit without any at all. The engines were flexing as well and some cedes engines in 2001 after all, in spite of intensive negotiations. And then Nick Heidfeld, who had slowly regained confidence shattered since the start of the season, had his 13th-fastest time disallowed for being underweight. Blame and counter-claims flew like confetti, again, rather publicly.

The car had been twitchy and nervous at the rear from the start. There was no high-speed grip from the aero-dynamics, but early in the season Barnard developed a new front wing which gave some feel back to the car and Alesi was much in favour. It helped him claim the year's best qualifying position, seventh at Monaco. But the car basically suffered instability and however much the suspension and set-up were fine-tuned, it would just

disguise the problem. Peugeot's withdrawal meant that engine development petered out after mid-season.

By this stage, Alan Jenkins had already left the company after Alain Prost felt unable to support him on a personnel decision. Without putting too fine a point on it, insiders claim that the rapid expansion of the team from 65 to 230 people in three years has overtaken the management structure, which mainly consists of Ligier throwbacks managing new Prost.

With Alain Prost's relative inexperience at running a team, and reacting in the face of a problem-filled season such as 2000, things can only improve. But fairly drastic changes may have to be made. Alesi has even named the names...

Bob Constanduros

Top left: Funeral fire. Peugeot finally pulled the plug on their Formula 1 involvement after seven largely disappointing seasons with three teams.

Top right: Jean Alesi grappled manfully with a car unworthy of his talent.

Above left: In spite of the difficulties, Alesi gave his best and his support for his friend and team boss, Alain Prost.

Above centre: Alain Prost came close to selling out mid-season, but the Prost badge remains with Ferrari power promised for 2000.

MIKA SALO

PEDRO DINIZ

16 SAUBER 17

SAUBER find themselves in that massive midfield bunch which is usually led by Jordan, Williams and sometimes BAR and which then also includes Arrows, Benetton and Jaguar. With the top two teams scooping maximum points or at least the podium, it was up to these seven teams to pick up the crumbs that they left – usually fourth to sixth.

That is the region of the grid where Sauber resided, picking up points when they could, capitalising on the reliability of their chassis and the well tried and tested Petronas engine which Ferrari had used throughout the previous year.

The problem is always trying to find an advantage. Each team is of a different status: three using full works engines in 2000, all except Sauber using dedicated engines in 2001. This is the jungle where it's easy to drop out of the bunch like Prost and end up fighting for last place, and incredibly difficult to move up to join the big two. Remember how it used to be the big four?

It is also a world of constant social climbing: getting a better engine deal than the next team, having your own wind tunnel, a bigger engineering staff, a development that no one else has. A hydraulic differential that the drivers like!

This is Sauber's world, and here they certainly kept their heads above water in 2000 and can be proud of usually being ahead of Prost with their works Peugeots, Jaguar with Ford support (once enjoyed by Sauber) and Arrows looking forward to their new AMT engines.

Sauber made steps forward in 2000. Jean Alesi went to Prost and was replaced by Mika Salo for his five races with them in 1999, prior to moving to Toyota. Pedro Diniz remained with the team. They kept the Ferrari engine, but the engineering staff was re-organised, with Leo Ress standing down as technical director and being replaced in March by Sauber returnee Willy Rampf who initially came back as head of

track engineering. Sergio Rinland joined as chief designer, head of the 35-strong design team but specialising mainly in composites.

Ress, however, was responsible for the C19. It appeared early in the winter and responded well to the set-up changes made to it. 'We felt on the pace with this car,' Rampf admitted. 'We ran early, which gave us the chance to sort out all the reliability problems.' However, testing revealed the odd problem on the horizon: there were two rear wing breakages.

The season got off to a shaky start. Salo started a fine 10th on the grid in Australia, and frustratedly followed home Villeneuve to sixth place, but was then disqualified for an illegal front wing. The team put that one behind them, and moved on to Brazil, but here, Salo suffered a rear wing failure on Saturday morning and there was another one that afternoon.

After a swift examination, it was decided that the team couldn't afford to jeopardise safety and race with

what they had, and both cars were withdrawn. It was scarcely an encouraging start to the season.

And it had far-reaching effects. 'The problem in Brazil where the rear wing broke put us back two months,' explained Rampf. 'We had to redesign the rear wing and, for safety reasons, look at all the structural parts, the wing elements and redesign all the wings. That took up a lot of capacity in design and manufacturing which meant that we couldn't work on other developments.'

But both cars finished at Imola – Salo again behind Villeneuve but in the points – and also in Britain. Salo finished seventh in Spain while it was Diniz's turn to finish seventh at the Nürburgring, having out-qualified his team-mate.

Salo scored his usual points in Monaco while a new engine spec, the only modification during the year, appeared for Montreal: more powerful and less weight. Smaller developments appeared throughout the year.

SAUBER C19-PETRONAS

Sponsors: Red Bull, Petronas, Parmalat, Compaq, Bridgestone, Catia Solutions, Brastemp

Team principal: Peter Sauber **Technical director:** Willy Rampf **Team manager:** Beat Zehnder **Chief mechanic:** Urs Kuratle

ENGINE   Type: Petronas (Ferrari) SPE 04A **No. of cylinders (vee angle):** V10 (80°) **Sparking plugs:** not given **Electronics:** Magneti Marelli **Fuel:** Petronas **Oil:** Petronas

TRANSMISSION   Gearbox: Sauber seven-speed longitudinal semi-automatic **Driveshafts:** Sauber **Clutch:** Sachs

CHASSIS   Front suspension: double wishbones, pushrod **Rear suspension:** double wishbones, pushrod **Suspension dampers:** Sachs

Wheel diameter: front: 13 in. rear: 13 in. **Wheels:** OZ **Tyres:** Bridgestone **Brake discs:** Carbone Industrie **Brake pads:** Carbone Industrie **Brake calipers:** Brembo

Steering: Sauber **Radiators:** not given **Fuel tanks:** ATL **Battery:** Magneti Marelli **Instruments:** Magneti Marelli

DIMENSIONS   Wheelbase: 3020 mm **Track:** front: 1470 mm rear: 1410 mm **Formula weight:** 1322.8 lb/600 kg including driver **Fuel capacity:** not given

Once the post-Brazil beefing-up process had been completed, a slimming exercise was initiated. 'The whole suspension was completely revised during the year,' said Rampf. 'We started by trying to make each composite part 10 to 20 per cent lighter. The monocoque was the only thing that wasn't modified. It was a new but necessary pace of development, one that has been lacking in the past.

Like all teams, Sauber concentrated on aerodynamic developments. Each time there was a different downforce configuration, there would be a change of aerodynamic package. The team had also worked on an hydraulic differential early in the season, and once the wing problem had been solved, that was restarted, although it was never raced.

However, as the season progressed, the Sauber drivers slipped a little further down the grid, as they had in years passed. Austria and Hungary were exceptions, with Salo finishing in the points in Austria and Germany. They frequently complained of a car that was difficult to balance, of a lack of traction and not enough grip in cornering. When it was well balanced at the start of the weekend, they could deliver the goods but actually working towards a good balance seemed more difficult.

Salo was generally the stronger of the pair, in spite of Diniz's continued enthusiasm. The Finn tried hard to integrate himself within the team, finding an apartment in Zurich. 'He pushes the team, and his experience with Ferrari meant he brought good useful ideas with him,' he said. 'He can never wait. Two weeks is too long for him,' said Rampf.

But after the announcement that the Finn was going to Toyota there were signs of decreased interest. Overall, the atmosphere was better within the team, but life will get harder for the Swiss concern, in spite of Peter Sauber's efforts to secure a dedicated engine deal.

Bob Constanduros

Top left: Mika Salo picked up occasional points, but spent the season largely in mid-field anonymity.

Top centre: Peter Sauber managed to keep his team in touch, but is still chasing a dedicated engine deal.

Top right: Salo decided an offer from Toyota was too good to pass up.

Photographs: Bryn Williams/Words & Pictures

Above: Pedro Diniz failed to score a single championship point for the first time since his 1995 debut year.

Paul-Henri Cahier

JOS VERSTAPPEN

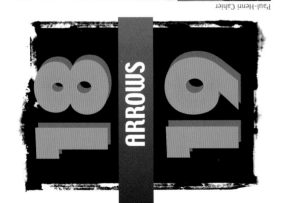

PEDRO DE LA ROSA

Paul-Henri Cahier

18 ARROWS 19

A FTER closing down his own F1 operation which had been based round Brian Hart's compact, if underpowered V10, Arrows boss Tom Walkinshaw decided the only way forward was to lease Supertec V10s for the new season in an effort to vault his Leafield-based team into the front rank.

It almost worked. Although the Supertec engine was struggling for power in absolute terms against the likes of Ferrari, Mercedes-Ilmor and even Cosworth, it was still a very user-friendly power unit which was generally reliable and unquestionably easy to install in the chassis.

Yet drivers Pedro de la Rosa and Jos Verstappen failed to unlock the A21's full potential, due largely to a succession of generally trifling mechanical failures which caused retirements from races where the Arrows cars seemed poised to score championship points. Despite this, 2000 was generally an encouraging season for the British team which did much to

enhance its overall credibility in the pit lane.

Arrows Technical Director Mike Coughlan, aided by aerodynamicist Eghbal Hamidy, came up with an effective and straightforward design in the A21 which was unusual in that it featured pullrod – rather than pushrod – front suspension, the first time this configuration had been used in F1 for a decade.

'There was obviously a big push to get everything in the car as low as possible,' said Coughlan, 'but I have to say that I was surprised that nobody else tried it, even though there were some downside issues which I think we handled quite well, knowing that it was not necessarily something of a compromise.'

Coughlan went this way in an effort to lower the centre of gravity of the car as much as possible and, from the very first test at Jerez, it seemed that the car was endowed with excellent mechanical grip. Its fuel tank was on the small side which made one-stop options at

places like Canada and Hockenheim a little too marginal for comfort, but the car displayed great wet-weather form, most notably in the hands of Pedro de la Rosa at Nürburgring where the Spaniard finished sixth.

'Yes, I think we'd basically got quite good mechanical grip,' said Coughlan, 'but, that said, we struggled at Monaco and Hungaroring. But both cars flew at Nürburgring and we were always at our best when the softer tyre compound was the preferred choice. On harder rubber, we tended to struggle.'

Hamidy had joined the team from Stewart in the summer of 1999 by which time the A21's basic concept was already finalised. 'He tidied up the aero package,' said Coughlan. 'He is a clever and very nice bloke.' However, by the end of the 2000 season Hamidy's future with the team was uncertain as, although bound by a contract with Arrows until the end of 2001, he had received a significant offer to join Jordan Grand Prix. It was

a matter which Tom Walkinshaw and Eddie Jordan would eventually have to sort out between them.

Coughlan admits that the switch from the Arrows-badged Hart V10 to the Renault-based Supertec unit saw the team change up a gear in terms of its expectations.

'I was very impressed,' he said. 'Working with the Supertec people raised our game considerably. Whenever we asked a question, they gave us more information in return that we'd ever expected from an engine supplier. They had huge reserves of experience and resource.'

Yet to achieve seventh place in the constructors' championship was less by far than Arrows believed it should have managed. 'Taking the season as a whole, I would have to say that we were encouraged, but ultimately very disappointed,' said Coughlan.

'We definitely underperformed. Overall, we should have been challenging for fifth place in the Championship and I believe the A21 was

ARROWS A21-SUPERTEC

Sponsors: Orange, Eurobet, Lost Boys, UPC/Chello, SGI, European Aviation

Team principal: Tom Walkinshaw **Technical director:** Mike Coughlan **Team manager:** Steve Nielsen **Chief mechanic:** Stuart Cowie

ENGINE **Type:** Supertec FB07 **No. of cylinders (vee angle):** V10 (71°) **Sparking plugs:** Champion **Electronics:** Magneti Marelli **Fuel:** Repsol **Oil:** Repsol

TRANSMISSION **Gearbox:** Arrows/Xtrac carbon-fibre six-speed longitudinal semi-automatic **Driveshafts:** Arrows **Clutch:** Arrows (hand-operated)

CHASSIS **Front suspension:** double wishbones, in-board spring dampers, pullrod **Rear suspension:** double wishbones, in-board spring dampers, pushrod

Suspension dampers: not given **Wheel diameter:** front: not given rear: not given **Wheels:** BBS **Tyres:** Bridgestone **Brake pads:** not given **Brake discs:** Hitco

Brake calipers: AP Racing **Steering:** Arrows **Radiators:** Secan/IMI Marston **Fuel tanks:** ATL **Battery:** not given **Instruments:** not given

DIMENSIONS **Wheelbase:** not given **Track:** front: not given rear: not given **Formula weight:** 1322.8 lb/600 kg including driver **Fuel capacity:** not given

basically a better car than the Benetton, the other Supertec user. Our end result was not really indicative of our potential. In my view, we should have been up there challenging Jordan.

'So often we would wind up perhaps seventh and ninth at the end of Saturday morning free qualifying only to slip to 11th or 12th when it mattered. I think to some extent we also suffered because it was the first season we were using the Supertec engine. We gave away some development time prior to the start of the season when we were just coming to terms with installation issues.'

Verstappen and de la Rosa were highly regarded within the team. 'Great blokes,' said Coughlan. 'Not

Schumacher and Häkkinen, but much better than most people give them credit for. I think Jos, in particular, will be much stronger in 2001 than he was this year now that he realises just how physically fit one has to be in F1 these days.'

Two of the most frustrating retirements came at Austria and Germany. At the A1-Ring de la Rosa was heading for third place on a one-stop strategy when a gearbox oil pipe failed and he had to retire. At Hockenheim a fortnight later he spun into a gravel trap while on course for a rostrum finish.

'That Austrian result was particularly disappointing,' reflects Coughlan. 'Pedro told me he was cruising, just cruising. To be sidelined by the

failure of a bought-out component which had never failed before was really hard to take.'

Next year Arrows will be switching engines yet again, replacing the Supertecs with Peugeot V10s now licensed to Asia Motor Technologies. First tests have been encouraging and Coughlan believes that the prospects for 2001 are very promising indeed. But he and his engineering team will be relying on the lessons of the past season in a bid to be better prepared from the first race as they seek to prove that this year's campaign was a stepping stone on the path to greater things in the future.

Alan Henry

Top left: The future's bright... Team boss Tom Walkinshaw oversaw a huge improvement in Arrows's fortunes.

Top right: The Supertec engine was well-suited to the fleet A21 chassis.

Above: Pedro de la Rosa looked set for a podium finish at Hockenheim. Unfortunately the popular Spaniard spun into retirement.

All photographs: Paul-Henri Cahier

MARC GENE

GASTON MAZZACANE

MINARDI 20 21

THE biggest thing that happened to Minardi in 2000 was that it was sold to Miami-based communications company Pan-American Sports Network (PSN). Its sale, said team principal and 68% stakeholder Gabriele Rumi, was essential to the future of the team. 'We can't continue as we are at the moment,' he admitted. 'We can't rival other teams given the finances that they have.'

Speaking in June, Minardi's principal shareholder since 1998 added: 'We have to find a power unit and then the sale will be done. It would be wrong for someone to buy the team without an engine deal. The trouble is that those who supply engines know that I need one, and the deal is expensive!'

By mid-September, the engine deal had been done, and Minardi announced the sale. Rumi was gone. He had personally kept the team alive for some five years, and was now no longer required. F1, for him, was a thing of the past. Veteran sporting director Cesare Fiorio had also left earlier in a disagreement about the team's

direction, so Giancarlo Minardi, still with a shareholding, once again controlled the team that bore his name.

At the time of the sale, Rumi said that the new owner couldn't be an individual such as he, because 'I don't think an individual could finance a team that could rival the others. It has to be a big company which has a global interest in commmunication, because current Formula 1 isn't about making cars that go quickly, but about communication. It's communication that runs the sport.'

However, it would be wrong to suggest that Rumi didn't appreciate the tremendous steps forward made by his team in 2000. However much McLaren drivers complained of being held up by Minardis – and neither of them could overtake Minardis for several laps at Indianapolis – the team did make considerable progress in 2000. They were never under threat of non-qualification from the 107 per cent and on one occasion were only a tiny 2.5s behind pole position in qualifying. Much of the credit went to technical

director Gustav Brunner, head of Minardi's nine-strong drawing office. It was his second car for the team but, once again, it was delayed by a late engine decision. After Ford had stated that they would no longer run customer engines, in September they were persuaded to supply to Minardi the same unit as the year before, rebadged Fondmetal, but the deal wasn't signed until mid-December.

That engine weighed in at 129 kg, probably 20 kg more than anyone else's and was as much as 80, maybe 100 bhp down on most others. It started the year exactly as it finished 1999 apart from one update for the Spanish GP which comprised a new cylinder head, which was a little better in mid-range, included better driveability, and was a few kilos lighter.

Brunner explained that the car's concept was pretty much the same as the previous year's, but refined. The progress made was with the aerodynamics, almost non-existent the previous year due to another late engine decision. In 2000, Minardi did some of

the aerodynamic work themselves, rather than rely on Jean-Claude Migeot at Fondmetal. But this is also a big concern for the future,' explains Brunner. 'Other teams have big wind tunnel crews, working in shifts. We don't have the same structure or money. Our handicap is the aerodynamics.'

Brunner also 'designed quite a lot of ballast into the monocoque. It's pretty solid at the bottom end. Last year we started off with 60 kg ballast, but this year we're down to half that, some of it integrated into the floor of the monocoque. It's safer and helps us to have a strong chassis.'

The team also broke new ground in F1 by designing its own titanium gearbox to save around six kilos. 'It's a lot stiffer,' explained Brunner, 'it stands up to temperature because it is the right material and it is smaller which helps the aerodynamics. Quite a few teams are looking at this technology. I'm not so sure how many will achieve it for next year but it's probably the direction to go rather than a carbon gearbox.'

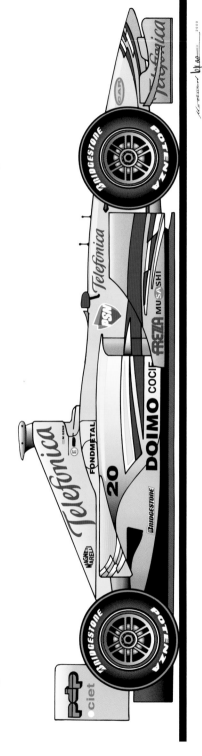

MINARDI M02-FONDMETAL

Sponsors: Telefonica, Fondmetal, PSN, Doimo, PDP, CAR, Bridgestone, Magneti Marelli, Musashi

Team principal: Giancarlo Minardi **Technical director:** Gustav Brunner **Chief mechanic:** Gabriele Pagliarini

ENGINE Type: Fondmetal Cosworth **No. of cylinders (vee angle):** V10 (72°) **Sparking plugs:** Champion **Electronics:** Magneti Marelli **Fuel:** Elf **Oil:** Elf

TRANSMISSION Gearbox: Minardi titanium six-speed longitudinal semi-automatic **Driveshafts:** Minardi **Clutch:** AP Racing (hand-operated)

CHASSIS Front suspension: double wishbones, pushrod **Rear suspension:** double wishbones, pushrod **Suspension dampers:** Sachs

Wheel diameter: front: 13 in. rear: 13. **Wheels:** Fondmetal **Tyres:** Bridgestone **Brake pads:** not given **Brake discs:** CCR **Brake calipers:** Brembo

Steering: Minardi **Radiators:** Secan **Fuel tanks:** ATL **Battery:** FIAMM **Instruments:** Magneti Marelli

DIMENSIONS Wheelbase: not given **Track:** front: 1459 mm rear: 1421 mm **Formula weight:** 1322.8 lb/600 kg including driver **Fuel capacity:** not given

Minardi began with a magnesium gearbox casing but introduced the titanium version after about a quarter of the season, running it ever since. It had a new crash structure and new rear suspension. They also made four or five types of front wing, but not in the wind tunnel. There were two updates on the diffuser and a few other updates on bodywork, side pods, bargeboards and brake ducts.

The team also developed an active differential which wasn't raced until Monza, but it was technology that several other teams couldn't get to grips with. So for a small team production was pretty busy. And it wasn't through lack of ideas that it wasn't busier; it was a lack of development in the wind tunnel and then time to produce those ideas.

Testing was again limited. 'After getting our own wind tunnel, our next priority is to create a test team,' admits Brunner. 'At the moment, if the T-car isn't used on the Sunday morning of a race, the guys go directly to the next circuit and carry on there as our test team. We did around 5,000 km, which is at least half, maybe a third less than the next least. The top teams are doing 25,000–30,000 km.'

Even so, reliability was mainly good. 'All our reliability problems were silly mistakes, finger trouble,' he said. 'We had no structural failures this year. We never had a mechanical failure.' That reliability was vital. 'Prost are behind us in the constructors' championship and that means dollars. They may be slightly quicker, but less reliable. Those dollars help the budget.'

The drivers certainly did their bit as well. Debutant Gaston Mazzacane was 'better than expected, he's cool and keeps cool. He was very close to Gene in some races.' His finishing record was good too. 'We expected slightly better from Gene, because he kicked off the season well, but later on he began to worry about his future. Telefonica changed their management and that unsettled his mind. He probably wasn't 100 per cent concentrated so I think he could have done better. But his race in Australia was probably the best of the year. His lap times were very competitive.'

Minardi now enters a new era of ownership and perhaps management when their aim, once again, will be to get off the bottom of the grid. 'We are still alive and you have to be optimistic in this game,' says the ever-cheerful Brunner. 'Things do change for everyone. We have also the great support of Mr Ecclestone. He likes to see this team survive.'

Bob Constanduros

Top left: Giancarlo Minardi was forced to spend much of his time seeking finance to keep the Faenza team in touch with the profoundly wealthier teams.

Top centre: Gaston Mazzacane performed creditably in his debut season.
Both photographs: Bryn Williams/Words & Pictures

Top right: Fondmetal's Gabriele Rumi finally called time on his patronage.
Paul-Henri Cahier

Above: Marc Gene was less impressive this season than in his 1999 debut year.
Bryn Williams/Words & Pictures

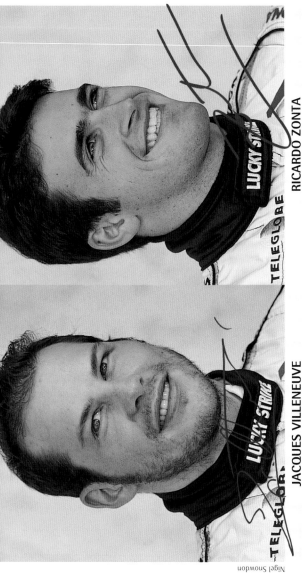

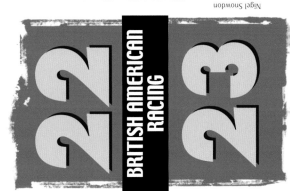

Nigel Snowdon

RICARDO ZONTA

JACQUES VILLENEUVE

22

23

BRITISH AMERICAN RACING

WHAT a difference a year makes. 'The starting point was the first race in Melbourne, because that was a true indication of our potential this year. We finished fourth in that race, and that's the position that we're attacking at the end of the championship.'

That was BAR team principal Craig Pollock's assessment of the team's second year after emerging from a disastrous first season. It is normally the second year that is worst, but then it simply couldn't be in BAR's case. Massive lessons were learned and, with stability of major personnel now ensured, the team was able to make progress and score points reasonably regularly as they battled with Williams, Benetton and Jordan for supremacy amongst the midfield bunch.

Of course, it wasn't just a case of title sponsors BAT pushing them in the background. Honda's smooth-running V10s had replaced the vibrating Supertec units which in turn caused a weight-saving programme during the year. But that was just one of the positives after a year of negatives.

'Honda pushed us tremendously, not just to be competitive but to set up logical systems in the structure,' explained Pollock. 'There's extra power, extra driveability but most of all learning to work with an outside organisation which isn't the easiest in the world to communicate with and therefore we've had to put in extra controls into our structure and logic into that. They are very integrated into every project that we have, because the better they have that, the better they can work with us.'

Pollock goes on to be refreshingly honest about the team's shortcomings. 'We were still a little overly arrogant at the start of the season, and this bit us on a number of occasions,' he admitted. 'We didn't seize the opportunities that were there. We made our mistakes at the start, and we're making a far fewer now which is a good sign, because that learning curve is still going in the right direction.

'One of the big turning points for us was Canada where we had our best opportunity of the season. We could have won the race, but through – I wouldn't say stupidity – but making mistakes we shot ourselves in the foot, which again was a huge pity but it served as a lesson to us and it refocused the whole team.

'We have cut out as much of the politics as humanly possible. Certainly there has been nothing which has prevented us from focusing on what we should be doing, coming to a race track and competing. One of our main weaknesses is understanding how the car works and maybe a little bit on the engineering side.'

Technical director Malcolm Oastler again designed a car that appeared early in the off-season, December. 'Last year's car came together with a new design team which hadn't married as a team,' he confessed, 'and the car didn't really marry either, with an engine that was quite difficult to cope with on its vibration level.

'We couldn't fix last year's car, but the problems weren't going to go away. All that was put into this year's car with a view to making it simply, tidier, more reliable, easy to service as well as being faster.'

Chief race engineer Steve Farrell takes up the story; 'the feature this year was a lot more go-faster parts were made instead of the reliability parts that we were having to fire-fight with last year. We had a major update for the Kyalami test in February, for instance. There were minor updates for Melbourne. 'One of our objectives was to go there with a reliable car, knowing that even if we weren't that quick, we would pick up points, and as it happens, it worked out beautifully.' Fourth and sixth his result.

'We built an over-heavy car for 2000 because the Supertec vibrated massively, but the Honda is the limousine

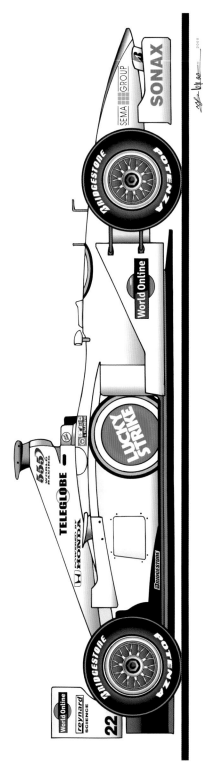

BRITISH AMERICAN RACING BAR 02–HONDA

Sponsors: Lucky Strike (BAT), Teleglobe/Excel, Sonex, K-Way, Beetrade.com, World Online, ART, Koni, Technogym, Bridgestone, Lincoln Electrics, Spire Telecom

Team principal: Craig Pollock **Technical director:** Malcolm Oastler **Team manager:** Ron Meadows **Chief engineer:** Alastair Gibson

ENGINE **Type:** Honda RA100E **No. of cylinders (vee angle):** V10 (not given) **Sparking plugs:** NGK **Electronics:** Honda PGM-F1 **Fuel:** Nisseki Mitsubishi **Oil:** Nisseki Mitsubishi

TRANSMISSION **Gearbox:** Six-speed longitudinal semi-automatic, sequential **Driveshafts:** BAR **Clutch:** AP Racing triple-plate carbon (hand-operated)

CHASSIS **Front suspension:** double wishbones, pushrod/torsion springs/rockers, mechanical anti-roll bar **Rear suspension:** double wishbones, pushrod/torsion springs/rockers, mechanical anti-roll bar **Suspension dampers:** Koni **Wheel diameter:** front: 13 in. rear: 13 in. **Wheel rim widths:** front: 12 in. rear: 13.7 in. **Wheels** OZ

Tyres: Bridgestone **Brake pads:** Brembo/Carbone Industrie **Brake discs:** Brembo/Carbone Industrie **Brake calipers:** AP Racing **Steering:** BAR **Radiators:** BAR

Fuel tanks: ATL **Battery:** 12 V 5AL lead-acid **Instruments:** Pi Research

DIMENSIONS **Wheelbase:** 120.8 in./3020 mm **Track:** front: 72 in./1800 mm rear: 72 in./1800 mm **Formula weight:** 1322.8 lb/600 kg including driver

Fuel capacity: 22 gallons/100 litres

version and we realised then we could backtrack on the heavyweight stuff,' he continued.

At Imola, there were 20 new components on the car, some of which were now weight-saving. Honda introduced a new version of the engine, by this stage in the season they were already up to Evo 3B. The biggest update of the year was the Evo 4 engine for Silverstone, where the team reverted to steel lower wishbones after Ricardo Zonta's massive testing accident.

The modifications came thick and fast, new featherweight bargeboards for Barcelona, cast front uprights in titanium (copied from Minardi) and new gearbox internals which had been troublesome but not fatal in previous races.

Monaco proved to be a difficult race, simply because of set-up, but it added to the team's reputation of having a low-downforce car. In reality, it was more because the team couldn't get the right set-up for high-downforce circuits — until Hungary.

In Montreal, the team started to use their own power steering system, although Honda had developed one in parallel. There were new disc bells

front and rear after the previous ones failed on Zonta at Monza resulting in another huge accident. Typical of progress made was the appearance of a new aerodynamic package for Austria, but '[the] production [department] got ahead of themselves,' says Farrell, 'and most of it was ready for the race before, Magny-Cours.'

Honda introduced the Evo 5 engine at Hockenheim, while the team were now concentrating on set-up. At Hungary, they used Honda's power steering system for the first time. 'On balance, theirs was better,' admitted Farrell explaining that Zonta largely pooh-poohed it, only adopting it in Suzuka.

Again, the low-downforce appraisal was levelled at the team after Villeneuve qualified 16th and Zonta 18th. 'Nobody really noticed, but we had a lousy qualifying session, we then made two changes to Jacques' car and transformed it,' said Farrell.

'We were setting top-three times in the race. We meant to set it up to Y by mistake which was the best all year. But it did have better efficiency in lower-downforce setting.'

Bob Constanduros

At Spa, the team started to use a third spring and revised front suspension geometry to take advantage of the power steering. Lightweight items appeared at Indianapolis while Honda brought a new S-spec engine to Suzuka for qualifying and the race, earning sixth place.

However, in spite of two test drivers supplementing the efforts of the two race drivers, BAR looks to be adopting the Ferrari course of a one-driver team. Zonta was treated very averagely, even though he usually qualified within three or four places of his team-mate, and twice out-qualified him altogether. His best was sixth in Austria. Villeneuve's fourth in Italy.

With results such as these, Pollock and his team had reason to be proud of the turn-around since 1999. They had worked hard and in the right direction, scoring points in a hard year as a result of a dedicated and increasingly 'married' team, to use Malcolm Oastler's words.

Top left: Jacques Villeneuve checks over his car. The French-Canadian has signed up to British American Racing for the next three seasons.
Mark Thompson/Allsport

Top right: BAR's partnership with Honda provided immediate results.
Bryn Williams/Words & Pictures

Above left: Jacques Villeneuve drove with all his usual commitment.
Bryn Williams/Words & Pictures

Above centre right: Craig Pollock can take pride in the progress made by his team after a disastrous debut season in 1999.
Paul-Henri Cahier

Above: Ricardo Zonta was very much the number two driver behind Villeneuve. Nevertheless the talented Brazilian showed more than enough to suggest that he could still have an F1 future.
Bryn Williams/Words & Pictures

BRITISH AMERICAN RACING

JS FRASER Oxford LTD

SPECIALIST MOTORSPORT TRAILER MANUFACTURER

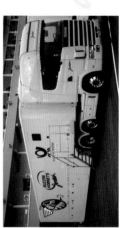

winning transport solutions

Tel: +44 (0)1865 880600   Fax: +44 (0)1865 883875   Email: sales@jsfraser.com

Visit our Website at www.jsfraser.com

2000

AUSTRALIAN
grand prix

Left: Mika Häkkinen had the spectre of Michael Schumacher right behind him at the pre-practice press conference.
Clive Mason/Allsport

Below left: After a perfect start to his championship quest, Michael Schumacher conducts celebrations from the podium.
Mark Thompson/Allsport

M. SCHUMACHER
BARRICHELLO
R. SCHUMACHER
VILLENEUVE
FISICHELLA
ZONTA

AS McLaren's pace-setting MP4/15s faltered, so Ferrari turned the tables and pressed home its attack to post a dramatic and convincing 1-2 in the opening race of the season round Melbourne's picturesque Albert Park. The previous two years had seen Ferrari's early season lack of pace and/or mechanical reliability enable the Silver Arrows to gain a crucial early advantage. But this time Michael Schumacher and his new Maranello running mate Rubens Barrichello made it first blood for the Prancing Horse.

Perhaps even more significantly, the pace of the new Ferrari F1-2000 lived up to Schumacher's pre-season predictions that it would be in a position to win races on merit from the start of the campaign.

The two Ferraris stormed home in first and second places just 11.4s apart to launch the Italian team's World Championship onslaught for the new millennium on the best possible note. Yet, in the final analysis, this was a victory achieved thanks to durability rather than unchallenged speed and the weekend finished with the jury still out over whether Schumacher was in a position consistently to beat the McLarens of Mika Häkkinen and David Coulthard in a straight fight.

In the F1 opener, the McLarens were running in their familiar 1-2 formation in the early phase of the race only to be sidelined with failures of seals in their pneumatic valvegear systems. Two similar failures had interrupted the McLarens' progress during Saturday free practice, but they still qualified in 1-2 formation with Häkkinen bagging the 22nd pole position of his career.

Ilmor Engineering pledged a major investigation into how this series of failures occurred and re-doubled their efforts to rectify the situation in time for the Brazilian Grand Prix at Interlagos, but Mika and David went to the starting line with their fingers firmly crossed.

Schumacher qualified fourth, but he was still confident the race would be different. 'When I came in and saw Häkkinen standing on his car celebrating pole position, I said to myself enjoy yourself while you can, because I'll be doing that tomorrow after winning the race.' Michael was as good as his word.

Only ten of the original 22 starters made it to the chequered flag in what was an extremely gruelling first race of the season. Into third place came Ralf Schumacher in the new Williams FW22-BMW which displayed praiseworthy mechanical reliability on its maiden competitive outing.

In fact, at one point both Schumacher and his young team-mate Jenson Button were running in the top six but the young Englishman retired with engine failure in the closing stages after an assured and extremely impressive F1 debut.

Fourth place fell to Jacques Villeneuve's BAR-Honda, the Canadian finally notching up the first ever title points for the team, while Giancarlo Fisichella's Benetton and Mika Salo's Sauber completed the top six in a tight chase to the chequered flag.

Häkkinen took an immediate lead from the start with Coulthard slotting in behind as the Canadian defended his line aggressively from Schumacher, forcing the Brazilian to back off which allowed Frentzen's Jordan to dive through into third place.

Schumacher keeps them guessing

MICHAEL Schumacher took the opportunity at Melbourne to hint that he would certainly race on beyond the expiry of his current contract with Ferrari at the end of the 2002 season when he will be almost 34 years old.

Yet whether he remains with the famous Italian team seemed, for the moment, to be quite another matter. 'I have a contract with them until the end of 2002 and I am very happy to continue with them,' he said. 'But after that? Well, I certainly want to continue racing, but how does anybody know what they will be doing in 2002?'

This tantalisingly ambiguous assurance, made on the eve of first practice for the first Grand Prix of the new millennium seemed likely to have a profound effect on possible driver contract negotiations amongst rival teams over the next two seasons.

Yet in reality, the current F1 status quo meant that it looked unlikely Schumacher would switch teams at the end of his current contract. It seemed virtually certain that he would race on with Ferrari not least because he wants to reap the dividend from all the effort he has expended since joining Ferrari at the start of 1996.

For his part, Schumacher reaffirmed that his new team-mate Rubens Barrichello would have to play a subordinate role this year as the displaced Eddie Irvine did last.

It is clear that he believed that beating the McLarens from the first race of the year was a realistic possibility for himself and Ferrari.

'I reckon him quite fast,' he said in the tone of one who sought to damn with faint praise. 'You can't make someone slower by contract. I don't think his [Barrichello's] situation is different from Eddie's [last year]. If he's faster, he's faster. And whoever is faster is going to be the number one.'

FERRARI

Ferrari's latest F1-2000 represented the technical summit of the joint design efforts of Ross Brawn and Rory Byrne over the four years they have been working at Maranello. Brawn summed it up as 'the first Ferrari F1 car to be conceived entirely in our new wind tunnel. In the area of aerodynamics, we have made the biggest step forward since I joined Ferrari.' Powered by a totally new Type 049 version of the Ferrari V10 engine, now opened out to an 89-degree vee angle in the interests of better packaging and lower centre of gravity, the new unit developed in excess of 770 bhp at the start of the year. A totally revised power steering and fuel system was incorporated and Byrne predicted that drivers Michael Schumacher and new signing Rubens Barrichello would be able to extract even more from its Bridgestone rubber thanks to its improved aerodynamics and front and rear suspension.

McLAREN-MERCEDES

Another subtly evolutionary version of the well-proven McLaren-Mercedes package from the design team steered by Adrian Newey, the MP4/15 was powered by a totally new Mercedes FO110J engine which originally ran on the dynamometer on 2 November and tested in one of the 1999 cars at the start of December. The new unit offered better driveability and power and there were changes to the gearbox and hydraulic systems in an effort to eliminate some of the technical problems which had bugged the team during the previous season. Driver line-up of Mika Häkkinen and David Coulthard remained unchanged, but supplemented by 1996 Monaco GP winner Olivier Panis as full-time test driver.

JORDAN-MUGEN HONDA

New Jordan EJ10s carrying new type number to celebrate Eddie Jordan's tenth season in F1, the new car started the season being tipped as a notable step forward over its immediate predecessor with considerable progress claimed by technical director Mike Gascoyne in terms of aerodynamic efficiency. Totally new layout run pushrod/torsion bar front suspension and lighter six-speed longitudinal gearbox heavily revised. The Mugen Honda MF301HE engine developed around 760 bhp, thus starting the season pretty well where it left off at the end of 1999 in terms of power output. Former Prost driver Jarno Trulli joined to replace Damon Hill as Frentzen's team-mate.

JAGUAR-COSWORTH

Re-launched amidst much expectation, glitz and razzmatazz, the Jaguar Racing team was in fact the Stewart-Ford squad sprayed green and expanded from its taut and leanly organised former self into a corporate monolith into which there was much finger-poking by Ford and Jaguar hierarchy who should have been kept at arm's length. Much understandably expected of Jaguar, of course. An evolutionary version of last year's Stewart SF3, the re-branded British Racing Green Jaguar R1 was a honed, refined and developed version of that promising machine. In reality, technical snags during testing with the oil system used for the uprated Cosworth V10 engine were destined to cause lingering problems. Former Ferrari man Eddie Irvine recruited as de facto team leader running alongside 1999 European GP winner Johnny Herbert gave the Jaguar squad a suitably patriotic all-British feel.

WILLIAMS-BMW

Dawn of totally new alliance between Williams and German car maker BMW saw all-new, Munich-built BMW type E41 V10 engine installed in much aerodynamically improved Williams FW22. Huge British interest surrounding 20-year-old

Jenson Button's inclusion in the team alongside Ralf Schumacher with new major sponsorship portfolio including Compaq and Reuters replacing backing from Rothmans tobacco sources which the team had enjoyed since the start of 1994.

BENETTON-PLAYLIFE

Much simpler new B200 chassis concept owing much of its configuration to former Honda R&D engineer Tim Densham who replaced Nick Wirth as Benetton chief designer late in 1999. Front torque transfer system and twin clutch gearbox amongst trick items shelved on aerodynamically improved new car. Giancarlo Fisichella and Alexander Wurz remained on driving strength, hoping to benefit from promisingly uprated Supertec FB02 V10 engine – still carrying the Playlife identification – which had more power than 1999 unit.

PROST-PEUGEOT

Chief designer Alan Jenkins and his team designed a visually quite distinctive car in the new AP03 with a shorter wheelbase and more obviously classical proportions for Prost's all-new driver line-up of veteran Jean Alesi and F3000 champion Nick Heidfeld. The latest Peugeot A20 engine started the year nudging the 800 bhp mark, and was mated to a new seven-speed gearbox in place of last year's six-speed unit. Whole programme inevitably clouded by Peugeot's perceived lack of interest in F1 generally and even at the first race there were rumours that Prost was trying to secure a Mercedes engine deal for the 2001 season.

SAUBER-PETRONAS

New C19 challenger benefited from engineering input of highly experienced new chief designer Sergio Rinland and preliminary testing indicated more than expected promise. Powered by developed versions of Ferrari's 1999-spec V10, with Mika Salo joining driver line-up alongside Pedro Diniz, Sauber seemed to be making a bigger effort than usual to escape from its traditional midfield placing.

ARROWS-MECACHROME

Discarding its own engine programme in favour of customer Supertec V10s after acrimonious split with former engine partner Brian Hart, Arrows boss Tom Walkinshaw had a bigger budget available than in recent years and strengthened technical director Mike Coughlan's design team notably by recruiting former Williams and Stewart aerodynamicist Eghbal Hamedy. New A21 design notable for its pullrod front suspension – unique in the 2000 F1 field – and its good handling qualities in the hands of Jos Verstappen and Pedro de la Rosa.

MINARDI-FONDMETAL

Characteristically neat Gustav Brunner-designed M02 chassis powered by Ford Zetec-R V10 engine now maintained by sub-contractor outside Cosworth orbit and co-badged Fondmetal. Marc Gene now joined in driver line-up by enthusiastic Argentine pay-driver Gaston Mazzacane.

BRITISH AMERICAN RACING-HONDA

Seeking to exorcise painful memories of disastrous maiden season, British American Racing started second F1 season on more confident, if lower key, note with evolutionary new BAR02 chassis powered by compact, powerful works Honda RA100E V10 engine claimed to be developing around 800 bhp at start of season. Drivers Jacques Villeneuve and Ricardo Zonta benefiting from close technical alliance between BAR and Honda which sees Japanese car maker also involved on chassis development programmes.

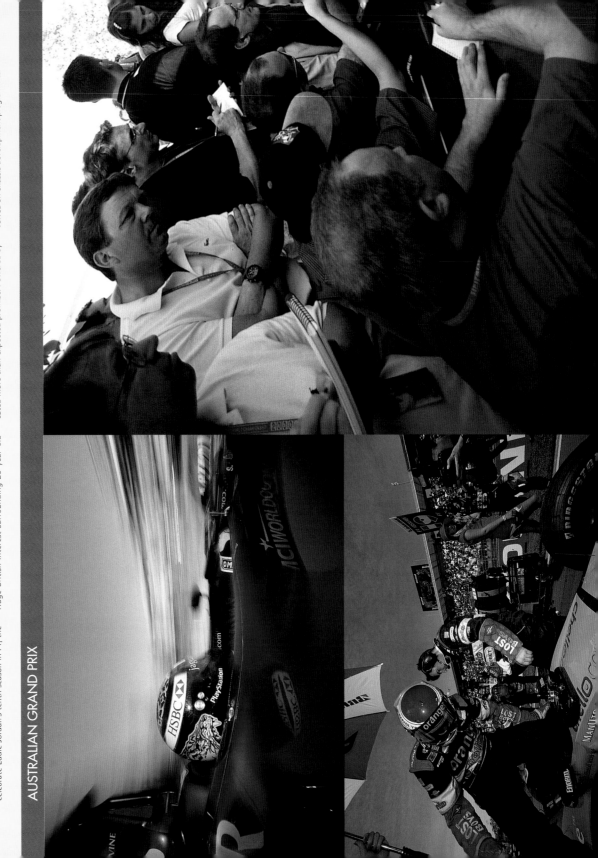

December 1999

Toyota formally confirms its upcoming F1 programme, due to start testing in 2001 and racing in 2002.

Michelin announces return to F1 in 2001 with the BMW Williams team and also Toyota when the Japanese company makes its Grand Prix debut.

British rising star Darren Manning is signed by British American Racing as test driver.

January 2000

Nicola Foulston quits as chief executive of Brands Hatch Leisure.

The BRDC holds major strategy meeting with its members to clarify its approach to negotiations to retain the British GP at Silverstone beyond 2001.

Jenson Button signs for BMW Williams after team reaches agreement to terminate Alex Zanardi's ongoing contract.

Jackie Stewart retires as Chief Executive Officer of Jaguar Racing.

February 2000

FIA President Max Mosley blasts EU for making a 'hopeless muddle of the facts' and being 'completely confused about the regulation and general functioning of motor sport.'

Dario Franchitti is seriously hurt after crashing his Team KOOL Green Reynard-Honda during pre-season CART testing at Florida's Homestead oval track.

Allan McNish signs to drive in Audi Le Mans challenge.

Brazilian rising star Tony Kanaan signs to drive Reynard-Mercedes for new CART team organised by ex-Ganassi star engineer Morris Nunn.

Bernie Ecclestone completes deal to sell 37.5 per cent of his F1 business to Hellman & Friedman, a San Francisco-based private equity firm.

Far left: Eddie Irvine (top) samples new horizons with Jaguar, and Jos Verstappen (bottom) hops into the promising Arrows A21 for another F1 comeback.
Both photographs: Paul-Henri Cahier

Left: Jenson Button found himself the centre of attention.
Paul-Henri Cahier

MELBOURNE QUALIFYING

Using the softer-compound Bridgestone rubber to best effect seemed poised to be the biggest on-track challenge of the Melbourne weekend. It didn't take long for persuasive evidence to confirm that running on worn rubber offered the best solution in terms of grip and consistency. But for the McLaren team, Saturday morning's free practice session produced a potentially disastrous setback.

Accelerating away from the pits on his out lap, Häkkinen's engine cut out and he rolled to a halt at the trackside. The pneumatic valvegear had malfunctioned, losing him half the session and when the car was retrieved the decision was taken to install a fresh Mercedes V10, a task which was carried out in a record 40 minutes.

Simultaneously, it was also decided to change the engine in Coulthard's car as it was smoking slightly due to a similar failure. This was achieved in 45 minutes, but only Mika got out again briefly before the end of the session.

Short on track time, it really was beginning to look as if the McLarens were about to go down to a pole position defeat at the hands of Schumacher's new Ferrari. Yet the McLaren lads kept their nerve and beat off the challenge from the highly motivated German ace yet again.

Mika and DC each stayed on a single set of rubber throughout the session, whereas Michael — seemingly inexplicably — opted to throw four sets of tyres at his Ferrari. It didn't pay off. He looked as much on the ragged edge as he'd been on Friday when he trashed his originally designated race car in a high-speed shunt which ripped off its left-hand suspension.

Eventually, with Mika comfortably ensconced on pole with a 1m 30.556s, it was Coulthard who crashed heavily attempting to fend off a potential challenge from the Ferrari team leader. Battling for chassis balance, David radioed in on his last run to ask whether there was any chance of a quick extra stop to make another set-up change.

No way, his pit crew replied, stay out. Going into the same fast right-hander that had claimed Schumacher the previous day, Coulthard clipped the inside kerb as he battled to keep his excessive understeer under control, found himself pitched into a spin and smartly removed the McLaren's left rear wheel against the retaining wall.

On came the red lights and the session was aborted with only a few moments left to run. That in turn thwarted 'Schuey's' final bid to get on terms with the Silver Arrows, although, in any case, it all looked pretty seamless for McLaren, with Coulthard managing a 1m 30.910s to join Mika on the front row, but Ron Dennis reckoned it had been a bitty, truncated affair. 'You might find it hard to believe, but we are not happy with our performance today,' he said. 'We might be by tomorrow evening, but we are not at the moment.'

From the touchlines, it all looked pretty seamless for McLaren, with Mugen Honda V10s lagging some 30 bhp or so behind the pace-setting Mercs, this was certainly a good effort. Trulli had fitted in well in the Jordan environment and the atmosphere seemed exceedingly positive and congenial.

Schumacher (1m 31.075s) and Barrichello (1m 31.102s) were pretty content with their own efforts, while the third row was buttoned up by the Jordan EJ10s of Heinz-Harald Frentzen (1m 31.359s) and new boy Jarno Trulli (1m 31.504s), the Italian arrival having a frustrating time with clutch and gearbox sensor problems for much of Saturday.

In reality, the Jordans looked in good shape.

On the inside of row four sat Eddie Irvine in the distinctive green Jaguar R1 on 1m 31.514s. The former Ferrari driver had got away relatively lightly from the whirlwind of technical problems which seemed to besiege the team in general — and his team-mate Johnny Herbert in particular.

'I am pleasantly surprised,' said Irvine. 'I really did not think we could qualify that high up. We changed the engine after morning practice and it made a huge difference to the performance which amounted to about four tenths of a second.'

Yet Herbert just seemed to suffer a succession of engine failures. These were caused by the need to reduce oil tank size on the Jaguar R1 in order to accommodate an enlarged fuel cell after some close calls on consumption with last year's Stewart-Ford SF3.

Unfortunately the smaller oil tank proved too marginal for the Cosworth CR2 V10's engine scavenging problems and Jaguar-badged engines were either popping like firecrackers or quietly rolling to a halt when their automatic shutdown systems intervened before they broke.

Herbert also suffered with power steering failure on the spare car which weaved ominously on the straight and almost pitched him into the wall. 'It has been a total nightmare,' shrugged the Englishman. 'After all the testing, I just don't need a race weekend like this.' He wound up 20th on 1m 33.638s.

For his part, although Jacques Villeneuve was basically heartened with the feel of the BAR-Honda, he confessed he was rather disappointed that his eighth-fastest 1m 31.968s hadn't put him closer behind the leaders. At least he was happier than team-mate Ricardo Zonta who finished 16th on 1m 33.173 after grappling with gearbox problems and a spin.

Giancarlo Fisichella was the quickest of the Benettons in ninth place ahead of a satisfied Mika Salo while Ralf Schumacher took 11th on 1m 32.220s in his Williams FW22, complaining that he had too much oversteer for his taste.

New boy Jenson Button, who'd spun hard into the wall during free practice on Friday, now found himself obliged to abandon his repaired FW22 due to fuel pressure problems and had to face the first start of his F1 career from 21st on the grid on 1m 33.828s. His frustration was compounded when he caught the red flag. In the Arrows camp, Pedro de la Rosa and Jos Verstappen were a little disappointed with 12th and 13th places — a starting position in the top ten had seemed a realistic ambition for both throughout much of free practice. Meanwhile, in 15th and 17th places respectively, the Prost-Peugeots of Nick Heidfeld and Jean Alesi continued what amounted to the French team's pre-race test and development programme to moderately promising effect.

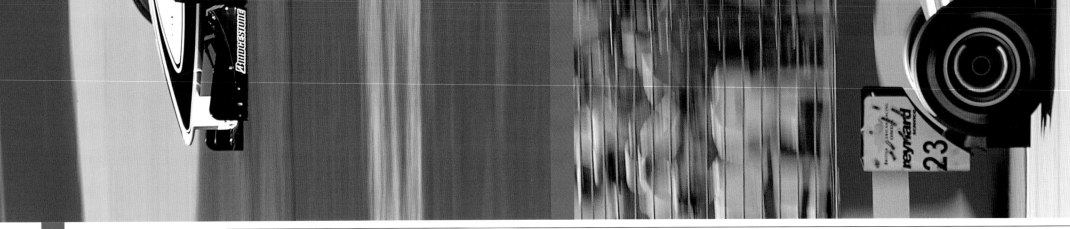

Right: **Ralf Schumacher's third-placed Williams-BMW is profiled against the colourful Melbourne back-drop.**
Mark Thompson/Allsport

Below right: **Brake discs aglow, Ricardo Zonta heads towards his first ever World Championship point in the BAR-Honda.**
Bryn Williams/Words & Pictures

By the end of the opening lap Häkkinen was already 0.5s ahead of Coulthard, but Schumacher was keeping pace with the two McLarens quite easily and the close-running trio quickly opened a 5.3s gap back to Frentzen as early as the third lap.

Michael claimed he was conserving his car and did not want to push too hard too soon, saving both tyres and fuel. He wanted to be in good shape when it came to the refuelling stops when he planned to press home his advantage and make a bid for the lead. But he did not have to bother, as things transpired.

The first setback for the McLarens came on lap seven when Pedro de la Rosa's Arrows A21, running in tenth place ahead of Eddie Irvine's Jaguar, crashed heavily due to a steering arm failure. Irvine tried to dodge the flying debris, but also spun off into retirement as he did so. With Herbert's Jaguar having already retired with clutch failure, it was a dreadful end to the Jaguar F1 debut.

Almost simultaneously, Jos Verstappen's ninth-place Arrows A21 was struck by the same problem. 'I had a scary moment due to a problem with the front steering arm,' said the Dutchman. 'I had to come in and the team changed that part, but when Pedro got back to the pits [after his accident] the team decided to pull me out of the race so as not to risk the driver or the car.'

The safety car was deployed to slow the field while this debris was cleared away, the race proper resuming on lap ten with Häkkinen again piling on the pressure at the front of the field. Then on lap 11 Coulthard came into the pits with a misfire. The engineers tried to adjust the engine mapping, but the problem was clearly more serious. He accelerated back into the fray but soon stopped with engine problems.

Häkkinen, meanwhile, was left to lead the field, but when he also succumbed to engine failure on lap 19, Schumacher's Ferrari was left storming away virtually unchallenged with a 16.5s lead over Frentzen.

Barrichello was the red meat in a Jordan sandwich, now, with Trulli right behind, while there was a big gap back to Jacques Villeneuve's BAR, Mika Salo's well-driven Sauber C19, Giancarlo Fisichella's Benetton and Ralf Schumacher's Williams.

Even though he had shadowed the McLarens from the start, Schumacher believed he was in total control of the race. 'I was driving pretty easily from the beginning,' he said.

'I would have preferred to race them to the end, to prove how really good we are. But I think there will be plenty of opportunities for us to do this again all through the year.'

Häkkinen, who started 2000 with the aim of becoming the first man since the legendary Juan Manuel Fangio to win a hat trick of World Championships, took the disappointment in a stoically philosophical fashion. Yet for David Coulthard, who was seeking to reverse his disappointing run of luck and make a credible title bid, this was almost a disappointment too far.

'I made a good start and was feeling comfortable in second place when the engine developed a misfire,' he said. 'I went into the pits to change the engine mapping but the problem could not be cured and unfortunately that was the end of my race.'

Coulthard's retirement left Häkkinen cruising round in a comfortable lead, but then the same mechanical jinx struck down the Finn and McLaren were left to contemplate the end of the opening race of the year with no constructors' championship points.

Meanwhile, further back Heinz-Harald was finding it quite difficult to fend off Barrichello for what the McLarens' retirement had turned into a battle over second place as his Jordan was oversteering with a heavy fuel load.

Things improved somewhat as the fuel was consumed, but the fact of the matter was that Barrichello was capable of running a second a lap quicker than the Jordan and Ferrari team manager Ross Brawn opted for a switch of strategy from a one- to two-stop schedule even as Rubens was swinging into the pit lane to make his first stop at the end of lap 33.

'I was talking to the team on the radio and we decided to switch to a two-stop to get me ahead,' said Barrichello. 'My only problem was when I got neutral as I was leaving the pits.' In fact, as things transpired, this change of strategy would not prove necessary. On lap 36 Frentzen came in for his pit stop and the Jordan remained stationary for an agonising 23.4s when the refuelling nozzle would not uncouple from the car.

On closer examination, the mathematics of the changed strategy for Barrichello represented an outside chance and nothing more. But as Ross Brawn rightly pointed out, they had to take the chance. By sticking to a one-stop strategy they were never going to beat Frentzen unless he hit trouble. Which, of course, he did.

Nor was that the end of it for Heinz-Harald. 'After my pit stop I had a problem selecting gears,' he explained. 'I tried to keep going by driving in one gear, but it became impossible so I had to come into the pits.' The problem was traced to an hydraulic leak.

After that Barrichello was through and away into the distance, moving up into second place when Ralf Schumacher made his scheduled refuelling

stop on lap 38. Meanwhile, Trulli's exhaust broke which damaged the engine electrical system due to localised overheating.

Michael, who had stopped on lap 30 without problems, could now ease back and allow Rubens to close up and then race through into the lead on the start/finish straight coming up to complete lap 45. Next time round Barrichello dived into the pits again for a quick 4.5s 'splash and dash' before resuming in second place. Now Ferrari's 1-2 victory was guaranteed.

For his part, Ralf Schumacher, who drove the spare FW22, was well satisfied with third place although the BMW Williams team was disappointed that Jenson Button retired with engine failure after a bold and confident F1 debut.

'My start wasn't the best in the world, but some people had worse, so it wasn't bad,' said the baby of the F1 pack. 'My first lap was very hectic and I tried to stay out of trouble. It was a nice steady race, apart from a little mistake on the fifth lap. I just wish it had lasted another 20 laps!'

In the closing stages of the race the battle from fourth to eighth place – Villeneuve, Fisichella, Zonta, Salo and Wurz – was absolutely nose-to-tail with Salo forcing his Sauber ahead of Zonta's BAR to take what looked like sixth place with just eight laps to run.

Unfortunately, at post-race scrutineering, the Finn's Sauber was disqualified owing to a front wing dimensional mix-up. The rather red-faced team later admitted it had fitted the nose wing from last year's C18 – and not checked its clearance. That drama promoted Zonta to a fortuitous sixth place, starting the new season on a very positive note for British American Racing with its first double helping of championship points.

'This was the fifth time we have tried to win in Australia and to be competitive at the start of the season,' said Schumacher. 'The first time I sat in the car I knew I would be able to fight for the championship right from the start. I am particularly looking forward to the next race at Interlagos. We have a car which will be competitive everywhere. And we know how to develop it.'

Schumacher might well have added that not since he won the 1994 Brazilian Grand Prix at the wheel of a Benetton-Ford had he triumphed in the opening race of a new season. That year he went on to win the World Championship.

As far as the 2000 season was concerned, this was indeed early days, but the expression of unbridled elation on Michael's face as he climbed the winner's rostrum at the Albert Park circuit signalled his confident belief that F1 history was poised to repeat itself.

MELBOURNE
10–12 MARCH 2000
ROUND 1

QANTAS AUSTRALIAN grand prix

MELBOURNE — ALBERT PARK
CIRCUIT LENGTH: 3.295 miles/5.303 km

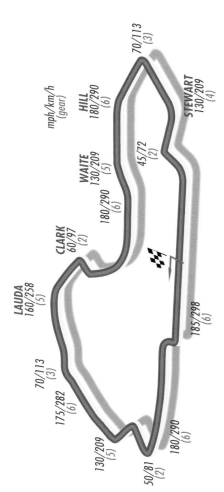

Track map speeds (mph/km/h, gear):
- HILL 180/290 (6)
- WAITE 130/209 (5)
- CLARK 60/97 (2)
- LAUDA 160/258 (5)
- STEWART 130/209 (4)
- 70/113 (3)
- 45/72 (2)
- 180/290 (6)
- 185/298 (6)
- 130/209 (5)
- 180/290 (6)
- 50/81 (2)
- 175/282 (6)
- 70/113 (3)

RACE DISTANCE: 58 laps, 191.117 miles/307.574 km   RACE WEATHER: Dry, hot and sunny

Pos.	Driver	Nat.	No.	Entrant	Car/Engine	Laps	Time/Retirement	Speed (mph/km/h)
1	Michael Schumacher	D	3	Scuderia Ferrari Marlboro	Ferrari F1-2000-049 V10	58	1h 34m 01.967s	121.946/196.254
2	Rubens Barrichello	BR	4	Scuderia Ferrari Marlboro	Ferrari F1-2000-049 V10	58	1h 34m 13.402s	121.700/195.858
3	Ralf Schumacher	D	9	BMW WilliamsF1 Team	Williams FW22-BMW E41 V10	58	1h 34m 21.996s	121.516/195.561
4	Jacques Villeneuve	CDN	22	Lucky Strike BAR Honda	BAR 02-Honda RA100E V10	58	1h 34m 46.434s	120.993/194.720
5	Giancarlo Fisichella	I	11	Mild Seven Benetton Playlife	Benetton B200-Playlife V10	58	1h 34m 47.152s	120.978/194.696
DQ	Mika Salo	SF	17	Red Bull Sauber Petronas	Sauber C19-Petronas SPE 04A V10	58	Illegal front wing	
6	Ricardo Zonta	BR	23	Lucky Strike BAR Honda	BAR 02-Honda RA100E V10	58	1h 34m 48.455s	120.950/194.651
7	Alexander Wurz	A	12	Mild Seven Benetton Playlife	Benetton B200-Playlife V10	58	1h 34m 48.902s	120.941/194.636
8	Marc Gene	ESP	20	Telefonica Minardi Fondmetal	Minardi M02-Fondmetal Ford Zetec-R V10	57		
9	Nick Heidfeld	D	15	Gauloises Prost Peugeot	Prost AP03-Peugeot A20 V10	56		
	Jenson Button	GB	10	BMW WilliamsF1 Team	Williams FW22-BMW E41 V10	46	Engine	
	Pedro Diniz	BR	16	Red Bull Sauber Petronas	Sauber C19-Petronas SPE 04A V10	41	Transmission	
	Gaston Mazzacane	ARG	21	Telefonica Minardi Fondmetal	Minardi M02-Fondmetal Ford Zetec-R V10	40	Gearbox	
	Heinz-Harald Frentzen	D	5	Benson & Hedges Jordan	Jordan EJ10-Mugen Honda MF301HE V10	39	Hydraulic leak	
	Jarno Trulli	I	6	Benson & Hedges Jordan	Jordan EJ10-Mugen Honda MF301HE V10	35	Exhaust	
	Jean Alesi	F	14	Gauloises Prost Peugeot	Prost AP03-Peugeot A20 V10	27	Hydraulics	
	Mika Häkkinen	SF	1	West McLaren Mercedes	McLaren MP4/15-Mercedes FO110J V10	18	Engine	
	Jos Verstappen	NL	19	Arrows Supertec	Arrows A21-Supertec FB02 V10	16	Track rod	
	David Coulthard	GB	2	West McLaren Mercedes	McLaren MP4/15-Mercedes FO110J V10	11	Engine	
	Pedro de la Rosa	ESP	18	Arrows Supertec	Arrows A21-Supertec FB02 V10	6	Track rod/accident	
	Eddie Irvine	GB	7	Jaguar Racing	Jaguar R1-Cosworth CR2 V10	6	Spun off	
	Johnny Herbert	GB	8	Jaguar Racing	Jaguar R1-Cosworth CR2 V10	1	Clutch	

Fastest lap: Barrichello, on lap 41, 1m 31.481s, 129.671 mph/208.685 km/h.

Lap record: Heinz-Harald Frentzen (F1 Williams FW19-Renault V10), 1m 30.585s, 130.929 mph/210.710 km/h (1997).

Lap chart

Grid order	1	2	3	4	5	6	7	8	9	10	11	12	13	14	15	16	17	18	19	20	21	22	23	24	25	26	27	28	29	30	31	32	33	34	35	36	37	38	39	40	41	42	43	44	45
1 HÄKKINEN	1	1	1	1	1	1	1	1	1	1	1	1	1	1	1	1	1	1																											
2 COULTHARD	2	2	2	2	2	2	2	2	2	2	2																																		
3 M. SCHUMACHER	3	3	3	3	3	3	3	3	3	3	3	3	3	3	3	3	3	3	3	3	3	3	3	3	22	3	3	3	4	3	3	3	3	3	3	3	3	3	3	3	3	3	3	3	3
4 BARRICHELLO	5	5	5	5	5	5	5	6	6	6	22	22	22	22	22	11	11	11	11	9	4	23	12	12	12	10	4	23	12	12	12	16	16	16	21	21	20	20	20	15	15				
5 FRENTZEN	4	4	4	4	4	4	4	22	17	17	17	17	17	17	17	23	23	23	9	23	12	12	10	10	10	23	12	12	10	10	10	20	20	20	15	15	15	15	15						
7 IRVINE	6	6	6	6	6	6	6	17	11	11	11	11	11	11	11	9	9	9	23	12	10	10	17	17	14	14	14	16	16	16	16	15	15	15											
22 VILLENEUVE	22	22	22	22	22	22	22	11	9	9	9	9	9	9	9	12	12	12	12	10	23	17	14	14	15	16	16	14	14	20	20														
11 FISICHELLA	17	17	17	17	17	17	17	9	23	23	23	23	23	23	23	10	10	10	10	17	17	14	15	15	16	15	15	20	20	15	15														
17 SALO	7	19	19	19	19	19	19	23	12	12	12	12	12	12	12	17	17	17	17	14	14	15	16	16	20	20	20	15	15																
9 R. SCHUMACHER	19	7	18	18	18	7	23	12	10	10	10	10	10	10	10	14	14	14	14	16	16	16	20	20																					
18 DE LA ROSA	11	18	7	7	7	11	12	10	14	14	14	14	14	14	14	16	16	16	16	20	20	20																							
19 VERSTAPPEN	18	11	11	11	11	12	10	14	16	16	16	16	16	16	16	20	20	20	20																										
12 WURZ	9	9	9	9	9	23	14	16	20	20	20	20	20	20	20	21	21	21																											
15 HEIDFELD	23	23	23	23	23	12	16	20	21	21	21	21	21	21	21																														
23 ZONTA	10	10	12	12	12	10	20	21																																					
14 ALESI	12	12	10	10	10	16	21																																						
20 GENE	16	16	16	16	16	15																																							
16 DINIZ	15	15	14	14	15	21																																							
8 HERBERT	21	21	21	21	21	14																																							
10 BUTTON	14	14	15	15	20	20																																							
21 MAZZACANE	8	20	20	20	19	19																																							
	20																																												

Pit stop
One lap behind leader

STARTING GRID

Pos	No	Driver	Team
1	1	HÄKKINEN	McLaren
2	2	COULTHARD	McLaren
3	3	M. SCHUMACHER	Ferrari
4	4	BARRICHELLO	Ferrari
5	5	FRENTZEN	Jordan
6	6	TRULLI	Jordan
7	7	IRVINE	Jaguar
8	22	VILLENEUVE	BAR
9	9	R. SCHUMACHER	Williams
10	18	DE LA ROSA	Arrows
11	11	FISICHELLA	Benetton
12	17	SALO	Sauber
13	19	VERSTAPPEN	Arrows
14	12	WURZ	Benetton
15	15	HEIDFELD	Prost
16	23	ZONTA	BAR
17	16	DINIZ	Sauber
18	8	HERBERT	Jaguar
19	14*	ALESI	Prost
20	20	GENE	Minardi
21	10	BUTTON	Williams
22	21	MAZZACANE	Minardi

*started from pit lane

FOR THE RECORD

First Grand Prix start
Jenson Button
Gaston Mazzacane

First Grand Prix points
Nick Heidfeld

British American Racing
Ricardo Zonta

TIME SHEETS

QUALIFYING
Weather: Dry, hot and sunny

Pos.	Driver	Car	Laps	Time
1	Mika Häkkinen	McLaren-Mercedes	11	1m 30.556s
2	David Coulthard	McLaren-Mercedes	11	1m 30.910s
3	Michael Schumacher	Ferrari	11	1m 31.075s
4	Rubens Barrichello	Ferrari	9	1m 31.102s
5	Heinz-Harald Frentzen	Jordan-Mugen Honda	12	1m 31.359s
6	Jarno Trulli	Jordan-Mugen Honda	8	1m 31.504s
7	Eddie Irvine	Jaguar-Cosworth	11	1m 31.968s
8	Jacques Villeneuve	BAR-Honda	10	1m 31.514s
9	Giancarlo Fisichella	Benetton-Playlife	11	1m 31.992s
10	Ralf Schumacher	Williams-BMW	9	1m 32.018s
11	Mika Salo	Sauber-Petronas	11	1m 32.220s
12	Pedro de la Rosa	Arrows-Supertec	11	1m 32.323s
13	Jos Verstappen	Arrows-Supertec	11	1m 32.477s
14	Alexander Wurz	Benetton-Playlife	11	1m 32.775s
15	Nick Heidfeld	Prost-Peugeot	11	1m 33.024s
16	Ricardo Zonta	BAR-Honda	10	1m 33.117s
17	Jean Alesi	Prost-Peugeot	11	1m 33.197s
18	Marc Gene	Minardi-Fondmetal	11	1m 33.261s
19	Johnny Herbert	Jaguar-Cosworth	11	1m 33.378s
20	Pedro Diniz	Sauber-Petronas	9	1m 33.638s
21	Jenson Button	Williams-BMW	11	1m 33.828s
22	Gaston Mazzacane	Minardi-Fondmetal	12	1m 34.705s

FRIDAY FREE PRACTICE
Weather: Dry, hot and sunny

Pos.	Driver	Laps	Time
1	Michael Schumacher	15	1m 32.130s
2	David Coulthard	32	1m 32.144s
3	Rubens Barrichello	30	1m 32.482s
4	Mika Häkkinen	24	1m 32.702s
5	Jacques Villeneuve	36	1m 33.525s
6	Pedro Diniz	34	1m 33.597s
7	Heinz-Harald Frentzen	35	1m 33.698s
8	Alexander Wurz	33	1m 33.718s
9	Ricardo Zonta	38	1m 33.847s
10	Eddie Irvine	24	1m 33.899s
11	Mika Salo	35	1m 33.940s
12	Gaston Mazzacane	35	1m 33.988s
13	Giancarlo Fisichella	30	1m 34.049s
14	Pedro de la Rosa	30	1m 34.060s
15	Jarno Trulli	20	1m 34.151s
16	Ralf Schumacher	15	1m 34.158s
17	Johnny Herbert	11	1m 34.414s
18	Jenson Button	40	1m 34.547s
19	Marc Gene	22	1m 34.696s
20	Jos Verstappen	19	1m 34.708s
21	Jean Alesi	18	1m 35.613s
22	Nick Heidfeld	23	1m 35.997s

SATURDAY FREE PRACTICE
Weather: Dry, hot and sunny

Pos.	Driver	Laps	Time
1	Michael Schumacher	25	1m 30.439s
2	David Coulthard	18	1m 30.958s
3	Heinz-Harald Frentzen	15	1m 31.020s
4	Rubens Barrichello	29	1m 31.366s
5	Ralf Schumacher	32	1m 31.602s
6	Jarno Trulli	27	1m 31.692s
7	Pedro de la Rosa	25	1m 31.898s
8	Jos Verstappen	25	1m 32.073s
9	Jacques Villeneuve	29	1m 32.113s
10	Mika Häkkinen	19	1m 32.131s
11	Johnny Herbert	29	1m 32.260s
12	Eddie Irvine	28	1m 32.345s
13	Giancarlo Fisichella	29	1m 32.382s
14	Marc Gene	30	1m 32.441s
15	Alexander Wurz	33	1m 32.654s
16	Pedro Diniz	29	1m 32.921s
17	Gaston Mazzacane	31	1m 33.039s
18	Mika Salo	10	1m 33.074s
19	Jean Alesi	19	1m 33.287s
20	Ricardo Zonta	4	1m 33.675s
21	Jenson Button	11	1m 33.791s
22	Nick Heidfeld	16	1m 33.826s

WARM-UP
Weather: Dry, hot and sunny

Pos.	Driver	Laps	Time
1	Rubens Barrichello	10	1m 31.225s
2	Jenson Button	11	1m 32.798s
3	Mika Häkkinen	12	1m 32.918s
4	David Coulthard	13	1m 33.034s
5	Jos Verstappen	8	1m 33.189s
6	Giancarlo Fisichella	14	1m 33.263s
7	Jean Alesi	14	1m 33.491s
8	Michael Schumacher	11	1m 33.557s
9	Pedro de la Rosa	7	1m 33.928s
10	Mika Salo	12	1m 33.967s
11	Jarno Trulli	15	1m 33.981s
12	Ralf Schumacher	12	1m 34.031s
13	Ricardo Zonta	13	1m 34.200s
14	Jacques Villeneuve	14	1m 34.200s
15	Alexander Wurz	12	1m 34.214s
16	Pedro Diniz	16	1m 34.345s
17	Marc Gene	14	1m 34.378s
18	Eddie Irvine	14	1m 34.541s
19	Heinz-Harald Frentzen	13	1m 35.092s
20	Gaston Mazzacane	6	1m 35.663s
21	Nick Heidfeld	12	1m 37.022s
22	Johnny Herbert	5	1m 48.934s

RACE FASTEST LAPS
Weather: Dry, hot and sunny

Driver	Time	Lap
Rubens Barrichello	1m 31.481s	41
Michael Schumacher	1m 31.752s	28
Heinz-Harald Frentzen	1m 32.110s	15
David Coulthard	1m 32.433s	29
Mika Häkkinen	1m 32.525s	18
Ralf Schumacher	1m 32.977s	50
Pedro Diniz	1m 33.185s	38
Jacques Villeneuve	1m 33.223s	28
Jarno Trulli	1m 33.231s	54
Marc Gene	1m 33.351s	36
Jenson Button	1m 33.435s	34
Giancarlo Fisichella	1m 33.449s	33
Ricardo Zonta	1m 33.459s	34
Alexander Wurz	1m 33.471s	51
Eddie Irvine	1m 33.653s	7
Mika Salo	1m 33.675s	53
Jean Alesi	1m 33.287s	19
Jos Verstappen	1m 33.791s	4
Nick Heidfeld	1m 33.826s	16

CHASSIS LOG BOOK

No	Driver	Chassis
1	Häkkinen	McLaren MP4/15/1
2	Coulthard	McLaren MP4/15/2
	spare	McLaren MP4/15/3
3	M. Schumacher	Ferrari F1-2000/200
4	Barrichello	Ferrari F1-2000/199
	spare	Ferrari F1-2000/198
5	Frentzen	Jordan EJ10/4
6	Trulli	Jordan EJ10/3
	spare	Jordan EJ10/2
7	Irvine	Jaguar R1/4
8	Herbert	Jaguar R1/1
	spare	Jaguar R1/3
9	R. Schumacher	Williams FW22/3
10	Button	Williams FW22/1
	spare	Williams FW22/2
11	Fisichella	Benetton B200/2
12	Wurz	Benetton B200/3
	spare	Benetton B200/1
14	Alesi	Prost AP03/1
15	Heidfeld	Prost AP03/2
	spare	Prost AP03/3
16	Diniz	Sauber C19/4
17	Salo	Sauber C19/2
	spare	Sauber C19/1
18	de la Rosa	Arrows A21/3
19	Verstappen	Arrows A21/1
	spare	Arrows A21/2
20	Gene	Minardi M02/3
21	Mazzacane	Minardi M02/2
	spare	Minardi M02/1
22	Villeneuve	BAR 02/3
23	Zonta	BAR 02/4
	spare	BAR 02/1

POINTS TABLES

DRIVERS

	Driver	Pts
1	Michael Schumacher	10
2	Rubens Barrichello	6
3	Ralf Schumacher	4
4	Jacques Villeneuve	3
5	Giancarlo Fisichella	2
6	Ricardo Zonta	1

CONSTRUCTORS

	Team	Pts
1	Ferrari	16
2 =	Williams	4
2 =	BAR	4
4	Benetton	2

BRAZILIAN
grand prix

FIA WORLD CHAMPIONSHIP • ROUND 2

Previous spread: Michael Schumacher's Ferrari dominated the race in Brazil.
Paul-Henri Cahier

Left: Heinz-Harald Frentzen's perseverance was rewarded with a third place after David Coulthard's disqualification.
Bryn Williams/Words & Pictures

TWO races, two wins, Michael Schumacher drove with his customary measured brilliance to score his second win of the season in the Brazilian Grand Prix at Interlagos, his quest for a third world title yet again aided by unreliability on the part of Mika Häkkinen's McLaren-Mercedes MP4/15 which looked on course for a probable victory before being sidelined with engine failure.

Worse still, David Coulthard's dogged run to second place, hobbled by gearchange problems, proved a wasted effort. At post-race scrutineering excessive wear on his McLaren's front wing end plates resulted in his exclusion from the results.

The team lodged an appeal, but an FIA tribunal duly rejected it eight days later. It was a bitter blow for F1's established pace-setters who returned from São Paulo without a single championship point to their credit.

For his part, Schumacher harnessed a two-stop refuelling strategy to brilliant effect, bursting through ahead of Häkkinen to take the lead at the end of the opening lap and pulling away relentlessly. Initial impressions may have suggested that Michael was on course to beat the McLarens with such a strategy, but the McLaren team was confident its one-stop approach for Häkkinen would pay off handsomely.

As it was, Mika was running confidently in the lead — yet to make his one refuelling stop — when his oil pressure faded and he retired at the end of lap 30. That left Coulthard to pick up the fallen McLaren standard, but, hobbled by gearchange problems from early in the race, the Scot was simply unable to press home his attack.

From the start it had seemed that Coulthard, who was on course for a long opening stint — he made his sole refuelling stop with 43 of the race's 71 laps run — was in good shape as a possible race winner, but things soon started to unravel for the Scot.

This was Schumacher's 37th career victory, his 18th since joining Ferrari at the start of the 1996 season, and one which emphatically underlined the fact that the latest Ferrari F1-2000 can sustain a consistent challenge at the front of the field.

Unfortunately his team-mate, local hero Rubens Barrichello, was unable to deliver the result the other Brazilian fans were craving and retired the other Ferrari F1-2000 with hydraulic failure after 27 laps.

Schumacher was understandably elated by this second straight win which gave him a huge tactical advantage over the McLaren drivers with only two of the season's 17 races completed.

'We made an obvious improvement to our starting strategy,' said Michael. 'I was able to catch Mika but I didn't want to take a risk too soon and of course he was not keen to let me pass. I enjoyed our battle — it's been a long time since there was a good fight and overtaking for the lead.'

Even so, Michael could count himself fortunate. In the closing stages his pit told him to ease back, worried that the Ferrari V10 had an oil pressure problem. Had Coulthard's car been in perfect fettle, it might have rendered him uncomfortably vulnerable. In the

Renault buys Benetton F1 team

THE Benetton family signalled its intention to quit F1 after 15 seasons with the news that it was selling out to Renault for a reputed £75 million. To that end, the team was directed and managed as from the Brazilian Grand Prix by the charismatic Flavio Briatore, the Italian entrepreneur who ran it on behalf of the Benetton family from 1989 up until 1997.

As part of the deal, Benetton will remain as the team's official sponsor until the end of 2001. In the longer term this move looked set to deprive the World Championship scene of an enthusiastic, colourful and promotionally imaginative team whose hard results have disappointingly failed to live up to its lively and charismatic profile over the past few seasons.

At the same time, Renault's decision to return to Formula 1 in such a manner represented another decisive step towards the domination of the World Championship by the world's major motor manufacturers. In that respect, Luciano Benetton, president of the Benetton group, made it clear that the financial requirements of a modern F1 team were now beyond his company's capabilities.

'Today globalisation means that it must be the specialists in each sector who compete in their own market,' he said. 'We have invested a great deal of effort in Formula 1 and it has brought us more satisfaction than we could have imagined.

'Now, to guarantee the development the team deserves in this new scenario, it is appropriate to pass the baton to Renault.'

INTERLAGOS QUALIFYING

A major investigation was promised by the FIA after qualifying for the Brazilian Grand Prix had to be red-flagged to a halt no fewer than three times in an hour when parts of an advertising hoarding collapsed onto the circuit. Eventually an official inquiry held in Paris fined the organisers a relatively modest $100,000.

The third time the hoarding fell apart, debris hit the hapless Jean Alesi's Prost AP03 as it approached the first left-hander at Interlagos at around 170 mph.

This sequence of events turned the qualifying session into an utter and complete fiasco. It was perhaps ironic that the collapse of a jerry-built Marlboro gantry should have caused the Marlboro-backed Ferraris to both be thwarted on what would have been pole-challenging quick runs.

'The interruptions caused by the advertising boards did not do any favours to our sport,' commented Eddie Jordan with masterly understatement.

Other team owners were more direct, feeling that an unacceptable exception is continually being made for the Brazilian track by the FIA with the result that the teams have to put up with paddock facilities which would result in the circuit being dropped from the calendar if it were almost anywhere else in the world. To add to everybody's frustrations, a heavy rain storm washed out the balance of the qualifying session with 17 minutes still left to run.

Moreover, the track's unacceptably bumpy surface — resurfaced this year, but still bumpy as hell — resulted in the Saubers having to be withdrawn from the race after a couple of extremely worrying wing failures.

Picking his way through the chaos, Mika Häkkinen took command from the outset and his eventual best of 1m 14.111s was an amazing 2.5s inside the 1999 pole-position time, a terrific effort even allowing for the fact that the circuit had recently been resurfaced.

David Coulthard was just 0.17s adrift in second place, prompting McLaren chief Ron Dennis to comment: 'I was very impressed with David's performance. I think he even may have a better handle on the characteristics of the circuit than Mika.'

Mercedes was confident that its Melbourne engine problems had now been licked. The problem had been the failure of a filter protecting a one-way valve which charges the pneumatic valvegear system on the Ilmor-built V10. This had allowed debris to enter the valve, causing it to stick open with the result that the air pressure leaked away.

'I have to apologise to the whole team and the guys who worked so hard,' said Norbert Haug, the Mercedes motor sport director. 'After so much testing it is something that should not have happened, and in the last 30 races it is something that has happened too often to us.

'But our commitment was to push, to go for race speed. We didn't expect it to happen to us again this year, but there is a long season ahead of us and I must say I feel quite confident.' Prescient words?

Michael Schumacher slammed his Ferrari F1-2000 round to take third place on the grid despite sliding off course on his second run, badly damaging the underside of his race chassis and switching to the spare to post 1m 14.508s. Barrichello had briefly stormed into second place, but his third run was thwarted by red flags and he had to be content with fourth in the final line-up.

'The car went well and the set-up was good,' said Rubens. 'We can be very competitive in the race and this is a track where you can overtake.'

Outside the exclusive top four, Giancarlo Fisichella worked out a really good chassis balance for his Benetton B200, posting a confident 1m 15.375s to line up fifth ahead of Eddie Irvine's Jaguar R1 on 1m 15.425s. Despite a succession of minor technical glitches the Jaguars thankfully showed no more signs of the acute oil consumption problems which had blighted the latest Cosworth CR2 V10 in the Australian Grand Prix.

'In the first race you learn about 50 per cent of the story as to how your season is going to develop,' said Irvine in cautiously optimistic tone.

'The second race gives you another 25 per cent knowledge and I am expecting by the third race at Imola [in a fortnight's time] we will really know about 85 per cent of our potential.'

In the Jordan camp, qualifying proved something of a disappointment. Heinz-Harald Frentzen never quite managed to get into the swing of things during the afternoon, ending up seventh on 1m 15.455s, while Jarno Trulli was a distant 12th after spinning off early on in his race car and then switched to the spare, later losing time with an electronic control box problem which affected the gearchange operation.

Eighth place on the grid was well earned by Ricardo Zonta on the first anniversary of his massive Interlagos practice accident, two places ahead of team-mate Jacques Villeneuve on this occasion. 'I was badly affected by the chaos,' shrugged Jacques, 'which was a shame, because I was expecting to qualify fifth or sixth.'

In the Williams-BMW camp, Jenson Button (1m 15.490s) and Ralf Schumacher (1m 15.561s) qualified 9th and 11th. Button's car required an engine change between Saturday practice and qualifying while Schumacher admitted he went in slightly the wrong direction on chassis set-up.

'The rear end of my car was a bit too stiff,' he admitted. 'Even though we changed this during qualifying, eventually I couldn't manage to achieve anything better than 11th.' Ralf added, however, that he felt confident for the race.

As in Melbourne, the Arrows A21 had displayed an impressive turn of speed for much of free practice, but things went wrong in qualifying with Jos Verstappen and Pedro de la Rosa trailing 14th and 16th.

'Obviously I am very disappointed,' said Verstappen, 'because I was really looking forward to the last run.' De la Rosa agreed that they had got it wrong, in his case he got badly embroiled in heavy traffic. But it certainly looked promising enough.

Separating the Arrows was Jean Alesi's Prost while the luckless Herbert's Jaguar ended up 17th ahead of the two Minardi M02s which, in turn, found themselves sandwiching Nick Heidfeld's Prost at the back of what — in the absence of the Saubers — was a 20-car starting grid.

DIARY

Bernie Ecclestone attacks British Prime Minister Tony Blair for 'third rate behaviour' over publicizing the £1 million gift the F1 supremo gave to the Labour Party when it came to power in 1997.

Dario Franchitti is passed fit to take part in the first race of the CART season at Homestead.

The works Audi team scores a 1-2 success in the Sebring 12-hour sports car race.

Planning for the long-awaited Silverstone village bypass is approved by the local council.

Williams technical director Patrick Head denies speculation that he and Frank Williams might sell the team to engine supplier BMW.

event he could cruise home without any pressure.

Once practice at Interlagos began, the Ferrari team's confident assertion that Barrichello would have a fair chance to bid for victory in his home Grand Prix began to look like a charmingly indulgent, rather academic gesture to their new driver in front of his adoring Brazilian crowd.

Such a strategy was always going to depend on 27-year-old Barrichello, who was still seeking his first F1 win, being quick enough to beat Michael Schumacher in a straight fight. Increasingly this was looking as much of a dream as it did to the previous incumbent Eddie Irvine who spent four seasons battling to get on terms with Schumacher's magical talent.

Yet none of this could alter the fact that Interlagos was a sell-out, fans queuing for miles for much of the night prior to the race in an outpouring of nationalistic emotion which transcended anything produced by the heydey of Emerson Fittipaldi or, come to that, the late Ayrton Senna. For the emotional *Paulistas* the chance to cheer their beloved *Rubinho* was an opportunity simply too good to miss.

For Barrichello, returning to race in his home Grand Prix as the first Brazilian to drive a factory F1 Ferrari

represented an unashamedly emotional moment for the boy who had spent much of his childhood living in a house overlooking the track.

'I was probably six years old when my grandfather gave me my first kart,' he said. 'I lived by the track and went to school at Interlagos. Sometimes when I wave to someone in the grandstand here it is because I recognise them as an old school friend.'

At the start, Häkkinen took an immediate lead from Schumacher's Ferrari, Coulthard and Barrichello. Further back there had been a few worrying moments prior to the parade lap when Alexander Wurz's Benetton was stranded when the engine suddenly died.

'On the formation lap I had a problem with the engine so I couldn't pull away,' he explained. 'Then at the start the same thing happened again, so I had to start from the pits. When I got onto the straight I found I could only pull fifth gear, so I knew it was just a question of time until I had to stop.' The Austrian eventually pulled in to retire after six laps.

At the end of the opening lap, Schumacher took his Ferrari diving up the inside of Häkkinen as they braked for the first corner after the pits. A few lengths further back Barrichello

darted inside Coulthard for third place.

By the end of lap three Michael was just over 3s ahead of Häkkinen and an amazing 8.7s in front of Eddie Irvine's Jaguar which was now running in fifth place as best of the rest. Then came the Jordan EJ10 of Heinz-Harald Frentzen, the impressive Pedro de la Rosa's Arrows, Ricardo Zonta's BAR, Jarno Trulli's Jordan and Jacques Villeneuve in the other BAR.

By lap six Schumacher had opened a 6.0s advantage over Häkkinen who now had his hands full with Barrichello on his tail, but Coulthard was fading fast in fourth place.

'I thought the team finally wasn't speaking to me,' he later recounted. 'I wasn't getting any response to my questions and it didn't take long to work out that my radio had failed.

'My third gear also failed, after two or three laps, which forced me to do the whole race, except for the pit stop, using fourth, fifth, sixth and seventh. I think it is a miracle that I was able to finish the race at all, because fourth gear was [also] starting to give me some difficulties later in the race.'

By lap ten Schumacher was 10.2s clear in the lead just as Nick Heidfeld retired his Prost AP03 from a distant 17th with engine failure. Two laps

Right: Giancarlo Fisichella had a good race, in spite of pronounced understeer resulting from his Benetton's initial heavy fuel load, finishing an eventual second.

Below: Coulthard's McLaren is checked in the scrutineering bay.
Both photographs: Paul-Henri Cahier

FIA Court upholds Coulthard's disqualification

DAVID Coulthard was disqualified from second place at Interlagos some hours after the race when, following a lengthy period of scrutineering during which his McLaren was examined and re-examined many times over, the FIA technical delegate Jo Bauer concluded that the front wing of the second-place McLaren-Mercedes was 7 mm too low according to the regulations.

The matter was reported to the stewards who duly disqualified the Scot from the race, after which McLaren immediately lodged an appeal which was heard by the FIA Court in Paris eight days after the race.

As expected, the Court refused to accept any mitigating circumstances from McLaren's lawyer who cited the deplorable condition of the track surface at São Paulo's Interlagos circuit as one of the reasons why Coulthard's McLaren was found to have infringed the front wing dimensions.

'The team is disappointed with the decision of the FIA Court of Appeal to refuse the team's appeal against the ruling of the stewards of the Brazilian Grand Prix,' said an official statement from the team immediately after the hearing.

'David Coulthard's McLaren-Mercedes MP4/15 started the Brazilian Grand Prix in fully legal trim. However, due to the nature of the circuit and the harshness of the bumps, substantial damage was encountered to the underside of the car and the front wing end plate moved on its axis. These factors resulted in the distance between the reference plane and the lowest part on the front wing being two millimetres less than permissible.

'The measurements taken at the end of the race represented a minor discrepancy, the causes of which were beyond the team's control.'

The FIA took the view that all other cars managed to finish the race in legal trim despite tackling the bumps which had apparently caught out the McLaren.

However, the decision to confirm Coulthard's exclusion certainly raised more than a few eyebrows in the F1 paddock from those who believe that the FIA's ruling flew in the face of its decision to reinstate the Ferraris of Eddie Irvine and Michael Schumacher to first and second places in last year's Malaysian Grand Prix.

On that occasion the issue centred around the dimensions of the bargeboards on the side of the Ferrari which were initially found to be illegal. The court of appeal decreed that they were within the prescribed tolerance, even though most F1 technical directors believed up until that moment that the 'tolerance' permitted referred only to the vertical plane – and not the horizontal plane permitted by the court.

On that occasion, the Maranello team won the appeal when it was

established that a 5 mm tolerance was allowed on such components. Unfortunately, the wing on David Coulthard's McLaren MP4/15 was well outside that tolerance.

later his team-mate Jean Alesi dropped out with a similar problem, having just moved up to ninth place, thereby capping another disastrous weekend for the beleaguered French outfit.

Starting lap 15, Barrichello finally pulled off the move he'd been building up to over the previous few laps, diving through inside Häkkinen's McLaren to take second place going into the first corner. He was now just over 17s behind Schumacher who came into the pits for a first 10.1s refuelling stop at the end of lap 20, dropping to third place.

Further back, lap 21 had seen Irvine spin off while running strongly in sixth place. 'Thinking I was slower than I actually was, I was pushing harder than I should have been and just lost the back end,' he said. 'I didn't really have a clear picture of just how competitive we are in a race situation before today, but I have to say I am impressed because I feel we can mix it at the top end.'

The Jaguar team leader boosted the team's confidence by suggesting he would have finished ahead on the rostrum, running as he was ahead of Fisichella and both Jordans in the opening stages.

Barrichello went through into the lead for two laps before making his own 10.7s first stop at the end of lap 22. That left Häkkinen running 7.4s ahead of Schumacher and the Finn gradually eased open the gap to 12.7s before engine failure intervened to end his hopes for the second place race.

'Obviously the word disappointed can't describe how I feel,' shrugged Häkkinen afterwards. 'We have been quick throughout the weekend, so I'm not happy to leave Brazil without any points. We certainly have some work to do before the start of the European season.'

Soon after Barrichello resumed the race in fourth place after his refuelling stop he began to experience steering and throttle control problems. Then his Ferrari began to trail an ominous smoke haze, signalling the first signs of what many onlookers took to be imminent engine failure. In fact this was leaking hydraulic fluid and he eventually stopped for good with 27 laps completed.

On lap 35, Jos Verstappen made his sole refuelling stop, dropping from third to ninth, allowing Giancarlo Fisichella's Benetton B200 to move up to third place ahead of Frentzen and Trulli. On lap 41 Frentzen made his only refuelling stop, dropping from fourth to seventh, while two laps later Coulthard came in for his 8.8s stop, resuming 38.8s behind Schumacher's leading Ferrari.

On lap 51 Schumacher made his second refuelling stop and resumed 24.4s ahead of the troubled Coulthard while, further back, Fisichella – who had run an incredibly long opening stint – arrived for a 7.1s 'splash and dash' which would see him back into the race with third place intact.

'It's a great result for the team,' said the Italian. 'The car was very difficult at the start of the race with a very heavy fuel level and a lot of understeer. Then after about 15 laps the behaviour and grip levels became much better, so I was able to keep pushing until the end.'

In fourth and fifth places came the Jordans of Frentzen and Trulli, the Italian benefiting in particular from the two-stop strategy which vaulted him up from 12th in the starting order, while Heinz-Harald ran a single-stop strategy.

'I was a bit disappointed that I couldn't keep up with Fisichella in the middle of the race,' said Trulli. 'Unfortunately my rear tyres took a lot of wear and I had to come in for an early pit stop to change them.' At the chequered flag he was just 2.3s behind the Benetton.

In sixth and seventh places, the Williams-BMWs of Ralf Schumacher and the impressive Jenson Button proved hearteningly reliable, if not particularly quick. What was impressive was the manner in which Button again tracked his team-mate after fluffing his first lap and dropping from ninth to 14th.

For many laps Button was locked in a wheel-to-wheel battle with Jos Verstappen's promising Arrows A21, eventually slicing through ahead of the Dutchman in what was quite a bold and decisive move mid-way round the 56th lap.

Moreover, the manner in which Button relentlessly harried Verstappen prior to making the move was extremely impressive, given that Verstappen is no soft touch himself, even though the Arrows driver later frankly admitted that he was not really fit enough.

Even so, there is a bold and audacious streak in the young Englishman, tempered by remarkable maturity and self-control. In many ways, Button's was the most telling individual performance of the race.

INTERLAGOS
24–26 MARCH 2000

ROUND 2

grande premio
MARLBORO do
BRAZIL

INTERLAGOS, SÃO PAOLO
AUTODROMO CARLOS PACE

CIRCUIT LENGTH: 2.677 miles/4.309 km

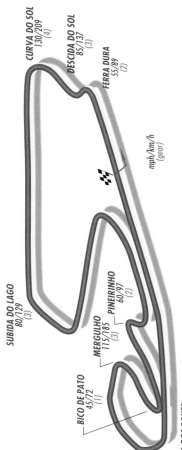

SUBIDA DO LAGO 80/129 (3)
CURVA DO SOL 130/209 (4)
DESCIDA DO SOL 85/137 (3)
FERRA DURA 55/89 (2)
MERGULHO 115/185 (3)
PINEIRINHO 60/97 (2)
BICO DE PATO 45/72 (1)
SUBIDA DOS BOXES 160/258 (5)
mph/km/h (gear)

RACE DISTANCE: 71 laps, 190.083 miles/305.909 km   RACE WEATHER: Dry, hot and sunny

Pos.	Driver	Nat.	No.	Entrant	Car/Engine	Laps	Time/Retirement	Speed (mph/km/h)
1	Michael Schumacher	D	3	Scuderia Ferrari Marlboro	Ferrari F1-2000-049 V10	71	1h 31m 35.271s	124.524/200.403
DQ	David Coulthard	GB	2	West McLaren Mercedes	McLaren MP4/15-Mercedes FO110J V10	71	Illegal front wing	
2	Giancarlo Fisichella	I	11	Mild Seven Benetton Playlife	Benetton B200-Playlife V10	71	1h 32m 15.169s	123.627/198.959
3	Heinz-Harald Frentzen	D	5	Benson & Hedges Jordan	Jordan EJ10-Mugen Honda MF301HE V10	71	1h 32m 17.539s	123.574/198.873
4	Jarno Trulli	I	6	Benson & Hedges Jordan	Jordan EJ10-Mugen Honda MF301HE V10	71	1h 32m 48.051s	122.897/197.784
5	Ralf Schumacher	D	9	BMW WilliamsF1 Team	Williams FW22-BMW E41 V10	70		
6	Jenson Button	GB	10	BMW WilliamsF1 Team	Williams FW22-BMW E41 V10	70		
7	Jos Verstappen	NL	19	Arrows Supertec	Arrows A21-Supertec FB02 V10	70		
8	Pedro de la Rosa	ESP	18	Arrows Supertec	Arrows A21-Supertec FB02 V10	70		
9	Ricardo Zonta	BR	23	Lucky Strike BAR Honda	BAR 02-Honda RA100E V10	69		
10	Gaston Mazzacane	ARG	21	Telefonica Minardi Fondmetal	Minardi M02-Fondmetal Ford Zetec-R V10	69		
	Johnny Herbert	GB	8	Jaguar Racing	Jaguar R1-Cosworth CR2 V10	51	Gearbox	
	Marc Gene	ESP	20	Telefonica Minardi Fondmetal	Minardi M02-Fondmetal Ford Zetec-R V10	31	Engine	
	Mika Häkkinen	SF	1	West McLaren Mercedes	McLaren MP4/15-Mercedes FO110J V10	30	Oil pressure	
	Rubens Barrichello	BR	4	Scuderia Ferrari Marlboro	Ferrari F1-2000-049 V10	27	Hydraulics	
	Eddie Irvine	GB	7	Jaguar Racing	Jaguar R1-Cosworth CR2 V10	20	Spun off	
	Jacques Villeneuve	CDN	22	Lucky Strike BAR Honda	BAR 02-Honda RA100E V10	16	Gearbox	
	Jean Alesi	F	14	Gauloises Prost Peugeot	Prost AP03-Peugeot A20 V10	11	Engine	
	Nick Heidfeld	D	15	Gauloises Prost Peugeot	Prost AP03-Peugeot A20 V10	9	Engine	
	Alexander Wurz	A	12	Mild Seven Benetton Playlife	Benetton B200-Playlife V10	6	Gearbox	
WDN	Pedro Diniz	BR	16	Red Bull Sauber Petronas	Sauber C19-Petronas SPE 04A V10			
WDN	Mika Salo	SF	17	Red Bull Sauber Petronas	Sauber C19-Petronas SPE 04A V10			

Fastest lap: M. Schumacher, on lap 48, 1m 14.755s, 128.940 mph/207.509 km/h (record).
Previous lap record: Jacques Villeneuve (F1 Williams FW19-Renault V10), 1m 18.397s, 122.465 mph/197.089 km/h (1997).

Grid order

	Grid order
1	HÄKKINEN
2	COULTHARD
3	M. SCHUMACHER
4	BARRICHELLO
11	FISICHELLA
7	IRVINE
5	FRENTZEN
23	ZONTA
10	BUTTON
22	VILLENEUVE
9	R. SCHUMACHER
6	TRULLI
19	VERSTAPPEN
14	ALESI
18	DE LA ROSA
8	HERBERT
20	GENE
15	HEIDFELD
21	MAZZACANE
12	WURZ

Pit stop
One lap behind leader

STARTING GRID

Pos	Driver	Team
1	HÄKKINEN	McLaren
2	COULTHARD	McLaren
3	M. SCHUMACHER	Ferrari
4	BARRICHELLO	Ferrari
11	FISICHELLA	Benetton
5	FRENTZEN	Jordan
23	ZONTA	BAR
10	BUTTON	Williams
22	VILLENEUVE	BAR
6	TRULLI	Jordan
9	R. SCHUMACHER	Williams
14	ALESI	Prost
12*	WURZ	Benetton
19	VERSTAPPEN	Arrows
18	DE LA ROSA	Arrows
8	HERBERT	Jaguar
7	IRVINE	Jaguar
20	GENE	Minardi
15	HEIDFELD	Prost
21	MAZZACANE	Minardi

* started from the pit lane

Lap Chart (laps 57–71)

	57	58	59	60	61	62	63	64	65	66	67	68	69	70	71
	3	3	3	3	3	3	3	3	3	3	3	3	3	3	3
	2	2	2	2	2	2	2	2	2	2	2	2	2	2	2
	1	1	1	1	1	1	1	1	1	1	1	1	1	1	1
	5	5	5	5	5	5	5	5	5	5	5	5	5	5	5
	6	6	6	6	6	6	6	6	6	6	6	6	6	6	6
	11	11	11	11	11	11	11	11	11	11	11	11	11	11	11
	10	10	10	10	10	10	10	10	10	10	10	10	10	10	10
	19	19	19	19	19	19	19	19	19	19	19	19	19	19	19
	18	18	18	18	18	18	18	18	18	18	18	18	18	18	18
	23	23	23	23	23	23	23	23	23	23	23	23	23	23	23
	21	21	21	21	21	21	21	21	21	21	21	21	21	21	21

FOR THE RECORD

First Grand Prix point

Jenson Button

TIME SHEETS

QUALIFYING
Weather: Cloudy, hot, eventual heavy rain

Pos.	Driver	Car	Time
1	Mika Häkkinen	McLaren-Mercedes	1m 14.111s
2	David Coulthard	McLaren-Mercedes	1m 14.285s
3	Michael Schumacher	Ferrari	1m 14.508s
4	Rubens Barrichello	Ferrari	1m 14.636s
5	Giancarlo Fisichella	Benetton-Playlife	1m 15.375s
6	Heinz-Harald Frentzen	Jordan-Mugen Honda	1m 15.455s
7	Ricardo Zonta	BAR-Honda	1m 15.484s
8	Jenson Button	Williams-BMW	1m 15.490s
9	Jacques Villeneuve	BAR-Honda	1m 15.515s
10	Jarno Trulli	Jordan-Mugen Honda	1m 15.561s
11	Ralf Schumacher	Williams-BMW	1m 15.627s
12	Jean Alesi	Prost-Peugeot	1m 15.664s
13	Alexander Wurz	Benetton-Playlife	1m 15.704s
14	Jos Verstappen	Arrows-Supertec	1m 15.715s
15	Pedro de la Rosa	Arrows-Supertec	1m 16.002s
16	Johnny Herbert	Jaguar-Cosworth	1m 16.250s
17	Eddie Irvine	Jaguar-Cosworth	1m 16.380s
18	Marc Gene	Minardi-Fondmetal	1m 17.112s
19	Nick Heidfeld	Prost-Peugeot	1m 17.178s
20	Pedro Diniz*	Sauber-Petronas	1m 17.512s
21	Gaston Mazzacane	Minardi-Fondmetal	1m 18.703s
22	Mika Salo*	Sauber-Petronas	

* subsequently withdrawn from race

FRIDAY FREE PRACTICE
Weather: Dry, hot and sunny

Pos.	Driver	Laps	Time
1	Mika Häkkinen	30	1m 15.896s
2	Michael Schumacher	28	1m 16.375s
3	David Coulthard	24	1m 16.606s
4	Rubens Barrichello	30	1m 16.613s
5	Pedro de la Rosa	22	1m 17.217s
6	Jean Alesi	39	1m 17.468s
7	Jos Verstappen	32	1m 17.641s
8	Jarno Trulli	33	1m 17.642s
9	Jacques Villeneuve	47	1m 17.654s
10	Giancarlo Fisichella	43	1m 17.831s
11	Heinz-Harald Frentzen	39	1m 17.920s
12	Mika Salo	39	1m 17.933s
13	Eddie Irvine	26	1m 17.971s
14	Ralf Schumacher	29	1m 18.024s
15	Marc Gene	34	1m 18.248s
16	Gaston Mazzacane	46	1m 18.280s
17	Ricardo Zonta	23	1m 18.289s
18	Pedro Diniz	38	1m 19.081s
19	Alexander Wurz	21	1m 19.129s
20	Jenson Button	27	1m 19.303s
21	Johnny Herbert	22	1m 19.575s
22	Nick Heidfeld	19	1m 20.364s

SATURDAY FREE PRACTICE
Weather: Cloudy and hot

Pos.	Driver	Laps	Time
1	Mika Häkkinen	29	1m 14.159s
2	Rubens Barrichello	31	1m 14.442s
3	David Coulthard	32	1m 14.502s
4	Michael Schumacher	13	1m 14.546s
5	Jarno Trulli	33	1m 14.604s
6	Giancarlo Fisichella	43	1m 15.156s
7	Jacques Villeneuve	38	1m 15.404s
8	Jos Verstappen	38	1m 15.509s
9	Ralf Schumacher	34	1m 15.594s
10	Heinz-Harald Frentzen	26	1m 15.724s
11	Pedro de la Rosa	28	1m 15.831s
12	Alexander Wurz	29	1m 15.947s
13	Ricardo Zonta	24	1m 16.110s
14	Johnny Herbert	26	1m 16.212s
15	Eddie Irvine	21	1m 16.284s
16	Jean Alesi	26	1m 16.457s
17	Marc Gene	26	1m 16.477s
18	Jenson Button	20	1m 16.709s
19	Nick Heidfeld	36	1m 16.863s
20	Mika Salo	16	1m 17.079s
21	Pedro Diniz	17	1m 17.949s
22	Gaston Mazzacane	5	1m 27.776s

WARM-UP
Weather: Cloudy and hot

Pos.	Driver	Laps	Time
1	Mika Häkkinen	12	1m 16.343s
2	Michael Schumacher	17	1m 16.348s
3	David Coulthard	17	1m 17.008s
4	Rubens Barrichello	13	1m 17.102s
5	Jos Verstappen	16	1m 17.665s
6	Ralf Schumacher	14	1m 17.691s
7	Jacques Villeneuve	14	1m 17.738s
8	Marc Gene	15	1m 17.761s
9	Giancarlo Fisichella	16	1m 17.766s
10	Ricardo Zonta	17	1m 18.112s
11	Pedro de la Rosa	18	1m 18.130s
12	Jarno Trulli	17	1m 18.288s
13	Heinz-Harald Frentzen	17	1m 18.642s
14	Jenson Button	14	1m 18.700s
15	Alexander Wurz	12	1m 18.879s
16	Gaston Mazzacane	14	1m 19.050s
17	Johnny Herbert	15	1m 19.216s
18	Eddie Irvine	11	1m 19.358s
19	Jean Alesi	6	1m 20.514s
20	Nick Heidfeld	6	1m 20.789s

RACE FASTEST LAPS
Weather: Dry, hot and sunny

Pos.	Driver	Time	Lap
1	Michael Schumacher	1m 14.755s	48
2	Heinz-Harald Frentzen	1m 15.192s	71
3	Ralf Schumacher	1m 15.456s	28
4	Mika Häkkinen	1m 15.632s	19
5	Rubens Barrichello	1m 15.633s	68
6	David Coulthard	1m 16.002s	68
7	Giancarlo Fisichella	1m 16.375s	50
8	Jarno Trulli	1m 16.379s	41
9	Jenson Button	1m 16.398s	50
10	Marc Gene	1m 16.658s	31
11	Gaston Mazzacane	1m 16.967s	62
12	Johnny Herbert	1m 16.975s	61
13	Ricardo Zonta	1m 17.174s	67
14	Pedro de la Rosa	1m 17.380s	65
15	Jos Verstappen	1m 17.696s	20
16	Mika Salo	1m 17.792s	16
17	Nick Heidfeld	1m 18.379s	36
18	Alexander Wurz	1m 18.381s	16
19	Jean Alesi	1m 19.765s	31
20	Pedro Diniz	1m 27.776s	5

POINTS TABLES

DRIVERS

Pos	Driver	Pts
1	Michael Schumacher	20
2	Giancarlo Fisichella	8
3 =	Rubens Barrichello	6
3 =	Ralf Schumacher	6
5	Heinz-Harald Frentzen	4
6 =	Jacques Villeneuve	3
6 =	Jarno Trulli	3
8 =	Ricardo Zonta	1
8 =	Jenson Button	1

CONSTRUCTORS

Pos	Team	Pts
1	Ferrari	26
2	Benetton	8
3 =	Williams	7
3 =	Jordan	7
5	BAR	4

CHASSIS LOG BOOK

No.	Driver	Chassis
1	Häkkinen	McLaren MP4/15/1
2	Coulthard	McLaren MP4/15/2
spare		McLaren MP4/15/3
3	M. Schumacher	Ferrari F1-2000/201
4	Barrichello	Ferrari F1-2000/199
spare		Ferrari F1-2000/198
5	Frentzen	Jordan E10/4
6	Trulli	Jordan E10/3
spare		Jordan E10/2
7	Irvine	Jaguar R1/4
8	Herbert	Jaguar R1/1
spare		Jaguar R1/3
9	R. Schumacher	Williams FW22/3
10	Button	Williams FW22/1
spare		Williams FW22/2
11	Fisichella	Benetton B200/2
12	Wurz	Benetton B200/3
spare		Benetton B200/1
14	Alesi	Prost AP03/1
15	Heidfeld	Prost AP03/2
spare		Prost AP03/3
16	Diniz	Sauber C19/4
17	Salo	Sauber C19/2
spare		Sauber C19/1
18	de la Rosa	Arrows A21/3
19	Verstappen	Arrows A21/1
spare		Arrows A21/2
20	Gene	Minardi M02/3
21	Mazzacane	Minardi M02/2
spare		Minardi M02/1
22	Villeneuve	BAR 02/3
23	Zonta	BAR 02/4
spare		BAR 02/1

SAN MARINO *grand prix*

M. SCHUMACHER
HÄKKINEN
COULTHARD
BARRICHELLO
VILLENEUVE
SALO

Paul-Henri Cahier

Imola may look a relatively straightforward circuit from the touchlines, but it is extremely bumpy in places and a driver has to use its kerbs to the maximum in order to wring a really quick lap out of his car.

Yet he must guard against pushing too hard, a pitfall which has caught out even the most distinguished of F1 exponents in the past. In particular, Mika Häkkinen arrived at the Autodromo Enzo e Dino Ferrari determined not to repeat his error in the 1999 race which robbed him of what could have been another race win.

On that occasion the Finn was surging away in the lead when he got onto a wobble over the left-hand kerb coming out onto the start/finish straight.

The wobble turned into a full-blown fishtail and the next thing Mika knew, he was in the wall with a wheel ripped off his McLaren-Merc. 'You need to use the kerbs to get a quick lap,' he winked knowingly this time after taking the 24th pole position of his career, 'but if you get greedy, it can be very dangerous.'

In Friday's free practice, Schumacher and Barrichello had given the passionate *tifosi* exactly what they had been yearning for in the form of a Ferrari 1–2. Coulthard and Häkkinen were only third and sixth, but Michael was certainly not making any premature assumptions. Ignoring McLaren on the basis of its performance in a Friday practice session would be tempting fate indeed.

Although Mika survived a neat 360-degree spin he finished the day in an unflustered and quietly confident frame of mind. McLaren, as usual, followed its long-established policy of ignoring what the opposition was up to during Friday practice, preferring to work through a structured programme of race preparation rather than going for quick times.

Nevertheless, Schumacher was clearly in an upbeat frame of mind. 'I am reasonably happy as we have got through all the work we set out to do today,' he said.

'We have had a better first day than we did at the first two races. I am sure we will be even quicker tomorrow. We can get pole position here, just as we could have done in Australia and Brazil!'

With a 20-point championship lead over both McLaren drivers, neither of whom had previously managed to score so far this season, Schumacher was obviously seeking a hat trick of victories which would immeasurably aid his quest to become the first driver in 21 years to win a World Championship at the wheel of a Ferrari.

However, Coulthard, who had won here in 1998, was determined to make up for his acute disappointment at being disqualified from second place in the Brazilian Grand Prix a fortnight before. Nothing less than a win would be good enough for him.

Inevitably, perhaps, qualifying turned out to be a three-way fight between Schumacher and the two McLarens. Mika opted for the softer of the two available, and closely matched, Bridgestone tyre compounds whereas Coulthard and both Ferraris went for the harder 'medium' choice. It contributed to the infinitesimal edge displayed by the reigning champion.

Coulthard set the serious ball rolling by posting a 1m 25.425s best some 23 minutes into the hour-long session, pipping Häkkinen's 1m 25.889s which was the Finn's fastest to that point. Mika hadn't been satisfied with his McLaren's handling on Friday and some major set-up changes had been made overnight. Then he made another change during qualifying which turned out to be a defining moment.

All three front runners were absolutely on the ragged edge, using kerb, rumble strips and sometimes a slice of the grassy run-off area as they strained every sinew through Imola's sequence of tricky turns. Häkkinen was the first to dip below the 1m 25s mark with 1m 24.830s then Michael went second on 1m 24.860s.

With 15 minutes to go, just as his brother Ralf's Williams-BMW rolled to a halt with engine failure, Michael accelerated his scarlet machine back onto the circuit. Yet although a brilliantly judged 1m 24.805s set Luca di Montezemolo punching the air with unbridled delight on the pit wall, it turned out that the Ferrari president's celebrations were premature.

Almost as Maranello was uncorking the champagne, Häkkinen came back with a 1m 24.714s best to top the timing sheets. Coulthard was close behind in third place, both he and Schumacher explaining that they had made slight mistakes on the exit of the second Rivazza left-hander on their final runs.

Schumacher, in particular, looked especially glum at the end of the session. 'I am very upset with myself because I made a bad mistake at Rivazza on my third run,' he said. 'Up to that point it had been a very exciting lap and I was four tenths up. I could have easily been on pole today.'

Meanwhile, Rubens Barrichello settled for fourth place, although many onlookers who studied the television

monitors were utterly convinced that he'd set his quickest lap during a period when yellow flags were displayed, a clear breach of the rules.

The official stewards, however, did not share the view and Rubens's time went unchallenged, even though the Brazilian was not happy with his performance. 'I was unable to find the right balance for any of my runs,' he admitted.

Ralf Schumacher's Williams-BMW FW22 wound up an excellent fifth fastest on 1m 25.871s. 'I was very happy with the car and I believe I could have picked up another 0.2s,' he said. By contrast, Jenson Button confessed that he had not mastered the technique of using the kerbs to best effect and languished well down the grid in a distant 18th place as a result.

The Jordan-Mugen Hondas of Heinz-Harald Frentzen (1m 25.892s) and Jarno Trulli (1m 26.002s) qualified sixth and eighth. 'I was fighting for every thousandth of a second,' said Frentzen. 'We are good enough for the third row, which is what we expected.' Trulli reported that his car was fine but he lost time on two runs with traffic and a yellow flag respectively.

Splitting the Jordans, Eddie Irvine was quite happy with his seventh-fastest time of 1m 25.929s in the Jaguar R1, using the softer of the two Bridgestone tyre options, but Johnny Herbert, 17th on 1m 27.051s, simply could not make the harder tyre choice work to his advantage.

Jacques Villeneuve wound up 9th in his BAR-Honda, both he and team-mate Ricardo Zonta (14th) believing that they were paying the price for time lost earlier in the day.

Pedro Diniz was happy with his race set-up in tenth place, but Giancarlo Fisichella (19th) admitted he probably made the wrong tyre choice for his Benetton while team-mate Alexander Wurz (11th) was much happier with his car.

Pedro de la Rosa wound up 13th, happy with the balance of his Arrows A21 while Marc Gene spun off in his Minardi and had to take over Gaston Mazzacane's car as the third M02 had been damaged when Gene crashed at the fast Piratella right-hander during the morning's free practice session, knocking off a wheel.

Jean Alesi had gearchange problems in his Prost-Peugeot on his way to 15th place in the grid order and Nick Heidfeld had to take over the spare AP03, set up for Alesi, after his own car would not start after a pit stop. He only managed eight laps and wound up a disappointed 22nd as a result.

SAN MARINO GRAND PRIX

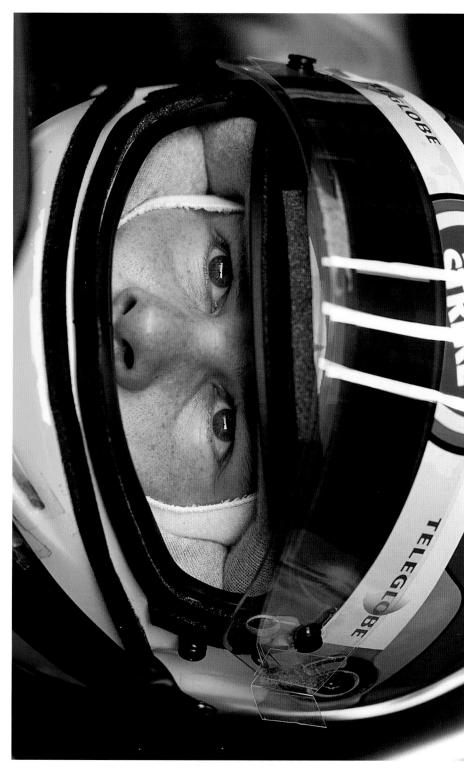

Below left: David Coulthard and his McLaren MP4/15 at speed.

Paul-Henri Cahier

Below: Jacques Villeneuve was in the points once again.

Clive Mason/Allsport

MICHAEL Schumacher defeated the reigning World Champion Mika Häkkinen in a ferociously close-fought San Marino Grand Prix, maintaining his unchallenged winning record so far during the 2000 season and further tightening what was beginning to look like an unassailable grip on the drivers' World Championship.

The German driver took his scarlet F1-2000 past the chequered flag to the accompaniment of hysterical cheering from the emotionally charged capacity crowd who had crammed into the evocatively titled Autodromo Enzo e Dino Ferrari for what unfolded into an epic confrontation.

It was the perfect end to a day which had started on a worrying note when Schumacher knocked down Ferrari mechanic Massimo Trebbi whilst coming in for a practice pit stop during the half-hour warm-up. Happily, Trebbi suffered no injuries after being bowled over by the German ace.

The passionate Ferrari fans were treated to a long-overdue first straight confrontation of the year between F1's two superstars, on this occasion both running to the same race strategy with two refuelling stops scheduled over the 62-lap race.

Yet although Häkkinen's McLaren-Mercedes MP4/15 led from the start, in reality the battle was just too close to call and it was clear from the outset

that a lucky break in traffic or a slightly misjudged pit strategy would tip the balance one way or the other.

The turning point came when Häkkinen made his second refuelling stop on lap 44. Schumacher, who had been trailing the McLaren by just over 2s at that point, stayed out for another four laps before making his own second stop and squeezing back into the race ahead of his rival.

'That was an exciting race and I hope the *tifosi* are happy with the result,' said Schumacher. 'I made a very bad start with massive wheelspin, but I managed to keep my second position. Our strategy remained as [originally planned].

'We did not know what Mika would do and we had to guess. The four laps before the second pit stop was the decisive moment when I pushed very hard.'

However, Häkkinen's race was compromised by a handling imbalance caused by running over debris on the circuit which damaged his car's underwing. He also lost a couple of seconds when a momentary malfunction of his car's electronic management system computer threw the McLaren into neutral and made him think his race was over.

'I thought the game was over,' said Häkkinen, 'but fortunately it came alive again and I could continue.'

Although Häkkinen and his team-

mate David Coulthard, who finished a strong third in the other McLaren-Mercedes, were relieved to get their championship scores off the ground following Häkkinen's engine failure in Brazil and Coulthard's disqualification, there was no hiding the Finn's abject disappointment at failing to post his first win of the year.

Häkkinen had surged into a commanding lead at the start, leaving Schumacher to make up for a very poor start by weaving ruthlessly at Coulthard and forcing him to back off, losing him crucial momentum and dropping him behind Rubens Barrichello in the second Ferrari F1-2000. He also very nearly took his brother Ralf's Williams-BMW, which made a fast start from the third row of the grid, out of the race at the same moment.

It was perhaps asking too much to expect race stewards to censure a Ferrari driver on Italian soil for this very uncharitable – but not strictly illegal – piece of manoeuvring, so Schumacher got away scot-free to chase off after Häkkinen's McLaren.

Barrichello now settled down to hold up Coulthard and the rest of the field while Schumacher made good his escape in second place.

In fact Barrichello's pace was so slow that onlookers concluded that his Ferrari must be full of fuel, scheduled for a one-stop race, but it only

later became clear that he was on the same two-stop strategy as Häkkinen, Schumacher and Coulthard.

Truth be told, the Brazilian was unhappy with the feel of his car and also had to grapple with one of his seat belts working loose. 'The set-up was not ideal and it was hard work,' said Rubens later.

'We tried to change yesterday's [qualifying] settings, but it did not help much. I was a bit unlucky at the second pit stop, when Coulthard passed me. He was quicker than me, but I could have kept him behind me as it is virtually impossible to pass here.

'I also had a problem with the lower part of my belts and could not maintain a good pace as my legs were moving around too much.'

In the opening stages, Häkkinen seemed able to assert the upper hand, albeit only slightly. Once the race settled down, he gradually extended his lead to 1.6s after ten laps, to 3.3s after 20 laps by which time Barrichello's third-place Ferrari was another 23.3s further back.

Early casualties included Heinz-Harald Frentzen's Jordan, which dropped out with gearbox problems after only four laps, while next time round Button's Williams-BMW blew up going into the Villeneuve chicane just before Tosa. Unfortunately the Williams-BMW dropped an oil slick on which the unfortunate Marc Gene's

SAN MARINO GRAND PRIX

Left: Mika Salo gained a point in the Sauber-Petronas.

Below left: Rubens Barrichello's Ferrari fends off the McLaren of Coulthard and Villeneuve's BAR-Honda after the start.
Both photographs: Paul-Henri Cahier

Minardi pirouetted out of the contest and into retirement.

Behind Coulthard, Jacques Villeneuve was doing a terrific job in fifth place with the BAR-Honda ahead of Jarno Trulli's Jordan and the Jaguar of Eddie Irvine which had suffered clutch problems at the start and briefly lost time as a result.

On lap 21 Irvine suddenly slowed, losing two places to Ralf Schumacher's Williams and Mika Salo's Sauber. It seemed as though the Ulsterman was poised to retire, but almost immediately picked up speed.

Later it emerged that the Jaguar's Cosworth V10 engine had started to misfire, the malfunction of a sensor in the exhaust system having caused it to run excessively rich. Over the radio from the pit wall Irvine was told to switch off the sensor and the problem was instantly rectified.

Häkkinen kept his lead through the first spate of refuelling stops, both he and Schumacher coming in for the first time together on lap 27. Mika was stationary for just 7.6s, Michael for 9.9s and they were 4.4s apart — when they came round again at the end of lap 28.

Even so, Häkkinen was now being troubled by the worsening aerodynamic imbalance caused by the leading edge of the floor starting to detach itself after the McLaren had smashed over some unidentified debris on the circuit.

By lap 32 Häkkinen was 5.1s ahead, but that was slashed to 3.9s next time round after the Finn got balked lapping Pedro de la Rosa's 15th-placed Arrows A21. But Mika still seemed to have the measure of the situation and teased the gap open to 4.8s.

On lap 43 Häkkinen suddenly lost an apparently inexplicable 2s which, in reality, didn't show up as too much of a drama on the timing screens as — by bizarre coincidence — Schumacher lost virtually the same amount of time when he had to back off at Acque Minerali as Pedro Diniz made a slight fist of allowing the Ferrari to lap his Sauber.

'He tried to be nice and let me pass, but it was the wrong place and 1 very nearly hit him,' explained Schumacher.

Häkkinen's problem was similarly fleeting, if perhaps more difficult to understand. It appeared that an 'electronic spike' caused the car's electronics program to reset itself as the engine revs faltered and threw the car momentarily into neutral. It later emerged that a malfunction of the

ignition timing trigger had caused the engine to falter and, when the revs dropped below a pre-set level, the whole system momentarily shut itself down and went into recalibration mode.

In reality, this had more of an unsettling effect on Häkkinen than it did in terms of time lost, but he was still 2.6s in the lead when he made his own second refuelling stop in 8.3s at the end of lap 44.

Schumacher now put the hammer down. In the extra four laps he stayed out before bringing the Ferrari in for its own second stop, he pulled back 2s on the McLaren and then

made another 3s on the overall lap in which he came into the pits. The fact that Häkkinen had drifted off the pace slightly at this point in the race allowed Michael to accelerate back into the fray 3.7s in front. From that moment on, it was all over bar the shouting.

During this period Ralf Schumacher's race also came to an end on lap 46 when a fuel pick-up problem stranded his Williams-BMW out on the circuit while he was running fifth.

'Unfortunately after the start I had to slow up, lost four places and dropped to ninth,' he shrugged. 'After that I gradually moved up to fifth and

DIARY

A new F1 cockpit safety system, developed jointly by Mercedes-Benz, McLaren and the FIA as an alternative to airbags, is unveiled at Imola. The HANS [Head and Neck Support] system consists of a rigid, collar-shaped carbon-fibre shell which is held onto the upper body by the seat belts and is fastened to the helmet with appropriate tethers.

BAR boss Craig Pollock hints that his number one driver Jacques Villeneuve has received an approach from McLaren for the 2001 season.

Jaguar Racing denies rumours that Johnny Herbert will be replaced in their F1 line-up by test driver Luciano Burti after the International F3000 championship at Imola.

Australia's Mark Webber wins the opening round of the British Grand Prix championship at Imola.

Mosley ignites F1 controversy

FIA president Max Mosley chose a media conference at the San Marino Grand Prix as tactically the right moment to fire a brisk warning salvo across the bows of the competing teams by announcing a crackdown on illegal control systems which he believes could be hidden within the electronics of the current generation of F1 cars.

There are beginning to be signs of a culture of cheating in Formula 1 and we are absolutely determined to stop it,' he said. 'We believe that one team may have been competing last year with an illegal car.

'As the governing body we have to be able to look all the team owners in the face and tell them that they are competing evenly with their rivals. And this is what we will do,' Mosley's plain speaking was intended to confront the issues of teams hiding illegal traction control systems in the electronic software programs fitted to the cars. In particular, he reflected an absolute determination to ban automatic limiters which control the cars' speed in the pit lane and which the FIA technical department believed were capable of masking a traction control function.

Traction control — the system whereby the teams use sensors fitted to each wheel to limit wheelspin by means of computer controls — was officially banned at the end of 1993 along with such other esoteric accessories as active suspension and anti-lock brakes.

Since then, Mosley has always been passionately committed to ensuring that Formula 1 remains primarily a driver's sport and is not swamped by technical overkill which reduces the input of the man behind the wheel.

Yet the suggestion that one team was cheating last year inevitably put all the competitors under an unwelcome spotlight. 'It is the prerogative of the president of the FIA to say what he has said,' commented Eddie Jordan.

'If he has said openly that he believes that one team has been cheating, it is then up to him to decide whether he will name them. Either way, it is certainly a clear indication of which direction he is coming from.'

Jordan flatly denied speculation that his team had somehow breached the technical rules last year. McLaren managing director Ron Dennis also specifically rejected any contention that McLaren was the team under scrutiny.

However, Patrick Head, the technical director of the BMW Williams team — who also denied any deliberate cheating — stated that the issue was not as straightforward as it may seem at first glance.

'It is very easy to put out general comments of innuendo with reference to cheating,' he said. 'Sometimes the interpretation of the regulations is developed and changed.

'Every team has to try and make the most competitive car. It is too easy to say that people are cheating, but in truth these things should be manageable behind closed doors and not sorted out in an aggressive, public way.'

Mosley was demanding that the teams made these changes to their electronic systems prior to the British Grand Prix at Silverstone on 23 April. Head and most of his fellow technical directors believed that this meant the FIA was effectively changing the engine regulations which have guaranteed stability until 2007 and cannot be altered simply by a decree from the governing body.

Mosley retorted that this was not a rule change, merely the application of a regulation which put the onus firmly on the competing teams to ensure that their cars comply with the regulations at all times throughout a race weekend. In other words, that they do not have illegal systems such as traction control.

after Jacques Villeneuve went in for his pit stop [on lap 43] I could push a little harder, but then I experienced my problems.'

In the closing phase of the race, although Häkkinen piled on the pressure, setting fastest race lap with only two laps to go, Michael's Ferrari held on to win by just over a second. McLaren boss Ron Dennis later denied that the team had made a tactical error by failing to run a longer second stint with the McLaren car, blaming the time lost by the Finn onto his technical tribulations.

Coulthard, meanwhile, had spent the first 46 laps boxed in behind Barrichello, only getting ahead of the Brazilian's Ferrari at their second refuelling stop, after which the McLaren driver pulled away comfortably to claim third spot on the victory podium.

'1 first of all found myself in fourth place because it was very close trying to pass Michael in the first corner and I had to back off to avoid touching him,' said the Scot.

'1 knew I was quicker than him [Barrichello], so it was just a question of staying close and hoping that I would be called in a lap or two later than he was planning to do. In the end, we stopped on the same lap and, thanks to my mechanics I got back into the race in front of him.'

Barrichello trailed home a rather disgruntled fourth, ahead of Jacques Villeneuve's BAR and Mika Salo's Sauber, the Finn deserving a pat on the back for getting out of Schumacher's way with brisk efficiency as the Ferrari team leader came up to lap him.

Villeneuve's fifth place was a just reward for a great performance even though he was lapped by the winners shortly before the end and there were only four cars on the same lap at the chequered flag.

Irvine was quite buoyed by his seventh place for Jaguar, while Pedro Diniz finished eighth ahead of Alexander Wurz's Benetton and Johnny Herbert in the other Jaguar. Fisichella's Benetton trailed Herbert by just 0.5s at the flag with Ricardo Zonta's BAR, Gaston Mazzacane's Minardi and Jos Verstappen's Arrows A21 posted as the only remaining finishers.

Frankly, this was a race which McLaren should have won, but Michael Schumacher's relentless focus was the key factor which had swung the advantage back in Maranello's direction. Yet at least second and third places had got McLaren's constructors' points tally off the deck. But there was still a long way to go.

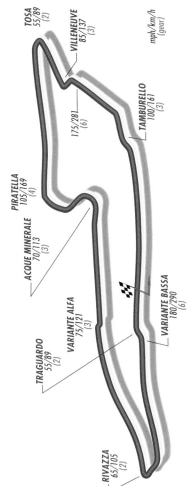

IMOLA

7–9 APRIL 2000

gran premio
WARSTEINER di SAN MARINO

IMOLA — AUTODROMO DINO E ENZO FERRARI
CIRCUIT LENGTH: 3.065 miles/4.933 km

Circuit turn labels: TOSA 55/89 (2) · VILLENEUVE 85/137 (3) · TAMBURELLO 100/161 (3) · 175/281 (6) · PIRATELLA 105/169 (4) · ACQUE MINERALE 70/113 (3) · VARIANTE ALFA 75/121 (3) · TRAGUARDO 55/89 (2) · VARIANTE BASSA 180/290 (6) · RIVAZZA 65/105 (2) · mph/km/h (gear)

RACE DISTANCE: 62 laps, 189.897 miles/305.609 km   RACE WEATHER: Dry, warm and overcast

Pos.	Driver	Nat.	No.	Entrant	Car/Engine	Laps	Time/Retirement	Speed (mph/km/h)
1	Michael Schumacher	D	3	Scuderia Ferrari Marlboro	Ferrari F1-2000-049 V10	62	1h 31m 39.776s	124.301/200.043
2	Mika Häkkinen	SF	1	West McLaren Mercedes	McLaren MP4/15-Mercedes FO110J V10	62	1h 31m 40.944s	124.274/200.000
3	David Coulthard	GB	2	West McLaren Mercedes	McLaren MP4/15-Mercedes FO110J V10	62	1h 32m 30.784s	123.158/198.204
4	Rubens Barrichello	BR	4	Scuderia Ferrari Marlboro	Ferrari F1-2000-049 V10	62	1h 33m 09.052s	122.315/196.847
5	Jacques Villeneuve	CDN	22	Lucky Strike BAR Honda	BAR 02-Honda RA100E V10	61		
6	Mika Salo	SF	17	Red Bull Sauber Petronas	Sauber C19-Petronas SPE 04A V10	61		
7	Eddie Irvine	GB	7	Jaguar Racing	Jaguar R1-Cosworth CR2 V10	61		
8	Pedro Diniz	BR	16	Red Bull Sauber Petronas	Sauber C19-Petronas SPE 04A V10	61		
9	Alexander Wurz	A	12	Mild Seven Benetton Playlife	Benetton B200-Playlife V10	61		
10	Johnny Herbert	GB	8	Jaguar Racing	Jaguar R1-Cosworth CR2 V10	61		
11	Giancarlo Fisichella	I	11	Mild Seven Benetton Playlife	Benetton B200-Playlife V10	61		
12	Ricardo Zonta	BR	23	Lucky Strike BAR Honda	BAR 02-Honda RA100E V10	60		
13	Gaston Mazzacane	ARG	21	Telefonica Minardi Fondmetal	Minardi M02-Fondmetal Ford Zetec-R V10	59		
14	Jos Verstappen	NL	19	Arrows Supertec	Arrows A21-Supertec FB02 V10	58	Gearbox	
15	Jarno Trulli	I	6	Benson & Hedges Jordan	Jordan EJ10-Mugen Honda MF301HE V10	49	Spun off/gearbox	
	Pedro de la Rosa	ESP	18	Arrows Supertec	Arrows A21-Supertec FB02 V10	45	Fuel pick-up	
	Ralf Schumacher	D	9	BMW WilliamsF1 Team	Williams FW22-BMW E41 V10	25	Hydraulics	
	Jean Alesi	F	14	Gauloises Prost Peugeot	Prost AP03-Peugeot A20 V10	22	Hydraulics	
	Nick Heidfeld	D	15	Gauloises Prost Peugeot	Prost AP03-Peugeot A20 V10	5	Engine	
	Jenson Button	GB	10	BMW WilliamsF1 Team	Williams FW22-BMW E41 V10	5	Spun off	
	Marc Gene	ESP	20	Telefonica Minardi Fondmetal	Minardi M02-Fondmetal Ford Zetec-R V10	5	Spun off	
	Heinz-Harald Frentzen	D	5	Benson & Hedges Jordan	Jordan EJ10-Mugen Honda MF301HE V10	4	Gearbox	

Fastest lap: Häkkinen, on lap 60, 1m 26.523s, 127.536 mph/205.249 km/h.

Lap record: Heinz-Harald Frentzen (F1 Williams FW19-Renault V10), 1m 25.531s, 128.936 mph/207.503 km/h (1997).

Lap chart — Grid order:

Grid order
1 HÄKKINEN
3 M. SCHUMACHER
2 COULTHARD
4 BARRICHELLO
9 R. SCHUMACHER
5 FRENTZEN
7 IRVINE
6 TRULLI
22 VILLENEUVE
16 DINIZ
12 WURZ
17 SALO
18 DE LA ROSA
23 ZONTA
14 ALESI
19 VERSTAPPEN
8 HERBERT
10 BUTTON
11 FISICHELLA
21 MAZZACANE
20 GENE
15 HEIDFELD

Legend: ▢ Pit stop · One lap behind leader

STARTING GRID

Pos	Driver	Team
1	HÄKKINEN	McLaren
3	M. SCHUMACHER	Ferrari
2	COULTHARD	McLaren
4	BARRICHELLO	Ferrari
9	R. SCHUMACHER	Williams
5	FRENTZEN	Jordan
7	IRVINE	Jaguar
6	TRULLI	Jordan
8	HERBERT	Jaguar
10	BUTTON	Williams
14	ALESI	Prost
19	VERSTAPPEN	Arrows
18	DE LA ROSA	Arrows
23	ZONTA	BAR
22	VILLENEUVE	BAR
16	DINIZ	Sauber
12	WURZ	Benetton
17	SALO	Sauber
11	FISICHELLA	Benetton
21	MAZZACANE	Minardi
20	GENE	Minardi
15*	HEIDFELD	Prost

* started from pit lane

FOR THE RECORD

100th Grand Prix start
Heinz-Harald Frentzen
Eddie Irvine

TIME SHEETS

QUALIFYING

Weather: Dry, hot and sunny

Pos.	Driver	Car	Laps	Time
1	Mika Häkkinen	McLaren-Mercedes	12	1m 24.714s
2	Michael Schumacher	Ferrari	11	1m 24.805s
3	David Coulthard	McLaren-Mercedes	12	1m 25.014s
4	Rubens Barrichello	Ferrari	12	1m 25.242s
5	Ralf Schumacher	Williams-BMW	9	1m 25.871s
6	Heinz-Harald Frentzen	Jordan-Mugen Honda	12	1m 25.892s
7	Eddie Irvine	Jaguar-Cosworth	12	1m 25.929s
8	Jarno Trulli	Jordan-Mugen Honda	12	1m 26.002s
9	Jacques Villeneuve	BAR-Honda	12	1m 26.124s
10	Pedro Diniz	Sauber-Petronas	12	1m 26.238s
11	Alexander Wurz	Benetton-Playlife	12	1m 26.281s
12	Mika Salo	Sauber-Petronas	12	1m 26.336s
13	Pedro de la Rosa	Arrows-Supertec	12	1m 26.349s
14	Ricardo Zonta	BAR-Honda	11	1m 26.814s
15	Jean Alesi	Prost-Peugeot	12	1m 26.824s
16	Jos Verstappen	Arrows-Supertec	11	1m 26.845s
17	Johnny Herbert	Jaguar-Cosworth	11	1m 27.051s
18	Jenson Button	Williams-BMW	11	1m 27.135s
19	Giancarlo Fisichella	Benetton-Playlife	11	1m 27.253s
20	Gaston Mazzacane	Minardi-Fondmetal	12	1m 28.161s
21	Marc Gene	Minardi-Fondmetal	11	1m 28.333s
22	Nick Heidfeld	Prost-Peugeot	8	1m 28.361s

FRIDAY FREE PRACTICE

Weather: Cool and bright

Pos.	Driver	Laps	Time
1	Michael Schumacher	28	1m 26.944s
2	Rubens Barrichello	21	1m 27.317s
3	David Coulthard	26	1m 27.372s
4	Heinz-Harald Frentzen	31	1m 27.730s
5	Jarno Trulli	33	1m 27.795s
6	Mika Häkkinen	33	1m 28.021s
7	Johnny Herbert	23	1m 28.139s
8	Giancarlo Fisichella	43	1m 28.236s
9	Ralf Schumacher	25	1m 28.372s
10	Pedro de la Rosa	41	1m 28.444s
11	Mika Salo	30	1m 28.555s
12	Eddie Irvine	25	1m 28.566s
13	Alexander Wurz	42	1m 28.771s
14	Jean Alesi	26	1m 28.950s
15	Gaston Mazzacane	42	1m 28.952s
16	Jos Verstappen	32	1m 28.976s
17	Ricardo Zonta	37	1m 29.097s
18	Nick Heidfeld	27	1m 29.113s
19	Pedro Diniz	18	1m 29.307s
20	Jenson Button	36	1m 29.326s
21	Marc Gene	33	1m 29.412s
22	Jacques Villeneuve	6	1m 53.474s

SATURDAY FREE PRACTICE

Weather: Cool and bright

Pos.	Driver	Laps	Time
1	Mika Häkkinen	27	1m 24.973s
2	Michael Schumacher	31	1m 25.085s
3	David Coulthard	31	1m 25.090s
4	Jarno Trulli	33	1m 25.852s
5	Heinz-Harald Frentzen	34	1m 26.097s
6	Rubens Barrichello	23	1m 26.357s
7	Mika Salo	31	1m 26.428s
8	Jacques Villeneuve	31	1m 26.551s
9	Eddie Irvine	22	1m 26.566s
10	Pedro Diniz	32	1m 26.634s
11	Johnny Herbert	29	1m 26.729s
12	Ralf Schumacher	17	1m 26.807s
13	Alexander Wurz	26	1m 26.855s
14	Giancarlo Fisichella	28	1m 26.964s
15	Jos Verstappen	19	1m 27.188s
16	Jean Alesi	29	1m 27.195s
17	Pedro de la Rosa	16	1m 27.312s
18	Jenson Button	12	1m 27.453s
19	Nick Heidfeld	22	1m 27.464s
20	Ricardo Zonta	15	1m 27.791s
21	Marc Gene	26	1m 28.155s
22	Gaston Mazzacane	27	1m 28.276s

WARM-UP

Weather: Sunny and warm

Pos.	Driver	Laps	Time
1	Mika Häkkinen	13	1m 27.418s
2	David Coulthard	12	1m 27.475s
3	Michael Schumacher	10	1m 27.620s
4	Rubens Barrichello	12	1m 28.220s
5	Heinz-Harald Frentzen	13	1m 28.426s
6	Jarno Trulli	17	1m 28.506s
7	Giancarlo Fisichella	14	1m 28.590s
8	Marc Gene	14	1m 28.618s
9	Eddie Irvine	15	1m 28.694s
10	Jean Alesi	13	1m 28.730s
11	Jenson Button	12	1m 28.835s
12	Nick Heidfeld	14	1m 28.836s
13	Jacques Villeneuve	14	1m 28.871s
14	Mika Salo	14	1m 28.900s
15	Ricardo Zonta	12	1m 28.929s
16	Ralf Schumacher	14	1m 28.942s
17	Jos Verstappen	13	1m 28.988s
18	Pedro de la Rosa	12	1m 29.100s
19	Pedro Diniz	14	1m 29.121s
20	Johnny Herbert	20	1m 29.247s
21	Alexander Wurz	21	1m 29.351s
22	Gaston Mazzacane	22	1m 30.261s

RACE FASTEST LAPS

Weather: Dry, warm and overcast

Driver	Time	Lap
Mika Häkkinen	1m 26.523s	60
Michael Schumacher	1m 26.774s	58
David Coulthard	1m 27.014s	54
Ralf Schumacher	1m 27.339s	45
Pedro Diniz	1m 27.814s	61
Rubens Barrichello	1m 27.899s	46
Mika Salo	1m 28.336s	40
Eddie Irvine	1m 28.387s	57
Jarno Trulli	1m 28.754s	28
Ricardo Zonta	1m 28.787s	39
Jacques Villeneuve	1m 28.816s	54
Jos Verstappen	1m 28.842s	54
Giancarlo Fisichella	1m 28.884s	59
Johnny Herbert	1m 29.049s	59
Alexander Wurz	1m 29.180s	55
Nick Heidfeld	1m 29.350s	16
Jean Alesi	1m 29.370s	42
Pedro de la Rosa	1m 29.719s	17
Gaston Mazzacane	1m 30.030s	15
Heinz-Harald Frentzen	1m 31.503s	3
Marc Gene	1m 31.524s	5
Jenson Button	1m 31.912s	4

POINTS TABLES

DRIVERS

	Driver	Pts
1	Michael Schumacher	30
2	Rubens Barrichello	9
3	Giancarlo Fisichella	8
4=	Mika Häkkinen	6
4=	Ralf Schumacher	6
4=	Jacques Villeneuve	6
7=	Heinz-Harald Frentzen	4
7=	David Coulthard	4
9	Jarno Trulli	3
10=	Ricardo Zonta	1
10=	Jenson Button	1
10=	Mika Salo	1

CONSTRUCTORS

	Team	Pts
1	Ferrari	39
2	McLaren	10
3	Benetton	8
4=	Williams	7
4=	Jordan	7
6	BAR	6
7	Sauber	1

CHASSIS LOG BOOK

No.	Driver	Chassis
1	Häkkinen	McLaren MP4/15/1
2	Coulthard	McLaren MP4/15/2
spare		McLaren MP4/15/3
3	M. Schumacher	Ferrari F1-2000/200
4	Barrichello	Ferrari F1-2000/199
spare		Ferrari F1-2000/198
5	Frentzen	Jordan EJ10/4
6	Trulli	Jordan EJ10/3
spare		Jordan EJ10/2
7	Irvine	Jaguar R1/4
8	Herbert	Jaguar R1/1
spare		Jaguar R1/3
9	R. Schumacher	Williams FW22/3
10	Button	Williams FW22/4
spare		Williams FW22/2
11	Fisichella	Benetton B200/2
12	Wurz	Benetton B200/5
spare		Benetton B200/3
14	Alesi	Prost AP03/3
15	Heidfeld	Prost AP03/4
spare		Prost AP03/1
16	Diniz	Sauber C19/4
17	Salo	Sauber C19/2
spare		Sauber C19/1
18	de la Rosa	Arrows A21/3
19	Verstappen	Arrows A21/1
spare		Arrows A21/2
20	Gene	Minardi M02/4
21	Mazzacane	Minardi M02/2
23	Zonta	BAR 02/6
22	Villeneuve	BAR 02/1
spare		BAR 02/4

BRITISH

grand prix

David Coulthard *(main picture)* took his McLaren to a convincing second-successive British Grand Prix win.

Below: Michael Schumacher was relieved to gain third place on the podium with his McLaren rivals.

Both photographs: Paul-Henri Cahier

COULTHARD
HÄKKINEN
M. SCHUMACHER
R. SCHUMACHER
BUTTON
TRULLI

SILVERSTONE QUALIFYING

Coulthard had featured strongly in the dramatic conditions during Friday practice when he stopped out on the circuit in a torrential rain storm. The Land Rover which was sent to retrieve his McLaren MP4/15 then became bogged down in the mud and the session had to be red-flagged in order that a tractor could finally rescue both machines.

Many drivers believed that the conditions were bad enough for the session to be cancelled, by implication heaping more embarrassment on the Silverstone organisers who never wanted this early date in the first place.

However, Coulthard used the opportunity to offer a robust defence of the track owners. 'No circuit I have raced on has spent as much on safety as Silverstone has,' he said. 'Their profits have not been put into other people's pockets, but invested in the circuit.

'As far as the conditions today are concerned, I don't know any circuit on which aquaplaning would not be a problem in conditions like we experienced today.'

Qualifying was a similarly unpredictable lottery on a drying track, the secret clearly being to keep one's nerve and hold back from one's final run as late as possible. With nine minutes to go, Jacques Villeneuve took his BAR out on a clear track to post a 1m 27.205s which, for a fleeting moment, looked as though it might be good enough for pole.

Five minutes later, rush hour suddenly erupted with a vengeance with 22 cars storming out onto the circuit as the racing line continued to dry. Eddie Irvine's Jaguar immediately posted a 1m 26.818s, then Jos Verstappen's promising Arrows A21 vaulted to the top of the timing screens on 1m 26.793s, followed in quick succession by Heinz-Harald Frentzen's Jordan (1m 25.706s), Coulthard (1m 26.088s) and finally Barrichello (below) on 1m 25.703s.

'I feel pretty good about this,' said Barrichello afterwards. 'I am particularly proud because in last week's test I only had two days here in the wet, so apart from the two laps I did yesterday, I had no experience with the car here in the dry.

'I went out quite early for my first run, which meant I was a little offset from the main group. I knew the car was good, and I knew I could do a good job, so I had to go out for my last run with the main group and pray not to have traffic.'

For his part, Frentzen was well satisfied to have grabbed second place on the front row of the grid. 'Well, I have to say that yesterday it would have been a bit too optimistic for me to say I was expected to be on the front row,' he grinned.

'But the team gave me a good car and we have been making improvements all weekend. We wanted to sort out some of these improvements in time for the race and it seems they are working well, so we can be proud of ourselves to be on the front row.'

Michael Schumacher missed getting into his final lap when he caught the chequered flag two seconds late and had to be content with fifth place on the grid as a consequence. This would be pivotal to the outcome of the race as the Ferrari team leader lined up alongside the highly impressive Jenson Button's Williams FW22, the young Brit outqualifying team-mate Ralf Schumacher by a single place.

Häkkinen was far from delighted after qualifying third and was characteristically cagey about his performance. 'We were more or less on a compromise set-up,' he said. 'Let's not go into too many details.' Coulthard was also philosophical. 'Considering that on my last run I was slowed down by a Jordan and was then running behind a Williams, fourth place isn't so bad,' he said.

Jos Verstappen's Arrows A21 wound up an excellent eighth before spinning off quite heavily shortly before the end of the session, while his team-mate Pedro de la Rosa was disappointed to have dropped back to 19th.

Eddie Irvine only managed ninth-fastest time in what started the day as the spare Jaguar R1, the Ulsterman failing to get past the chequered flag into his final lap by five seconds. Johnny Herbert wound up 14th, held up on his last run by a yellow flag.

During the morning's free practice session Irvine had slid into a gravel trap and collided with Jenson Button's Williams which had arrived there a couple of seconds earlier. The impact only seemed like a light tap, but it was enough to write off the Jaguar's monocoque. That meant that the spare R1 was now pressed into service as Eddie's race chassis and the team kept its fingers firmly crossed that a replacement would not be called upon again before a fresh spare was readied for race morning.

Jacques Villeneuve qualified tenth on 1m 27.025s. 'I expected to end up sixth, but unfortunately completed my last lap under the yellow flag,' he said. 'I am very happy with the car.' Giancarlo Fisichella was unhappy with the balance of his Benetton (12th) while Pedro Diniz and Mika Salo admitted the timing of their runs with the Sauber C19s. Nick Heidfeld took the spare Prost AP03 to set 17th-fastest time, preferring its choice of gear ratios to his original race car. Marc Gene and Gaston Mazzacane predictably shared the back row of the grid for Minardi.

DAVID Coulthard took a leaf out of Nigel Mansell's book with a memorably bold overtaking manoeuvre to cap the race of his life at Silverstone and post his second straight victory in the British Grand Prix, a record last achieved by Mansell here in 1991 and '92. He took the chequered flag just 1.4s ahead of his McLaren-Mercedes team-mate Mika Häkkinen, after a flawless performance which vaulted him into second place in the drivers' World Championship behind Ferrari's Michael Schumacher who finished third.

The golden moment for the 29-year-old Scot came on lap 31 of the hotly contested fourth round of the World Championship when Coulthard was shadowing the leading Ferrari F1-2000 of Rubens Barrichello which had started from pole position.

The Brazilian driver suffered a slight gearchange glitch going through the daunting 140-mph Becketts ess-bend and Coulthard got a run at him coming out onto the 190-mph Hangar Straight. In a manoeuvre which mimicked Mansell's epic victory over his Williams-Honda team-mate Nelson Piquet here 13 years before, Coulthard forced his way round the outside of the Ferrari to take the lead.

It was a performance which brought the crowds to their feet in delighted approval and helped take their mind off the chaotic traffic jams and muddy car parks which had blighted their weekend so far and been the prime topic of conversation for much of the weekend.

'After Rubens made that small mistake coming out of Becketts I found myself thinking of that move Nigel pulled on Nelson Piquet those few years ago and thought, right, let's give it a go,' he said.

It was an upbeat end to a weekend which had seen Silverstone virtually flooded out to the point where the public car parks had to be closed for Saturday qualifying in a vain attempt to improve things for race day. Yet such a step could not forestall the inevitable outpourings of acrimony which swirled round the organisers, circuit owners and the FIA, the governing body in particular coming under much fire for sanctioning the unseasonable Easter date for the British race rather than its regular July place on the calendar.

On race day, things got even worse. The combination of a capacity crowd and the slow process of gaining access to the spectator car parks caused total seizure of the traffic flow around the Northampton circuit. Despite warnings from the police not even to try joining the 15-mile traffic jams to gain entry to the circuit, a 60,000-strong crowd displayed remarkable grit and determination to gain access to a venue which looked more like the Glastonbury rock festival than a round of a high-profile international sport.

Coulthard's success made their single-mindedness seem all worthwhile in addition to exorcising the painful memory of his disqualification from second place in the Brazilian Grand Prix following a trifling front wing infringement.

'I feel absolutely delighted,' he said. 'I had such a long time out there [in the lead] to think about it, but I developed a small gearbox problem and was preparing to cry in the car because I did not need that. I am thankful it held together and we got both cars home in first and second places, which is fantastic.'

Behind Schumacher, the dramatically improving Williams-BMWs of Ralf Schumacher and British rising star Jenson Button took fourth and fifth places while Jarno Trulli's Jordan completed the points-scoring top six after an heroic effort from Jacques Villeneuve in the BAR ended four laps from the finish with gearbox problems.

If Coulthard's victory in last year's race had been recalled a slightly fortuitous success, benefiting as it did from Eddie Irvine's Ferrari overshooting its pit during a refuelling stop and Häkkinen's McLaren losing a wheel, there were certainly no ifs and buts hanging over this top-drawer performance.

Rubens Barrichello's Ferrari leads from pole into Copse with Heinz-Harald Frentzen's Jordan just behind.
Paul-Henri Cahier

BRITISH GRAND PRIX

Far left: Gerhard Berger keeps an anxious watch on the skies.
Bryn Williams/Words & Pictures

Centre left: Taxis ferry spectators to the Northamptonshire circuit.
Graham Chadwick/Allsport

Left: Max Mosley and Jackie Stewart had differences of opinion regarding the Silverstone débâcle.
Paul-Henri Cahier

Below left: Doughty photographers braved the elements during practice.
Bryn Williams/Words & Pictures

The Silverstone fiasco: whose fault was it all?

THREE-times World Champion Jackie Stewart — the man who later in the year would replace Ken Tyrrell as the President of the British Racing Drivers' Club which owns Silverstone — held motor racing's governing body to blame over the fiasco which resulted in the public being turned away from the Saturday qualifying session for Britain's round of the FIA Formula 1 World Championship.

Describing the sequence of events which led up to rescheduling Britain's round of the World Championship as 'scandalous' he said that the whole episode was a major disaster for the sport as a whole.

'It is terrible for F1,' said Stewart who recently retired from his post as chairman of Jaguar Racing. 'It is terrible for the corporate partners of the team, terrible for the fans and bad for all our industry.

'But this is not Silverstone's fault. The governing body chooses the dates, not Silverstone. All major professional sporting events follow the sun. I don't care whether you are talking about the Masters, the Kentucky Derby, Ascot or the British Grand Prix.

'Would they put the Italian Grand Prix on in April? Of course, they wouldn't. Why? Because it would probably be pouring with rain as it is here.'

Even as Stewart delivered his carefully judged critique, a forlorn, windswept poster on the exit road to Silverstone optimistically touted a July date for the 2001 British Grand Prix 'subject to confirmation' — an ironic twist on a weekend where torrential rain forced the race organisers to turn away Saturday's spectators due to the glutinous state of the near-flooded public car parks.

Against this backdrop of shock, anger and disbelief within the motor racing community, there was a lighter moment during Friday morning's free practice session at Silverstone which somehow seemed to put the whole awful dilemma of the rain-soaked British Grand Prix into perspective.

F1 powerbroker Bernie Ecclestone was striding down the paddock, not really watching where he was going as he talked earnestly to one of his acolytes, when he stepped in the only deep puddle within 20 metres.

Apart from the fact that puddles are not generally permitted within the exclusive environs of the Formula 1 paddock — and the fact that one is not privileged to know how much Mr Ecclestone pays for his footwear — this seemed an appropriate reward for the multi-billionaire who many believe should shoulder much of the blame for the rescheduling of the British race which has led to all these problems.

Yet this may be a harsh judgement on Ecclestone, for had Silverstone been blessed with a fine Easter weekend the fact that the race had been moved from its traditional July date would not have mattered in the slightest.

Even giving Bernie the benefit of the doubt, the fact is that moving the British Grand Prix from its summer date amounts to a major disruption of the British sporting eco-system. Along with Royal Ascot, Henley and Wimbledon, Britain's round of the World Championship is associated with sunny afternoons and long evenings. Not cold miserable rain.

'It's not my fault,' said Ecclestone firmly. 'Don't blame me. Internal [motor racing] politics caused the change of date. It is disappointing for the spectators, but not something which Silverstone could have done anything about.

'Someone had to have this date in the calendar and Silverstone agreed to it. But it didn't work. Don't blame them for not knowing that the weather was going to be like this.'

However, Stewart's former F1 entrant Ken Tyrrell clearly felt that Ecclestone knew exactly the implications of the change of date.

'What we're seeing here this weekend must surely tell everyone — even Bernie — that the time for the British Grand Prix is certainly not in April,' he said. 'And I think even Bernie recognizes that if the race was held at Brands Hatch or Donington Park at the same time, it would be raining there as well.'

McLaren managing director Ron Dennis took a more conciliatory line, insisting that while this was not Silverstone's fault, the decision to reschedule the race 'was not malicious.'

He added: 'It has rained pretty well consistently for 15 days which was always going to give any promoter a major problem. But it has to be said that whoever has the challenge of putting the international calendar together has a juggling job to do.'

Some cynics have reflected on the reaction of the organisers of the 1993 European Grand Prix at Donington as an example of what Silverstone should have done. Faced with similarly torrential rain in the run-up to the Easter Sunday race, Donington's owner Tom Wheatcroft started a crash programme to tarmac all his public car parks only days before the race.

Even so, he lost a reputed three million pounds on the race and Formula 1 has not been back to Donington since. However, the point is surely that most of the races on the European calendar would have faced the same dilemma with sodden car parks had their races taken place in such inhospitable conditions.

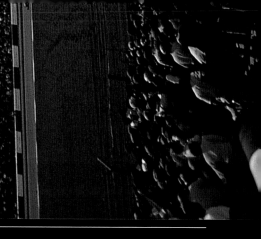

DIARY

Ferrari president Luca di Montezemolo visits the British Grand Prix and warns that F1 must continue to have a stable European heartland.

Bernie Ecclestone says he hopes that Silverstone and Brands Hatch can cut a deal to ensure the British Grand Prix remains at the Northamptonshire track from 2002.

Darren Manning wins Formula 3000 race supporting the British Grand Prix at Silverstone.

Jenson Button reminded by Williams that the onus is on him to keep Juan Pablo Montoya out of the team for 2001.

Top: A little bit of sunshine: Rubens Barrichello poses for a photo with a young fan in the paddock as the sun puts in a weak appearance.
Paul-Henri Cahier

Above right: Jenson Button led team-mate Ralf Schumacher early on, and they finished in fifth and fourth respectively.
Mark Thompson/Allsport

Above: Jos Verstappen qualified well in eighth, but his race ended after only 20 laps.
Bryn Williams/Words & Pictures

Right: The cars set out on the warm-up lap under sunny skies.
Paul-Henri Cahier

Two laps after passing Barrichello, Coulthard came in to make his first refuelling stop which dropped him back to fourth place behind the Brazilian, Michael Schumacher and Heinz-Harald Frentzen's hard-charging Jordan which had started from second place on the front row of the grid.

On lap 35 Barrichello was preparing to come in for his sole routine refuelling stop when an unexpected hydraulic problem pitched him into a spin on the final corner before the pit lane entry. He managed to regain control, splashing his way over the sodden grassy infield before regaining the tarmac and driving straight into the pits to retire.

Thereafter Schumacher led briefly until he made his own refuelling stop on lap 38, after which Coulthard was never headed all the way to the chequered flag. In the closing stages the McLaren pit signalled to Häkkinen that he should hold second place and not move in to challenge Coulthard for the lead. Under the circumstances, the team had no intention of risking its first 1-2 finish of the 2000 season with a show of unwanted heroics.

Häkkinen finished the race in a resigned, slightly disappointed frame of mind after wrestling with poor handling balance throughout the race. An engine problem in the crucial pre-race warm-up had severely restricted his laps and, despite some last-moment chassis adjustments before the start, but it wasn't enough, because we are talking here about what should have been bigger changes than just a bit of tuning.'

As the two McLarens sailed past the chequered flag five lengths apart, Michael Schumacher was pounding through the last few corners, counting his blessings with third place for Ferrari, a quite remarkable rescue job after coming round eighth at the end of the opening lap.

'At the start I took the option of going through the grass,' he said. 'It should have worked, but after so much rain in the past days the grass was so wet that I found myself just sitting there and going nowhere with the wheels spinning.

'Later round that lap I was having a good fight with my brother Ralf, but had to back off at Bridge corner first time round and he seemed to be very keen to close the door!

'But I am absolutely satisfied. For most of the race I was running eighth and wondering how the race would develop and how many points I was going to lose. I am quite happy with third place.'

In the early stages of the race Jacques Villeneuve had been running ahead of Schumacher's Ferrari in seventh place. Barrichello was leading from Heinz-Harald Frentzen, Coulthard and Häkkinen, the Jordan driver

having a two-stop strategy in mind, as had the two Williams-BMW drivers who were running ahead of the boxed-in Schumacher from the start.

Unfortunately Barrichello was keeping the pace of the race down to a level where it might have aided Schumacher had Michael been able to get ahead of Villeneuve. That had the effect of undermining the two-stop strategies, with the result that Frentzen – having failed to get away in the lead from the start with his lighter fuel load – had no choice but to sit and watch any potential advantage ebbing away.

Schumacher got ahead of Villeneuve by harnessing a well used strategy. Jacques stopped from third place on lap 33 – the same as Coulthard – but Michael stayed out for another five laps, slamming in a sequence of quick times which enabled him to emerge comfortably ahead of the BAR.

Ralf Schumacher got ahead of Button for fourth place at his first refuelling stop, both Williams-BMWs sounding very rough towards the end of the race, an apparent broken exhaust masking potentially more serious technical problems. They both made it home in the points, though, after two of the most impressive performances of the afternoon.

Frentzen's hopes of a top-six finish were thwarted when his Jordan jammed in sixth gear and he had to pull off with just six laps to go. Villeneuve was also frustrated, aiming for sixth place when he was struck by a similar affliction.

'The car was jumping out of gear for several laps before I came in and then the transmission just packed up,' he shrugged. 'I am very unhappy, because we threw away a point today that could turn out to be valuable at the end of the season.'

That handed Jarno Trulli sixth place ahead of Giancarlo Fisichella's Benetton B200. 'At the beginning of the race Trulli hit a piece of bodywork in front of me and it flew up and damaged the nose of my car,' he said. 'I thought it would be more of a problem, but in fact we left it as it was for the rest of the race and it wasn't a big problem.'

Mika Salo wound up eighth in the Sauber C19, reasonably satisfied with his climb from 18th on the grid despite excessive understeer on his last set of tyres, to finish just ahead of Alexander Wurz's Benetton. Jean Alesi's Prost AP03 finished tenth ahead of Pedro Diniz's Sauber.

Schumacher's satisfaction at a job well done was certainly not shared by the beleaguered Jaguar team which was tugging at the heart strings of its British motor sporting heritage with their first F1 outing on home soil.

Johnny Herbert and Eddie Irvine trailed home a distant 12th and 13th after the engines of both cars stalled at the second refuelling stops. The team tried to put an upbeat gloss on their reliability, but it was a pretty dismal performance to round off what many spectators still regarded as a pretty dismal weekend, albeit brightened towards the end by Coulthard's emotional success.

BRITISH GRAND PRIX

SILVERSTONE — GRAND PRIX CIRCUIT

CIRCUIT LENGTH: 3.195 miles/5.141 km

mph/km/h (gear)

- COPSE 140/225 (5)
- MAGGOTTS 170/274 (5)
- BECKETTS 130/209 (5)
- CHAPEL 95/153 (4)
- HANGAR STRAIGHT 190/305 (6)
- STOWE CORNER 100/161 (4)
- THE VALE 165/266 (5)
- CLUB CORNER 70/113 (2)
- ABBEY CURVE 75/121 (2)
- PRIORY 95/153 (4)
- LUFFIELD 60/97 (2)
- BROOKLANDS 50/81 (2)
- BRIDGE 155/250 (5)
- WOODCOTE 155/250 (5)

All results and data © FIA 2000

RACE DISTANCE: 60 laps, 191.604 miles/308.356 km **RACE WEATHER: Dry, warm and sunny**

Pos.	Driver	Nat.	No.	Entrant	Car/Engine	Laps	Time/Retirement	Speed (mph/km/h)
1	David Coulthard	GB	2	West McLaren Mercedes	McLaren MP4/15-Mercedes FO110J V10	60	1h 28m 50.108s	129.410/208.266
2	Mika Häkkinen	SF	1	West McLaren Mercedes	McLaren MP4/15-Mercedes FO110J V10	60	1h 28m 51.585s	129.374/208.208
3	Michael Schumacher	D	3	Scuderia Ferrari Marlboro	Ferrari F1-2000-049 V10	60	1h 29m 10.025s	128.928/207.490
4	Ralf Schumacher	D	9	BMW WilliamsF1 Team	Williams FW22-BMW E41 V10	60	1h 29m 31.420s	128.415/206.664
5	Jenson Button	GB	10	BMW WilliamsF1 Team	Williams FW22-BMW E41 V10	60	1h 29m 47.867s	128.023/206.033
6	Jarno Trulli	I	6	Benson & Hedges Jordan	Jordan EJ10-Mugen Honda MF301HE V10	60	1h 30m 09.381s	127.514/205.214
7	Giancarlo Fisichella	I	11	Mild Seven Benetton Playlife	Benetton B200-Playlife V10	59		
8	Mika Salo	SF	17	Red Bull Sauber Petronas	Sauber C19-Petronas SPE 04A V10	59		
9	Alexander Wurz	A	12	Mild Seven Benetton Playlife	Benetton B200-Playlife V10	59		
10	Jean Alesi	F	14	Gauloises Prost Peugeot	Prost AP03-Peugeot A20 V10	59		
11	Pedro Diniz	BR	16	Red Bull Sauber Petronas	Sauber C19-Petronas SPE 04A V10	59		
12	Johnny Herbert	GB	8	Jaguar Racing	Jaguar R1-Cosworth CR2 V10	59		
13	Eddie Irvine	GB	7	Jaguar Racing	Jaguar R1-Cosworth CR2 V10	59		
14	Marc Gene	ESP	20	Telefonica Minardi Fondmetal	Minardi M02-Fondmetal Ford Zetec-R V10	59		
15	Gaston Mazzacane	ARG	21	Telefonica Minardi Fondmetal	Minardi M02-Fondmetal Ford Zetec-R V10	59		
16	Jacques Villeneuve	CDN	22	Lucky Strike BAR Honda	BAR 02-Honda RA100E V10	56	Gearbox	
17	Heinz-Harald Frentzen	D	5	Benson & Hedges Jordan	Jordan EJ10-Mugen Honda MF301HE V10	54	Gearbox	
	Nick Heidfeld	D	15	Gauloises Prost Peugeot	Prost AP03-Peugeot A20 V10	51	Engine	
	Ricardo Zonta	BR	23	Lucky Strike BAR Honda	BAR 02-Honda RA100E V10	36	Spun off	
	Rubens Barrichello	BR	4	Scuderia Ferrari Marlboro	Ferrari F1-2000-049 V10	35	Hydraulics	
	Pedro de la Rosa	ESP	18	Arrows Supertec	Arrows A21-Supertec FB02 V10	26	Electronics	
	Jos Verstappen	NL	19	Arrows Supertec	Arrows A21-Supertec FB02 V10	20	Electronics	

Fastest lap: Häkkinen, on lap 56, 1m 26.217s, 133.385 mph/214.663 km/h.

Previous lap record: Michael Schumacher (F1 Ferrari F310B-V10), 1m 24.475s, 136.109 mph/219.047 km/h (1997).

Lap chart

Grid order	1	2	3	4	5	6	7	8	9	10	11	12	13	14	15	16	17	18	19	20	21	22	23	24	25	26	27	28	29	30	31	32	33	34	35	36	37	38	39	40	41	42	43	44	45	46	47
4 BARRICHELLO	4	4	4	4	4	4	4	4	4	4	4	4	4	4	4	4	4	4	4	4	4	4	4	2	2	2	2	2	2	2	2	2	2	2	2	2	2	2	2	2	2	2	2	2	2	2	2
5 FRENTZEN	5	5	5	5	5	5	5	5	5	5	5	5	5	5	5	5	5	5	5	5	5	5	5	5	5	5	1	1	1	1	1	1	1	1	1	1	1	1	1	1	1	1	1	1	1	1	1
1 HÄKKINEN	2	2	2	2	2	2	2	2	2	2	2	2	2	2	2	2	1	1	1	1	1	1	1	10	22	22	3	3	3	3	3	3	3	3	3	3	3	3	3	5	5	5	5	5	5	5	5
2 COULTHARD	1	1	1	1	1	1	1	1	1	1	1	1	1	1	1	1	22	22	22	22	22	22	22	22	3	5	22	9	9	10	1	1	6	22	11	11	7	23	14	16	8	16	15	12	14	14	16
3 M. SCHUMACHER	10	10	10	10	10	10	10	10	10	10	10	10	10	10	10	10	10	10	10	10	10	10	10	3	10	3	5	22	22	22	6	6	22	11	7	7	14	14	16	8	16	8	12	15	12	12	14
10 BUTTON	22	22	22	22	22	22	22	22	22	22	22	22	22	22	22	22	3	3	3	3	3	3	3	5	9	9	9	5	5	6	22	22	11	7	23	14	23	16	8	14	12	12	8	8	8	8	8
9 R. SCHUMACHER	9	9	9	9	9	9	9	9	9	9	9	9	9	9	9	9	9	9	9	9	9	9	9	9	1	10	10	10	6	11	11	11	7	23	14	23	16	8	12	12	14	14	14	14	15	15	15
19 VERSTAPPEN	19	19	19	19	19	19	19	19	19	19	6	6	6	6	6	6	6	6	6	6	6	6	6	6	6	6	6	6	11	7	7	7	23	14	16	16	8	12	15	15	15	15	16	16	16	16	12
7 IRVINE	6	6	6	6	6	6	6	6	6	6	11	11	11	11	11	11	11	11	11	11	11	11	11	11	11	11	11	11	7	23	23	23	14	16	8	8	12	15	7	7	7	7	7	7	7	7	7
22 VILLENEUVE	11	11	11	11	11	11	11	11	11	11	7	7	7	7	7	7	7	7	7	7	7	7	14	14	14	14	14	14	23	14	14	14	16	8	12	12	15	7									
6 TRULLI	7	7	7	7	7	7	7	7	7	7	14	14	14	14	14	14	14	14	14	14	14	14	23	23	23	23	23	23	14	16	16	16	8	12	15	15											
11 FISICHELLA	14	14	14	14	14	14	14	14	14	14	23	23	23	23	23	23	23	23	23	23	23	23	8	8	8	8	8	8	16	8	8	8	12	15													
16 DINIZ	23	23	23	12	23	23	23	23	23	23	18	18	18	18	16	16	16	16	16	16	16	16	15	15	15	15	15	15	8	12	12	12	15														
8 HERBERT	17	17	17	17	17	17	17	17	17	17	16	16	16	16	18	18	18	8	8	8	8	8	16	16	16	16	16	16	12	15	15	15															
14 ALESI	14	14	14	14	14	14	14	12	12	12	12	23	12	12	15	15	15	15	15	15	15	15	20	20	20	20	20	20	15																		
23 ZONTA	23	23	12	23	12	12	12	18	18	18	18	12	8	8	8	8	8	20	21	21	21	21	21	21	21	21	21	21	20																		
17 SALO	16	16	16	16	16	16	16	16	16	16	8	8	15	15	17	17	20	21	20	20	20	20	17	17	17	17	17	17	21	21																	
18 DE LA ROSA	8	8	8	8	8	8	8	15	15	15	15	15	20	20	20	20	21	12	12	12	12	12	12	12	12	12	12	12																			
12 WURZ	15	15	15	15	15	15	15	20	20	20	20	20	21	21	21	21	12	17	17	17	17	17	18	18	18	18	18	18	18	18	18	18															
20 GENE	20	20	20	20	20	20	20	21	21	21	21	21	17	17	12	12	17																														
21 MAZZACANE	21	21	21	21	21	21	21	21	21	21	21	21	21	21	21	21	21	21	21	21	21	21	21	21	21	21	21	21	21	21	21	21	21	21	21	21	21	21	21	19							

Pit stop (shaded)

One lap behind leader (shaded)

STARTING GRID

1 HÄKKINEN McLaren	**2 COULTHARD** McLaren
4 BARRICHELLO Ferrari	**5 FRENTZEN** Jordan
3 M. SCHUMACHER Ferrari	
9 R. SCHUMACHER Williams	**10 BUTTON** Williams
7 IRVINE Jaguar	
6 TRULLI Jordan	**11 FISICHELLA** Benetton
22 VILLENEUVE BAR	**19 VERSTAPPEN** Arrows
16 DINIZ Sauber	**8 HERBERT** Jaguar
15 ALESI Prost	**23 ZONTA** BAR
17 HEIDFELD Prost	**18 SALO** Sauber
14 DE LA ROSA Arrows	**12 WURZ** Benetton
20 GENE Minardi	**21 MAZZACANE** Minardi

FOR THE RECORD

100th Grand Prix start
Jordan

Lap Chart

```
        48 49 50 51 52 53 54 55 56 57 58 59 60
         2  2  2  2  2  2  2  2  2  2  2  2  2
         5  5  5  5  5  5  5  5  5  5  5  5  5
        10 10 10 10 10 10 10 10 10 10 10 10 10
        22 22 22 22 22 22 22 22 22 22 22 22 22
         6  6  6  6  6  6  6  6  6  6  6  6  6
         1  1  1  1  1  1  1  1  1  1  1  1  1
        11 11 11 11 11 11 11 11 11 11 11 11 11
         8  8  8  8  8  8  8  8  8  8  8  8  8
        17 17 17 17 17 17 17 17 17 17 17 17 17
         9  9  9  9  9  9  9  9  9  9  9  9  9
        15 15 15 15 15 15 15 15 15 15 15 15 15
        14 14 14 14 14 14 14 14 14 14 14 14 14
        13 13 13 13 13 13 13 13 13 13 13 13 13
        16 16 16 16 16 16 16 16 16 16 16 16 16
         7  7  7  7  7  7  7  7  7  7  7  7  7
        20 20 20 20 20 20 20 20 20 20 20 20 20
        21 21 21 21 21 21 21 21 21 21 21 21 21
```

TIME SHEETS

QUALIFYING

Weather: Drying circuit, sunny

Pos.	Driver	Car	Laps	Time
1	Rubens Barrichello	Ferrari	11	1m 25.703s
2	Heinz-Harald Frentzen	Jordan-Mugen Honda	10	1m 25.706s
3	Mika Häkkinen	McLaren-Mercedes	10	1m 25.741s
4	David Coulthard	McLaren-Mercedes	12	1m 26.088s
5	Michael Schumacher	Ferrari	11	1m 26.161s
6	Jenson Button	Williams-BMW	12	1m 26.733s
7	Ralf Schumacher	Williams-BMW	10	1m 26.786s
8	Jos Verstappen	Arrows-Supertec	12	1m 26.793s
9	Eddie Irvine	Jaguar-Cosworth	12	1m 26.818s
10	Jacques Villeneuve	BAR-Honda	11	1m 27.025s
11	Jarno Trulli	Jordan-Mugen Honda	11	1m 27.164s
12	Giancarlo Fisichella	Benetton-Playlife	12	1m 27.253s
13	Pedro Diniz	Sauber-Petronas	12	1m 27.301s
14	Johnny Herbert	Jaguar-Cosworth	12	1m 27.461s
15	Jean Alesi	Prost-Peugeot	12	1m 27.559s
16	Ricardo Zonta	BAR-Honda	12	1m 27.772s
17	Nick Heidfeld	Prost-Peugeot	12	1m 27.806s
18	Mika Salo	Sauber-Petronas	11	1m 28.135s
19	Pedro de la Rosa	Arrows-Supertec	12	1m 28.205s
20	Alexander Wurz	Benetton-Playlife	12	1m 28.253s
21	Marc Gene	Minardi-Fondmetal	11	1m 28.533s
22	Gaston Mazzacane	Minardi-Fondmetal	12	1m 29.174s

FRIDAY FREE PRACTICE

Weather: Drying circuit, then heavy rain

Pos.	Driver	Laps	Time
1	Heinz-Harald Frentzen	27	1m 27.683s
2	Eddie Irvine	18	1m 28.169s
3	David Coulthard	20	1m 28.525s
4	Mika Häkkinen	23	1m 28.659s
5	Jarno Trulli	25	1m 28.705s
6	Jacques Villeneuve	24	1m 28.845s
7	Rubens Barrichello	23	1m 29.083s
8	Alexander Wurz	22	1m 29.111s
9	Giancarlo Fisichella	21	1m 29.214s
10	Marc Gene	23	1m 29.537s
11	Jenson Button	24	1m 29.775s
12	Pedro Diniz	26	1m 30.214s
13	Pedro de la Rosa	16	1m 30.279s
14	Jos Verstappen	28	1m 30.313s
15	Ralf Schumacher	14	1m 30.593s
16	Mika Salo	26	1m 30.643s
17	Jean Alesi	20	1m 30.656s
18	Nick Heidfeld	23	1m 31.006s
19	Gaston Mazzacane	24	1m 31.250s
20	Ricardo Zonta	20	1m 31.322s
21	Michael Schumacher	27	1m 36.425s
22	Johnny Herbert	10	1m 39.690s

SATURDAY FREE PRACTICE

Weather: Rain, then slowly drying

Pos.	Driver	Laps	Time
1	Mika Häkkinen	25	1m 33.132s
2	Michael Schumacher	30	1m 33.360s
3	David Coulthard	31	1m 33.414s
4	Rubens Barrichello	29	1m 33.587s
5	Ralf Schumacher	29	1m 33.906s
6	Giancarlo Fisichella	18	1m 34.466s
7	Heinz-Harald Frentzen	34	1m 34.709s
8	Jos Verstappen	25	1m 34.787s
9	Jarno Trulli	36	1m 34.855s
10	Mika Salo	30	1m 34.926s
11	Pedro de la Rosa	27	1m 35.114s
12	Nick Heidfeld	32	1m 35.130s
13	Pedro Diniz	21	1m 35.166s
14	Jacques Villeneuve	33	1m 35.313s
15	Ricardo Zonta	34	1m 35.679s
16	Jean Alesi	18	1m 35.858s
17	Alexander Wurz	33	1m 36.013s
18	Johnny Herbert	24	1m 36.020s
19	Marc Gene	25	1m 36.305s
20	Gaston Mazzacane	32	1m 37.187s
21	Jenson Button	4	1m 41.870s
22	Eddie Irvine	4	1m 44.323s

WARM-UP

Weather: Dry, warm and sunny

Pos.	Driver	Laps	Time
1	David Coulthard	14	1m 26.800s
2	Pedro de la Rosa	12	1m 26.844s
3	Michael Schumacher	14	1m 26.905s
4	Ralf Schumacher	8	1m 27.012s
5	Mika Häkkinen	14	1m 27.134s
6	Rubens Barrichello	13	1m 27.404s
7	Jenson Button	12	1m 27.525s
8	Gaston Mazzacane	12	1m 27.598s
9	Marc Gene	14	1m 27.640s
10	Jos Verstappen	15	1m 27.740s
11	Johnny Herbert	14	1m 27.769s
12	Pedro Diniz	16	1m 27.801s
13	Jean Alesi	11	1m 27.997s
14	Giancarlo Fisichella	15	1m 28.001s
15	Jacques Villeneuve	13	1m 28.144s
16	Ricardo Zonta	13	1m 28.245s
17	Heinz-Harald Frentzen	16	1m 28.397s
18	Eddie Irvine	16	1m 28.514s
19	Alexander Wurz	15	1m 28.590s
20	Jarno Trulli	13	1m 28.918s
21	Nick Heidfeld	11	1m 28.994s
22	Mika Salo	5	5m 44.173s

RACE FASTEST LAPS

Weather: Dry, warm and sunny

Driver	Time	Lap
Mika Häkkinen	1m 26.217s	56
Michael Schumacher	1m 26.428s	59
Ralf Schumacher	1m 26.998s	49
David Coulthard	1m 27.093s	31
Heinz-Harald Frentzen	1m 27.286s	41
Rubens Barrichello	1m 27.496s	34
Jenson Button	1m 27.631s	44
Alexander Wurz	1m 27.655s	27
Jarno Trulli	1m 27.824s	36
Johnny Herbert	1m 28.001s	53
Eddie Irvine	1m 28.009s	54
Pedro Diniz	1m 28.037s	52
Jean Alesi	1m 28.093s	32
Jacques Villeneuve	1m 28.116s	32
Giancarlo Fisichella	1m 28.093s	27
Mika Salo	1m 28.178s	44
Nick Heidfeld	1m 28.388s	34
Gaston Mazzacane	1m 28.487s	43
Marc Gene	1m 28.557s	39
Alexander Wurz	1m 28.665s	34
Nick Heidfeld	1m 28.803s	54
Pedro de la Rosa	1m 28.867s	25
Jos Verstappen	1m 29.546s	12

CHASSIS LOG BOOK

	Driver	Chassis
1	Häkkinen	McLaren MP4/15/1
2	Coulthard	McLaren MP4/15/2
	spare	McLaren MP4/15/3
3	M. Schumacher	Ferrari F1-2000/200
4	Barrichello	Ferrari F1-2000/199
	spare	Ferrari F1-2000/198
5	Frentzen	Jordan EJ10/4
6	Trulli	Jordan EJ10/3
	spare	Jordan EJ10/2
7	Irvine	Jaguar R1/4
8	Herbert	Jaguar R1/1
	spares	Jaguar R1/3 & 2
9	R. Schumacher	Williams FW22/3
10	Button	Williams FW22/4
	spare	Williams FW22/2
11	Fisichella	Benetton B200/5
12	Wurz	Benetton B200/3
	spare	Benetton B200/4
14	Alesi	Prost AP03/3
15	Heidfeld	Prost AP03/4
	spare	Prost AP03/1
16	Diniz	Sauber C19/4
17	Salo	Sauber C19/2
	spare	Sauber C19/1
18	de la Rosa	Arrows A21/4
19	Verstappen	Arrows A21/2
	spare	Arrows A21/1
20	Gene	Minardi M02/3
21	Mazzacane	Minardi M02/2
	spare	Minardi M02/1
22	Villeneuve	BAR 02/5
23	Zonta	BAR 02/1
	spare	BAR 02/4

POINTS TABLES

DRIVERS

Pos.	Driver	Points
1	Michael Schumacher	34
2	David Coulthard	14
3	Mika Häkkinen	12
4 =	Rubens Barrichello	9
4 =	Ralf Schumacher	9
6 =	Giancarlo Fisichella	8
6 =	Jacques Villeneuve	8
8	Heinz-Harald Frentzen	5
9	Jarno Trulli	4
10	Jenson Button	3
11 =	Ricardo Zonta	1
11 =	Mika Salo	1

CONSTRUCTORS

Pos.	Team	Points
1	Ferrari	43
2	McLaren	26
3	Williams	12
4 =	Benetton	8
4 =	Jordan	8
6	BAR	6
7	Sauber	1

SPANISH

grand prix

FIA WORLD CHAMPIONSHIP • ROUND 5

HÄKKINEN

COULTHARD

BARRICHELLO

R. SCHUMACHER

M. SCHUMACHER

FRENTZEN

Previous spread: Michael Schumacher (inset, left) appears philosophical whilst the blistered Bridgestone tyre on his Ferrari tells its own tale (main picture), and a relieved Häkkinen (inset, right) grabbed his first win of the season.

All photographs: Paul-Henri Cahier

Right: Michael Schumacher bottles up Mika Häkkinen, Ralf Schumacher, David Coulthard and Rubens Barrichello at the first corner.

Paul-Henri Cahier

CATALUNYA QUALIFYING

After three days of testing work in Barcelona the previous week, the teams returned to experience a familiar situation; track conditions had changed quite dramatically and the priority on Friday was to re-learn as much as possible without squandering unnecessary sets of tyres.

Despite this, in the Ferrari camp Michael Schumacher's laid-back confidence emphasised his underlying belief that he could beat the McLarens in a straight fight for pole position. With a perfectly timed run in 1m 20.974s – a full second faster than last year's fastest qualifying time – he buttoned up his 24th career pole, and the first of the 2000 season. Apart from the two Arrows drivers, Michael was the only competitor to opt for the harder of the two Bridgestone tyre options.

'The increase in wind and temperature made it a bit more difficult towards the end,' he said. 'I was not completely happy with the car, even though I had a clean run, so we made some adjustments but they did not [quite] work out the way I wanted.'

Rubens Barrichello never completely managing to get all three sectors of the lap quite correct. For his part, Coulthard certainly looked like a potential pole winner from the start. From Friday's first free practice session he seemed to have the upper hand over teammate Mika Häkkinen who complained, right through to the end of Saturday morning, that his MP4/15 suffered from too much oversteer.

David started qualifying buoyed to have received a touching message from the father of one of the pilots who had been killed in the Learjet crash. Tell David to put it on pole,' was the message sent via McLaren boss Ron Dennis. He certainly tried.

Unfortunately his efforts would be thwarted as early as his first run when a slight misfire caused him to steer straight into the pit lane rather than complete the lap. The car had developed a fuel pick-up problem which meant he had to run with around 10 litres extra for the balance of the session to prevent a recurrence.

The unwanted additional weight was just enough to shade his efforts on this circuit where there is traditionally a fine balance between extra weight and tyre degradation, dropping him to fourth as Häkkinen vaulted through to second ahead of Barrichello.

In fifth place, Ralf Schumacher posted a 1m 21.605s with the Williams FW22-BMW. 'If somebody had told us at the beginning of the season that at this race we would be only two-tenths behind a Ferrari, we wouldn't have believed it,' grimned Ralf. The car was really quite good, even though I was still losing some time in the third sector of the lap with a touch of oversteer.'

Jenson Button lined up 11th. 'It was not my best qualifying session,' he said. The wind made the car slightly unstable which lost me a bit of confidence.'

Jacques Villeneuve qualified his BAR-Honda sixth on 1m 21.963s, the Canadian squeezing in ahead of the Jordans of Jarno Trulli and Heinz-Harald Frentzen.

Trulli echoed Button's sentiments when he noted: 'The windy conditions made it difficult to put three good sector times together; one minute there was no wind, then a big gust and the next minute a gust from the other direction.'

In ninth place, Pedro de la Rosa produced an excellent showing at the wheel of the Arrows A21. 'Well, we've finally made it in the top ten,' he said with an enthusiasm which proved unfortunately premature.

'The car was very good from first thing this morning. The set-up was very good, which shows in the end result, and the car was very consistent during qualifying. I hope tomorrow will be as successful.'

Unfortunately, at a post-qualifying check, a sample of fuel taken from the Spaniard's Arrows was found not to match the sample lodged with the FIA prior to the race. Whilst it appeared that contaminants had caused the anomaly – there was no suggestion of deliberate cheating – de la Rosa's time was disallowed and he was relegated to last place on the grid.

'When we get back to base, the team will carry out a full review with our fuel supplier,' said team chief Tom Walkinshaw. 'We are confident that the fuel manufacturing process is correct and that the contamination occurred in transportation.'

In the Jaguar camp there was also a mood of disappointment prevailing. Eddie Irvine and Johnny Herbert qualified 10th and 15th respectively, neither able to consolidate any worthwhile progress in terms of track performance.

'I felt that we'd made a step forward in testing,' said Irvine, 'but after today we need to examine why it didn't work out that way. We tried a few set-up changes this morning, and made some headway, but it didn't feel the same this afternoon.'

For his part, Herbert's car lost its front wing-mounted camera when he clipped a kerb early on and admitted to a slight mistake on his final run which cost him badly. 'We tried a few things and improved the car,' he shrugged, 'but we've still got a lot of work to do.'

Separating the two Jaguars were Button, Jos Verstappen's Arrows, Mika Salo's understeering Sauber and the Benetton of Giancarlo Fisichella. The Italian reported that the balance of his car felt much improved, but that there was insufficient grip. His teammate Alexander Wurz languished down in 19th place, admitting that he'd lost his way after making changes to his car's set-up.

In the Prost-Peugeot camp Jean Alesi wound up 18th, the Frenchman unable to complete a third run after his race chassis suffered hydraulic problems. His team-mate Nick Heidfeld had earlier taken the spare AP03 after his own had suffered engine failure, so it wasn't available for Alesi's use.

M IKA Häkkinen simply could not conceal his relief as he climbed from the cockpit of his McLaren-Mercedes MP4/15 after it rolled to a halt in the scrutineering area at the Circuit de Catalunya. After 65 gruelling laps he had finally nailed down his first win of the new millennium. The fact that he had also headed the third straight McLaren-Mercedes 1–2 in this race was almost of secondary importance. Overwhelmingly, he was just happy to have posted his first win of the year. And it had taken him five races.

Yet the most vocal applause was reserved for David Coulthard who drove a brilliant race to finish second under circumstances which were extremely stressful, from both a physical and psychological standpoint.

As he drove into the scrutineering bay his fiancée Heidi Wichlinski cut a lonely, relieved figure as she stood by the barrier and watched him brake

the silver McLaren-Mercedes to a standstill.

Only five days had passed since she, David, and his trainer Andy Matthews, had been passengers in a chartered Learjet which crashed whilst making an emergency landing at Lyon Satolas airport, killing both its pilots.

Not being one to make a fuss, Coulthard made only passing reference to the discomfort caused by his bruised ribcage. It was only when Dennis later made mention of the acute pain from his driver had been suffering from half-distance onwards that those outside McLaren began to appreciate the magnitude of his achievement in handling the pummelling G-forces which are part and parcel of driving a Formula 1 car on the limit for an hour and a half.

'I do have some injuries to both my sides,' he said, modestly shrugging aside the discomfort later officially attributed to cracked ribs. 'As Heidi and Andy have got better each day, so I got worse each day. I am looking forward to having some time off next week and I think I may not do the test planned for this week.'

Häkkinen's victory moved him into second place in the World Championship 14 points behind Ferrari team leader Michael Schumacher who had a troubled run to finish fifth. Yet at the end of the race the Finn slowed right down and let the entire field overtake him, allowing Coulthard's to be the first car to enter the scrutineering bay where McLaren chairman Ron Dennis and Mercedes board director Professor Jürgen Hubbert were waiting for the Scot with a bottle of water and quiet congratulations.

At the start, Michael Schumacher made a slowish getaway from pole position, moving straight across to block Häkkinen's McLaren. This in turn gave an added boost to the fast-starting Ralf Schumacher's Williams FW22 which came surging up the inside from fifth

place on the grid to clip Häkkinen's right rear wheel from third place as the pack jostled into the first right-hander.

Häkkinen just managed to keep control, although he later confessed he was worried that his McLaren might have suffered some sort of suspension damage, finishing the opening lap 1.1s behind the Ferrari team leader. Then came Ralf, David Coulthard, Rubens Barrichello's Ferrari F1-2000, Jacques Villeneuve's BAR-Honda and Heinz-Harald Frentzen's Jordan EJ10.

At the tail of the field Pedro Diniz had already pirouetted his Sauber C19 into retirement, while the second lap yielded two more casualties. Battling for 17th place, Pedro de la Rosa clearly got carried away by the emotion of the moment, racing as he was on home soil in a competitive car.

He attempted to muscle his way past Jean Alesi's Prost AP03 going into the fast left-hander at the end of the back straight and the two cars collided.

'I was last on the grid, so had to take some risks,' said de la Rosa. 'I had a good start, pushed hard on the first lap and had a quicker car than most of the guys around me. Alesi was blocking me like crazy, so I went to overtake him and had three-quarters of the car inside him, but he just closed the door.' Needless to say, Alesi did not accept this interpretation. He reckoned de la Rosa had simply driven into the side of him.

Initially Häkkinen fell away, dropping to 3.4s adrift by lap ten, after which he gradually narrowed Schumacher's advantage again, moving up to 1.9s adrift by lap 17. Ralf Schumacher was under pressure from Coulthard with Barrichello next up and Villeneuve's BAR-Honda already a massive 20.8s further back in sixth.

Villeneuve made the first of his two planned refuelling stops at the end of lap 21. Unfortunately, as he accelerated back into the fray the throttle stopped

working and his race was at an end. 'It's a shame, because we could have made sixth place today,' he shrugged. 'The car is a definite improvement on previous races and I don't feel I was holding anybody up behind me.'

There followed a rush of refuelling stops. Jarno Trulli's Jordan came in from seventh at the end of lap 22, resuming 17th after unfortunately stalling his engine. Then on lap 23 Ralf Schumacher made his first stop in 7.3s, dropping from third to fifth, while next time round his elder brother made a rather more spectacular first stop in his Ferrari.

Michael felt a bump from the rear of the car as he accelerated away, but was not fully aware that he had knocked over his British chief mechanic Nigel Stepney, leaving him writhing in pain with a broken ankle after the team's 'lollipop man' Federico Uguzzoni, waved Michael back into the race a fraction of a second

DIARY

The FIA summons the organisers of the British Grand Prix to explain the chaotic conditions surrounding the 2000 race to a meeting of its World Council on June 21 in Warsaw.

Damon Hill denies that he has received an approach to become involved with the forthcoming Toyota F1 team.

Jaguar team chief Neil Ressler denies that an approach has been made to Ross Brawn, the Ferrari technical director.

Brazilian driver Mario Haberfeld escapes without injury from a 130-mph testing accident during qualifying for the F3000 race at Barcelona.

before Stepney – who was refuelling the car – moved clear of the right rear wheel.

Nevertheless, Michael retained first place but when he led Häkkinen in for their second stop on lap 41 there was a problem with the Ferrari refuelling nozzle which delayed him sufficiently for Häkkinen to take a lead he would never lose.

On lap 25 Barrichello made his first refuelling stop (9.3s) dropping from second to fourth, while Häkkinen came in next time round, dropping from first to second after a 7.8s stop. Further back, Frentzen also made his first stop, dropping from sixth to eighth, while Jos Verstappen's Arrows A21 retired with gearbox problems.

By lap 28 Häkkinen was really pressing Schumacher's Ferrari very hard while brother Ralf was under a lot of pressure from Barrichello and Coulthard. 11 laps later the second round of stops began with Coulthard making a 7.5s stop dropping from fourth to fifth, retaking Ralf Schumacher round the outside of the first corner as he resumed.

Next time round, Ralf and Rubens both stopped, rejoining behind Coulthard, while on lap 41 came the decisive moment of the race as Schumacher's Ferrari and Häkkinen's McLaren came into the pits nose-to-tail for their second stops. Mika was in and out in 8.1s, but Michael was stationary for 17.5s, handing the lead decisively to his rival.

Meanwhile, Coulthard, who lost time at his first refuelling stop when he selected the wrong gear, found

himself on the receiving end of what he regarded as Michael Schumacher's unacceptable driving tactics when he came up to challenge the Ferrari for second place at the start of lap 47.

'I don't think that first manoeuvre of Michael's was at all fair,' he said after Michael squeezed him to the right as they went into the braking area for the first right-hander at 190 mph.

'I was very surprised how later he made the decision to move over [on me]. You are allowed [by the rules] to make one move, but I had momentum on him and he made the move incredibly late.

'Die-hards will say "well, that's racing, don't be a pansy" but I didn't think it was fair. We arrived at the corner right on the limit and I must say it was a relief to get away with

that one. It was incredibly close.' On the following lap he successfully overtook the Ferrari on the outside instead.

By now Michael was grappling with a slow puncture and Ralf tried to squeeze through to take third place at the same point on the circuit where Alesi and de la Rosa had earlier come to grief. Michael wasn't having any of it, pushing him wide so that the Williams-BMW was now on the outside of the following right-hander.

Barrichello immediately capitalised on this sudden outburst of sibling rivalry to slice through into third place. Michael then headed for the pit lane, leaving his fuming brother demoted to fourth which he held to the chequered flag.

'I would prefer to watch the video of Barrichello overtaking me before saying anything more about this manoeuvre', said the Williams team leader, tactfully dodging any overt criticism of his brother who eventually finished fifth behind him after that unscheduled third stop.

Jenson Button lost a worthy sixth place when his Williams-BMW suffered engine failure with just four laps to go, leaving Frentzen sixth for Jordan. Mika Salo took seventh ahead of Ricardo Zonta in the BAR, but the Brazilian was harrying the Sauber all the way to the flag.

'I was able to close the gap to him at about a second a lap,' said Zonta, 'but I was probably going to need another lap to have a chance to pass him.'

In ninth and tenth places came the Benetton B200s of Giancarlo Fisichella and Alexander Wurz, the Austrian losing time at his second stop with a right rear wheel problem. 'Another race to forget,' said MD Flavio Briatore crisply.

Irvine and Herbert struggled home 11th and 13th, sandwiching Trulli's delayed Jordan, while the Minardis of Marc Gene and Gaston Mazzacane, plus Heidfeld's Prost were the only other cars running at the chequered flag.

It was a great day for McLaren and a rare disappointment for Michael Schumacher. The Ferrari ace rounded off the day receiving a degree of censure from Ron Dennis.

'That behaviour at the start is the second time that Michael has pushed things right to the edge,' said the McLaren boss, pointedly reflecting on the Ferrari driver's similar weaving at the start of last month's San Marino Grand Prix.

'You don't win these races by having a passive approach, certainly, but there are limits which should not be crossed.'

Cool Coulthard returns after air crash escape

If you hadn't known that David Coulthard had come within inches of death in the torn wreckage of an out-of-control private jet as it skidded off the runway at a French airport just two days earlier, you certainly wouldn't have guessed it from his characteristically calm and controlled demeanour when he arrived in the paddock at the Circuit de Catalunya for the first time on the Thursday prior to the race.

Composed without being too laid back, cordial without any artificial chumminess, the 29-year-old Scot was handling the after-effects of the crash which killed the two pilots of his leased jet at Lyon on Tuesday with the same reserve which he brings to bear on his life as a professional racing driver.

On closer examination he may have looked a little pale and hollow-eyed, but he was certainly not showing any signs of anxiety after a 55-minute flight by private jet from Nice to Barcelona earlier that same morning. If there were any demons dancing in his sub-conscious, you would never have known.

Yet that is the whole thing about Coulthard. His combination of understated good manners and Scottish phlegm always leaves you with the very clear impression of what he has done, if not what he inwardly feels about it.

So it was in the official FIA media conference on the Thursday afternoon. Rubens Barrichello, Ralf Schumacher and Pedro Diniz were amongst the drivers alongside him on the stage, but Coulthard was inevitably the centre of attention. And not because of his masterly victory in the British Grand Prix at Silverstone.

Coulthard read from a prepared script in an effort to give the press corps what they wanted, but one ended up feeling there was more for him to reflect about.

'First of all, I wish to express our heartfelt sympathies to the families of the two pilots, David Saunders and Dan Worley, who behaved with the utmost professionalism throughout the incident,' he said.

'The background to the flight is that I chartered a Lear 35. This is an

aircraft with which I am familiar, although it was neither the aircraft nor the crew which I used on a regular basis. We left Farnborough at lunchtime on Tuesday, to return to Monaco.

'During the flight the co-pilot informed us that we had an engine problem and would have to make an emergency landing from Lyon, which would be in about ten minutes' time. Prior to landing, we had time to prepare ourselves in the 'brace' position.

'On impact, a wing tank ruptured and there was a fire on the right side of the aircraft. When the plane finally came to rest, the front of the cockpit had broken free from the main fuselage. At this point we established that the only way out was through the front of the aircraft. Andy led the way through the aircraft, and as this part of the aircraft was three or four feet above the ground, I followed Andy out so that we could help Heidi get down.

'Once we were all clear of the plane, I returned to see whether there was anything I could do for the pilots. But there was nothing to be done. In less than a minute the emergency services took over.'

He then made a plea for privacy for the rest of the weekend on behalf of his fiancée and trainer while he himself 'had professional obligations to try and win [Sunday's] grand prix as I fight for the World Championship.'

With that, Coulthard retired to the television studios to give a single interview on the subject along the same theme before beating a dignified retreat to the solitude of the McLaren team's motorhome.

One person not in the least surprised at Coulthard's relaxed demeanour was FIA medical delegate Professor Sid Watkins who gave the Scot a precautionary check over to confirm that he had little more than bruised ribs and elbows.

'These people are literally like fighter pilots,' said Watkins. They wouldn't be in this business if they were not like that. As far as David is concerned, the whole episode is over and done with.

'When I saw him for the first time, he was absolutely normal and greeted me with his usual mellow Scottish humour. He will be fine and should have no problem racing.'

Right: Ralf Schumacher locks a front wheel in his attempt to keep David Coulthard at bay.

Below right: Mika gives a joyous Rubens Barrichello a soaking.
Both photographs: Paul-Henri Cahier

CATALUNYA
ROUND 5 · 5–7 MAY 2000

gran premio MARLBORO de ESPAÑA

CATALUNYA CIRCUIT — BARCELONA

CIRCUIT LENGTH: 2.938 miles/4.728 km

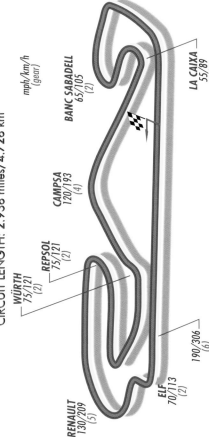

WÜRTH 75/121 (2)
REPSOL 75/121 (2)
RENAULT 130/209 (5)
190/306 (6)
ELF 70/113 (2)
CAMPSA 120/193 (4)
BANC SABADELL 65/105 (2)
LA CAIXA 55/89 (2)
mph/km/h (gear)

RACE DISTANCE: 65 laps, 190.962 miles/307.323 km **RACE WEATHER: Dry, warm and sunny**

Pos.	Driver	Nat.	No.	Entrant	Car/Engine	Laps	Time/Retirement	Speed (mph/km/h)
1	Mika Häkkinen	SF	1	West McLaren Mercedes	McLaren MP4/15-Mercedes FO110J V10	65	1h 33m 55.390s	121.990/196.324
2	David Coulthard	GB	2	West McLaren Mercedes	McLaren MP4/15-Mercedes FO110J V10	65	1h 34m 11.456s	121.643/195.765
3	Rubens Barrichello	BR	4	Scuderia Ferrari Marlboro	Ferrari F1-2000-049 V10	65	1h 34m 24.502s	121.363/195.315
4	Ralf Schumacher	D	9	BMW WilliamsF1 Team	Williams FW22-BMW E41 V10	65	1h 34m 32.701s	121.187/195.032
5	Michael Schumacher	D	3	Scuderia Ferrari Marlboro	Ferrari F1-2000-049 V10	65	1h 34m 43.373s	120.960/194.666
6	Heinz-Harald Frentzen	D	5	Benson & Hedges Jordan	Jordan EJ10-Mugen Honda MF301HE V10	65	1h 35m 17.315s	120.241/193.510
7	Mika Salo	SF	17	Red Bull Sauber Petronas	Sauber C19-Petronas SPE 04A V10	64		
8	Ricardo Zonta	BR	23	Lucky Strike BAR Honda	BAR 02-Honda RA100E V10	64		
9	Giancarlo Fisichella	I	11	Mild Seven Benetton Playlife	Benetton B200-Playlife V10	64		
10	Alexander Wurz	A	12	Mild Seven Benetton Playlife	Benetton B200-Playlife V10	64		
11	Eddie Irvine	GB	7	Jaguar Racing	Jaguar R1-Cosworth CR2 V10	64		
12	Jarno Trulli	I	6	Benson & Hedges Jordan	Jordan EJ10-Mugen Honda MF301HE V10	64		
13	Johnny Herbert	GB	8	Jaguar Racing	Jaguar R1-Cosworth CR2 V10	64		
14	Marc Gene	ESP	20	Telefonica Minardi Fondmetal	Minardi M02-Fondmetal Ford Zetec-R V10	63		
15	Gaston Mazzacane	ARG	21	Telefonica Minardi Fondmetal	Minardi M02-Fondmetal Ford Zetec-R V10	63		
16	Nick Heidfeld	D	15	Gauloises Prost Peugeot	Prost AP03-Peugeot A20 V10	62		
17	Jenson Button	GB	10	BMW WilliamsF1 Team	Williams FW22-BMW E41 V10	61	Engine	
	Jos Verstappen	NL	19	Arrows	Arrows A21-Supertec FB02 V10	25	Gearbox	
	Jacques Villeneuve	CDN	22	Lucky Strike BAR Honda	BAR 02-Honda RA100E V10	21	Engine	
	Jean Alesi	F	14	Gauloises Prost Peugeot	Prost AP03-Peugeot A20 V10	1	Collision with de la Rosa	
	Pedro de la Rosa	ESP	18	Arrows	Arrows A21-Supertec FB02 V10	1	Collision with Alesi	
	Pedro Diniz	BR	16	Red Bull Sauber Petronas	Sauber C19-Petronas SPE 04A V10	0	Spun off	

Fastest lap: Häkkinen, on lap 28, 1m 24.470s, 125.260 mph/201.586 km/h.
Lap record: Giancarlo Fisichella (F1 Jordan 197-Peugeot V10), 1m 22.242s, 128.919 mph/207.475 km/h (1997).

Pit stop
One lap behind leader

Grid order		
3	M. SCHUMACHER	
1	HÄKKINEN	
4	BARRICHELLO	
2	COULTHARD	
9	R. SCHUMACHER	
22	VILLENEUVE	
6	TRULLI	
5	FRENTZEN	
7	IRVINE	
10	BUTTON	
19	VERSTAPPEN	
17	SALO	
11	FISICHELLA	
8	HERBERT	
16	DINIZ	
23	ZONTA	
14	ALESI	
12	WURZ	
15	HEIDFELD	
20	GENE	
21	MAZZACANE	
18	DE LA ROSA	

STARTING GRID

3 M. SCHUMACHER — Ferrari	**1** HÄKKINEN — McLaren
4 BARRICHELLO — Ferrari	**2** COULTHARD — McLaren
9 R. SCHUMACHER — Williams	**22** VILLENEUVE — BAR
6 TRULLI — Jordan	**5** FRENTZEN — Jordan
7 IRVINE — Jaguar	**10** BUTTON — Williams
19 VERSTAPPEN — Arrows	**17** SALO — Sauber
11 FISICHELLA — Benetton	**8** HERBERT — Jaguar
15 ALESI — Prost	**12** WURZ — Benetton
16 DINIZ — Sauber	**23** ZONTA — BAR
15 HEIDFELD — Prost	**20** GENE — Minardi
21 MAZZACANE — Minardi	**18*** DE LA ROSA — Arrows

* times disallowed

Lap chart (laps 52–65) — race running-order chart

```
    52 53 54 55 56 57 58 59 60 61 62 63 64 65
 1   2  2  2  2  2  2  2  2  2  2  2  2  2  2
 2  10 10 10 10 10 10 10 10 10  3  3  3  3  3
 ...
(dense lap-by-lap position matrix)
```

FOR THE RECORD

150th Grand Prix start
Johnny Herbert

50th Grand Prix start
Jarno Trulli

QUALIFYING

Weather: Sunny and hot

Pos.	Driver	Car	Laps	Time
1	Michael Schumacher	Ferrari	10	1m 20.974s
2	Mika Häkkinen	McLaren-Mercedes	11	1m 21.052s
3	David Coulthard	McLaren-Mercedes	11	1m 21.416s
4	Rubens Barrichello	Ferrari	11	1m 21.422s
5	Ralf Schumacher	Williams-BMW	12	1m 21.605s
6	Jacques Villeneuve	BAR-Honda	12	1m 21.963s
7	Jarno Trulli	Jordan-Mugen Honda	12	1m 22.006s
8	Heinz-Harald Frentzen	Jordan-Mugen Honda	12	1m 22.135s
9*	Pedro de la Rosa	Arrows-Supertec	12	1m 22.185s
10	Eddie Irvine	Jaguar-Cosworth	11	1m 22.370s
11	Jenson Button	Williams-BMW	12	1m 22.385s
12	Jos Verstappen	Arrows-Supertec	12	1m 22.421s
13	Mika Salo	Sauber-Petronas	12	1m 22.443s
14	Giancarlo Fisichella	Benetton-Playlife	11	1m 22.569s
15	Johnny Herbert	Jaguar-Cosworth	12	1m 22.781s
16	Pedro Diniz	Sauber-Petronas	12	1m 22.841s
17	Ricardo Zonta	BAR-Honda	12	1m 22.882s
18	Jean Alesi	Prost-Peugeot	12	1m 22.894s
19	Alexander Wurz	Benetton-Playlife	12	1m 23.010s
20	Nick Heidfeld	Prost-Peugeot	6	1m 23.033s
21	Marc Gene	Minardi-Fondmetal	11	1m 23.486s
22	Gaston Mazzacane	Minardi-Fondmetal	12	1m 24.257s

* times disallowed due to fuel irregularities

FRIDAY FREE PRACTICE

Weather: Warm and overcast

Pos.	Driver	Laps	Time
1	Michael Schumacher	18	1m 21.982s
2	Ralf Schumacher	29	1m 22.509s
3	Rubens Barrichello	20	1m 22.549s
4	Jarno Trulli	11	1m 22.582s
5	Jenson Button	30	1m 23.119s
6	Mika Häkkinen	21	1m 23.266s
7	Heinz-Harald Frentzen	37	1m 23.394s
8	Pedro Diniz	3	1m 23.495s
9	Jacques Villeneuve	26	1m 23.582s
10	Jean Alesi	34	1m 23.868s
11	Giancarlo Fisichella	13	1m 24.026s
12	Jos Verstappen	28	1m 24.114s
13	Johnny Herbert	28	1m 24.161s
14	Alexander Wurz	25	1m 24.346s
15	Eddie Irvine	23	1m 24.451s
16	Nick Heidfeld	28	1m 24.461s
17	Ricardo Zonta	27	1m 24.582s
18	Mika Salo	37	1m 24.767s
19	Gaston Mazzacane	33	1m 24.948s
20	Jacques Villeneuve	22	1m 25.166s
21	Pedro de la Rosa	9	1m 25.189s

SATURDAY FREE PRACTICE

Weather: Sunny and warm

Pos.	Driver	Laps	Time
1	Michael Schumacher	27	1m 21.088s
2	David Coulthard	26	1m 21.370s
3	Rubens Barrichello	22	1m 21.372s
4	Mika Häkkinen	19	1m 21.593s
5	Ralf Schumacher	18	1m 21.604s
6	Jarno Trulli	21	1m 21.911s
7	Heinz-Harald Frentzen	26	1m 22.162s
8	Pedro de la Rosa	29	1m 22.206s
9	Jacques Villeneuve	29	1m 22.386s
10	Jenson Button	26	1m 22.465s
11	Jos Verstappen	20	1m 22.468s
12	Giancarlo Fisichella	22	1m 22.493s
13	Alexander Wurz	22	1m 22.605s
14	Eddie Irvine	20	1m 22.642s
15	Mika Salo	22	1m 22.749s
16	Nick Heidfeld	35	1m 22.810s
17	Jean Alesi	25	1m 22.815s
18	Marc Gene	26	1m 22.944s
19	Johnny Herbert	24	1m 23.173s
20	Pedro Diniz	15	1m 23.644s
21	Ricardo Zonta	27	1m 23.942s
22	Gaston Mazzacane	30	1m 24.866s

WARM-UP

Weather: Hot and overcast

Pos.	Driver	Laps	Time
1	Michael Schumacher	13	1m 22.855s
2	Mika Häkkinen	12	1m 23.214s
3	Rubens Barrichello	11	1m 23.427s
4	David Coulthard	11	1m 23.517s
5	Jenson Button	7	1m 24.076s
6	Pedro de la Rosa	13	1m 24.132s
7	Heinz-Harald Frentzen	13	1m 24.248s
8	Jarno Trulli	14	1m 24.334s
9	Ralf Schumacher	10	1m 24.545s
10	Jos Verstappen	10	1m 24.556s
11	Jacques Villeneuve	16	1m 24.877s
12	Jean Alesi	9	1m 24.923s
13	Eddie Irvine	13	1m 24.925s
14	Ricardo Zonta	14	1m 24.985s
15	Giancarlo Fisichella	15	1m 25.149s
16	Johnny Herbert	12	1m 25.210s
17	Nick Heidfeld	11	1m 25.702s
18	Alexander Wurz	15	1m 25.989s
19	Marc Gene	12	1m 26.184s
20	Gaston Mazzacane	15	1m 26.258s
21	Mika Salo	12	1m 26.516s
22	Pedro Diniz	13	1m 26....

RACE FASTEST LAPS

Weather: Dry, warm and sunny

Pos.	Driver	Time	Lap
1	Mika Häkkinen	1m 24.470s	28
2	Michael Schumacher	1m 24.517s	2
3	David Coulthard	1m 24.648s	26
4	Jenson Button	1m 24.729s	20
5	Heinz-Harald Frentzen	1m 25.183s	28
6	Rubens Barrichello	1m 25.288s	24
7	Ralf Schumacher	1m 25.288s	25
8	Jarno Trulli	1m 25.326s	24
9	Mika Salo	1m 25.806s	29
10	Marc Gene	1m 25.896s	24
11	Alexander Wurz	1m 26.147s	19
12	Eddie Irvine	1m 26.239s	64
13	Ricardo Zonta	1m 26.241s	20
14	Jean Alesi	1m 26.352s	34
15	Giancarlo Fisichella	1m 26.663s	19
16	Nick Heidfeld	1m 26.701s	8
17	Johnny Herbert	1m 27.152s	18
18	Jos Verstappen	1m 27.538s	24

POINTS TABLES

DRIVERS

1	Michael Schumacher	36
2	Mika Häkkinen	22
3	David Coulthard	20
4	Rubens Barrichello	13
5	Ralf Schumacher	12
6	Giancarlo Fisichella	8
7 =	Heinz-Harald Frentzen	5
7 =	Jacques Villeneuve	5
9	Jarno Trulli	4
10	Jenson Button	3
11 =	Ricardo Zonta	1
11 =	Mika Salo	1

CONSTRUCTORS

1	Ferrari	49
2	McLaren	42
3	Williams	15
4	Jordan	9
5	Benetton	8
6	BAR	6
7	Sauber	1

CHASSIS LOG BOOK

	Driver	Chassis
1	Häkkinen	McLaren MP4/15/4
2	Coulthard	McLaren MP4/15/5
	spare	McLaren MP4/15/1
3	M. Schumacher	Ferrari F1-2000/200
4	Barrichello	Ferrari F1-2000/199
	spare	Ferrari F1-2000/198
5	Frentzen	Jordan E10/6
6	Trulli	Jordan E10/3
	spare	Jordan E10/4
7	Irvine	Jaguar R1/4
8	Herbert	Jaguar R1/1
	spare	Jaguar R1/3
9	R. Schumacher	Williams FW22/6
10	Button	Williams FW22/5
	spare	Williams FW22/4
11	Fisichella	Benetton B200/5
12	Wurz	Benetton B200/2
	spare	Benetton B200/3
14	Alesi	Prost AP03/3
15	Heidfeld	Prost AP03/4
	spare	Prost AP03/1
16	Diniz	Sauber C19/4
17	Salo	Sauber C19/2
	spare	Sauber C19/1
18	de la Rosa	Arrows A21/3
19	Verstappen	Arrows A21/4
	spare	Arrows A21/2
20	Gene	Minardi M02/3
21	Mazzacane	Minardi M02/4
	spare	Minardi M02/1
22	Villeneuve	BAR 02/5
23	Zonta	BAR 02/1
	spare	BAR 02/2

M. SCHUMACHER
HÄKKINEN
COULTHARD
BARRICHELLO
FISICHELLA
DE LA ROSA

EUROPEAN
grand prix

FIA WORLD CHAMPIONSHIP • ROUND 6

Previous spread: The changeable weather once again dominated proceedings on the Eifel circuit.

Left: David Coulthard was only able to convert his pole position into third place in the race.
Both photographs: Paul-Henri Cahier

Below left: Pedro de la Rosa was mightily impressive in the Arrows.
Mark Thompson/Allsport

MICHAEL Schumacher showcased his genius as F1's rain master *par excellence* with a flawless European Grand Prix victory in front of his drenched, but delighted fans at the circuit deep in the Eifel mountains where motor racing tradition hangs in the air like the mists in the surrounding pine forests.

Schumacher and Häkkinen were in a class of their own, lapping every other car in the field as they continued what was increasingly assuming the appearance of a two-horse battle for the title crown. With six of the season's 17 races completed, Schumacher's fourth win of the year left him 18 points ahead of his rival who had a lone victory at Barcelona to his credit so far.

It was also the 39th win of Schumacher's career, consolidating his third place in the all-time grands prix winner's stakes and leaving him just two wins short of the late Ayrton Senna's career total.

By any standards, Schumacher's performance raised nostalgic memories of heady drives on the adjacent, epic 14-mile Nürburgring circuit which now lies as a silent and abandoned epitaph to a past era of grand prix racing adjacent to the current circuit.

The 'new Nürburgring' is hardly the stuff of which legends are made, but Schumacher's drive to victory here certainly was. Despite a race-long battle with Häkkinen, whom he displaced from the lead with a decisive overtaking move after 11 of the race's 67 laps, Schumacher asserted a decisive edge which became dramatically accentuated as a light shower developed into a relentless downpour.

Häkkinen's dramatic sprint into the lead at the start left Schumacher far from delighted as the McLaren-Mercedes gave his Ferrari's left front wheel a firm tap as it accelerated through from the second row of the grid. Michael later commented that he thought this was all a little unnecessary, an observation which many onlookers judged a trifle ironic, given the Ferrari team leader's inclination towards weaving in front of his rivals to protect his own advantage while accelerating away from the grid.

Further back, Jarno Trulli's Jordan EJ10 became the first casualty of the race when he was hit from behind by Giancarlo Fisichella's Benetton. 'My car was completely damaged and I was lucky to keep driving, as otherwise it would have been very dangerous,' said Trulli. 'I am obviously very disappointed as we knew we were capable of getting a good result here.'

Fisichella was lucky to be able to continue. 'The incident with Ralf Schumacher and Trulli wasn't my fault,' he shrugged, 'but luckily my car was only very slightly damaged, so I was able to drive it without problems.' Trulli pulled off gently with a damaged left rear wheel and suspension.

By the end of the opening lap Häkkinen led by 0.5s from Schumacher with Coulthard third ahead of Barrichello. Already a gap was opening back to Jacques Villeneuve in fifth place while, further back, Pedro de la Rosa overtook Arrows team-mate Jos Verstappen for ninth and Jean Alesi squeezed ahead of Jenson Button's Williams for 15th.

It certainly wasn't a good race for Eddie Jordan's lads. Compounding Trulli's misfortune, Heinz-Harald Frentzen found himself forced to take to the grass at the first corner in order to avoid another collision. He dropped to 12th and was steeling himself for a long slog back through the pack when his Mugen Honda V10 expired on the third lap.

'I had escaped being caught up in a collision at the first corner, and I was feeling in control, running on a high fuel load which was our strategy decision, when my engine blew,' he explained.

On the fourth lap Jenson Button overtook Ralf Schumacher to take sixth, just as Eddie Irvine's Jaguar was displaced from eighth by de la Rosa. It took only a couple of laps before Fisichella was challenging Villeneuve — the BAR already 5.9s down on Barrichello's Ferrari as rain began falling seriously on lap five — while de la Rosa was quick to move ahead of Ralf Schumacher's Williams for seventh.

Despite having a heavier fuel load than Schumacher's Ferrari, Häkkinen repulsed his rival until lap 11 when Michael neatly outbraked him to take the lead going into the tight chicane just before the pits.

By now the rain was absolutely sheeting down, badly hampering visibility for all the competitors, and when the Ferrari and McLaren returned to the race Schumacher really began to extend his advantage.

Häkkinen admitted that he was perhaps too tentative here, although it was clear that he was originally running a heavier fuel load than Schumacher, but his efforts to run a longer opening stint than the Ferrari were sluiced away with the rain.

'I didn't want to push too hard and risk spinning off on the slippery track,' he shrugged. Meanwhile, Michael was pressing on hard, pleasantly surprised that his harder compound rubber was giving him such consistent grip.

At that first stop Michael was stationary for 12.1s, but a sticking rear wheel delayed Mika 3s longer. By the time Schumacher was back in the race he was 11.58s ahead of the McLaren, now with Coulthard between them.

From then on, any potential for a decisive counter-attack, trickled away from Häkkinen. Sure enough, for many laps in the torrential rain during the middle of the race he proved easily capable of trading fastest laps with Michael. But it wasn't enough.

'Everything was perfect and the car worked well in the rain,' said Schumacher. 'The only critical point was when it started to rain. None of us in front [of the field] wanted to pit as it was not clear that this [rain] was for real. But as soon as we saw the others going faster on rain tyres, then I came in immediately.'

The tactically astute Ferrari team subsequently brought Schumacher in for his second stop at the end of lap 35, allowing Häkkinen to surf back through into the lead. But although the Finn managed to open out a 25s advantage by lap 43, the McLaren team's failure to bring him in two laps earlier meant that he was only 21s in front

NÜRBURGRING QUALIFYING

Jenson Button had stopped the clocks with fastest time for the BMW Williams squad in Friday free practice, a performance which understandably sent the UK tabloid media into a frenzy of excitement. The mature young 20-year-old was sufficiently levelheaded to acknowledge, albeit obliquely, that this had little to do with the dazzling level of talent attributed to him by his supporters, more to do with a light fuel load and a fresh set of tyres shortly before the chequered flag.

'I don't want to get too excited, as it's not qualifying,' he said. 'A lot is going to change, even if I must admit it would be nice to be among those at the very top tomorrow at this time. My target is to qualify in the top 10, as close as possible to Ralf [Schumacher's] time.'

Sadly, Jenson's hopes were not to be realised. On Saturday morning, he touched a slippery kerb with a rear wheel and rumpled his Williams FW22 against a tyre barrier, wrecking front and rear suspension, wings and nose section. Come qualifying, he would line up 11th, 0.4s adrift his team-mate Ralf Schumacher who took fifth on the grid, best of the rest behind the established heavy hitters.

Instead, David Coulthard took over as top Brit when it mattered, guiding his McLaren-Mercedes to a well-deserved — and long overdue — pole position, his first since Montreal two years ago. Still nursing uncomfortably cracked ribs as a lingering legacy of his Learjet crash at Lyon almost three weeks earlier, the Scot produced an immaculate performance on an intermittently wet circuit to ease out Michael Schumacher's Ferrari F1-2000 by 0.138s.

Bridgestone had brought along both soft and super-soft tyre compounds, but the real problem in the cool conditions was that the latter choice tended to grain very quickly, aggravating the incipient understeer on a track surface which had been washed clean of any coating of rubber by heavy overnight rain.

'It's also important to set your car up for qualifying to get the best out of new rubber, because there is a big difference between that and old tyres,' said Ferrari's Rubens Barrichello who wound up fourth behind Coulthard, Schumacher and Häkkinen.

The World Championship points leader was happy at least to be ahead of Häkkinen, the man he privately acknowledged as his sole title rival. 'I am sure I could have gone quicker, especially as I made a mistake at turn five on my quick run,' he said. 'Starting from the front row will allow us to work out a good strategy for the race.'

Along with Jacques Villeneuve's BAR and Jos Verstappen's Arrows A21, the Ferrari drivers were the only ones who opted for the softer of the two available tyre compounds.

'Most of the drivers chose the extra-soft specification as we expected,' said Bridgestone technical manager Yoshihiko Ichikawa. 'However, they may find that they have more understeer compared with their rivals using the soft compound.'

'Everybody will be making a big effort to overcome any understeer problems and in the race the solution may be to use scrubbed tyres.'

In the Jordan camp, Heinz-Harald Frentzen finished the day storming out of the circuit in a temper after making something of a mess of his qualifying efforts. The pole-sitter in last year's European GP, 'H-H' reckoned he could put the Jordan EJ10 on the second row this time round, but everything went wrong in the changeable conditions.

Balked badly by Verstappen's Arrows on what he hoped would be his best run, he failed to improve late in the session and had to be content with tenth on 1m 18.830s, his frustration heightened by the fact that team-mate Jarno Trulli vaulted through to sixth fastest in the final minute.

Giancarlo Fisichella had mixed feelings about winding up seventh on 1m 18.697s. 'It is quite a good result, but I am angry at losing a position because of Ralf Schumacher,' he fumed.

'He braked hard on the last corner and slowed me down so I didn't get past the chequered flag for my last flying lap. He didn't only ruin my last lap, but there were two or three other cars, including Villeneuve, behind me too. There had been a small problem on starting my engine, which meant the last lap was cut quite fine, but still I know I could have improved my time.'

Eddie Irvine gave the Jaguar team's morale something of a boost by qualifying eighth, nine places ahead of Johnny Herbert who was starting his 150th Grand Prix at the Nürburgring.

'Eddie did a solid job and could probably have found another couple of tenths to put him fifth or sixth,' said technical director Gary Anderson.

'He was adamant that he couldn't see any rain coming when our spotters told him it was on the way. After I suggested that maybe he should keep his eye on the road and that we'd watch the weather, he put in a really good lap.'

Behind Button, de la Rosa and Verstappen qualified their Arrows A21s 12th and 13th ahead of a disappointed Alexander Wurz, the Austrian complaining of excessive understeer on his Benetton. Next up were Diniz and Herbert.

The beleaguered Prost-Peugeot team also found qualifying turning into a bitter disappointment, with Nick Heidfeld being disqualified from the morning after his AP03 tipped the scales 3 kg below the all-up 600 kg weight minimum. Team-mate Jean Alesi qualified 18th after crashing his spare car on a wet patch of circuit and then suffering a gearbox failure before his race car

EUROPEAN GRAND PRIX

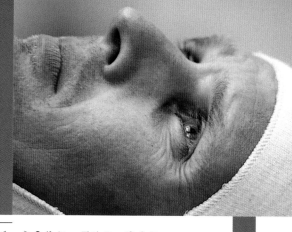

Far left and centre left: Anything you can do! McLaren and Ferrari defended their garage entrances with screens.

Left: In contrast to his victory the previous year, Johnny Herbert's European GP was not a happy one.

Below left: Michael Schumacher's Ferrari steps out of shape in the treacherous conditions.

All photographs: Paul-Henri Cahier

EUROPEAN GRAND PRIX

---

when he made his second stop at the end of lap 45.

In reality, Häkkinen needed a 32s lead if he was to be sure of resuming the race ahead of Schumacher, but the fact remained that this delay cost at least 5s, a chunk of precious extra time he might have used to good effect to press the winning Ferrari even harder during the closing stages.

'If I hadn't caught those backmarkers before the finish, I would certainly have got very close,' said Häkkinen. 'But naturally I also understand that Michael could have pushed harder too. Obviously there are improvements to be made [by the team in signalling] the backmarkers, and today that situation didn't help me too much.'

On lap 30, Eddie Irvine and Jos Verstappen, battling for seventh, collided at the first corner. The Jaguar was pitched into a spin and tagged by Ralf Schumacher's Williams, the German driver struggling with a heavy fuel load on a one-stop strategy.

'My car developed brake problems,' said Ralf, 'and on the straights I had to pump the pedal, which caused me a couple of off-track moments. I saw the accident coming between Irvine and Verstappen, but I expected them to both slide off onto the inside. As Irvine's rear moved onto the right in front of me, I was already accelerating and could not avoid hitting it.'

Irvine momentarily resumed, but his damaged rear wing flew off the Jaguar almost immediately and he spun off going into the next corner. Verstappen also failed to survive the skirmish, crashing heavily further round the same lap.

Jacques Villeneuve also had a disappointing afternoon. Having run fifth in the early stages, a first tyre change to wets on lap 15 dropped him briefly to 13th, but he was back up again to seventh before he retired on lap 46.

'I was coming in for my second pit stop and on my in lap I was told just to bring the car in and switch off — I guess there must have been a problem that showed up on the telemetry,' said the frustrated Canadian after another good drive.

In third place, meanwhile, Coulthard was frustrated by an acute nervousness at the back of his McLaren which made it very difficult to drive and the Scot counted himself lucky to have scraped home third ahead of Rubens Barrichello.

'There wasn't anything I could do,' said Coulthard whose car had been set up for drier conditions in a bet-hedging exercise and was therefore short on aerodynamic downforce.

'It was up to him [Barrichello] whether he felt able to pass me or not. I drove the

whole race as fast as I was able to, considering the balance of the car.'

Commented Barrichello: 'I am a bit disappointed as I could have done better than fourth. The race was difficult mainly because of the lack of visibility caused by the rain, but the car was good except that I had a small problem with my down-shifts.

'My initial thought [in retrospect] is that maybe I stayed out one lap too long on dry tyres; the three-stop strategy which meant I had to overtake slower cars in poor visibility was not ideal, but it was definitely the quickest way to make up lost time. Maybe I should have been on the podium today.'

Giancarlo Fisichella drove a superb race in the Benetton B200 to take fifth place at the chequered flag ahead of the outstanding Pedro de la Rosa who put the potential of the impressive Arrows A21 on public display to claim the team's first point of the season.

Williams ended the day very disappointed, with Patrick Head admitting that it was a very poor performance by the team as a whole. 'We may have been guilty of letting the car out for too long on the dry tyres,' said the Williams technical chief, 'but there was clearly plenty of potential for points today.'

After handling himself with supreme confidence and assurance in his first wet F1 race, Button bumped the rear of Johnny Herbert's Jaguar — which was later pushed off by Alexander Wurz's Benetton — in heavy traffic which exposed the nose of his Williams. The best assessment was that water then leaked into the front of the chassis and caused some sort of electrical shut-down three laps from the chequered flag.

Time and again Button had attempted to pull out and overtake Herbert's Jaguar

— only to find that the low ride height of his Williams was causing the central underbody 'plank' to bog down in standing water and actually lose him speed.

For his part, Herbert — who had scored the Stewart-Ford team's sole GP victory under similarly unpredictable circumstances on this same circuit barely eight months earlier — remained philosophical about his own misfortune.

'As it began to rain, I radioed that I was coming in, but I stayed out for another lap on grooves [dry tyres] because I wanted to be absolutely sure it was the right decision,' he said.

'As it turned out, the extra lap all alone on wets would have been to my advantage. A point was always going to be out of reach. To be honest, finishing seventh is no use, so the incident with Wurz doesn't matter too much. It felt good to make the right decision on the tyres again, and it was a good race up until the sudden ending.'

Herbert's abrupt departure from the fray left Pedro Diniz in seventh place with the Sauber C19, his team-mate Mika Salo having departed the fray much earlier with gearbox problems.

'I have to be satisfied with seventh, because I was last after I spun on lap three,' said the Brazilian. 'In the wet conditions I had a lot of understeer, visibility was really bad and it was hard to catch and pass several other cars.'

Yet at the end of it all, this was another remarkable day which belonged totally to Michael Schumacher. His relentless consistency and iron nerve had broken Häkkinen's resolve in absolutely appalling conditions. It was becoming difficult to see just how this title chase would go down to the wire at the final race of the season.

No truth in Häkkinen retirement rumours

WORLD Champion Mika Häkkinen confirmed at the Nürburgring that speculation surrounding his possible retirement at the end of the season was totally groundless.

'The rumours are not true, I am not planning to retire,' said Häkkinen who has a firm contract with McLaren for at least the next two seasons. 'I am intending to continue racing. That's the plan at the moment.'

The Finn also declined to comment on speculation — which proved true — that his wife Erja was pregnant with their first child. 'It is a private matter which I don't want to talk about,' he said.

McLaren International managing director Martin Whitmarsh admitted that Häkkinen had been so worried about the rumours that last week he wrote an open letter to the entire McLaren workforce reaffirming his total commitment to the team.

'Mika made it clear that he was extremely concerned about these rumours and assured the staff that the is committed to winning races and championships for us this year, next year and for some time beyond,' said Whitmarsh.

'There wasn't anything I could do,' said Norbert Haug, the Mercedes-Benz motor sport director, also offered a ringing endorsement of the present McLaren driver line-up and confirmed that he wanted to continue with Häkkinen and Coulthard in the future.

DIARY

Mercedes-Benz quashes speculation that it might supply the Prost F1 team with engines in 2001 with confirmation that it would continue its exclusive deal with McLaren.

Michael and Ralf Schumacher insist that any bad blood between them following their wheel-banging skirmish in the Spanish Grand Prix was whipped up by the media.

Global insurance giant Allianz announces a collaborative programme with the BMW Williams team and the FIA to develop the transfer of F1 safety technology into a road application.

The Ferrari team takes delivery of a top-of-the-range Piaggio Executive P180 Avanti private aircraft for use in ferrying senior company personnel.

165

NÜRBURGRING
19–21 MAY 2000

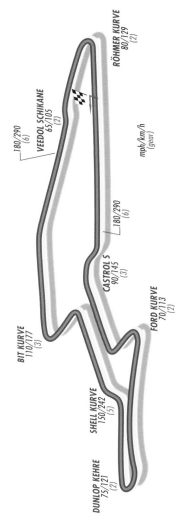

ROUND 6

WARSTEINER
grand prix of
EUROPE

NÜRBURGRING — GRAND PRIX CIRCUIT

CIRCUIT LENGTH: 2.831 miles/4.556 km

- BIT KURVE 110/177 (3)
- VEEDOL SCHIKANE 65/105 (2)
- RÖHMER KURVE 80/129 (2)
- 180/290 (6)
- CASTROL S 90/145 (3)
- FORD KURVE 70/113 (2)
- SHELL KURVE 150/242 (5)
- DUNLOP KEHRE 75/121 (2)
- 180/290 (6)
- mph/km/h (gear)

RACE DISTANCE: 67 laps, 189.664 miles/305.235 km **RACE WEATHER: Dry and cloudy, followed by heavy rain**

Pos.	Driver	Nat.	No.	Entrant	Car/Engine	Laps	Time/Retirement	Speed (mph/km/h)
1	Michael Schumacher	D	3	Scuderia Ferrari Marlboro	Ferrari F1-2000-049 V10	67	1h 42m 00.307s	111.561/179.540
2	Mika Häkkinen	SF	1	West McLaren Mercedes	McLaren MP4/15-Mercedes FO110J V10	67	1h 42m 14.129s	111.310/179.136
3	David Coulthard	GB	2	West McLaren Mercedes	McLaren MP4/15-Mercedes FO110J V10	66		
4	Rubens Barrichello	BR	4	Scuderia Ferrari Marlboro	Ferrari F1-2000-049 V10	66		
5	Giancarlo Fisichella	I	11	Mild Seven Benetton Playlife	Benetton B200-Playlife V10	66		
6	Pedro de la Rosa	ESP	18	Arrows	Arrows A21-Supertec FB02 V10	66		
7	Pedro Diniz	BR	16	Red Bull Sauber Petronas	Sauber C19-Petronas SPE 04A V10	65		
8	Gaston Mazzacane	ARG	21	Telefonica Minardi Fondmetal	Minardi M02-Fondmetal Ford Zetec-R V10	65		
9	Jean Alesi	F	14	Gauloises Prost Peugeot	Prost AP03-Peugeot A20 V10	65		
10	Jenson Button	GB	10	BMW WilliamsF1 Team	Williams FW22-BMW E41 V10	62	Electrics	
11	Johnny Herbert	GB	8	Jaguar Racing	Jaguar R1-Cosworth CR2 V10	61	Collision with Wurz	
12	Alexander Wurz	A	12	Mild Seven Benetton Playlife	Benetton B200-Playlife V10	61	Collision with Herbert	
	Ricardo Zonta	BR	23	Lucky Strike BAR Honda	BAR 02-Honda RA100E V10	51	Spun off	
	Marc Gene	ESP	20	Telefonica Minardi Fondmetal	Minardi M02-Fondmetal Ford Zetec-R V10	47	Throttle pedal	
	Jacques Villeneuve	CDN	22	Lucky Strike BAR Honda	BAR 02-Honda RA100E V10	46	Engine	
	Eddie Irvine	GB	7	Jaguar Racing	Jaguar R1-Cosworth CR2 V10	29	Collision with R. Schumacher	
	Jos Verstappen	NL	19	Arrows	Arrows A21-Supertec FB02 V10	29	Accident	
	Ralf Schumacher	D	9	BMW WilliamsF1 Team	Williams FW22-BMW E41 V10	29	Collision with Irvine	
	Mika Salo	SF	17	Red Bull Sauber Petronas	Sauber C19-Petronas SPE 04A V10	27	Drive shaft	
	Heinz-Harald Frentzen	D	5	Benson & Hedges Jordan	Jordan EJ10-Mugen Honda MF301HE V10	2	Engine	
	Jarno Trulli	I	6	Benson & Hedges Jordan	Jordan EJ10-Mugen Honda MF301HE V10	0	Collision with Fisichella	
EXC	Nick Heidfeld	D	15	Gauloises Prost Peugeot	Prost AP03-Peugeot A20 V10		Underweight in qualifying	

Fastest lap: M. Schumacher, on lap 8, 1m 22.269s, 123.879 mph/199.365 km/h.

Lap record: Heinz-Harald Frentzen (F1 Williams FW19-Renault V10), 1m 18.805s, 129.325 mph/208.128 km/h (1997).

Lap chart

Grid order	1	2	3	4	5	6	7	8	9	10	11	12	13	14	15	16	17	18	19	20	21	22	23	24	25	26	27	28	29	30	31	32	33	34	35	36	37	38	39	40	41	42	43	44	45	46	47	48	49	50	51	52	53
2 COULTHARD	1	1	1	1	1	1	1	1	1	1	1	1	1	1	1	1	1	1	3	3	3	3	3	3	3	3	3	3	3	3	3	3	3	3	3	3	3	3	3	3	3	3	3	3	3	3	3	3	3	3	3	3	3
3 M. SCHUMACHER	3	3	3	3	3	3	3	3	3	3	3	3	3	3	3	3	3	3	1	1	1	1	1	1	2	2	2	2	2	2	1	1	1	1	1	1	1	1	1	1	1	1	1	1	1	1	1	1	1	1	1	1	1
1 HÄKKINEN	2	2	2	2	2	2	2	2	2	2	2	2	2	2	2	2	2	2	2	2	2	2	2	2	1	1	1	1	1	1	2	2	2	2	2	2	2	2	2	2	2	2	2	2	2	2	2	2	2	2	2	2	2
4 BARRICHELLO	4	4	4	4	4	4	4	4	4	4	4	4	4	4	4	4	4	4	4	4	4	4	4	4	4	4	4	4	4	4	4	4	4	4	4	4	4	4	4	4	4	4	4	4	4	4	4	4	4	4	4	4	4
9 R. SCHUMACHER	22	22	22	22	22	22	11	11	11	11	11	11	11	18	18	18	18	18	8	8	8	8	8	8	8	8	8	8	8																								
6 TRULLI	9	9	9																																																		
11 FISICHELLA	11	11	11	11	11	11	22	22	22	22	22	22	22	4	7	7	7	7	19	19	19	4	4	4	10	10	10	12	12	12	12	12	12	23	23	23	23	16	16	16	16	20	20	20	21	21	21	21	21				
7 IRVINE	7	7	7	7	7	7	7	7	7	9	9	9	9	9	9	9	9	9	9	9	22	22	22	22	14	14	14	14	14																								
22 VILLENEUVE	19	18	18	18	18	18	18	18	18	7	7	7	7	12	12	12	12	12	23	23	23	23	23	14	18	18	18	10	10	10	10	10	10	10	12	12	12	12	23	23	23	23	23	16	16	16	20						
5 FRENTZEN	18	19	19	19	19	19	9	9	9																																												
10 BUTTON	12	12	12	12	12	12	12	12	12	12	12	12	12	7	4	4	4	4	4	4	4	10	10	10	12	12	12	16	16	16	16	16	16	16	16	16	16	20	20	20	20	16	16										
18 DE LA ROSA	5	5	14	14	14	14	14	14	14	14	14	14	14	10	10	10	10	10	12	12	12	12	12	12	23	23	23	23	23	23	23	23	23	12	20	20	20	23	12	12	12	12	12	23	23	23	16	16	16	16	16	16	16
19 VERSTAPPEN	10	14	10	10	10	10	10	10	10	20	20	20	20	20	20	20	20	20	20	20	20	20	20	20	20	20	20	20	20	20	20	20	20	20	23	23	23																
12 WURZ	14	10	20	20	20	20	20	20	20	23	23	23	23	23	23	23	23	23	10	10	10	16	16	16	16	16	16	21	21	21	21	14	14	14	14	14	14	21	21	21	21	21	21	12	12	12	12	12					
16 DINIZ	16	16	17	17	17	17	23	23	23	16	16	16	16	16	16	16	16	16	16	16	16	21	21	21	21	21	21	23	23	23	23	21	21	21	21	21	21	16	16	16	16	23	23	21	20	20	23	23	23	21	21	21	21
8 HERBERT	17	17	16	16	16	16	16	16	16	17	17	17	17	17	17	17	17	17	17	17	17	23	14	23	16	16	16	20	20	20	20	23	23	23	16	16	16	14	14	14	14	14	14	14	14	14							
14 ALESI	20	20	20	23	23	23	17	17	17	8	8	8	8	8	8	8	8	8	7	7	7	7	7	7	7	7	7	16	16	16	14	14	14	16	16	16	20	20	20	20	20	20	20	20									
23 ZONTA	8	8	21	21	21	21	21	21	21	21	21	21	21	21	21	21	21	21	21	21	21	21	21	21	14	14	14	14	14	14	21	21	20	20	20	20	14	14	14	14	14												
17 SALO	23	23	16	16	16	16	16	16	16	16	16	16	16	16	16	16	16	16	16	16	16	16	16	16	16																												
20 GENE	21	21																																																			
21 MAZZACANE	21	21																																																			

Pit stop · One lap behind leader

STARTING GRID

	2 COULTHARD McLaren		3 M. SCHUMACHER Ferrari
	1 HÄKKINEN McLaren		4 BARRICHELLO Ferrari
	9 R. SCHUMACHER Williams		6 TRULLI Jordan
	11 FISICHELLA Benetton		7 IRVINE Jaguar
	10 BUTTON Williams		5 FRENTZEN Jordan
	22 VILLENEUVE BAR		18 DE LA ROSA Arrows
	19 VERSTAPPEN Arrows		12 WURZ Benetton
	16 DINIZ Sauber		8 HERBERT Jaguar
	14 ALESI Prost		23 ZONTA BAR
	17 SALO Sauber		20 GENE Minardi
	21 MAZZACANE Minardi		

Lap chart (leader/position progression, laps 53–67):

Lap	53	54	55	56	57	58	59	60	61	62	63	64	65	66	67
	3	3	3	3	3	3	3	3	3	3	3	3	3	3	3
	1	1	1	1	1	1	1	1	1	1	1	1	1	1	1
	2	2	2	2	2	2	2	2	2	2	2	2	2	2	2
	4	4	4	4	4	4	4	4	4	4	4	4	4	4	4
	18	18	18	18	18	18	18	18	18	18	18	18	18	18	18
	11	11	11	11	11	11	11	11	11	11	11	11	11	11	11
	10	10	10	10	10	10	10	10	10	10	16	16	16	16	16
	12	12	12	12	16	16	16	16	16	16	21	21	21	21	21
	16	16	16	16	12	12	21	21	21	21	12	12	14	14	14
	14	14	14	14	14	14	14	14	14	14	14	14	14	14	14

TIME SHEETS

QUALIFYING

Weather: Wet track at start, light rain mid-session

Pos.	Driver	Car	Laps	Time
1	David Coulthard	McLaren-Mercedes	8	1m 17.529s
2	Michael Schumacher	Ferrari	8	1m 17.667s
3	Mika Häkkinen	McLaren-Mercedes	9	1m 17.785s
4	Rubens Barrichello	Ferrari	9	1m 18.227s
5	Ralf Schumacher	Williams-BMW	9	1m 18.515s
6	Jarno Trulli	Jordan-Mugen Honda	9	1m 18.612s
7	Giancarlo Fisichella	Benetton-Playlife	8	1m 18.697s
8	Eddie Irvine	Jaguar-Cosworth	9	1m 18.703s
9	Jacques Villeneuve	BAR-Honda	9	1m 18.742s
10	Heinz-Harald Frentzen	Jordan-Mugen Honda	8	1m 18.830s
11	Jenson Button	Williams-BMW	11	1m 18.887s
12	Pedro de la Rosa	Arrows-Supertec	8	1m 19.024s
13*	Nick Heidfeld	Prost-Peugeot	10	1m 19.147s
14	Jos Verstappen	Arrows-Supertec	11	1m 19.378s
15	Alexander Wurz	Benetton-Playlife	8	1m 19.422s
16	Pedro Diniz	Sauber-Petronas	9	1m 19.638s
17	Johnny Herbert	Jaguar-Cosworth	11	1m 19.651s
18	Jean Alesi	Prost-Peugeot	8	1m 19.766s
19	Ricardo Zonta	BAR-Honda	9	1m 19.814s
20	Mika Salo	Sauber-Petronas	10	1m 20.162s
21	Marc Gene	Minardi-Fondmetal	7	1m 20.715s
22	Gaston Mazzacane	Minardi-Fondmetal	11	1m 21.015s

* excluded from meeting for being underweight

FRIDAY FREE PRACTICE

Weather: Cool and bright, drying track

Pos.	Driver	Laps	Time
1	Jenson Button	42	1m 19.808s
2	Alexander Wurz	36	1m 20.248s
3	Mika Häkkinen	25	1m 20.300s
4	David Coulthard	25	1m 20.507s
5	Michael Schumacher	35	1m 20.519s
6	Ralf Schumacher	14	1m 20.548s
7	Jarno Trulli	21	1m 20.609s
8	Ricardo Zonta	32	1m 20.709s
9	Nick Heidfeld	37	1m 20.751s
10	Jacques Villeneuve	30	1m 20.786s
11	Marc Gene	35	1m 20.801s
12	Pedro Diniz	34	1m 20.850s
13	Giancarlo Fisichella	32	1m 20.862s
14	Rubens Barrichello	33	1m 20.891s
15	Heinz-Harald Frentzen	18	1m 20.992s
16	Eddie Irvine	24	1m 21.246s
17	Johnny Herbert	22	1m 21.323s
18	Jean Alesi	32	1m 21.442s
19	Jos Verstappen	23	1m 21.655s
20	Pedro de la Rosa	30	1m 21.659s
21	Gaston Mazzacane	42	1m 22.135s
22	Mika Salo	24	1m 22.161s

SATURDAY FREE PRACTICE

Weather: Cool and bright, damp track

Pos.	Driver	Laps	Time
1	Michael Schumacher	36	1m 18.527s
2	Rubens Barrichello	26	1m 18.754s
3	Mika Häkkinen	28	1m 18.761s
4	David Coulthard	25	1m 18.907s
5	Heinz-Harald Frentzen	34	1m 19.011s
6	Giancarlo Fisichella	29	1m 19.038s
7	Jacques Villeneuve	38	1m 19.225s
8	Ralf Schumacher	26	1m 19.302s
9	Pedro de la Rosa	25	1m 19.333s
10	Jarno Trulli	35	1m 19.409s
11	Ricardo Zonta	29	1m 19.667s
12	Johnny Herbert	33	1m 19.745s
13	Jenson Button	15	1m 19.756s
14	Nick Heidfeld	36	1m 19.833s
15	Jean Alesi	27	1m 19.894s
16	Alexander Wurz	27	1m 19.902s
17	Eddie Irvine	29	1m 19.914s
18	Mika Salo	28	1m 19.991s
19	Marc Gene	27	1m 20.262s
20	Pedro Diniz	27	1m 20.283s
21	Jos Verstappen	11	1m 20.382s
22	Gaston Mazzacane	33	1m 21.177s

WARM-UP

Weather: Damp and overcast

Pos.	Driver	Laps	Time
1	Michael Schumacher	16	1m 20.251s
2	Mika Häkkinen	16	1m 20.260s
3	Heinz-Harald Frentzen	16	1m 20.899s
4	Rubens Barrichello	15	1m 21.042s
5	Jos Verstappen	19	1m 21.451s
6	David Coulthard	14	1m 21.604s
7	Pedro de la Rosa	13	1m 21.725s
8	Jacques Villeneuve	15	1m 21.760s
9	Eddie Irvine	17	1m 21.847s
10	Jarno Trulli	15	1m 22.046s
11	Pedro Diniz	14	1m 22.130s
12	Marc Gene	14	1m 22.137s
13	Alexander Wurz	15	1m 22.246s
14	Mika Salo	16	1m 22.277s
15	Jean Alesi	17	1m 22.305s
16	Ralf Schumacher	14	1m 22.437s
17	Giancarlo Fisichella	13	1m 22.521s
18	Jenson Button	15	1m 22.703s
19	Ricardo Zonta	13	1m 23.144s
20	Johnny Herbert	13	1m 23.410s
21	Gaston Mazzacane	13	1m 23.746s

RACE FASTEST LAPS

Weather: Dry and cloudy, followed by heavy rain

Pos.	Driver	Time	Lap
1	Michael Schumacher	1m 22.269s	8
2	Rubens Barrichello	1m 22.288s	8
3	Mika Häkkinen	1m 22.289s	7
4	David Coulthard	1m 22.339s	8
5	Pedro de la Rosa	1m 23.125s	8
6	Giancarlo Fisichella	1m 23.255s	5
7	Jos Verstappen	1m 23.369s	8
8	Jacques Villeneuve	1m 23.390s	8
9	Jenson Button	1m 23.485s	8
10	Alexander Wurz	1m 23.688s	8
11	Ralf Schumacher	1m 23.802s	9
12	Jean Alesi	1m 23.898s	7
13	Eddie Irvine	1m 24.008s	8
14	Marc Gene	1m 24.018s	8
15	Mika Salo	1m 24.346s	5
16	Ricardo Zonta	1m 24.715s	8
17	Johnny Herbert	1m 24.772s	4
18	Gaston Mazzacane	1m 24.798s	8
19	Pedro Diniz	1m 24.937s	2
20	Heinz-Harald Frentzen		2

CHASSIS LOG BOOK

1	Häkkinen	McLaren MP4/15/4
2	Coulthard	McLaren MP4/15/5
spare		McLaren MP4/15/1
3	M. Schumacher	Ferrari F1-2000/200
4	Barrichello	Ferrari F1-2000/202
spare		Ferrari F1-2000/199
5	Frentzen	Jordan E10/6
6	Trulli	Jordan E10/5
spare		Jordan E10/4
7	Irvine	Jaguar R1/4
8	Herbert	Jaguar R1/1
spare		Jaguar R1/5
9	R. Schumacher	Williams FW22/5
10	Button	Williams FW22/4
spare		Williams FW22/3
11	Fisichella	Benetton B200/4
12	Wurz	Benetton B200/2
spare		Benetton B200/6
14	Alesi	Prost AP03/3
15	Heidfeld	Prost AP03/1
spare		Prost AP03/4
16	Diniz	Sauber C19/4
17	Salo	Sauber C19/2
spare		Sauber C19/1
18	de la Rosa	Arrows A21/3
19	Verstappen	Arrows A21/4
spare		Arrows A21/2
20	Gene	Minardi M02/3
21	Mazzacane	Minardi M02/4
spare		Minardi M02/1
22	Villeneuve	BAR 02/2
23	Zonta	BAR 02/1
spare		BAR 02/4

POINTS TABLES

DRIVERS

1	Michael Schumacher	46
2	Mika Häkkinen	28
3	David Coulthard	24
4	Rubens Barrichello	16
5	Ralf Schumacher	12
6	Giancarlo Fisichella	10
7 =	Jacques Villeneuve	5
7 =	Heinz-Harald Frentzen	5
9	Jarno Trulli	4
10	Jenson Button	3
11 =	Ricardo Zonta	1
11 =	Mika Salo	1
11 =	Pedro de la Rosa	1

CONSTRUCTORS

1	Ferrari	62
2	McLaren	52
3	Williams	15
4	Benetton	10
5	Jordan	9
6	BAR	6
7 =	Sauber	1
7 =	Arrows	1

MONACO

grand prix

FIA WORLD CHAMPIONSHIP • ROUND 7

West
Mercedes-Benz
Mobil 1
BOSS
West

COULTHARD
BARRICHELLO
FISICHELLA
IRVINE
SALO
HÄKKINEN

Paul-Henri Cahier

MONTE CARLO QUALIFYING

Qualifying at Monte Carlo is inevitably a nerve-wracking affair. The tension builds inexorably through the free practice sessions, drivers initially grumbling that they can't see anything in their mirrors, that their differential settings have left them with too much understeer and that they can't find a gap in the traffic to squeeze in a clear lap.

Meanwhile the engineers are screwing on as much wing as they can muster at this highest of downforce circuits on the F1 calendar. And there is also the question of engine cooling to keep in mind, particularly with the ambient temperature climbing to around 27 degrees during that frantic Saturday hour of qualifying.

In general terms, reducing an F1 engine's operating temperature by between two and three degrees involves degrading the car's aerodynamic efficiency by around 0.2 per cent. Not much, you might think, but in this close-fought world of wafer-thin performance margins, a tricky balancing act to get right.

Then there was the potentially crucial issue of tyre choice. Monaco has a very low-grip surface and always starts out in a very dirty and greasy state due to its use as an everyday road for the rest of the year. On the face of it, that might have inclined most teams towards choosing the softer of the two Bridgestone compounds. However, testing tended to suggest the harder compound simply because it was better suited to sharp and constant changes of direction.

Again, it looked as though this would be a close call, but what had become very evident by Saturday morning was that worn rubber offered a better and more progressive handling balance than new tyres. This proved to be something of a factor in undermining the traditional head-to-head between Schumacher's Ferrari and Häkkinen's McLaren through the streets of the Mediterranean principality.

At the end of Thursday free practice, the Finn just managed to emerge with the upper hand, taking full advantage of the grippier track surface as the rubber went down to lap just 0.09s faster than Michael's best as the chequered flag came out.

Yet things became somewhat unravelled for Häkkinen and his team-mate David Coulthard when it came to qualifying. Schumacher, brimful of confidence and relishing the challenge of this confined little circuit, slammed in a succession of quick laps to clinch the 25th pole position of his career with a 1m 19.475s best — 1.1s quicker than Häkkinen's pole time a year earlier.

Joining him on the front row was Trulli's Jordan, a brilliant effort from the Italian driver seeing him just 0.3s shy of the Ferrari team leader. The weekend had started out really badly for us when we discovered [on Thursday] that we could not use the new front suspension we had here,' said Trulli.

'On this track you need maximum steering angle, and the wheel was touching inside, so we had to go back to the previous suspension. Unfortunately for me the settings were completely wrong, so step by step, we had to work really hard. Although I didn't expect to do too well, for qualifying the car was pretty good.'

Under the circumstances, Trulli would do an excellent job in the race keeping Coulthard under control considering that he freely admitted that he didn't expect to be able to win the race or even get on terms with Schumacher and the McLarens.

Such an attitude in itself gave a flavour of the invincibility which seemed to surround Schumacher and the Ferrari team this season. With that in mind, it certainly made a change to see the Ferrari team leader checking out before the chequered flag. But it was not something his rivals could reasonably expect to depend on again.

Heinz-Harald Frentzen was happy with his fourth-fastest 1m 19.961s. He was very happy with the car, but criticised the way in which Irvine apparently slowed suddenly in the tunnel when right ahead of him — with an obvious technical problem — as unacceptable.

'I am annoyed by the unsporting behaviour of Eddie Irvine,' said the Jordan driver. 'He ought to have the experience not to slow down to 30 mph in the tunnel at the end of the session when his car clearly had a mechanical problem and he cannot benefit by continuing on the racing line. This not only endangers other drivers but in this case also ruined the final qualifying run for Jarno [Trulli] and me.'

David Coulthard (1m 19.888s) and Mika Häkkinen (1m 20.241s) wound up third and fifth on the grid. Coulthard commented: 'I had expected to be better than that because I had been very confident with the car on Thursday. I got a waved yellow flag in Casino Square, although I couldn't see another car, then another at the chicane for Wurz. I felt I had the potential to be quicker again and feel pretty good about the race.'

Häkkinen suffered traffic and understeer on the second sector of his lap, but pulled up from 17th to 5th on his final run. Jean Alesi was satisfied with seventh fastest on 1m 20.494s in the Prost AP03, despite alternator problems on his race car early in the session which forced him to switch to his spare AP03 for his remaining laps. Nick Heidfeld (18th) continued to be frustrated by lack of grip and understeer.

In the Benetton camp, Giancarlo Fisichella wound up eighth fastest, reporting that his Benetton's handling had badly deteriorated since the morning untimed session. Ralf Schumacher (9th) reported that his Williams-BMW had excessive understeer and that Irvine got in his way on his best lap.

Jenson Button (14th) also got caught by yellow flags on his best lap while Irvine himself (10th) had power steering failure on his flying lap, he and Johnny Herbert both commenting on too much oversteer with their Jaguars.

Jacques Villeneuve was disappointed with 17th place in the final line-up, having been forced to abandon his race car out on the circuit after a Honda engine failure obliged him to attack the entire qualifying session in the spare car.

'Unfortunately the spare car had been sitting in the sun and it was quite hot when I climbed into it,' said Jacques. 'My first run was OK, but on the second someone spun and I did a slow out lap with the result that my tyre pressures dropped.

'On my next run I spun, but I had enough fuel for a final attempt. Unfortunately, on the way into the pits, I was stopped at the weighbridge and there wasn't enough time left to go out again. Quite honestly, whether it's 17th or 14th position makes very little difference.'

Things would certainly go better for Villeneuve come the race.

DAVID Coulthard radiated an aura of calm serenity as he ascended the winners' rostrum after a flawless drive to victory in the Monaco Grand Prix at the end of an afternoon which saw only nine of the original 22 starters completing a race which, even by its own challenging standards, had proved a particularly punishing affair.

Criticized in the past for his share of unforced errors, on this occasion Coulthard displayed peerless form to steer his silver and black McLaren-Mercedes with meticulous precision through the corridor of unyielding guard rails behind which was strewn the wreckage of many rival cars whose drivers had failed to match his deft and confident touch.

For once, the equable Scot found himself the beneficiary of the misfortunes of his rivals. He surged into the lead when Michael Schumacher's dominant Ferrari was forced into retirement with broken rear suspension with only 23 of the race's 78 laps to go.

'I gladly seize this win and I don't feel sorry for Michael at all,' beamed the Scot as he relished the eighth Grand Prix victory of his career, 'because I've had more than my fair share of reliability problems and I think it's about time he had some!'

Coulthard took the chequered flag 15.9s ahead of Rubens Barrichello in the sole surviving Ferrari while Giancarlo Fisichella's Benetton was third ahead of Eddie Irvine who scored the first points for the newly branded Jaguar F1 team.

Even in success, Coulthard has often been rather clipped and stilted when it comes to handling post-race press conferences. This time he appeared more assured than ever, tanned and relaxed despite the physical effort involved in his drive to victory and his admission that he had been forced to have a dose of painkillers to mask the lingering discomfort to his ribs, injured in last month's air crash.

He also reiterated that he had his sights on the World Championship on a day when his team-mate Mika Häkkinen could only finish sixth, troubled by brake and gearbox problems.

'I have never been psyched by the achievements of Mika or Michael, or anybody against whom I am competing,' he said. 'I have always believed that I had more to give and, slowly, as my confidence grows, I am giving more and more all the time.'

The start of the race turned out to be a chaotic episode. Pedro Diniz's Sauber was left stranded on the grid immediately prior to the formation lap

MONACO GRAND PRIX

Right: Jackie Stewart with Indianapolis Motor Speedway president Tony George.
Paul-Henri Cahier

Centre right: Giancarlo Fisichella once again finished on the podium.
Mark Thompson/Allsport

Far right: BAR senior race engineer Jock Clear and Jacques Villeneuve contemplate the problems of inadequate downforce.
Paul-Henri Cahier

Below right: Eddie Irvine took Jaguar into the points for the first time with a hard-won fourth place.
Paul-Henri Cahier

when its engine stalled. It seemed as though the Brazilian would inevitably be consigned to the back of the grid, but as the cars took their final position in the line-up, Alexander Wurz's Benetton suffered a sudden engine failure with the result that the start was aborted.

At the first restart Schumacher accelerated straight into the lead only for an electrical problem associated with the race timing computer software to trigger the 'abort start' procedure and flash the appropriate red warning strips on all the timing screens.

Red flags were not immediately shown all round the circuit, only at the start/finish line, so the pack plunged onwards round the opening lap. At the Grand Hotel – formerly Loews – hairpin, Pedro de la Rosa tried to run round the outside of Jenson Button only for the Williams inadvertently to tip the Arrows into a spin, the two cars shuddering to a halt and blocking the circuit.

Button, Ricardo Zonta, Nick Heidfeld, Pedro Diniz and Marc Gene all had to run back to take spare cars but Gaston Mazzacane and Jacques Villeneuve were able to drive back. De la Rosa was left unable to start after earlier trashing another Arrows A21 at Tabac during the warm-up.

All this drama at least helped Wurz's cause. 'Initially I couldn't restart in the spare car as it was set up for Giancarlo,' he explained. 'Then after the red flag, we had a chance to adapt the car for me for the restart, but we didn't have time fully to change the set-up.'

Meanwhile, Schumacher was dishing out a repeat performance immediately as the lights went out to signal the second restart. This time everybody negotiated the opening lap with no drama, the Ferrari team leader bursting into view past the royal box already 2.3s ahead of Trulli's Jordan, David Coulthard's McLaren, Heinz-Harald Frentzen's Jordan and Mika Häkkinen's McLaren.

Over the opening five laps Schumacher slammed in a sequence of quick times to build up a 5.8s lead over the second-place Jordan. By this time Häkkinen was 10.5s adrift in fifth place with Eddie Irvine's Jaguar R1 leading the pursuit, the Finn now dropping away from the leading Ferrari at around a second a lap.

Behind Häkkinen, Ralf Schumacher's Williams was being pursued with some zeal by Jean Alesi's Prost, the Frenchman holding a strongly impressive seventh place. 'I was keeping a good pace, waiting for the right

moment to start attacking,' said Jean. Unfortunately his fine run ended after 29 laps when the transmission broke, the legacy, he felt, of the three starts he'd put the car through on this particular afternoon.

Another early retirement was Button, who'd been obliged to take the spare Williams FW22 after jogging back from his initial skirmish with de la Rosa. Running 19th, his first Monaco GP ended when the engine started playing up and he retired on his 17th lap with fading oil pressure.

By this time the circuit at Ste Dévote was getting particularly slippery. Wurz crashed the spare Benetton there on lap 19, to be followed three laps later by tail-ender Gaston Mazzacane's Minardi. On lap 31, Diniz lost control, almost teased the Sauber round safely, but clanged the left rear wheel rim against the barrier and shuddered to a standstill.

For Häkkinen, meanwhile, the mathematics of the championship made it look as though it was 'Monte Carlo or Bust' for the stoic Finn. As things turned out, he had a wretched time, struggling to an eventual sixth behind Mika Salo's Sauber. From the start, the reigning champion was fighting hard for fifth place between Heinz-Harald Frentzen's Jordan and Ralf Schumacher's Williams-BMW.

Suddenly on lap 36 Häkkinen slowed dramatically and came into the pits, warning his engineers over the radio that his brakes had suddenly started to feel very strange.

As he pulled to a halt, the mechanics opened the access hatch in the front of the monocoque to find that an engine telemetry sender – mounted inside the monocoque 'roof below the little aerial in front of the cockpit – had dropped down and jammed behind the pedals. It was quickly ripped out and Mika resumed 14th.

For his part, Schumacher was 34s in the lead by the time Jarno Trulli's Jordan, which had qualified second and run ahead of Coulthard from the start, dropped out with gearbox problems on lap 37. That left Coulthard with a clear track between him and the Ferrari and he set about whittling down Schumacher's advantage by posting a succession of fastest laps.

'I thought there would be an opportunity to pass Jarno and it was just a matter of how far down the road it would be,' he said. 'I thought I would wait until after the pit stops to have a try, which I would have done, although it would have involved him giving me room at the tightest hairpin. 'Once ahead, I didn't honestly think

I could take 36 seconds off Michael, but I had a quick car and wasn't going to sit back. In those circumstances you push hard and see what happens as an opportunity may come which you can take.'

By this stage the field had been further decimated with accidents, Ralf Schumacher in particular crashing his Williams at Ste Dévote on lap 38, suffering a badly cut leg.

'I don't actually know where this injury came from,' joked the German driver. 'After crashing into the barrier, I jumped out, but did not look at the damaged car and therefore did not realise that my leg was hurt.

'I went off the circuit, because

disastrously overheated by a cracked exhaust.

Subsequently two other drivers would testify to the fact that they saw Schumacher lightly brush the barriers on a couple of occasions, but there was no suggestion that these minor slips contributed to his eventual retirement.

That left Coulthard to surge through to a commanding victory ahead of Rubens Barrichello, the surviving Ferrari driver being told to back off in the closing stages by engineers worried that he might fall victim to a fault similar to that which sidelined his team-mate.

'Basically, having started from where

Häkkinen was coming out of the pits and I went on the left side of the track to overtake him. But the line was dirty there and I didn't manage to brake sufficiently and finished in the barrier.'

Soon to follow his example, Heinz-Harald Frentzen's Jordan, Jos Verstappen's Arrows and Ricardo Zonta's BAR also eventually strayed terminally from the straight and narrow.

On lap 49, Schumacher made his sole refuelling stop and resumed 11.1s ahead of Coulthard who had yet to come in. The Scot's McLaren then closed to 1.5s before surging through into the lead on lap 56 as the leading Ferrari's rear suspension broke after its carbon-fibre components had been

I did, I spent the race catching up,' said Rubens. 'Towards the end I backed off because I was told to drop my revs, but I spent a lot of the race conserving tyres and fuel.'

In third place, Giancarlo Fisichella was understandably delighted with the outcome of the race. 'I was optimistic to get in the points, but didn't think I would be able to get on the podium from my starting position,' he said.

'I was pushing hard behind Barrichello, then on about the 46th lap I got a puncture in one of my rear tyres and lost about six or seven seconds. I had to come in ten laps early for my stop, but after that the balance was good and I could push till the end.'

Eddie Irvine's dogged run to fourth place was a huge morale-booster for the Milton Keynes-based team on a day when Ford president Jac Nasser was spectating from the pits.

'It was a big struggle,' admitted Irvine, 'one of the hardest races of my life. The steering was getting very heavy towards the end, and I was suffering from dehydration because my drink bottle wasn't working and my foot is badly blistered. But I'll worry about that tomorrow.

'It's great to put Jaguar's name on the scoreboard. If we continue to put all the jigsaw pieces in place on a regular basis, the points will come our way again for sure.'

Mika Salo fended off Häkkinen for fifth, the McLaren driver also frustrated by gearbox problems in the closing stages, while Jacques Villeneuve finished a good seventh ahead of Nick Heidfeld's Prost and Johnny Herbert's Jaguar.

For Schumacher, this was a potentially disastrous setback on a day when he could have all-but closed down the McLaren-Mercedes challenge for the World Championship. Having qualified commandingly on pole position, he seemed to be surging away towards what promised to be his fifth victory in seven races.

For his part, Schumacher reacted somewhat haughtily to his disappointment, indicating that he still regarded Häkkinen rather than Coulthard as his main title rival. 'It is true that I could have picked up ten points today but the driver I consider my main rival could also have done so,' he said.

Had he won for Ferrari, he could well have extended his 18-point advantage by up to another ten points over the McLaren drivers. Now Coulthard was only 12 points behind, driving as well as he had ever done and determined to make a fight of it all the way to the end of the season.

Right: Johnny Herbert and Michael Schumacher cruise down the narrow Monaco pit lane.
Bryn Williams/Words & Pictures

Below left: McLaren mechanics work on David Coulthard's car in cramped conditions in the pit area.
Paul-Henri Cahier

DIARY

Jenson Button collects a £500 ticket for speeding at 141 mph en route to Monaco in his BMW diesel saloon.

Alain Prost parts company from his design chief Alan Jenkins after a difficult season so far.

Rockingham Speedway, near Corby, wins its battle to become the first British oval track to be awarded a round of the CART championship, the date scheduled for 2001.

Juan Montoya scores Toyota's first CART victory at Milwaukee at the wheel of the Ganassi team's Lola.

The Penske team pledges it will return to the Indy 500 in 2001.

Monaco is out of step claims McLaren boss

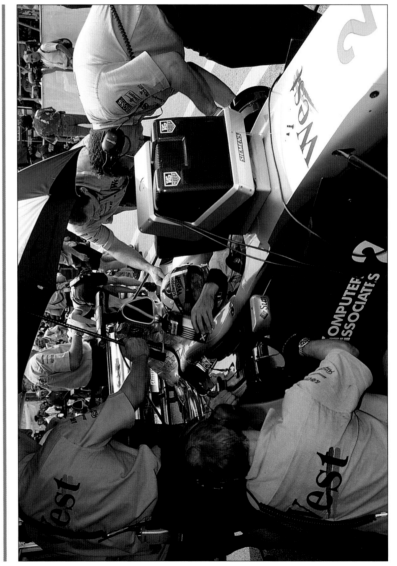

McLAREN team chief Ron Dennis put the Monaco Grand Prix organisers under pressure by stating that the temporary pit facilities at the race were no longer acceptable by the current standards of F1.

'This Grand Prix carries with it strange pressures,' he said. 'How can we really be expected to tolerate not having proper garages and pits here? It makes for a very unpleasant working environment for the whole team with excessive noise and excessive heat. It makes life very difficult indeed.'

Given the huge amount of revenue which the Grand Prix generates for the Principality, Dennis insisted that the organisers take steps to improve things in the future – particularly at a time

when Silverstone has been castigated for allegedly poor facilities by the sport's governing body.

'I don't have any particular agenda here,' said Dennis, 'but every single circuit is expected to improve its facilities on a year-on-year basis. I appreciate the speed at which marshals remove damaged cars and so on, but I fail to understand why we have to put up with these facilities when other circuits have high standards imposed on them.

'Problems are there to be solved. We treasure the Monaco Grand Prix for what it is. But they just have to get to grips with that particular problem.'

MONACO — MONTE CARLO GRAND PRIX CIRCUIT

CIRCUIT LENGTH: 2.094 miles/3.370 km

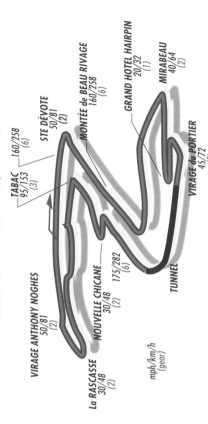

VIRAGE ANTHONY NOGHES 50/81 (2)
La RASCASSE 30/48 (2)
NOUVELLE CHICANE 30/48 (2)
STE DÉVOTE 50/81 (2)
MONTÉE de BEAU RIVAGE 160/258 (6)
TABAC 95/153 (3)
160/258 (6)
175/282 (6)
TUNNEL
VIRAGE du PORTIER 45/72 (2)
GRAND HOTEL HAIRPIN 20/32 (1)
MIRABEAU 40/64 (2)
MONTÉE de BEAU RIVAGE 160/258 (6)
mph/km/h [gear]

RACE DISTANCE: 78 laps, 163.333 miles/262.860 km   RACE WEATHER: Dry hot and sunny

Pos.	Driver	Nat.	No.	Entrant	Car/Engine	Laps	Time/Retirement	Speed (mph/km/h)
1	David Coulthard	GB	2	West McLaren Mercedes	McLaren MP4/15-Mercedes FO110J V10	78	1h 49m 28.213s	89.522/144.072
2	Rubens Barrichello	BR	4	Scuderia Ferrari Marlboro	Ferrari F1-2000-049 V10	78	1h 49m 44.102s	89.306/143.724
3	Giancarlo Fisichella	I	11	Mild Seven Benetton Playlife	Benetton B200-Playlife V10	78	1h 49m 46.735s	89.270/143.666
4	Eddie Irvine	GB	7	Jaguar Racing	Jaguar R1-Cosworth CR2 V10	78	1h 50m 34.137s	88.632/142.640
5	Mika Salo	SF	17	Red Bull Sauber Petronas	Sauber C19-Petronas SPE 04A V10	78	1h 50m 48.988s	88.434/142.321
6	Mika Häkkinen	SF	1	West McLaren Mercedes	McLaren MP4/15-Mercedes FO110J V10	77		
7	Jacques Villeneuve	CDN	22	Lucky Strike BAR Honda	BAR 02-Honda RA100E V10	77		
8	Nick Heidfeld	D	15	Gauloises Prost Peugeot	Prost AP03-Peugeot A20 V10	77		
9	Johnny Herbert	GB	8	Jaguar Racing	Jaguar R1-Cosworth CR2 V10	76		
10	Heinz-Harald Frentzen	D	5	Benson & Hedges Jordan	Jordan EJ10-Mugen Honda MF301HE V10	70	Accident	
	Jos Verstappen	NL	19	Arrows	Arrows A21-Supertec FB02 V10	60	Accident	
	Michael Schumacher	D	3	Scuderia Ferrari Marlboro	Ferrari F1-2000-049 V10	55	Broken pushrod	
	Ricardo Zonta	BR	23	Lucky Strike BAR Honda	BAR 02-Honda RA100E V10	48	Accident	
	Ralf Schumacher	D	9	BMW WilliamsF1 Team	Williams FW22-BMW E41 V10	37	Accident	
	Jarno Trulli	I	6	Benson & Hedges Jordan	Jordan EJ10-Mugen Honda MF301HE V10	36	Gearbox	
	Pedro Diniz	BR	16	Red Bull Sauber Petronas	Sauber C19-Petronas SPE 04A V10	30	Accident	
	Jean Alesi	F	14	Gauloises Prost Peugeot	Prost AP03-Peugeot A20 V10	29	Transmission	
	Gaston Mazzacane	ARG	21	Telefonica Minardi Fondmetal	Minardi M02-Fondmetal Ford Zetec-R V10	22	Accident	
	Marc Gene	ESP	20	Telefonica Minardi Fondmetal	Minardi M02-Fondmetal Ford Zetec-R V10	21	Gearbox	
	Alexander Wurz	A	12	Mild Seven Benetton Playlife	Benetton B200-Playlife V10	18	Accident	
	Jenson Button	GB	10	BMW WilliamsF1 Team	Williams FW22-Playlife V10	16	Oil pressure	
DNS	Pedro de la Rosa	ESP	18	Arrows	Arrows A21-Supertec FB02 V10			

Fastest lap: Häkkinen, on lap 57, 1m 21.571s, 92.416 mph/148.729 km/h (record).
Previous lap record: Mika Häkkinen (F1 McLaren MP4/14-Mercedes V10), 1m 22.259s, 91.562 mph/147.355 km/h (1999).

Grid order:

Grid order	
3	M. SCHUMACHER
6	TRULLI
2	COULTHARD
5	FRENTZEN
1	HÄKKINEN
4	BARRICHELLO
14	ALESI
11	FISICHELLA
9	R. SCHUMACHER
7	IRVINE
8	HERBERT
17	SALO
10	BUTTON
19	VERSTAPPEN
18	DE LA ROSA
15	HEIDFELD
16	DINIZ
23	ZONTA
20	GENE
21	MAZZACANE

Pit stop
One lap behind leader

STARTING GRID

No.	Driver	Team
3	M. SCHUMACHER	Ferrari
6	TRULLI	Jordan
2	COULTHARD	McLaren
5	FRENTZEN	Jordan
1	HÄKKINEN	McLaren
4	BARRICHELLO	Ferrari
14	ALESI	Sauber
11	FISICHELLA	Benetton
7	R. SCHUMACHER	Williams
9	IRVINE	Jaguar
12*	WURZ	Benetton
8	HERBERT	Jaguar
15*	VILLENEUVE	BAR
10*	BUTTON	Williams
17	SALO	Sauber
18**	DE LA ROSA	Arrows
19	VERSTAPPEN	Arrows
16***	DINIZ	Sauber
23	ZONTA	BAR
21	MAZZACANE	Minardi
20*	GENE	Minardi
—	HEIDFELD	Prost

* started from the pit lane
** did not start
*** started from the back of the grid

FOR THE RECORD

First Grand Prix points
Jaguar

TIME SHEETS

QUALIFYING
Weather: Dry, hot and sunny

Pos.	Driver	Car	Laps	Time
1	Michael Schumacher	Ferrari	12	1m 19.475s
2	Jarno Trulli	Jordan-Mugen Honda	11	1m 19.746s
3	David Coulthard	McLaren-Mercedes	12	1m 19.888s
4	Heinz-Harald Frentzen	Jordan-Mugen Honda	11	1m 19.961s
5	Mika Häkkinen	McLaren-Mercedes	11	1m 20.241s
6	Rubens Barrichello	Ferrari	12	1m 20.416s
7	Jean Alesi	Prost-Peugeot	11	1m 20.494s
8	Giancarlo Fisichella	Benetton-Playlife	12	1m 20.703s
9	Ralf Schumacher	Williams-BMW	12	1m 20.742s
10	Eddie Irvine	Jaguar-Cosworth	11	1m 20.743s
11	Johnny Herbert	Jaguar-Cosworth	12	1m 20.792s
12	Alexander Wurz	Benetton-Playlife	11	1m 20.871s
13	Mika Salo	Sauber-Petronas	11	1m 21.561s
14	Jenson Button	Williams-BMW	12	1m 21.605s
15	Jos Verstappen	Arrows-Supertec	12	1m 21.738s
16	Pedro de la Rosa	Arrows-Supertec	10	1m 21.832s
17	Jacques Villeneuve	BAR-Honda	12	1m 21.848s
18	Nick Heidfeld	Prost-Peugeot	12	1m 22.017s
19	Pedro Diniz	Sauber-Petronas	12	1m 22.136s
20	Ricardo Zonta	BAR-Honda	12	1m 22.324s
21	Marc Gene	Minardi-Fondmetal	12	1m 23.721s
22	Gaston Mazzacane	Minardi-Fondmetal	11	1m 23.794s

THURSDAY FREE PRACTICE
Weather: Hot and sunny

Pos.	Driver	Laps	Time
1	Mika Häkkinen	28	1m 21.387s
2	Michael Schumacher	36	1m 21.486s
3	David Coulthard	29	1m 22.098s
4	Eddie Irvine	27	1m 22.260s
5	Heinz-Harald Frentzen	33	1m 22.497s
6	Ralf Schumacher	25	1m 22.700s
7	Jean Alesi	25	1m 22.708s
8	Pedro de la Rosa	39	1m 22.944s
9	Jarno Trulli	30	1m 23.066s
10	Rubens Barrichello	35	1m 23.095s
11	Mika Salo	37	1m 23.356s
12	Jacques Villeneuve	42	1m 23.438s
13	Jenson Button	42	1m 23.578s
14	Giancarlo Fisichella	15	1m 23.783s
15	Johnny Herbert	20	1m 23.828s
16	Pedro Diniz	26	1m 23.872s
17	Ricardo Zonta	48	1m 23.876s
18	Jos Verstappen	25	1m 24.552s
19	Jacques Villeneuve	25	1m 24.587s
20	Alexander Wurz	21	1m 25.325s
21	Nick Heidfeld	23	1m 25.462s
22	Gaston Mazzacane	24	1m 27.031s

SATURDAY FREE PRACTICE
Weather: Hot and sunny

Pos.	Driver	Laps	Time
1	David Coulthard	25	1m 20.405s
2	Michael Schumacher	34	1m 20.503s
3	Giancarlo Fisichella	40	1m 20.599s
4	Jarno Trulli	30	1m 20.863s
5	Mika Häkkinen	22	1m 20.910s
6	Rubens Barrichello	30	1m 20.998s
7	Jean Alesi	24	1m 21.072s
8	Alexander Wurz	27	1m 21.213s
9	Heinz-Harald Frentzen	22	1m 21.249s
10	Ralf Schumacher	24	1m 21.366s
11	Pedro de la Rosa	29	1m 21.401s
12	Eddie Irvine	27	1m 21.411s
13	Johnny Herbert	28	1m 22.023s
14	Jenson Button	31	1m 22.206s
15	Mika Salo	30	1m 22.338s
16	Pedro Diniz	25	1m 22.488s
17	Ricardo Zonta	30	1m 22.634s
18	Jos Verstappen	31	1m 22.642s
19	Jacques Villeneuve	40	1m 22.971s
20	Nick Heidfeld	21	1m 23.088s
21	Marc Gene	34	1m 23.631s
22	Gaston Mazzacane	39	1m 24.246s

WARM-UP
Weather: Hot and sunny

Pos.	Driver	Laps	Time
1	Rubens Barrichello	15	1m 22.251s
2	Michael Schumacher	16	1m 22.307s
3	David Coulthard	15	1m 22.471s
4	Ralf Schumacher	12	1m 22.745s
5	Jarno Trulli	17	1m 23.034s
6	Mika Häkkinen	14	1m 23.111s
7	Jenson Button	16	1m 23.245s
8	Giancarlo Fisichella	16	1m 23.600s
9	Eddie Irvine	16	1m 23.628s
10	Alexander Wurz	13	1m 24.091s
11	Heinz-Harald Frentzen	18	1m 24.115s
12	Jean Alesi	12	1m 24.158s
13	Johnny Herbert	15	1m 24.380s
14	Pedro Diniz	14	1m 24.413s
15	Mika Salo	15	1m 24.455s
16	Marc Gene	15	1m 24.887s
17	Jos Verstappen	12	1m 24.931s
18	Jacques Villeneuve	17	1m 25.090s
19	Pedro de la Rosa	9	1m 25.135s
20	Ricardo Zonta	16	1m 25.397s
21	Nick Heidfeld	15	1m 25.515s
22	Gaston Mazzacane	14	1m 26.028s

RACE FASTEST LAPS
Weather: Dry, hot and sunny

Driver	Time	Lap
Mika Häkkinen	1m 21.571s	57
David Coulthard	1m 21.787s	54
Giancarlo Fisichella	1m 21.905s	58
Jarno Trulli	1m 21.910s	73
Michael Schumacher	1m 21.912s	45
Rubens Barrichello	1m 22.123s	68
Heinz-Harald Frentzen	1m 22.338s	20
Eddie Irvine	1m 22.424s	67
Jos Verstappen	1m 22.488s	25
Jenson Button	1m 22.634s	58
Jacques Villeneuve	1m 23.245s	32
Nick Heidfeld	1m 23.261s	67
Johnny Herbert	1m 23.393s	35
Mika Salo	1m 23.466s	73
Ralf Schumacher	1m 23.514s	48
Ricardo Zonta	1m 23.769s	35
Jean Alesi	1m 23.949s	27
Marc Gene	1m 24.351s	18
Pedro Diniz	1m 24.486s	35
Pedro de la Rosa	1m 24.590s	30
Gaston Mazzacane	1m 23.657s	34
Alexander Wurz	1m 25.740s	14

POINTS TABLES

DRIVERS

Pos.	Driver	Points
1	Michael Schumacher	46
2	David Coulthard	34
3	Mika Häkkinen	29
4	Rubens Barrichello	22
5	Giancarlo Fisichella	14
6	Ralf Schumacher	12
7 =	Heinz-Harald Frentzen	5
7 =	Jacques Villeneuve	5
9	Jarno Trulli	4
10 =	Eddie Irvine	3
10 =	Jenson Button	3
10 =	Mika Salo	3
13 =	Ricardo Zonta	1
13 =	Pedro de la Rosa	1

CONSTRUCTORS

Pos.	Team	Points
1	Ferrari	68
2	McLaren	63
3	Williams	15
4	Benetton	14
5	Jordan	9
6	BAR	6
7 =	Jaguar	3
7 =	Sauber	3
9	Arrows	1

CHASSIS LOG BOOK

No.	Driver	Chassis
1	Häkkinen	McLaren MP4/15/4
2	Coulthard	McLaren MP4/15/5
	spares	McLaren MP4/15/1 & 2
3	M. Schumacher	Ferrari F1-2000/198
4	Barrichello	Ferrari F1-2000/202
	spares	Ferrari F1-2000/199 & 200
5	Frentzen	Jordan EJ10/6
6	Trulli	Jordan EJ10/5
	spares	Jordan EJ10/1 & 4
7	Irvine	Jaguar R1/4
8	Herbert	Jaguar R1/1
	spares	Jaguar R1/3 & 5
9	R. Schumacher	Williams FW22/5
10	Button	Williams FW22/4
	spares	Williams FW22/3
11	Fisichella	Benetton B200/4
12	Wurz	Benetton B200/2
	spares	Benetton B200/3
14	Alesi	Prost AP03/3
15	Heidfeld	Prost AP03/4
	spares	Prost AP03/1
16	Diniz	Sauber C19/3
17	Salo	Sauber C19/5
	spares	Sauber C19/4
18	de la Rosa	Arrows A21/3
19	Verstappen	Arrows A21/4
	spares	Arrows A21/2
20	Gene	Minardi M02/3
21	Mazzacane	Minardi M02/4
	spares	Minardi M02/1
22	Villeneuve	BAR 02/2
23	Zonta	BAR 02/1
	spares	BAR 02/4 & 7

CANADIAN
grand prix

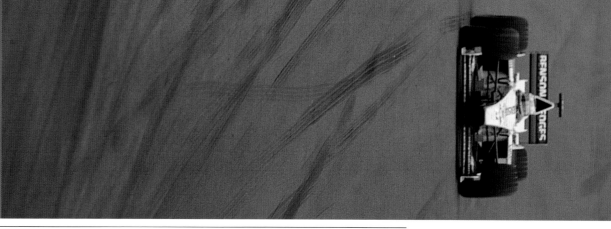

Main photo: Michael Schumacher takes the lead at the start with David Coulthard in second spot. Rubens Barrichello locks up his Ferrari's brakes behind Mika Häkkinen.
Bryn Williams/Words & Pictures

Left: Look into my eyes. Michael strikes a Svengali-like pose.
Clive Mason/Allsport

1	M. SCHUMACHER
2	BARRICHELLO
3	FISICHELLA
4	HÄKKINEN
5	VERSTAPPEN
6	TRULLI

D AVID Coulthard's bid to sustain his Monaco-winning momentum was dashed seconds before the start of the Canadian Grand Prix when he stalled the engine of his McLaren-Mercedes MP4/15 and incurred a 10-second stop-go penalty after his mechanics remained working on his car on the starting grid beyond the permitted time limit.

It was a slip which effectively left the path wide open for Michael Schumacher to post Ferrari's fifth victory of the season, although the race which started with the German race comfortably dominating proceedings in dry conditions ended in torrential rain, Schumacher pushing his car along as gently as he dared, nursing what turned out to be a problem with a front wheel bearing. Had Coulthard been close behind, instead of delayed by the penalty, he could well have been the unexpected beneficiary of the Ferrari's problems.

F1 rules prohibit the mechanics from working on the cars within 15 seconds of the start of the final formation lap and the McLaren mechanics spilled over into this time frame as they worked to coax David's machine into life. This contravened Article 139 of the sporting regulations and made a penalty inevitable.

'I wanted to reposition my car on the grid and stalled the engine,' said Coulthard. 'We had to move the car slightly in order to engage the external starter and that meant that we strayed into the 15 seconds just before the parade lap.'

Instead, the Scot found himself trailing home a dejected and sodden seventh as Schumacher and Rubens Barrichello surfed to a commanding 1-2 victory in conditions of spray and deteriorating visibility which tightened their hold on the title battle with eight of the season's 17 races completed.

After a qualifying session which saw Coulthard swapping fastest times with Schumacher's Ferrari in a close-fought battle for pole position ended with the Scot clinching second place on the front row of the grid, Coulthard was frustrated by that last-minute glitch in those final few moments before the cars moved away.

'I guessed that there was something going on because his mechanics were going on the grid later than the 15-second limit,' said Schumacher, 'but David was not close enough to attack me. After he had gone, I eased up to avoid any mistakes.'

Schumacher also admitted that he had a suspected technical problem during the race which the team initially believed was a brake sensor malfunction, prompting him to make his routine refuelling stop slightly earlier than originally scheduled.

In order to rectify the problem, Schumacher wound the brake balance towards the front wheels. That cost him a slide across the gravel trap at the first corner when the rain was at its heaviest. 'It was no problem,' he said. 'I just steered across the run-off and regained the circuit.'

Schumacher also paid tribute to Barrichello for the way in which he shadowed him protectively in the closing stages when he was taking it easy. 'He is a good man, and one day I will pay him back,' he said.

McLaren had come to Montreal determined to celebrate their 500th grand prix outing with a victory, but were left trying to put a stoic face on their acute disappointment as Häkkinen salvaged fourth place at the end of an action-packed race given additional spice by the dismal conditions which prevailed from half-distance onwards, leaving cars skating in all directions.

At the start, Schumacher made a copy-book getaway to lead Coulthard into the first corner, but the sensation of those first few yards was Jacques Villeneuve, the Canadian hero blasting his BAR-Honda through into third place from sixth on the grid, squeezing out Mika Häkkinen's McLaren as he did so.

Unlike previous years when the field has invariably been embroiled in a multiple shunt at the first corner, on this occasion everybody managed to squeeze through intact, with Schumacher already piling on the pressure to make an early break from the rest of the pack.

By the end of the opening lap the Ferrari team leader was a full second ahead of Coulthard, with a gap already opening to Villeneuve, Rubens Barrichello's Ferrari, Häkkinen, Frentzen and the impressive Pedro de la Rosa in the Arrows A21.

Second time round, Coulthard set the fastest lap to trim Schumacher's advantage back to 0.9s as de la Rosa overtook Frentzen for sixth place. Further back, the Jaguar squad had already sustained a major blow after Eddie Irvine's Jaguar had to be pushed from the starting grid and eventually joined in two laps down from the pit lane.

'I could feel there was something not quite right with the clutch on the parade lap,' said Irvine. 'At the start it just dropped, the car stalled and that was that.' He spent the rest of the afternoon trailing round at the back, effectively using the race as a truncated test session.

In the opening phase of the race, Schumacher settled down to shadow Coulthard, confident in the knowledge that Villeneuve was keeping Barrichello, Häkkinen and the rest of the potential challengers boxed in behind his BAR which was losing a second a lap to the leading duo.

It was only on lap ten that the timing screens flashed up Coulthard's penalty, by which time Villeneuve was 12s behind him in third place, David duly came in to take his punishment at the end of lap 14, resuming in 10th place, now out of the winning equation.

Characteristically, the Scot took the blame. 'I'm the biggest fault,' he said. 'I stalled as we tried to get me repositioned. I wanted to pull the car forward onto the yellow line, but it was slightly off-centre to get the external starter engaged.

'Rules are rules, but perhaps in this situation there should be a clause to take into account what's good for the race. To put you out for that, in hindsight, spoiled the race. We are now back into the same position as before Monaco. You can't change what has happened.'

Presented with Ferrari's metronomic consistency, McLaren was always going to face an uphill struggle making up for its early season run of unreliability. Yet Coulthard claimed he was confident he had the legs of Schumacher's Ferrari as he shadowed the Italian car in the opening stages of Sunday's race, prior to his penalty.

'I was just trying to probe how much he had got in hand when I had to come in to take my stop-go,' said Coulthard. 'I think we were quicker than Michael on certain parts of the circuit.'

Coulthard's delay left Villeneuve, whose BAR-Honda had been ideally suited to the low-downforce aerodynamic requirements of the Montreal track, running second ahead of Barrichello's Ferrari.

On lap 23 the first spots of rain began to fall and, next time round, Jarno Trulli's Jordan overtook Ricardo Zonta's BAR for sixth place. Verstappen slid wide at the chicane on the return leg and Coulthard, right behind, was also pitched into a harmless spin, dropping from ninth to 11th. The Dutchman's Arrows immediately came in for the first of its two refuelling stops.

On lap 32 Zonta overtook Frentzen for sixth place only for the Jordan to retire next time round. 'Things were

DIARY

TAG McLaren Chairman Ron Dennis is awarded the CBE in the Queen's Birthday Honours list.

Helio Castroneves wins first CART victory of his career at Detroit with the Penske team Reynard-Honda.

Dario Franchitti tipped for Jaguar F1 test drive.

Andrew Craig resigns as Chief Executive Officer of CART to be replaced in the interim by former Indy 500 winner and team owner Bobby Rahal.

MONTREAL QUALIFYING

Whereas Monte Carlo calls for the highest downforce levels, the Circuit Gilles Villeneuve is at the opposite end of the aerodynamic scale. F3-style rear wings are part of the package in everybody's quest for the ultimate straight-line speed. That – and dramatically effective braking – are the keys to a good lap.

With track temperatures nudging 36 degrees on Friday morning, the choice of tyre compounds would be crucial. Bridgestone tests at Monza the previous week had yielded valuable data for F1's sole tyre supplier and it was quickly clear that the softer of the two proposed compounds would be ideal for the Canadian race.

Tyre degradation is not a big problem on the Montreal track surface, with the result that the performance differential between new and used rubber is almost zero. 'In reality, it just comes down to driver preference,' said Jordan technical director Mike Gascoyne. 'They usually go for what they feel most comfortable with on their first lap.'

However, several of the teams, including pace-setters Ferrari and McLaren, opted to qualify using worn front tyres paired with fresh rears. The combination offered significantly better chassis balance and enhanced precise turn-in, particularly on the tighter corners. New front tyres brought with them too much understeer.

Buoyed by his Monaco victory, Coulthard looked formidable from the outset. The Canadian track is one of his favourites and always seems to bring out the best in him.

He finished Friday's free practice session fastest and, if anything, seemed a touch more confident than Häkkinen, in qualifying the Finn looking slightly adrift on this track where there are no really daunting corners on which to demonstrate his heroic, raw car control. In fact, when Mika's car was examined in detail, it was found to have a seized linear bearing on one of its rear shock absorbers.

Coulthard was again fastest on Saturday morning, despite losing half the session with an electronic problem which prompted the team to carry out a precautionary engine change. He certainly looked a likely candidate for pole position and prepared to battle all the way to ensure he got it.

Michael Schumacher's 1999 pole-winning 1m 19.298s lap was the yardstick at which to aim and it was Häkkinen who really started the ball seriously rolling, setting an early pace on 1m 19.570s. Three minutes later Coulthard improved to 1m 19.128s, an impressive effort indeed since Schumacher could only post a second-fastest 1m 19.301s on his first run with the Ferrari.

At 1.30 p.m. Häkkinen counter-attacked dramatically, lowering the barrier to 1m 18.985s. Coulthard came back with a 1m 18.826s and – yet again – Michael could only claw back to second with a 1m 18.840s. Seconds later, Jos Verstappen rumpled his Arrows A21 into a barrier, ripping off the right side suspension, and the red flag brought the session to a temporary end while the debris was cleared away.

In the final rush, Barrichello momentarily vaulted his Ferrari up to second place on 1m 18.801s, but then Coulthard seemingly consolidated his best time on 1m 18.537s. But the remarkable Schumacher clinched his 26th career pole by taking the Ferrari round in 1m 18.439s as the chequered flag fluttered at the start-line. It promised to be quite a race.

There were also broad grins in the Jordan camp after qualifying at the Circuit Gilles Villeneuve after Heinz-Harald Frentzen qualified fifth, just two places ahead of his amenable team-mate Jarno Trulli.

Jordan had always performed well at Montreal, their cars' efficiency under hard braking being a formidable asset at this circuit where retardation is almost more important than unfettered acceleration. In particular, Frentzen was particularly satisfied, perhaps feeling he had gone some way towards making amends for the unforced error at Monte Carlo which had seen him throw his EJ10 challenger into the wall – and out of the race.

Trulli was less satisfied with the balance of his car, but one of the surprises of the hour-long session was the performance of the two BAR-Hondas which qualified sixth and eighth in the hands of Jacques Villeneuve and Ricardo Zonta.

'The team did a great job today and the possibility of scoring points is looking very good, although I'm sure we can fight for a podium as well because the car is very good on old tyres,' said Villeneuve who was revelling in the fact that this grid position proved just how effective the BAR 02 could be in low-downforce aerodynamic trim.

Pedro de la Rosa's Arrows A21 wound up ninth on 1m 19.912s, the Spanish driver reporting he was very happy with the feel of his car. Jos Verstappen also said his race chassis handled well, but he hit the barrier on a fast left-hander on the return leg of the circuit causing the red flag to come out. He took his spare A21 (13th) but was not happy with its handling.

Tenth place in the line-up was taken by Giancarlo Fisichella's Benetton B200 (1m 19.932s), the Italian complaining of excessive understeer and lack of traction. Alexander Wurz lost time when he caught the red flags for Verstappen's accident and then had more traffic, having to be content with 14th overall.

In the BMW Williams camp Ralf Schumacher was back in the cockpit after badly cutting his leg in that Monaco shunt, but the German driver was disappointed with his FW22's lack of grip and lined up 12th, six places ahead of team-mate Jenson Button's car which had fuel pick-up problems on its third and fourth runs.

Mika Salo's Sauber C19 was 15th, the Finn frustrated by downshift problems shortly before the end of the session, while Jean Alesi's Prost-Peugeot suffered engine failure and Gaston Mazzacane crashed heavily, first taking the spare Minardi M02 and then his team-mate Marc Gené's car in order to make the 107 per cent qualifying cut.

CANADIAN GRAND PRIX

Main picture: Jacques Villeneuve made a lightning start to leap into third ahead of Rubens Barrichello, but crashed later.
Clive Mason/Allsport

Bottom left: Paul Newman *(second from right)* was a high-profile guest of Jaguar.
Paul-Henri Cahier

Below: Gaston Mazzacane and Nick Heidfeld concentrate on their struggles in tail-end cars.

Photographs: Mark Thompson and Clive Mason/Allsport

CANADIAN GRAND PRIX

New British Grand Prix threat

THE British Grand Prix stood to be dropped from the 2001 World Championship unless the organisers could satisfy motor racing's international governing body that they could address and rectify the organisational shortcomings which blighted this year's event.

That was the firm message from the FIA's World Motor Sport Council, meeting in Warsaw three days after the Montreal race, following a detailed examination of this year's race over Easter weekend which saw unprecedented traffic chaos as more than 100,000 spectators attempted to gain access to Silverstone.

Definite inclusion on the calendar depended on confirmation from FIA safety delegate Charlie Whiting that changes proposed to the procedures in the Silverstone race control have been implemented and that satisfactory plans be submitted to show how the circuit and police authorities will ensure that there will be no repetition of the traffic problems which arose in 2000.

Furthermore, the FIA demanded a report detailing how ticket-holding spectators who could not enter the circuit have been compensated. In particular this referred to the crowds who were turned away from Saturday qualifying after the promoters closed the sodden public car parks in a last-ditch attempt to improve conditions for race day.

However, the Motor Sports Association, Britain's national club, and Silverstone's owners, the British Racing Drivers' Club, both felt confident of meeting the FIA's exacting requirements in time for the next world council meeting on October 4.

'The MSA, Silverstone and the BRDC accept the conclusion of the hearing of the FIA world council in Warsaw today,' said a spokesperson.

'The conditions attached to next year's Grand Prix are indeed those which Silverstone would have considered in any event. All provisions will be complied with in good time for the world motor sport council meeting in October.'

The 2001 fixture at Silverstone was to be the last under the current contract, from 2002 the contract for the event passing to Brands Hatch Leisure which had still to obtain planning permission to up-rate its circuit. Most F1 insiders believed that Brands Hatch would have liked to strike a partnership with the BRDC to run the race at Silverstone.

However, the FIA's hard line dismayed Jackie Stewart, the former triple World Champion who would be elected to the position of President of the BRDC the following month.

'I am very disappointed that the July date has not been restored,' he said, 'because it has been traditional for a great number of years. Since Britain is the capital of motor sport it seems to me wrong that our race has not been given a time more suitable.

'However, I am sure that the MSA and the BRDC will ensure that all of the appropriate conditions to run the race will be provided, as they have been all these years until the extreme conditions which prevailed at this year's race which was held on a date demanded by the FIA.'

going fine until I started to have a problem with the brake pressure,' said Heinz-Harald. 'We tried to see if we could solve the problem, but eventually I had to retire.'

On lap 34 Schumacher made his early first refuelling stop in 9.5s, allowing Barrichello through into the lead. Next time round Häkkinen slipped through into third place ahead of Villeneuve and stayed there for the next seven laps before dropping to fifth with a 9.4s refuelling stop on lap 42. On lap 43, Barrichello refuelled from the lead in 8.7s and resumed second behind Schumacher.

Villeneuve, meanwhile, had fended off the Ferrari challenge until Barrichello squeezed ahead on lap 25, but Villeneuve's prospects of a deserved place on the podium evaporated on lap 44 when he came in for his routine re-fuelling stop only to find that his crew fitted another set of dry weather tyres, so he had to come back for wet rubber

next time round. This mix-up dropped Villeneuve to tenth place, now with no chance of a finish in the points.

'In fact, Villeneuve was a complete, total mobile chicane,' said McLaren boss Ron Dennis, venting his frustration over the manner in which Jacques had forced the BAR ahead of Häkkinen's McLaren going into the first corner.

'He had nothing to lose. He was in Canada, pumped up and going for it. The die of the race was cast when he made the very aggressive move he took at the start, coming past Mika and Rubens Barrichello. He was a man on a mission.'

Many people felt this was wide of the mark, highlighting the fact that F1's technical rules were in urgent need of a makeover to make overtaking easier rather than showing Villeneuve in any sort of irresponsible light. Dennis's remarks also tended to overlook the very obvious point that

had the Finn qualified higher than fourth on the grid, he might not have been so vulnerable to Villeneuve's bold challenge at the first corner.

By lap 40 the rain was falling heavily and both Ferrari drivers were keen on making their second stops for wet tyres and Barrichello duly followed Michael into the pit road at the end of lap 45. It was the Brazilian's choice, but because he was second in the queue he found himself waiting for 21.0s compared to Schumacher's 6.7s. Clearly, without that delay, Rubens could have won on this occasion.

'After the race at the Nürburgring, where I lost a lot of time coming in late for my pit stop, I discussed the situation with the team,' said Barrichello later. 'I said that even if I had to make an extra stop if the rain stopped, it would be quicker to come in immediately.

'So I was given the option to come in behind Michael. I have no problem

with backing off to protect Michael when I am asked to do so by the team. In any case, I had a clutch problem.

In the Benetton camp, Giancarlo Fisichella was delighted with his eventual third place after a perfectly timed single stop on lap 44. 'Our strategy had always been to stop late in the race, so I had a very high fuel load from the start,' he explained.

'When it started to rain I got on the radio, and then after one more lap I came in which was perfect timing for our stop.' Fisichella resumed second, and although he was overtaken by Barrichello, the Italian managed to keep ahead of Häkkinen to the chequered flag.

After an excellent, planned two-stop run, Verstappen's Arrows finished a fine fifth ahead of Jarno Trulli's Jordan, Coulthard, Zonta, Alexander Wurz's Benetton and Pedro Diniz in the Sauber.

Unfortunately Villeneuve's enthusiasm to shine carried him beyond the bounds of propriety in the closing stages of the race. On lap 65 he came slamming down the inside of the hairpin, punting Ralf Schumacher's Williams-BMW into unexpected retirement.

'It was one hell of an impact,' said Coulthard, whose McLaren had been overtaken by the BAR seconds earlier. Ralf reacted philosophically. 'He apologised immediately, and the matter is closed for me,' he said.

Bottom: Giancarlo Fisichella continued his early season form with another visit to the podium.

Rubens Barrichello (*right*) deferred to his team-mate Michael Schumacher, and settled for second place.

Below right: Jos Verstappen confirmed Arrows promise with fifth spot.

MONTREAL

16–18 JUNE 2000

grand prix
AIR
CANADA

MONTREAL — CIRCUIT GILLES VILLENEUVE
CIRCUIT LENGTH: 2.747 miles/4.421 km

155/250 (5)

70/113 (2)

180/290 (6) 60/97 (2)

L'ÉPINGLE 35/56 (1)

55/89 (2)

60/97 (2)

SENNA HAIRPIN 40/64 (2) 180/290 (6)

195/314 (6)

mph/km/h (gear)

RACE DISTANCE: 69 laps, 189.549 miles/305.049 km   RACE WEATHER: Dry and cloudy, followed by heavy rain

Pos.	Driver	Nat.	No.	Entrant	Car/Engine	Laps	Time/Retirement	Speed (mph/km/h)
1	Michael Schumacher	D	3	Scuderia Ferrari Marlboro	Ferrari F1-2000-049 V10	69	1h 41m 12.313s	112.374/180.849
2	Rubens Barrichello	BR	4	Scuderia Ferrari Marlboro	Ferrari F1-2000-049 V10	69	1h 41m 12.487s	112.371/180.844
3	Giancarlo Fisichella	I	11	Mild Seven Benetton Playlife	Benetton B200-Playlife V10	69	1h 41m 27.678s	112.091/180.393
4	Mika Häkkinen	SF	1	West McLaren Mercedes	McLaren MP4/15-Mercedes FO110J V10	69	1h 41m 30.874s	112.032/180.298
5	Jos Verstappen	NL	19	Arrows	Arrows A21-Supertec FB02 V10	69	1h 42m 04.521s	111.417/179.308
6	Jarno Trulli	I	6	Benson & Hedges Jordan	Jordan EJ10-Mugen Honda MF301HE V10	69	1h 42m 14.000s	111.245/179.031
7	David Coulthard	GB	2	West McLaren Mercedes	McLaren MP4/15-Mercedes FO110J V10	69	1h 42m 14.529s	111.235/179.015
8	Ricardo Zonta	BR	23	Lucky Strike BAR Honda	BAR 02-Honda RA100E V10	69	1h 42m 22.768s	111.085/178.775
9	Alexander Wurz	A	12	Mild Seven Benetton Playlife	Benetton B200-Playlife V10	69	1h 42m 32.212s	110.915/178.501
10	Pedro Diniz	BR	16	Red Bull Sauber Petronas	Sauber C19-Petronas SPE 04A V10	69	1h 42m 41.857s	110.741/178.221
11	Jenson Button	GB	10	BMW WilliamsF1 Team	Williams FW22-BMW E41 V10	68		
12	Gaston Mazzacane	ARG	21	Telefonica Minardi Fondmetal	Minardi M02-Fondmetal Ford Zetec-R V10	68		
13	Eddie Irvine	GB	7	Jaguar Racing	Jaguar R1-Cosworth CR2 V10	66		
14	Ralf Schumacher	D	9	BMW WilliamsF1 Team	Williams FW22-BMW E41 V10	64	Collision with Villeneuve	
15	Jacques Villeneuve	CDN	22	Lucky Strike BAR Honda	BAR 02-Honda RA100E V10	64	Collision with R. Schumacher	
16	Marc Gene	ESP	20	Telefonica Minardi Fondmetal	Minardi M02-Fondmetal Ford Zetec-R V10	64	Spun off	
	Pedro de la Rosa	ESP	18	Arrows	Arrows A21-Supertec FB02 V10	48	Collision with Diniz	
	Mika Salo	SF	17	Red Bull Sauber Petronas	Sauber C19-Petronas SPE 04A V10	42	Engine	
	Jean Alesi	F	14	Gauloises Prost Peugeot	Prost AP03-Peugeot A20 V10	38	Hydraulics	
	Nick Heidfeld	D	15	Gauloises Prost Peugeot	Prost AP03-Peugeot A20 V10	34	Engine fire	
	Heinz-Harald Frentzen	D	5	Benson & Hedges Jordan	Jordan EJ10-Mugen Honda MF301HE V10	32	Brakes	
	Johnny Herbert	GB	8	Jaguar Racing	Jaguar R1-Cosworth CR2 V10	14	Gearbox	

All results and data © FIA 2000

Fastest lap: Häkkinen, on lap 37, 1m 19.049s, 125.105 mph/201.338 km/h (record).

Previous lap record: Michael Schumacher (F1 Ferrari F300-V10), 1m 19.379s, 124.586 mph/200.501 km/h (1998).

Grid order	1	2	3	4	5	6	7	8	9	10	11	12	13	14	15	16	17	18	19	20	21	22	23	24	25	26	27	28	29	30	31	32	33	34	35	36	37	38	39	40	41	42	43	44	45	46	47	48	49	50	51	52	53	54
3 M. SCHUMACHER	3	3	3	3	3	3	3	3	3	3	3	3	3	3	3	3	3	3	3	3	3	3	3	3	3	3	3	3	3	3	3	3	3	4	4	4	4	4	4	4	4	3	3	3	3	3	3	3	3	3	3	3	3	3
2 COULTHARD	2	2	2	2	2	2	2	2	2	2	2	2	22	22	22	22	22	22	22	22	22	22	22	22	4	4	4	4	4	4	4	4	4	3	3	3	3	3	3	4	4	1	11	4	4	4	4	4	4	4	4			
4 BARRICHELLO	22	22	22	22	22	22	22	22	22	22	22	22	4	4	4	4	4	4	4	4	4	4	22	22	22	22	22	22	22	22	22	22	1	1	1	1	1	1	22	22	1	11	4	11	11	11	11	11	11	11	11			
1 HÄKKINEN	4	4	4	4	4	4	4	4	4	4	4	4	1	1	1	1	1	1	1	1	1	1	1	1	1	1	1	1	1	1	1	1	22	22	22	22	22	22	23	11	11	4	1	1	1	1	1	1	1	1				
5 FRENTZEN	1	1	1	1	1	1	1	1	1	1	1	1	18	18	18	18	18	5	5	5	5	5	5	5	5	5	6	6	6	6	6	6	6	6	23	23	23	11	1	22	6	6	6	6	6	6	6	6						
22 VILLENEUVE	5	18	18	18	18	18	18	18	18	18	18	18	5	5	5	5	5	23	23	23	6	6	6	5	5	5	23	23	23	23	23	23	11	11	11	2	12	6	12	12	12	12	12	12	12	12								
6 TRULLI	18	5	5	5	5	5	5	5	5	5	5	5	23	23	23	23	23	6	6	6	23	23	23	23	23	23	5	11	11	11	11	11	11	9	9	9	1	6	23	22	22	19	19	19	19	19	19							
23 ZONTA	23	23	23	23	23	23	23	23	23	23	23	23	6	6	6	6	6	19	19	19	11	11	11	11	11	11	11	11	9	9	9	9	9	2	2	2	12	23	2	19	19	9	9	9	9	9	9							
18 DE LA ROSA	6	6	6	6	6	6	6	6	6	6	6	6	19	19	19	19	19	2	2	2	9	9	9	9	9	9	14	14	14	2	2	2	12	12	12	6	2	9	9	2	2	2	2	2	2									
11 FISICHELLA	11	11	11	19	19	19	19	19	19	19	19	19	2	2	2	2	2	11	11	11	14	14	14	14	14	14	2	2	12	12	12	18	16	16	9	9	16	2	22	22	22	22	22	23										
8 HERBERT	19	19	19	11	11	11	11	11	11	11	11	11	11	11	11	11	11	9	9	9	2	2	2	2	2	2	12	12	2	18	18	17	6	19	19	18	23	23	23	23	23	23	23											
9 R. SCHUMACHER	8	8	8	8	8	8	8	8	8	8	8	8	9	9	9	14	14	12	12	12	12	12	12	12	12	18	18	17	17	17	16	16	19	16	16	12	16	18	16	16	16	16	16												
19 VERSTAPPEN	9	9	9	9	9	9	9	9	9	9	9	8	14	14	14	14	18	12	12	18	18	18	18	18	18	17	17	16	16	6	19	17	17	18	19	18	18	16	16	20	20	20	20	20											
12 WURZ	12	12	12	12	12	12	12	12	12	12	12	12	12	12	12	12	17	18	18	17	17	17	17	17	17	16	16	10	10	10	10	10	17	18	18	10	20	20	20	20	20	10	10	10	10										
17 SALO	14	14	14	14	14	14	14	14	14	14	14	8	17	17	17	17	12	17	17	18	16	16	16	16	16	15	15	15	15	15	15	15	10	20	20	18	10	10	10	10	10	21	21	21	21	21									
7 IRVINE	17	17	17	17	17	17	17	17	17	17	17	14	16	16	16	16	16	15	15	15	15	15	15	15	15	10	10	20	20	19	19	19	20	20	21	21	21	7	7	7	7	7	7	7											
14 ALESI	16	16	16	16	16	16	16	16	16	16	16	17	15	15	15	15	15	16	16	16	10	10	10	10	10	20	19	19	21	21	14	21	21	21	21	7	7	7	7	7														
10 BUTTON	15	15	15	15	15	15	15	15	15	15	15	10	10	10	10	10	10	10	10	10	20	20	20	20	20	19	21	21	14	14	21	7	7	7	7																			
16 DINIZ	10	10	10	10	10	10	10	10	10	10	10	16	16	20	20	20	20	20	20	20	19	19	19	19	19	19	19	19	21	15	7	7	7	7																					
20 GENE	20	20	20	20	20	20	20	20	20	20	20	20	21	21	21	21	21	21	21	21	21	21	21	21	21	7	7																											
15 HEIDFELD	21	21	21	21	21	21	21	21	21	21	21	21	7	7	7	7	7	7	7	7	7	7	7	7	7	7	7																											
21 MAZZACANE	7	7	7	7	7	7	7	7	7	7	7	7	7																																									

Pit stop
One lap behind leader

3 M. SCHUMACHER Ferrari		2 COULTHARD McLaren	
4 BARRICHELLO Ferrari		1 HÄKKINEN McLaren	
5 FRENTZEN Jordan		22 VILLENEUVE BAR	
6 TRULLI Jordan		23 ZONTA BAR	
18 DE LA ROSA Arrows		11 FISICHELLA Benetton	
8 HERBERT Jaguar		9 R. SCHUMACHER Williams	
19 VERSTAPPEN Arrows		12 WURZ Benetton	
17 SALO Sauber		7 IRVINE Jaguar	
14 ALESI Prost		10 BUTTON Williams	
16 DINIZ Sauber		20 GENE Minardi	
15 HEIDFELD Prost		21 MAZZACANE Minardi	

55	56	57	58	59	60	61	62	63	64	65	66	67	68	69	
3	3	3	3	3	3	3	3	3	3	3	3	3	3	3	1
4	4	4	4	4	4	4	4	4	4	4	4	4	4	4	2
11	11	11	11	11	11	11	11	11	11	11	11	11	11	11	3
1	1	1	1	1	1	1	1	1	1	1	1	1	1	1	4
6	6	6	6	6	19	19	19	19	19	19	19	19	19	19	5
12	12	19	19	19	6	6	6	6	6	6	6	6	6	6	6
19	19	12	12	12	12	12	12	12	12	12	12	12	2	2	
9	9	9	9	9	9	9	9	9	9	2	2	2	23	23	
2	2	2	2	2	2	2	2	2	2	23	23	23	12	12	
22	22	22	22	22	22	22	22	22	22	16	16	16	16	16	
23	23	23	23	23	23	23	23	23	23	10	10	10	10		
16	16	16	16	16	16	16	16	16	16	21	21	21	21		
20	20	20	20	20	20	20	20	10	10	7	7				
10	10	10	10	10	10	10	10	20	20						
21	21	21	21	21	21	21	21	21							
7	7	7	7	7	7	7	7	7							

40th Grand Prix win
Michael Schumacher

500th Grand Prix start
McLaren

QUALIFYING

Weather: Dry, hot and sunny

Pos.	Driver	Car	Laps	Time
1	Michael Schumacher	Ferrari	11	1m 18.439s
2	David Coulthard	McLaren-Mercedes	12	1m 18.537s
3	Rubens Barrichello	Ferrari	10	1m 18.801s
4	Mika Häkkinen	McLaren-Mercedes	12	1m 18.985s
5	Heinz-Harald Frentzen	Jordan-Mugen Honda	11	1m 19.483s
6	Jacques Villeneuve	BAR-Honda	12	1m 19.544s
7	Jarno Trulli	Jordan-Mugen Honda	12	1m 19.581s
8	Ricardo Zonta	BAR-Honda	12	1m 19.742s
9	Pedro de la Rosa	Arrows-Supertec	12	1m 19.912s
10	Giancarlo Fisichella	Benetton-Playlife	12	1m 19.932s
11	Johnny Herbert	Jaguar-Cosworth	11	1m 19.954s
12	Ralf Schumacher	Williams-BMW	12	1m 20.073s
13	Jos Verstappen	Arrows-Supertec	12	1m 20.107s
14	Alexander Wurz	Benetton-Playlife	12	1m 20.113s
15	Mika Salo	Sauber-Petronas	11	1m 20.445s
16	Eddie Irvine	Jaguar-Cosworth	11	1m 20.500s
17	Jean Alesi	Prost-Peugeot	8	1m 20.512s
18	Jenson Button	Williams-BMW	10	1m 20.534s
19	Pedro Diniz	Sauber-Petronas	12	1m 20.692s
20	Marc Gene	Minardi-Fondmetal	11	1m 21.058s
21	Nick Heidfeld	Prost-Peugeot	12	1m 21.680s
22	Gaston Mazzacane	Minardi-Fondmetal	11	1m 22.091s

FRIDAY FREE PRACTICE

Weather: Hot and sunny

Pos.	Driver	Laps	Time
1	David Coulthard	34	1m 20.602s
2	Michael Schumacher	37	1m 20.611s
3	Rubens Barrichello	32	1m 20.623s
4	Johnny Herbert	40	1m 21.174s
5	Mika Häkkinen	36	1m 21.370s
6	Jarno Trulli	29	1m 21.380s
7	Mika Salo	30	1m 21.487s
8	Eddie Irvine	38	1m 21.592s
9	Giancarlo Fisichella	39	1m 21.687s
10	Jacques Villeneuve	31	1m 21.846s
11	Jean Alesi	39	1m 22.022s
12	Jos Verstappen	51	1m 22.065s
13	Marc Gene	31	1m 22.176s
14	Pedro de la Rosa	41	1m 22.176s
15	Heinz-Harald Frentzen	38	1m 22.262s
16	Jenson Button	42	1m 22.343s
17	Pedro Diniz	34	1m 22.507s
18	Alexander Wurz	37	1m 22.582s
19	Gaston Mazzacane	47	1m 22.606s
20	Ricardo Zonta	19	1m 22.668s
21	Ralf Schumacher	18	1m 22.933s
22	Nick Heidfeld	13	1m 23.543s

SATURDAY FREE PRACTICE

Weather: Warm and breezy

Pos.	Driver	Laps	Time
1	David Coulthard	28	1m 18.654s
2	Michael Schumacher	32	1m 18.873s
3	Rubens Barrichello	35	1m 18.909s
4	Mika Häkkinen	44	1m 19.115s
5	Jarno Trulli	38	1m 19.342s
6	Ralf Schumacher	39	1m 19.536s
7	Jacques Villeneuve	40	1m 19.569s
8	Heinz-Harald Frentzen	28	1m 19.619s
9	Mika Salo	38	1m 19.763s
10	Giancarlo Fisichella	42	1m 19.847s
11	Jenson Button	30	1m 19.918s
12	Jos Verstappen	35	1m 19.988s
13	Alexander Wurz	43	1m 20.005s
14	Johnny Herbert	37	1m 20.008s
15	Jean Alesi	33	1m 20.021s
16	Eddie Irvine	31	1m 20.052s
17	Ricardo Zonta	32	1m 20.306s
18	Nick Heidfeld	30	1m 20.486s
19	Pedro Diniz	26	1m 20.546s
20	Pedro de la Rosa	32	1m 20.552s
21	Marc Gene	38	1m 20.914s
22	Gaston Mazzacane	38	1m 21.309s

WARM-UP

Weather: Cool and overcast

Pos.	Driver	Laps	Time
1	Michael Schumacher	15	1m 18.932s
2	Rubens Barrichello	15	1m 19.055s
3	Mika Häkkinen	14	1m 19.838s
4	David Coulthard	17	1m 19.895s
5	Jarno Trulli	18	1m 20.388s
6	Pedro de la Rosa	18	1m 20.486s
7	Giancarlo Fisichella	18	1m 20.580s
8	Marc Gene	15	1m 20.811s
9	Mika Salo	15	1m 20.834s
10	Jacques Villeneuve	16	1m 21.125s
11	Jos Verstappen	14	1m 21.132s
12	Heinz-Harald Frentzen	18	1m 21.143s
13	Alexander Wurz	16	1m 21.211s
14	Gaston Mazzacane	15	1m 21.388s
15	Jean Alesi	13	1m 21.480s
16	Johnny Herbert	14	1m 21.516s
17	Pedro Diniz	8	1m 21.627s
18	Eddie Irvine	13	1m 21.627s
19	Ralf Schumacher	16	1m 21.716s
20	Jenson Button	8	1m 22.417s
21	Nick Heidfeld	7	1m 22.810s
22	Ricardo Zonta		no time

RACE FASTEST LAPS

Weather: Dry and cloudy, followed by heavy rain

Driver	Time	Lap
Mika Häkkinen	1m 19.049s	37
Rubens Barrichello	1m 19.235s	38
Michael Schumacher	1m 19.812s	30
David Coulthard	1m 19.947s	38
Giancarlo Fisichella	1m 20.399s	37
Jarno Trulli	1m 20.479s	31
Pedro Diniz	1m 20.494s	36
Ralf Schumacher	1m 20.520s	38
Jacques Villeneuve	1m 20.533s	39
Marc Gene	1m 20.547s	38
Alexander Wurz	1m 20.625s	39
Ricardo Zonta	1m 20.686s	38
Jos Verstappen	1m 20.693s	34
Eddie Irvine	1m 20.693s	34
Mika Salo	1m 20.696s	37
Jenson Button	1m 20.781s	37
Pedro de la Rosa	1m 20.842s	35
Jean Alesi	1m 20.889s	20
Nick Heidfeld	1m 21.096s	31
Heinz-Harald Frentzen	1m 21.110s	21
Gaston Mazzacane	1m 21.196s	37
Johnny Herbert	1m 22.369s	10

1	Häkkinen	McLaren MP4/15/6
2	Coulthard	McLaren MP4/15/5
	spare	McLaren MP4/15/2
3	M. Schumacher	Ferrari F1-2000/203
4	Barrichello	Ferrari F1-2000/202
	spare	Ferrari F1-2000/198
5	Frentzen	Jordan EJ10/6
6	Trulli	Jordan EJ10/5
	spare	Jordan EJ10/4
7	Irvine	Jaguar R1/4
8	Herbert	Jaguar R1/6
	spare	Jaguar R1/5
9	R. Schumacher	Williams FW22/5
10	Button	Williams FW22/4
	spare	Williams FW22/3
11	Fisichella	Benetton B200/4
12	Wurz	Benetton B200/2
	spare	Benetton B200/3
14	Alesi	Prost AP03/3
15	Heidfeld	Prost AP03/1
	spare	Prost AP03/4
16	Diniz	Sauber C19/4
17	Salo	Sauber C19/6
	spare	Sauber C19/2
18	de la Rosa	Arrows A21/3
19	Verstappen	Arrows A21/4
	spare	Arrows A21/2
20	Gene	Minardi M02/3
21	Mazzacane	Minardi M02/4
	spare	Minardi M02/1
22	Villeneuve	BAR 02/4
23	Zonta	BAR 02/1
	spare	BAR 02/2

DRIVERS

1	Michael Schumacher	56
2	David Coulthard	34
3	Mika Häkkinen	32
4	Rubens Barrichello	28
5	Giancarlo Fisichella	18
6	Ralf Schumacher	12
7 =	Heinz-Harald Frentzen	5
7 =	Jacques Villeneuve	5
7 =	Jarno Trulli	5
10 =	Eddie Irvine	3
10 =	Jenson Button	3
10 =	Mika Salo	3
13	Jos Verstappen	2
14 =	Ricardo Zonta	1
14 =	Pedro de la Rosa	1

CONSTRUCTORS

1	Ferrari	84
2	McLaren	66
3	Benetton	18
4	Williams	15
5	Jordan	10
6	BAR	6
7 =	Jaguar	3
7 =	Sauber	3
7 =	Arrows	3

FRENCH

grand prix

COULTHARD
HÄKKINEN
BARRICHELLO
VILLENEUVE
R. SCHUMACHER
TRULLI

FIA WORLD CHAMPIONSHIP • ROUND 9

Mobil **ⵏ**

David Coulthard (*right*) shows his
irritation with Michael Schumacher's
defensive tactics as the pair battle for
the lead.
Paul-Henri Cahier

DIARY

Honda confirms it will provide Jordan with works F1 engines on a par with those used by British American Racing from the start of the 2001 season.

Johnny Herbert and Jaguar agree they will part company at the end of the current season.

Olivier Panis in talks with BAR about the prospect of a drive alongside Jacques Villeneuve in 2001.

Arrows poised to switch from Supertec V10 deal in 2001 to use Peugeot V10s under the Asia Motor Technologies banner, the French car maker having sold this corporation the rights to its F1 engine programme.

MAGNY-COURS QUALIFYING

Coulthard had his hands full from the start of the weekend, even though he was well on the pace from the outset. On Friday morning he had a mechanical fuel pump failure, then in the afternoon a cracked carbon-fibre oil tank thwarted his progress. Thanks to the liberal application of tank tape and araldite, the leak was quenched for long enough for him to finish the day with the fastest time.

Yet this was only the beginning of a remarkable catalogue of misfortune. On Saturday morning his race car suffered another split oil tank. As he nursed it gently back to the pits, the engine oil level fell to a dangerously low level, so it was decided to install a fresh Mercedes V10 for qualifying.

As the engine was being changed, the mechanics now found that the electric fuel pump had failed. Since the fuel pumps on the MP4/15 are situated inside the fuel cell itself, rectifying the problem was clearly not going to be the work of a moment.

Consequently the McLaren mechanics were faced with the prospect of working their fingers to the bone, not to mention against the clock, to change all Häkkinen's settings on the spare car in order that Coulthard could use it in qualifying.

This was far more complicated than adjusting pedal, seat and shock absorber settings because Mika and David were using very different mechanical set-ups at this race, with variations between such basic components as pushrods and steering rack.

On the face of it, the odds seemed to be stacked pretty heavily against the McLaren lads getting everything finished in time, but they all knuckled down brilliantly to get David out on the circuit for his first run in the spare with just 25 minutes to go. This also produced the unusual sight of his distinctive blue helmet poking out of a car carrying 'Mika' labels at this unbranded race where cigarette advertising is not permitted.

Immediately David was right on the pace. Five minutes earlier Schumacher had clinched the 27th pole position of his career with a 1m 15.632s, but the McLaren driver was determined to make a fight of it, coming close on 1m 16.176s.

Then he went back into the pit lane to take the now-readied race car, surviving a spin and another run spoiled when he came up behind Ralf Schumacher's Williams which was exiting the pit lane, before slamming in a 1m 15.734s best to clinch second spot on the front row. To make things even more difficult, Coulthard was twice stopped at the random pit lane weight check.

'I have to take my hat off to all the mechanics who had to work hard under very pressured conditions and did a good job,' he said.

For all the Scot's heroics, Michael remained characteristically unruffled. 'My first run was spot-on and that's the main reason I took pole,' he said, 'because others improved on their later runs. So far the weekend is going well, largely because of the good work we did here in testing last week.'

In the second McLaren, Häkkinen seemed a shade off the pace. Time was when one expected Mika to pull a miracle out of the bag in the closing seconds of the session and push Schumacher's Ferrari off pole. Not this time, and the Finn had to manage with a best of 1m 16.050s.

Third up to the final moments of the session, Mika was bumped back to fourth by Barrichello's Ferrari (1m 16.047s) on the Brazilian's final lap. Häkkinen smiled weakly and talked vaguely about a touch too much understeer and problems pitching the car into the slower corners.

Barrichello believed that only ill-fortune prevented him from bagging second on the grid. 'We had a bit of difficulty as we tried to change the set-up after the first run, which wasn't bad, and then we made further changes for the next two,' he said.

'But when we checked the ride height we did not get the result we expected. We went back to the original set-up for the final run, but by then the track was hotter and slower.'

Ralf Schumacher wound up a delighted, and slightly surprised, fifth fastest on 1m 16.291s in his Williams FW22-BMW. 'I got the maximum out of the car,' he said. 'I eventually managed the perfect lap after slight mistakes on the first three runs.' Jenson Button had to be satisfied with tenth on 1m 16.905s. 'By the time I got out for my second and third runs the conditions were too hot,' he said.

Eddie Irvine managed a strong sixth-fastest time (1m 16.399s) in the Jaguar R1, reporting no particular problems. Johnny Herbert wound up 11th on 1m 17.176s. 'I didn't get the balance right and could not attack the faster corners,' he said.

Jacques Villeneuve was also extremely satisfied with seventh-fastest time in the BAR-Honda, but Ricardo Zonta stopped on the circuit possibly with an engine failure, and then had to take over the spare car without the latest aerodynamic package.

Heinz-Harald Frentzen (8th) and Jarno Trulli (9th) were disappointed. 'I had expected a top six place, but somewhere the lap time just slipped away from us,' said Frentzen. Mika Salo (12th) continued to wrestle with his Sauber's driveability while Pedro Diniz took the spare car after a gearbox problem. Pedro de la Rosa took the spare Arrows A21 after his race car developed an electrical problem while both Benetton drivers reported consistently poor grip and balance.

Right: Ralf Schumacher qualified an impressive fifth on the grid and carried on the good work in the race.

Below right: Jarno Trulli took the final points-scoring position.
Both photographs: Paul-Henri Cahier

DAVID Coulthard dramatically revitalised his challenge for the World Championship with a decisive victory in the French Grand Prix during the course of which he elbowed his McLaren-Mercedes ahead of Michael Schumacher's Ferrari to take the lead in a symbolic assertion to take on the German driver head-to-head over the remaining eight races of the season.

Only two days after the McLaren team confirmed that the 29-year-old Scot would be staying in its line-up alongside Mika Häkkinen for the 2001 season, Coulthard's success firmly endorsed the team's strategy to defuse their future plans of any element of uncertainty.

After climbing from the winner's rostrum following his 14.7s victory over Mika Häkkinen in second place, Coulthard launched a brisk attack on what he clearly regarded as Schumacher's unsporting tactics, thus ensuring that the controversial question of driving etiquette was lobbed firmly back into the court of the sport's governing body.

'I won the race and I am delighted about that, but I just don't think Michael is very sporting in the way he drives on the track,' he said. 'I know people will say sour grapes, or whatever, but trying to drive people off the circuit is not within the rules.

'I'm delighted that our team has got first and second places, because we did it in the most sporting way and deserved it more.'

At first glance, this seemed to have the potential to become an embarrassing issue for the FIA president Max Mosley who used the occasion of the French Grand Prix to launch a new European road safety initiative which rides on the back of the supposed high standards of driving showcased by the F1 fraternity.

The 'one move' technique – whereby a driver is permitted to manoeuvre his car once in a specific direction while defending his line – is not a rule as such, but a factor which will be taken into account by the stewards when it comes to assessing blame in the event of an incident.

The paddock was divided over its legitimacy, some people feeling that it was a means of validating dangerous driving. Coulthard clearly felt it had been deployed by Schumacher at Magny-Cours in a manner which took it far beyond the normal boundaries of permissible sportsmanship.

Having qualified second on the grid, Coulthard had to back off going into the first corner when Schumacher deliberately swerved across his bows.

'The rules allow him to make one change of position, so he's within the rules,' said Coulthard, 'but once again I had to lift and weave to one side because of a car veering across in front of me.

'I think that my start was a little better than Michael's, but when he cut across me I had to back off. I didn't try to drive Rubens [Barrichello] off the track and he won the corner. It should be done in a sporting way, not in a you-move-or-we're-going-to-crash situation.'

It was probably the best drive of Coulthard's career and, like so many things in F1, was underpinned by a seemingly minor, but crucial technical decision made as the Scot's McLaren-Mercedes MP4/15 was lined up on the starting grid alongside Schumacher's pole-winning Ferrari F1-2000.

During the warm-up, Coulthard had been worried about the long-term prospects of slight understeer on the long 180-degree Estoril right-hander beyond the pits which leads out onto the long back straight. With the entire field opting for Bridgestone's super soft compound – and the track washed raw of its coating of rubber by an overnight storm – there was a premium on having the best balanced car possible in an effort to minimise tyre wear.

With this in mind, David and his engineer Pat Fry decided to remove the gurney flap from the rear wing – the narrow tailplane which is used to fine-tune the car's aerodynamic downforce. After a few laps he knew it was the right decision.

The first traces of understeer quickly vanished as the car settled into its stride and the fractionally reduced drag bonus gave him slightly improved top speed as he approached the Adelaide hairpin at around 190 mph. Thus armed, he convincingly delivered the goods.

Thanks to the chop he received from Schumacher, Coulthard dropped to an initial third place behind Rubens Barrichello in the other Ferrari. But the McLaren driver fought back doggedly, displaying great flair and determination as he first hunted down the Brazilian, overtaking him with 22 of the race's 72 laps completed.

After the first flurry of refuelling stops, Coulthard had a clear track to Schumacher's Ferrari and piled on the pressure. From 5.3s behind on lap 26, he reduced it to 4.9s, 3.6s, 2.5s, 1.2s and then down to 0.5s by lap 32.

From then on the gloves were off and David was determined to get the lead. On one lap his frustration

Below right: Bernie was in the pink after his mega-deal.

Left: Jean Alesi smokes the Bridgestones on his Prost.

Below left: Alain Prost and Jean Alesi sum up the mood in the French team's camp.
All photographs: Paul-Henri Cahier

brimmed over as he attempted to run round the outside of the Adelaide hairpin at the end of the back straight, only for Schumacher to squeeze him out.

The in-car camera on the rollover bar of McLaren number two suddenly bore witness to a hand waving in an abusive gesture to Schumacher. Sheepishly, and with great dignity, Coulthard apologised for this momentary lapse of taste once the race was over.

On lap 40, finally it was all over. Coulthard dived down the inside of the Ferrari at the same point, they rubbed wheels and the McLaren was through, accelerating away on a surge of adrenalin, carrying the Scot on towards the ninth grand prix victory of his career and his third this season so far.

Commented the Ferrari team leader: 'The tyres on my car seemed to suffer a drop in performance earlier on than the others. This problem was at its worst after the first pit stop. At first I could control the situation, but then the tyres went off and I tried to look after them, knowing that there were still a lot of laps to go. Then I started to slow and Coulthard managed to get past me.'

For his part, Schumacher was now denied any points in the torrid heat of central France. After grappling with premature deterioration of grip on his second set of tyres, he eventually stopped after 58 laps with a rare engine failure.

Häkkinen's second place was worthy enough, but somehow the Finn's dashing driving style lacked its fine edge yet again. He now only had a single win to his credit this season and Coulthard was increasingly looking like a man set to deprive him of his World Championship crown.

Third at the chequered flag, Barrichello also suffered from premature loss of tyre grip. He additionally lost 10s at his second refuelling stop when there was a problem with his front right wheel which effectively wiped out all chance of launching a serious counter-attack against Häkkinen.

'It was a shame,' said Rubens, 'because I heard that Häkkinen had a so-so pit stop as well.'

For British American Racing, sent reeling with Honda's decision to also supply Jordan next year, the race proved a welcome respite from much criticism. Jacques Villeneuve fought tooth and nail against Ralf Schumacher's Williams for the distinction of being 'best of the rest' and won the scrap by just over 2s at the finish. Schumacher was also dogged by slight overheating in the closing stages; it later emerged that one of his 'tear off' visors had lodged in a radiator duct.

'At the start I lost two positions to Villeneuve and Frentzen,' he shrugged. 'I had the feeling that I could have been faster than Heinz-Harald, but it was impossible to overtake him.

'Luckily, the team had a good pit-stop strategy so that I could overtake Heinz after the first stop. Later I managed to overtake Trulli and got close to Villeneuve, but didn't want to risk too much and slowed down a bit to save the valuable two points.'

For his part, of course, Villeneuve was elated. 'The start was so good that I even surprised myself,' he grinned. 'I settled into fifth and was also surprised that the first four didn't pull away from us.

'We were running with more fuel than was necessary to give us flexibility over when to make our stops. I had a good battle with Ralf towards the end. He was better in the corners, but I was quicker on the straights.'

Jacques also had the satisfaction of out-classing both Jordans on this occasion. Jarno Trulli heading Heinz-Harald Frentzen home for sixth place after a tense moment when the two cars touched at the hairpin before the pits. For both men, the revised aerodynamic package and an up-rated Mugen Honda V10 scheduled for the next race in Austria could not arrive quickly enough.

Jenson Button drove well to take eighth ahead of Giancarlo Fisichella's Benetton and Mika Salo's Sauber. The Benetton B200s looked moderately respectable in the race, Fisichella pulling up from 16th to ninth although there was another disappointing outcome for Alexander Wurz who ended up in a gravel trap after 34 laps.

Further back, the Prosts of Nick Heidfeld and Jean Alesi wound up 12th and 14th after a fraught race in which the young German driver pitched his team-mate into a spin and later had to make an extra stop to recharge the engine's pneumatic valve-gear reservoir.

'My car understeered at Estoril,' explained Heidfeld, 'so Jean overtook me. So did Fisichella two laps later, even though I was quicker.

'I tried to out-brake Fisichella in the hairpin, but I was a bit late on the brakes and touched Jean, who spun, for which I am really sorry.'

The two Prosts were separated by a frustrated Eddie Irvine who had to make two extra unscheduled stops with the Jaguar R1 to top up with fuel after the rigs short-changed him on two previous pit visits. 'We can't continue to qualify in the top six and walk away empty handed,' shrugged Irvine. 'It's just another chance missed.'

For Schumacher, it had been two retirements in three races. Although he still led the championship stakes, McLaren-Mercedes were piling on the pressure. It would become even more relentless yet.

Yet the day overwhelmingly belonged to Coulthard. After the embarrassment of stalling on the grid before the start in Canada two weeks earlier, he had now delivered a flawless, top-drawer performance which added more lustre to his status as a genuine World Championship contender.

Ecclestone's sale of the century

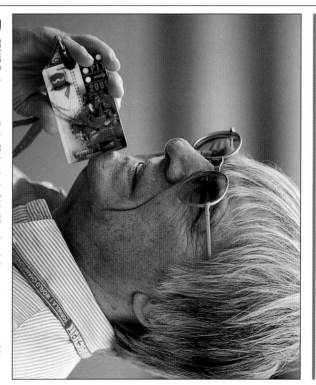

BERNIE Ecclestone pulled off the deal of his life when it began to emerge at Magny-Cours that his Formula One Management group had extended its stranglehold on grand prix racing's commercial rights for another 100 years beyond their current expiry in 2011.

Although the FIA general assembly overwhelmingly voted to extend those rights until 31 December 2111 in exchange for a payment of around £211.76 million, Ecclestone's business might only have to pay £1.76 million per year over the balance of the contract. However, should Ecclestone successfully float his business on the stock exchange, the payment scheduled to the FIA will be speeded up.

'Bernie bought some rights from the FIA and if it makes sense for both parties, then that's fine,' said Flavio Briatore, managing director of the Benetton team and a close personal friend of Ecclestone. 'I believe it is properly done.'

The precise details of the new contract had yet to be communicated to the competing teams. 'We are just chaff in the wind,' shrugged Frank Williams. 'Bernie has told us he is negotiating with Max to buy the rights, but we don't know how much is involved.'

Ferrari sporting director Jean Todt mirrored Williams's obvious concern. 'We are aware, we are informed, but it is up to the FIA and the owner of the rights to make any comments,' he said.

The long-term implications for the teams' income were less clear. The 11 F1 entrants currently share 47 per cent of the income derived from television and other marketing rights under the terms of the Concorde agreement, a complex protocol which has governed the commercial and technical administration of grand prix racing since 1982.

However, it seemed questionable that the new arrangement would have the unqualified support of McLaren and Williams, two of the sport's blue riband teams who have won more races between them over the past two decades than the rest of the competitors put together.

The negotiating clout of McLaren chairman Ron Dennis and Sir Frank Williams forced Ecclestone and the FIA to change the terms of the newly renegotiated Concorde agreement in 1997 when it became clear to these two team owners that Ecclestone was taking too large a slice of the commercial cake.

The current Concorde agreement expires in 2007 and it is clear that the teams will be looking for another pay hike from Ecclestone's kitty when it comes to negotiating fresh terms.

More immediately, however, the European Union competition commissioner Mario Monti had given the green light to this new F1 arrangement. He had previously complained that by having a stake in the income from the World Championship, the FIA was in an unfairly monopolistic situation. Now the governing body was being seen to isolate itself from Ecclestone's commercial operation and thereby theoretically remove itself from further legal criticism.

It was also believed that this ruling could affect the manner in which other major sports, such as football, are administered. There was speculation, for example, that UEFA television contracts could come under the anti-monopolistic scrutiny of the EU competition commissioner as a direct consequence of Formula 1's commercial reorganisation.

In a separate development, the FIA was planning to move its headquarters back to Paris from Geneva. It moved to Switzerland in early 1999 after a row with the French government over its tax status. That was now apparently close to being resolved.

Mobil 1
grand prix de
FRANCE

CIRCUIT DE NEVERS — MAGNY-COURS

CIRCUIT LENGTH: 2.640 miles/4.248 km

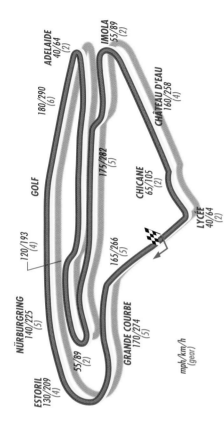

- NÜRBURGRING 140/225 (5)
- ESTORIL 130/209 (4)
- 55/89 (2)
- 120/193 (4)
- GOLF
- ADELAIDE 40/64 (2)
- IMOLA 55/89 (2)
- 180/290 (6)
- 175/282 (5)
- CHÂTEAU D'EAU 160/258 (4)
- 165/266 (5)
- GRANDE COURBE 170/274 (5)
- CHICANE 65/105 (2)
- LYCÉE 40/64 (2)
- mph/km/h [gear]

RACE DISTANCE: 72 laps, 190.069 miles/305.886 km RACE WEATHER: Dry, hot and sunny

Pos.	Driver	Nat.	No.	Entrant	Car/Engine	Laps	Time/Retirement	Speed (mph/km/h)
1	David Coulthard	GB	2	West McLaren Mercedes	McLaren MP4/15-Mercedes FO110J V10	72	1h 38m 05.538s	116.258/187.100
2	Mika Häkkinen	SF	1	West McLaren Mercedes	McLaren MP4/15-Mercedes FO110J V10	72	1h 38m 20.286s	115.968/186.633
3	Rubens Barrichello	BR	4	Scuderia Ferrari Marlboro	Ferrari F1-2000-049 V10	72	1h 38m 37.947s	115.622/186.076
4	Jacques Villeneuve	CDN	22	Lucky Strike BAR Honda	BAR 02-Honda RA100E V10	72	1h 39m 06.860s	115.060/185.171
5	Ralf Schumacher	D	9	BMW WilliamsF1 Team	Williams FW22-BMW E41 V10	72	1h 39m 09.519s	115.008/185.088
6	Jarno Trulli	I	6	Benson & Hedges Jordan	Jordan EJ10-Mugen Honda MF301HE V10	72	1h 39m 21.143s	114.784/184.727
7	Heinz-Harald Frentzen	D	5	Benson & Hedges Jordan	Jordan EJ10-Mugen Honda MF301HE V10	71		
8	Jenson Button	GB	10	BMW WilliamsF1 Team	Williams FW22-BMW E41 V10	71		
9	Giancarlo Fisichella	I	11	Mild Seven Benetton Playlife	Benetton B200-Playlife V10	71		
10	Mika Salo	SF	17	Red Bull Sauber Petronas	Sauber C19-Petronas SPE 04A V10	71		
11	Pedro Diniz	BR	16	Red Bull Sauber Petronas	Sauber C19-Petronas SPE 04A V10	71		
12	Nick Heidfeld	D	15	Gauloises Prost Peugeot	Prost AP03-Peugeot A20 V10	71		
13	Eddie Irvine	GB	7	Jaguar Racing	Jaguar R1-Cosworth CR2 V10	70		
14	Jean Alesi	F	14	Gauloises Prost Peugeot	Prost AP03-Peugeot A20 V10	70		
15	Marc Gene	ESP	20	Telefonica Minardi Fondmetal	Minardi M02-Fondmetal Ford Zetec-R V10	70		
	Michael Schumacher	D	3	Scuderia Ferrari Marlboro	Ferrari F1-2000 049 V10	58	Engine	
	Pedro de la Rosa	ESP	18	Arrows	Arrows A21-Supertec FB02 V10	45	Gearbox	
	Alexander Wurz	A	12	Mild Seven Benetton Playlife	Benetton B200-Playlife V10	34	Spun off	
	Gaston Mazzacane	ARG	21	Telefonica Minardi Fondmetal	Minardi M02-Fondmetal Ford Zetec-R V10	31	Spun off	
	Jos Verstappen	NL	19	Arrows	Arrows A21-Supertec FB02 V10	25	Gearbox	
	Johnny Herbert	GB	8	Jaguar Racing	Jaguar R1-Cosworth CR2 V10	20	Clutch	
	Ricardo Zonta	BR	23	Lucky Strike BAR Honda	BAR 02-Honda RA100E V10	16	Brakes	

Fastest lap: Coulthard, on lap 28, 1m 19.479s, 119.644 mph/192.548 km/h
Lap record: Nigel Mansell (F1 Williams FW14B-Renault V10), 1m 17.070s, 123.355 mph/198.521 km/h (1992).

Grid order	1	2	3	4	5	6	7	8	9	10	11	12	13	14	15	16	17	18	19	20	21	22	23	24	25	26	27	28	29	30	31	32	33	34	35	36	37	38	39	40	41	42	43	44	45	46	47	48	49	50	51	52	53	54	55
3 M. SCHUMACHER	3	3	3	3	3	3	3	3	3	3	3	3	3	3	3	3	3	3	3	3	3	3	3	3	2	3	3	3	3	2	2	2	2	2	2	2	2	2	2	2	2	2	2	2	2	2	2	2	2	2	2	2	2	2	2
2 COULTHARD	4	4	4	4	4	4	4	4	4	4	4	4	4	4	4	4	4	4	4	2	2	2	4	2	3	4	4	4	4	3	3	3	4	4	4	4	4	4	4	1	1	1	1	1	1	1	1	1	1	1	1	1	1	1	1
4 BARRICHELLO	2	2	2	2	2	2	2	2	2	2	2	2	2	2	4	2	4	2	4	4	4	4	3	4	4					4	4	4	3	3	3	3	3	3	3	4	4	4	4	4	4	4	4	4	4	4	4	4	4	4	4
1 HÄKKINEN	1	1	1	1	1	1	1	1	1	1	1	1	1	1	1	1	1	1	1	1	1	1	22	10	1	1	1	1	1	1	1	1	1	1	9	9	9	22	22	22	9	9	9	9	9	9	9	2	2	2	2	2	2	2	2
9 R. SCHUMACHER	22	22	22	22	22	22	22	22	22	22	22	22	22	22	22	22	22	22	22	22	22	22	1	22	9	9	9	9	9	9	22	22	22	22	22	22	22	9	9	9	22	22	22	22	22	9	9	9	9	9	9	9	9	9	9
22 VILLENEUVE	9	9	9	5	5	5	5	5	5	5	5	5	5	5	5	5	5	5	5	5	5	10	5	5	5	5	5	5	5	5	9	9	9	9	5	5	5	5	5	5	5	10	10	10	10	22	22	22	22	22	22	22	22	22	22
5 FRENTZEN	6	6	6	9	9	9	9	9	9	9	9	9	9	9	9	6	6	6	6	6	6	6	10	6	6	6	6	6	10	9	17	5	5	5	5	11	11	11	11	11	5	5	5	5	5	5	5	5	5	5	5	5	5	5	5
6 TRULLI	17	17	17	17	17	17	17	17	17	7	7	7	7	7	7	10	10	10	10	10	10	6	17	9	17	7	6	10	10	10	10	10	10	11	11	6	6	6	6	6	6	6	6	6	6	6	6	6	6	6	6	6	6	6	6
10 BUTTON	10	10	10	10	10	10	10	10	10	10	10	10	10	10	10	7	7	7	7	7	7	17	6	17	7	17	17	17	17	17	5	17	17	10	10	10	10	10	10	10	10	11	11	11	11	10	10	10	10	10	10	10	10	10	10
17 HERBERT	8	8	8	8	8	8	8	8	8	8	8	8	8	8	8	8	8	18	18	18	18	18	7	8	8	8	8	8	8	8	6	18	16	17	17	17	17	17	16	16	16	16	16	16	17	16	15	15	15	15	15	7	16	16	16
18 DE LA ROSA	18	18	18	18	18	18	18	18	18	18	18	18	18	18	18	15	15	15	15	15	15	19	19	7	19	19	11	11	11	11	11	11	11	16	16	16	16	16	17	17	17	17	17	17	16	15	7	16	16	16	16	16	15	15	15
11 FISICHELLA	12	12	12	12	12	12	12	12	12	12	12	11	11	11	11	11	11	11	11	11	19	15	16	19	12	12	12	16	12	16	16	16	15	15	15	15	15	15	15	15	15	15	15	15	15	7	16	7	7	7	7	
16 DINIZ	16	16	16	16	16	16	16	16	16	16	16	16	16	16	16	16	16	16	16	16	16	11	11	16	16	16	16	12	16	12	12	15	7	7	7	7	7	7	7	7	7	7	7	7	7										
12 WURZ	19	19	19	19	19	19	19	19	19	19	19	19	19	19	19	19	19	19	19	19	11	16	15	15	15	15	15	15	15	15	15	7	12	12	12	12																			
15 HEIDFELD	23	23	23	23	23	23	23	23	14	14	14	14	14	14	14	14	14	14	14	14	14	14	14	14	14	14	14	14	14	20	20	21	21	21	21	21																			
14 ALESI	14	14	14	14	14	14	14	14	23	23	23	23	23	23	23	23	23	23	23	23	23	23	14	21	21	20	20	20	20	14	14	20	20	20	20	20																			
23 ZONTA	16	16	16	16	16	16	16	16	16	16	16	16	16	16	16	16	16	16	16	16	12	12	12	12	20	21	21	21	21	21	21																								
19 VERSTAPPEN	12	12	12	12	12	12	12	12	12	12	12	12	12	12	12	12	12	12	12	12	20	20	20	20																															
20 GENE	20	20	20	20	20	20	20	20	20	20	20	20	20	20	20	20	20	20	20	20	14	14	8	8																															
21 MAZZACANE	21	21	21	21	21	21	21	21	21	21	21	21	21	21	21	21	21	21	21	21	21	21	7																															

Pit stop
One lap behind leader

STARTING GRID

Pos	Driver	Team		Pos	Driver	Team
3	M. SCHUMACHER	Ferrari		2	COULTHARD	McLaren
1	HÄKKINEN	McLaren		4	BARRICHELLO	Ferrari
9	R. SCHUMACHER	Williams		7	IRVINE	Jaguar
5	FRENTZEN	Jordan		22	VILLENEUVE	BAR
10	BUTTON	Williams		6	TRULLI	Jordan
17	SALO	Sauber		8	HERBERT	Jaguar
11	FISICHELLA	Benetton		18	DE LA ROSA	Arrows
15	HEIDFELD	Prost		16	DINIZ	Sauber
14	WURZ	Benetton		18	ALESI	Prost
23	ZONTA	BAR		19	VERSTAPPEN	Arrows
20	GENE	Minardi		21	MAZZACANE	Minardi

Lap chart header:

```
57 58 59 60 61 62 63 64 65 66 67 68 69 70 71 72
```

TIME SHEETS

QUALIFYING
Weather: Hot and sunny

Pos.	Driver	Car	Laps	Time
1	Michael Schumacher	Ferrari	8	1m 15.632s
2	David Coulthard	McLaren-Mercedes	10	1m 15.734s
3	Mika Häkkinen	McLaren-Mercedes	12	1m 16.047s
4	Rubens Barrichello	Ferrari	12	1m 16.050s
5	Ralf Schumacher	Williams-BMW	12	1m 16.291s
6	Eddie Irvine	Jaguar-Cosworth	12	1m 16.399s
7	Jarno Trulli	Jordan-Mugen Honda	11	1m 16.653s
8	Heinz-Harald Frentzen	Jordan-Mugen Honda	12	1m 16.658s
9	Jenson Button	Williams-BMW	11	1m 16.905s
10	Johnny Herbert	Jaguar-Cosworth	11	1m 17.176s
11	Jacques Villeneuve	BAR-Honda	11	1m 17.223s
12	Mika Salo	Sauber-Petronas	12	1m 17.279s
13	Pedro de la Rosa	Arrows-Supertec	10	1m 17.299s
14	Giancarlo Fisichella	Benetton-Playlife	12	1m 17.317s
15	Pedro Diniz	Sauber-Petronas	12	1m 17.361s
16	Nick Heidfeld	Prost-Peugeot	12	1m 17.374s
17	Alexander Wurz	Benetton-Playlife	12	1m 17.408s
18	Jean Alesi	Prost-Peugeot	12	1m 17.569s
19	Ricardo Zonta	BAR-Honda	12	1m 17.668s
20	Jos Verstappen	Arrows-Supertec	12	1m 17.933s
21	Marc Gene	Minardi-Fondmetal	11	1m 18.130s
22	Gaston Mazzacane	Minardi-Fondmetal	12	1m 18.302s

FRIDAY FREE PRACTICE
Weather: Hot and sunny

Pos.	Driver	Laps	Time
1	David Coulthard	9	1m 16.253s
2	Michael Schumacher	25	1m 16.474s
3	Mika Häkkinen	23	1m 16.687s
4	Rubens Barrichello	13	1m 16.757s
5	Mika Salo	30	1m 17.371s
6	Heinz-Harald Frentzen	31	1m 18.032s
7	Giancarlo Fisichella	9	1m 18.041s
8	Nick Heidfeld	34	1m 18.125s
9	Ralf Schumacher	22	1m 18.148s
10	Jarno Trulli	7	1m 18.156s
11	Eddie Irvine	23	1m 18.235s
12	Jean Alesi	32	1m 18.262s
13	Johnny Herbert	20	1m 18.586s
14	Alexander Wurz	32	1m 18.718s
15	Pedro Diniz	30	1m 18.819s
16	Pedro de la Rosa	30	1m 18.862s
17	Jenson Button	30	1m 18.869s
18	Jacques Villeneuve	29	1m 19.130s
19	Jos Verstappen	22	1m 19.550s
20	Marc Gene	36	1m 19.567s
21	Ricardo Zonta	17	1m 19.697s
22	Gaston Mazzacane	44	1m 20.061s

SATURDAY FREE PRACTICE
Weather: Hot and sunny

Pos.	Driver	Laps	Time
1	Michael Schumacher	27	1m 15.965s
2	Mika Häkkinen	24	1m 16.144s
3	Rubens Barrichello	25	1m 16.679s
4	Ralf Schumacher	16	1m 16.827s
5	Jarno Trulli	30	1m 16.956s
6	Heinz-Harald Frentzen	23	1m 16.983s
7	Eddie Irvine	29	1m 16.993s
8	David Coulthard	21	1m 17.060s
9	Jenson Button	27	1m 17.104s
10	Johnny Herbert	28	1m 17.135s
11	Giancarlo Fisichella	25	1m 17.372s
12	Pedro de la Rosa	26	1m 17.446s
13	Mika Salo	32	1m 17.500s
14	Jacques Villeneuve	30	1m 17.580s
15	Alexander Wurz	28	1m 17.660s
16	Jos Verstappen	26	1m 17.744s
17	Ricardo Zonta	31	1m 17.870s
18	Nick Heidfeld	22	1m 17.909s
19	Pedro Diniz	31	1m 18.046s
20	Jean Alesi	26	1m 18.211s
21	Gaston Mazzacane	28	1m 18.759s
22	Marc Gene	31	1m 18.778s

WARM-UP
Weather: Rain, then drying, sunny

Pos.	Driver	Laps	Time
1	Mika Häkkinen	13	1m 19.329s
2	David Coulthard	14	1m 19.507s
3	Michael Schumacher	14	1m 19.960s
4	Jarno Trulli	17	1m 20.124s
5	Rubens Barrichello	14	1m 20.270s
6	Eddie Irvine	16	1m 20.289s
7	Heinz-Harald Frentzen	15	1m 20.442s
8	Ricardo Zonta	16	1m 20.723s
9	Giancarlo Fisichella	15	1m 20.864s
10	Mika Salo	17	1m 20.993s
11	Pedro de la Rosa	14	1m 21.133s
12	Johnny Herbert	14	1m 21.150s
13	Jacques Villeneuve	16	1m 21.184s
14	Jos Verstappen	13	1m 21.366s
15	Marc Gene	15	1m 21.377s
16	Nick Heidfeld	13	1m 21.384s
17	Ralf Schumacher	12	1m 21.392s
18	Pedro Diniz	13	1m 21.506s
19	Jenson Button	11	1m 21.585s
20	Jean Alesi	9	1m 21.868s
21	Gaston Mazzacane	15	1m 22.011s
22	Alexander Wurz	11	1m 22.518s

RACE FASTEST LAPS
Weather: Dry, hot and sunny

Pos.	Driver	Time	Lap
1	David Coulthard	1m 19.479s	28
2	Michael Schumacher	1m 19.656s	4
3	Eddie Irvine	1m 19.708s	61
4	Mika Häkkinen	1m 19.746s	29
5	Rubens Barrichello	1m 20.225s	42
6	Heinz-Harald Frentzen	1m 20.857s	3
7	Jacques Villeneuve	1m 20.908s	27
8	Ralf Schumacher	1m 20.958s	45
9	Giancarlo Fisichella	1m 21.071s	26
10	Jarno Trulli	1m 21.115s	62
11	Nick Heidfeld	1m 21.151s	14
12	Jenson Button	1m 21.255s	4
13	Ricardo Zonta	1m 21.506s	4
14	Pedro de la Rosa	1m 21.725s	26
15	Mika Salo	1m 21.753s	30
16	Pedro Diniz	1m 21.901s	3
17	Jean Alesi	1m 22.293s	2
18	Johnny Herbert	1m 22.420s	2
19	Marc Gene	1m 22.481s	27
20	Alexander Wurz	1m 22.498s	23
21	Jos Verstappen	1m 22.563s	5
22	Gaston Mazzacane	1m 22.639s	25

POINTS TABLES

DRIVERS

Pos	Driver	Points
1	Michael Schumacher	56
2	David Coulthard	44
3	Mika Häkkinen	38
4	Rubens Barrichello	32
5	Giancarlo Fisichella	18
6	Ralf Schumacher	14
7 =	Jarno Trulli	8
7 =	Jacques Villeneuve	8
9	Heinz-Harald Frentzen	6
10	Eddie Irvine	5
10 =	Mika Salo	3
10 =	Jenson Button	3
13	Jos Verstappen	2
14 =	Ricardo Zonta	1
14 =	Pedro de la Rosa	1

CONSTRUCTORS

Pos	Constructor	Points
1	Ferrari	88
2	McLaren	82
3	Benetton	18
4	Williams	17
5	Jordan	14
6	BAR	9
7	Jaguar	5
7 =	Sauber	3
7 =	Arrows	3

CHASSIS LOG BOOK

No.	Driver	Chassis
1	Häkkinen	McLaren MP4/15/6
2	Coulthard	McLaren MP4/15/5
spare		McLaren MP4/15/2
3	M. Schumacher	Ferrari F1-2000/203
4	Barrichello	Ferrari F1-2000/202
spare		Ferrari F1-2000/198
5	Frentzen	Jordan EJ10/6
6	Trulli	Jordan EJ10/5
spare		Jordan EJ10/3
7	Irvine	Jaguar R1/4
8	Herbert	Jaguar R1/6
spare		Jaguar R1/5
9	R. Schumacher	Williams FW22/2
10	Button	Williams FW22/4
spare		Williams FW22/3
11	Fisichella	Benetton B200/4
12	Wurz	Benetton B200/2
spare		Benetton B200/5
14	Alesi	Prost AP03/3
15	Heidfeld	Prost AP03/5
spare		Prost AP03/1
16	Diniz	Sauber C19/7
17	Salo	Sauber C19/5
spare		Sauber C19/1
18	de la Rosa	Arrows A21/3
19	Verstappen	Arrows A21/4
spare		Arrows A21/2
20	Gene	Minardi M02/3
21	Mazzacane	Minardi M02/4
spare		Minardi M02/1
22	Villeneuve	BAR 02/4
23	Zonta	BAR 02/1
spare		BAR 02/2

AUSTRIAN
grand prix

FIA WORLD CHAMPIONSHIP • ROUND 10

HÄKKINEN

COULTHARD

BARRICHELLO

VILLENEUVE

BUTTON

SALO

Left: With Michael Schumacher's Ferrari beached in the foreground, the way was open for Mika Häkkinen *(inset)* to take the honours.

MIKA Häkkinen proved that a rest was as good as a change at the A1-Ring when he returned from a ten-day holiday recharging his batteries at his Monaco home to totally dominate the Austrian Grand Prix and set himself up for a possible World Championship hat trick.

Yet within hours of taking the chequered flag, Häkkinen's second win of the 2000 season was under threat. At post-race scrutineering, the Finn's McLaren-Mercedes MP4/15 was found to be missing one of the official paper FIA seals on its electronic control box which controls a wide range of the operating parameters of its Mercedes V10-cylinder engine.

The programs contained in such control boxes have a huge influence over the performance of the engine and the rules insist that once these programs are approved and lodged with the governing body they must not be altered without permission.

Although there was no obvious suggestion that there was anything amiss with Häkkinen's car, the fact that the seal was missing amounted to an offence in itself. It also meant there would be several days' delay before the result could be confirmed while the FIA electronics expert put the control box through a rigorous check before reporting his findings.

Ron Dennis, the McLaren chairman, said he was satisfied that the software was legal on Häkkinen's car. 'We are satisfied that it complies with the regulations,' he said.

However, FIA president Max Mosley would not be drawn into the issue. 'I cannot make any comment at this stage,' he said on the Monday after the race.

The rival Ferrari team took a harder line, sending a missive to the race stewards suggesting that Coulthard's second-place McLaren should also be excluded. The existence of this letter only became public a fortnight later, when the teams arrived at Hockenheim for the German Grand Prix, and would cause more than a passing degree of tension between McLaren and Ferrari as a result.

'Ferrari did not send a secret letter to the FIA and, quite rightly, the FIA passed it on to the stewards who, in turn, showed it to McLaren prior to the meeting when they were to make their decision,' claimed Luca di Montezemolo later.

'I understand how our rivals feel. This year they have been penalised twice for not having respected the technical regulations, which are extremely clear.

'They were the ones in the past who have always said "the technical regulations must be respected." If I put myself in their shoes, I quite understand them, but I find the comments made by their team manager wide of the mark, to say the least.'

However Ron Dennis refused to be drawn into a protracted war of words, but a McLaren insider said: 'We have seen the letter and know its contents.'

In the event, the FIA moved quickly to resolve the situation. Its electronics people satisfied themselves that there had been no tampering with the car's ECU and this fact was reported to a reconvened meeting of the Austrian Grand Prix stewards held in London ten days later.

Häkkinen was allowed to retain his drivers' championship points, but McLaren lost its constructors' points and was fined $50,000, the maximum financial penalty which the race stewards are empowered to impose.

The decision meant that the Finn could at least breathe again. With his McLaren-Mercedes team-mate David Coulthard freely admitting he settled for a safe second place on a day when Michael Schumacher's Ferrari crashed out on the first corner, the result dramatically threw the title battle wide open with seven of the season's 17 races still to run.

The German driver still led the title chase with 56 points, but Coulthard

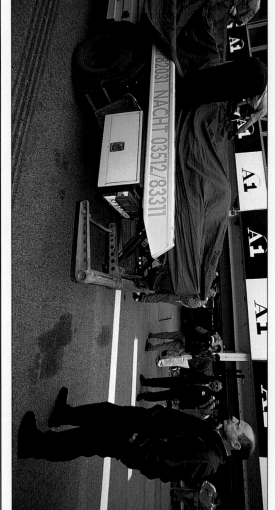

Paul-Henri Cahier

Much curiosity surrounded Häkkinen's potential form for what promised to be a crucial race for the Finn. The cumulative efforts of the past two years had finally caught up with him at Magny-Cours, leaving him so stressed out that Ron Dennis agreed he should have a mid-season break and do nothing for ten days following the French GP.

While some cynics reckoned this was precious beyond belief, it was a shrewd move. Mika returned with a fresh spring in his step and, aided by the use of Coulthard's chassis set-up, blitzed his way to pole position. More than that, he ran three laps during qualifying which would have been good enough for pole. By any standards it was an impressive performance.

McLaren had come to Austria off the back of a productive test session at Mugello during which Olivier Panis had been so impressive at the wheel of the MP4/15 that even Michael Schumacher was heard to comment that he was glad the Frenchman wasn't racing against him as well.

Bridgestone brought both medium- and soft-compound rubber to the A1-Ring and it was certainly a close call as to whether new or used tyres were the best choice. In the McLaren camp, Häkkinen did his first qualifying run on used fronts and rears while Coulthard initially tried used fronts and new rears in a bid to minimise incipient understeer.

After that the MP4/15s ran on new front and rears for their remaining qualifying laps. 'Achieving the ultimate [chassis] balance here is somewhat of an art because the first sector is slow corners, the second sector is quicker corners and the third sector is slow again,' said McLaren technical director Adrian Newey.

'The soft tyres tend to be OK for one lap and then the grooves open up and that initially causes some understeer. Then they eventually come back again. So there's a period between lap three and lap ten when you have a bit more understeer. Here the tyres are better when they are fresh, which is why we qualified on new tyres.'

In the event, most of the field opted for the softer compound with only the two Williams-BMW drivers, the Arrows team-mates and Heinz-Harald Frentzen selecting the medium compound.

Häkkinen was understandably content with his own performance in securing the 27th pole position of his career, while Coulthard concealed his disappointment well after being pipped at the post by just 0.385s.

'The set-up was definitely better, unfortunately I was worse,' he said. 'On my last run I didn't quite get the first corner right. Normally the first sector has been quite strong for me, but I just tried to sneak a little bit more at the entrance to the first corner. But I clipped the kerb and lost almost two tenths by the time I got to the second corner.'

In the Ferrari camp, there was huge disappointment that

A1-RING QUALIFYING

Michael Schumacher could only manage to line up fourth fastest on 1m 11.046s, 0.2s behind team-mate Rubens Barrichello. From the word go Michael seemed to be struggling for balance and had a spin and a couple of lurid slides as he tried to over-compensate for an obvious performance deficiency.

'I seemed to lose out to the others in the first and third sectors and was only really competitive in the second one,' he shrugged. 'I could have been quicker, but not quick enough for the front row.'

The third row of the grid threw up an impressive pairing with Jarno Trulli's Jordan EJ10 alongside Ricardo Zonta's BAR-Honda. Trulli reported that his car's balance was just about perfect for much of the weekend and by saving his run to later in the session comprehensively out-flanked his team-mate Frentzen who admitted that he made his runs too soon and had to be content with a distant 15th.

Zonta was absolutely delighted to have pipped team-mate Jacques Villeneuve who lined up right behind him, both BAR drivers surviving lurid spins during the course of qualifying. 'I was a bit disappointed with the outcome,' said Jacques, 'because we went for a final four-timed-lap run and it was a bit too much for the tyres. But it's a great result for the team, though, because the times are very tight.'

Eighth-fastest Giancarlo Fisichella wrestled all weekend long with wayward handling balance on his Benetton B200, but pipped Mika Salo's Sauber C19 and Jos Verstappen's Arrows A21 who rounded off the top ten, the Dutchman being very happy with the feel of his car despite slightly too much understeer.

In the Prost camp Nick Heidfeld qualified well in 13th, using new rear tyres and scrubbed fronts on his fourth – and best – run, while in the Jaguar camp, Eddie Irvine was obliged to withdraw from the race on Friday afternoon after suffering recurring abdominal pains which caused him to fly back to London for specialist medical treatment. His place in the team was taken by F3 ace Luciano Burti, Jaguar's test driver, who qualified in spectacularly in 21st place, just 2.4s away from Häkkinen's pole time on his GP debut.

Meanwhile, Johnny Herbert's Jaguar R1 suffered a broken left rear suspension in qualifying while Burti continued his learning process. 'I'm thoroughly disappointed because I think we could have popped our nose into the top ten today, but we never got the chance on the last run because of the suspension problem,' said Herbert as he reflected on his eventual 16th place on the grid. 'It's a shame because the car felt good up to that point.'

There was also no joy in the Williams camp where the FW22s showed their usual aversion to low-grip circuits, Jenson Button and Ralf Schumacher lining up 18th and 19th as they struggled for mechanical grip particularly in the slow corners.

Black magic. Another flawless pit stop from the McLaren crew fuelled Mika Häkkinen to victory once again.

Mark Thompson/Allsport

Major car makers poised to take slice of F1 action

RUMBLINGS of discontent amongst F1 teams regarding Bernie Ecclestone's increasing stranglehold on the FIA World Championship seemed likely to be silenced if five of the world's major motor manufacturers eventually decide to purchase a one-third stake in Bernie Ecclestone's SLEC empire.

Reports in British business circles suggested strongly that Ford, DaimlerChrysler and Toyota – plus two others, presumably including Ferrari's owners Fiat – were keen to buy a stake in SLEC from EMTV, the German media company which purchased a 50 per cent stake in SLEC earlier this year.

Speculation intensified after the Austrian Grand Prix that if the major motor companies buy a stake in F1 they would not only become locked in for a long period, but that fact in itself would prevent anybody from even contemplating a rival series – something which has been muttered about by some F1 entrants if they fail to cut a financial deal more beneficial to themselves when it comes to re-negotiating the Concorde agreement which expires in 2007.

This development came on the back of the decision by the FIA to lease Ecclestone the commercial rights attached to the FIA Formula 1 World Championship for another 100 years beyond the current expiry of his present arrangement in 2011.

Nick Samengo-Turner – who heads Cambridge Capital Partners, an investment banking boutique specialising in the motor industry and whose family backed the Parnell Racing F1 team in the early 1960s – commented: 'The important issue is, will the teams go along with signing the new TV rights agreement?'

Another F1 insider commented wryly: 'A deal like this would tie the elephants and clowns down so they cannot leave the circus.'

In October 1999 Ecclestone sold 12.5 per cent of SLEC for £235 million to Morgan Grenfell Private Equity, a venture capital arm of Deutsche Bank. They tried to syndicate another 37.5 per cent of SLEC to other investors, but instead the American venture capital firm Hellman & Friedman snapped up the stake in February 2000.

A month later EMTV, whose previous claim to fame was that it owned the 'muppets', bought the stakes from the two venture capitalists for a total of £1.3 billion – which ensured that Hellman & Friedman had doubled its money in four weeks.

Right: Luciano Burti, a last-minute replacement for the indisposed Eddie Irvine, took a steady approach on his grand prix debut.

Below right: Jenson Button congratulates the Brazilian after the race.
Both photographs: Paul-Henri Cahier

---

and Häkkinen were closing in on 50 and 48 points respectively. As an added bonus, McLaren surged ahead of Ferrari in the constructors' points table for the first time this season with 98 points to the Italian team's 92. Until the stewards' decision, that is.

Having been beaten to pole position by the revitalised Häkkinen, Coulthard was just squeezed back into second place as the pack braked hard for the first corner. But as the McLarens got through cleanly in first and second places, Schumacher suddenly found his Ferrari pitched sideways in third place after a nudge from Ricardo Zonta's fast-starting BAR immediately behind it.

In a split second cars were scattering in all directions with Schumacher out of the race on the spot despite half-hearted efforts to stagger back on the circuit which some cynics interpreted as a bid to get the race red-flagged to a halt.

In the middle of the mêlée, Pedro Diniz swerved his Sauber to avoid Jos Verstappen's Arrows, and pushed Fisichella's Benetton into the barrier. Both Saubers then bumped into each other and Jarno Trulli's Jordan collided with Schumacher's spun Ferrari. The safety car was deployed to slow the field for a lap while the debris was cleared, leaving Häkkinen ahead of Coulthard, Mika Salo's Sauber, Pedro de la Rosa's Arrows and the rest of the pack.

The safety car pulled into the pit lane on lap three, after which the two McLarens were left to surge majestically away from their rivals, leaving Schumacher to walk back to the pits in company with an equally disappointed Jarno Trulli who had qualified his Jordan fifth only for his car to end up nose-to-nose with the Ferrari team leader in the gravel trap.

'Being on the inside of the corner you are never quite sure how much grip is there,' said Coulthard. 'I went as deep as I dared, but I was quite happy with the outcome of the opening lap when I saw Michael was out.

'Then I thought "what's the point of risking everything when I'm pulling back six points on Michael?" so I chose to consider the big picture. Although Mika was a little quicker than me in the early stages because I had a slightly heavier fuel load, the race was over after about ten laps when I decided not to take the big risk.'

As early as lap 20 of the 71-lap race the McLaren pit was showing 'SHIFT REVS' signals to the reigning World Champion, indicating that it was already time to cut his revs, change up early and conserve the machinery.

In fact, the first corner pile-up delivered a double bonus to the McLaren duo. Not only did it remove Schumacher from the equation, but Rubens Barrichello also found his other Ferrari handling badly after being forced to dodge around over the debris in order to get through the corner.

Schumacher was philosophical. 'I was going into the first corner when Zonta hit me, sending me into a spin,' he said. 'It is as simple as that. Of course, I am very disappointed. Ricardo overestimated his own abilities and underestimated his speed, but I am sure there was nothing intentional about his actions.

'He was given a stop-go penalty, so I am sure he will admit it was his fault.'

In the opening phase of the race, Barrichello found his Ferrari handling so badly that he was unable to make any impression on the impressive Pedro de la Rosa whose Arrows A21 held a strong third place through to its retirement with engine problems on lap 32.

'I didn't see much of what happened at the start,' said Barrichello. 'I made a good one and braked quite late, but saw the nose of Michael's car on my inside. But then I was hit by somebody and went wide onto the gravel, but I managed to power out of it. I was lucky to survive.

'The car was almost undriveable because the floor was damaged, then at the pit stop the team made some adjustments, but by then it was too late. All in all, I was lucky to finish third.'

With the first four runners stringing out in distant formation during the early laps of the race, Mika Salo's Sauber ran fifth ahead of Johnny Herbert's Jaguar and Jenson Button's Williams-BMW, both the British drivers enjoying an unexpected opportunity to showcase their talents after making many places dodging through the first-corner carnage.

In the event, it was Jacques Villeneuve who stormed through to snatch fourth place from Button, vaulting ahead of the 20-year-old at his refuelling stop at the end of lap 49 and then opening a 3.5s margin at the chequered flag.

Jacques, who'd dropped to a distant 15th after the first-corner chaos, was well satisfied with the BAR-Honda's performance. 'I really didn't think I'd get in the points today,' he admitted, 'so it was a good result.

'We obviously had a terrible start to the race, but then our pit-stop strategy was good – we pitted late – and that's what allowed us to finish fourth. I didn't have any problems in the race other than with [Nick] Heidfeld, who was driving like when he was in Formula 3000, just putting everyone in the grass.

'When you're running 14th and 15th, that sort of driving is very difficult to accept. All told, though, a good outcome.'

Criticism from Villeneuve pretty well rounded off what, for Heidfeld, was a fairly ghastly day. Battling for 13th place with his Prost-Peugeot team-mate Jean Alesi, the young German's race ended on lap 42 when the two French cars collided and pirouetted into retirement at the first corner.

'I had been in eighth place when I made my one and only pit stop,' said Nick. 'Jean was [then] very close behind me after the stop and he was a lot quicker because he still had to stop a second time.

'At the first corner, he touched me trying to overtake me on the inside. I saw him on the straight, but not when he was beside me in the corner. It's a shame, because I was well placed and neither of us was able to continue.'

Alesi was equally philosophical. 'I didn't realise that Nick was unable to see me,' he shrugged. 'I'm very disappointed.'

For Jenson Button, the Austrian Grand Prix was a huge success, ending with fifth place on a day when team-mate Ralf Schumacher was delayed by brake problems and spent the latter part of the race as little more than a test session.

'It was a hard race,' said Button. 'The first corner was pretty tough to find a way through and I'm not quite sure how I came out of it at the end. The team did a good job with my pit stop, but unfortunately Jacques was able to just pop out of the pits in front of me.'

Herbert, who will be replaced in the Jaguar squad next season, missed out on the last championship point by less than half a second as he tailed Salo past the chequered flag.

'I was pretty pleased with the way I drove today, so it's frustrating finishing seventh after pushing so hard for the entire race as it means no reward,' he shrugged. His thoughts as he was lapped by the imperious Häkkinen, whom he partnered in the struggling Lotus team almost a decade ago, were not recorded.

AUSTRIAN GRAND PRIX

A1-RING
14–16 JULY 2000

grösser A1 preis von ÖSTERREICH

ZELTWEG — A1-RING
CIRCUIT LENGTH: 2.688 miles/4.326 km

REMUS KURVE 40/64 (1)
175/282 (6)
175/282 (6)
NIKI LAUDA KURVE 100/161 (4)
GÖSSER KURVE 60/97 (2)
JOCHEN RINDT KURVE 120/193 (4)
145/233 (4)
170/274 (6)
POWER HORSE KURVE 110/177 (4)
mph/km/h (gear)
MOBILKOM KURVE 90/145 (3)
CASTROL KURVE 75/121 (2)

RACE DISTANCE: 71 laps, 190.852 miles/307.146 km   RACE WEATHER: Dry, hot and sunny

Pos.	Driver	Nat.	No.	Entrant	Car/Engine	Laps	Time/Retirement	Speed (mph/km/h)
1	Mika Häkkinen	SF	1	West McLaren Mercedes	McLaren MP4/15-Mercedes FO110J V10	71	1h 28m 15.818s	129.737/208.792
2	David Coulthard	GB	2	West McLaren Mercedes	McLaren MP4/15-Mercedes FO110J V10	71	1h 28m 28.353s	129.431/208.299
3	Rubens Barrichello	BR	4	Scuderia Ferrari Marlboro	Ferrari F1-2000-049 V10	71	1h 28m 46.613s	128.987/207.585
4	Jacques Villeneuve	CDN	22	Lucky Strike BAR Honda	BAR 02-Honda RA100E V10	70		
5	Jenson Button	GB	10	BMW WilliamsF1 Team	Williams FW22-BMW E41 V10	70		
6	Mika Salo	SF	17	Red Bull Sauber Petronas	Sauber C19-Petronas SPE 04A V10	70		
7	Johnny Herbert	GB	8	Jaguar Racing	Jaguar R1-Cosworth CR2 V10	70		
8	Marc Gene	ESP	20	Telefonica Minardi Fondmetal	Minardi M02-Fondmetal Ford Zetec-R V10	70		
9	Pedro Diniz	BR	16	Red Bull Sauber Petronas	Sauber C19-Petronas SPE 04A V10	70		
10	Alexander Wurz	A	12	Mild Seven Benetton Playlife	Benetton B200-Playlife V10	70		
11	Luciano Burti	BR	7	Jaguar Racing	Jaguar R1-Cosworth CR2 V10	69		
12	Gaston Mazzacane	ARG	21	Telefonica Minardi Fondmetal	Minardi M02-Fondmetal Ford Zetec-R V10	68		
	Ricardo Zonta	BR	23	Lucky Strike BAR Honda	BAR 02-Honda RA100E V10	58	Engine	
	Ralf Schumacher	D	9	BMW WilliamsF1 Team	Williams FW22-BMW E41 V10	52	Brakes	
	Nick Heidfeld	D	15	Gauloises Prost Peugeot	Prost AP03-Peugeot A20 V10	41	Collision with Alesi	
	Jean Alesi	F	14	Gauloises Prost Peugeot	Prost AP03-Peugeot A20 V10	41	Collision with Heidfeld	
	Pedro de la Rosa	ESP	18	Arrows	Arrows A21-Supertec FB02 V10	32	Gearbox	
	Jos Verstappen	NL	19	Arrows	Arrows A21-Supertec FB02 V10	14	Loss of power	
	Heinz-Harald Frentzen	D	5	Benson & Hedges Jordan	Jordan EJ10-Mugen Honda MF301HE V10	4	Engine	
	Michael Schumacher	D	3	Scuderia Ferrari Marlboro	Ferrari F1-2000 049 V10	0	Accident	
	Jarno Trulli	I	6	Benson & Hedges Jordan	Jordan EJ10-Mugen Honda MF301HE V10	0	Accident	
	Giancarlo Fisichella	I	11	Mild Seven Benetton Playlife	Benetton B200-Playlife V10	0	Accident	

Fastest lap: Coulthard, on lap 67, 1m 11.783s, 134.808 mph/216.953 km/h (record).

Previous lap record: Jacques Villeneuve (F1 Williams FW19-Renault V10), 1m 11.814s, 134.657 mph/216.709 km/h (1997).

Grid order	1	2	3	4	5	6	7	8	9	10	11	12	13	14	15	16	17	18	19	20	21	22	23	24	25	26	27	28	29	30	31	32	33	34	35	36	37	38	39	40	41	42	43	44	45	46	47	48	49	50	51	52	53	54	55
1 HÄKKINEN	1	1	1	1	1	1	1	1	1	1	1	1	1	1	1	1	1	1	1	1	1	1	1	1	1	1	1	1	1	1	1	1	1	1	1	1	1	1	2	2	2	2	1	1	1	1	1	1	1	1	1	1	1	1	1
2 COULTHARD	2	2	2	2	2	2	2	2	2	2	2	2	2	2	2	2	2	2	2	2	2	2	2	2	2	2	2	2	2	2	2	2	2	2	2	2	2	2	1	1	1	1	2	2	2	2	2	2	2	2	2	2	2	2	2
4 BARRICHELLO	17	17	17	18	18	18	18	18	18	18	18	18	18	18	18	18	18	18	18	18	18	18	18	18	18	18	18	18	18	18	18	18	4	4	4	4	4	4	4	4	4	4	4	4	4	4	4	4	4	4	4	4	4	4	4
3 M. SCHUMACHER	18	18	18	17	17	17	4	4	4	4	4	4	4	4	4	4	4	4	4	4	4	4	4	4	4	4	4	4	4	4	18	17	17	17	17	17	17	17	17	17	17	17	8	10	10	22	22	22	22	22	22	22	22	22	22
6 TRULLI	19	8	8	8	4	4	17	17	17	17	17	17	17	17	17	17	17	17	17	17	17	17	17	17	17	8	8	8	8	8	8	22	10	12	12	10	10	10	8	22	10	12	12	10	10	10	10	10	10	10	10	10	10	10	10
23 ZONTA	8	10	4	4	8	8	8	8	8	8	8	8	8	8	8	8	8	8	8	8	8	8	8	8	8	8	8	8	8	8	10	10	10	10	10	10	10	10	10	10	10	10	17	22	12	12	10	10	17	17	17	17	17	17	17
22 VILLENEUVE	10	4	5	5	10	10	10	10	10	10	10	10	10	10	10	10	10	10	10	10	10	10	10	10	10	10	10	10	10	10	20	20	20	20	20	20	20	20	20	22	22	22	12	17	17	17	17	8	8	8	8	8	8	8	8
11 FISICHELLA	4	5	10	10	20	20	20	20	20	20	20	20	20	20	20	20	20	20	20	20	20	20	20	20	20	20	20	20	20	20	12	15	15	15	15	15	22	22	22	20	20	12	17	8	8	8	8	20	20	20	20	20			
17 SALO	5	20	20	20	12	12	12	12	12	12	12	12	12	14	14	14	14	14	14	14	14	14	12	12	12	12	12	12	12	15	22	22	22	22	22	15	15	12	12	12	23	23	20	20	20	12	12	12	12	12	12			
19 VERSTAPPEN	20	12	12	12	15	15	14	14	14	14	14	14	14	12	12	12	12	12	12	12	12	12	15	22	12	12	12	12	12	7	7	16	23	20	20	16	16	16	16	16	16	16	16	16											
16 DINIZ	12	21	15	15	14	14	15	15	15	15	15	15	15	15	15	15	15	15	15	15	15	15	22	22	22	22	22	22	22	7	7	7	7	7	7	16	16	16	23	16	16	23	23	23	23	23	23	23							
18 DE LA ROSA	21	15	14	14	22	22	22	22	22	22	22	22	22	22	22	22	22	22	22	22	22	22	7	7	7	7	7	7	7	14	14	14	16	16	16	23	23	7	7	7	7	7	7	7	7	7	7	7							
15 HEIDFELD	15	19	22	22	23	23	23	23	23	23	23	23	23	23	23	7	7	7	7	7	7	7	14	14	14	14	14	14	14	16	16	23	23	23	15	15	21	21	21	21	21	21	21	21	21	21	21	21							
12 WURZ	14	14	7	7	7	7	7	7	7	7	16	16	16	16	16	21	21	21	21	21	21	16	16	16	16	16	16	16	23	23	14	14	14	14	14	9	9	9	9	9	9	9	9	9	9										
5 FRENTZEN	22	22	16	16	16	16	16	16	16	16	7	7	7	7	21	21	21	16	16	16	16	21	21	21	21	21	21	21	21	21																									
8 HERBERT	7	7	9	21	21	21	16	21	21	21	21	21	21	21	16	16	16	16	16	21	21	21	21	21	9	9	9	9	9	9																									
14 ALESI	23	23	21	21	16	16	16	9	19	19	19	19	21	19	9	9	9	9	9	9	9	9	9	9																															
10 BUTTON	9	9	16	16	19	19	19	19	9	9	9	9	9																																										
9 R. SCHUMACHER	16	16	19	19																																																			
20 GENE																																																							
7 IRVINE																																																							
21 MAZZACANE																																																							

Pit stop

One lap behind leader

STARTING GRID

1 HÄKKINEN McLaren	**2 COULTHARD** McLaren
4 BARRICHELLO Ferrari	**3 M. SCHUMACHER** Ferrari
6 TRULLI Jordan	**23 ZONTA** BAR
22 VILLENEUVE BAR	**11 FISICHELLA** Benetton
17 SALO Sauber	**19 VERSTAPPEN** Arrows
15 HEIDFELD Prost	**12 WURZ** Benetton
5 FRENTZEN Jordan	**8 HERBERT** Jaguar
14 ALESI Prost	**10 BUTTON** Williams
9 R. SCHUMACHER Williams	**20 GENE** Minardi
7* BURTI Jaguar	**21 MAZZACANE** Minardi
16 DINIZ Sauber	**18 DE LA ROSA** Arrows

* started from pit lane

Lap chart (laps 56–71)

```
   56 57 58 59 60 61 62 63 64 65 66 67 68 69 70 71
    2  2  2  2  2  2  2  2  2  2  2  2  2  2  2  2
    1  1  1  1  1  1  1  1  1  1  1  1  1  1  1  1
    4  4  4  4  4  4  4  4  4  4  4  4  4  4  4  4
   22 22 22 22 22 22 22 22 22 22 22 22 22  4  4  4
   10 10 10 10 10 10 10 10 10 10 10 10 10 10 10 10
   17 17 17 17 17 17 17 17 17 17 17 17 17 17 17 17
    8  8  8  8  8  8  8  8  8  8  8  8  8  8  8  8
   20 20 20 20 20 20 20 20 20 20 20 20 20 20 20 20
   12 12 12 12 12 12 12 12 12 12 16 16 16 16 12 12
   16 16 16 16 16 16 16 16 16 16 12 12 12 12 16 16
   23 23 23 23 23 23 23 23 23 23 23 23 23 23 23 23
    7  7  7 21 21 21 21 21 21 21 21 21 21 21 21 21
   21 21 21  7  7  7  7  7  7  7  7  7  7  7  7  7
```

FOR THE RECORD

100th Grand Prix start
David Coulthard

First Grand Prix start
Luciano Burti

TIME SHEETS

QUALIFYING
Weather: Overcast, light rain

Pos.	Driver	Car	Laps	Time
1	David Coulthard	McLaren-Mercedes	12	1m 10.410s
2	Mika Häkkinen	McLaren-Mercedes	12	1m 10.795s
3	Rubens Barrichello	Ferrari	12	1m 10.844s
4	Michael Schumacher	Ferrari	12	1m 11.046s
5	Jarno Trulli	Jordan-Mugen Honda	11	1m 11.640s
6	Ricardo Zonta	BAR-Honda	12	1m 11.647s
7	Jacques Villeneuve	BAR-Honda	12	1m 11.649s
8	Giancarlo Fisichella	Benetton-Playlife	12	1m 11.761s
9	Mika Salo	Sauber-Petronas	10	1m 11.905s
10	Jos Verstappen	Arrows-Supertec	12	1m 11.931s
11	Pedro Diniz	Sauber-Petronas	11	1m 11.978s
12	Pedro de la Rosa	Arrows-Supertec	12	1m 12.007s
13	Nick Heidfeld	Prost-Peugeot	11	1m 12.037s
14	Alexander Wurz	Benetton-Playlife	12	1m 12.038s
15	Heinz-Harald Frentzen	Jordan-Mugen Honda	12	1m 12.043s
16	Johnny Herbert	Jaguar-Cosworth	12	1m 12.238s
17	Jean Alesi	Prost-Peugeot	12	1m 12.304s
18	Jenson Button	Williams-BMW	11	1m 12.337s
19	Ralf Schumacher	Williams-BMW	12	1m 12.347s
20	Marc Gene	Minardi-Fondmetal	11	1m 12.722s
21	Luciano Burti	Jaguar-Cosworth	12	1m 12.822s
22	Gaston Mazzacane	Minardi-Fondmetal	12	1m 13.419s

FRIDAY FREE PRACTICE
Weather: Overcast and warm

Pos.	Driver	Laps	Time
1	David Coulthard	28	1m 12.464s
2	Mika Häkkinen	21	1m 12.711s
3	Mika Salo	42	1m 12.786s
4	Michael Schumacher	40	1m 12.823s
5	Ricardo Zonta	49	1m 13.052s
6	Jarno Trulli	43	1m 13.146s
7	Rubens Barrichello	38	1m 13.359s
8	Jacques Villeneuve	43	1m 13.463s
9	Pedro Diniz	39	1m 13.548s
10	Giancarlo Fisichella	55	1m 13.596s
11	Jos Verstappen	40	1m 13.638s
12	Jean Alesi	35	1m 13.648s
13	Nick Heidfeld	45	1m 13.794s
14	Marc Gene	42	1m 13.807s
15	Pedro de la Rosa	33	1m 13.815s
16	Johnny Herbert	44	1m 13.878s
17	Gaston Mazzacane	54	1m 14.030s
18	Heinz-Harald Frentzen	47	1m 14.042s
19	Alexander Wurz	48	1m 14.136s
20	Jenson Button	44	1m 14.351s
21	Eddie Irvine	22	1m 14.603s
22	Ralf Schumacher	13	1m 15.572s

SATURDAY FREE PRACTICE
Weather: Overcast, light rain

Pos.	Driver	Laps	Time
1	Mika Häkkinen	33	1m 11.336s
2	David Coulthard	35	1m 11.416s
3	Michael Schumacher	37	1m 11.605s
4	Rubens Barrichello	36	1m 11.754s
5	Jacques Villeneuve	25	1m 12.007s
6	Johnny Herbert	33	1m 12.082s
7	Heinz-Harald Frentzen	37	1m 12.084s
8	Mika Salo	27	1m 12.142s
9	Giancarlo Fisichella	27	1m 12.208s
10	Pedro de la Rosa	29	1m 12.230s
11	Jos Verstappen	47	1m 12.342s
12	Jarno Trulli	35	1m 12.404s
13	Jenson Button	36	1m 12.430s
14	Ricardo Zonta	30	1m 12.434s
15	Ralf Schumacher	30	1m 12.525s
16	Pedro Diniz	27	1m 12.529s
17	Nick Heidfeld	27	1m 12.698s
18	Alexander Wurz	45	1m 12.822s
19	Gaston Mazzacane	28	1m 13.114s
20	Jean Alesi	27	1m 13.141s
21	Marc Gene	32	1m 13.706s
22	Luciano Burti	18	1m 14.149s

WARM-UP
Weather: Dry and overcast

Pos.	Driver	Laps	Time
1	Rubens Barrichello	15	1m 12.480s
2	David Coulthard	16	1m 12.677s
3	Mika Häkkinen	16	1m 12.754s
4	Jos Verstappen	17	1m 12.785s
5	Michael Schumacher	16	1m 13.281s
6	Ricardo Zonta	20	1m 13.608s
7	Pedro Diniz	17	1m 13.625s
8	Ralf Schumacher	16	1m 13.632s
9	Jacques Villeneuve	17	1m 13.735s
10	Pedro de la Rosa	13	1m 13.785s
11	Jenson Button	13	1m 13.827s
12	Heinz-Harald Frentzen	14	1m 13.852s
13	Mika Salo	17	1m 14.003s
14	Nick Heidfeld	18	1m 14.013s
15	Marc Gene	17	1m 14.167s
16	Jarno Trulli	18	1m 14.234s
17	Alexander Wurz	19	1m 14.349s
18	Giancarlo Fisichella	15	1m 14.466s
19	Johnny Herbert	16	1m 14.785s
20	Gaston Mazzacane	15	1m 14.795s
21	Luciano Burti	13	1m 15.277s
22	Jean Alesi	9	1m 15.407s

RACE FASTEST LAPS
Weather: Dry, hot and sunny

Driver	Time	Lap
David Coulthard	1m 11.783s	67
Mika Häkkinen	1m 11.837s	27
Rubens Barrichello	1m 11.887s	68
Jacques Villeneuve	1m 12.630s	44
Ralf Schumacher	1m 12.811s	42
Jarno Trulli	1m 12.855s	44
Pedro Diniz	1m 12.955s	63
Jenson Button	1m 12.964s	46
Nick Heidfeld	1m 13.317s	65
Pedro de la Rosa	1m 13.490s	25
Jean Alesi	1m 13.593s	38
Johnny Herbert	1m 13.613s	70
Marc Gene	1m 13.626s	41
Mika Salo	1m 13.674s	69
Gaston Mazzacane	1m 13.733s	67
Alexander Wurz	1m 14.039s	41
Luciano Burti	1m 14.098s	39
Jos Verstappen	1m 14.227s	9
Heinz-Harald Frentzen	1m 16.588s	4

POINTS TABLES

DRIVERS

1	Michael Schumacher	56
2	David Coulthard	50
3	Mika Häkkinen	48
4	Rubens Barrichello	36
5	Giancarlo Fisichella	18
6	Ralf Schumacher	14
7	Jacques Villeneuve	11
8	Jarno Trulli	6
9 =	Heinz-Harald Frentzen	5
9 =	Jenson Button	5
11	Mika Salo	4
12	Eddie Irvine	3
13	Jos Verstappen	2
14 =	Ricardo Zonta	1
14 =	Pedro de la Rosa	1

CONSTRUCTORS

1	Ferrari	92
2	McLaren	88
3	Williams	19
4	Benetton	18
5	BAR	12
6	Jordan	11
7	Sauber	4
8 =	Jaguar	3
8 =	Arrows	3

CHASSIS LOG BOOK

	Driver	Chassis
1	Häkkinen	McLaren MP4/15/6
2	Coulthard	McLaren MP4/15/7
	spare	McLaren MP4/15/2
3	M. Schumacher	Ferrari F1-2000/204
4	Barrichello	Ferrari F1-2000/202
	spare	Ferrari F1-2000/198
5	Frentzen	Jordan EJ10/6
6	Trulli	Jordan EJ10/5
	spare	Jordan EJ10/4
7	Burti	Jaguar R1/4
8	Herbert	Jaguar R1/6
	spare	Jaguar R1/5
9	R. Schumacher	Williams FW22/2
10	Button	Williams FW22/3
	spare	Williams FW22/4
11	Fisichella	Benetton B200/4
12	Wurz	Benetton B200/2
	spare	Benetton B200/5
16	Diniz	Sauber C19/7
17	Salo	Sauber C19/5
	spare	Sauber C19/6
15	Heidfeld	Prost AP03/3
14	Alesi	Prost AP03/2
	spare	Prost AP03/1
18	de la Rosa	Arrows A21/3
19	Verstappen	Arrows A21/4
	spare	Arrows A21/2
20	Gene	Minardi M02/3
21	Mazzacane	Minardi M02/4
	spare	Minardi M02/1
22	Villeneuve	BAR 02/4
23	Zonta	BAR 02/1
	spare	BAR 02/2

GERMAN *grand prix*

Clockwise from top left:
Michael Schumacher ends up
in the gravel after tangling
with Fisichella on the run into
the first corner.
Mark Thompson/Allsport

An emotional Rubens
Barrichello on the top step of
the podium; and taking the
flag for the first victory in his
123-race F1 career.
Both photographs: Paul-Henri Cahier

BARRICHELLO
HÄKKINEN
COULTHARD
BUTTON
SALO
DE LA ROSA

HOCKENHEIM QUALIFYING

Friday free practice ended with a thunderstorm *(below)* of such Wagnerian proportions that the official press conference was cancelled after the voices of the participants were literally drowned out by the rain beating on the aluminium roof of the media centre. It set the tone for the rest of the weekend.

This circuit through the pine forests near Heidelberg is also one of the most demanding on machinery – around 60 per cent of the 4.241-mile lap sees the cars running on absolutely full throttle – and, by definition, is also very hard on the brakes as competitors call for dramatic retardation from almost 200 mph on three occasions every lap.

Schumacher finished the first day just 0.043s ahead of his old adversary Heinz-Harald Frentzen who the previous week signed a two-year extension of his contract with the Jordan team and who was confident that he could run with the leading bunch on his home turf.

Jordan arrived at Hockenheim with a raft of aerodynamic improvements which were tested with positive results at Silverstone the previous week. Yet when it came to Saturday qualifying, Heinz-Harald tried to be a little too clever. And paid a most unfortunate price.

As qualifying started, so did the rain. Everybody queued up at the end of the pit lane on dry rubber, determined to make the most of the first few laps. Frentzen decided to straight-line the first chicane in order to get ahead of a Sauber and a Prost immediately ahead of him.

This slice of enterprise produced a clear track – and a penalty. 'H–H' found his best dry-weather time disallowed and his second flying lap was spoiled when Jacques Villeneuve's BAR spun in front of him at the Ostkurve. For much of the session that left him outside the 107 per cent qualifying cut-off, but he eventually squeezed in 17th on 1m 49.280s.

As Frentzen quietly seethed, the McLaren MP4/15s of David Coulthard and Mika Häkkinen were trading fastest times with Michael Schumacher's Ferrari for those first few frantic laps. Frentzen did a 1m 48.819s – which quickly went out of the window. Moments later Jarno Trulli got down to 1m 48.121s. Then Schumacher went quickest on 1m 47.163s before Coulthard plucked a startlingly brave 1m 45.697s out of the hat. It would keep the Scot at the top of the timing screens for the rest of the afternoon.

The main issue was always going to be fought out between McLaren and Ferrari. The Italian cars arrived at Hockenheim with a totally new low-downforce aero package while McLaren brought a few subtle bodywork changes and lightweight brake calipers to help their qualifying efforts.

Yet on Saturday morning Schumacher ran into problems, spinning off into a tyre barrier after his car's undertray became detached. The impact removed its rear wing and right suspension, so it was prepared for Rubens Barrichello's use in qualifying as Michael switched to the spare.

'Qualifying was a lottery and we didn't quite get it right', admitted Ferrari technical director Ross Brawn after Michael vaulted from fourth to second in the closing moments of the session, still in precarious wet/dry conditions.

'It was a disaster for Rubens who stopped on the circuit with an electrical problem. We were already trying to repair Michael's crashed car but then had to try and change all the pedals around as well because Rubens brakes with his right foot and Michael with his left. To change the pedals takes a long time which is why we missed the little dry spell at the start of the session.' In the end the Brazilian had to be satisfied with 18th.

Giancarlo Fisichella used the spare Benetton B200 to great effect after spinning off in his race car. 'On my first lap, I spun off because the kerbs were wet and I thought that was the end of the session for me because we expected it to rain any minute,' he said.

As things turned out, he delivered a perfect 1m 47.130s which looked good enough to secure second place alongside Coulthard on the front row until Schumacher simply stunned everybody with a 1m 47.063s on dry tyres while the track was still significantly wet on the second sector of the lap.

Häkkinen was out shortly afterwards, but failed to match this superb effort, the Finn having to be content with fourth on 1m 47.162s which meant that he lined up behind Coulthard in the other MP4/15.

The jumbled grid order immediately behind the World Champion reflected some opportunistic driving during that brief spell when the circuit was dry. Pedro de la Rosa (1m 47.786s) emerged an excellent fifth in the Arrows A21 ahead of Jarno Trulli's Jordan (1m 47.833s) and Benetton's Alexander Wurz.

In ninth place Jacques Villeneuve's BAR was sandwiched by the Jaguar R1s of Johnny Herbert (1m 48.078s) and Eddie Irvine (1m 48.305s). Two well timed runs and a strong showing from the promising new Project 2 Cosworth V10 engines understandably left a smile on the corporate face of the Jaguar squad.

'It's nice to have a change of luck,' said Herbert. 'Even this morning I had problems with water pressure which cost me some preparation time, but the rain arrived at the right time for us during qualifying. Our strategy paid off so I'm pleased with the position.'

Jacques Villeneuve lined up ninth in his BAR-Honda, taking the spare car after a spin, while team-mate Ricardo Zonta wound up 12th after a fresh Honda V10 was installed in his car prior to the start of the session. Unfortunately he then came up behind Alesi coming into the stadium on his best lap.

Nick Heidfeld qualified strongly in 13th place with the Prost AP03-Peugeot after a late run, but team-mate Jean Alesi languished in 20th place. In the BMW Williams camp Ralf Schumacher admitted that he had not chosen the best chassis set-up and could only manage 14th, two places ahead of Jenson Button.

'My first lap was fast,' said Jenson, 'but in the first corner Fisichella went off the track into the gravel and came straight back across the circuit almost twice, so I had to lift off quite a bit and lost some time.

'When Fisichella went out for his second run, the track was in good condition and there was nobody out there. He really had perfect timing! We went out just after, but it started raining. In my last run the track was too wet for any improvement.'

Giancarlo Fisichella's fortunes continued to wane when he was involved in the first-corner accident with Michael Schumacher.
Mark Thompson/Allsport

RUBENS Barrichello posted the first victory of his F1 career at Hockenheim against a backdrop of ever-changing fortunes which effectively distilled as much action as is usually produced across two seasons into a little over one hour and twenty minutes.

From the moment Michael Schumacher's Ferrari F1-2000 collided with Giancarlo Fisichella's Benetton B200 on the sprint to the first corner, leaving the two rivals to pirouette into the tyre barriers, the 11th round of the title chase offered just about everything a spectator could have wanted. And considerably more.

It was also a race which yielded a deserved and universally popular winner. There may have been question marks over Barrichello's ultimate speed when he signed for Ferrari for a head-to-head with Michael Schumacher, but the pleasant and civilised Brazilian is a genuinely likeable fellow with no side to his character and a pleasant manner.

It was therefore with great delight that the paddock celebrated the success of this demonstrably good guy who, on his 123rd Grand Prix start, dodged every hazard and drove brilliantly in dramatically changing wet/dry track conditions to capture a brilliant win.

In F1 terms, this was the equivalent of Tiger Woods coming from ten strokes down to win the Open. The popular driver from São Paulo never put a wheel wrong in conditions which caught out some of the most celebrated names in the business and the Brazilian national anthem rang out over the winner's rostrum for the first time since Barrichello's hero Ayrton Senna won at Adelaide seven years earlier at the wheel of a McLaren.

The emotion of the moment was almost too much for Rubens, who stood with tears coursing down his cheeks flanked by Mika Häkkinen and David Coulthard who finished second and third in their McLaren-Mercedes MP4/15s.

As if to add a final bizarre touch to the proceedings, the F1 fraternity was also treated to the remarkable sight of a spectator who had dodged the marshals and security men to stand on the grass alongside the 190 mph straight leading out of the stadium in what was apparently an unconventional, one-man protest against Mercedes-Benz.

He was identified as a 47-year-old Frenchman who claimed he'd been dismissed by Mercedes for health reasons after working there for 22 years. He was later charged with trespass and appeared before the public prosecutor at Mannheim on the Monday after the race.

As the stadium area of the circuit was lashed by torrential rain in the closing stages, Barrichello bravely stayed out in the lead of the race on dry-weather tyres, rightly figuring that he was making up as much on the dry sections as he was losing in the wet.

'Ross Brawn [Ferrari's technical director] told me, "Mika is coming in" and I said "I want to keep an eye on things, let's stay out for another lap,"' said Barrichello.

'After that lap Ross said "just keep going Rubens, because you're going to win if you keep up that pace." I feel just great.'

He eventually took the chequered flag 7.4s ahead of Mika Häkkinen's McLaren-Mercedes with David Coulthard taking third place in a result which moved him to just two points behind Schumacher in the drivers' World Championship.

Jenson Button wound up a splendid fourth after a great race in which he beat Mika Salo's Sauber in a straight fight, while the Arrows A21 of the impressive Pedro de la Rosa took the final point for sixth place.

Starting from 18th on the grid, Barrichello's car carried a light fuel load to help him overtake the midfield competitors as quickly and efficiently as possible. This would mean him having to make two stops to the McLarens' one, but it was the quickest way to help him make up ground.

Coulthard had qualified on pole position ahead of Schumacher's Ferrari, but it was Häkkinen who came sprinting through from fourth place on the grid to lead into the first corner. A few yards further back, Schumacher dodged across the track and collided with Giancarlo Fisichella's Benetton which had qualified a promising third.

'It all happened so fast,' said Fisichella. 'I think we should really decide in the rules about whether a driver should stick to his line or not because like this it's just a waste of a race.'

By the end of the opening lap Häkkinen led from Coulthard with Jarno Trulli straining every sinew to keep up, with his Jordan EJ10 in third place. Next up was Pedro de la Rosa's Arrows, followed by the Jaguar R1s of Eddie Irvine and Johnny Herbert and Jos Verstappen's Arrows. Further back, Barrichello had already made eight places on his starting position, coming round for the first time in tenth place.

By lap 15 the two McLarens pulled out a lead of 13s over Barrichello's Ferrari, the Brazilian having climbed through the pack in a neatly disciplined flowing style, picking off his rivals in methodical and decisive fashion under hard braking.

At the end of lap 17 Barrichello made his first refuelling stop, dropping from third to sixth. Seven laps later the peculiar interloper appeared on the edge of the circuit and the safety car was soon deployed to slow

the field. Track marshals were obviously extremely reluctant to make a rush at the unwelcome visitor as they were worried he might do something really dramatic such as stepping out in front of a car.

Once he was eventually taken into custody, it emerged that he had already been on the circuit earlier in the day in an attempt to disrupt proceedings. He had actually made his way onto the starting grid in a one-man protest, but was bundled away moments before the cars departed on their formation lap. Quite why he was released to disrupt proceedings again was not satisfactorily explained.

Mika now came in for his first stop which took 8.7s. Next time round David was in for his 9.0s stop which put him back into the queue in sixth with Trulli now second ahead of Barrichello, de la Rosa and Heinz-Harald Frentzen's Jordan.

Trulli then found himself collecting a 10s stop-go penalty after he accelerated round the right-hander after the pits just as Barrichello was accelerating out of the pit lane following his second refuelling stop on lap 26. Amazingly, Barrichello complained over his radio and Jean Todt e-mailed race control from the pit wall with a complaint, on the basis of which flimsy information Trulli was called in.

'It seems I was penalised for passing Barrichello as he came out of the pits,' shrugged the young Italian, 'but to me he and I were side by side and I was on the racing line, so I cannot understand this decision.'

An FIA official later commented 'but it would have spoiled Barrichello's race,' clearly unaware of the irony of his remark. It didn't do much for Trulli's, of course, and the Italian finished the day in ninth place at the end of a day which should have seen him take a worthy position on the rostrum.

His team-mate Heinz-Harald Frentzen stormed through the field from 17th to sixth place before making his first stop, holding his place and later battled for second place with Coulthard before problems with his car's telemetry system heralded more serious electronic problems which eventually caused his retirement with only six laps to the finish.

On lap 29 an accident between Jean Alesi and Pedro Diniz caused the safety car to be deployed once more, until lap 31. Two laps later heavy rain began falling in the stadium section and Mika pitted from the lead to change to wet tyres in 6.8s at the end of lap 35, leaving Barrichello ahead of David.

Commented Mika: 'I made one of

DIARY

Tomas Enge and Tomas Scheckter score a convincing 1-2 victory for the McLaren junior team in the Hockenheim F3000 race.

Brazilian Cristiano da Matta takes first CART win of his career at Chicago, beating Michael Andretti by 1.6s.

Tom Kristensen has first run in an F1 Jaguar trying out Michelin tyres.

McLaren confirms it will not appeal against the loss of its 10 constructors' World Championship points after Mika Häkkinen's disqualification from the Austrian Grand Prix.

Paul-Henri Cahier

Right: **Mika Salo again showed his liking for Hockenheim, taking fifth place.**

Below: **Pedro de la Rosa deserved better than sixth place after an impressive performance in the Arrows.**
Both photographs: Paul-Henri Cahier

Villeneuve 'will walk away' if BAR fails to deliver

JACQUES Villeneuve's new contract with British American Racing, announced in Germany, seemed like a dream deal for the Canadian because he can leave the team and seek pastures new if the BAR-Honda proves uncompetitive in the long-term.

After fending off bids from Benetton, Villeneuve (above) confirmed he would be staying with BAR for another three seasons. He will be paid $16 million dollars next season, then $17 million in 2001 and $18 million in 2002.

It is understood that Benetton boss Flavio Briatore offered him a package which would earn him $40 million dollars over three years, plus a maximum of another $5 million in bonuses. Pollock described as 'absolute bullshit' rumours that the deal fell through because they also wanted Renault, who bought Benetton earlier this year, to buy out their 15 per cent shareholding in BAR.

'The team has to perform,' said Jacques firmly. 'If the team does not perform, then I will walk away. Everything in life is possible.

'I also know where I stand here, whereas to have changed teams would have involved going on the basis of promises again. That can be great, and it can turn out well.

'As far as winning is concerned, I think that either team [BAR or Benetton] would have been a viable option. Now I am positive that this team can do it.'

It is believed that Villeneuve's contract allows him to leave at the end of 2002 unless BAR finishes in the top four in the constructors' championship.

the best starts to go from fourth to leading into the first corner. I felt in control of the race until the safety car came out. When the rain started to fall heavily I pitted for wets. I might have won the race if I had remained on slicks. However, the risk of spinning off was too big. I had to be careful with the wets in the fast dry sections not to ruin them and make them useless for the wet parts.'

David was running second when he made a 7.6s stop to change to wet tyres at the end of lap 38, resuming fifth, then climbing to third, which he held to the finish.

'Obviously I didn't get the perfect start,' he said. 'When the safety car came out on the lap I was meant to have my pit stop, and seeing Mika entering the pit lane, I stayed out for an-

other lap which put me back to sixth.

'When the rain began I stayed out for a long time to see what sort of difference wet tyres made on lap times. I only decided to come in for wets one corner before the pit lane, so it was a late call. However, I'm happy to settle for points today and close the gap to the championship leader considerably.'

Button was understandably elated with his fourth place, considering that he had been obliged to start at the back of the grid when his Williams-BMW refused to fire up prior to the formation lap and he was unable to regain his grid position.

Superb Williams pit-wall strategy saw him make perfectly timed stops on laps 27 and 34, switching to rain tyres at the latter visit.

'The team made an excellent job

calling me in at the right time to switch to wet tyres,' he said. 'It was very difficult to drive at that moment, because at the back of the circuit it was dry, yet in the pit lane it was raining. It was also a very exciting moment when I passed Mika Salo's Sauber to take fourth just two laps before the end of the race.'

Williams technical director Patrick Head described the young Englishman's run to fourth as 'a brilliant result for Jenson' on a day when Ralf Schumacher struggled home seventh, his FW22's diffuser damaged by an unfortunate nudge from Ricardo Zonta's BAR.

De la Rosa's run to sixth place capped off a dramatic race day for the Arrows team which had started when Jos Verstappen spun on his installation lap at the start of the morning warm-up session and collided with Jacques Villeneuve's BAR.

The Dutchman suffered a slightly grazed hand and forearm, but he managed to get out again later in the session in the spare car. Meanwhile, de la Rosa ran over a Prost engine cover which had flown off onto the track and his A21 sustained a puncture and damaged front wing.

In the race Pedro came on strongly in the dry conditions, but just before he came in for wet tyres he made a mistake, missing his braking point as he came back into the stadium. 'I was third at that point, but lost two positions and should have finished higher up,' he said. 'Nevertheless, it was a good effort by the team and I'm happy for them.'

For his part, Verstappen spun off in the closing stages leaving Ralf Schumacher to take seventh ahead of Jacques Villeneuve's BAR, who over-exuberant team-mate Ricardo Zonta. 'It was a stupid accident,' said Jacques. 'Since the beginning of the year he has gone off in every other race because he drives over his limit. Today I paid for it.'

In ninth and tenth places came the hapless Trulli and Eddie Irvine in the sole surviving Jaguar which had been struggling for grip through the stadium during the early stages. Johnny Herbert eventually suffered another transmission problem and again failed to finish.

It had been a great day for Ferrari, yet for Michael Schumacher the spectre of having dropped a potential 20 points over two races looked like a self-inflicted wound the knock-on effects of which could cause him continuing pain in the months to come. How much pain there was no way of knowing.

GERMAN GRAND PRIX

Faces around the paddock.

Nick Heidfeld and Ricardo Zonta *(top and above left).*

Left to right: **Flavio Briatore, Eddie Irvine and Eddie Jordan.**

Above right: **Jenson Button continued his stunning progress in F1 with another top-notch drive.**

All photographs: Paul-Henri Cahier

grösser Mobil 1 preis von DEUTSCHLAND

HOCKENHEIM
CIRCUIT LENGTH: 4.241 miles/6.825 km

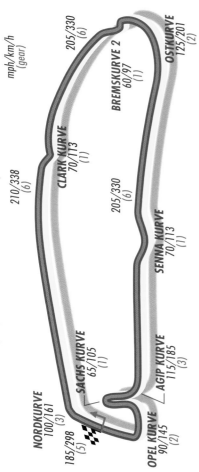

NORDKURVE 100/161 (3)
185/298 (5)
SACHS KURVE 65/105 (1)
AGIP KURVE 115/185 (3)
OPEL KURVE 90/145 (2)
SENNA KURVE 70/113 (11)
SACHS KURVE
210/338 (6)
CLARK KURVE 70/113 (11)
205/330 (6)
BREMSKURVE 2 60/97 (1)
205/330 (6)
OSTKURVE 125/201 (2)

mph/km/h (gear)

RACE DISTANCE: 45 laps, 190.839 miles/307.125 km   RACE WEATHER: Cloudy, with rain at end of race

Pos.	Driver	Nat.	No.	Entrant	Car/Engine	Laps	Time/Retirement	Speed (mph/km/h)
1	Rubens Barrichello	BR	4	Scuderia Ferrari Marlboro	Ferrari F1-2000-049 V10	45	1h 25m 34.418s	133.806/215.340
2	Mika Häkkinen	SF	1	West McLaren Mercedes	McLaren MP4/15–Mercedes FO110J V10	45	1h 25m 41.870s	133.612/215.028
3	David Coulthard	GB	2	West McLaren Mercedes	McLaren MP4/15–Mercedes FO110J V10	45	1h 25m 55.586s	133.257/214.456
4	Jenson Button	GB	10	BMW WilliamsF1 Team	Williams FW22–BMW E41 V10	45	1h 25m 57.103s	133.217/214.393
5	Mika Salo	SF	17	Red Bull Sauber Petronas	Sauber C19–Petronas SPE 04A V10	45	1h 26m 01.530s	133.103/214.209
6	Pedro de la Rosa	ESP	18	Arrows	Arrows A21–Supertec FB02 V10	45	1h 26m 03.498s	133.053/214.128
7	Ralf Schumacher	D	9	BMW WilliamsF1 Team	Williams FW22–BMW E41 V10	45	1h 26m 05.316s	133.006/214.052
8	Jacques Villeneuve	CDN	22	Lucky Strike BAR Honda	BAR 02–Honda RA100E V10	45	1h 26m 21.955s	132.579/213.365
9	Jarno Trulli	I	6	Benson & Hedges Jordan	Jordan EJ10–Mugen Honda MF301HE V10	45	1h 26m 25.319s	132.492/213.226
10	Eddie Irvine	GB	7	Jaguar Racing	Jaguar R1–Cosworth CR2 V10	45	1h 26m 54.082s	131.762/212.050
11	Gaston Mazzacane	ARG	21	Telefonica Minardi Fondmetal	Minardi M02–Fondmetal Ford Zetec-R V10	45	1h 27m 03.922s	131.514/211.651
12	Nick Heidfeld	D	15	Gauloises Prost Peugeot	Prost AP03–Peugeot A20 V10	40	Alternator	
	Heinz-Harald Frentzen	D	5	Benson & Hedges Jordan	Jordan EJ10–Mugen Honda MF301HE V10	39	Low battery voltage	
	Jos Verstappen	NL	19	Arrows	Arrows A21–Supertec FB02 V10	39	Spun off	
	Ricardo Zonta	BR	23	Lucky Strike BAR Honda	BAR 02–Honda RA100E V10	37	Spun off	
	Marc Gene	ESP	20	Telefonica Minardi Fondmetal	Minardi M02–Fondmetal Ford Zetec-R V10	33	Engine	
	Alexander Wurz	A	12	Mild Seven Benetton Playlife	Benetton B200–Playlife V10	31	Gearbox	
	Pedro Diniz	BR	16	Red Bull Sauber Petronas	Sauber C19–Petronas SPE 04A V10	29	Collision with Alesi	
	Jean Alesi	F	14	Gauloises Prost Peugeot	Prost AP03–Peugeot A20 V10	29	Collision with Diniz	
	Johnny Herbert	GB	8	Jaguar Racing	Jaguar R1–Cosworth CR2 V10	12	Gearbox	
	Michael Schumacher	D	3	Scuderia Ferrari Marlboro	Ferrari F1-2000 049 V10	0	Collision with Fisichella	
	Giancarlo Fisichella	I	11	Mild Seven Benetton Playlife	Benetton B200–Playlife V10	0	Collision with M. Schumacher	

Fastest lap: Barrichello, on lap 20, 1m 44.300s, 146.376 mph/235.570 km/h (record).

Previous lap record: David Coulthard (F1 McLaren MP4/14–Mercedes V10), 1m 45.270s, 144.985 mph/233.331 km/h (1999).

Grid order	1	2	3	4	5	6	7	8	9	10	11	12	13	14	15	16	17	18	19	20	21	22	23	24	25	26	27	28	29	30	31	32	33	34	35	36	37	38	39	40	41	42	43	44	45
2 COULTHARD	2	1	1	1	1	1	1	1	1	1	1	1	1	1	1	1	1	1	1	1	1	2	2	1	1	1	1	1	1	1	1	1	1	1	4	4	4	4	4	4	4	4	4	4	4
3 M. SCHUMACHER																																													
11 FISICHELLA	6	6	6	6	6	6	6	6	6	6	6	6	6	6	6	6	6	6	4	4	4	4	4	6	6	6	4	4	2	2	2	2	2	2	2	2	2	2	2	2	2	2	2	2	2
1 HÄKKINEN	18	18	18	18	18	4	4	4	4	4	4	4	4	4	4	4	4	18	18	18	18	18	18	4	4	4	5	5	5	1	17	10	10	10	10	17	17	10	10	10	17	1	1	1	1
18 DE LA ROSA	7	8	8	8	4	18	18	18	18	18	18	18	18	18	18	18	18	4	5	5	2	5	5	18	18	18	18	18	18	18	18	17	17	17	17	10	10	17	17	17	10	10	10	10	10
6 TRULLI	8	19	19	4	8	8	8	8	8	8	5	8	19	19	19	19	9	5	2	2	5	22	22	23	10	9	9	18	9	9	22	18	5	2	5	2	2	9	18	18	18	18	18	18	18
8 HERBERT	22	4	7	7	19	19	19	19	8	5	8	19	8	8	8	9	5	19	19	22	22	23	10	9	9	2	2	23	17	17	5	5	23	5	2	5	9	6	18	9	9	9	9	9	9
22 VILLENEUVE	23	22	22	22	22	22	22	22	22	19	19	5	22	22	22	22	22	22	22	23	23	10	9	22	22	22	23	9	23	23	23	23	9	23	9	9	6	18	9	22	22	22	22	22	22
7 IRVINE	4	23	23	23	23	23	9	5	19	22	22	22	5	5	9	5	23	23	23	9	10	9	23	10	23	23	17	17	10	10	9	9	6	9	23	6	18	22	22	6	6	7	7	7	7
19 VERSTAPPEN	9	9	9	9	5	9	5	23	23	23	23	23	9	9	5	23	17	17	9	10	9	17	17	17	17	17	10	10	19	19	19	6	7	6	6	18	22	7	7	7	7	21	15	21	21
23 ZONTA	12	12	12	12	12	5	12	9	5	9	9	9	23	23	23	17	12	9	10	17	17	10	20	19	19	19	19	19	6	6	6	7	21	15	21	21	7	15	21	15	21	15	21	15	
9 R. SCHUMACHER	15	15	5	5	9	12	12	12	12	12	12	12	12	12	12	12	16	16	17	20	19	19	19	20	20	20	20	6	7	7	7	21	15	21	15	15	21	21	15	21	15				
17 SALO	16	5	17	17	17	17	17	17	17	17	17	17	16	16	16	16	16	16	20	19	20	20	14	14	14	10	6	7	21	15	21	15	21	7	7	7	15								
5 FRENTZEN	5	16	16	16	16	16	16	16	16	16	16	16	20	20	20	20	20	20	16	14	14	14	21	21	21	21	21	21	15	21	15														
4 BARRICHELLO	4	23	23	23	23	9	23	20	20	20	20	20	14	14	14	14	14	14	14	21	21	21	15	15	15	15	15	15	21																
14 DINIZ	14	14	14	14	14	14	14	14	14	14	14	14	21	21	21	21	21	21	21	15	15	15																							
14 ALESI	10	10	10	10	10	10	10	10	10	10	10	21	21	21	21	21	21	21	15	15	15																								
21 MAZZACANE	21	21	21	21	21	21	21	21	21	21	21	21	21	21	21	21	21	21	21	21	21																								
20 GENE																																													
10 BUTTON																																													

Paul-Henri Cahier

STARTING GRID

	Pole
2 COULTHARD McLaren	3 M. SCHUMACHER Ferrari
11 FISICHELLA Benetton	1 HÄKKINEN McLaren
18 DE LA ROSA Arrows	6 TRULLI Jordan
12 WURZ Benetton	8 HERBERT Jaguar
22 VILLENEUVE BAR	7 IRVINE Jaguar
19 VERSTAPPEN Arrows	23 ZONTA BAR
15 HEIDFELD Prost	9 R. SCHUMACHER Williams
17 SALO Sauber	10* BUTTON Williams
16 DINIZ Sauber	14 ALESI Prost
21 MAZZACANE Minardi	20 GENE Minardi
5 FRENTZEN Jordan	4 BARRICHELLO Ferrari

* started from back of grid

TIME SHEETS

QUALIFYING

Weather: Damp with intermittent rain

Pos.	Driver	Car	Laps	Time
1	David Coulthard	McLaren-Mercedes	6	1m 45.697s
2	Michael Schumacher	Ferrari	10	1m 47.063s
3	Giancarlo Fisichella	Benetton-Playlife	8	1m 47.130s
4	Mika Häkkinen	McLaren-Mercedes	9	1m 47.162s
5	Pedro de la Rosa	Arrows-Supertec	7	1m 47.786s
6	Jarno Trulli	Jordan-Mugen Honda	7	1m 47.833s
7	Alexander Wurz	Benetton-Playlife	7	1m 48.037s
8	Johnny Herbert	Jaguar-Cosworth	6	1m 48.078s
9	Jacques Villeneuve	BAR-Honda	7	1m 48.121s
10	Eddie Irvine	Jaguar-Cosworth	9	1m 48.305s
11	Jos Verstappen	Arrows-Supertec	7	1m 48.321s
12	Ricardo Zonta	BAR-Honda	10	1m 48.665s
13	Nick Heidfeld	Prost-Peugeot	11	1m 48.690s
14	Ralf Schumacher	Williams-BMW	9	1m 48.841s
15	Mika Salo	Sauber-Petronas	8	1m 49.204s
16	Jenson Button	Williams-BMW	8	1m 49.215s
17	Heinz-Harald Frentzen	Jordan-Mugen Honda	11	1m 49.280s
18	Rubens Barrichello	Ferrari	10	1m 49.544s
19	Pedro Diniz	Sauber-Petronas	10	1m 49.936s
20	Jean Alesi	Prost-Peugeot	9	1m 50.289s
21	Gaston Mazzacane	Minardi-Fondmetal	9	1m 51.611s
22	Marc Gene	Minardi-Fondmetal	7	1m 53.094s

FRIDAY FREE PRACTICE

Weather: Overcast, damp patches

Pos.	Driver	Laps	Time
1	Michael Schumacher	36	1m 43.532s
2	Heinz-Harald Frentzen	28	1m 43.575s
3	Mika Häkkinen	27	1m 44.120s
4	Rubens Barrichello	29	1m 44.128s
5	David Coulthard	29	1m 44.379s
6	Jarno Trulli	17	1m 44.521s
7	Ricardo Zonta	35	1m 44.906s
8	Jacques Villeneuve	25	1m 44.985s
9	Giancarlo Fisichella	37	1m 45.048s
10	Mika Salo	30	1m 45.094s
11	Nick Heidfeld	24	1m 45.229s
12	Pedro de la Rosa	33	1m 45.433s
13	Jean Alesi	21	1m 45.520s
14	Ralf Schumacher	26	1m 45.542s
15	Johnny Herbert	16	1m 45.664s
16	Jenson Button	33	1m 45.791s
17	Pedro Diniz	34	1m 45.884s
18	Eddie Irvine	27	1m 45.901s
19	Alexander Wurz	33	1m 46.573s
20	Marc Gene	27	1m 46.995s
21	Jos Verstappen	20	1m 47.000s
22	Gaston Mazzacane	10	1m 48.062s

SATURDAY FREE PRACTICE

Weather: Damp with intermittent rain

Pos.	Driver	Laps	Time
1	Mika Häkkinen	20	1m 41.658s
2	Michael Schumacher	26	1m 41.932s
3	David Coulthard	27	1m 41.971s
4	Rubens Barrichello	23	1m 42.340s
5	Heinz-Harald Frentzen	22	1m 42.446s
6	Giancarlo Fisichella	24	1m 42.613s
7	Jenson Button	21	1m 42.617s
8	Mika Salo	21	1m 42.877s
9	Jacques Villeneuve	27	1m 42.878s
10	Jarno Trulli	27	1m 42.903s
11	Jos Verstappen	24	1m 43.175s
12	Pedro de la Rosa	22	1m 43.438s
13	Ricardo Zonta	22	1m 43.534s
14	Pedro Diniz	23	1m 43.554s
15	Alexander Wurz	22	1m 43.623s
16	Eddie Irvine	24	1m 44.049s
17	Nick Heidfeld	12	1m 44.174s
18	Jean Alesi	8	1m 44.515s
19	Marc Gene	23	1m 44.591s
20	Gaston Mazzacane	30	1m 45.000s
21	Johnny Herbert	20	1m 45.234s
22	Ralf Schumacher	9	1m 52.141s

WARM-UP

Weather: Cloudy and mild

Pos.	Driver	Laps	Time
1	David Coulthard	12	1m 44.065s
2	Mika Häkkinen	10	1m 44.227s
3	Pedro de la Rosa	11	1m 44.636s
4	Michael Schumacher	11	1m 44.782s
5	Heinz-Harald Frentzen	12	1m 44.809s
6	Pedro Diniz	13	1m 45.361s
7	Giancarlo Fisichella	12	1m 45.363s
8	Jacques Villeneuve	12	1m 45.363s
9	Rubens Barrichello	12	1m 45.490s
10	Jarno Trulli	13	1m 45.538s
11	Jos Verstappen	5	1m 45.668s
12	Ricardo Zonta	13	1m 45.692s
13	Jean Alesi	10	1m 45.867s
14	Mika Salo	14	1m 45.921s
15	Alexander Wurz	11	1m 46.012s
16	Ralf Schumacher	12	1m 46.088s
17	Eddie Irvine	11	1m 46.396s
18	Johnny Herbert	12	1m 46.543s
19	Marc Gene	10	1m 46.619s
20	Nick Heidfeld	13	1m 47.168s
21	Gaston Mazzacane	11	1m 47.291s
22	Jenson Button	7	1m 47.463s

RACE FASTEST LAPS

Weather: Cloudy with rain at end of race

Driver	Time	Lap
Rubens Barrichello	1m 44.300s	20
David Coulthard	1m 44.579s	24
Heinz-Harald Frentzen	1m 44.614s	20
Mika Häkkinen	1m 44.698s	23
Jarno Trulli	1m 45.754s	30
Pedro de la Rosa	1m 46.243s	21
Jacques Villeneuve	1m 46.374s	24
Pedro Diniz	1m 46.629s	24
Ralf Schumacher	1m 46.685s	24
Jean Alesi	1m 47.001s	23
Jenson Button	1m 47.073s	23
Mika Salo	1m 47.129s	32
Nick Heidfeld	1m 47.140s	23
Jos Verstappen	1m 47.156s	25
Marc Gene	1m 47.158s	33
Alexander Wurz	1m 47.248s	33
Ricardo Zonta	1m 47.248s	33
Johnny Herbert	1m 47.269s	24
Eddie Irvine	1m 47.332s	9
Gaston Mazzacane	1m 47.448s	22
Eddie Irvine	1m 47.570s	18

CHASSIS LOG BOOK

No.	Driver	Chassis
1	Häkkinen	McLaren MP4/15/4
2	Coulthard	McLaren MP4/15/5
	spare	McLaren MP4/15/2
3	M. Schumacher	Ferrari F1-2000/200
4	Barrichello	Ferrari F1-2000/202
	spare	Ferrari F1-2000/198
5	Frentzen	Jordan E10/6
6	Trulli	Jordan E10/5
	spare	Jordan E10/4
7	Irvine	Jaguar R1/5
8	Herbert	Jaguar R1/6
	spare	Jaguar R1/1
9	R. Schumacher	Williams FW22/2
10	Button	Williams FW22/4
	spare	Williams FW22/3
11	Fisichella	Benetton B200/4
12	Wurz	Benetton B200/2
	spare	Benetton B200/5
16	Diniz	Sauber C19/7
17	Salo	Sauber C19/5
	spare	Sauber C19/6
14	Alesi	Prost AP03/5
15	Heidfeld	Prost AP03/2
	spare	Prost AP03/1
18	de la Rosa	Arrows A21/3
19	Verstappen	Arrows A21/4
	spare	Arrows A21/2
22	Villeneuve	BAR 02/4
23	Zonta	BAR 02/1
	spare	BAR 02/2
20	Gene	Minardi M02/3
21	Mazzacane	Minardi M02/4
	spare	Minardi M02/1

POINTS TABLES

DRIVERS

1	Michael Schumacher	56
2 =	David Coulthard	54
2 =	Mika Häkkinen	54
4	Rubens Barrichello	46
5	Giancarlo Fisichella	18
6	Ralf Schumacher	14
7	Jacques Villeneuve	11
8 =	Jenson Button	8
8 =	Jarno Trulli	8
9 =	Mika Salo	6
11	Heinz-Harald Frentzen	6
12	Eddie Irvine	3
13 =	Jos Verstappen	2
13 =	Pedro de la Rosa	2
15	Ricardo Zonta	1

CONSTRUCTORS

Pos.	Constructor	Points
1	Ferrari	102
2	McLaren	98
3	Williams	22
4	Benetton	18
5	BAR	12
6	Jordan	11
7	Sauber	6
8	Arrows	4
9	Jaguar	3

FOR THE RECORD

First Grand Prix win
Rubens Barrichello

HUNGARIAN
grand prix

FIA WORLD CHAMPIONSHIP ● ROUND 12

HÄKKINEN
M. SCHUMACHER
COULTHARD
BARRICHELLO
R. SCHUMACHER
FRENTZEN

Mika Häkkinen took the lead at the start from Michael Schumacher and assumed complete control of the race.

Paul-Henri Cahier

DIARY

Premier 1 Grand Prix, a new category using 4-litre Dallara-Judd single-seaters in a unique commercial partnership with major European football clubs, announces its plans for 2002.

Olivier Panis signs deal to join Jacques Villeneuve at British American Racing for 2001.

Jenson Button signs for Benetton.

Tomas Scheckter tests F1 Jaguar at Silverstone.

Bruno Junqueira closes on F3000 title with his fourth win of the season at the Hungaroring.

HUNGARORING QUALIFYING

In many ways the Hungaroring is an unremarkable circuit. Tight and acrobatic with straights that seem too short, it traditionally marks a turning point in the summer, a tedious follow-my-leader event to be endured before the F1 fraternity stretches its legs on epic circuits such as Spa-Francorchamps, Monza and Suzuka.

Yet it is the very confined nature of this sun-baked circuit, about 12 miles from the centre of Budapest, which has traditionally played so dramatically into Schumacher's hands. The Ferrari team leader is a driver whose magical touch enables him to overtake when others think twice about it and whose very presence in his rivals' mirrors has the same intimidating effect as that exerted a decade ago by the late Ayrton Senna.

Twice Schumacher has won here at Budapest – and on both occasions he has outsmarted his rivals by gambling on three refuelling stops instead of two in order to emerge triumphant.

In 1994 he drove his Benetton-Ford B194 to a commanding victory over Damon Hill's Williams-Renault FW16, then four years later repeated that success with a brilliant win for Ferrari ahead of Coulthard's McLaren-Mercedes.

This rare ability to deliver up blisteringly quick laps to order are just part of the package which makes Schumacher such a formidable performer. Moreover, his speed on the laps both entering and leaving the pits during the course of refuelling stops is also consistently impressive.

Of course, Hungaroring is a crucially tyre-sensitive event, particularly with track temperatures nudging into the low 30-degree bracket as they were on this particular weekend. The track has notoriously poor grip and is particularly dirty off-line, but even so Bridgestone's super-soft tyre choice was clearly the way to go as tyre degradation in itself is not a major factor at this circuit.

It was Coulthard who took the fight to the Ferrari team leader from the word go. He seemed more confident in his McLaren MP4/15 set-up from the outset than Häkkinen, posting fastest time in Friday's free practice.

Nor was he troubled by any lingering after-effects resulting from a 160-mph smash during testing last week at the Valencia circuit in southern Spain.

The McLaren team's technical director Adrian Newey put a philosophical face on the rear suspension failure which had caused a rear wheel to rip back and remove the car's rear wing at high speed. Coulthard spun five times before slamming into the tyre barrier, emerging shaken but thankfully unhurt.

'One always strives to avoid such incidents, but inevitably one is not always successful,' said Newey. 'It is very difficult to have 100 per cent success in avoiding such technical problems.'

For the Hungarian race the McLarens had strengthened steel rear suspension wishbones after the errant component failed after around 7,600 km of running due to a fatigue failure at a welded joint, some 2,500 km short of its life rating.

Yet, for all Coulthard's confidence, there was nothing he could do about Schumacher. Ferrari's latest high-downforce configuration enabled Michael to pile on the pressure from the outset. Häkkinen set the early pace on 1m 19.291s with the track temperature up to a blazing 43 degrees, but the Finn was only checking out a major set-up change.

At 13.22 Ralf Schumacher's Williams FW22, benefiting from a slightly up-rated BMW V10, revised diffuser and improved all-round set-up, went fastest on 1m 19.115s. Coulthard came back with 1m 18.155s and then Schumacher took the Ferrari round in a stunning 1m 17.514s to equal the legendary Juan Manuel Fangio's career tally of 28 pole positions.

'It felt pretty good, but not perfect,' said Schumacher. 'You don't get much rest on this circuit. It has a variation of corners. You have bumps and high-speed/low-speed corners. There's a bit of everything, which makes it difficult to find the optimum set-up, although, to be honest, the race set-up is not too much different to that we use in qualifying.'

Coulthard duly wound up third on 1m 17.886s ahead of Mika on 1m 17.922s. 'I didn't optimise my car on low fuel,' said Coulthard, 'but I was happier when it had a heavier load. It's quite well balanced compared with previous years, but there is still too much understeer on the first and second sectors.'

Häkkinen commented; 'I haven't been very happy with the car all weekend, to be honest. We made some radical changes which is why I went out on my first run early. We continued making changes throughout the session and it was quite good by the end.'

Ralf Schumacher's Williams FW22-BMW qualified fourth, his best grid position of the season. 'The revised aerodynamics and up-rated BMW engine have improved things a lot,' he said. Jenson Button was satisfied with eighth place on his first visit to Hungaroring. 'Tomorrow I think championship points are possible,' he said.

Heinz-Harald Frentzen's Jordan-Mugen Honda (1m 18.523s) completed the top half-dozen, still grappling with excessive understeer in the second and third sectors. Jarno Trulli was a disappointed 12th, also complaining of dire understeer. He changed his car's nose section in the closing stages of the session which changed its handling balance but did not improve things.

Giancarlo Fisichella's Benetton B200 wound up seventh fastest (1m 18.607s), the Italian complaining that Michael Schumacher blocked him on his fastest lap – for which Ross Brawn later apologised on behalf of the Ferrari team – while Alexander Wurz finished 11th, using Fisichella's chassis settings for this session.

Mika Salo (9th) was satisfied with his best time on his Sauber C19's second run but Pedro Diniz (13th) struggled for a good set-up. Eddie Irvine managed a moderately encouraging 10th in his Jaguar R1, but Johnny Herbert (17th) struggled with a huge amount of understeer and spun near the end of the session.

In the Arrows and BAR camps, the drivers were battling as expected in high-downforce configuration while Nick Heidfeld (19th) switched to the spare Prost AP03 for his fourth run but still complained of too much understeer.

In many respects it was the most significant race of the season so far. From third place on the starting grid, Mika Häkkinen vaulted his McLaren-Mercedes MP4/15 to the left round the outside of his slow-starting team-mate David Coulthard, then jinked back across to the right and dived inside Michael Schumacher's Ferrari F1-2000 as they went into the first corner.

Schumacher momentarily tried to squeeze Häkkinen out, but there was no way. By any standards, it was a fair cop. Mika was clearly set on coming through, whatever Michael thought about it and the Ferrari ace was clearly aware of this. Coulthard, hidebound by the traditional problem of having to start from the dusty inside line close to the pit wall, was left in third place at the first turn. Which was where he finished.

That was the end of the story. Mika led commandingly throughout, his McLaren clearly having a better balance in race trim than its Italian rival. Having spent two days comprehensively re-adjusting his car's set-up – right down to making a minor change on the grid seconds before the formation lap – the Finn was just too fast for Schumacher to handle on this occasion.

'I knew that the start would be crucial, because it's almost impossible to overtake here,' said Mika. 'Normally the perfect start doesn't happen more than once a year and after my getaway two weeks ago at Hockenheim I thought that my quota had been used up.

'Once I took the lead I was comfortable throughout the race and the entire team has done a fantastic job the whole weekend. I'm extremely happy to win and also to take the lead in the World Championship.'

Sure enough, Michael kept up for the first few laps, getting more grip from his scrubbed Bridgestones than the new rubber on Mika's McLaren. But once the World Champion caught his stride, there was no contest. Michael was left to battle with Coulthard over second place, just getting the verdict by less than a second at the chequered flag.

Coulthard lost his chance of a strong second place behind Häkkinen with the timing of his second refuelling stop. Having harried Schumacher for many laps, he was faced with a tantalisingly empty track when the Ferrari peeled off into the pit lane for Schumacher's own second stop on lap 50.

Owing to a clutch of slower cars ahead, rather than allow Coulthard his head in a demonstrably faster car for a few more laps in order to close the gap, the McLaren team brought him in for his second stop on the next lap. The net result was that the Scot just failed by a matter of feet to squeeze back into the race ahead of his rival and thereafter spent the balance of a frustrating race staring at Schumacher's rear wing.

'I didn't get a perfect getaway today and was unhappy with the balance until my first pit stop after which I felt I could really join in the race,' said Coulthard.

'I was so close to Michael after my stop and really piling on the pressure, but, just like at Monaco, you are unable to get really close to other cars round here. A couple of times I was held up unnecessarily by the Minardis, but when I came out after my second stop behind Michael I just had no chance to be second.'

Häkkinen led the opening lap by 0.4s while Ralf Schumacher very nearly squeezed ahead of Coulthard to take third place as the pack exited the tricky downhill right-hander after the start. The first lap also caught out Jacques Villeneuve's BAR and Pedro de la Rosa's Arrows, the two cars colliding and limping back to the pits for repairs.

'For once I had a pretty bad start with too much wheelspin,' said Jacques. 'I was on the outside of de la Rosa at the chicane and he braked very late. I did as well, but hit the back of his car.'

With six laps completed Häkkinen was 2.6s ahead of Schumacher's Ferrari which was being closely shadowed by Coulthard, after which came a further 3.4s gap back to Ralf Schumacher's

---

Left: Olivier Panis's stint as McLaren test driver paved the way for his return to the grid in 2001 with the British American Racing team.

Opposite page: Ready for battle. The McLaren of Coulthard and the Ferrari of Schumacher await final preparations on the grid before the start.

All photographs: Paul-Henri Cahier

Right: **Damage limitation: Schumacher held off Coulthard's challenge to take second place behind Häkkinen.**
Bryn Williams/Words & Pictures

Below: **Heinz-Harald Frentzen's Jordan scraped home in sixth spot.**
Paul-Henri Cahier

Williams in fourth. Two laps later Fisichella's Benetton slid off at the first corner, dropping from seventh to 14th, while Jenson Button also had a moment and dropped behind Eddie Irvine rather than making up a place at the Benetton driver's expense.

Meanwhile Jean Alesi was in trouble with the Prost AP03, coming in from 16th place at the end of lap nine to investigate why his steering seemed to be pulling ominously to one side. 'But the wheel had already changed its alignment too much,' he shrugged, 'and the car had totally lost its balance.' He resumed for two more laps before throwing in the towel.

Prost's dismal fortune continued on lap 22 when Nick Heidfeld became the race's second retirement. 'The car was definitely better than in all the practice sessions this weekend,' he explained, 'but it is difficult to say how much better because I was held up by [Ricardo] Zonta.

'Soon we detected a problem with the battery voltage, and when I came in for my first pit stop the team asked me to keep the engine at high revs. But I had to lower the revs to obtain first gear...' The car stalled and, despite a push from the mechanics, could not be coaxed back into life.

Meanwhile, up at the front of the field Häkkinen was 7.7s ahead of Schumacher's Ferrari by lap 20 and Michael decided to come in for a 7.3s refuelling stop on lap 27. Mika stayed out until lap 31 when he dodged in for a 7.0s stop, allowing Coulthard through into the lead before the Scot made a 6.9s stop next time round.

Then the rhythm of the race settled down with Häkkinen now 13.2s ahead of the Ferrari with Coulthard another 4.8s down. Next, Rubens Barrichello's Ferrari was now fourth ahead of Ralf

Schumacher and Heinz-Harald Frentzen's Jordan EJ10.

On lap 46 Marc Gene incurred a 10s stop-go penalty for balking in his Minardi and four laps later Schumacher's Ferrari came in for its second refuelling stop in 7.7s. Coulthard was in next time round, but just failed to get out ahead of the Ferrari, effectively spelling the end of his bid to complete a McLaren 1–2 on this tortuous circuit.

Again Häkkinen stayed out later than his key rival, diving in for a 6.8s second stop at the end of lap 53. The Finn was by now 43.3s ahead of the Ferrari when he entered the pit lane, so there was no need to hurry. He easily accelerated back into the race ahead of the Ferrari, writing the final paragraph to the Hungarian GP story.

Mika eventually won by 7.9s with Schumacher driving just as quickly as he needed to in order to keep Coulthard at bay to the chequered flag. 'All things considered, I am happy with second place,' said Michael. 'It was not such a bad start, but I could see Mika behind me and then he came inside me.

'I kept it tight, but he was there and in the end I had to open the door. Even if I had kept the lead, I think he would have passed me later or in the pit stops.'

Behind the disappointed Coulthard, Barrichello admitted that fourth was as good as he could have expected given that he didn't qualify particularly well. 'After that, it was impossible for me to overtake Ralf Schumacher, so I paid the price,' he reflected, 'but the pit crew did a fantastic job to put me ahead of him.'

Fifth place fell to Ralf Schumacher, best of the rest after the regular top four, while the Jordans of Frentzen and

Jarno Trulli wound up sixth and seventh. Frentzen stopped twice, but Trulli opted for a risky one-stop run which left him struggling with a fuel-heavy car in the opening phase of the race.

'But in the second part of the race the car became better and better and I was able to push hard,' he said with satisfaction. 'It was tough out there in the heat, but luckily I am extremely fit.'

A throttle problem caused Jenson to lose power in the closing stages, dropping him back to ninth behind Jarno Trulli's Jordan and Eddie Irvine's troubled Jaguar.

'Jenson drove an amazingly good defensive race,' said Williams technical chief Patrick Head admiringly, but he couldn't quite hold Trulli and Irvine back. 'Certainly I think he may have been in the points if he hadn't had that problem.'

For his part, Irvine seemed surprisingly satisfied. 'It's probably one of the best races I've driven without reward,' he said.

'I had a lot of fun out there, it was very entertaining, a good workout. We lost time for various reasons throughout the race. I had to pit early because we had a fuel pressure problem and then had to carry extra fuel for the remainder of the race as insurance.

'I got caught behind a Minardi at a crucial time in the race when I was dicing for seventh, which cost me about 20 seconds and ultimately two places. But I now feel we are getting there.'

Next up were Mika Salo's Sauber and Alexander Wurz's sole surviving Benetton, Giancarlo Fisichella having given up after his car became too difficult to drive.

Yet the bottom line to the weekend was that Häkkinen was back in command of the title struggle. Schumacher looked deeply concerned after the race over the manner in which his Ferrari had been outclassed by the McLaren team leader. In the short-term, it seemed as though that concern was not misplaced.

Bridgestone allays tyre fears for Indianapolis banking

F1 tyre suppliers Bridgestone moved to allay concerns over potential performance problems which may be encountered running on the banked section of the Indianapolis banked oval during the United States GP.

Computer simulations carried out by top teams revealed that from the point the cars rejoin the oval track, running clockwise from turn two back round turn one and to the right-hander after the pits, they would be on the throttle for around 28s.

Bridgestone had originally recommended teams to run the tyres at an extremely high 26 psi in order to handle the nine-degree banked right-hander. F1 tyres generally run in the region of 16–18 psi and teams were worried that the suggested high pressures would overheat the tyres and degrade their grip on the twisty infield section.

However Bridgestone technical manager Yoshihiko Ichikawa made it clear that the tyre maker was acutely aware of the technical challenge involved.

'We have a lot of experience of banked ovals through our CART programme through our Firestone brand,' he said.

'The challenge is that the higher the pressure, the smaller the tyre's contact patch and therefore the higher the temperature generated over a restricted area, with consequent potential for blistering.'

Mr Ichikawa also pointed out that the combination of lateral and vertical G-loadings on an F1 car's left rear corner on the banked turn at Indianapolis would amount to almost one ton sustained for up to five seconds.

HUNGARORING
11–13 AUGUST 2000

MARLBORO
MAGYAR
NAGYDIJ

HUNGARORING
CIRCUIT LENGTH: 2.470 miles/3.975 km

170/274 (6)

mph/km/h (gear)

90/145 (2)

105/169 (2)

60/97 (1)   70/113 (2)

120/193 (4)

95/153 (2)

140/225 (4)   90/145 (2)   80/129 (2)

120/193 (4)

60/97 (1)   140/225 (4)   110/177 (4)

RACE DISTANCE: 77 laps, 190.186 miles/306.075 km   RACE WEATHER: Dry, hot and sunny

Pos.	Driver	Nat.	No.	Entrant	Car/Engine	Laps	Time/Retirement	Speed (mph/km/h)
1	Mika Häkkinen	SF	1	West McLaren Mercedes	McLaren MP4/15-Mercedes FO110J V10	77	1h 45m 33.869s	108.096/173.964
2	Michael Schumacher	D	3	Scuderia Ferrari Marlboro	Ferrari F1-2000-049 V10	77	1h 45m 41.786s	107.961/173.747
3	David Coulthard	GB	2	West McLaren Mercedes	McLaren MP4/15-Mercedes FO110J V10	77	1h 45m 42.324s	107.952/173.732
4	Rubens Barrichello	BR	4	Scuderia Ferrari Marlboro	Ferrari F1-2000-049 V10	77	1h 46m 18.026s	107.348/172.760
5	Ralf Schumacher	D	9	BMW WilliamsF1 Team	Williams FW22-BMW E41 V10	77	1h 46m 24.306s	107.242/172.590
6	Heinz-Harald Frentzen	D	5	Benson & Hedges Jordan	Jordan EJ10-Mugen Honda MF301HE V10	77	1h 46m 41.968s	106.963/172.114
7	Jarno Trulli	I	6	Benson & Hedges Jordan	Jordan EJ10-Mugen Honda MF301HE V10	76		
8	Eddie Irvine	GB	7	Jaguar Racing	Jaguar R1-Cosworth CR2 V10	76		
9	Jenson Button	GB	10	BMW WilliamsF1 Team	Williams FW22-BMW E41 V10	76		
10	Mika Salo	SF	17	Red Bull Sauber Petronas	Sauber C19-Petronas SPE 04A V10	76		
11	Alexander Wurz	A	12	Mild Seven Benetton Playlife	Benetton B200-Playlife V10	76		
12	Jacques Villeneuve	CDN	22	Lucky Strike BAR Honda	BAR 02-Honda RA100E V10	75		
13	Jos Verstappen	NL	19	Arrows	Arrows A21-Supertec FB02 V10	75		
14	Ricardo Zonta	BR	23	Lucky Strike BAR Honda	BAR 02-Honda RA100E V10	75		
15	Marc Gene	ESP	20	Telefonica Minardi Fondmetal	Minardi M02-Fondmetal Ford Zetec-R V10	74		
16	Pedro de la Rosa	ESP	18	Arrows	Arrows A21-Supertec FB02 V10	73		
	Gaston Mazzacane	ARG	21	Telefonica Minardi Fondmetal	Minardi M02-Fondmetal Ford Zetec-R V10	68	Engine	
	Johnny Herbert	GB	8	Jaguar Racing	Jaguar R1-Cosworth CR2 V10	67	Gearshift	
	Pedro Diniz	BR	16	Red Bull Sauber Petronas	Sauber C19-Petronas SPE 04A V10	62	Engine	
	Giancarlo Fisichella	I	11	Mild Seven Benetton Playlife	Benetton B200-Playlife V10	31	Brakes	
	Nick Heidfeld	D	15	Gauloises Prost Peugeot	Prost AP03-Peugeot A20 V10	22	Battery voltage	
	Jean Alesi	F	14	Gauloises Prost Peugeot	Prost AP03-Peugeot A20 V10	11	Suspension	

Fastest lap: Häkkinen, on lap 33, 1m 20.028s, 111.108 mph/178.812 km/h.

Lap record: Nigel Mansell (F1 Williams FW14B-Renault V10), 1m 18.308s, 113.349 mph/182.418 km/h (1992).

Grid order	1	2	3	4	5	6	7	8	9	10	11	12	13	14	15	16	17	18	19	20	21	22	23	24	25	26	27	28	29	30	31	32	33	34	35	36	37	38	39	40	41	42	43	44	45	46	47	48	49	50	51	52	53	54	55	56	57	58	59	60
3 M. SCHUMACHER	1	1	1	1	1	1	1	1	1	1	1	1	1	1	1	1	1	1	1	1	1	1	1	1	1	1	1	1	1	1	1	2	1	1	1	1	1	1	1	1	1	1	1	1	1	1	1	1	1	1	1	1	1	1	1	1	1	1	1	1
2 COULTHARD	3	3	3	3	3	3	3	3	3	3	3	3	3	3	3	3	3	3	3	3	3	3	3	3	3	3	3	3	2	2	2	1	3	3	3	3	3	3	3	3	3	3	3	3	3	3	3	3	2	2	3	3	3	3	3	3	3	3	3	3
1 HÄKKINEN	2	2	2	2	2	2	2	2	2	2	2	2	2	2	2	2	2	2	2	2	2	2	2	2	2	2	2	2	4	3	3	3	2	2	2	2	2	2	2	2	2	2	2	2	2	2	2	2	3	2	2	2	2	2	2	2	2	2	2	2
9 R. SCHUMACHER	9	9	9	9	9	9	9	9	9	9	9	9	9	9	9	9	9	9	9	9	9	9	9	9	9	9	9	9	3	4	5	5	5	4	4	4	4	4	4	4	4	4	4	4	4	4	4	9	9	9	4	4	4	4	4	4	4	4	4	4
4 BARRICHELLO	4	4	4	4	4	4	4	4	4	4	4	4	4	4	4	4	4	4	4	4	4	4	4	4	4	9	5	10	10	4	9	9	9	9	9	9	9	9	9	9	9	9	9	9	4	4	5	5	5	5	5	9	9	9	9
5 FRENTZEN	5	5	5	5	5	5	5	5	5	5	5	5	5	5	5	5	5	5	5	5	5	5	5	5	5	5	10	4	4	9	5	5	5	5	5	5	5	5	5	5	5	5	5	5	9	9	9	9	9	5	5	5	5	5
11 FISICHELLA	11	11	11	11	11	11	11	11	11	7	7	7	7	7	7	7	7	7	7	7	7	7	7	10	10	10	10	10	9	9	9	10	10	10	10	10	10	10	10	10	10	10	10	10	10	10	10	10	10	10	10	10	10	10	10	10	10	10	10	10
10 BUTTON	10	10	10	10	10	10	10	10	10	10	10	10	10	10	10	10	10	10	10	10	10	10	7	12	12	12	12	12	12	12	12	7	7	7	7	7	7	7	7	7	7	7	7	7	7	7	7	7	16	16	16	6	6	6	6	6
17 SALO	7	7	7	7	7	7	7	12	12	12	12	12	12	12	12	12	12	12	12	12	12	12	12	17	17	17	17	17	7	7	6	6	6	6	6	6	6	6	17	17	17	16	16	16	16	7	6	6	6	16	16	16	16	16	16
7 IRVINE	12	12	12	12	12	12	12	17	17	17	17	17	17	17	17	17	17	17	17	17	17	17	17	16	16	16	16	7	6	6	17	17	17	17	17	17	17	17	12	12	16	17	6	6	6	6	7	7	7	7	7	7	7	7	7
12 WURZ	17	17	17	17	17	17	16	16	16	16	16	16	16	16	16	16	16	16	16	16	16	7	7	7	16	6	17	17	12	12	12	12	12	12	12	6	16	12	6	17	17	17	17	17	17	17	17	17	17	17	17	17	17	17	17
6 TRULLI	16	16	16	16	16	16	6	6	6	6	6	6	6	6	6	6	6	6	6	6	6	6	6	6	16	16	16	16	16	16	16	16	16	16	16	6	6	12	12	12	12	12	12	12	12	12	12	12	12
16 DINIZ	6	6	6	6	6	6	14	11	11	11	8	8	8	8	8	8	8	8	8	8	8	8	8	8	8	22	22	8	8	8	8	8	8	8	8	8	8	8	8	8	8	8	8	22	22	8	8	8	8	8	8	8	22	22
14 ALESI	14	14	14	14	14	14	11	8	8	8	11	11	11	23	23	23	23	23	23	23	23	23	23	23	8	19	19	19	19	19	19	19	19	19	19	19	19	19	19	19	19	22	8	22	22	22	22	22	22	22	8	8
18 DE LA ROSA	8	8	8	8	8	8	8	23	23	23	23	23	23	15	15	15	15	15	15	19	19	20	20	19	22	22	8	23	23	23	22	22	22	22	22	22	22	22	19	23	23	23	19	19	19	19	19	19	19	19
22 VILLENEUVE	23	23	23	23	23	23	23	14	15	15	15	15	15	19	19	19	19	19	19	20	19	22	22	8	23	20	23	22	22	22	23	23	23	23	23	23	23	23	23	23	23	23	23	23
8 HERBERT	15	15	15	15	15	15	15	15	19	19	19	19	20	20	20	20	20	20	20	22	22	19	19	20	20	23	20	20	20	20	20	20	20	20	20	20	20	20	20	20	20	20	21	20	20	20	20
23 ZONTA	19	19	19	19	19	19	19	19	20	20	20	20	20	21	21	21	22	22	21	21	20	21	21	21	21	21	21	21	21	21	21	21	21	21	21	21	21	21	21	21	21	20	20	21	21	21	21	21	21	21
15 HEIDFELD	20	20	20	20	20	20	20	20	21	21	21	21	21	11	11	11	21	21	11	11	11	11	11	18	18	18	18	18	18	18	18	18	18	18	18	18	18	18	18	18	18	18	18	18	18	18	18	18	18
19 VERSTAPPEN	21	21	21	21	21	21	21	21	22	22	22	22	22	22	22	22	11	11	11	11	18	18	18	11	11	11	11
20 GENE	22	18	18	18	18	18	18	22	18	18	18	18	18	18	18	18	18	18	18
21 MAZZACANE	18	22	22	22	22	22	22	22	18	14	14

Pit stop
One lap behind leader

STARTING GRID

Pos	No	Driver	Team
1	3	M. SCHUMACHER	Ferrari
2	2	COULTHARD	McLaren
3	1	HÄKKINEN	McLaren
4	9	R. SCHUMACHER	Williams
5	4	BARRICHELLO	Ferrari
6	5	FRENTZEN	Jordan
7	11	FISICHELLA	Benetton
8	10	BUTTON	Williams
9	17	SALO	Sauber
10	7	IRVINE	Jaguar
11	12	WURZ	Benetton
12	6	TRULLI	Jordan
13	16	DINIZ	Sauber
14	14	ALESI	Prost
15	18	DE LA ROSA	Arrows
16	22	VILLENEUVE	BAR
17	8	HERBERT	Jaguar
18	23	ZONTA	BAR
19	15	HEIDFELD	Prost
20	19	VERSTAPPEN	Arrows
21	20	GENE	Minardi
22	21	MAZZACANE	Minardi

Lap chart columns (laps 61–77): 61 62 63 64 65 66 67 68 69 70 71 72 73 74 75 76 77

TIME SHEETS

QUALIFYING
Weather: Dry, hot and sunny

Pos.	Driver	Car	Laps	Time
1	Michael Schumacher	Ferrari	9	1m 17.514s
2	David Coulthard	McLaren-Mercedes	12	1m 17.886s
3	Mika Häkkinen	McLaren-Mercedes	12	1m 17.922s
4	Ralf Schumacher	Williams-BMW	11	1m 18.321s
5	Rubens Barrichello	Ferrari	12	1m 18.330s
6	Heinz-Harald Frentzen	Jordan-Mugen Honda	12	1m 18.523s
7	Giancarlo Fisichella	Benetton-Playlife	11	1m 18.607s
8	Jenson Button	Williams-BMW	11	1m 18.699s
9	Mika Salo	Sauber-Petronas	12	1m 18.748s
10	Eddie Irvine	Jaguar-Cosworth	11	1m 19.008s
11	Alexander Wurz	Benetton-Playlife	12	1m 19.259s
12	Jarno Trulli	Jordan-Mugen Honda	12	1m 19.266s
13	Pedro Diniz	Sauber-Petronas	12	1m 19.451s
14	Jean Alesi	Prost-Peugeot	12	1m 19.626s
15	Pedro de la Rosa	Arrows-Supertec	12	1m 19.897s
16	Jacques Villeneuve	BAR-Honda	11	1m 19.937s
17	Johnny Herbert	Jaguar-Cosworth	11	1m 19.956s
18	Ricardo Zonta	BAR-Honda	12	1m 20.272s
19	Nick Heidfeld	Prost-Peugeot	12	1m 20.481s
20	Jos Verstappen	Arrows-Supertec	12	1m 20.609s
21	Marc Gene	Minardi-Fondmetal	12	1m 20.654s
22	Gaston Mazzacane	Minardi-Fondmetal	12	1m 20.905s

FRIDAY FREE PRACTICE
Weather: Dry, hot and sunny

Pos.	Driver	Laps	Time
1	David Coulthard	23	1m 18.792s
2	Mika Häkkinen	19	1m 18.943s
3	Michael Schumacher	25	1m 19.138s
4	Rubens Barrichello	29	1m 19.896s
5	Jarno Trulli	24	1m 20.104s
6	Giancarlo Fisichella	26	1m 20.304s
7	Ralf Schumacher	26	1m 20.307s
8	Jenson Button	32	1m 20.343s
9	Heinz-Harald Frentzen	26	1m 20.443s
10	Eddie Irvine	27	1m 20.713s
11	Nick Heidfeld	34	1m 20.803s
12	Mika Salo	32	1m 20.872s
13	Jean Alesi	24	1m 20.878s
14	Jacques Villeneuve	39	1m 21.243s
15	Pedro Diniz	26	1m 21.323s
16	Alexander Wurz	28	1m 21.381s
17	Pedro de la Rosa	27	1m 21.400s
18	Jos Verstappen	25	1m 21.803s
19	Marc Gene	36	1m 21.972s
20	Johnny Herbert	28	1m 22.015s
21	Ricardo Zonta	28	1m 22.169s
22	Gaston Mazzacane	23	1m 24.529s

SATURDAY FREE PRACTICE
Weather: Dry, hot and sunny

Pos.	Driver	Laps	Time
1	Michael Schumacher	30	1m 17.395s
2	David Coulthard	29	1m 18.025s
3	Rubens Barrichello	30	1m 18.268s
4	Heinz-Harald Frentzen	26	1m 18.411s
5	Ralf Schumacher	25	1m 18.430s
6	Mika Häkkinen	20	1m 18.467s
7	Jarno Trulli	23	1m 18.503s
8	Giancarlo Fisichella	30	1m 18.561s
9	Mika Salo	29	1m 18.793s
10	Pedro Diniz	23	1m 19.006s
11	Jenson Button	31	1m 19.024s
12	Eddie Irvine	27	1m 19.312s
13	Jacques Villeneuve	29	1m 19.560s
14	Jean Alesi	28	1m 19.951s
15	Johnny Herbert	30	1m 19.972s
16	Jos Verstappen	33	1m 20.049s
17	Pedro de la Rosa	30	1m 20.192s
18	Alexander Wurz	23	1m 20.403s
19	Ricardo Zonta	31	1m 20.515s
20	Nick Heidfeld	27	1m 20.682s
21	Marc Gene	27	1m 20.784s
22	Gaston Mazzacane	17	1m 21.069s

WARM-UP
Weather: Dry, hot and sunny

Pos.	Driver	Laps	Time
1	David Coulthard	15	1m 19.261s
2	Michael Schumacher	15	1m 19.381s
3	Rubens Barrichello	15	1m 19.961s
4	Ralf Schumacher	17	1m 20.438s
5	Mika Häkkinen	10	1m 20.464s
6	Heinz-Harald Frentzen	15	1m 20.682s
7	Pedro Diniz	15	1m 20.914s
8	Mika Salo	15	1m 21.016s
9	Jacques Villeneuve	15	1m 21.079s
10	Jenson Button	14	1m 21.220s
11	Jarno Trulli	15	1m 21.313s
12	Jos Verstappen	15	1m 21.568s
13	Pedro de la Rosa	18	1m 21.609s
14	Giancarlo Fisichella	17	1m 21.653s
15	Jean Alesi	11	1m 21.693s
16	Eddie Irvine	14	1m 21.714s
17	Ricardo Zonta	15	1m 21.728s
18	Johnny Herbert	13	1m 22.112s
19	Alexander Wurz	13	1m 22.279s
20	Marc Gene	10	1m 23.500s
21	Gaston Mazzacane	13	1m 23.853s
22	Nick Heidfeld	6	1m 24.220s

RACE FASTEST LAPS
Weather: Dry, hot and sunny

Driver	Time	Lap
Mika Häkkinen	1m 20.028s	33
Rubens Barrichello	1m 20.520s	42
Heinz-Harald Frentzen	1m 20.640s	58
David Coulthard	1m 20.641s	29
Michael Schumacher	1m 20.762s	22
Jacques Villeneuve	1m 21.163s	48
Ralf Schumacher	1m 21.211s	45
Jenson Button	1m 21.372s	32
Mika Salo	1m 21.423s	33
Jarno Trulli	1m 21.483s	71
Alexander Wurz	1m 21.483s	34
Jean Alesi	1m 21.491s	47
Pedro Diniz	1m 21.572s	70
Eddie Irvine	1m 21.609s	22
Jos Verstappen	1m 22.366s	27
Johnny Herbert	1m 22.439s	30
Ricardo Zonta	1m 22.633s	30
Giancarlo Fisichella	1m 22.933s	53
Marc Gene	1m 23.388s	16
Nick Heidfeld	1m 23.644s	4
Pedro de la Rosa	1m 23.820s	53
Gaston Mazzacane	1m 23.912s	4

CHASSIS LOG BOOK

No	Driver	Chassis
1	Häkkinen	McLaren MP4/15/7
2	Coulthard	McLaren MP4/15/6
spare		McLaren MP4/15/2
3	M. Schumacher	Ferrari F1-2000/203
4	Barrichello	Ferrari F1-2000/202
spare		Ferrari F1-2000/198
5	Frentzen	Jordan E10/6
6	Trulli	Jordan E10/5
spare		Jordan E10/4
9	R. Schumacher	Williams FW22/2
10	Button	Williams FW22/3
spare		Williams FW22/4
11	Fisichella	Benetton B200/5
12	Wurz	Benetton B200/2
spare		Benetton B200/3
16	Diniz	Sauber C19/7
17	Salo	Sauber C19/5
spare		Sauber C19/6
14	Alesi	Prost AP03/5
15	Heidfeld	Prost AP03/3
spare		Prost AP03/1
18	de la Rosa	Arrows A21/3
19	Verstappen	Arrows A21/4
spare		Arrows A21/2
22	Villeneuve	BAR 02/4
23	Zonta	BAR 02/5
spare		BAR 02/2
20	Gene	Minardi M02/3
21	Mazzacane	Minardi M02/4
spare		Minardi M02/1

POINTS TABLES

DRIVERS

Pos	Driver	Points
1	Mika Häkkinen	64
2	Michael Schumacher	62
3	David Coulthard	58
4	Rubens Barrichello	49
5	Giancarlo Fisichella	18
6	Ralf Schumacher	16
7	Jacques Villeneuve	11
8	Jenson Button	8
9=	Jarno Trulli	6
9=	Mika Salo	6
9=	Heinz-Harald Frentzen	6
12	Eddie Irvine	4
13=	Jos Verstappen	2
13=	Pedro de la Rosa	2
15	Ricardo Zonta	1

CONSTRUCTORS

Pos	Team	Points
1	McLaren	112
2	Ferrari	111
3	Williams	24
4	Benetton	18
5=	Jordan	12
5=	BAR	12
7	Sauber	6
8	Arrows	4
9	Jaguar	3

BELGIAN
grand prix

HÄKKINEN
M. SCHUMACHER
R. SCHUMACHER
COULTHARD
BUTTON
FRENTZEN

Left: Podium party. Häkkinen and the Schumacher brothers let off steam, and the bubbly, after the race.
Bryn Williams/Words & Pictures

Below left: Mika Häkkinen attacks Eau Rouge.
Paul-Henri Cahier

CONTEMPORARY grand prix racing has sometimes been criticised for being something of a processional affair, but every so often a set of very specific circumstances sets the stage for an epic confrontation that goes down in the pages of the sport's history books. So it was with this year's Belgian Grand Prix played out over the splendid Spa-Francorchamps circuit between F1's two acknowledged superstars, Mika Häkkinen and Michael Schumacher.

After an early spin on a slippery track surface while leading the race, Häkkinen fought back brilliantly to clinch victory in a dazzling overtaking manoeuvre which many onlookers believed would help catapult him towards the achievement of becoming the first F1 driver since Fangio to win three straight title crowns.

With just three laps of the race remaining, Häkkinen aimed his McLaren-Mercedes MP4/15 straight up the inside of backmarker Ricardo Zonta's BAR as leader Michael Schumacher momentarily dodged his Ferrari to the left of the startled Brazilian driver on the flat-out run towards the Les Combes right-hander here on this spectacular Belgian circuit.

For a fleeting second the three cars were in line abreast at 195 mph as Häkkinen used the slipstream of the slower car to vault ahead of his key rival. From then on the game was up and Häkkinen surged away to score the 18th victory of his career by 1.1s from the Ferrari team leader.

Zonta admitted that he was amazed by Häkkinen's move. 'When they came up behind me I saw Michael and slowed to let him pass me,' he said. 'It was only then that I saw the silver McLaren flashing past on the other side. When I went on the brakes, the McLaren went on going at full speed.'

Häkkinen now led the championship on 74 points, six ahead of Schumacher with David Coulthard, who finished fourth behind Ralf Schumacher's Williams, now trailing on 61 after a race in which an unfortunately timed first refuelling stop cost him to lose touch with the leading bunch.

Jenson Button drove another fine race to finish fifth after qualifying superbly in third place on his first F1 outing at the circuit. An early collision with Jarno Trulli's Jordan left the 20-year-old grappling with heavy steering on his Williams-BMW. He acknowledged: 'I could have achieved more today.'

Trulli had qualified his Jordan EJ10 superbly on the front row of the grid alongside Häkkinen, but was struggling to conserve his rear tyres on a heavy fuel load during the opening stages of the race.

Earlier, Giancarlo Fisichella had found the tyre barriers doing an excellent job during the rain-soaked warm-up when he crashed his Benetton B200 heavily at Stavelot, the car flipping over and being wrecked in the impact. Fisichella walked away from the spectacular incident without a scratch.

The warm-up also saw David Coulthard grappling with an unusual problem when he switched to the spare McLaren-Mercedes MP4/15 and the front wing covers were mistakenly left on as he accelerated away on his installation lap. A few moments after complaining over the radio that 'the aerodynamic balance feels very strange' one of the covers flew off as he slid onto the grass at Les Combes. 'There were a few red faces in our garage,' admitted Ron Dennis.

Heavy rain had doused the circuit during Sunday morning, but although the circuit was still pretty wet, it had not actually rained for two hours before the start. Nevertheless, after discussing the matter with the drivers, race director Charlie Whiting agreed to start the race behind the safety car. From the touchlines opinions were divided as to whether this was just pandering to the drivers' foibles – or a mature and balanced assessment of the risks in admittedly still very tricky track conditions.

At the end of the opening lap Häkkinen came through in formation just 0.8s ahead of the young Italian, but once the pack was unleashed he quickly stretched that to 2.1s at the end of lap two, then 3.8s and 9.1s. On lap four Button got himself slightly wrong-footed as Trulli slowed up dramatically, braking for the Bus Stop chicane and Schumacher, lurking in fourth place, took the opportunity to nip through to third on the spot, then second going into La Source.

Button then tried to follow the Ferrari through and nudged Trulli, who had taken a very wide entry in an effort to cut back inside Schumacher on the exit of the corner, into a spin as they exited the race on the spot.

'I think Jenson was a bit too aggressive too soon,' he said. 'He should have waited for a couple of laps as he would probably have got past me since I was struggling slightly. There was not enough room for Jenson to overtake me.' As Jenson sorted himself out after this incident, so Coulthard and Ralf

BELGIAN GRAND PRIX

SPA-FRANCORCHAMPS QUALIFYING

Spa-Francorchamps is a medium- to low-downforce circuit where the real challenge is balancing the requirement for absolute speed on the first and third sectors of the 4.33-mile lap against the need for added grip on the middle sector where there are more slow- and medium-speed corners.

There is also the question of raising the rear ride height in order to accommodate the huge vertical loadings sustained as the cars plunge through the daunting Eau Rouge corner.

Bridgestone brought along both soft and medium tyre compounds, all the teams eventually opting for the former despite concerns about higher levels of degradation. In part, this strategy was dictated by confident predictions that the weather on race day would probably be wet. Even if it remained dry, there was little likelihood of seeing a repeat of the 32-degree track temperatures which prevailed throughout qualifying.

David Coulthard arrived fresh from a mid-season holiday intended to recharge his competitive batteries. The Scot was slightly dismissive of the need for such a break even though it did the trick for Häkkinen who has had the upper hand at McLaren since taking two weeks off prior to winning last month's Austrian GP.

'I don't think the key to going faster is going on holiday,' he said. 'I am obviously anxious to win here, but I think as Mika proved in Hungary, this business is not necessarily about leading the front row of the grid – but leading out of the first corner of the race.'

Not that Mika had it all his own way. Some pretty high-profile opposition concentrated his mind from the moment he set the ball rolling with a 1m 51.680s fastest lap just ten minutes into the session. The result was a sensational qualifying session.

A few moments later the dauntless Jacques Villeneuve – a great Spa-lover – slammed round in 1m 52.857s in the BAR-Honda, while Ralf Schumacher then caught everybody's attention by slicing 0.1s off Häkkinen's best for the first sector of the lap.

It all translated into a second-fastest 1m 52.454s for the Williams-BMW driver, but the runner-up slot was thereafter occupied in quick succession by Jarno Trulli's Jordan (1m 51.948s) and Michael Schumacher's Ferrari (1m 51.894s) before Trulli briefly took pole on 1m 51.598s.

Yet Häkkinen didn't seem able to put a wheel wrong. Ultimately he stopped the clocks with a stunning 1m 50.646s, clinching the 26th pole of his career ahead of Trulli by 0.773s.

Jenson Button performed magnificently to snatch third on the grid from Michael Schumacher's slightly off-pace Ferrari F1-2000. While Michael spent two days struggling to work out a decent handling balance from Maranello's revised low-downforce aero package, the 20-year-old Brit was laying his Williams-BMW into the long corners with a measured precision which vividly reminded technical chief Patrick Head of Alain Prost's smooth, fluid driving style.

Jenson was beside himself. 'I'm absolutely ecstatic!' said Button. 'I thought I could only out-qualify Michael Schumacher if he had gone out or fallen off the track or something.'

For his part, Schumacher was very pensive. 'I can't honestly say this was an entirely satisfactory qualifying session for us,' he said. 'Being fourth, almost a second off the pole, is not what we expected.

'On my second run, which turned out to be my best, I was slowed by traffic in the second sector. Then on my third run, I had to slow again because of the yellow flags, as can be seen from my third sector time.'

Coulthard was a similarly disappointed fifth ahead of Ralf Schumacher (1m 51.743s) and Jacques Villeneuve's BAR-Honda (1m 51.799s).

For his part, Heinz-Harald Frentzen (above) wound up a frustrated eighth on 1m 51.926s, admitting that the first incident when he blocked Coulthard had certainly been his fault. 'It was my mistake,' he said. 'I saw him too late because I was having trouble with my radio.' Later he blamed David for twice blocking him. 'I thought that was a little unfair,' he added. On his third run he encountered traffic.

Johnny Herbert was moderately satisfied with ninth. Both Alexander Wurz and Giancarlo Fisichella suffered engine problems and had to share the spare Benetton B200. Jean Alesi's Prost-Peugeot spun at the chicane late in the session, bringing out the yellow flags.

In the Ferrari camp, Rubens Barrichello was extremely disappointed not to have improved on 10th place in the line-up. 'All weekend I have been unable to find the ideal set-up,' he shrugged.

'Finally, on my third run, the car seemed to be going better and I was setting a good time and could have made up a few important places on the grid. However, at the entry to the chicane, I locked the wheels and ended up spinning. Then when I came back to the pits I had to stop at scrutineering and lost further time.'

Schumacher both nipped by, demoting the young Williams driver to fifth.

Next time round Michael made a 6.3s stop to switch to dry tyres while brother Ralf also brought the Williams in and next time round Häkkinen (7.2s), Button (7.3s) and Eddie Irvine's fifth-placed Jaguar all came in for the same reason. On lap eight Häkkinen was just 7.2s ahead of Coulthard, who came in for a 7.2s switch to dry-weather rubber, so on lap nine Mika was left 6.2s ahead of Schumacher's Ferrari which was very clearly on the offensive.

On lap 11 Michael had trimmed the McLaren lead to 4.9s and it was down to 4.6s as they finished lap 12. Then, coming out of Stavelot on lap 13, Häkkinen's McLaren looped into a lazy spin coming out of Stavelot. Mika quickly regained control of his machine but now found himself 5.6s behind the leading Ferrari which began to pull away all the way through to its second (11.1s) stop at the end of lap 22 by which time Schumacher was almost 12s ahead.

Häkkinen stayed out until lap 27 by which time he was 15s ahead of Schumacher, but despite a quick 8.8s stop from the McLaren mechanics he returned to the race 5.8s behind the Ferrari.

A quick adjustment at that second pit stop improved the fine edge of the McLaren's handling and, from that moment onwards, he began to hunt down Schumacher's scarlet Ferrari.

On the face of it a straight fight between Schumacher and Häkkinen through the fast swerves of this most spectacular of grand prix circuits was the stuff of which legends are made.

Yet Schumacher's defensive tactics on the lap before Häkkinen pulled his successful overtaking move once again rekindled the lingering controversy as to just what level of driving etiquette is expected from the world's leading drivers.

As Schumacher battled to keep ahead on a drying track surface which swung a decisive performance advantage in favour of Häkkinen's McLaren, the Finn came swooping up the inside of the Ferrari as they approached Les Combes on lap 40.

Schumacher then chopped across Häkkinen so ruthlessly that the McLaren driver initially thought that his left front wheel had made contact with the Ferrari's right rear.

After the two cars had taken the chequered flag and pulled into the parc fermé, Häkkinen could be seen lecturing Schumacher quite firmly, his hand movements indicating that the topic of conversation was the first overtaking manoeuvre.

Yet under the relentless spotlight of the post-race media conference, Häkkinen retained his Nordic composure and weighed his words with meticulous precision.

'One tends to react to issues immediately and without thinking in these situations,' he said. 'I want to look at the video of the move to understand what happened, but I thought there was something going on that was not fair.'

Schumacher concealed his disappointment manfully. Characteristically, he brushed aside suggestions that he'd done anything that his competitors wouldn't have done to him without a moment's hesitation.

For his part, Schumacher finished the day worried about the Ferrari F1-2000's apparent drop-off in performance for the second straight race. Plagued by chassis balance problems throughout qualifying, the team decided to experiment by back-tracking to an earlier-spec front wing in the race morning warm-up. Yet the handling imbalance remained.

'I simply could not keep Mika back,' he confessed later. 'As for the passing move, usually there is only room for two cars on the track, but Mika made an outstanding move. If he had not passed me there, he would have done it later.'

Initially it looked the way to go, but as the track dried out in the closing stages so Schumacher's Bridgestones degraded faster than Häkkinen's, notwithstanding a front flap adjustment at his second pit stop. In the laps immediately before Häkkinen made his bid to overtake, Schumacher was running up towards Les Combes hard over to the right of the circuit, desperately attempting to cool his overworked tyres as the McLaren driver relentlessly closed on him.

Ralf Schumacher finished third after a relatively lonely race while Coulthard took fourth, having spent many laps shadowing Heinz-Harald Frentzen before the McLaren crew successfully vaulted him ahead of the Jordan when they both came in to refuel at the end of lap 28.

Rubens Barrichello had a disappointing day, his Ferrari F1-2000 running out of fuel as he came into the pit lane while running fourth at the end of lap 33. Another brutally disappointing retirement was that of Jean Alesi in the Prost-Peugeot, the Frenchman having vaulted up into the top six thanks to a brilliantly timed early change to dry tyres at the end of lap four, one lap ahead of the rush hour.

Left: Heinz-Harald Frentzen short-cuts the kerb at the Bus Stop chicane.

Right: Bad luck for Jarno Trulli as the Italian's Jordan is nudged into a spin by Jenson Button's Williams.

Below right: Another strong performance by Jacques Villeneuve in the BAR-Honda saw him lead Barrichello and Frentzen before eventually just slipping out of a points-scoring position.

Right: 'I use my 'ead, no?' Ricardo Zonta in conversation.
Bryn Williams/Words & Pictures

Far right: Jenson Button put in another brilliant performance at Spa.
Paul-Henri Cahier

Bottom right: Ralf Schumacher scored yet another podium place in the Williams FW22-BMW.
Paul-Henri Cahier

Bottom: Gaston Mazzacane in the Minardi M02.
Clive Mason/Allsport

DIARY

Brazilian Ricardo Zonta and Germany's Nick Heidfeld are tipped to drive for the Sauber-Petronas team in 2001.

Bruno Junquiera clinches F3000 championship despite finishing out of the points in the Spa finale which was won by Fernando Alonso.

The Porsche Super Cup race at Spa was cancelled after wear rates and temperature levels, following problems in practice.

CART team owner Barry Green is tipped to take over from Craig Pollock as chief of British American Racing.

He was storming along in fifth place, seemingly set to score the Prost team's first points of the year, when his engine wilted on lap 33 and he had to call it a day.

Button was a mildly disappointed fifth ahead of Frentzen's Jordan while Jacques Villeneuve in the BAR and Johnny Herbert in the Jaguar R1 finished seventh and eighth. 'It was an enjoyable race,' said Herbert, 'but unfortunately I was on my own most of the time so wasn't actually racing with anybody apart from when Mika Salo was catching me at the end.' He held off the Sauber by 0.8s at the chequered flag.

Irvine was tenth, disappointed that his Jaguar's balance deteriorated when he switched to dry-weather tyres, while Diniz, Zonta and Wurz followed him across the line.

As the McLaren team celebrated, so Schumacher was left to ponder his seemingly dramatic defeat at the hands of the reigning World Champion.

'We do not feel we have lost the championship,' he said firmly. 'Everyone is still pushing very hard in the team and the championship is still alive. But Häkkinen was simply much faster today, even though we improved the car from yesterday to today and from the last race to this one.'

Dramatically – perhaps unexpectedly – that would change.

Mosley attends Toyota F1 launch

FIA president Max Mosley attended the formal announcement of the Toyota team's F1 programme at Spa on the Thursday before the race and paid tribute to the Japanese company's boldness in taking on the challenge of building its own car and engine at its base in Cologne from which it will race from the start of 2002.

'My job is to welcome Toyota to the FIA F1 World Championship,' he said. 'It is certainly a rare occasion when a new team comes into F1 committed to building its own car and engine, so this must be seen as a very courageous step.

'This is a very specialised business which requires particular skills, so for one of the three biggest car companies in the world to come in without the assistance of an established team is certainly very brave and should be applauded.'

Tsutomu Tomita, Toyota Motorsport's chairman, offered an upbeat assessment of the team's future programme. 'The Toyota F1 project is more than just a management dream, it has been a long-lasting dream of the whole company.'

The first Toyota V10 engine was expected to run on the dynamometer in September (it met that deadline) and the first prototype car will start testing during the spring of 2001.

Test driving will be carried out by Allan McNish and Mika Salo, the Finn taking the bold decision to leave Sauber in order to be ready to race the new Toyota F1 in 2002.

'My decision to test instead of race next year was not taken lightly or easily,' said Salo, 'but having seen how much effort is going into the Toyota F1 project, I'm happy to take this step.'

Mark Thompson/Allsport

BELGIAN GRAND PRIX

FOSTER'S BELGIUM grand prix

ROUND 13

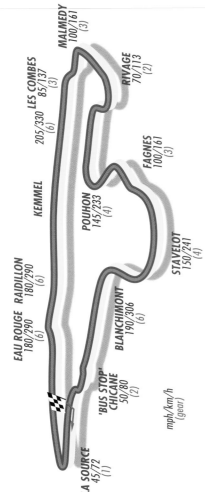

SPA-FRANCORCHAMPS
CIRCUIT LENGTH: 4.330 miles/6.968 km

LA SOURCE 45/72 (1)
EAU ROUGE 180/290 (6)
RAIDILLON 180/290 (6)
KEMMEL 205/330 (6)
LES COMBES 85/137 (3)
MALMEDY 100/161 (3)
RIVAGE 70/113 (2)
POUHON 145/233 (4)
FAGNES 100/161 (3)
STAVELOT 150/241 (4)
BLANCHIMONT 190/306 (6)
'BUS STOP' CHICANE 50/80 (2)

mph/km/h (gear)

All results and data © FIA 2000

RACE DISTANCE: 44 laps, 190.507 miles/306.592 km **RACE WEATHER: Wet at first, then drying, warm and sunny**

Pos.	Driver	Nat.	No.	Entrant	Car/Engine	Laps	Time/Retirement	Speed (mph/km/h)
1	Mika Häkkinen	SF	1	West McLaren Mercedes	McLaren MP4/15-Mercedes FO110J V10	44	1h 28m 14.494s	129.535/208.467
2	Michael Schumacher	D	3	Scuderia Ferrari Marlboro	Ferrari F1-2000-049 V10	44	1h 28m 15.598s	129.508/208.424
3	Ralf Schumacher	D	9	BMW WilliamsF1 Team	Williams FW22-BMW E41 V10	44	1h 28m 52.590s	128.610/206.978
4	David Coulthard	GB	2	West McLaren Mercedes	McLaren MP4/15-Mercedes FO110J V10	44	1h 28m 57.775s	128.485/206.777
5	Jenson Button	GB	10	BMW WilliamsF1 Team	Williams FW22-BMW E41 V10	44	1h 29m 04.408s	128.325/206.520
6	Heinz-Harald Frentzen	D	5	Benson & Hedges Jordan	Jordan EJ10-Mugen Honda MF301HE V10	44	1h 29m 10.478s	128.180/206.286
7	Jacques Villeneuve	CDN	22	Lucky Strike BAR Honda	BAR 02-Honda RA100E V10	44	1h 29m 26.874s	127.789/205.656
8	Johnny Herbert	GB	8	Jaguar Racing	Jaguar R1-Cosworth CR2 V10	44	1h 29m 42.302s	127.422/205.066
9	Mika Salo	SF	17	Red Bull Sauber Petronas	Sauber C19-Petronas SPE 04A V10	44	1h 29m 43.164s	127.401/205.033
10	Eddie Irvine	GB	7	Jaguar Racing	Jaguar R1-Cosworth CR2 V10	44	1h 29m 46.049s	127.334/204.924
11	Pedro Diniz	BR	16	Red Bull Sauber Petronas	Sauber C19-Petronas SPE 04A V10	44	1h 29m 48.617s	127.273/204.826
12	Ricardo Zonta	BR	23	Lucky Strike BAR Honda	BAR 02-Honda RA100E V10	43		
13	Alexander Wurz	A	12	Mild Seven Benetton Playlife	Benetton B200-Playlife V10	43		
14	Marc Gene	ESP	20	Telefonica Minardi Fondmetal	Minardi M02-Fondmetal Ford Zetec-R V10	43		
15	Jos Verstappen	NL	19	Arrows	Arrows A21-Supertec FB02 V10	43		
16	Pedro de la Rosa	ESP	18	Arrows	Arrows A21-Supertec FB02 V10	42		
17	Gaston Mazzacane	ARG	21	Telefonica Minardi Fondmetal	Minardi M02-Fondmetal Ford Zetec-R V10	42		
	Rubens Barrichello	BR	4	Scuderia Ferrari Marlboro	Ferrari F1-2000-049 V10	32	Fuel pressure	
	Jean Alesi	F	14	Gauloises Prost Peugeot	Prost AP03-Peugeot A20 V10	32	Fuel pressure	
	Nick Heidfeld	D	15	Gauloises Prost Peugeot	Prost AP03-Peugeot A20 V10	12	Engine	
	Giancarlo Fisichella	I	11	Mild Seven Benetton Playlife	Benetton B200-Playlife V10	8	Electrics	
	Jarno Trulli	I	6	Benson & Hedges Jordan	Jordan EJ10-Mugen Honda MF301HE V10	4	Collision with Button	

Fastest lap: Barrichello, on lap 30, 1m 53.803s, 136.964 mph/220.423 km/h.
Lap record: Alain Prost (F1 Williams FW15C-Renault V10), 1m 51.095s, 140.424 mph/225.990 km/h (1993).

● Pit stop
One lap behind leader

Grid order	1	2	3	4	5	6	7	8	9	10	11	12	13	14	15	16	17	18	19	20	21	22	23	24	25	26	27	28	29	30	31	32	33	34	35	36	37	38	39	40	41	42	43	44
1 HÄKKINEN	1	1	1	1	1	1	1	1	1	1	1	3	3	3	3	3	1	1	1	1	1	1	1	1	1	1	1	1	1	1	1	1	1	1	1	1	1	1	1	1	1	1	1	1
6 TRULLI	6	6	6	6																																								
10 BUTTON	10	10	10	3	3	2	10	9	10	9	22	5	22	14	5	5	5	22	22	14	8	22	22	8	8	8	8	8	8	8	8	8	8	8	8	8	8	8	8	8	8	8	8	8
3 M. SCHUMACHER	3	3	3	2	2	2	2	14	14	14	14	14	14	2	2	2	22	5	5	5	22	8	8	17	17	17	7	7	16	16	16	16	16	23	23	23	23	23	23	23	23	23	23	23
2 COULTHARD	2	2	2	9	9	9	9	2	2	2	5	22	5	5	22	22	8	4	8	8	16	16	16	16	16	7	17	16	7	12	12	12	12	12	12	12	12	12	12	12	12	12	12	12
9 R. SCHUMACHER	9	9	9	22	7	9	22	5	5	5	2	2	2	22	14	14	4	8	4	4	4	4	4	7	7	16	16	17	12	18	18	18	18	18	18	18	18	18	18	18	18	18	18	18
22 VILLENEUVE	22	22	22	5	22	17	5	22	22	22	9	9	8	8	8	8	14	14	14	22	5	5	5	5	18	18	18	18	18	7	19	19	19	19	21	21	21	21	21	21	21	21	21	21
5 FRENTZEN	5	5	5	5																																								
8 HERBERT	8	4	4	4	8	8	8	8	8	8	4	4	4	4	4	16	16	16	16	16	7	7	7	18	12	12	12	12	19	19	7	7	7	7	20	20	20	20	20	20	20	20	20	20
4 BARRICHELLO	4	8	8	11	11	4	4	4	4	4	8	8	9	9	9	9	7	7	7	7	12	12	12	12	23	23	23	23	23	20	20	20	20	20	19	19	19	19	19	19	19	19	19	19
7 FISICHELLA	11	11	11	11																																								
7 IRVINE	7	7	7	23	23	23	17	17	17	17	17	17	7	7	7	7	23	23	23	23	23	23	23	23	20	20	20	20	20	21	21	21	21	21										
23 ZONTA	23	23	23	17	17	18	23	23	23	23	23	23	17	17	16	12	12	12	12	12	18	18	18	20	21	21	21	21	21															
15 HEIDFELD	15	15	15	14	14	16	16	16	16	16	16	16	16	16	12																													
16 DINIZ	18	18	18	18	16	14	14	12	12	12	12	12	12	12	17	17	17	17	18	18	20	20	20	21																				
18 DE LA ROSA	16	14	14	16	18	19	18	18	18	18	18	18	18	18	18	18	18	18	17	17	21	21	21																					
17 ALESI	17	19	19	19	12	12	12	19	19	19	19	19	19	19	19	19	19	19	19	19	17	17																						
12 SALO	12	12	12	12																																								
19 WURZ	19	20	20	15	15	15	15	20	20	20	20	20	20	20	20	20	20	20	20	20	19	19	19	19																				
20 VERSTAPPEN	20	21	21	21																																								
12 GENE	19	20	20	20	21	21	21	21	21	21	21	21	21	21	21	21	21	21	21	21																								
21 MAZZACANE	21	16	16	16																																								

STARTING GRID

Pos	No.	Driver	Team
1	1	HÄKKINEN	McLaren
2	6	TRULLI	Jordan
3	3	M. SCHUMACHER	Ferrari
4	10	BUTTON	Williams
5	9	R. SCHUMACHER	Williams
6	2	COULTHARD	McLaren
7	5	FRENTZEN	Jordan
8	22	VILLENEUVE	BAR
9	4	BARRICHELLO	Ferrari
10	8	HERBERT	Jaguar
11	7	IRVINE	Jaguar
12	11	FISICHELLA	Benetton
13	15	HEIDFELD	Prost
14	23	ZONTA	BAR
15	18	DE LA ROSA	Arrows
16	16	DINIZ	Sauber
17	17	SALO	Sauber
18	14	ALESI	Prost
19	19	VERSTAPPEN	Arrows
20	12	WURZ	Benetton
21	21	MAZZACANE	Minardi
22	20	GENE	Minardi

FOR THE RECORD

350th Grand Prix start — Arrows
250th Grand Prix start — Minardi

TIME SHEETS

QUALIFYING
Weather: Sunny and very hot

Pos.	Driver	Car	Laps	Time
1	Mika Häkkinen	McLaren-Mercedes	11	1m 50.646s
2	Jarno Trulli	Jordan-Mugen Honda	12	1m 51.419s
3	Jenson Button	Williams-BMW	12	1m 51.444s
4	Michael Schumacher	Ferrari	12	1m 51.552s
5	David Coulthard	McLaren-Mercedes	11	1m 51.587s
6	Ralf Schumacher	Williams-BMW	12	1m 51.743s
7	Jacques Villeneuve	BAR-Honda	12	1m 51.799s
8	Heinz-Harald Frentzen	Jordan-Mugen Honda	11	1m 51.926s
9	Johnny Herbert	Jaguar-Cosworth	12	1m 52.242s
10	Rubens Barrichello	Ferrari	12	1m 52.444s
11	Giancarlo Fisichella	Benetton-Playlife	5	1m 52.756s
12	Eddie Irvine	Jaguar-Cosworth	11	1m 52.885s
13	Ricardo Zonta	BAR-Honda	11	1m 53.002s
14	Nick Heidfeld	Prost-Peugeot	12	1m 53.193s
15	Pedro de la Rosa	Arrows-Supertec	11	1m 53.211s
16	Pedro Diniz	Sauber-Petronas	11	1m 53.237s
17	Jean Alesi	Prost-Peugeot	11	1m 53.309s
18	Mika Salo	Sauber-Petronas	11	1m 53.357s
19	Alexander Wurz	Benetton-Playlife	12	1m 53.403s
20	Jos Verstappen	Arrows-Supertec	11	1m 53.912s
21	Marc Gene	Minardi-Fondmetal	12	1m 54.680s
22	Gaston Mazzacane	Minardi-Fondmetal	12	1m 54.784s

FRIDAY FREE PRACTICE
Weather: Sunny and very hot

Pos.	Driver	Laps	Time
1	David Coulthard	14	1m 53.398s
2	Mika Häkkinen	17	1m 53.919s
3	Johnny Herbert	24	1m 53.945s
4	Jacques Villeneuve	31	1m 54.136s
5	Michael Schumacher	21	1m 54.226s
6	Alexander Wurz	27	1m 54.266s
7	Jos Verstappen	19	1m 54.338s
8	Giancarlo Fisichella	20	1m 54.350s
9	Rubens Barrichello	26	1m 54.502s
10	Jarno Trulli	24	1m 54.666s
11	Marc Gene	29	1m 54.832s
12	Ralf Schumacher	23	1m 55.209s
13	Jenson Button	26	1m 55.270s
14	Pedro Diniz	25	1m 55.312s
15	Ricardo Zonta	26	1m 55.546s
16	Eddie Irvine	22	1m 55.645s
17	Heinz-Harald Frentzen	19	1m 55.750s
18	Mika Salo	28	1m 55.847s
19	Gaston Mazzacane	32	1m 56.125s
20	Pedro de la Rosa	15	1m 56.252s
21	Jean Alesi	16	1m 56.508s
22	Nick Heidfeld	30	1m 56.857s

SATURDAY FREE PRACTICE
Weather: Sunny and very hot

Pos.	Driver	Laps	Time
1	Mika Häkkinen	20	1m 51.043s
2	Jenson Button	23	1m 51.367s
3	Jarno Trulli	21	1m 51.545s
4	Heinz-Harald Frentzen	12	1m 51.821s
5	Ralf Schumacher	24	1m 51.998s
6	David Coulthard	20	1m 52.088s
7	Michael Schumacher	26	1m 52.282s
8	Jacques Villeneuve	27	1m 52.335s
9	Rubens Barrichello	21	1m 52.553s
10	Johnny Herbert	23	1m 52.769s
11	Jean Alesi	12	1m 52.830s
12	Giancarlo Fisichella	18	1m 53.085s
13	Nick Heidfeld	24	1m 53.278s
14	Alexander Wurz	19	1m 53.306s
15	Eddie Irvine	24	1m 53.395s
16	Pedro de la Rosa	22	1m 53.778s
17	Pedro Diniz	25	1m 53.799s
18	Ricardo Zonta	27	1m 54.262s
19	Mika Salo	23	1m 54.334s
20	Marc Gene	21	1m 54.587s
21	Gaston Mazzacane	23	1m 54.804s
22	Jos Verstappen	9	1m 54.969s

WARM-UP
Weather: Intermittent rain

Pos.	Driver	Laps	Time
1	Mika Häkkinen	11	2m 03.392s
2	Michael Schumacher	12	2m 03.562s
3	Jenson Button	9	2m 03.564s
4	Rubens Barrichello	9	2m 03.744s
5	David Coulthard	13	2m 04.120s
6	Mika Salo	13	2m 04.279s
7	Johnny Herbert	12	2m 04.528s
8	Ralf Schumacher	10	2m 04.958s
9	Jarno Trulli	12	2m 05.017s
10	Jacques Villeneuve	10	2m 05.050s
11	Heinz-Harald Frentzen	12	2m 05.340s
12	Eddie Irvine	10	2m 05.600s
13	Ricardo Zonta	10	2m 05.737s
14	Jean Alesi	9	2m 06.475s
15	Nick Heidfeld	11	2m 06.768s
16	Jos Verstappen	16	2m 06.789s
17	Alexander Wurz	10	2m 06.865s
18	Pedro Diniz	9	2m 07.585s
19	Pedro de la Rosa	6	2m 08.184s
20	Giancarlo Fisichella	10	2m 08.414s
21	Gaston Mazzacane	10	2m 08.801s
22	Marc Gene	9	

RACE FASTEST LAPS
Weather: Wet, then drying, warm and sunny

Pos.	Driver	Time	Lap
1	Rubens Barrichello	1m 53.803s	30
2	David Coulthard	1m 54.131s	32
3	Michael Schumacher	1m 54.252s	18
4	Giancarlo Fisichella	1m 54.469s	32
5	Mika Häkkinen	1m 54.966s	33
6	Heinz-Harald Frentzen	1m 55.110s	30
7	Mika Salo	1m 55.153s	42
8	Pedro Diniz	1m 55.425s	33
9	Jenson Button	1m 55.473s	24
10	Ralf Schumacher	1m 55.511s	41
11	Jacques Villeneuve	1m 55.603s	31
12	Johnny Herbert	1m 55.603s	42
13	Eddie Irvine	1m 55.954s	15
14	Jean Alesi	1m 56.726s	42
15	Alexander Wurz	1m 56.770s	29
16	Jarno Trulli	1m 57.261s	19
17	Ricardo Zonta	1m 57.263s	29
18	Gaston Mazzacane	1m 57.269s	34
19	Jos Verstappen	1m 57.432s	42
20	Nick Heidfeld	1m 58.831s	12
21	Pedro de la Rosa	2m 02.148s	8
22	Marc Gene	2m 07.154s	3

CHASSIS LOG BOOK

No.	Driver	Chassis
1	Häkkinen	McLaren MP4/15/6
2	Coulthard	McLaren MP4/15/7
	spare	McLaren MP4/15/2
3	M. Schumacher	Ferrari F1-2000/205
4	Barrichello	Ferrari F1-2000/202
	spare	Ferrari F1-2000/200
5	Frentzen	Jordan EJ10/6
6	Trulli	Jordan EJ10/5
	spare	Jordan EJ10/4
9	R. Schumacher	Williams FW22/2
10	Button	Williams FW22/4
	spare	Williams FW22/3
11	Fisichella	Benetton B200/5
12	Wurz	Benetton B200/2
	spare	Benetton B200/3
14	Alesi	Prost AP03/5
15	Heidfeld	Prost AP03/2
	spare	Prost AP03/1
16	Diniz	Sauber C19/7
17	Salo	Sauber C19/5
	spare	Sauber C19/6
18	de la Rosa	Arrows A21/5
19	Verstappen	Arrows A21/4
	spare	Arrows A21/1
22	Villeneuve	BAR 02/4
23	Zonta	BAR 02/5
	spares	BAR 02/2 & 3
20	Gene	Minardi M02/3
21	Mazzacane	Minardi M02/4
	spare	Minardi M02/1

POINTS TABLES

DRIVERS
1	Mika Häkkinen	74
2	Michael Schumacher	68
3	David Coulthard	61
4	Rubens Barrichello	49
5	Ralf Schumacher	20
6	Giancarlo Fisichella	18
7	Jacques Villeneuve	11
8	Jenson Button	10
9	Heinz-Harald Frentzen	7
10=	Jarno Trulli	6
10=	Mika Salo	6
12	Eddie Irvine	3
13=	Jos Verstappen	2
13=	Pedro de la Rosa	2
15	Ricardo Zonta	1

CONSTRUCTORS
	Team	Points
1	McLaren	125
2	Ferrari	117
3	Williams	30
4	Benetton	18
5	Jordan	13
6	BAR	12
7	Sauber	6
8	Arrows	4
9	Jaguar	3

ITALIAN
grand prix

FIA WORLD CHAMPIONSHIP • ROUND 14

CAMPARI

ITALIAN GRAND PRIX

MONZA QUALIFYING

As expected, the home team pulled something extra out of the bag in the Friday free practice session where Barrichello just pipped Schumacher for fastest time. The Ferraris ran with a metronomic consistency which contrasted dramatically with the excursions and setbacks which befell their rivals at McLaren, David Coulthard's efforts ending prematurely in the gravel trap after sliding off the road at the 140-mph Lesmo right-hander.

'I'm not sure whether I made a mistake or there was a problem with the car, but the team is analysing the data,' said Coulthard diplomatically after his car returned to the pits on a breakdown truck with its left rear wheel dangling forlornly.

Closer examination revealed a rear wishbone on the McLaren had broken, the brand new component having failed due to a manufacturing fault.

Coulthard's team-mate Mika Häkkinen also lost most of the morning session with a clutch problem which prevented him from completing valuable chassis set-up work on a circuit which had been changed significantly since last year's race with the inclusion of a dramatically re-profiled first chicane plus minor changes to the second chicane after Curva Grande.

The fastest cars were slamming into the braking area at 210 mph, slowing to 50 mph in 4.3s between first lifting from the throttle and shaving the apex of the corner. Consistent and dependable braking performance was an absolutely crucial element of the competitive equation.

The drivers' reaction to this revision was mixed, with most agreeing that it would be fine once the race was underway although there would be the inevitable traffic jam there on the opening lap. Some observers also wryly noted that the revised kerbs at the chicanes seemed calculated to deprive McLaren of their proven ability to ride high kerbs with relative impunity and, as a result of these modifications, swing the performance balance into Ferrari's favour.

Coulthard and Heinz-Harald Frentzen had both expressed their reservations about the revised track layout during the previous week's Monza test, but Michael Schumacher, perhaps predictably, offered a different perspective.

'Personally I rate it safer than what we had before,' he said. 'If you go through the races throughout the year, you will find places like Monaco, or wherever, where we have very tight corners.

'I think it is a point of discipline between the drivers not to be crazy and just to use the space that is available but no more than that.'

Come qualifying and Schumacher put in a simply dominant performance, his Ferrari seeming to sustain a small, but crucial edge over the McLarens throughout the hour-long session. There were no obvious high-speed imbalance problems and in low-downforce trim the F1-2000s certainly looked more convincing than they had done during qualifying at Hockenheim, the previous low-downforce, high-speed circuit on the calendar.

All the competitors preferred Bridgestone's medium tyre compound – the softer of the two available options – and although there were a few concerns expressed about possible blistering problems, all the teams seemed relaxed with their choice. However, this was a softer compound than last year's Bridgestone preferred tyre choice at Monza, so with exposure to added wear under higher-speed braking for the new corner beyond the pits, some thoughts turned to the possibility of a two-stop strategy.

Rubens Barrichello admitted that he was pretty satisfied with his second-fastest 1m 23.797s. 'I am much happier here than at the last two races where I was a bit unlucky,' he said.

'I think I could have gone a bit quicker, but at the end I had some problems in traffic.'

Meanwhile Häkkinen's McLaren-Mercedes suffered a glitch in a fuel pressure sensor which briefly caused a misfire on the Finn's out lap, but it cleared when he got up to racing speeds even as the mechanics were preparing the spare MP4/15 for his emergency use.

'I thought I got the maximum out of the car in terms of driving, but its handling could have been better,' said the Finn. Coulthard, meanwhile, dropped to fifth in the final order after failing to string together three quick sector times into a single lap. He was also briefly – and inadvertently – balked by Frentzen and made a discreet visit to the Jordan pit gently to compare notes on the unfortunate incident.

Separating the two McLarens in fourth place on the grid came Jacques Villeneuve on a splendid 1m 24.238s best in the BAR-Honda. Team-mate Ricardo Zonta, by contrast, stopped out on the circuit with gearbox problems and had to take over the spare car, which had Villeneuve's cockpit set-up. He lined up a distant 17th.

In the Jordan camp, Saturday morning's free practice session brought with it much in the way of problems. Heinz-Harald Frentzen slid into the tyre barrier at Parabolica, damaging his car's front suspension and steering rack, while Jarno Trulli suffered a hydraulic fuel pump problem.

Under the circumstances, they did well to qualify sixth and eighth, sandwiching Ralf Schumacher's Williams-BMW, although Frentzen reckoned, even then, that he lost 0.4s when he came up behind de la Rosa's Arrows.

Fisichella lined up ninth ahead of de la Rosa and Jos Verstappen, both of whom were cautiously optimistic about their prospects in the Arrows A21s.

The outcome of the race itself was destined to be particularly disappointing for the Jaguar team. Eddie Irvine had been highly encouraged by the performance of the Jaguar R1, even though he only managed 14th on the grid. 'The balance has been quite good, but we need more speed,' he said.

Previous spread: The Ferrari team celebrates on the pit wall as Michael Schumacher takes the flag, with Mika Häkkinen following in second place.
Paul-Henri Cahier

Right: Jos Verstappen drove a strong race in the Arrows to finish fourth.

Below right: Fifth place for Alexander Wurz was a welcome boost for the Benetton team.

Below left: Handshake for Luciano Burti from Neil Ressler as Jaguar announced the current test driver's elevation to full-time team member for 2001.

AFTER two demoralising defeats in Hungary and Belgium, Michael Schumacher and the Ferrari team reversed what was beginning to seem a dominant trend to deliver a commanding victory in the Italian Grand Prix at Monza.

Yet the sheer emotional effort proved a little too much for Schumacher. At the post-race media conference his 'ice man' image unexpectedly melted and he was reduced to sobbing uncontrollably after storming to his sixth victory of the year with a 3.8s win over Mika Häkkinen's McLaren.

It was a success which not only took him to within two points of the FIA Formula 1 World Championship lead with three races remaining on the calendar but, perhaps even more significantly, brought his career tally to 41 wins, matching that of the late Ayrton Senna with whom he now held joint second place in the all-time winner's stakes behind Alain Prost.

'I think it is obvious why I am so emotional,' said Schumacher. 'The victory was here in Italy in front of the Ferrari home crowd, we have obviously been in some difficulty over the past few races where we haven't been on the pace, but now we're back on the road.

'This success simply came a lot more close to me – I cannot put it into words.'

Schumacher's win came at the end of a race blighted by a tragic first-lap accident which cost the life of a trackside marshal. At the start Häkkinen had moved off the grid slightly faster only for Schumacher to move right to block him and then move back to the left to take his line into the first corner.

The leading runners got through without problems, but in the middle of the pack Mika Salo's Sauber and Eddie Irvine's Jaguar collided, forcing Pedro Diniz to go straight on in avoidance and his Sauber collided with one of the polystyrene blocks placed in the escape road of the newly profiled corner.

Irvine was out of the race on the spot while Salo suffered a punctured tyre and continued at reduced speed. A few seconds later, on the approach to the second chicane, Heinz-Harald Frentzen was slightly wrong-footed as Rubens Barrichello braked his Ferrari earlier than the Jordan driver expected.

Frentzen – who was two-stopping, had a lighter fuel load and intent on making up ground as quickly as possible – tagged the side of his team-mate Jarno Trulli and the two cars spun into Rubens Barrichello's Ferrari which was braking hard just in front of him. Suddenly all hell broke loose with Coulthard

ITALIAN GRAND PRIX

left: The back half of the field scramble round the first chicane largely unscathed. The second chicane was to be the scene of tragedy.

Bryn Williams/Words & Pictures

Bottom left: Brakes red-hot, Pedro Diniz lines up his Sauber-Petronas for one of Monza's controversial new chicanes.

Paul-Henri Cahier

Coulthard claims race should have been stopped

DAVID Coulthard called for heavy penalties to be imposed on the organisers of the Italian Grand Prix after the death of a trackside fire marshal hit by flying debris from the multiple accident in which he was one of the victims and as a result of which his challenge for the World Championship was effectively ended.

The McLaren-Mercedes driver said he believed that the race should have been stopped while the seriously injured Paolo Ghislimberti was attended by the emergency medical team.

'I think the race should have been stopped — not continued while he lay at the side of the track receiving emergency medical treatment,' he said.

Meanwhile, the sport's governing body promised an urgent review of grand prix circuit safety standards in the wake of the tragedy.

FIA president Max Mosley was quick to acknowledge that the question of breaking up the flow of circuits with chicanes certainly contributed towards the 'bunching up' of F1 cars which could be potentially hazardous.

'We have kept the question of chicanes under close scrutiny for some years now,' he said, 'and we will look at the issues again in the light of this accident.'

Mosley added that the entire sport had been stunned by the fatal accident to Ghislimberti.

'It is absolutely ghastly that a voluntary official should be killed in this way,' he said. 'The only real way of ensuring this never happens again is for track marshals effectively to regard their jobs as if they were soldiers coming under fire in a war.

'But I don't think it is realistic to suggest they crouch down behind the trackside barriers at eye level and only raise their heads above the parapet when they need to go into action. In those circumstances it would soon become very difficult to recruit any marshals at all.'

'In his situation I can understand his feelings, especially driving a Ferrari at Monza, but as he well knows the reasons for any accident are not as simple as he would like everyone to believe.

'As the stewards' enquiry showed after they had reviewed all the evidence, it was a racing incident, the sort that happens several times a year, but fortunately without the same tragic result.'

From a purely pragmatic viewpoint, this was also the end of the road for David Coulthard's World Championship hopes. 'To say I am disappointed is an understatement, really,' he said.

'I've had less obstacles on the track this year, but I am still tripping at the last hurdle. I've got to do my best in these last few races, then try again next year.'

The safety car was immediately deployed with Schumacher, who had led from pole position, now reduced to cruising round behind the silver Mercedes shadowed by Häkkinen's

'When you have cars tightly bunched at over 300 km/h all braking hard for a slow chicane, accidents are sometimes inevitable. I heard after the race that Barrichello was blaming me for the accident.

'The first lap is always the most risky part of any race and it is inevitable that circumstances sometimes come together which result in an accident.

'I think everyone who knows me and my racing career knows that I am not the sort of driver to take unnecessary risks at the start of a race and I don't have a reputation for being involved in accidents,' he said.

Once the atmosphere calmed, Frentzen vigorously rebutted those accusations while at the same time striking a commendably conciliatory note.

Barrichello, in particular, was extremely shaken as there were marks on the top of his helmet to indicate just what a close call he had experienced. In the immediate aftermath of the race the Brazilian blamed Frentzen for triggering the accident and called for the Jordan driver to be suspended from ten races.

also being bundled into the gravel trap and Pedro de la Rosa's Arrows first clipping the rear of Ricardo Zonta's BAR before somersaulting over the back of Johnny Herbert's Jaguar.

Wheels flew and shredded carbon-fibre debris from disintegrating front wings exploded in all directions, during which debris from Frentzen's car hit a marshal, 30-year-old Paolo Ghislimberti, who unfortunately sustained major head and chest injuries from which he later died in hospital.

Once the pack was unleashed again the Italian GP developed into a two-horse race with Schumacher edging away from Häkkinen and Jacques Villeneuve's BAR, which had qualified an excellent fourth, pulling off after another three laps with electronic failure.

On the same lap Jos Verstappen moved up to fourth place, his Arrows A21 moving ahead of Giancarlo Fisichella's Benetton B200, while Mika Salo moved ahead of Sauber teammate Pedro Diniz for 11th.

It was clear that on this occasion Häkkinen's McLaren MP4/15 simply did not have the speed to stay with the leading Ferrari. By the end of lap 13 Schumacher was 2.1s ahead and had pulled out another second by lap 16, was 7.0s ahead on lap 25 and 8.5s to the good by lap 30.

Schumacher duly led to his refuelling stop on lap 39, allowing Häkkinen through into the lead before the Finn stopped on lap 42. By then he was only 13.7s ahead of the Ferrari, an insufficient margin to get in and out

McLaren, Jacques Villeneuve's BAR, Ralf Schumacher's Williams-BMW and Giancarlo Fisichella's Benetton.

The safety car's flashing lights were turned off as it led the pack round lap 11, signalling to the pursuing field that it would be pulling into the pits at the end of that lap and that the race would be resumed.

Coming down the back straight towards Parabolica, the final corner before the start/finish line, Schumacher slowed suddenly as he tried to warm up his tyres and brakes after all those miles of running below racing speeds. The cars behind him braked hard and, Jenson Button, running in sixth place, suddenly found himself faced with the rear end of Fisichella's slowing Benetton and lurched onto the grass in avoidance.

The impact damaged Button's left rear suspension and he slid off into the gravel trap at the next corner. Several other drivers found themselves wrong-footed by Schumacher who later apologised for his behaviour.

'I was going to warm up my brakes and I think I did a mistake in the way I did it,' he said. 'I am sorry for whoever suffered for this.'

Button was unamused. 'I am very annoyed,' he admitted. 'I got told off for overtaking under the safety car, but I think I avoided quite a big accident.

'Jacques stood on the brakes so as not to overtake the people in front and I had nowhere to go. I just missed a marshal who was standing at the side of the circuit.'

ITALIAN GRAND PRIX

DIARY

Bernie Ecclestone says that Brands Hatch is 'a non-event now' after the Department of the Environment announced that it would review the circuit's application for planning permission.

McLaren boss Ron Dennis denies he has any ambitions to run F1 racing after FIA president Max Mosley expressed just such a belief in a politically charged letter written to Frank Williams and circulated to other team owners.

Luciano Burti signs a contract to replace Johnny Herbert in the 2001 Jaguar F1 line-up.

The Penske team Reynard-Hondas of Helio Castroneves and Gil de Ferran finish first and second in the CART round at Laguna Seca, California.

of the pits again without Schumacher going back ahead.

On his second set of tyres Häkkinen found his McLaren's handling balance was much improved and began to close the gap towards the finish, but Schumacher had everything under control and duly took the chequered flag to the unbridled delight of the capacity 125,000-strong crowd after what had been a distinctly processional race.

'We made some modifications to the car during the pit stop, and it made the balance of the car better,' said Häkkinen, declining an invitation to confirm that an adjustment had been made to the differential settings.

'But it was obviously not enough, and the gap to Michael was too much. It was impossible to catch him, and the backmarkers [made it even more difficult].

'There were a couple of Minardis who were quite a pain; they wouldn't let me overtake very easily and I lost two or three seconds because of that. But at the end of the day that is not an excuse. I believe that Michael had no reason to push any more, so...'

The decimation amongst the front runners allowed some unfamiliar faces to occupy points-scoring positions behind Ralf Schumacher's third-place Williams-BMW. Jos Verstappen (Arrows), Alexander Wurz (Benetton) and Ricardo Zonta (BAR) completed the top six in a race which saw just 12 of its original 22 starters taking the chequered flag.

Ralf Schumacher was certainly well satisfied with his performance from seventh on the grid, even though it was aided by the number of cars eliminated in the first-lap shunt.

'We always knew that some of the others were on a light-weight [low-fuel] strategy,' he said, 'but at Monza it's the ones on the longer [range] strategy who usually have the upper hand. We were quicker than Verstappen at the end of the day and I knew we could be quicker than Zonta, so I didn't worry much.'

Fisichella was running a strong fourth behind the Williams-BMW when he followed Ralf in for his sole refuelling stop at the end of lap 43. While the Williams got away cleanly after a

neat 6.4s stop, the Benetton was stationary for an agonisingly long time.

Fisichella explained later: 'I'm really disappointed with the race. I really wanted to get some points, particularly here at my home race in Monza. We developed a problem with the clutch early on in the race, but it was OK whilst I was on the track. I just had to be careful when I changed down.

'Then when I came in for the pit stop I tried to engage first gear and the engine stalled. We finally managed to get the car restarted but then I was in 11th place rather than fourth.'

That left Jos Verstappen to finish a strong fourth ahead of Alexander Wurz and Ricardo Zonta with the Sauber and Minardi duos completing the top ten, albeit one lap down on the leaders.

Zonta's performance proved particularly noteworthy. Having qualified a lowly 17th he stormed through the field after being forced into the pits at the end of the opening lap to replace a tyre punctured when Pedro de la Rosa's Arrows made momentary contact with his wheel.

The Brazilian made two more scheduled refuelling stops to take his second point of the season. 'If it hadn't been for that, I would have finished right in front of Verstappen in the race,' he said optimistically.

At the end of the day the mood in the paddock was sombre in the extreme, the elation surrounding this memorable home victory for Michael Schumacher and the Ferrari team tempered by the tragedy of the marshal's death. Police officers appeared everywhere and all the cars involved in the first-lap accident at the second chicane were duly impounded by the authorities.

They would all be released back to their teams by late the following afternoon. The race stewards soon concluded that the fatality had been a racing accident, unfortunate and unforeseeable, but an accident none the less. It was a sobering thought that the hitherto unknown Paolo Ghislimberti had ended his life by becoming the first F1 fatality since Ayrton Senna was killed at Imola in the San Marino Grand Prix six years earlier.

Below: The worshipful *tifosi* congregate in front of the podium.

Below: Yes! Michael Schumacher was back on top at Monza. Ralf was content to share in his brother's emotional triumph.

ROUND 14
MONZA
8–10 SEPTEMBER 2000

gran premio CAMPARI d'ITALIA

MONZA — GRAND PRIX CIRCUIT
CIRCUIT LENGTH: 3.600 miles/5.793 km

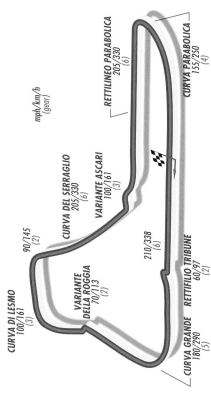

- CURVA DI LESMO 100/161 (3)
- 90/145 (2)
- CURVA DEL SERRAGLIO 205/330 (6)
- VARIANTE DELLA ROGGIA 70/113 (2)
- VARIANTE ASCARI 100/161 (3)
- RETTILINEO PARABOLICA 205/330 (6)
- CURVA PARABOLICA 155/250 (4)
- 210/338 (6)
- RETTIFILIO TRIBUNE 60/97 (2)
- CURVA GRANDE 180/290 (5)
- mph/km/h (gear)

RACE DISTANCE: 53 laps, 190.614 miles/306.764 km **RACE WEATHER: Dry, hot and sunny**

Pos.	Driver	Nat.	No.	Entrant	Car/Engine	Laps	Time/Retirement	Speed (mph/km/h)
1	Michael Schumacher	D	3	Scuderia Ferrari Marlboro	Ferrari F1-2000-049 V10	53	1h 27m 31.638s	130.665/210.286
2	Mika Häkkinen	SF	1	West McLaren Mercedes	McLaren MP4/15-Mercedes FO110J V10	53	1h 27m 35.448s	130.571/210.134
3	Ralf Schumacher	D	9	BMW WilliamsF1 Team	Williams FW22-BMW E41 V10	53	1h 28m 24.070s	129.374/208.208
4	Jos Verstappen	NL	19	Arrows	Arrows A21-Supertec FB02 V10	53	1h 28m 31.576s	129.191/207.913
5	Alexander Wurz	A	12	Mild Seven Benetton Playlife	Benetton B200-Playlife V10	53	1h 28m 39.064s	129.010/207.621
6	Ricardo Zonta	BR	23	Lucky Strike BAR Honda	BAR 02-Honda RA100E V10	53	1h 28m 40.931s	128.964/207.548
7	Mika Salo	SF	17	Red Bull Sauber Petronas	Sauber C19-Petronas SPE 04A V10	52		
8	Pedro Diniz	BR	16	Red Bull Sauber Petronas	Sauber C19-Petronas SPE 04A V10	52		
9	Marc Gene	ESP	20	Telefonica Minardi Fondmetal	Minardi M02-Fondmetal Ford Zetec-R V10	52		
10	Gaston Mazzacane	ARG	21	Telefonica Minardi Fondmetal	Minardi M02-Fondmetal Ford Zetec-R V10	52		
11	Giancarlo Fisichella	I	11	Mild Seven Benetton Playlife	Benetton B200-Playlife V10	52		
12	Jean Alesi	F	14	Gauloises Prost Peugeot	Prost AP03-Peugeot A20 V10	51		
	Nick Heidfeld	D	15	Gauloises Prost Peugeot	Prost AP03-Peugeot A20 V10	15	Spun off	
	Jacques Villeneuve	CDN	22	Lucky Strike BAR Honda	BAR 02-Honda RA100E V10	14	Electrics	
	Jenson Button	GB	10	BMW WilliamsF1 Team	Williams FW22-BMW E41 V10	10	Accident	
	Johnny Herbert	GB	8	Jaguar Racing	Jaguar R1-Cosworth CR2 V10	1	Collision with de la Rosa	
	Rubens Barrichello	BR	4	Scuderia Ferrari Marlboro	Ferrari F1-2000-049 V10	0	Accident	
	David Coulthard	GB	2	West McLaren Mercedes	McLaren MP4/15-Mercedes FO110J V10	0	Accident	
	Jarno Trulli	I	6	Benson & Hedges Jordan	Jordan EJ10-Mugen Honda MF301HE V10	0	Accident	
	Heinz-Harald Frentzen	D	5	Benson & Hedges Jordan	Jordan EJ10-Mugen Honda MF301HE V10	0	Accident	
	Pedro de la Rosa	ESP	18	Arrows	Arrows A21-Supertec FB02 V10	0	Accident	
	Eddie Irvine	GB	7	Jaguar Racing	Jaguar R1-Cosworth CR2 V10	0	Accident	

Fastest lap: Häkkinen, on lap 50, 1m 25.595s, 151.394 mph/243.645 km/h (record for new circuit configuration).

Lap chart

Grid order	1	2	3	4	5	6	7	8	9	10	11	12	13	14	15	16	17	18	19	20	21	22	23	24	25	26	27	28	29	30	31	32	33	34	35	36	37	38	39	40	41
3 M. SCHUMACHER	3	3	3	3	3	3	1	1	1	1	1	3	3	3	3	3	3	1	1	1	1	1	1	1	1	1	1	1	1	1	1	1	1	1	1	1	1	1	1	1	1
4 BARRICHELLO	1	1	1	1	1	1	3	3	3	3	3	1	1	1	1	1	1	3	3	3	3	3	3	3	3	3	3	3	3	3	3	3	3	3	3	3	3	3	3	3	3
1 HÄKKINEN	22	22	22	22	22	22	9	9	9	9	9	9	9	9	9	9	9	9	9	9	9	9	9	9	9	9	9	9	9	9	9	9	9	9	9	9	9	9	9	9	9
22 VILLENEUVE	9	9	9	9	9	9	19	19	23	23	19	19	11	11	11	11	11	12	12	12	12	12	12	20	16	16	20	20	16	23	19	16	23	17	17	20	20	20	20	19	19
6 COULTHARD	11	11	11	11	11	11	11	11	12	12	12	11	12	12	12	12	12	20	20	20	20	16	16	16	17	20	16	16	23	16	16	23	16	23	19	12	12	12	12	12	12
9 R. SCHUMACHER	12	12	12	12	12	12	12	12	20	20	20	12	20	20	15	23	20	16	17	21	16	20	20	17	20	17	17	17	16	20	23	20	20	16	16	23	23	23	23	23	23
5 FRENTZEN	19	19	19	19	19	19	20	20	15	15	15	20	15	15	23	16	16	17	16	16	17	17	17	21	21	21	21	23	17	17	17	17	17	20	20	16	17	17	17	17	17
11 FISICHELLA	20	20	20	20	20	20	15	15	16	16	16	15	16	16	16	17	17	21	21	17	21	21	21	16	23	23	23	21	20	21	21	21	21	21	23	17	16	16	16	16	16
18 DE LA ROSA	15	15	15	15	15	15	16	16	17	17	17	16	17	23	17	21	21	23	23	23	23	23	23	23	16	16	16	16	21	20	20	20	20	20	20	20	20	20	20	20	20
19 VERSTAPPEN	21	21	21	21	21	21	17	17	21	21	21	17	21	17	21	14	23	16	16	16	16	16	16	16	21	21	21	20	21	21	21	21	21	21	21	21	21	21	21	21	21
10 BUTTON	16	16	16	16	16	16	21	21	14	14	23	21	23	21	14	14	14	14	14	14	14	14	14	14	14	14	14	14	11	11	11	11	11	11	11	11	11	11	11	11	11
12 WURZ	23	23	23	23	23	23	23	23	16	16	14	23	14	14	14	17	14	14	14	14	14	14	14	14	14	14	14	14	14	14	14	14	14	14	14	14	14	14	14	14	14
7 IRVINE	17	17	17	17	17	17	14	14																																	
17 SALO	8	14	14	14	14	14																																			
23 ZONTA	14																																								
8 HERBERT																																									
14 ALESI																																									
15 HEIDFELD																																									
20 GENE																																									
21 MAZZACANE																																									

Pit stop
One lap behind leader

STARTING GRID

Pos	No	Driver	Team
1	3	M. SCHUMACHER	Ferrari
2	4	BARRICHELLO	Ferrari
3	1	HÄKKINEN	McLaren
4	22	VILLENEUVE	BAR
5	2	COULTHARD	McLaren
6	6	TRULLI	Jordan
7	9	R. SCHUMACHER	Williams
8	5	FRENTZEN	Jordan
9	11	FISICHELLA	Benetton
10	18	DE LA ROSA	Arrows
11	12	WURZ	Benetton
12	7	IRVINE	Jaguar
13	19	VERSTAPPEN	Arrows
14	10	BUTTON	Williams
15	17	SALO	Sauber
16	16	DINIZ	Sauber
17	23	ZONTA	BAR
18	8	HERBERT	Jaguar
19	14	ALESI	Prost
20	15	HEIDFELD	Prost
21	20	GENE	Minardi
22	21	MAZZACANE	Minardi

Lap Chart

42	43	44	45	46	47	48	49	50	51	52	53
3	3	3	3	3	3	3	3	3	3	3	3
1	1	1	1	1	1	1	1	1	1	1	1
9	9	9	9	9	9	9	9	9	9	9	9
19	19	19	19	19	19	19	19	19	19	19	19
12	12	12	12	12	12	12	12	12	12	12	12
23	23	23	23	23	23	23	23	23	23	23	23
17	17	17	17	17	17	17	17	17	17	17	17
16	16	16	16	16	16	16	16	16	16	16	16
20	20	20	20	20	20	20	20	20	20	20	20
16	16	16	16	16	16	16	16	16	16	16	16
21	21	21	21	21	21	21	21	21	21	21	21
14	14	14	14	14	14	14	14	14	14	14	

TIME SHEETS

QUALIFYING

Weather: Dry, hot and sunny

Pos.	Driver	Car	Laps	Time
1	Michael Schumacher	Ferrari	10	1m 23.770s
2	Rubens Barrichello	Ferrari	12	1m 23.797s
3	Mika Häkkinen	McLaren-Mercedes	12	1m 23.967s
4	Jacques Villeneuve	BAR-Honda	12	1m 24.238s
5	David Coulthard	McLaren-Mercedes	12	1m 24.290s
6	Jarno Trulli	Jordan-Mugen Honda	12	1m 24.477s
7	Ralf Schumacher	Williams-BMW	10	1m 24.516s
8	Heinz-Harald Frentzen	Jordan-Mugen Honda	12	1m 24.786s
9	Giancarlo Fisichella	Benetton-Playlife	12	1m 24.789s
10	Pedro de la Rosa	Arrows-Supertec	12	1m 24.814s
11	Jos Verstappen	Arrows-Supertec	11	1m 24.820s
12	Jenson Button	Williams-BMW	12	1m 24.907s
13	Alexander Wurz	Benetton-Playlife	10	1m 25.150s
14	Eddie Irvine	Jaguar-Cosworth	12	1m 25.251s
15	Mika Salo	Sauber-Petronas	11	1m 25.322s
16	Pedro Diniz	Sauber-Petronas	11	1m 25.324s
17	Ricardo Zonta	BAR-Honda	11	1m 25.337s
18	Johnny Herbert	Jaguar-Cosworth	12	1m 25.388s
19	Jean Alesi	Prost-Peugeot	12	1m 25.558s
20	Nick Heidfeld	Prost-Peugeot	12	1m 25.625s
21	Marc Gene	Minardi-Fondmetal	12	1m 26.336s
22	Gaston Mazzacane	Minardi-Fondmetal	12	1m 27.360s

FRIDAY FREE PRACTICE

Weather: Dry, hot and sunny

Pos.	Driver	Laps	Time
1	Rubens Barrichello	26	1m 25.057s
2	Michael Schumacher	36	1m 25.117s
3	Jarno Trulli	35	1m 25.390s
4	Mika Häkkinen	22	1m 25.553s
5	David Coulthard	18	1m 25.796s
6	Eddie Irvine	31	1m 25.907s
7	Pedro de la Rosa	31	1m 25.912s
8	Pedro Diniz	28	1m 25.981s
9	Jos Verstappen	26	1m 26.020s
10	Mika Salo	32	1m 26.293s
11	Jenson Button	29	1m 26.452s
12	Johnny Herbert	33	1m 26.634s
13	Marc Gene	34	1m 26.638s
14	Heinz-Harald Frentzen	26	1m 26.763s
15	Giancarlo Fisichella	35	1m 26.809s
16	Jacques Villeneuve	37	1m 26.906s
17	Ricardo Zonta	37	1m 27.070s
18	Alexander Wurz	15	1m 27.093s
19	Nick Heidfeld	44	1m 27.135s
20	Gaston Mazzacane	29	1m 27.468s
21	Ralf Schumacher	33	1m 27.852s
22	Jean Alesi	23	1m 27.904s

SATURDAY FREE PRACTICE

Weather: Dry, hot and sunny

Pos.	Driver	Laps	Time
1	Michael Schumacher	31	1m 23.904s
2	Mika Häkkinen	22	1m 24.142s
3	Rubens Barrichello	29	1m 24.199s
4	David Coulthard	33	1m 24.292s
5	Ralf Schumacher	31	1m 24.352s
6	Jenson Button	27	1m 24.515s
7	Giancarlo Fisichella	27	1m 24.644s
8	Ricardo Zonta	33	1m 24.672s
9	Jacques Villeneuve	32	1m 24.780s
10	Eddie Irvine	31	1m 25.064s
11	Mika Salo	31	1m 25.179s
12	Jos Verstappen	11	1m 25.198s
13	Jean Alesi	27	1m 25.299s
14	Pedro Diniz	22	1m 25.407s
15	Nick Heidfeld	32	1m 25.431s
16	Johnny Herbert	32	1m 25.473s
17	Pedro de la Rosa	30	1m 25.508s
18	Jarno Trulli	31	1m 25.776s
19	Heinz-Harald Frentzen	7	1m 26.272s
20	Marc Gene	33	1m 26.295s
21	Gaston Mazzacane	22	1m 27.234s
22	Alexander Wurz	5	8m 45.695s

WARM-UP

Weather: Dry, hot and sunny

Pos.	Driver	Laps	Time
1	Ricardo Zonta	15	1m 26.448s
2	Mika Häkkinen	13	1m 26.513s
3	Michael Schumacher	8	1m 26.593s
4	David Coulthard	15	1m 26.611s
5	Jos Verstappen	13	1m 26.718s
6	Mika Salo	16	1m 27.097s
7	Rubens Barrichello	8	1m 27.233s
8	Jacques Villeneuve	12	1m 27.321s
9	Jenson Button	12	1m 27.339s
10	Jean Alesi	14	1m 27.398s
11	Pedro de la Rosa	14	1m 27.457s
12	Heinz-Harald Frentzen	17	1m 27.538s
13	Alexander Wurz	16	1m 27.692s
14	Eddie Irvine	15	1m 27.711s
15	Johnny Herbert	12	1m 27.775s
16	Giancarlo Fisichella	17	1m 27.833s
17	Jarno Trulli	16	1m 27.919s
18	Pedro Diniz	12	1m 27.984s
19	Ralf Schumacher	12	1m 28.198s
20	Gaston Mazzacane	14	1m 28.388s
21	Marc Gene	14	1m 28.534s
22	Nick Heidfeld	12	1m 29.501s

RACE FASTEST LAPS

Weather: Dry, hot and sunny

Driver	Time	Lap
Mika Häkkinen	1m 25.595s	50
Michael Schumacher	1m 25.663s	36
Ricardo Zonta	1m 26.433s	22
Ralf Schumacher	1m 26.636s	49
Giancarlo Fisichella	1m 26.731s	46
Alexander Wurz	1m 26.869s	44
Jos Verstappen	1m 27.033s	31
Pedro Diniz	1m 27.215s	44
Mika Salo	1m 27.297s	26
Jean Alesi	1m 27.978s	47
Jacques Villeneuve	1m 28.038s	31
Marc Gene	1m 28.131s	49
Gaston Mazzacane	1m 28.299s	14
Nick Heidfeld	1m 29.580s	14
Jenson Button	2m 27.131s	8

CHASSIS LOG BOOK

No	Driver	Chassis
1	Häkkinen	McLaren MP4/15/6
2	Coulthard	McLaren MP4/15/7
	spare	McLaren MP4/15/2
3	M. Schumacher	Ferrari F1-2000/205
4	Barrichello	Ferrari F1-2000/202
	spare	Ferrari F1-2000/200
5	Frentzen	Jordan E110/6
6	Trulli	Jordan E110/5
	spare	Jordan E110/4
7	Irvine	Jaguar R1/5
8	Herbert	Jaguar R1/4
	spare	Jaguar R1/4
9	R. Schumacher	Williams FW22/2
10	Button	Williams FW22/3
	spare	Williams FW22/2
11	Fisichella	Benetton B200/5
12	Wurz	Benetton B200/2
	spare	Benetton B200/3
14	Alesi	Prost AP03/5
15	Heidfeld	Prost AP03/2
	spare	Prost AP03/1
16	Diniz	Sauber C19/7
17	Salo	Sauber C19/5
	spare	Sauber C19/6
18	de la Rosa	Arrows A21/5
19	Verstappen	Arrows A21/4
	spare	Arrows A21/1
22	Villeneuve	BAR 02/4
23	Zonta	BAR 02/5
	spares	BAR 02/2 & 3
20	Gene	Minardi M02/3
21	Mazzacane	Minardi M02/4
	spare	Minardi M02/1

POINTS TABLES

DRIVERS

Pos	Driver	Points
1	Mika Häkkinen	80
2	Michael Schumacher	78
3	David Coulthard	61
4	Rubens Barrichello	49
5	Ralf Schumacher	24
6	Giancarlo Fisichella	18
7	Jacques Villeneuve	11
8	Jenson Button	10
9	Heinz-Harald Frentzen	7
10=	Jarno Trulli	6
10=	Mika Salo	6
12	Jos Verstappen	5
13	Eddie Irvine	3
14=	Alexander Wurz	3
14=	Ricardo Zonta	2
14=	Eddie Irvine	2
14=	Pedro de la Rosa	2

CONSTRUCTORS

Pos	Team	Points
1	McLaren	131
2	Ferrari	127
3	Williams	34
4	Benetton	20
5	Jordan	13
5=	BAR	13
7	Arrows	7
7	Sauber	7
9	Jaguar	6
		3
		2

UNITED STATES
grand prix

INDIANAPOLIS MOTOR SPEEDWAY

FIA WORLD CHAMPIONSHIP • ROUND 15

M. SCHUMACHER

BARRICHELLO

FRENTZEN

VILLENEUVE

COULTHARD

ZONTA

UNITED STATES GRAND PRIX

INDIANAPOLIS QUALIFYING

It was terrific to see the display of genuine tactical driving in qualifying as Rubens Barrichello helped tow Michael Schumacher out of reach from the marauding David Coulthard, seconds before Mika Häkkinen attempted to tow 'DC' into contention in the battle for occupancy of the front row.

Michael had forced the Ferrari F1-2000 round in 1m 14.492s, but was worried that the McLarens might go quicker, even though the MP4/15s were running a touch more downforce than their key rivals. So out he went behind Barrichello whose sister car he slipstreamed out onto the start/finish straight as he began his next flying lap. The result was a 1m 14.266s. And it was just as well.

Later in the session Häkkinen, who'd run out of laps and had to come in immediately after launching Coulthard on his way, did precisely the same with the result that David improved to 1m 14.392s. It would have been good enough for pole before Michael made his improvement.

Interestingly, Mika was not too worried about dropping back onto the second row of the grid. Pragmatic to the end, he noted: 'I wasn't really too disappointed to drop to third. Maybe the second row is not too bad because the guys on the front row might lose traction over the bricks.'

His optimism was misplaced. Thanks to lobbying from Ferrari sporting director Jean Todt, who was concerned that Schumacher might be slightly disadvantaged by starting on the traditional brick strip on the startline which dates back to the days when the entire speedway was so paved, the front row was moved back by 17 ft.

Some F1 insiders argued that the demands of the challenging infield section meant that the cars were not displayed to their most impressive effect on the banking. The need to run in 85 per cent high-downforce configuration for the infield sliced the top end off their straight line speed. In qualifying, at least.

Yet not even the challenge of a banked corner on a brand new circuit could upset the customary symmetry of the front two rows of the grid. Even so, after bagging his 30th career pole position, Michael Schumacher confessed to appreciating just what a potential challenge a banked track could be.

'It's a good feeling going round the banking, but because our entry speed is not so great we do not experience being on the limit,' he said. 'But you can imagine if you would go much faster how much the banking would help and satisfy you, but on the other hand you have the wall right next to you.

'With the wall so close, I wouldn't want to experience that. You know, we Europeans are probably a bit more chicken than Americans!'

Behind Barrichello's fourth-place Ferrari, Jarno Trulli drove superbly in the Jordan EJ10 to wind up best of the rest on 1m 15.006s while Jenson Button – who had been second quickest to Häkkinen in the damp Saturday morning session – produced a fine sixth-fastest 1m 15.017s in the Williams FW22-BMW. This was really a terrific effort on a weekend when it was confirmed that his place in the team's line-up would be taken by Juan Pablo Montoya from the start of next season.

By contrast, Ralf Schumacher struggled with a wheel bearing

failure, a spin and was unable to get the right balance out of his FW22, winding up tenth.

'I am very happy,' said Button. 'I was optimistic that I might improve further, but I lost time with the yellow flag when Jean Alesi spun and pushed too hard on my final run.'

Jacques Villeneuve was really buoyed up at the prospect of returning to the scene of his 1995 Indianapolis 500 victory which he scored at the wheel of Barry Green's Reynard-Ford when he lapped the banked oval as a matter of course at around 220 mph. He was certainly not intimidated by the prospect of racing on the new circuit in the wet.

'At least in the wet the speed will be lower, which will help things,' he said. 'The champ cars do not race on ovals in the wet, so that will be something of a new attraction for the spectators.'

'What you've got to understand is that the Indy drivers go through there at 230 mph in the dry. Our F1 cars won't be doing anywhere near that, so I don't think the banking, wet or dry, will be any problem.'

Villeneuve also gave a qualified green light to the revised circuit which now blends part of the banking with a twisting infield loop to produce a circuit more suitable for Formula 1 machinery.

'The track looks quite good, although there are a couple of corners which I don't think needed to be so tight,' he said. 'But as an event, it will be an interesting contrast to the Indy 500 which is the biggest race in itself, almost a world championship bound up in a single race. The Grand Prix is just a single race in the championship.

'For myself, when I raced here five years ago my car was more competitive than my BAR is at the moment. I left here with great memories in 1995 – and haven't been back since – so I think I had rather forgotten just how impressive the whole place looks.'

When it came to his own qualifying efforts, Jacques was frustrated to have spun on his best lap. 'When I spun, I was just trying too hard and went into the hairpin too fast,' he shrugged. The BAR team briefly attracted severe disapproval and censure from Bridgestone for running their tyres at pressures lower than the minimum recommended level. On Saturday, however, Bridgestone relented and reduced the pressure recommendations, much to Villeneuve's satisfaction.

Villeneuve had to be content with eighth place on the grid ahead of Pedro Diniz's Sauber, Ralf Schumacher and Alexander Wurz who had certainly come to terms with Indianapolis more positively and effectively than team-mate Giancarlo Fisichella.

The Italian was well off the pace and lined up 15th, attracting much criticism from Benetton team chief Flavio Briatore for a general lack of motivation and focus.

Ricardo Zonta qualified his BAR just outside the top ten, 12th on 1m 15.784s which was one place ahead of Jos Verstappen's Arrows A21, the cars from Leafield not quite living up to the pace that might have been expected from them, given their reputation for excellent straight line speed.

'We've got a general lack of grip on the infield,' shrugged technical director Mike Coughlan.

Previous spread: Making history: Michael Schumacher powers to victory on the famous Indy banked oval.
Paul-Henri Cahier

Right: The empty track stretches out ahead of the packed grid just before the start of the first U.S. Grand Prix since 1991.

Below right: No quarter: Michael Schumacher hustles his Ferrari round the outside of David Coulthard's McLaren at turn one to take the lead.

Below left: Michelin's Pierre Dupasquier in conversation with Alain Prost.

MICHAEL Schumacher took a giant, possibly decisive, stride to becoming Ferrari's first World Champion driver in 21 years when he stormed to a dominant victory in the first United States Grand Prix to be held in a decade and the first to be staged on a new circuit at the spectacular Indianapolis motor speedway.

It was the German driver's 42nd F1 career victory in a Ferrari 1-2 ahead of his team-mate Rubens Barrichello on a day when the McLaren-Mercedes challenge faltered uncharacteristically and dramatically. Despite a spin just four laps from the end – by his own admission an unforced error – he kept control to beat the Brazilian by just 12.1s.

David Coulthard, who had qualified alongside Schumacher on the front row of the grid, finished a distant fifth after being penalised for a jumped start, while reigning World Champion Mika Häkkinen retired with a fiery engine failure as he closed relentlessly on Schumacher's Ferrari just before half distance.

At the end of a race of dramatically changing fortunes, it was Heinz-Harald Frentzen who just squeezed his Jordan EJ10 across the line third ahead of Jacques Villeneuve's BAR-Honda and Coulthard.

Schumacher now led the championship by eight points from Häkkinen with only two races and 20 points remaining to be raced for to the end of the season.

A morning of steady rain had abated by the time the famed Indianapolis fever got into top gear with bands, a rendition of The Star-Spangled Banner and the prayers for the safety of the drivers all raising the tension before the cars trickled out onto the gradually drying circuit for the first time.

In the event it was Coulthard who got the jump on the Ferrari from second spot on the front row of the grid, storming his McLaren-Mercedes into an immediate lead as the pack sprinted away to the first right-hander a quarter of a mile away up the corridor of concrete.

By the end of the opening lap Coulthard was already 1.2s ahead of Schumacher, but even by this early stage the stewards were examining video footage of the Scot's getaway from the grid which looked over-optimistic, to say the least. Häkkinen was third ahead of Rubens Barrichello's Ferrari, Jarno Trulli's Jordan and the impressive Jenson Button in the Williams-BMW.

All the leading competitors had

UNITED STATES GRAND PRIX

DIARY

Prost team confirms a two-year deal to use customer Ferrari engines starting in 2001.

Juan Pablo Montoya is officially confirmed as Jenson Button's successor for 2001 in the BMW WilliamsF1 team.

Antonio Pizzonia clinches British F3 title after finishing second at Spa-Francorchamps.

Bernd Schneider consolidates lead in DTM 2000 series with another win for Mercedes at Oschersleben.

UNITED STATES GRAND PRIX

Far left: Mika Häkinen's race ended with an engine failure just when he seemed set to challenge for the lead.
Bryn Williams/Words & Pictures

Left: Ferrari mechanics rush down the pit lane to congratulate Schumacher and Barrichello.
Paul-Henri Cahier

Below left: Heinz-Harald Frentzen ended a slump in Jordan's recent fortunes with third place.
Paul-Henri Cahier

started on rain tyres because although the main straight and the banked corner leading onto it were drying fast, the tight infield section was still extremely wet and slippery. This made judging the precise moment to make the switch to dry-weather tyres difficult to call and it was certainly clear that Häkinen came in too early when he elected to stop at the end of lap seven.

By contrast, Michael Schumacher decided to stay out in the lead until lap 16 by which time it looked as though he'd broken the back of the McLaren challenge.

Mid-way round the second lap Button's brimming cup of confidence lured him into a bold overtaking move on Trulli. He squeezed inside the Italian, but Trulli wasn't going to be a soft touch and the two cars rubbed wheels, briefly spinning off the road before crawling into the pits for their punctured tyres to be changed.

Button was extremely calm and philosophical about the whole situation, but Trulli was less generous in his assessment of the manoeuvre. 'Jenson Button, he is really an idiot at the moment,' he said. 'He is driving like crazy. He was pushing me hard and tried to outbrake me, but it is too late. I think he needs to cool down.'

Trulli had a long stop for his car to be checked over, then resumed only to stop out on the circuit with what was initially thought to be a gearbox problem. A subsequent detailed examination revealed that a water temperature sensor, positioned low in the Mugen Honda engine bay, had failed as a result of the long stop and its automatic shutdown system had turned off the engine.

Ironically Button also recovered and was climbing back into contention on dry-weather rubber when his Williams's ignition switch was knocked to the off position as the car bottomed out over a particularly vicious bump and the FW22 rolled to a silent standstill just beyond the start/finish line.

By lap five the first three were absolutely nose-to-tail with Coulthard taking some creative lines through the slower corners to keep Schumacher's Ferrari behind him. Häkinen was now poised right behind the Italian car, but Michael wasn't about to be ruffled by his two rivals and expertly sliced past Coulthard to take the lead down the outside of the first corner at the start of lap seven.

Coulthard tried to keep out of the Ferrari's way as Schumacher squeezed round the outside of his McLaren, but the two cars momentarily rubbed

F1 return to the U.S.A. judged a huge success

AS Michael Schumacher and the Ferrari team celebrated their dominant victory in Sunday's inaugural U.S. Grand Prix at the Indianapolis motor speedway, America awoke to review the success of F1's return to its shores for the first time in nine years. The general consensus was a resounding thumbs-up.

In terms of media coverage, Schumacher's triumph grabbed a respectable, if not lavish, share of the column inches on a day that the Green Bay Packers dealt out a 29–3 drubbing to the St. Louis Cardinals in the National Football League and Tony Stewart scored an impressive NASCAR stock car win on the demanding mile oval at Dover Downs, Delaware.

Perhaps helpfully, it was also a day on which the U.S. public gave a thumbs down to deferred T.V. coverage of the Olympic Games on the basis that they knew the results long before they were screened.

Former Indy 500 winners A.J. Foyt, Johnny Rutherford, Rodger Ward, Emerson Fittipaldi, Mario Andretti and new Jaguar Formula 1 chief executive officer Bobby Rahal also gave their approval to the grand prix after spectating there on Sunday.

'It was a fantastic day for motor racing,' said Fittipaldi. 'I think it starts a new era of F1 in America.'

Rahal agreed. 'It was a great race,' he agreed. 'It will also raise the stature of Indianapolis even more. I think this can now be a successful event for a long time, definitely not a one-off.'

For Indianapolis speedway president Tony George, who was accorded the privilege of waving the chequered flag as Schumacher tore out of the famous final banked corner for the last time, it was a £30-million

gamble which paid off. That was the estimated cost of up-rating the famous Brickyard to F1 specification, but before he paid Bernie Ecclestone the £9-million annual fee for staging the race.

Yet this was nickels and dimes for the Hulman–George dynasty which owns the speedway. The family may not appear in any list of the top-100 richest families in the U.S.A., but their wealth is estimated at around £2.5 billion with huge commercial interests in Coca Cola bottling, banking and real estate in addition to their 55-year-old ownership of the speedway.

They are also at the absolute epi-centre of U.S. motor racing politics and the arrival of the U.S. Grand Prix at Indianapolis left their position dramatically strengthened in other areas.

In that respect, Tony George and Bernie Ecclestone were working the same agenda.

Five years ago George split the U.S. domestic racing scene asunder when he invented his own Indy Racing League series to promote traditional oval track events of which the Indy 500 was the jewel in the crown.

George had been under pressure to engineer a rapprochement with CART. Instead he chose to cut the key deal with Ecclestone to bring Formula 1 to Indianapolis. Paradoxically, that has strengthened the IRL because Indianapolis now had enough going for it without needing to patch up its quarrel with CART.

By the same token, CART was at one time regarded as a potential challenge to Formula 1 on the international stage. Hand-in-glove with George, Ecclestone had now headed it off.

Right: Michael Schumacher and Rubens Barrichello hug each other after Ferrari's crushing 1–2 finish.

the track was drying sufficiently for dry-weather tyres to become a realistic option. Häkkinen came in to make the change at the end of the eighth lap just after Coulthard came in to take his inevitable 10s stop–go penalty.

'I knew I jumped the start,' said Coulthard. 'It's unfortunate. I was ready to go and they weren't, so you have to pay the penalty. You set a rhythm of when you expect the lights to change. Obviously, you're trying to anticipate. It seemed to me that they were a bit longer than normal [making the decision] but rules are rules and I have to accept the punishment.

'I planned to get a better start and have been good enough, but I made a mistake and you pay the penalty. I am

disappointed in myself. I moved, I tried to stop, but then the lights changed, so I went.'

This left Schumacher with a comfortable 12.9s lead over Frentzen's Jordan and Pedro Diniz's Sauber, after which the capacity crowd was treated to the remarkable sight of Argentine pay-driver Gaston Mazzacane in the Minardi M02 hanging on ahead of Häkkinen's McLaren for six laps before coming in to change to dry-weather tyres at the end of lap 14.

Schumacher kept the Ferrari out in the lead until the end of lap 16, diving in for a 7.0s tyre change before resuming 10.9s ahead of Häkkinen. On the face of it one might have been forgiven for thinking that Schumacher

now had it in the bag, but Häkkinen then began rattling off a succession of fastest laps, slashing the German driver's advantage from 10.9s on lap 17 to 4.1s on lap 25.

Just as it looked as though the fans would be treated to a dramatic head-to-head between the two championship contenders, Häkkinen suddenly slowed on his 26th lap as flames began to flicker from beneath his McLaren's engine bay. He trickled slowly into the pit entry lane and stopped with a major engine failure.

Now Michael's brother Ralf took up the chase in his Williams-BMW, but despite steadying the gap to the leading Ferrari he was written out of the front-running equation when an unscheduled pit stop dropped him to the tail of the field on lap 42. He eventually retired with suspected loss of pneumatic valve pressure after 58 laps.

This left Frentzen battling with Barrichello for second place but the Brazilian successfully leap-frogged his Jordan rival to take second at their second refuelling stops and from then on Ferrari's American grand slam was all but guaranteed.

In the closing stages Jacques Villeneuve launched an heroic challenge on Frentzen's third-placed Jordan, the Canadian outbraking the Jordan at the end of the pit straight but then flying straight on over the grass. Villeneuve regained his composure for another attack, but eventually had to be satisfied with fourth place just half a second behind.

Coulthard finished fifth, frustrated by poor performance from his third set of tyres, one of which was worn down to the canvass by the time he took the chequered flag.

Ricardo Zonta completed the top six for the BAR-Honda squad with Eddie Irvine just missing out on a point in seventh and Pedro Diniz's Sauber next up from Nick Heidfeld's Prost-Peugeot, the sole surviving French machine after Jean Alesi pirouetted into retirement after his engine seized.

One of the most impressive performances came from Jaguar's Johnny Herbert who was the only one to start on dry-weather rubber and stormed through to fifth only to lose a huge chunk of time after clouting a wheel gun in the pit lane which damaged his front wing.

He wound up 11th after losing 20s changing the nose section. In the early stages Herbert's Jaguar had been the second-fastest car on the circuit at Indianapolis. Not bad for a guy who was being shown the door at the end of the year.

wheels and the Scot received a dressing down from his rival.

'As he is not fighting for the World Championship, and I have been trying to do this, I don't know what his thoughts were and whether the situation was different to the way I see it,' said Schumacher.

'I passed him, but he did not take the tightest line to avoid me.'

In response, Coulthard later remarked: 'At the end of the day I didn't drive into anybody and Michael pulled off a good move. I don't think there is a rule which says if you are not in the hunt for the championship you are not allowed to race and you have to let people past.'

By this stage it was also clear that

SAP UNITED STATES GRAND PRIX
INDIANAPOLIS 2000

INDIANAPOLIS
22–24 SEPTEMBER 2000
ROUND 15

SAP UNITED STATES grand prix

INDIANAPOLIS — GRAND PRIX CIRCUIT
CIRCUIT LENGTH: 2.605 miles/4.192 km

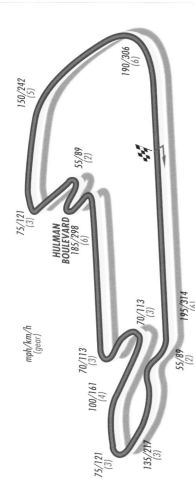

mph/km/h (gear)

75/121 (3)
150/242 (5)
190/306 (6)
55/89 (2)
185/298 (6)
HULMAN BOULEVARD
70/113 (3)
100/161 (4)
195/314 (6)
55/89 (2)
135/217 (3)
75/121 (3)

RACE DISTANCE: 73 laps, 190.139 miles/305.999 km RACE WEATHER: Cool and cloudy, infield wet at start

Pos.	Driver	Nat.	No.	Entrant	Car/Engine	Laps	Time/Retirement	Speed (mph/km/h)
1	Michael Schumacher	D	3	Scuderia Ferrari Marlboro	Ferrari F1-2000-049 V10	73	1h 36m 30.883s	118.203/190.229
2	Rubens Barrichello	BR	4	Scuderia Ferrari Marlboro	Ferrari F1-2000-049 V10	73	1h 36m 43.001s	117.956/189.832
3	Heinz-Harald Frentzen	D	5	Benson & Hedges Jordan	Jordan EJ10-Mugen Honda MF301HE V10	73	1h 36m 48.251s	117.849/189.660
4	Jacques Villeneuve	CDN	22	Lucky Strike BAR Honda	BAR 02-Honda RA100E V10	73	1h 36m 48.819s	117.838/189.642
5	David Coulthard	GB	2	West McLaren Mercedes	McLaren MP4/15-Mercedes FO110J V10	73	1h 36m 59.696s	117.617/189.287
6	Ricardo Zonta	BR	23	Lucky Strike BAR Honda	BAR 02-Honda RA100E V10	73	1h 37m 22.577s	117.157/188.546
7	Eddie Irvine	GB	7	Jaguar Racing	Jaguar R1-Cosworth CR2 V10	73	1h 37m 41.998s	116.769/187.921
8	Pedro Diniz	BR	16	Red Bull Sauber Petronas	Sauber C19-Petronas SPE 04A V10	72		
9	Nick Heidfeld	D	15	Gauloises Prost Peugeot	Prost AP03-Peugeot A20 V10	72		
10	Alexander Wurz	A	12	Mild Seven Benetton Playlife	Benetton B200-Playlife V10	72		
11	Johnny Herbert	GB	8	Jaguar Racing	Jaguar R1-Cosworth CR2 V10	72		
12	Marc Gene	ESP	20	Telefonica Minardi Fondmetal	Minardi M02-Fondmetal Ford Zetec-R V10	72		
	Jean Alesi	F	14	Gauloises Prost Peugeot	Prost AP03-Peugeot A20 V10	64	Engine	
	Gaston Mazzacane	ARG	21	Telefonica Minardi Fondmetal	Minardi M02-Fondmetal Ford Zetec-R V10	59	Engine	
	Ralf Schumacher	D	9	BMW WilliamsF1 Team	Williams FW22-BMW E41 V10	58	Engine	
	Pedro de la Rosa	ESP	18	Arrows	Arrows A21-Supertec FB02 V10	45	Gearbox	
	Giancarlo Fisichella	I	11	Mild Seven Benetton Playlife	Benetton B200-Playlife V10	44	Engine	
	Jos Verstappen	NL	19	Arrows	Arrows A21-Supertec FB02 V10	34	Slid off	
	Mika Häkkinen	SF	1	West McLaren Mercedes	McLaren MP4/15-Mercedes FO110J V10	25	Engine	
	Mika Salo	SF	17	Red Bull Sauber Petronas	Sauber C19-Petronas SPE 04A V10	18	Spun off	
	Jenson Button	GB	10	BMW WilliamsF1 Team	Williams FW22-BMW E41 V10	14	Engine	
	Jarno Trulli	I	6	Benson & Hedges Jordan	Jordan EJ10-Mugen Honda MF301HE V10	12	Engine	

Fastest lap: Coulthard, on lap 40, 1m 14.711s, 125.513 mph/201.994 km/h (record established).

Lap chart

Legend: shaded = Pit stop; lighter shade = One lap behind leader

Grid order	1	2	3	4	5	6	7	8	9	10	11	12	13	14	15	16	17	18	19	20	21	22	23	24	25	26	27	28	29	30	31	32	33	34	35	36	37	38	39	40	41	42	43	44	45	46	47	48	49	50	51	52	53	54	55
3 M. SCHUMACHER	2	2	2	2	2	2	2													5	5	5	5	5	5	19	19	19	8	22	22	22	22	4	4	4	4	16	16	16	16	16	16	18	18	2	2	7	7	23	23	23	23	3	3
2 COULTHARD	3	3	3	3	2	2	2									5	5	5	5	19	19	19	19	8	22	22	22	2	4	4	4	16	16	7	7	7	7	23	23	20	15	14	14	9	15	15	9	15	12	12	12	8	20	20	
1 HÄKKINEN	1	1	1	1	1	1	1			5	5	5	5	5	5	19	19	19	16	8	22	22	22	4	4	16	16	16	18	18	18	2	7	23	23	23	20	14	14	15	21	21	15	9	12	12	12	8	8	20	20				
4 BARRICHELLO	4	4	4	4	4	22	22	22		9	16	16	16	16	9	8	8	18	18	23	7	7	7	20	20	14	14	14	15	21	15	9	12	12	8	8	20	20																	
6 TRULLI	6	22	22	22	16	16	16	16	9	18	18	18	18	23	23	7	7	20	20	14	14	14	15	21	15	12	12	8	8	20	20																								
10 BUTTON	10	5	5	5	5	9	18	18	23	7	7	20	20	14	14	15	21	21	15	12	12	8	8	6																															
5 FRENTZEN	5	16	16	16	16	19	19	4	18	23	23	14	14	2	2	12	12	12	12	8	8	6	6																																
22 VILLENEUVE	22	9	9	9	9	4	4	19	4	20	20	21	21	15	15	14				6	6																																		
16 DINIZ	16	19	19	19	19	8	8	8	2	14	14	15	15	21	12	6																																							
9 R. SCHUMACHER	9	23	23	16	18	18	7	20	20	15	15	12	12	12	6																																								
12 WURZ	12	7	7	18	23	23	20	14	14	12	12	6	6	6																																										
23 ZONTA	23	18	18	12	7	20	14	15	15	11	11	11																																												
19 VERSTAPPEN	19	12	12	7	20	14	15	21	11																																															
17 SALO	17	15	15	20	14	21	21	11																																																
15 FISICHELLA	15	17	17	14	21	11	11																																																	
7 IRVINE	7	14	14	21	11																																																			
18 DE LA ROSA	18	11	20	11																																																				
8 HERBERT	8	20	8																																																				
14 ALESI	14	21	21																																																				
21 MAZZACANE	21	10	10																																																				
20 GENE	20	8	6	6	6	6																																																	

Pit stop

One lap behind leader

STARTING GRID

3 M. SCHUMACHER — Ferrari	**2** COULTHARD — McLaren
1 HÄKKINEN — McLaren	**4** BARRICHELLO — Ferrari
6 TRULLI — Jordan	**10** BUTTON — Williams
5 FRENTZEN — Jordan	**22** VILLENEUVE — BAR
11 FISICHELLA — Benetton	**15** HEIDFELD — Prost
19 VERSTAPPEN — Arrows	**17** SALO — Sauber
7 IRVINE — Jaguar	**18** DE LA ROSA — Arrows
12 WURZ — Benetton	**23** ZONTA — BAR
16 DINIZ — Sauber	**9** R. SCHUMACHER — Williams
8 HERBERT — Jaguar	**14** ALESI — Prost
21 MAZZACANE — Minardi	**20** GENE — Minardi

FOR THE RECORD
50th Grand Prix start
Alexander Wurz

TIME SHEETS

QUALIFYING
Weather: Warm and overcast, very light rain

Pos.	Driver	Car	Laps	Time
1	Michael Schumacher	Ferrari	12	1m 14.266s
2	David Coulthard	McLaren-Mercedes	12	1m 14.392s
3	Mika Häkkinen	McLaren-Mercedes	12	1m 14.428s
4	Rubens Barrichello	Ferrari	12	1m 14.600s
5	Jarno Trulli	Jordan-Mugen Honda	12	1m 15.006s
6	Jenson Button	Williams-BMW	12	1m 15.017s
7	Heinz-Harald Frentzen	Jordan-Mugen Honda	11	1m 15.067s
8	Jacques Villeneuve	BAR-Honda	10	1m 15.317s
9	Pedro Diniz	Sauber-Petronas	12	1m 15.418s
10	Ralf Schumacher	Williams-BMW	11	1m 15.484s
11	Alexander Wurz	Benetton-Playlife	12	1m 15.762s
12	Ricardo Zonta	BAR-Honda	12	1m 15.784s
13	Jos Verstappen	Arrows-Supertec	12	1m 15.808s
14	Mika Salo	Sauber-Petronas	12	1m 15.881s
15	Giancarlo Fisichella	Benetton-Playlife	12	1m 15.907s
16	Nick Heidfeld	Prost-Peugeot	12	1m 16.060s
17	Eddie Irvine	Jaguar-Cosworth	12	1m 16.098s
18	Pedro de la Rosa	Arrows-Supertec	12	1m 16.143s
19	Johnny Herbert	Jaguar-Cosworth	12	1m 16.225s
20	Jean Alesi	Prost-Peugeot	11	1m 16.471s
21	Gaston Mazzacane	Minardi-Fondmetal	11	1m 16.809s
22	Marc Gene	Minardi-Fondmetal	11	1m 17.161s

FRIDAY FREE PRACTICE
Weather: Warm and overcast

Pos.	Driver	Laps	Time
1	David Coulthard	13	1m 14.561s
2	Mika Häkkinen	31	1m 14.695s
3	Michael Schumacher	53	1m 14.927s
4	Rubens Barrichello	42	1m 15.144s
5	Jarno Trulli	45	1m 15.226s
6	Ralf Schumacher	36	1m 15.249s
7	Heinz-Harald Frentzen	42	1m 15.646s
8	Jenson Button	44	1m 15.741s
9	Marc Gene	45	1m 15.806s
10	Jacques Villeneuve	49	1m 16.147s
11	Alexander Wurz	43	1m 16.345s
12	Eddie Irvine	42	1m 16.546s
13	Jos Verstappen	30	1m 16.572s
14	Nick Heidfeld	32	1m 16.626s
15	Ricardo Zonta	50	1m 16.656s
16	Mika Salo	38	1m 16.660s
17	Johnny Herbert	42	1m 16.670s
18	Pedro de la Rosa	42	1m 16.787s
19	Gaston Mazzacane	47	1m 16.838s
20	Giancarlo Fisichella	41	1m 16.902s
21	Pedro Diniz	23	1m 17.053s
22	Jean Alesi	15	1m 18.213s

SATURDAY FREE PRACTICE
Weather: Warm and bright

Pos.	Driver	Laps	Time
1	Michael Schumacher	34	1m 14.804s
2	Rubens Barrichello	32	1m 15.014s
3	David Coulthard	35	1m 15.139s
4	Jenson Button	33	1m 15.153s
5	Mika Häkkinen	34	1m 15.293s
6	Heinz-Harald Frentzen	32	1m 15.399s
7	Giancarlo Fisichella	34	1m 15.626s
8	Jacques Villeneuve	30	1m 15.637s
9	Ralf Schumacher	32	1m 15.738s
10	Jarno Trulli	32	1m 16.077s
11	Pedro Diniz	34	1m 16.169s
12	Ricardo Zonta	29	1m 16.180s
13	Jos Verstappen	33	1m 16.260s
14	Johnny Herbert	28	1m 16.308s
15	Nick Heidfeld	36	1m 16.363s
16	Alexander Wurz	34	1m 16.368s
17	Pedro de la Rosa	33	1m 16.508s
18	Mika Salo	34	1m 16.542s
19	Gaston Mazzacane	33	1m 16.653s
20	Eddie Irvine	33	1m 16.662s
21	Jean Alesi	31	1m 17.100s
22	Marc Gene	30	1m 17.317s

WARM-UP
Weather: Light rain

Pos.	Driver	Laps	Time
1	David Coulthard	13	1m 23.144s
2	Mika Häkkinen	11	1m 23.706s
3	Michael Schumacher	11	1m 23.922s
4	Jacques Villeneuve	14	1m 24.012s
5	Jarno Trulli	14	1m 24.038s
6	Jos Verstappen	13	1m 24.119s
7	Rubens Barrichello	12	1m 24.517s
8	Giancarlo Fisichella	13	1m 24.622s
9	Pedro de la Rosa	14	1m 24.626s
10	Jenson Button	12	1m 24.675s
11	Ricardo Zonta	11	1m 24.692s
12	Heinz-Harald Frentzen	13	1m 24.719s
13	Ralf Schumacher	12	1m 24.720s
14	Eddie Irvine	13	1m 24.765s
15	Alexander Wurz	15	1m 25.135s
16	Johnny Herbert	16	1m 25.199s
17	Marc Gene	16	1m 25.369s
18	Jean Alesi	14	1m 25.373s
19	Nick Heidfeld	14	1m 25.387s
20	Gaston Mazzacane	11	1m 25.831s
21	Pedro Diniz	13	1m 26.126s
22	Mika Salo	7	1m 27.098s

RACE FASTEST LAPS
Weather: Cool and cloudy, infield wet at start

Driver	Time	Lap
David Coulthard	1m 14.711s	40
Rubens Barrichello	1m 14.822s	51
Michael Schumacher	1m 14.901s	48
Jacques Villeneuve	1m 15.117s	68
Pedro Diniz	1m 15.305s	69
Heinz-Harald Frentzen	1m 15.521s	69
Alexander Wurz	1m 15.560s	70
Eddie Irvine	1m 15.598s	55
Mika Salo	1m 15.675s	72
Ricardo Zonta	1m 15.812s	48
Mika Häkkinen	1m 15.773s	25
Jos Verstappen	1m 15.812s	69
Jenson Button	1m 16.074s	72
Ralf Schumacher	1m 16.044s	44
Johnny Herbert	1m 15.825s	72
Nick Heidfeld	1m 16.124s	69
Marc Gene	1m 16.234s	72
Jean Alesi	1m 16.252s	42
Giancarlo Fisichella	1m 16.276s	55
Gaston Mazzacane	1m 16.653s	33
Eddie Irvine	1m 16.662s	33
Pedro de la Rosa	1m 17.317s	30

POINTS TABLES

DRIVERS

Pos.	Driver	Points
1	Michael Schumacher	88
2	Mika Häkkinen	80
3	David Coulthard	63
4	Rubens Barrichello	55
5	Ralf Schumacher	24
6	Giancarlo Fisichella	18
7	Jacques Villeneuve	14
8	Heinz-Harald Frentzen	11
9	Jarno Trulli	10
10=	Jenson Button	6
10=	Mika Salo	6
12	Jos Verstappen	5
13=	Eddie Irvine	3
13=	Ricardo Zonta	3
15=	Alexander Wurz	2
15=	Pedro de la Rosa	2

CONSTRUCTORS

Pos.	Constructor	Points
1	Ferrari	143
2	McLaren	133
3	Williams	34
4	Benetton	20
5=	Jordan	17
5=	BAR	17
7	Arrows	7
8	Sauber	6
9	Jaguar	3

CHASSIS LOG BOOK

1	Häkkinen	McLaren MP4/15/4
2	Coulthard	McLaren MP4/15/5
	spares	McLaren MP4/15/6 & 2
3	M. Schumacher	Ferrari F1-2000/205
4	Barrichello	Ferrari F1-2000/203
	spares	Ferrari F1-2000/198 & 204
5	Frentzen	Jordan EJ10/6
6	Trulli	Jordan EJ10/5
	spare	Jordan EJ10/4
7	Irvine	Jaguar R1/5
8	Herbert	Jaguar R1/4
	spare	Jaguar R1/6
9	R. Schumacher	Williams FW22/6
10	Button	Williams FW22/4
	spare	Williams FW22/3
11	Fisichella	Benetton B200/5
12	Wurz	Benetton B200/3
	spare	Benetton B200/6
14	Alesi	Prost AP03/3
15	Heidfeld	Prost AP03/2
	spare	Prost AP03/1
16	Diniz	Sauber C19/7
17	Salo	Sauber C19/5
	spare	Sauber C19/6
18	de la Rosa	Arrows A21/2
19	Verstappen	Arrows A21/4
	spare	Arrows A21/1
22	Villeneuve	BAR 02/4
23	Zonta	BAR 02/1
	spares	BAR 02/3 & 5
20	Gene	Minardi M02/3
21	Mazzacane	Minardi M02/4
	spare	Minardi M02/1

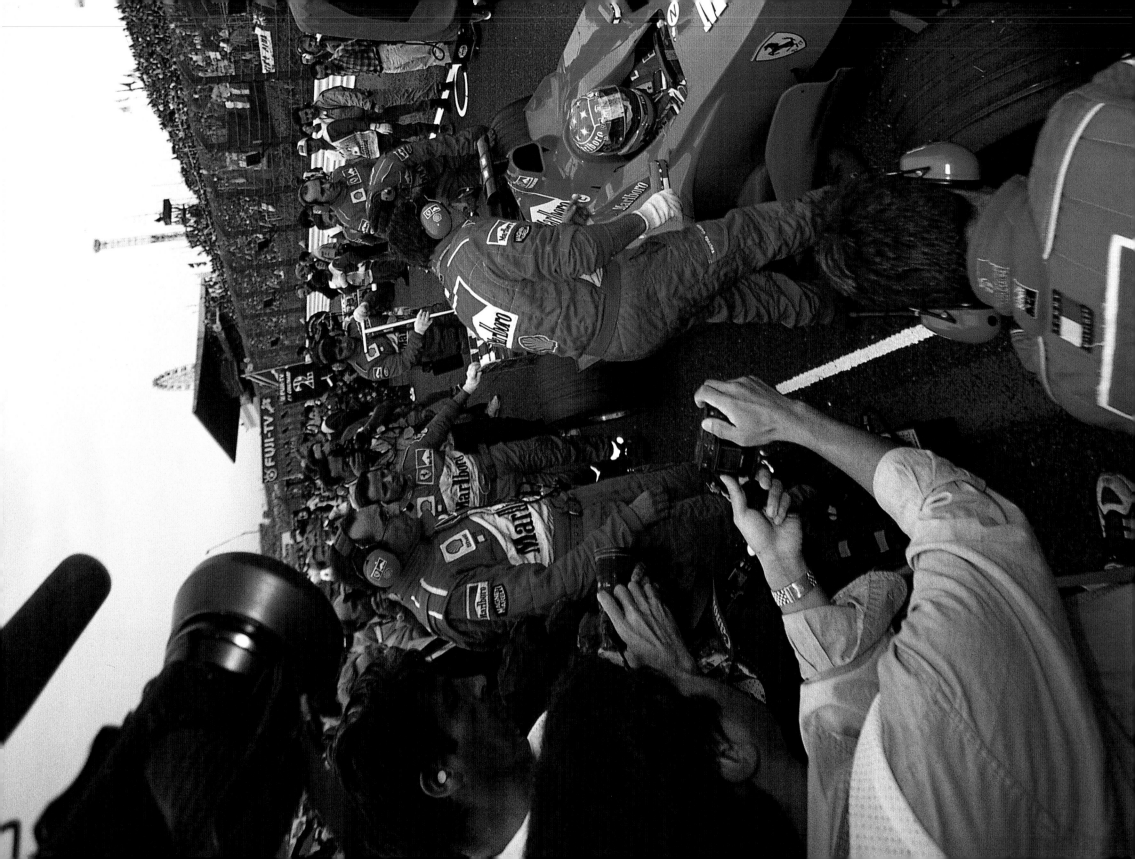

JAPANESE *grand prix*

M. SCHUMACHER

HÄKKINEN

COULTHARD

BARRICHELLO

BUTTON

VILLENEUVE

The moment of truth nears for Michael Schumacher as his besieged Ferrari is prepared on the grid before the start of the race.

Paul-Henri Cahier

SUZUKA QUALIFYING

Qualifying on this superbly challenging 5.864 km circuit was always going to be a highly charged affair between the two title contenders. Ferrari had spent the previous week at Mugello and Fiorano piling on the miles with Bridgestone's medium-hard compound Suzuka tyre which, unusually, was not supplemented with an alternative back-up choice.

Ferrari also benefited from a new front wing which was tried in the Mugello test, this being a development of the one first used at Spa. Schumacher also started his set-up work with Mugello chassis settings which proved a pretty good baseline from which to work.

The hour-long session on Saturday afternoon proved to be an electrifying affair with Häkkinen and Schumacher trading fastest times at the head of the pack. Although Coulthard set the ball rolling with a 1m 36.633s best – already 0.8s inside Schumacher's 1999 pole time – Schumacher came storming into contention with a 1m 36.094s on his first run.

Häkkinen countered almost immediately with a 1m 36.168s which moved him up to second, then at 13.37 slammed in a 1m 36.075s to go quickest. Six minutes later Michael's scarlet Ferrari edged back down the pit lane and onto the circuit to dip below the 1m 36s mark with a 1m 35.900s.

Michael went even quicker with six minutes to go, raising the stakes with a 1m 35.825s, his Ferrari looking amazingly stable under hard traction out of even the tightest corners, an enviable quality remarked on repeatedly by just about every commentator in the place.

Finally, with just 28s to go before the chequered flag was shown, it was Mika's turn to try again in an effort which seemed set to earn him his first ever Japanese GP pole. Mid-way round the lap he had to lap Jos Verstappen's Arrows, the Dutchman keeping well out of the way, but in the second sector the chance of further improvement seemed to slip away from him.

Fishtailing under hard acceleration out of the final chicane, Häkkinen sprinted towards the line but failed by 0.009s to get the job done. That amounted to a difference of 55 cm in terms of distance travelled between the two cars and both men were obviously elated by their efforts.

Inevitably it was a matter of much speculation as to whether McLaren had been disadvantaged by the lack of a softer tyre choice.

'The qualifying times go to show that these new medium-specification tyres are actually softer than the soft compound tyres we brought here last year,' said Bridgestone's technical manager Yoshihiko Ichikawa. 'Therefore it is obvious that if we had brought the soft tyre here, everyone would have chosen the medium compound.'

This viewpoint was not unreservedly shared by McLaren technical director Adrian Newey. 'The tyres are good, although a little harder than we'd like,' he said.

'The medium-compound tyre is comparable to the hard tyre that Bridgestone brought here in 1998. At that time we ran on the soft tyres.'

Coulthard wound up third fastest, admitting that he'd been unable to run quickly enough to stay with the leaders. 'The balance has been about as good as it's ever been round here,' he shrugged, 'but maintaining the grip has been the problem.' David briefly tried a different nose section and wing during Saturday free practice in an effort to improve his car's turn-in, but struggled to pick up the necessary extra pace.

After Barrichello beached his Ferrari in a gravel trap on Saturday, technical director Ross Brawn phoned Maranello to despatch a messenger to Japan with a third new-spec nose section just in case the team should run short of spares. In fact, Rubens hadn't damaged the front wing, but had another spin on Saturday and lined up a slightly unsettled fourth.

Button not only stormed round to take fifth on the grid, but his 1m 36.628s best outdid his team-mate Ralf Schumacher's best by 0.1s, the two men sharing the third row of the grid. 'It's one of the best moments of the season for me,' he enthused. 'It's amazing.'

Had it not been for Button's outstanding run, or that of the Englishman's team-mate Ralf Schumacher, Eddie Irvine would have earned first prize in his battle to be 'best of the rest' with the Jaguar R1. The Cosworth-engined cars looked more convincing than ever with 'Irv' bagging seventh place and Johnny Herbert just three places further back.

'Maybe a perfect lap would have given me [another] couple of tenths, but there's no such thing as a perfect lap round here,' said Irvine who was celebrating the seventh anniversary of his F1 debut here at Suzuka.

'The softer tyres literally transformed the car. We couldn't hope to have done better than this.'

In the BAR camp, Jacques Villeneuve qualified ninth, happy with the balance of his Honda-engined car's chassis but concerned like Coulthard about lack of grip.

'I am having a hard time with the tyres we have here,' said the Canadian. 'They've got a different characteristic to drive on and I'm having a hard time adapting to that.'

As the Honda factory's two works-backed runners for the 2001 season, there was obviously much rivalry between BAR and Jordan and while Heinz-Harald Frentzen managed to get his EJ10 qualified one place ahead of Villeneuve, the Silverstone brigade was not without its problems.

Jarno Trulli, by contrast, lost much track time after spinning on Pedro Diniz's oil which had the knock-on effect of a handling balance problem throughout qualifying which itself was aggravated by a power steering problem.

Meanwhile, Alexander Wurz lined up in 11th place, and in 12th Giancarlo Fisichella reported that his Benetton B200 did not feel as good as it did in the morning. Pedro de la Rosa's Arrows A21 (13th) suffered hydraulic problems and Jean Alesi's Prost AP03 (17th) was handling little better. Mika Salo took the spare Sauber-Petronas after his race machine suffered an alternator problem, but in general terms it was business as usual in the second half of the grid.

FERRARI'S £70-million investment in Michael Schumacher over the past five seasons finally paid off in brilliant style at Suzuka as the 31-year-old German became the famous Italian team's first World Champion driver since South Africa's Jody Scheckter in 1979.

By winning the Japanese Grand Prix, Schumacher also became only the eighth driver in 50 years to win the championship in a Ferrari and the first to take the title since the death of company founder Enzo Ferrari in 1988.

It was an epic success won in peerless style by the man acknowledged as the very best of his F1 generation. Pitched head-to-head against his most formidable rival Mika Häkkinen, Schumacher had to shadow the Finn for much of the race before vaulting ahead after his second refuelling stop with just 13 of the race's 53 laps left to run.

As Schumacher crossed the line just 1.8s ahead of his arch-rival Mika Häkkinen, the Ferrari pit crew erupted into a huge outpouring of tangled elation and emotion.

The team's normally reserved sporting director Jean Todt gave his number one driver a bear hug on the rostrum before he himself was soaked in champagne by Schumacher, runner-up Häkkinen and third-place man David Coulthard who had kept ahead of the other Ferrari of Rubens Barrichello to the finish.

'It is difficult to find the words to say how it feels,' said Schumacher. 'It is similar to Monza, but don't expect me to cry. I felt an outbreak of emotion as I crossed the line and it was great to finish with a win after a fight to the last corner, thanks to Mika.

'The crucial moment of the race was when we saw Mika going in for his second stop and I still had two laps to go.

'Then a Benetton spun in front of me as I was coming into the pits and I didn't think I had done enough. But as I went down the pit lane, Ross Brawn [Ferrari's technical director] was saying over the radio "it's looking good, it's looking good, it's looking bloody good." It was the most amazing moment of my racing career.'

Todt saluted Schumacher's efforts on behalf of the team. 'This is a joyous moment,' he said. 'I am happy and feel honoured to work with such a fantastic team and such an exceptional driver as Michael.

'Today's win came after an exciting race with a worthy opponent. Häkkinen is a great driver and a champion, both as a man and a professional.'

In fact, from the outset it looked as though Häkkinen might turn the prevailing tide and prolong the title battle to the Malaysian GP on October 22. Although beaten to pole position, the McLaren-Mercedes team leader surged into an immediate lead at the start, refusing to be intimidated as Schumacher swerved towards him in typical style accelerating away from the grid.

Seconds earlier there had been a heart-stopping moment as Häkkinen's McLaren began to belch blue smoke on the grid and a dribble of fluid could be seen on the track below its gearbox.

In the pit lane Ilmor boss Mario Ilien walked over to examine the telemetry, but the problem was nothing more than excess hydraulic fluid burning away. The car had been slightly over-filled and, from that moment onwards, the McLaren, like the winning Ferrari, never missed a beat.

Mika led by 0.8s at the end of the opening lap and from then on it was a two-horse race. On the face of it one might have forgiven David Coulthard

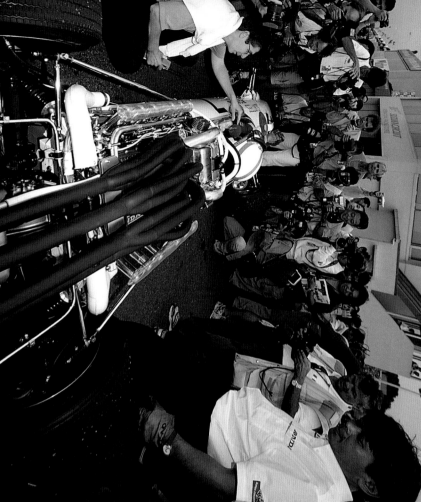

Honda piles pressure on BAR to deliver

HONDA'S president warned British American Racing that a failure to achieve good results in F1 could cause major economic problems for the Japanese car maker.

Speaking in Tokyo prior to the Japanese GP, Hiroyuki Yoshino cautioned: 'Unless we see tangible results in the F1 programme we may find ourselves in a difficult position as far as Honda's commercial activities are concerned.

'We are looking for hard results, not just next year, but in this race too.'

It is believed that Yoshino's remarks reflect the depth of a rift within the senior company's management structure about the usefulness of an F1 involvement as a marketing tool. Sources close to the company suggest that the factions are led by the intensely pro-F1 former president Nobuhiko Kawamoto on one side and Honda's sceptical – and highly profitable – U.S. operation on the other.

However Honda did commit itself to no let-up in its programme for the 2001 season. Honda F1 boss Takefumi Hosaka insisted that every effort would be made to ensure parity of supply between Honda and BAR, and that the chassis collaboration programme would continue with the latter.

'This year we are also supplying several teams in CART racing and taking care of them all on an individual basis,' he said. 'Based on that knowledge we do not expect any problems in supplying both [F1] teams.

'Performance-wise, we would like to push ahead of the other [leading] teams.'

Jacques Villeneuve leads Eddie Irvine to finish in sixth place and push BAR further up in the constructors' championship.

Bryn Williams/Words & Pictures

Below left: Passions rekindled. John Surtees was on hand to demonstrate the raucous 1967 V12 Honda.

Paul-Henri Cahier

DIARY

Japanese Grand Prix Friday free practice is hit by a minor earth tremor as fall-out from a major quake in the south west of the country.

British Grand Prix date is confirmed for 15 July 2001 by FIA World Council.

Speculation emerges that Bridgestone will quit F1 at the end of 2002.

Ricardo Zonta signs as Jordan F1 team test driver for 2001.

F3000 future is confirmed as supporting race for 2001 Brazilian Grand Prix.

for pacing himself carefully in third place as one of his priorities was to keep tabs on his opposite number at Ferrari, Rubens Barrichello. But his overall pace was disappointing and the Scot, who had been grappling to find grip for much of the weekend, was simply unable to offer any tactical assistance to Häkkinen.

Häkkinen successfully led through the first spate of refuelling stops, but lost the lead in the flurry of second stops as the circuit was brushed with a light rain shower. He stopped on lap 22 for a first 6.8s stop followed by Michael coming in next time round for a 7.4s refuelling visit.

Once Coulthard made his stop from what had originally been third place, so the original order was resumed at the head of the pack. Then on lap 29 it started to rain and Häkkinen was also briefly held up lapping Pedro de la Rosa's Arrows, a delay which cost another full second for the Finn.

Häkkinen was later critical – and de la Rosa's driving seemed to err uncomfortably close to the tactics which race director Charlie Whiting had indicated would be severely dealt with at the pre-race briefing – but the Spaniard was unapologetic.

'In the first two stints I was driving as hard as I could,' he explained, 'and Mika Häkkinen caught me at the wrong place through the Esses. That meant he lost some time because I was slow, but there wasn't much I could

do. You cannot let the leaders pass you when they are nearly three seconds behind.'

However, this delay had nothing to do with the fact that he lost an almost unaccountable five seconds on the out lap from his second stop on lap 36 compared with the dynamic Schumacher.

So what was the problem? Basically, his McLaren 'sliding around all over the place with no grip' on its third set of tyres. It was the defining moment of the race, because at that moment when the track was at its most greasy, Schumacher was still pressing on hard on nicely rubbed in, worn Bridgestones through to his own second stop on lap 40.

'I thought, for sure, this would be an advantage for Mika,' said Schumacher afterwards, 'because my tyres were worn out.' But Mika was wrestling to get temperature into his new dry tyres and, as the sky darkened although the expected heavy rain shower never materialised, the balance of the race shifted towards the Ferrari team leader.

From then on all Schumacher had to do was keep cool, but he admitted that Häkkinen simply wouldn't give him any respite. 'Mika could have certainly made it easier for me,' he said. 'I had to push hard all the way to the final corner.

'I knew there would be two crucial laps when Mika went to the pits [for

the second time] and I pushed really hard. Then one of the Benettons [Wurz] spun in front of me and as I came into the pits I thought it was not going to be enough.'

Overwhelmingly this was a duel which served to underline that Schumacher and Häkkinen are consistently in a class of their own in the ranks of contemporary grand prix drivers. For Michael's part, although he has no great sense of history and tradition, he could hardly fail to be impressed by the fact that he'd now become only the eighth driver in 50 years to win a World Championship in one of the famous scarlet cars.

For the McLaren-Mercedes squad, the outcome of the race was clearly a massive disappointment, Ron Dennis and the team's technical director Adrian Newey watching with impassive detachment as Häkkinen took the chequered flag shortly behind the Ferrari.

'Next year's World Championship starts in Malaysia,' said Mercedes motor sport director Norbert Haug crisply.

Into third and fourth places came Coulthard and Barrichello, on this day neither in the same class as their respective team-mates, while Jenson Button rounded off his first visit to Suzuka on a brilliant note with fifth place.

'My start was quite disastrous, actually,' he admitted. 'Having started fifth, I dropped back to seventh, but kept pushing. The car was well balanced and worked very well. I was putting in

quite good times, although obviously not as good as Ferrari or McLaren.'

By contrast, Ralf Schumacher had a pretty dismal time with three off-course excursions during the course of the race, the last of which ended in a gravel trap and called time on his efforts. He was coming up to lap Marc Gene at the time and the Spaniard braked too heavily, unsettling the pursuing Williams driver. 'I appreciate he came to apologise after the race,' said Schumacher.

Into sixth place came Jacques Villeneuve after a heady run through the field during which he pulled a couple of really good overtaking manoeuvres on the Jaguars, the Cosworth-powered R1s showing themselves to be particularly pitch-sensitive and nervous under hard retardation for the chicane.

BAR could take some satisfaction from the fact that their performance was a whole lot more impressive than Jordan's. Heinz-Harald Frentzen retired after 29 laps with an hydraulic failure, while Jarno Trulli struggled home a distant 13th after starting on a three-stop strategy and then being switched to a two-stop, a decision which left him with a car which was bottoming out badly with more fuel aboard than had originally been intended.

Taken as a whole, after their decent qualifying performance, Jaguar faded slightly in the race. Irvine ran a strong fifth from the start, but a sticking right rear wheel nut at his first refuelling drop cost him 3s which dropped him out of contention.

The knock-on effect of this was to lose him an eventual seventh place to Johnny Herbert as the F1 veteran squeezed out ahead of the pits ahead of him. Thereafter the two Jaguars ran in close company to the chequered flag.

Irvine was philosophical. 'Our pit stops were atrocious, and have been all year,' he announced. 'Within four laps of fitting fresh tyres my times had dropped almost a second a lap and the rear end was very loose. We have to sharpen up everything. If we'd had a good first stop we would have finished ahead of Button.'

12 months previously, Irvine had finished a close second to Häkkinen in the World Championship which Michael Schumacher was supposed to win. How did he feel now that his old Ferrari colleague had finally nailed down that success?

'Brilliant,' beamed Irvine. 'He thoroughly deserved it, just as he's deserved it every year since he last won it. Basically he's just the best.'

On this occasion, it would certainly have been difficult to contradict Irvine's conclusion.

Right: Mika Häkkinen leads Schumacher early in the race. The Flying Finn eventually had to settle for second place in the race and the championship.

Below right: Michael Schumacher celebrates his third World Championship crown with his wife Corinna and Ferrari team colleagues.

Below left: Jenson Button put in another impressive performance to finish in fifth place on his first ever visit to the Suzuka track.

FUJI TELEVISION
JAPANESE
grand prix

SUZUKA RACING CIRCUIT
CIRCUIT LENGTH: 3.644 miles/5.864 km

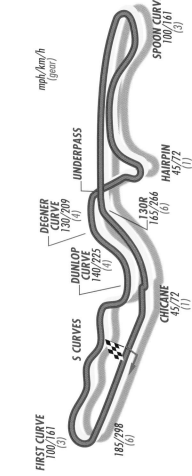

FIRST CURVE 100/161 (3)
185/298 (6)
S CURVES
DUNLOP CURVE 140/225 (4)
DEGNER CURVE 130/209 (4)
130R 165/266 (6)
UNDERPASS
HAIRPIN 45/72 (1)
CHICANE 45/72 (1)
SPOON CURVE 100/161 (3)
mph/km/h (gear)

RACE DISTANCE: 53 laps, 192.995 miles/310.596 km   **RACE WEATHER: Cool and overcast, with very light rain towards the end**

Pos.	Driver	Nat.	No.	Entrant	Car/Engine	Laps	Time/Retirement	Speed (mph/km/h)
1	Michael Schumacher	D	3	Scuderia Ferrari Marlboro	Ferrari F1-2000-049 V10	53	1h 29m 53.435s	128.820/207.316
2	Mika Häkkinen	SF	1	West McLaren Mercedes	McLaren MP4/15-Mercedes FO110J V10	53	1h 29m 55.272s	128.776/207.245
3	David Coulthard	GB	2	West McLaren Mercedes	McLaren MP4/15-Mercedes FO110J V10	53	1h 31m 03.349s	127.171/204.663
4	Rubens Barrichello	BR	4	Scuderia Ferrari Marlboro	Ferrari F1-2000-049 V10	53	1h 31m 12.626s	126.956/204.316
5	Jenson Button	GB	10	BMW WilliamsF1 Team	Williams FW22-BMW E41 V10	53	1h 31m 19.129s	126.805/204.073
6	Jacques Villeneuve	CDN	22	Lucky Strike BAR Honda	BAR 02-Honda RA100E V10	52		
7	Johnny Herbert	GB	8	Jaguar Racing	Jaguar R1-Cosworth CR2 V10	52		
8	Eddie Irvine	GB	7	Jaguar Racing	Jaguar R1-Cosworth CR2 V10	52		
9	Ricardo Zonta	BR	23	Lucky Strike BAR Honda	BAR 02-Honda RA100E V10	52		
10	Mika Salo	SF	17	Red Bull Sauber Petronas	Sauber C19-Petronas SPE 04A V10	52		
11	Pedro Diniz	BR	16	Red Bull Sauber Petronas	Sauber C19-Petronas SPE 04A V10	52		
12	Pedro de la Rosa	ESP	18	Arrows	Arrows A21-Supertec FB02 V10	52		
13	Jarno Trulli	I	6	Benson & Hedges Jordan	Jordan EJ10-Mugen Honda MF301HE V10	52		
14	Giancarlo Fisichella	I	11	Mild Seven Benetton Playlife	Benetton B200-Playlife V10	52		
15	Gaston Mazzacane	ARG	21	Telefonica Minardi Fondmetal	Minardi M02-Fondmetal Ford Zetec-R V10	51		
	Marc Gene	ESP	20	Telefonica Minardi Fondmetal	Minardi M02-Fondmetal Ford Zetec-R V10	46	Engine	
	Ralf Schumacher	D	9	BMW WilliamsF1 Team	Williams FW22-BMW E41 V10	41	Spun off	
	Nick Heidfeld	D	15	Gauloises Prost Peugeot	Prost AP03-Peugeot A20 V10	41	Broken rear suspension	
	Alexander Wurz	A	12	Mild Seven Benetton Playlife	Benetton B200-Playlife V10	37	Spun off	
	Heinz-Harald Frentzen	D	5	Benson & Hedges Jordan	Jordan EJ10-Mugen Honda MF301HE V10	29	Hydraulics	
	Jean Alesi	F	14	Gauloises Prost Peugeot	Prost AP03-Peugeot A20 V10	19	Engine	
	Jos Verstappen	NL	19	Arrows	Arrows A21-Supertec FB02 V10	9	Gearbox	

Fastest lap: Häkkinen, on lap 26, 1m 39.189s, 132.246 mph/212.830 km/h.

Lap record: Heinz-Harald Frentzen (F1 Williams FW19- Renault V10), 1m 38.942s, 132.576 mph/213.361 km/h (1997).

Grid order	1	2	3	4	5	6	7	8	9	10	11	12	13	14	15	16	17	18	19	20	21	22	23	24	25	26	27	28	29	30	31	32	33	34	35	36	37	38	39	40	41
3 M. SCHUMACHER	1	1	1	1	1	1	1	1	1	1	1	1	1	1	1	1	1	1	1	1	1	1	3	3	1	1	1	1	1	1	1	1	3	3	3	3	1	1	1	1	1
1 HÄKKINEN	3	3	3	3	3	2	2	2	2	2	2	2	2	2	2	2	2	2	2	2	2	2	1	1	3	3	3	3	3	3	3	3	1	1	1	1	2	2	2	2	2
2 COULTHARD	2	2	2	2	2	9	9	9	9	9	9	9	9	4	4	4	4	4	4	4	4	4	4	4	2	2	2	2	2	2	2	2	2	2	2	2	3	3	3	3	3
4 BARRICHELLO	9	9	9	9	9	4	4	4	4	4	4	4	4	10	10	4	4	4	4	4	4	4	4	4	4	4	4	4	4	4	4	4	4	4	4	4	4	4	4	4	4
10 BUTTON	4	4	4	4	4	4	10	10	10	10	10	10	7	7	7	10	10	10	10	10	10	10	10	10	10	10	10	10	10	10	10	10	10	10	10	10	10	10	10	10	10
9 R. SCHUMACHER	10	10	10	10	10	10	7	22	22	22	22	22	22	22	22	7	7	22	22	22	22	22	22	22	9	9	9	9	9	22	22	22	22	22	22	22	22	22	22	22	22
7 IRVINE	8	8	8	8	8	8	22	8	8	8	8	8	8	8	8	22	22	7	7	7	7	8	8	8	22	22	22	22	22	9	9	9	8	8	8	7	7	7	8	8	8
5 FRENTZEN	22	22	22	22	22	22	8	5	5	7	7	7	14	23	23	8	8	8	8	8	8	7	7	7	8	8	8	8	8	8	8	8	7	7	7	8	8	8	7	7	7
22 VILLENEUVE	19	19	19	19	19	6	6	6	6	6	6	6	6	6	6	5	5	5	23	23	23	23	23	23	23	23	23	23	23	23	23	23	23	23	23	23	23	23	23	23	23
8 HERBERT	5	5	5	5	5	5	5	7	7	5	5	18	18	18	18	6	6	6	6	6	6	6	6	6	17	17	17	17	17	17	17	17	17	17	17	17	17	17	17	17	17
12 WURZ	6	6	6	6	6	18	18	18	18	18	18	12	12	12	12	18	18	18	18	18	16	16	16	16	16	16	16	16	16	16	16	16	16	16	16	16	16	16	16	16	16
11 FISICHELLA	18	18	18	18	18	12	12	12	12	12	12	14	23	6	16	12	12	12	12	12	18	18	18	18	18	18	18	6	6	6	11	11	11	11	18	18	18	18	18	18	18
18 DE LA ROSA	12	12	12	12	12	17	17	17	17	17	17	23	6	16	5	23	23	23	14	14	12	12	12	12	6	6	6	11	11	11	6	6	6	6	6	11	11	11	11	11	11
19 VERSTAPPEN	14	14	14	14	14	14	14	14	14	14	14	6	16	5	14	14	14	14	15	15	14	14	14	14	11	11	11	18	18	18	18	18	18	18	11	6	6	6	6	6	
7 TRULLI	15	15	15	15	15	15	15	15	15	15	15	16	5	14	6	15	15	15	11	11	15	15	15	15	12	12	12	12	12	12	12	12	12	12	12	12	12	12	12	12	
15 HEIDFELD	23	23	23	23	23	23	23	23	23	23	23	5	15	15	15	16	16	16	16	16	6	11	11	11	15	15	20	20	20	20	20	20	20	20	20	20	20	20	20	20	
14 ALESI	16	16	16	16	16	16	16	16	16	16	16	15	11	11	11	11	11	11	6	6	11	20	20	20	20	20	15	15	15	15	15	15	15	15	21	21	21	21	21	21	
23 ZONTA	11	11	11	11	11	11	11	11	11	11	11	11	20	20	20	20	20	20	20	20	20	15	21	21	21	21	21	21	21	21	21	21	21	21	15	15	15	15	15	15	
17 SALO	20	20	20	20	20	20	20	20	20	20	20	20	16	16	16	21	21	21	21	21	21	21																			
16 DINIZ	21	21	21	21	21	21	21	21	21	21	21	21	21	21	21																										
20 GENE																																									
21 MAZZACANE																																									

Pit stop
One lap behind leader

STARTING GRID

3 M. SCHUMACHER Ferrari	1 HÄKKINEN McLaren
2 COULTHARD McLaren	4 BARRICHELLO Ferrari
10 BUTTON Williams	9 R. SCHUMACHER Williams
7 IRVINE Jaguar	5 FRENTZEN Jordan
22 VILLENEUVE BAR	8 HERBERT Jaguar
12 WURZ Benetton	11 FISICHELLA Benetton
18 DE LA ROSA Arrows	19 VERSTAPPEN Arrows
14 ALESI Prost	23 ZONTA BAR
6 TRULLI Jordan	15 HEIDFELD Prost
17 SALO Sauber	16 DINIZ Sauber
20 GENE Minardi	21 MAZZACANE Minardi

Lap chart

42	43	44	45	46	47	48	49	50	51	52	53
1	1	1	1	1	1	1	1	1	1	1	1
3	3	3	3	3	3	3	3	3	3	3	3
2	2	2	2	2	2	2	2	2	2	2	2
4	4	4	4	4	4	4	4	4	4	4	4
10	10	10	10	10	10	10	10	10	10	10	10
22	22	22	22	22	22	22	22	22	22	22	5
7	7	8	8	8	8	8	8	8	8	7	6
8	8	7	7	7	7	7	7	7	7	16	4
11	11	16	16	16	16	16	16	16	16	17	3
16	16	17	17	17	17	17	17	17	17	23	2
17	17	23	23	23	23	23	23	23	23	6	1
23	23	6	6	6	6	6	6	6	6		●
										5	
										4	
										3	
										2	
										1	

TIME SHEETS

QUALIFYING

Weather: Warm and bright

Pos.	Driver	Car	Laps	Time
1	Michael Schumacher	Ferrari	9	1m 35.825s
2	Mika Häkkinen	McLaren-Mercedes	12	1m 35.834s
3	David Coulthard	McLaren-Mercedes	12	1m 36.236s
4	Rubens Barrichello	Ferrari	12	1m 36.330s
5	Jenson Button	Williams-BMW	10	1m 36.628s
6	Ralf Schumacher	Williams-BMW	11	1m 36.788s
7	Eddie Irvine	Jaguar-Cosworth	12	1m 36.899s
8	Heinz-Harald Frentzen	Jordan-Mugen Honda	12	1m 37.243s
9	Jacques Villeneuve	BAR-Honda	11	1m 37.267s
10	Johnny Herbert	Jaguar-Cosworth	12	1m 37.329s
11	Alexander Wurz	Benetton-Playlife	12	1m 37.348s
12	Giancarlo Fisichella	Benetton-Playlife	12	1m 37.479s
13	Pedro de la Rosa	Arrows-Supertec	11	1m 37.652s
14	Jos Verstappen	Arrows-Supertec	11	1m 37.674s
15	Jarno Trulli	Jordan-Mugen Honda	11	1m 37.679s
16	Nick Heidfeld	Prost-Peugeot	11	1m 38.141s
17	Jean Alesi	Prost-Peugeot	12	1m 38.209s
18	Ricardo Zonta	BAR-Honda	9	1m 38.269s
19	Mika Salo	Sauber-Petronas	6	1m 38.490s
20	Pedro Diniz	Sauber-Petronas	12	1m 38.576s
21	Marc Gene	Minardi-Fondmetal	9	1m 39.972s
22	Gaston Mazzacane	Minardi-Fondmetal	12	1m 40.462s

FRIDAY FREE PRACTICE

Weather: Warm and bright

Pos.	Driver	Laps	Time
1	Michael Schumacher	26	1m 37.728s
2	Mika Häkkinen	31	1m 38.339s
3	Rubens Barrichello	19	1m 38.537s
4	David Coulthard	31	1m 39.010s
5	Jenson Button	37	1m 39.111s
6	Jarno Trulli	26	1m 39.261s
7	Heinz-Harald Frentzen	28	1m 39.529s
8	Pedro de la Rosa	26	1m 39.547s
9	Jacques Villeneuve	34	1m 39.669s
10	Ricardo Zonta	37	1m 39.887s
11	Eddie Irvine	26	1m 40.014s
12	Ralf Schumacher	24	1m 40.166s
13	Pedro Diniz	30	1m 40.328s
14	Nick Heidfeld	37	1m 40.403s
15	Mika Salo	31	1m 40.431s
16	Giancarlo Fisichella	30	1m 40.520s
17	Jos Verstappen	28	1m 40.523s
18	Johnny Herbert	27	1m 40.824s
19	Alexander Wurz	10	1m 40.985s
20	Jean Alesi	24	1m 41.014s
21	Marc Gene	26	1m 41.670s
22	Gaston Mazzacane	16	1m 45.238s

SATURDAY FREE PRACTICE

Weather: Warm and bright

Pos.	Driver	Laps	Time
1	Mika Häkkinen	21	1m 37.037s
2	Michael Schumacher	27	1m 37.176s
3	Jenson Button	28	1m 37.244s
4	Rubens Barrichello	21	1m 37.260s
5	Ralf Schumacher	25	1m 37.493s
6	David Coulthard	28	1m 37.503s
7	Giancarlo Fisichella	28	1m 37.739s
8	Eddie Irvine	24	1m 37.893s
9	Alexander Wurz	25	1m 38.257s
10	Jacques Villeneuve	20	1m 38.422s
11	Pedro de la Rosa	21	1m 38.438s
12	Jarno Trulli	13	1m 38.471s
13	Jos Verstappen	21	1m 38.578s
14	Johnny Herbert	29	1m 38.590s
15	Nick Heidfeld	29	1m 38.758s
16	Ricardo Zonta	22	1m 38.868s
17	Heinz-Harald Frentzen	17	1m 38.872s
18	Mika Salo	31	1m 38.921s
19	Jean Alesi	23	1m 39.225s
20	Pedro Diniz	6	1m 39.960s
21	Marc Gene	25	1m 40.185s
22	Gaston Mazzacane	29	1m 41.210s

WARM-UP

Weather: Warm and overcast

Pos.	Driver	Laps	Time
1	Michael Schumacher	12	1m 38.005s
2	Mika Häkkinen	13	1m 38.526s
3	Rubens Barrichello	13	1m 38.758s
4	David Coulthard	13	1m 38.820s
5	Jenson Button	8	1m 39.620s
6	Jarno Trulli	13	1m 39.626s
7	Ralf Schumacher	14	1m 39.844s
8	Jacques Villeneuve	14	1m 39.957s
9	Mika Salo	13	1m 40.053s
10	Pedro Diniz	13	1m 40.089s
11	Eddie Irvine	13	1m 40.171s
12	Giancarlo Fisichella	14	1m 40.201s
13	Jos Verstappen	14	1m 40.264s
14	Johnny Herbert	11	1m 40.330s
15	Jean Alesi	10	1m 40.332s
16	Ricardo Zonta	12	1m 40.341s
17	Alexander Wurz	15	1m 40.646s
18	Pedro de la Rosa	13	1m 40.651s
19	Heinz-Harald Frentzen	13	1m 41.231s
20	Nick Heidfeld	12	1m 41.272s
21	Marc Gene	11	1m 42.110s
22	Gaston Mazzacane	6	1m 42.815s

RACE FASTEST LAPS

Weather: Cool and overcast, then very light rain

Driver	Time	Lap
Mika Häkkinen	1m 39.189s	26
Michael Schumacher	1m 39.443s	27
David Coulthard	1m 40.058s	26
Rubens Barrichello	1m 40.218s	26
Jenson Button	1m 40.699s	23
Jacques Villeneuve	1m 40.739s	18
Ralf Schumacher	1m 40.900s	23
Jarno Trulli	1m 40.967s	12
Ricardo Zonta	1m 40.980s	26
Pedro Diniz	1m 41.002s	25
Eddie Irvine	1m 41.154s	18
Heinz-Harald Frentzen	1m 41.185s	15
Johnny Herbert	1m 41.226s	17
Mika Salo	1m 41.634s	15
Pedro de la Rosa	1m 42.079s	26
Jos Verstappen	1m 42.356s	23
Nick Heidfeld	1m 42.416s	14
Giancarlo Fisichella	1m 42.737s	19
Jean Alesi	1m 42.786s	8
Alexander Wurz	1m 42.795s	15
Marc Gene	1m 43.997s	15

CHASSIS LOG BOOK

1	Häkkinen	McLaren MP4/15/6
2	Coulthard	McLaren MP4/15/7
	spares	McLaren MP4/15/2 & 4
3	M. Schumacher	Ferrari F1-2000/205
4	Barrichello	Ferrari F1-2000/203
	spares	Ferrari F1-2000/198 & 204
5	Frentzen	Jordan EJ10/6
6	Trulli	Jordan EJ10/5
	spare	Jordan EJ10/4
7	Irvine	Jaguar R1/5
8	Herbert	Jaguar R1/6
	spare	Jaguar R1/4
9	R. Schumacher	Williams FW22/6
10	Button	Williams FW22/4
	spare	Williams FW22/3
11	Fisichella	Benetton B200/5
12	Wurz	Benetton B200/3
	spare	Benetton B200/6
14	Alesi	Prost AP03/1
15	Heidfeld	Prost AP03/2
	spare	Prost AP03/3
16	Diniz	Sauber C19/7
17	Salo	Sauber C19/5
	spare	Sauber C19/6
18	de la Rosa	Arrows A21/2
19	Verstappen	Arrows A21/4
	spare	Arrows A21/1
20	Gene	Minardi M02/3
21	Mazzacane	Minardi M02/4
	spares	Minardi M02/1
22	Villeneuve	BAR 02/4
23	Zonta	BAR 02/1
	spares	BAR 02/3 & 5

POINTS TABLES

DRIVERS

1	Michael Schumacher	98
2	Mika Häkkinen	86
3	David Coulthard	67
4	Rubens Barrichello	58
5	Ralf Schumacher	24
6	Giancarlo Fisichella	18
7	Jacques Villeneuve	15
8	Jenson Button	12
9	Heinz-Harald Frentzen	11
10=	Jarno Trulli	6
10=	Mika Salo	6
12	Jos Verstappen	5
13=	Eddie Irvine	3
13=	Ricardo Zonta	3
15=	Alexander Wurz	2
15=	Pedro de la Rosa	2

CONSTRUCTORS

1	Ferrari	156
2	McLaren	143
3	Williams	36
4	Benetton	20
5	BAR	18
6	Jordan	17
7	Arrows	7
8	Sauber	6
9	Jaguar	3

MALAYSIAN
grand prix

FIA WORLD CHAMPIONSHIP • ROUND 17

M. SCHUMACHER

COULTHARD

BARRICHELLO

HÄKKINEN

VILLENEUVE

IRVINE

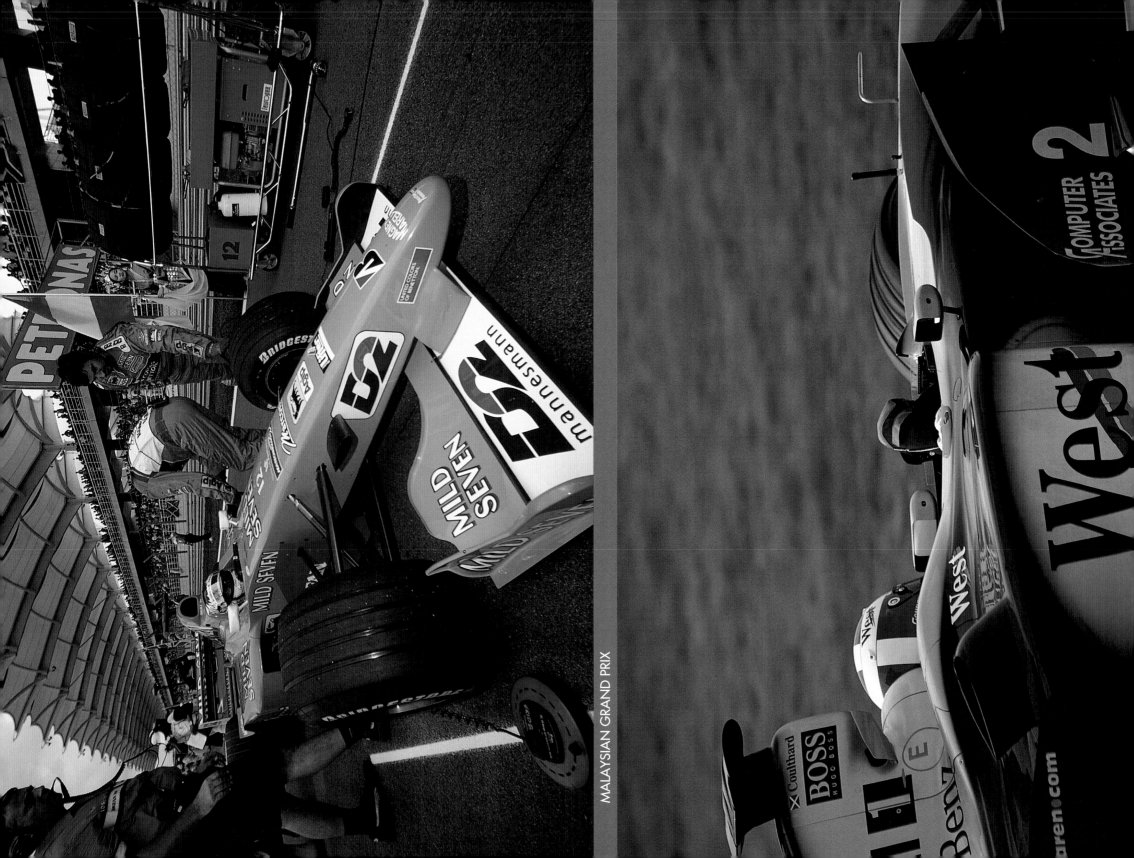

Previous spread: The end of a 21-year wait for Ferrari as Michael Schumacher finally delivered the drivers' World Championship for Maranello.
Paul-Henri Cahier

Below left: Alexander Wurz made great use of the qualifying car to put his Benetton fifth on the grid.
Paul-Henri Cahier

Left: David Coulthard fought hard to push Schumacher all the way.

MICHAEL Schumacher completed an historic double for the Ferrari team with a memorable 44th career victory in the Malaysian Grand Prix at Kuala Lumpur's impressive Sepang circuit, an achievement which boosted his number of victories this season to nine, equalling the one-year record established by Nigel Mansell back in 1992.

To clinch the constructors' championship Ferrari only needed to add another three points to its existing total, so even if the rival McLaren-Mercedes squad had managed to post a 1-2 success it would almost certainly not have been sufficient to get the job done.

Despite this, McLaren-Mercedes drivers Mika Häkkinen and David Coulthard attacked the final race of the season with tremendous gusto, successfully edging Michael's pole position Ferrari back to third place in his sprint to the first corner. Both men had a great chance of winning, yet both made slight slips which cost them dear and allowed the flawless Schumacher through to another close victory.

Unfortunately Häkkinen moved before the starting lights went out and thus surged into the lead going down to the first corner almost certain in his own mind — correctly, as it turned out — that he would incur a 10s stop-go penalty. Nevertheless he kept his head down to lead the pack through the first corner with Coulthard's sister car coming round the outside of Schumacher to take an immediate second place.

Rubens Barrichello was fourth in his Ferrari F1-2000 ahead of Alexander Wurz's Benetton B200 and Jacques Villeneuve's BAR-Honda. Unfortunately, further back down the pack there was big trouble brewing, and as Pedro de la Rosa's Arrows A21, Nick Heidfeld's Prost AP03 and Pedro Diniz's Sauber C19 funnelled into the second corner, they all collided in a spectacular cloud of shredded bodywork and bouncing wheels.

The incident also involved Jean Alesi, but while the Frenchman's Prost AP03 continued the other three immediately retired. Further round the opening lap Ralf Schumacher's Williams ran wide onto the grass and dropped to the tail of the field. Meanwhile Jarno Trulli also brushed the rear of another car — he reckoned it was Eddie Irvine's Jaguar — and had to come in at the end of the opening lap for a replacement nose section to be fitted.

Häkkinen led by 1.1s at the end of the opening lap, but by then the safety car had been deployed to slow the field as the debris from the three-car pile-up was swiftly cleared away. At the start of lap three the safety car was withdrawn and Häkkinen, mindful of his penalty, first allowed Coulthard through into the lead and quickly afterwards dropped behind Schumacher and Barrichello, not wishing to be accused later of holding up any rivals without justification.

On lap five the outgoing World Champion duly stopped for his penalty while on the same lap Heinz-Harald Frentzen went autocrossing in his Jordan EJ10 and had to come in for repairs. It seemed that bouncing across the outfield caused an electrical connection to fail and, although Heinz went out for another lap, he was in to retire for good at the end of lap seven when the power steering packed up due to hydraulic failure.

This all left Coulthard leading by 3.6s and he really looked confident, opening the gap over Schumacher's Ferrari steadily to 4.8s on lap 10 and 5.4s on lap 12. But on lap 13 came disaster for the Scot. 'I had managed to move from third to second at the start and took the lead when the team told Mika to move over on lap three as they realised he had jumped the start,' said Coulthard. 'Unfortunately I went wide at the exit of turn six, picking up some grass, which went into the radiator inlets causing the temperature to rise. As a result the team decided to call me in for my pit stop early to remove the grass.

'I rejoined the race and was stuck behind Michael but was putting him under as much pressure as I could without getting into the dirty air created by his car.'

David pitted on lap 17 in 7.0s, allowing Michael a clear run to rattle off a succession of fastest laps. On lap 18 he cut a 1m 39.571s, then a 1m 39.369s, a 1m 39.344s and a 1m 39.064s. He then made his own first refuelling stop on lap 24 in 7.1s, allowing Barrichello through momentarily into the lead before he himself came in next time round. When the race settled down again lap 26 saw Schumacher leading Coulthard by 4.9s. As far as the outcome of the race was concerned, that was effectively that.

Coulthard opted for new front tyres at his second stop which left him grappling with a little more understeer than he could have expected on scrubbed rubber. At his second stop on lap 38 he fitted scrubbed tyres which gave him more front-end bite for the balance of the race. Yet Schumacher retained the upper hand. 'We wanted to win with the constructors' championship and we have done it, not just by winning and getting three points but by winning and coming

DIARY

Speculation intensifies that Adrian Reynard will raise the £65 million needed to purchase a controlling interest in British American Racing by selling his Reynard empire to Prodrive's David Richards.

The Prost team loses an estimated £1 million in F1 travel benefits after finishing 11th and last in the constructors' World Championship.

Telefonica announces withdrawal from F1 after two seasons with Minardi.

Asia Motor Technologies claims its budget to bankroll development of the Peugeot V10 engine will be increased by about 60 per cent over Peugeot's 2000 budget for the 2001 season.

SEPANG QUALIFYING

From the outset, qualifying seemed set to unfold as a close-fought affair between McLaren and Ferrari, the Italian team only having to add three more points to its total in order to clinch the constructors' title, irrespective of what Häkkinen and Coulthard could manage. From the outset, the cards were stacked in Maranello's favour.

Anybody who imagined that Schumacher might ease up now that he'd bagged his third World Championship was set to be severely disappointed. Fresh from ten days' holiday on a tropical island, Michael was on pin-sharp form and confidently out-ran the McLarens to take his ninth pole position of the season.

In company with most of the field, Schumacher used old front tyres and new rears, this deemed the most effective way of keeping understeer to a minimum. Even though the front-running pace was 2s faster than at last year's inaugural race at Sepang, tyre degradation levels were encouragingly low.

'This session was not as easy as it might have looked,' said Schumacher. 'My first run was not spot-on, then we tried changing the rear wing for the second run, but it was the wrong decision, so we went back to the original settings for my final attempt.

'Apart from a small mistake in the first sector, it was just right.'

By contrast, his team-mate Rubens Barrichello was acutely disappointed. With second place on the grid apparently comfortably in the bag, the Brazilian had already removed his helmet in the scrutineering bay only to watch the timing screen send the stark message that Häkkinen (1m 37.860s) and Coulthard (1m 37.889s) had bumped him back to fourth place.

'I was at the limit of the car as it was today,' shrugged Häkkinen. 'At this circuit you need to have a car which is very stable on entry and exit of the corners and we weren't able to put that together today. We were struggling, particularly in the first and last sectors of the lap.

Coulthard added: 'I am disappointed to be so far from Michael's time. I changed the car after the first run and couldn't go as quickly as before, so for the last run I put the set-up back to where it had been — I went quicker, but not enough.

'Before the last run we also had a fuel line pop off. I had my helmet visor up at the time and fuel sprayed in my left eye. We also had a small fire which could have been very nasty — after all, the mechanics are in shorts and tee shirts.'

Best of the rest on this occasion was Alexander Wurz, the man who'd been formally confirmed as the McLaren team's new test driver the previous day. Perhaps as a fond farewell from the Benetton squad, his B200 was fitted with the one available Renault Sport-tweaked Supertec V10 — complete with special oil and fuel — and the lanky Austrian duly responded with a fine display of the form which made his F1 reputation in 1997 but which has been sadly lacking ever since.

Wurz had been begging Benetton team chief Flavio Briatore to be allowed a race weekend driving the development B200 chassis which had hitherto been the exclusive preserve of Giancarlo Fisichella. However, after Suzuka it appeared that Fisichella had turned his nose up at the car and indicated he wasn't really bothered whether or not he drove it again. Wurz therefore seized his opportunity with both hands and made the very best of his opportunity. It seemed as though, yet again, McLaren had hired a test driver with the 'right stuff'.

Jacques Villeneuve was moderately satisfied with sixth on the grid for the BAR-Honda squad, but Ricardo Zonta wound up 11th after explaining that he was losing time under braking.

'I'm disappointed,' said Villeneuve. 'On the first part of that last run the car was quick, then part way round the lap a cylinder must have gone down on the engine or something, and I lost a lot of power.' Subsequent examination revealed that the engine had unexpectedly switched to a lean fuel/air mixture which knocked off the fine edge of its performance.

Eddie Irvine made set-up changes to improve his Jaguar R1 en route to seventh-fastest time, but Johnny Herbert had too much understeer.

'It's strange to me how, after changing the engine for qualifying, the car can completely change,' said Herbert. 'I've gone from a well balanced car this morning to an understeering car this afternoon. My first runs were similar to Eddie's, but he managed to pull out a fast one whereas my car did not improve.'

Ralf Schumacher (8th) made a mistake at turn 14 on his best lap, losing 0.4s, while Jenson Button (16th) paid the knock-on penalty for his problems during the morning's free practice session when engine problems saw the Williams lads install a replacement BMW V10 in a record 50 minutes.

Meanwhile, Jos Verstappen had an off-track moment which damaged the undertray and radiator on his Arrows A21 and switched to the spare car set up for Pedro de la Rosa. Jarno Trulli (9th) found that scrubbed front tyres and new rears on his Jordan EJ10 still left him with too much understeer.

Clive Mason/Allsport

left: Ready for action, drivers leave the pre-race briefing. Visible *(from left to right)* are Alesi, Ralf Schumacher, Villeneuve, Verstappen, Irvine and Heidfeld.

Below left: Johnny Herbert makes his pass on Salo stick. Unfortunately for Johnny his last F1 race ended in the tyre wall after a rear suspension failure.

Right: Michael and Rubens are happy with their hairdos, Ross Brawn seems less convinced.

Paul-Henri Cahier

third [Barrichello],' he said with some elation after the race. 'It was a very tight and tough race and "DC" was pushing me all the way, so it was tough physically and on the car. I did not know Mika had jumped the start as I was concentrating on the lights.

'I did not have a very good start and struggled to get off the line and so I was third as David out-braked me round the outside. He was pulling away [in the early stages] and I was concerned, because I could not go any faster. At that point he was definitely quicker than me.'

After the race Coulthard took the chance to clear the tension which has festered between him and Schumacher for much of the season, particularly after Coulthard criticised his rival for his driving tactics in the French Grand Prix, which the McLaren driver eventually won. 'I apologised to Michael for the year,' said Coulthard. 'We have had some differences and I am embarrassed by some of the things I have said and done. I said he was a very worthy champion and that I am looking forward to racing against him next year.

'We all react in the heat of the moment and act in ways we regret. I always said I wouldn't get into speaking to someone via the press, but I did. I don't think that was fair on Michael and I wanted to apologise.'

Meanwhile, Häkkinen's penalty pushed him back to 16th place, 47.3s behind the leader. From that point he staged a storming comeback through to an eventual fourth at the chequered flag, a quite remarkable performance considering he started the race with insufficient fuel to run through to lap 35 of the 56-lap event before making his only refuelling stop.

Barrichello finished an excellent third, struggling to shrug off the effects of flu, although he lost time with a slight problem engaging first gear at his second refuelling stop. Rounding off the top four was the gallant Häkkinen who chiselled his way back to 35.2s behind the winning Ferrari at the finish.

During the course of the race Mika became embroiled in a brief, but dramatic tussle with Jacques Villeneuve which saw the BAR and McLaren passing and repassing as the Canadian driver struggled desperately to hang onto fourth. It would have been good enough to clinch fourth place for BAR in the constructors' championship; as it was, Jacques took fifth which left his team equal on points with Benetton who took the place with Giancarlo Fisichella's best result of the year — second in Brazil. 'I had a good race today, but it was a shame for the team's championship position that Ricardo wasn't able to turn a strong performance into that point that would have given us fourth place.' Shrugged Villeneuve. For his part, Zonta was extremely dejected. 'I was up behind Irvine after the first pit stop and we hit oil on the entry to turn six,' he explained. 'He lost the rear of the car, but managed to keep it on the track. I also slid on the oil and then the car went into the gravel.

'I then had to come in early for my second stop to have the radiators cleared since the engine was getting very hot. After the stop, I was catching the cars in front, in sixth, seventh and eighth places, but then the engine let go.'

Alexander Wurz ran strongly from the start of his final race for Benetton, but faded to a disappointing seventh with brake problems. Apart from his early efforts, amongst the midfield ruck, there was precious little in the way of signs that anybody is seriously emerging to challenge the Ferrari/McLaren axis. Both Williams-BMWs succumbed to engine-related failures after a weekend in which both Ralf Schumacher and Jenson Button had struggled for balance and grip but were aiming for a top-six finish out of their one-stop strategies. 'This obviously isn't a fairytale ending to a fantastic season,' said Dr Mario Theissen, BMW Motorsport's Director. 'We started the race with high-performance engines in both cars of the specification introduced at Spa, but unfortunately Jenson was stopped by an engine failure. In Ralf's car there was a malfunction in the engine oil supply system. In order to avoid an unnecessary failure, we called him in.'

For the Jaguar team, Eddie Irvine at least brought some sliver of consolation with sixth place and another championship point to round off a bruising season. Yet Johnny Herbert's F1 finale sadly amounted to a distillation of the setbacks which have dogged his 12-year front-line career.

Herbert's day ended on what could have been a tragic note with a high-speed accident in his Jaguar R1 from which he was extremely fortunate to emerge unscathed. Herbert was running a strong fourth prior to his first scheduled stop on lap 28 only for the refuelling nozzle to jam and prove reluctant to remove from the side of the fuel tank. That dropped him back to 12th, but he was back to 10th by lap 48 when a massive right rear suspension failure under braking from 170 mph saw the car slam sideways into a track-side tyre barrier.

Thankfully the 36-year-old veteran emerged from the wrecked car with nothing more than bruises and was released to return to his hotel after a check-up in hospital.

'I guess it was inevitable that because I began my [Formula 1] career being carried to the car, I would end it being carried out of it,' he chirped with remarkable good humour, referring to his debut for Benetton at Rio in 1989 when he was still recovering from serious leg injuries.

'There's nothing like ending your career with a bang, I'm O.K. I have a bit of pain from the left knee, but nothing too serious.'

Mosley and Dennis exchange letters over Suzuka stewards issue

FIA president Max Mosley circulated copies of a lengthy letter to McLaren chairman Ron Dennis at Sepang, chastising him roundly on a number of matters including what was perceived as his implied criticism of the Italian FIA steward Roberto Causo at the Japanese Grand Prix.

Prompted by an inquiry from a journalist, Dennis admitted that he was uneasy about the fact that there was an Italian steward at the race, the implication being that he was worried about possible partiality in favour of Michael Schumacher and the Ferrari team. Mosley responded with a robust tract in which he asked Dennis in future 'to think things through more carefully before expressing your opinions.

'Although I am sure you would not intend such a thing, your actions might also be seen as an attempt to intimidate our officials, something which is now a recognised problem in other sports. This all discourages new sponsors and new fans. Indeed at a certain level such conduct can be a breach of the International Sporting Code,' Mosley continued to suggest that Dennis write a letter of apology to Causo, but then launched into a further critique of the McLaren chief in connection with his attitude towards race director Charlie Whiting's driver briefing at Suzuka where he threatened heavy penalties for anyone who disrupted the race.

Mosley tried to draw an analogy between Michael Schumacher's obstructive driving in the 1999 Malaysian Grand Prix and David Coulthard's performance in the early stages of the 2000 U.S. Grand Prix at Indianapolis.

His letter then continued to speculate on various scenarios whereby drivers from different teams could gang up to affect the outcome of the World Championship:

'It was the FIA's plain duty in the highly charged atmosphere of that race [at Suzuka] to take the precaution of issuing an appropriate warning at the drivers' briefing, if only to reassure all other competitors. This is what Charlie Whiting did.'

Mosley then suggested that if Dennis did not like the way the current FIA F1 World Championship was run he should go away and start his own;

'What you should not do, however, is enter our F1 World Championship, on whose rule-making body you sit and whose regulations and procedures have been known to you for more than 30 years, and then undermine it by constantly complaining to anyone in the media who will listen.'

Dennis responded by issuing a copy of a well-reasoned reply to the FIA president, but decided to be drawn into a lengthy debate on the matter with the media.

SEPANG
20–22 OCTOBER 2000

ROUND 17

PETRONAS
MALAYSIAN grand prix

SEPANG

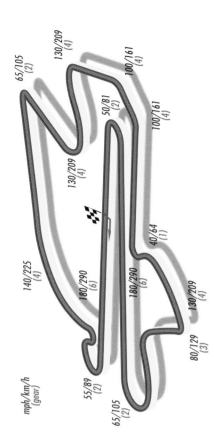

CIRCUIT LENGTH: 3.444 miles/5.543 km

mph/km/h (gear)

55/89 (2)
65/105 (2)
80/129 (3)
130/209 (4)
180/290 (6)
140/225 (4)
180/290 (6)
130/209 (4)
40/64 (1)
100/161 (4)
50/81 (2)
100/161 (4)
130/209 (4)
65/105 (2)
130/209 (4)

RACE DISTANCE: 56 laps, 192.879 miles/310.408 km **RACE WEATHER: Hot, humid and sunny**

Pos.	Driver	Nat.	No.	Entrant	Car/Engine	Laps	Time/Retirement	Speed (mph/km/h)
1	Michael Schumacher	D	3	Scuderia Ferrari Marlboro	Ferrari F1-2000-049 V10	56	1h 35m 54.235s	120.669m/194.199
2	David Coulthard	GB	2	West McLaren Marlboro	McLaren MP4/15-Mercedes FO110J V10	56	1h 35m 54.967s	120.654m/194.174
3	Rubens Barrichello	BR	4	Scuderia Ferrari Marlboro	Ferrari F1-2000-049 V10	56	1h 36m 12.679s	120.284m/193.578
4	Mika Häkkinen	SF	1	West McLaren Mercedes	McLaren MP4/15-Mercedes FO110J V10	56	1h 36m 29.504s	119.934m/193.016
5	Jacques Villeneuve	CDN	22	Lucky Strike BAR Honda	BAR 02-Honda RA100E V10	56	1h 37m 04.927s	119.205m/191.842
6	Eddie Irvine	GB	7	Jaguar Racing	Jaguar R1-Cosworth CR2 V10	56	1h 37m 06.803s	119.166m/191.780
7	Alexander Wurz	A	12	Mild Seven Benetton Playlife	Benetton B200-Playlife V10	56	1h 37m 23.549s	118.825/191.231
8	Mika Salo	SF	17	Red Bull Sauber Petronas	Sauber C19-Petronas SPE 04A V10	55		
9	Giancarlo Fisichella	I	11	Mild Seven Benetton Playlife	Benetton B200-Playlife V10	55		
10	Jos Verstappen	NL	19	Arrows	Arrows A21-Supertec FB02 V10	55		
11	Jean Alesi	F	14	Gauloises Prost Peugeot	Prost AP03-Peugeot A20 V10	55		
12	Jarno Trulli	I	6	Benson & Hedges Jordan	Jordan EJ10-Mugen Honda MF301HE V10	55		
13	Gaston Mazzacane	ARG	21	Telefonica Minardi Fondmetal	Minardi M02-Fondmetal Ford Zetec-R V10	50	Engine	
	Johnny Herbert	GB	8	Jaguar Racing	Jaguar R1-Cosworth CR2 V10	48	Suspension	
	Ricardo Zonta	BR	23	Lucky Strike BAR Honda	BAR 02-Honda RA100E V10	46	Engine	
	Ralf Schumacher	D	9	BMW WilliamsF1 Team	Williams FW22-BMW E41 V10	43	Engine	
	Marc Gene	ESP	20	Telefonica Minardi Fondmetal	Minardi M02-Fondmetal Ford Zetec-R V10	36	Broken wheel spline	
	Jenson Button	GB	10	BMW WilliamsF1 Team	Williams FW22-BMW E41 V10	18	Engine	
	Heinz-Harald Frentzen	D	5	Benson & Hedges Jordan	Jordan EJ10-Mugen Honda MF301HE V10	7	Steering	
	Pedro de la Rosa	ESP	18	Arrows	Arrows A21-Supertec FB02 V10	0	Accident	
	Nick Heidfeld	D	15	Gauloises Prost Peugeot	Prost AP03-Peugeot A20 V10	0	Accident	
	Pedro Diniz	BR	16	Red Bull Sauber Petronas	Sauber C19-Petronas SPE 04A V10	0	Accident	

Fastest lap: Häkkinen, on lap 34, 1m 38.543s, 125.826 mph/202.498 km/h (record).

Previous lap record: Michael Schumacher (F1 Ferrari F399 V10), 1m 40.267s, 123.640 mph/198.980 km/h (1999).

Lap chart

Legend: shaded = Pit stop; One lap behind leader.

Grid order	1	2	3	4	5	6	7	8	9	10	11	12	13	14	15	16	17	18	19	20	21	22	23	24	25	26	27	28	29	30	31	32	33	34	35	36	37	38	39	40	41	42	43	44
3 M. SCHUMACHER	1	1	2	2	2	2	2	2	2	2	2	2	2	4	4	4	4	3	3	3	3	3	3	3	3	3	3	3	3	1	1	1	1	1	1	1	1	1	1	1	1	1	1	1
1 HÄKKINEN	2	2	3	3	4	4	4	4	4	4	4	4	4	12	12	12	12	2	2	2	2	1	1	1	1	4	4	4	4	3	3	3	3	4	4	4	4	4	4	4	4	4	4	4
2 COULTHARD	3	3	4	1	1	1	1	1	1	1	1	1	1	1	1	1	1	1	1	1	1	22	22	22	22	2	2	2	2	2	2	2	2	2	2	2	2	2	2	2	2	2	2	2
4 BARRICHELLO	4	4	1	12	12	12	12	12	12	12	12	12	12	7	7	2	2	7	7	23	23	8	8	19	12	12	12	22	22	23	23	11	11	23	19	19	11	8	3	3	3	3	3	3
12 WURZ	12	12	12	22	22	22	22	22	22	22	22	22	22	12	12	12	12	12	12	12	12	12	12	12	22	22	23	23	11	11	17	17	17	7	7	11	11	11	17	17	7	7	7	7
22 VILLENEUVE	22	22	22	7	7	7	7	7	7	7	7	7	7	23	23	23	23	23	8	8	8	7	7	7	7	11	11	11	17	17	11	7	7	11	11	17	17	17	11	11	11	11	12	12
9 R. SCHUMACHER	9	9	5	9	9	9	9	9	9	9	9	9	9	9	9	9	9	9	9	9	9	9	9	9	9	17	17	17	23	7	7	12	12	17	17	7	7	7	7	7	17	17	11	11
7 IRVINE	7	7	7	8	8	8	8	8	8	8	8	8	8	8	8	8	8	8	23	7	7	11	11	11	11	23	22	12	12	12	12	22	22	12	12	12	12	12	12	12	12	12	17	17
6 TRULLI	5	5	8	5	5	5	5	23	23	23	23	23	23	11	11	11	11	11	11	11	11	23	23	23	23	19	19	19	19	22	22	23	23	19	23	23	23	6	6	6	6	6	6	6
5 FRENTZEN	8	8	9	23	23	23	23	17	17	17	17	17	17	17	17	17	17	17	17	17	17	17	17	17	17	6	6	6	6	6	6	19	19	6	6	6	6	14	14	14	14	14	14	14
23 ZONTA	23	23	23	11	11	11	11	11	11	11	11	11	11	19	19	19	19	19	19	19	19	19	19	6	6	14	14	14	14	14	14	6	6	14	14	14	14	21	21	21	21	21	21	21
8 HERBERT	11	11	11	17	17	17	17	19	19	19	19	19	19	20	20	20	20	20	20	14	14	14	14	14	14	21	21	21	21	21	21	21	21	21	21	21	21							
11 FISICHELLA	10	10	10	19	19	19	19	10	10	10	10	10	14	14	14	14	14	14	14	20	20	20	20	20	20																			
18 DE LA ROSA	17	17	17	10	10	10	10	14	14	14	14	14	20	10	10	10	10	10	10																									
19 VERSTAPPEN	19	19	19	20	20	20	14	20	20	20	20	20	10																															
10 BUTTON	20	20	20	14	14	14	20																																					
17 SALO	21	21	21	21	21	6	6	6	6	6	6	6	6	21	21	21	21	21	21	21	21	21	21	21	21																			
14 ALESI	14	14	14	6	6																																							
15 HEIDFELD	6	6	6																																									
16 DINIZ																																												
20 GENE																																												
21 MAZZACANE																																												

Pit stop
One lap behind leader

STARTING GRID

Pos	Driver	Team
3	M. SCHUMACHER	Ferrari
1	HÄKKINEN	McLaren
2	COULTHARD	McLaren
4	BARRICHELLO	Ferrari
7	WURZ	Benetton
12	VILLENEUVE	BAR
5	IRVINE	Jaguar
9	R. SCHUMACHER	Williams
6	TRULLI	Jordan
8	FRENTZEN	Jordan
23	ZONTA	BAR
11	HERBERT	Jaguar
11	FISICHELLA	Benetton
18	DE LA ROSA	Arrows
19	VERSTAPPEN	Arrows
10	BUTTON	Williams
17	SALO	Sauber
14	ALESI	Prost
15	HEIDFELD	Prost
16	DINIZ	Sauber
20	GENE	Minardi
21	MAZZACANE	Minardi

TIME SHEETS

QUALIFYING
Weather: Hot, humid and sunny

Pos.	Driver	Car	Laps	Time
1	Michael Schumacher	Ferrari	8	1m 37.397s
2	Mika Häkkinen	McLaren-Mercedes		1m 37.860s
3	David Coulthard	McLaren-Mercedes	11	1m 37.889s
4	Rubens Barrichello	Ferrari	11	1m 37.896s
5	Alexander Wurz	Benetton-Playlife	12	1m 38.644s
6	Jacques Villeneuve	BAR-Honda	11	1m 38.653s
7	Eddie Irvine	Jaguar-Cosworth	12	1m 38.696s
8	Ralf Schumacher	Williams-BMW	12	1m 38.739s
9	Jarno Trulli	Jordan-Mugen Honda	11	1m 38.909s
10	Heinz-Harald Frentzen	Jordan-Mugen Honda	11	1m 38.988s
11	Ricardo Zonta	BAR-Honda	11	1m 39.158s
12	Giancarlo Fisichella	Benetton-Playlife	12	1m 39.331s
13	Johnny Herbert	Jaguar-Cosworth	12	1m 39.387s
14	Pedro de la Rosa	Arrows-Supertec	12	1m 39.443s
15	Jos Verstappen	Arrows-Supertec	9	1m 39.489s
16	Jenson Button	Williams-BMW	10	1m 39.563s
17	Mika Salo	Sauber-Petronas	12	1m 39.591s
18	Jean Alesi	Prost-Peugeot	11	1m 40.065s
19	Nick Heidfeld	Prost-Peugeot	11	1m 40.148s
20	Pedro Diniz	Sauber-Petronas	11	1m 40.521s
21	Marc Gene	Minardi-Fondmetal	12	1m 40.662s
22	Gaston Mazzacane	Minardi-Fondmetal	12	1m 42.078s

FRIDAY FREE PRACTICE
Weather: Hot, humid and sunny

Pos.	Driver	Laps	Time
1	Mika Häkkinen	36	1m 40.262s
2	Michael Schumacher	28	1m 40.276s
3	David Coulthard	27	1m 40.498s
4	Rubens Barrichello	34	1m 40.877s
5	Jarno Trulli	31	1m 41.304s
6	Ralf Schumacher	35	1m 41.493s
7	Ricardo Zonta	39	1m 41.497s
8	Giancarlo Fisichella	35	1m 41.593s
9	Alexander Wurz	30	1m 41.679s
10	Heinz-Harald Frentzen	28	1m 41.751s
11	Jos Verstappen	28	1m 41.914s
12	Jenson Button	36	1m 42.012s
13	Johnny Herbert	28	1m 42.113s
14	Eddie Irvine	31	1m 42.141s
15	Pedro de la Rosa	31	1m 42.254s
16	Pedro Diniz	31	1m 42.457s
17	Jacques Villeneuve	17	1m 42.649s
18	Jean Alesi	33	1m 42.868s
19	Mika Salo	34	1m 43.284s
20	Gaston Mazzacane	29	1m 43.424s
21	Marc Gene	33	1m 43.655s
22	Nick Heidfeld	23	1m 43.786s

SATURDAY FREE PRACTICE
Weather: Hot, humid and sunny

Pos.	Driver	Laps	Time
1	David Coulthard	29	1m 38.109s
2	Michael Schumacher	30	1m 38.203s
3	Ralf Schumacher	32	1m 38.318s
4	Alexander Wurz	32	1m 38.348s
5	Rubens Barrichello	26	1m 38.955s
6	Mika Häkkinen	28	1m 38.955s
7	Eddie Irvine	24	1m 39.107s
8	Jenson Button	27	1m 39.110s
9	Jacques Villeneuve	34	1m 39.230s
10	Jarno Trulli	31	1m 39.337s
11	Johnny Herbert	29	1m 39.382s
12	Ricardo Zonta	32	1m 39.430s
13	Nick Heidfeld	32	1m 39.440s
14	Pedro de la Rosa	31	1m 39.794s
15	Jos Verstappen	28	1m 39.798s
16	Mika Salo	32	1m 39.812s
17	Giancarlo Fisichella	20	1m 39.839s
18	Pedro Diniz	30	1m 39.849s
19	Jean Alesi	27	1m 39.916s
20	Heinz-Harald Frentzen	10	1m 39.988s
21	Marc Gene	12	1m 40.551s
22	Gaston Mazzacane	21	1m 42.370s

WARM-UP
Weather: Hot, humid and sunny

Pos.	Driver	Laps	Time
1	Ricardo Zonta	13	1m 40.032s
2	Mika Häkkinen	12	1m 40.080s
3	Michael Schumacher	12	1m 40.246s
4	David Coulthard	12	1m 40.393s
5	Alexander Wurz	15	1m 40.916s
6	Rubens Barrichello	8	1m 41.161s
7	Jacques Villeneuve	14	1m 41.309s
8	Johnny Herbert	12	1m 41.332s
9	Eddie Irvine	11	1m 41.527s
10	Mika Salo	14	1m 41.559s
11	Pedro Diniz	14	1m 41.755s
12	Jenson Button	11	1m 41.791s
13	Jarno Trulli	14	1m 41.888s
14	Giancarlo Fisichella	13	1m 41.956s
15	Pedro de la Rosa	12	1m 42.104s
16	Marc Gene	12	1m 42.155s
17	Jos Verstappen	13	1m 42.155s
18	Jean Alesi	17	1m 42.177s
19	Heinz-Harald Frentzen	13	1m 42.282s
20	Ralf Schumacher	13	1m 42.372s
21	Nick Heidfeld	7	1m 42.731s
22	Gaston Mazzacane	11	1m 43.621s

RACE FASTEST LAPS
Weather: Hot, humid and sunny

Pos.	Driver	Time	Lap
1	Mika Häkkinen	1m 38.543s	34
2	Michael Schumacher	1m 39.064s	21
3	Rubens Barrichello	1m 39.302s	23
4	David Coulthard	1m 39.529s	36
5	Jacques Villeneuve	1m 40.160s	20
6	Eddie Irvine	1m 40.292s	18
7	Alexander Wurz	1m 40.312s	19
8	Ricardo Zonta	1m 40.498s	21
9	Johnny Herbert	1m 40.764s	14
10	Mika Salo	1m 40.896s	27
11	Giancarlo Fisichella	1m 40.925s	53
12	Jarno Trulli	1m 41.104s	27
13	Jenson Button	1m 41.262s	33
14	Jean Alesi	1m 41.634s	34
15	Ralf Schumacher	1m 41.729s	42
16	Marc Gene	1m 41.928s	27
17	Jos Verstappen	1m 42.146s	17
18	Pedro Diniz	1m 43.147s	27
19	Gaston Mazzacane	1m 43.726s	17
20	Heinz-Harald Frentzen	1m 44.557s	3

CHASSIS LOG BOOK

No.	Driver	Chassis
1	Häkkinen	McLaren MP4/15/4
2	Coulthard	McLaren MP4/15/5
	spares	McLaren MP4/15/6 & 2
3	M. Schumacher	Ferrari F1-2000/205
4	Barrichello	Ferrari F1-2000/203
	spares	Ferrari F1-2000/198 & 204
5	Irvine	Jaguar R1/5
6	Frentzen	Jordan EJ10/6
7	Trulli	Jordan EJ10/5
	spare	Jordan EJ10/4
8	Herbert	Jaguar R1/6
9	R. Schumacher	Williams FW22/6
10	Button	Williams FW22/4
	spare	Williams FW22/3
11	Fisichella	Benetton B200/5
12	Wurz	Benetton B200/3
	spare	Benetton B200/6
14	Alesi	Prost AP03/3
15	Heidfeld	Prost AP03/2
	spare	Prost AP03/1
16	Diniz	Sauber C19/7
17	Salo	Sauber C19/5
	spare	Sauber C19/6
18	de la Rosa	Arrows A21/2
19	Verstappen	Arrows A21/4
	spare	Arrows A21/1
20	Gene	Minardi M02/3
21	Mazzacane	Minardi M02/1
	spare	Minardi M02/2
22	Villeneuve	BAR 02/4
23	Zonta	BAR 02/1
	spares	BAR 02/3 & 5

POINTS TABLES

DRIVERS

Pos	Driver	Points
1	Michael Schumacher	108
2	Mika Häkkinen	89
3	David Coulthard	73
4	Rubens Barrichello	62
5	Ralf Schumacher	24
6	Giancarlo Fisichella	18
7	Jacques Villeneuve	17
8	Jenson Button	12
9	Heinz-Harald Frentzen	11
10=	Jarno Trulli	6
10=	Mika Salo	6
10=	Jos Verstappen	6
13	Eddie Irvine	4
14	Ricardo Zonta	3
15=	Alexander Wurz	2
15=	Pedro de la Rosa	2

CONSTRUCTORS

Pos	Constructor	Points
1	Ferrari	170
2	McLaren	152
3	Williams	36
4	Benetton	20
5	BAR	20
6	Jordan	17
7	Arrows	7
8	Sauber	6
9	Jaguar	4

DRIVERS' POINTS TABLE

Compiled by Nick Henry

Paul-Henri Cahier

Place	Driver	Nationality	Date of birth	Car	Australia	Brazil	San Marino	Britain	Spain	Europe	Monaco	Canada	France	Austria	Germany	Hungary	Belgium	Italy	U.S.A.	Japan	Malaysia	Points total
1	Michael Schumacher	D	3/1/69	Ferrari	1	1f	1	3	5p	1f	Rp	1p	Rp	R	R	2p	2	1p	1p	1p	1p	108
2	Mika Häkkinen	SF	28/9/68	McLaren-Mercedes	Rp	Rp	2p	2f	1f	2	6f	4f	2	1p	2	1f	1p	2f	R	2f	4f	89
3	David Coulthard	GB	27/3/71	McLaren-Mercedes	R	DQ	3	1	2	3p	1	7	1f	2f	3p	3	4	R	5f	3	2	73
4	Rubens Barrichello	BR	23/5/72	Ferrari	2f	R	4	Rp	3	4	R	4	3	R	1f	4	Rf	2	2	4	3	62
5	Ralf Schumacher	D	30/6/75	Williams-BMW	3	5	R	4	4	R	3	14*	5	R	7	5	3	3	3	R	R	24
6	Giancarlo Fisichella	I	14/1/73	Benetton-Playlife	5	2	11	7	9	5	3	2	9	R	R	12	R	R	R	14	9	18
7	Jacques Villeneuve	CDN	9/4/71	BAR-Honda	4	R	5	16*	R	R	7	15*	4	4	8	R	7	R	4	6	5	17
8	Jenson Button	GB	19/1/80	Williams-BMW	R	6	R	5	17*	10*	R	11	8	5	4	9	5	R	R	5	R	12
9	Heinz-Harald Frentzen	D	18/5/67	Jordan-Mugen Honda	R	3	R	17*	6	R	R	R	7	R	9	6	6	R	3	R	R	11
10=	Jarno Trulli	I	13/7/74	Jordan-Mugen Honda	R	4	15*	6	12	10*	10*	6	R	R	R	7	R	7	R	13	12	6
10=	Mika Salo	SF	30/11/66	Sauber-Petronas	DQ	WD	6	8	7	R	5	R	6	6	5	10	9	R	R	10	8	6
12	Jos Verstappen	NL	4/3/72	Arrows-Supertec	R	7	14	R	R	R	R	5	10	R	R	13	15	4	R	R	10	5
13	Eddie Irvine	GB	10/11/65	Jaguar-Cosworth	R	R	7	13	11	R	4	13	13	R	10	8	10	R	R	8	6	4
14	Ricardo Zonta	BR	23/3/76	BAR-Honda	6	9	12	R	8	R	R	8	R	R	R	14	12	6	R	9	R	3
15=	Alexander Wurz	A	15/2/74	Benetton-Playlife	7	R	9	9	10	12*	R	9	R	10	R	11	13	5	7	R	7	2
15=	Pedro de la Rosa	ESP	24/2/71	Arrows-Supertec	R	8	R	R	R	6	DNS	R	R	R	6	16	16	R	R	12	R	2
	Jean Alesi	F	11/6/64	Prost-Peugeot	R	R	R	10	R	9	R	R	14	R	R	16	R	12	R	11	11	0
	Luciano Burti	BR	5/3/75	Jaguar-Cosworth	-	-	-	-	-	-	-	-	-	11	-	-	-	-	-	-	-	0
	Pedro Diniz	BR	22/5/70	Sauber-Petronas	R	WD	8	11	R	7	R	10	11	9	R	R	11	8	8	11	R	0
	Marc Gene	ESP	29/3/74	Minardi-Fondmetal	8	R	R	14	14	R	R	16*	15*	8	R	15	14	9	12	R	R	0
	Nick Heidfeld	D	10/5/77	Prost-Peugeot	9	R	R	R	16	EXC	8	R	12	R	12*	R	R	R	R	R	R	0
	Johnny Herbert	GB	25/6/64	Jaguar-Cosworth	R	R	10	12	13	11*	R	R	R	12	11	R	R	R	R	7	15	0
	Gaston Mazzacane	ARG	8/5/75	Minardi-Fondmetal	R	10	13	15	15	R	R	R	R	R	11	R	17	R	R	15	13	0

KEY

p	pole position	R	retired	DNQ	did not qualify
f	fastest lap	DQ	disqualified	EXC	excluded
*	classified but not running at the finish	DNS	did not start	WD	withdrawn

Compiled by David Hayhoe

POINTS & PERCENTAGES

GRID POSITIONS: 2000

Pos.	Driver	Starts	Best	Worst	Average
1	Michael Schumacher	17	1	5	2.00
2	Mika Häkkinen	17	1	5	2.53
3	David Coulthard	17	1	5	2.71
4	Rubens Barrichello	17	1	18	4.82
5	Jarno Trulli	17	2	15	7.53
6	Heinz-Harald Frentzen	17	2	17	7.88
7	Ralf Schumacher	17	4	19	8.47
8	Jacques Villeneuve	17	4	17	8.71
9	Eddie Irvine	16	6	17	9.69
10	Giancarlo Fisichella	17	3	19	10.29
11	Jenson Button	17	3	21	11.82
12	Alexander Wurz	17	5	20	13.18
13	Pedro de la Rosa	17	5	22	13.82
14	Jos Verstappen	17	8	20	13.94
15	Johnny Herbert	17	8	20	14.12
16	Mika Salo	16	9	19	14.19
17	Ricardo Zonta	17	6	20	14.24
18	Pedro Diniz	16	9	20	15.50
19	Jean Alesi	17	7	20	16.47
20	Nick Heidfeld	16	13	22	17.31
21	Marc Gene	18	18	22	20.53
22	Luciano Burti	1	21	21	21.00
23	Gaston Mazzacane	17	20	22	21.53

CAREER PERFORMANCES: 2000 DRIVERS

Driver	Nationality	Races	Championships	Wins	2nd places	3rd places	4th places	5th places	6th places	Pole positions	Fastest laps	Points
Jean Alesi	F	184	—	1	16	15	11	14	2	2	4	236
Rubens Barrichello	BR	130	—	1	6	8	13	9	4	3	3	139
Luciano Burti	BR	1	—	—	—	—	—	—	—	—	—	—
Jenson Button	GB	17	—	—	—	—	1	4	1	—	—	12
David Coulthard	GB	107	—	9	21	11	5	7	5	10	14	294
Pedro de la Rosa	E	33	—	—	—	—	—	—	2	—	—	6
Pedro Diniz	BR	98	—	—	—	—	3	1	3	—	—	10
Giancarlo Fisichella	I	74	—	—	5	3	4	5	3	1	—	67
Heinz-Harald Frentzen	D	114	—	3	3	11	11	8	12	2	6	53
Marc Gene	E	33	—	—	—	—	—	1	—	—	—	1
Mika Häkkinen	FIN	145	2	18	14	16	10	9	7	26	22	383
Nick Heidfeld	D	16	—	—	—	—	—	—	—	—	—	—
Johnny Herbert	GB	162	—	3	1	3	11	6	5	—	—	98
Eddie Irvine	GB	113	—	4	6	14	9	6	6	—	1	177
Gaston Mazzacane	RA	17	—	—	—	—	—	—	—	—	—	—
Mika Salo	FIN	93	—	—	1	1	7	4	—	—	1	31
Michael Schumacher	D	145	3	44	24	15	6	4	—	32	41	678
Ralf Schumacher	D	66	—	2	7	—	11	3	—	1	—	86
Jarno Trulli	I	63	—	—	1	2	—	5	—	—	—	17
Jos Verstappen	NL	74	—	—	2	1	2	1	—	—	—	16
Jacques Villeneuve	CDN	82	1	11	5	7	6	4	—	13	9	197
Alexander Wurz	D	52	—	—	1	5	3	1	—	1	—	26
Ricardo Zonta	BR	29	—	—	—	—	—	3	—	—	—	3

Note: Drivers beginning the formation lap are deemed to have made a start

UNLAPPED: 2000

Number of cars on same lap as leader

Grand Prix	Starters	at 1/4 distance	at 1/2 distance	at 3/4 distance	at full distance
Australia	22	16	13	9	8
Brazil	20	13	9	5	5
San Marino	22	17	15	4	4
Britain	22	22	10	11	6
Spain	22	19	14	8	6
Europe	21	19	9	5	2
Monaco	22	19	7	5	2
Canada	22	20	18	12	10
France	22	21	12	9	6
Austria	22	14	3	3	3
Germany	22	17	11	NA	6
Hungary	22	20	18	12	11
Belgium	22	13	11	8	6
Italy	22	13	11	8	6
USA	22	20	11	8	6
Japan	22	17	15	12	7
Malaysia	22	17	15	12	7

NA not available

LAP LEADERS: 2000

Grand Prix	Michael Schumacher	Mika Häkkinen	David Coulthard	Rubens Barrichello	Heinz-Harald Frentzen	Total
Australia	33	18	—	—	—	58
Brazil	61	8	1	—	—	71
San Marino	18	44	—	—	—	62
Britain	3	—	21	33	3	60
Spain	38	27	—	—	—	65
Europe	46	20	1	—	—	67
Monaco	55	—	23	—	—	78
Canada	61	—	8	—	—	69
France	38	—	34	—	—	72
Austria	67	4	—	—	—	71
Germany	—	33	2	10	—	45
Hungary	—	76	1	—	—	77
Belgium	23	21	—	—	—	44
Italy	50	3	—	—	—	53
USA	67	—	—	6	—	73
Japan	19	33	1	—	—	53
Malaysia	36	2	15	3	—	56
Total	548	352	107	58	9	1,074
(Per cent)	51.0	32.8	10.0	5.4	0.8	(100)

RETIREMENTS: 2000

Number of cars to have retired

Grand Prix	Starters	at 1/4 distance	at 1/2 distance	at 3/4 distance	at full distance	percentage
Australia	22	4	7	11	12	54.5
Brazil	20	4	7	8	9	45.0
San Marino	22	3	5	6	8	36.4
Britain	22	—	2	4	5	22.7
Spain	22	3	4	5	5	22.7
Europe	21	2	6	8	12	57.1
Monaco	22	6	8	12	13	59.1
Canada	22	3	9	11	9	40.9
France	22	1	3	6	7	31.8
Austria	22	5	7	9	10	45.5
Germany	22	3	7	9	11	50.0
Hungary	22	3	5	6	10	45.5
Belgium	22	6	8	10	10	45.5
Italy	22	8	10	10	5	22.7
USA	22	5	6	8	6	27.3
Japan	22	1	2	4	7	31.8
Malaysia	22	5	6	7	10	45.5

BRUNO SHADES IT
OVER TEN ROUNDS

by Simon Arron

Left: Bruno Junqueira bounced back from the disappointment of missing out on a Formula 1 drive with Williams to claim the F3000 title.

Bottom left and centre: Anglophile Frenchman Nicolas Minassian emphasised his talent during a season-long battle with his Brazilian rival.

Bottom right: Junqueira looks set to follow 1998 F3000 Champion Juan Montoya's career path and chase success in the CART Fedex series.
All photographs: Paul-Henri Cahier

IF the FIA Formula 3000 Championship functioned as its creator had intended, Bruno Junqueira and Nicolas Minassian would have been swamped with offers from grand prix teams by the end of last season.

Between them, the Brazilian and the Frenchman won seven of 10 races in a championship that remains as closely contested as any in the world (and is supposed to be the final port of call for tomorrow's bright-eyed F1 brigade). Their reward? Junqueira, who nicked the title by three points, received offers from three middling F1 teams but Minassian's phone remained strangely silent. Both will consequently race in the United States-based champ car series in 2001. This trend has led people to mutter that F3000 isn't doing its job – that it's a let-down, in short.

But this is a flawed judgment.

F3000 is not failing in its primary role as a finishing school. Rather, it's a victim of circumstance – particularly when the number of available places in Formula 1 remains so regimentally finite. And a move to F1 at any cost is not necessarily a career benefit – just ask 1999 FIA F3000 champion Nick Heidfeld.

Anyone who has worked with the German in the past will tell you he is a very quick and technically gifted driver, yet the world at large knows only of a frustrated young man whose ambitions have been hamstrung by a dog-eared Prost during the past season. His once-glittering reputation has been tarnished and its restoration will be no easy matter.

Junqueira, a calm, bright 24-year-old with a mechanical engineering degree on his CV, has seen the warning signs. Does he do a flit to the States, where logic suggests he will be a front-runner, or sign up for a job in F1's midfield and risk sullying his reputation?

'Racing in F1 has always been my dream,' Junqueira says, 'and that's not something I want to give up. But as the season went on, more and more people kept saying to me, "Look, you might be better off doing something else if there are no decent drives available." The more I thought about it, the more I began to see their point of view.'

The Jenson Button factor has not helped F3000 drivers, of course. Williams's decision to promote the young Englishman directly to F1 from the British F3 series proved to be a spectacularly successful gamble – and has also led gainsayers to question F3000's purpose.

The fact is, however, that some exceptional talents are able to adapt – Alain Prost, Nelson Piquet, Ayrton Senna, Mika Häkkinen and Button are relatively recent examples that spring to mind. Others take time to mature. Would anyone have taken a second look at Juan Pablo Montoya on the basis of his F3 track record? Certainly not. His scintillating F3000 form in 1997 and 1998, however, made him a hot property and, with a champ car title and Indy 500 win subsequently acquired, he is finally to get his F1 break next year with Williams, ironically in Button's old seat.

F1 team managers might be faddish, but the simple truth is that there are no hard, fast rules. Some drivers get lucky breaks, others don't. And while rare as Ferrari winning the World Championship for drivers, aspiring grand prix stars have no option other than to be pragmatists. For Junqueira and Minassian, America is a necessary diversion. And until there are more than just a couple of competitive teams in F1, the driver exodus seems likely to increase.

Junqueira might have raced in F1 this season, of course, had Button not beaten him to the Williams drive for the sake of about one tenth of a second in a pre-season shoot-out.

That might have sapped lesser drivers' morale, but Junqueira has a steely streak that is not always obvious when he's outside the car. Benefiting from continuity in his second season with the Williams-affiliated Petrobras Junior team, he never let this early-season disappointment show.

'He was down for perhaps a couple of days,' team director Paul Jackson says, 'but then we went to do a test and he was saying, "Right. Come on guys, we've got a championship to win. Let's get on with it." He has great mental fortitude and has been an absolute joy to work with.'

The Brazilian's four wins came about through a blend of speed, opportunism, good old-fashioned common sense – and a little luck. In Barcelona he wasn't necessarily the fastest bloke on the track, but he was the most sensible. At the Nürburgring he won despite spinning twice in foul conditions, once while following the Safety Car and once while avoiding someone else's accident. On the second occasion, he looped across the grass and rejoined the circuit facing the right way after unintentionally cutting a corner and gaining a place or two. In Monaco both drivers clashed at the first corner – a gift he accepted gratefully. Champion's luck? Perhaps, but he also drove like a champ, too.

Back row: (from left) Ayari, Mikola, Gollin, Couto, Bourdais, Olivier, van Hooydonk, Alonso, Webber, Bernoldi, Minassian, Junqueira.

Middle row: Wilson, McGarrity, Mauricio, Maslov, Manning, Saelens, Goossens, Montagny, Haberfeld, Davies.

Front row: Kolby, Walfisch, Piccini, Leinders, Scheckter, Enge, Melo.

FORMULA 3000 REVIEW

Above: David Saelens spent his year largely in the shadow of team-mate Minassian.

Left: Although inconsistent in qualifying, Justin Wilson showed his potential in race situations.

Above right: Mark Webber made a successful return to single seaters after his spell with Mercedes in sports cars.

Right: Fabrice Walfisch was lucky to escape injury when he ran into the back of Tomas Enge at the Nürburgring.

All photographs: Paul-Henri Cahier

Far left: The F3000 competitors line up for the end of term photograph at Spa.

Left: Fast mover: Tomas Scheckter impressed with his raw speed after replacing the disappointing Sarrazin.

Below left: Thomas Enge took a memorable win for McLaren at Hockenheim.

Bottom left: Spanish youngster Fernando Alonso was the sensation in his first season. His crushing win at Spa marked him as a man to watch in 2001.

All photographs: Paul-Henri Cahier

His victory in Monte Carlo gave him a 20-point lead over Minassian (who had won the opening race in Imola), although the Frenchman never accepted that the fight was lost. The D2 Super Nova driver proved the point by winning the next two races at Magny-Cours and the A1-Ring, while Junqueira entered a three-race fallow period that allowed the Frenchman to draw level at the top.

At Hockenheim, Minassian failed by 0.19s to score the point that would have given him a slight lead and it came down to what Junqueira described as a 'two-race fight for the championship'.

In Hungary, when it really mattered, Junqueira dug deep, bagged pole position and drove faultlessly to lead all the way despite intense pressure from impressive Spanish teenager Fernando Alonso. Minassian was only fourth – which left him needing victory in the Spa finale to have any chance of the title.

Nicolas, a popular and amusing member of the F3000 community, sustained a nasty, self-inflicted knee injury during the race build-up, when he slipped while cleaning his car and gashed himself with a vacuum nozzle. The wound required several stitches but, limping noticeably, he never complained. Only eighth on the grid, he put in one of the drives of the season to take third place, which left him three points adrift.

Engine problems restricted Junqueira to ninth, but that didn't matter in the circumstances and he became the 16th man to win the title. 'It might not have been a glorious way to win,' Junqueira says, 'but the championship was our reward for what we did in ten races, not just one.'

Minassian was one of the first people to congratulate his title rival. Whichever way the dice had landed, the series was guaranteed a deserving champion.

Find of the season was Alonso, in whom Spain believes it has its first potential F1 champion – so long as they can keep him away from the long-term Minardi contract that has been threatened. In only his second season of car racing, the reigning Formula Nissan champion understandably took time to find his feet with Team Astromega; his speed was obvious, but so was his rawness. His victory in the Spa finale was immaculate; despite having completed only a handful of laps of the track in a touring car beforehand, he dominated with ease.

Mark Webber (European Arrows)

was another major discovery. Having spent much of the previous two seasons not doing very much sports car racing with Mercedes, he relished the return to the cutting edge of top-line single-seater racing and even led the championship briefly after a splendid win in the wet/dry second round of the series at Silverstone.

The only other winner was Czech Tomas Enge, who brought McLaren's mySAP-backed junior team – the reigning champion – a glimmer of relief when he won spectacularly at Hockenheim. Leading the race on wet tyres on a drying track, Enge pitted for slicks, carved his way back through the field, survived a late spin and passed team-mate Tomas Scheckter at the start of the final lap to record a memorable victory.

Scheckter, son of 1979 world champion Jody, was drafted into McLaren to replace Frenchman Stéphane Sarrazin, who was supposed to have been a serious title contender. After a difficult start to the year, however, he spoke out against the team in the French press, hoping that might be a catalyst for change. It was. They sacked him.

On a brighter note for the French, the nation's 1999 F3 champion Sébastien Bourdais (Gauloises Formula) showed flashes of real promise. He qualified on the front row in Monaco and Magny-Cours – and might have won on the streets of the principality if Minassian's fast-but-erratic team-mate David Saelens hadn't bundled him off at the first corner.

His future looks bright, as do those of Englishmen Justin Wilson (Nordic) and Darren Manning (Arden). In his second year at this level, Wilson always raced well but let himself down with inconsistent qualifying performances. His run from 11th to second at the A1-Ring was one of the year's highlights.

Back from a successful sabbatical in Japan, Manning lacked an accomplished team-mate to help him share development work – and that showed. He stays with Arden for a second year in 2001 and will benefit from this year's experience. Both he and Wilson are potential title winners.

The prize for the least productive season goes to Enrique Bernoldi (Red Bull Junior), who might have won at least twice. A puncture cost him the lead in Barcelona and suspension failure pitched him off when he appeared to have the Nürburgring race well in control. A sum total of five championship points does not reflect his consistent speed.

RISING SONS

by Marcus Simmons

Left: After a dominant start, Antonio Pizzonia overcame a mid-year slump to clinch the British F3 Championship in his maiden season.

Below left: Tomas Scheckter's efforts were diluted by his move up to F3000. The young South African now has a testing role with the Jaguar F1 team.

Right: Faces to watch: Brazilian, Antonio Pizzonia, and impressive Japanese hot shot, Takuma Sato.

Far right: French champion Jonathon Cochet took prestigious wins at the Zandvoort Marlboro Masters and Pau.

Photographs: Allsport
Lorenzo Bellanca/LAT Photographic

NO doubt about it, Formula 3 is going through one of its periodic peaks at the moment. The year 2000 saw this talent production line step up another couple of gears, with the British championship reaping probably its best harvest of future stars since the 1990/'91 era.

The funny thing is that opinions are divided on just who is the best prospect out of the three real aces which emerged from the constantly shuffling pack. Was it champion Antonio Pizzonia, runner-up Tomas Scheckter or third man Takuma Sato? Whatever your opinion, there was no question that, with these three all being rookies to the British F3 Championship's top division, this was a vintage year for newcomers.

Pizzonia, as everyone expected, began the season as the man to beat. The Brazilian was with reigning F3 champion team Manor Motorsport, the squad with which he won last year's Formula Renault title. Sure enough, he won the first two races, but surprisingly only three more were to follow. One of these, however, was a sublime performance on the Brands Hatch Grand Prix circuit, as sure an indicator of driving talent as any and on which Pizzonia was utterly dominant.

One reason for the champion's success not being as runaway as anticipated was that Scheckter and Sato each had spells as the men on form – the Japanese, in fact, was almost dominant through the closing few races. Another contributing factor was possibly Pizzonia's Formula 1 test work with Benetton. That went well enough to start with, but by mid-season 'Jungle Boy' – so named because of his Amazonian homeland – was in the middle of an alarming slump in F3 form amid rumours that things were not going well on the F1 front.

Manor worked hard to get his confidence back and Pizzonia duly repaid them with a win at Snetterton, but the form of the early season was still elusive.

Pizzonia, still only 20 years old, is a great talent. He does have a uniquely aggressive driving style, hurling his Dallara-Mugen into fast corners, but Manor managed to find a set-up to suit him before the season started. The team also suffered on the development front in the middle of the year, purely because its lead driver was so heavily involved in his F1 work.

Scheckter, just 10 days younger than Pizzonia, joined the crack Stewart Racing team, which had suffered a drop-off in form during 1999. There was no question that things were much better in 2000, so much so that the South African driver was able to pose a strong early title challenge to his Brazilian rival thanks to two mid-spring wins.

Things went a bit pear-shaped from then on. Having found a decent set-up on its Dallara-Mugens, Scheckter reckoned that the team tried to be a bit clever and ended up going slower. Following in the footsteps of father Jody, who mixed and matched formulae on his way up the racing ladder, Tomas then embarked on an extra-curricular Formula 3000 programme. While admiring his willingness to get stuck into anything, some might say that was counter-productive to the F3 campaign.

From early May onwards, Scheckter qualified on the front row only twice, which makes life rather hard in the difficult-to-overtake F3 category. But he frequently pulled it out of the fire with some blistering race performances.

Sato, a relatively elderly 23, had a sizeable fan club within the F3 paddock by the end of the season. A college cycling champion, this remarkably talented man only started karting in 1996, which makes his racing achievements more impressive still.

He hooked up with the Carlin Motorsport team for 2000, which would be just his second full season in car racing and his first in the U.K. During the early races there were mistakes from both team and driver which, coupled with a dose of good old-fashioned bad luck, conspired against Sato being in the running for the championship.

Even so, his progress was a fascinating aspect of the season. A frequent spinner and occasional heavy crasher in testing, Sato could then translate that into sensational race weekend performances. His pole lap at Spa, by more than 0.8 seconds (that's EIGHT TENTHS!!) was just one of his accomplishments that made you shake your head in sheer 'Did he really do that?' wonder. He took four wins, but it could have been more. At Spa, for instance, his Dallara-Mugen got stuck in third gear on the warm-up lap, but to his credit he rejoined nearly two laps down and drove as hard as he could to the finish.

Sato, a Honda protégé, has a massive future, but for the short-term that remains in F3 as he embarks on a second season in 2001.

There were others to show flashes of promise too, principally Dane Nicolas Kiesa, another F3 rookie who lined up with Italian championship defector RC Motorsport. The reigning British Formula Ford champion took a finely-judged mid-season win at Donington, the team's form improving as it visited circuits for the second time. Unfortunately, results tailed off towards the end of the year, Kiesa and RC not helped by some unreliability from their Opel-Spiess engines. The team had a world exclusive contract to use Spiess's latest powerplant, but might have been better off at times with the tried and trusted older Opel.

The other winner was Ben Collins, Sato's team-mate at Carlin. The Briton, returning for a third season of F3 after a one-year sabbatical in Indy Lights, is as fast as anyone on his day and took an impressive pole on the Brands GP circuit. His win, at Donington, was slightly fortuitous, but on balance well-deserved. Sometimes, however, he struggled to find form – occasionally through over-driving – and was also very unlucky with mechanical problems.

Best of the non-winners was Indian Narain Karthikeyan, who teamed up alongside Scheckter at Stewart. In a complete contrast to 1999, something of a win-or-bust season, the amiable and philosophical Madras ace was a virtual ever-present in the top 10, but never at the front. Ford India-backed Karthikeyan, just wasn't as happy at Stewart as he had been in the more homely Carlin environment in '99, and you often heard different stories from driver and team to explain any lack of pace.

Italian Gianmaria Bruni came to Britain with high hopes after beating Pizzonia to the Formula Renault Eurocup title. Unfortunately, F3 was a bit harder than he thought and he didn't impress for the first half of the season. Mid-year he sorted out his differences with the Fortec Motorsport team and a much happier partnership emerged, Bruni often racing into the top four. British team-mate Michael Bentwood, in his fifth season of F3, reaped the reward of his experience with some strong early showings. Although results faded, it was enough for him to be top home-grown driver in the points.

The Renault UK-backed Promatecme team had a disastrous season. Matt Davies was expected to challenge for the crown, but it was team-mate Andy Priaulx, an ex-powerboating and hillclimb champion, who impressed with some pole in the wet for the finale on the Silverstone GP circuit. Doubts over the Renault engines could never be fully

verified, meaning the team was often shooting in the dark. Similarly, Renault-powered was promising British Gary Paffett, who dominated the 'Class B' Scholarship Class for Fred Goddard Racing with 14 wins from 16 races.

The German championship was wide open, with four men shooting for the title going into the final meeting at Hockenheim. Italian Giorgio Pantano, in his first full season of car racing, was doing a great job to top the points for the KMS Dallara-Opel team, the Swiss squad looking for its first title since Pantano's compatriot Jarno Trulli did the deed in 1996.

Another rookie, André Lotterer, suffered from inconsistency in his Bertram Schafer Racing machine, but along with Pantano seems to be the driver expected to go far within the sport. Comparative veterans Pierre Kaffer (Hoffman Motorsport) and Alex Müller (Team Ghinzani) were the other drivers taking the destiny of the championship down to the wire.

Stefan Mücke, Austrian Patrick Friesacher, Italian Enrico Toccacelo and Japanese Toshihiro Kaneishi also won during a season which witnessed formidable strength in depth among the 30-car grids, all of them contemporary 'Class A' machinery.

French championship winner Jonathan Cochet had a stellar year which also included victories in the Pau Grand Prix and Marlboro Masters at Zandvoort, Europe's premier F3 races. In his third F3 season, Cochet gave the Dallara-Renault-equipped Signature Competition squad its first title and now deserves a Formula 3000 chance.

Portugal's Tiago Monteiro won three on the trot to end the year as the form man, the ASM driver adding a surprise success in the British championship round at Spa. Ryo Fukuda, another Japanese doing well in Europe, rivalled Cochet for much of the season before running out of money.

Ironically, it was a Frenchman who won the Japanese championship, Sébastien Philippe wrapping things up for the Dome Dallara-Mugen team with a round to go and some spare. Austrian Robert Lechner won a couple of times for TOM'S, while Yuji Ide and Seiji Ara were top locals.

In the South American championship, Vitor Meira was all set to wrap up the title for the Amir Nasr Racing team with one round to go at the time of writing. Only fellow Brazilian Joao de Oliveira offered a significant challenge.

AUDI, AUDI, AUDI!

by *Gary Watkins*

Left: Gold on silver at Le Mans for Audi as the German marque swept to a dominant 1-2-3 finish. Here, the R8 prototype of Kristensen, Biela and Pirro heads towards victory.
ker Robertson/Allsport

Bottom left: Allan McNish shields his eyes from the low sun in the second place Audi R8. The Scot (*bottom right*) has been the outstanding driver of the American Le Mans Series.

Bottom centre: Stéphane Ortelli and Laurent Aiello (*in car*) shared the driving duties with McNish at Le Mans.
Photographs: Peter J. Fox and Bryn Williams

RARELY does the Le Mans 24 Hours throw up a performance as dominant as this. Porsche's factory squad maintained a stranglehold on the 1982 event, while 10 years later Peugeot matched its clean sweep of the top three positions. This time it was Audi's turn to stamp its mark on sports car racing's blue riband by monopolising the podium. The German manufacturer's trio of works-run R8 prototypes were in a class of their own in 2000. Quite simply, the opposition didn't even get close.

But the question remains: was there any real opposition? Bar the works Panoz squad, the answer was in the negative. The American operation looked the only team capable of taking the fight to Audi, and promptly shot itself in the foot by putting 60-year-old racing legend Mario Andretti in its number one entry. Cadillac's much-hyped return to Le Mans was little short of an embarrassment, while Chrysler's move up to the prototype class was very much a toe-in-the-water affair. That was it as far as true factory participation went in the top LMP900 division.

Audi had it easy, there's no doubting that. But equally beyond doubt was the strength of the marque's second assault on the great race. An all-new chassis was designed to replace the previous year's slow but steady R8R. Audi's definitive Le Mans contender proved it was already the fastest sports car in the world when it finished 1-2 in the American Le Mans Series opener at Sebring in March and the car was subsequently honed into an ultra-reliable contender in the run-up to June's 24 Hours. It's almost certainly no exaggeration to say that the R8s competed more miles of endurance testing than the rest of the field put together.

Little was left to chance on the driver front, either. When Tom Kristensen and Allan McNish, Le Mans winners in 1997 and 1998 respectively, came on the market they were snapped up by Audi. And the whole campaign was masterminded by Reinhold Joest, a man who has probably forgotten more about winning Le Mans than most rival team bosses are ever likely to know.

There were hiccoughs along the way, as with any Le Mans assault. Two of the Audis lost time when they underwent pit stops to change the gearbox and rear suspension. The whole assembly was replaced on the two cars in six and eight minutes following their respective transmission and suspension problems, but that was enough to ensure the one undelayed R8 ran out the winner.

The victory laurels went to Kristensen, Frank Biela and Emanuele Pirro. McNish claimed pole position and led together with Laurent Aiello and Stéphane Ortelli until their unscheduled stop as night turned to day on Saturday evening. From then on boreto, Rinaldo Capello and Christian Abt needed their new rear end on Sunday morning, and that was that. McNish led the charge after the Kristensen car, but despite denials from Audi, team orders were clearly invoked in the final hours.

This strategy ensured that McNish was an unrepresentative full lap behind Pirro at the finish, with the third car a further nine laps down after experiencing further problems. The fourth-placed entry was more than 20 laps behind the winner, which proved there was no one able to exploit the chinks in the German squad's armour.

The lead Panoz mixed it with the Audis early on, and lead driver David Brabham even topped the order for a while. But the ageing front-engined design wasn't quite fleet enough to keep up, particularly when Andretti was driving. A gearbox change, an oil leak and then a late-race puncture that put Andretti into the barriers ruled out a decent finish, although two more Panoz made it home fifth and sixth.

Fourth place should have gone to Cadillac, not to the American factory team but the semi-works DAMS squad. The slick French operation avoided the transmission problems that blighted the works cars, only to lose the honour of calling itself 'best of the rest' a couple of hours from the end with suspension failure.

That left the team run by four-time Le Mans winner Henri Pescarolo to follow the Audis home. The French legend was making his seventeenth appearance in the race, but he showed he knows how to get a car to the end. His Courage-Peugeot was hardly quick, but it barely missed a beat in the hands of Emmanuel Clerico, Olivier Grouillard and Sébastien Bourdais.

Honours in the GTS class went to the ORECA Chrysler squad for the third year in succession despite the arrival of opposition in the form of works-backed Chevrolet Corvettes. Dick Barbour, a renowned sports car driver and entrant in the 1970s, reformed his team and won the 'baby' or GT class with his solo Porsche 911 GT3-R. The car was subsequently disqualified for a technical infringement, handing victory to the Japanese Taisan squad's similar car.

The majority of the top cars at Le Mans also compete in the ALMS with various degrees of frequency, where they were joined by the 1999 Le Mans-winning BMW squad. The Schnitzer-run Bimmer V12 LMRs won twice early on in the season when Audi reverted to the year-old R8R. But after Joest wheeled the pukka R8 back out, the opposition barely got a look in.

Panoz won in dire conditions at the Nürburgring, one of the two European rounds, but after that, McNish and ALMS team-mate Capello were the dominant force. Five wins from seven starts over the second half of the season enabled Formula 1-bound McNish to wrap up the title before the finale on the old Australian Grand Prix circuit in Adelaide at the end of December.

The ALMS was the definitive article in 2000, its sophomore season. It emerged as a true successor to the long-dead final incarnation of the World Sportscar Championship: the series took place on three continents; its three classes battled it out in each of its three categories; and it attracted the best sports car drivers in the world.

It wasn't all good news for the ALMS, though. A new domestic championship was set up by the organisers of the NASCAR Winston Cup, the France family. Grand American Road Racing, or Grand-Am, may have been only a qualified success, but it undoubtedly deprived its rival of entries.

The stalwart Dyson squad was the class act in Grand-Am, though poor reliability meant the prototype drivers' title remained open to the season finale. The team's number one driver, James Weaver, eventually notched up a hat trick of Stateside sports car titles having previously won the lower-level United States Road Racing Championship in 1998-'99.

Grand-Am was closely aligned with another series at odds with the ALMS. The European-based SportsRacing World Cup continued its slow but steady growth, a stated aim of its organisers. Grids in the prototype-only series were up, and so too was the quality of both the teams and drivers.

Perhaps the major disappointment for the World Cup organisers was the French JMB team won the championship for a third-successive year, scooping the honours in the team's David Terrien and Christian Pescatori Ferrari 333SP. There was no doubting, though, that JMB deserved its success, certainly the best driver pairing in the series, while the team was definitely the most proficient out there.

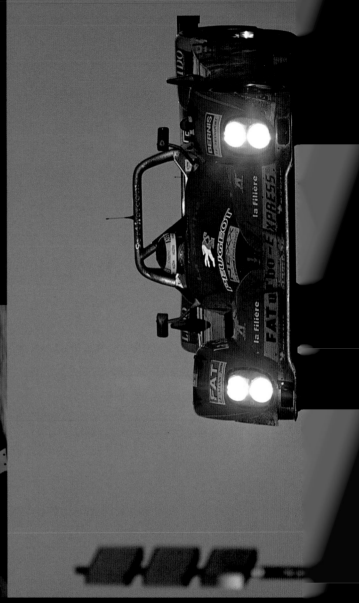

GT RACING REVIEW

Above: The BMW prototype of Jean-Marc Gounon holds a brief lead from the Panoz and Audi challengers at the start of the ALMS round at the Nürburgring.
Bryn Williams/Words & Pictures

Right: Is the message on the BMW aimed at its GT competitors?
Bryn Williams/Words & Pictures

Centre right: Dawn breaks over the Dunlop Bridge at Le Mans 2000.
Mike Hewitt/Allsport

Right: The Bourdais/Clerico/Grouillard Courage entered by Henri Pescarolo upheld French honour at Le Mans with a fine fourth place behind the Audis.
Mike Hewitt/Allsport

Top far right: The Panoz cars ran gamely throughout the ALMS season but were no match for the Audis.
Ker Robertson/Allsport

Far right: Olivier Beretta steps into the cockpit of the Chrysler Viper which he, Karl Wendlinger and Dominique Dupuy took to a GTS class win at Le Mans.
Bryn Williams/Words & Pictures

The success of the SRWC was acknowledged by the sport's governing body as the end of the season and renamed – for the second time in three years – the FIA Sports Car Championship. That put it on equal footing with the FIA GT Championship, which endured another rebuilding year in 2000.

The full-house GT1 cars disappeared at the end of 1998 and for the 2000 season so did the last of the manufacturer-backed factory teams. Far from ringing the death knell for the series, the latter sparked something of a resurgence. An influx of privateer teams and the addition of a secondary class, N-GT, for GT3-type cars ensured that grids were healthy in terms of quantity if not quality.

The drawback was that the series became the domain of the wealthy amateur, with only a handful of cars driven by two professionals. That meant it was no surprise that the British Lister team scooped drivers' honours with former grand prix racer Julian Bailey and Jamie Campbell-Walter. Lister's Jaguar-engined Storm was the fastest car in the field and the two Britons easily the best driver pairing. Only bad luck, combined with a system of success ballast, prevented Bailey and Campbell-Walter from wrapping up the title long before the final round.

Lister vowed that it would be back to defend its title, almost certainly against stronger opposition, in 2001.

The World Cup, too, looked set to continue its growth into the new season, though there was much speculation as to the future of sports car racing in Europe as 2000 drew to a close.

The man behind the ALMS, Don Panoz, confirmed that he would go ahead with plans for a stand-alone European Le Mans Series. Five races were announced in September, with two 'enduros' in the States and the Australian ALMS seasonal finale in Adelaide also counting. The future of an increasingly-crowded sports car scene remained unclear in the run-up to Christmas. As to whether Europe could support the ELMS, the rebadged World Cup and the FIA GT series, there was no answer.

Top left: Don Panoz, mastermind of the American Le Mans Series, proposed a stand-alone European Le Mans Series.
Ker Robertson/Allsport

Above: The Jamie Campbell-Walter/Julian Bailey Lister Storm was the class of the field in the FIA GT Championship.
Dave Cundy/Graphic Images (UK) Ltd

Below: The ORECA Chrysler Viper proved to be the fastest of the GTS-class machines once again.
Bryn Williams/Words & Pictures

BOOM AND BUST . . .

by Charles Bradley

AFTER a decade of boom, the touring car world entered the 21st Century treading a rocky road. Manufacturers no longer flocked around the flame of T.V.-friendly wheel-to-wheel action of the showroom-based machinery, which epitomised the 'win on Sunday, sell on Monday' motto more than any other racing category.

Now that once-thriving world is in crisis, thanks to the demise of its backbone: Super Touring. The two-litre formula, pioneered in Britain and replicated across Europe, the Far East, South America and Australia, is almost dead. Killed by spiralling costs and the need for cutting edge engineering skills, championships have struggled to stay afloat with all sorts of new regulations and variations on a theme.

Britain has new technical rules next year for smaller cars such as Ford's Focus, Peugeot's 307 and Vauxhall's Astra Coupe, as opposed to the 'repmobiles' that have been the staple diet of years past. It also has new promoters in the shape of British Motorsport Promoters, an amalgamation of the country's circuit owners which gazumped (and then purchased) Alan Gow's TOCA organisation for the rights to the BTCC for the next five years.

Currently, only Vauxhall and Peugeot have committed to the new-look regulations, and BMP will again run a Super Production (Group N) Class B element to bolster grids in 2001. That was one of the success stories of this season, as the much slower production saloon-style cars formed a mobile chicane for the rapid Super Tourers to negotiate.

Even the ice-cool Alain Menu

tripped over them on occasion, but that didn't stop him notching up his second BTCC title. The 33-year-old Swiss gave Ford its first drivers' championship victory since 1990, which spearheaded a clean sweep of the silverware as it picked up the manufacturers' and teams' crowns too. To rub salt into the opposition's wounds, Menu even won the Michelin Pit Stop Challenge for the quickest tyre changes over the entire season!

Ford's opposition was Honda and Vauxhall, who both fell short of matching the Prodrive-built and run machines. But that didn't make life easy for Menu, who acknowledged he had the two toughest team-mates of his entire career in the shape of 1998 champion Rickard Rydell and '98 runner-up Anthony Reid.

The season culminated in a downto-the-wire finale on a sultry Saturday evening at Silverstone. Title outsider Rydell won the Sprint race, giving him an unlikely shot at the crown after both Menu and Reid had crashed, but a water leak on the grid for the final round of the year cruelly ended his challenge. It summed up his season where: 'I had the pace, but not the luck.'

Menu was assured of the title when Reid, who unlike the Swiss was carrying a full 40-kilo quota of 'success ballast, was harpooned out of the race by Vincent Radermecker's Vauxhall with just a handful of laps remaining. Alain was noticeably more emotional than after his 1997 success with Williams-Renault but he, like Rydell and Reid, are now in the unenviable situation of not knowing what they're going to be racing next year. As soon

as it had wrapped up the manufacturers' title, the Blue Oval announced it was turning its back on the category, following the lead of previous champions Nissan, Volvo and Renault.

Vauxhall pushed Ford the hardest in the early part of the season, but fell away as the Vectra's engine just couldn't compete. Its lack of ability to generate heat in its tyres was a massive drawback, especially in one-lap qualifying, so it often had to come from behind. Its highlight should have been Thruxton in May, where the abrasive nature of the high-speed corners masked its failings. But there it scored a massive P.R. own goal by ordering Feature race leader Jason Plato to move aside for team leader Yvan Muller, and received a slating in the press for its tactics.

Muller and Plato finished the year fourth and fifth, just eight points apart, which proved the equality of their abilities behind the wheel. Next year they could be the only superstar players in the series – so expect another battle royal, hopefully without team orders.

Honda managed, once again, to shoot itself in the foot. It lined up a quality attack in the shape of Le Mans winner Tom Kristensen, former champ Gabriele Tarquini and James Thompson, the latter long overdue a BTCC title. The cars were run by West Surrey Racing (Kristensen and Thompson) and JAS Engineering (Tarquini), and built by Foss-Tech in York.

So far, so good. But somewhere along the line, various parties fell out. This lack of cohesion was further damaged when Thompson crashed violently in the season opener and missed the

next two race weekends while nursing injuries which had flared up from his 1995 testing crash at Knockhill.

It took until round eight at Knockhill for Tarquini to win, and victories trickled along until an end-of-season torrent that came far too late. Kristensen's crushingly dominant double at Silverstone was hardly noticed with all eyes focused on the title drama going on behind.

Super Touring will live on for a year at least, however, thanks to the enthusiasm for the formula of the Italians and the Swedes. After a merger with the German championship fell apart pre-season, Italy's teams clubbed together and made the brave decision to attempt to run a European series. Despite the added overheads of extra travel, the European Super Touring Cup proved to be the success story of the year, attracting extensive T.V. coverage from Eurosport and FIA backing for 2001.

Reigning Italian champion Fabrizio Giovanardi won the title, his Nordauto Engineering-run Alfa Romeo 156 outpointing the '99-spec, JAS-run Honda Accord of Holland's Peter Kox after a close, season-long battle which ended at the finale at Cerklje airfield in Slovenia. A first corner collision there helped Giovanardi to the crown, and left runner-up Kox in a huff.

The series also attracted drivers of the calibre of Gianni Morbidelli, Emanuele Naspetti (both BMWs) and Nicola Larini (Alfa). Even multiple touring car champion Johnny Cecotto was tempted out of retirement to contest the Vallelunga rounds, while a plethora of Audi A4 Quattros also helped boost the field.

In Sweden, which has become the retirement home for many BTCC race cars in recent years, it was fitting that former BTCC Independents' Cup champion Tommy Rustad took the title in last year's British series-winning Nissan Primera, run by Crawford Racing. It took until the final round for Tommy to see off the challenge of Fredrik Ekblom's Audi A4 Quattro, run by former European Rallycross star Tommy Kristoffersson, and even then he only just pipped him by eight points.

Mattias Ekström was also in the title hunt until the end of the season in his ex-Rickard Rydell Volvo S40, while Jens Edman marked himself out as a potential star of the future by finishing fourth, bagging a hat trick of race wins along the way, in an ancient Ford Mondeo.

Further afield, the South American Super Touring Championship was a shadow of its former self and run solely in Argentina. As we closed for press it was being led by 'Concho' Lopez in an Alfa Romeo 156, who had finished every race on the podium but was yet to win a race, ahead of former EuroBrun F1 driver Oscar Larrauri, who had won three races in his Alfa.

The South African Bankfin touring car series was again run to Super Production regs and, for the fourth time, was won by the Nissan Primera of Giniel de Villiers, despite a strong challenge in the second half of the year by the works Opel Vectra of Shaun Watson-Smith. The opposition struggled to keep up with the pace-setters. Audi suffered a lack of power from its A4's engine, while BMW's new-shape 318i was quick in qualifying

but was unable to challenge consistently for wins.

The TOCA-run Australian series switched its calendar from the winter to the summer, so it started in May, took a mid-season break and doesn't finish until February, 2001. Three-time champion Paul Morris had won all six races to date in his BMW and lay 60 points ahead of the Ford Mondeo of Alan Gurr.

Nearly all of these championships now face a lack of manufacturer interest and a dearth of nearly-new touring car hardware. Negotiations are on-going for many, including the promising European series, to adopt the new BTCC rules in future, a decision on which the future of this branch of the sport could rest.

While Britain has gone down the 'smaller cars, less power' route in its quest for cost cutting, Germany has taken another approach. The DTM series was resurrected this year, and rose like a phoenix from the flames.

Its 460 bhp, V8-powered monsters are costly to build, but the machines are then placed under strictly controlled regulations which reduce running costs to a bare minimum. For instance, the next two races from the back of the grid – as a result, only two engine problems were recorded all season and mechanical reliability was remarkably high.

Mercedes and Opel were the catalysts behind the rebirth and, just as in DTM and ITC years past, battled out the title with its lead drivers Bernd Schneider and Manuel Reuter respectively. They each ran eight cars with tin-top stars Joachim Winkelhock,

Above: Gabriele Tarquini returned to the BTCC with the JAS-run Honda Accord.
Graphic Images (UK) Ltd/Dave Cundy

Above left: The Ford driver triumvirate of Rickard Rydell, Anthony Reid and Alain Menu dominated the BTCC championship.
Malcom Griffiths/LAT Photographic

Far left: Alain Menu led a Ford clean sweep in BTCC with the Prodrive-prepared Mondeo.
John Overton

Left: Yvan Muller battled hard for Vauxhall.
Jeff Bloxham/LAT Photographic

Uwe Alzen and Klaus Ludwig being joined by a plethora of young guns such as Darren Turner, Thomas Jäger and Timo Scheider.

Audi also got involved via support for privateers Abt Sportsline, which enlisted BTCC Honda Accord builders Foss-Tech to produce a quartet of four TT-Rs in just 100 days. Its driving staff included reigning BTCC champ Laurent Aiello, former German STW Cup winner Christian Abt and James Thompson, but they struggled until late in the season to match the works cars, mainly due to a hurriedly-prepared aerodynamic package that just didn't produce enough downforce.

The DTM witnessed another case of history repeating as Schneider, the last man to win it in 1995, did so again. Despite his Mercedes lacking straight-line speed compared to the rival Opel V8 Coupes, although the Abt Audis were the swiftest on the straights thanks to their lack of downforce, Schneider scored over half a dozen wins for the AMG squad.

Reuter, the 1996 ITC champion, was the best of the rest for Opel, while 50-year-old Ludwig showed age is no barrier in touring cars, the triple Le Mans 24 Hours winner taking third in the series and a brace of wins at Sachsenring. Speaking of age, the most impressive junior drivers were Marcel Fässler from Switzerland and Scotland's Peter Dumbreck, the latter bouncing back from his horrific back-flip at Le Mans in 1999 to consistently finish in the top six.

Other race wins fell the way of Winkelhock, who won at the Norisring but also blotted his copybook by starting a

ten-car pile-up at Oschersleben, and Alzen, who won the restarted race after his colleague had taken out half of the opposition.

The DTM needs at least another manufacturer, however, to be called a true success story, but is a brave initiative that deserves to succeed. After the demise of its previous incarnation, due to the mega-bucks it took to contest, the DTM simply can't afford to fail again.

Also going down the V8-powered muscle car route was Octagon Motorsport, a division of marketing giant the Interpublic Group. It announced a new category for 2001 called Superstars, boasting an impressive pan-European calendar visiting some of the continent's finest race tracks and heralding itself as a four-wheel version of the highly successful World Superbike Championship.

Despite endorsement from Damon Hill, huge interest from teams and positive noises from Volvo for one, the ambitious series was postponed until 2002 due to a lack of manufacturer commitment.

The touring car waters have become so muddied that manufacturers simply don't have the faith to leap in at present. The European Commission's investigation into car pricing, the amalgamation of many marques, the likes of BMW, Toyota and Honda, not to mention the bewildering choice of rules and regulations, is enough to put anyone off.

The harsh reality is that the touring car world has to face up to the likelihood that only the strongest championships will survive.

WARS OF ATTRITION

AMERICAN RACING REVIEW

by Gordon Kirby

Left: Crowds may have dwindled somewhat in NASCAR, but a full house is still guaranteed at the Daytona 500.
Robert Laberge/Allsport USA

Below: Juan Montoya conquered the Indy 500 and humiliated his IRL competitors into the bargain.
Jon Ferrey/Allsport USA

Below: CART provided thrilling racing, none better than at the Michigan 500.

Bottom: Team owner Bobby Rahal took temporary charge of CART before moving to F1 with Jaguar.
Both photographs: Robert Laberge/Allsport USA

THE first year of the new millennium was a very sobering one for American motor racing. After years of dizzy, immensely profitable growth, NASCAR suddenly faced a dramatic decline in crowds and popularity, presenting a whole host of new, unexpected problems. Also, for the first time in six years, a driver was killed at a NASCAR race. In fact, three NASCAR drivers – Kenny Irwin, Adam Petty and Tony Roper – were killed in 2000, triggering a searching look for safety with both the cars and the tracks.

NASCAR's problems came rapidly, almost unexpectedly, at the same time that Bill France Jr., boss of American stock car racing since 1972, found himself in a serious battle with cancer. France's father Bill Sr. founded NASCAR in 1949 and he and his son built it step by step into America's most business-like and formidable sanctioning body. But NASCAR's third generation leader Brian France has stepped into a very different world.

During last year in particular, attendance figures began to fall at many tracks. T.V. ratings have also declined and everything is being wagered to turn things around on a new $400-million contract with NBC, a network with little experience covering motor racing.

The fact is that NASCAR is feeling the effects of too much growth. Too many tracks have been built with many more seats than most can fill. Steady increases in ticket prices have also driven away fans and because the France family's publicly-traded company ISC owns the majority of the tracks, the future looks challenging to say the least.

There's little question that NASCAR's upmarket push has failed, and that traditional NASCAR fans who used to attend eight or ten races each year, now go to only two or three. The NASCAR press has been full for years with complaints from fans about greed in the pricing of tickets, hotels and collectibles, and those warnings appear to have come home to roost.

Meanwhile, on the champ car racing scene, it became abundantly clear early in the year that new leadership was required in CART. The effects of the five-year-old split between CART and Indianapolis boss Tony George continue to weaken the sport and the split has turned into a war of attrition.

George's low-cost Indy Racing League (IRL) has not taken off and is no match for CART, but the split has seriously eroded the overall interest in open-wheeled racing in the States. All of CART's street or temporary circuit races and most road races remain very

healthy, but few oval races – CART or IRL – are attracting many fans.

Against this backdrop CART chairman Andrew Craig, who left the position in June, was replaced on an interim basis by the retired driver and team owner Bobby Rahal, who dealt with plenty of issues during his short tenure, quickly working out the 2001 calendar and settling on the engine rules for 2001 and 2002, as well as initiating new television contract talks.

In the meantime, the search began for a full-time C.E.O. with Long Beach promoter Chris Pook quickly emerging as the front runner. The team owners' decision on who would run their business in 2001 and beyond was due in mid-November, just days after the AUTOCOURSE copy deadline.

Penske bounces back

Meanwhile, CART's championship went down to the wire, to the final lap of the last race for the second year in a row. For most of the season it was anybody's championship. Not one driver was able to win more than three of 20 races or put together a string of wins, or even podium finishes. Of the record-setting 11 race winners, Paul Tracy was the only driver to win two in a row.

Momentum, as Ron Dennis would describe it, or any kind of F1-style domination, was entirely unknown. With five drivers and four teams still mathematically capable of winning the championship going into the final race, nobody could deny that this year's champ car title battle was anything but diabolically competitive.

Gil de Ferran finally eked-out the championship with just two wins, two seconds and three third places. In his first year with Roger Penske's thoroughly revamped team, the 32-year-old de Ferran didn't take the title lead until Laguna Seca in September, where he finished second to young teammate Helio Castroneves. Through the last four races de Ferran stayed ahead of the opposition with just a pair of third places and pole positions.

He won the title by finishing third in the season's last race, a nail-biting California 500 that took two days to run. De Ferran crossed the line two places ahead of Adrian Fernandez, his only remaining rival, who kept himself in the title hunt by finishing in the points, usually around sixth or seventh, in all but three races.

The rule of thumb in CART is that fifth place in every race will win the championship but de Ferran was more than 30 points off that pace and over

Far left: Gil de Ferran took the CART crown in a battle which ran for the whole of the 20-race series.
Robert Laberge/Allsport USA

Left: Back on top. Roger Penske revamped his team and ended a three-year barren spell in sensational fashion.
Al Bello/Allsport USA

Bottom far left: Helio Castroneves won three races for Marlboro Team Penske and the Brazilian looks every inch a future champion.
Jon Ferrey/Allsport USA

Bottom left: Life begins at 40. Roberto Moreno's first full-time ride with a top team brought third place in the final standings and the year's most popular victory at Cleveland.
Robert Laberge/Allsport USA

Below left: Adrian Fernandez may not have been one of the fastest drivers in CART, but his tactical approach paid dividends, taking him to the brink of the title.
Robert Laberge/Allsport USA

100 points shy of Alex Zanardi's record-setting 1998 season. In fact, this year's champion accumulated fewer points per race than any driver in CART's 22-year history.

It has to be said that de Ferran showed his mettle and speed by taking five poles during the year, second only to the mercurial 1999 champion Juan Montoya who finished fewer than half the races in 2000. Montoya took seven poles but de Ferran was there on the front row ten times and was right there with Montoya on pure speed.

Penske's team had suffered a tough time in recent years, of course. Totally dominant in 1994 with 12 wins, the team went three years from May 1997 to May 2000, without winning a race. After de Ferran finally posted that long-sought after 100th win for the team at Nazareth at the end of May, there were four more wins, another by de Ferran and three for Castroneves, and finally a tenth title for the team, its eighth in CART added to the two in USAC back in 1977 and '78.

Penske's tenth championship represented one of the greatest turnarounds in the sport's history. A year ago Penske was at its nadir as Al Unser Jr. sadly left the team. They then made the tough decision to change drivers, chassis and engines for 2000. Unser's contract wasn't renewed and the two Brazilian drivers were hired. Penske had originally signed Greg Moore as de Ferran's team-mate, but Moore's tragic death at Fontana in 1999 opened the door to the brilliantly talented Castroneves.

Penske also made the very deep decisions to turn his back on his own cars in favour of Reynards, and to renounce Mercedes-Benz engines for Hondas. These were tough calls indeed, for Penske Cars in Dorset had produced beautiful and more-often-than-not successful cars for more than 20 years, while back in 1984 Roger was a co-founder of Ilmor Engineering, builders of Mercedes' F1 and CART engines, and a business partner of DaimlerChrysler in the manufacture of diesel engines and car retailing.

Finally, Goodyear's withdrawal from CART at the end of 1999 meant Penske changed tyre brands as well, ending another long-standing, decades' old relationship. With a totally new package and a new team boss in Tim Cindric, hired from Rahal, the team has rebounded in style.

Cindric stepped quickly and comfortably into the new pair of shoes provided by Penske, running the team with utter efficiency in company with old hands Clive Howell and Tom Wurtz. And Penske Cars contributed a constant stream of aerodynamic and chassis development components to ensure that the team fielded cars that were very different from a standard Reynard.

After two years with Jim Hall's team and three more with Derrick Walker, de Ferran showed himself as a very adept and mature team leader for Penske. Gil has an engineer's analytical mind and an amusing personality which he used to immediately fuse together the re-mixed team. Team-mate Castroneves is extremely fast, one of the brightest new talents around, and proved himself an excellent team-mate as he scored the first win of his career at Detroit in June and added two more wins before summer's end.

It's interesting that the leading protagonists in this year's champ car war of attrition were the Penske and Patrick teams. Roger Penske and Pat Patrick were CART's co-founders, of course, and their teams are the most experienced in the business with roots stretching back to the 1960s.

Penske and Patrick are old friends and business partners, as well as genial competitors. Patrick has invested in the Penske corporation on a number of occasions and the pair of Michigan businessmen combined their resources to create CART in 1979. Yet retirement is the last thing on their minds.

Patrick's team has won 43 races over the years, as well as two championships, the last with Emerson Fittipaldi 11 years ago. Unlike Penske, in recent years the Patrick organisation has enjoyed an almost unchanged package of drivers, chassis, engines and tyres. Roberto Moreno this year replaced P.J. Jones and Jan Magnussen who shared Patrick's second car last year, but the Reynard-Ford-Firestone combination remained unchanged. So too has the team itself, a largely long-standing group of steady Eddies, led by veteran manager Jim McGee.

Fernandez joined Patrick in 1998 and won two races in each of the last three years. The 35-year-old Mexican won this year in Brazil and Australia, beating team-mate Moreno to second in the championship. Both drivers profited from their individual abilities to get excellent fuel mileage and from consequently keen pit strategy orchestrated by McGee.

Fernandez rarely qualified well, never better than third, and usually around 12th, but moved up doggedly in the races. Moreno wasn't much better in qualifying, although he took his first pole of his champ car career at

Far left: Paul Tracy matured enormously and took three victories for Team KOOL Green.
Robert Laberge/Allsport USA

Bottom far left: Always a racer, Michael Andretti has lost none of his speed, but typically still suffered from bad luck in his final season with Newman-Haas.
Jon Ferrey/Allsport USA

Left: Too many retirements meant Juan Montoya was unable to hold onto his crown, but he was still regarded as the fastest man in the series.
Jon Ferrey/Allsport USA

Below left: Kenny Bräck, Paul Tracy and Adrian Fernandez on the podium at Road America. The competitiveness and unpredictability of the series is one of its many attractions.
Robert Laberge/Allsport USA

Below centre left: Cristiano da Matta took a win for PPI Motorsports and has won a ride with Newman-Haas in 2001.
Jon Ferrey/Allsport USA

Bottom centre left: Kenny Bräck was top rookie and finished the series in a highly creditable fourth overall.
Jon Ferrey/Allsport USA

Cleveland in July and duly scored a dominant first victory the following day. Never spectacular, the sleuth-like Patrick team finished the year second and third in the championship, the best team result so far.

As stable as Patrick's team has been, some big changes are taking place for next season. Fernandez has departed to form his own team in partnership with Ganassi's long-time general manager Tom Anderson and Honda. His replacement is not yet known, although Oriol Servia is believed to have the job. Also, Toyota will replace Ford as Patrick's powerplant in 2001, ending a six-year partnership.

Seven teams won races in 2000. Penske was the strongest with five wins followed by Chip Ganassi's squad with four (three for Montoya, one for Jimmy Vasser). Three teams scored three wins apiece – Green (all by Tracy), Patrick (two for Fernandez, one for Moreno) and Newman-Haas (two for Michael Andretti, one for Christian Fittipaldi); Bobby Rahal's team won the season-opener with Max Papis, but never again, while Cal Wells's PPI team scored its only champ car win with Cristiano da Matta at Chicago in July.

After winning four consecutive titles from 1996–99 with Reynard-Hondas, Ganassi switched both chassis and engines to Lola-Toyotas in 2000. The move could by no means be called a failure, because '99 champion Montoya scored Toyota's first champ car victory at Milwaukee in June and went on to win two more races and lead more laps by far than any other driver. Vasser also won a race late in the year at Houston, but made the podium in only three other races.

Montoya finished only eight races and wound up ninth in the championship while Vasser finished sixth in the points. The hyper-talented Montoya now moves on to F1 with BMW Williams while Vasser also departs Ganassi's team after six years to join Mo Nunn's operation where he will be teamed with Tony Kanaan and again enjoy Honda engines. Filling their places will be F3000 stars Bruno Junqueira and Nicolas Minassian, Ganassi's first all-foreign driver pairing.

Barry Green's team won the 1995 title with Jacques Villeneuve and finished a close second with Dario Franchitti last year. Franchitti was a favourite for this year's championship but a pre-season testing accident put him out of action and side-tracked his programme.

It wasn't long before Dario was back to full strength, finishing second in Japan in May and qualifying on the front row at Milwaukee and Detroit. He was on pole at Elkhart Lake and again the following week in Vancouver, where he had his best chance all year only to stall in the pits and finish second to team-mate Paul Tracy. A miserable year finished with four DNFs in a row and a lowly 13th in the points.

Tracy had a much better year, winning three races and keeping his championship hopes alive into the season finale. Tracy led the championship from Long Beach in April through to Detroit in June, and after a mid-season slump, was back to second in the points after round 18 in Houston. He didn't finish at either Surfers Paradise or the California 500, however, falling to fifth in the points.

Michael Andretti was another pre-season championship favourite with one of Newman-Haas's Lola-Fords, but he all-too-typically ran into problem after problem. He won in Japan in May, in Toronto two months later and led the championship for five races in July and August. In the last seven races, however, Andretti scored just a single point and faded to eighth in the final rankings.

In August, Andretti went contract-shopping, deciding to leave Newman-Haas for an expanded three-car Team Green operation in 2001 with Tracy and Franchitti. Michael has spent ten of the last 12 years with Newman-Haas and his departure ends the Andretti family's 18-year relationship which extends back to its foundation in 1983 with father Mario driving.

Team-mate Christian Fittipaldi had even worse luck, although he frequently battled with Andretti and had a better qualifying record in 2000. Luck finally turned Christian's way in the final race of the year when his car ran faultlessly all the way and he scored his second win of the season, his first in a 500-miler. But it wasn't enough to push him into the points-scorers' top ten.

The other team to lead the championship was Bobby Rahal's squad of Reynard-Fords, with Max Papis and Kenny Bräck driving. Papis won the season-opener, but had little else to show for his efforts. Team-mate Bräck, on the other hand, enjoyed an excellent rookie year. The 1998 IRL champion and '99 Indy 500 winner easily took CART's rookie of the year award, finishing fourth in the championship. Although failing to win a race, Bräck threatened on a couple of occasions and made the podium four times.

The only other team to win a race was Cal Wells's PPI operation which ran two Reynard-Toyotas for da Matta

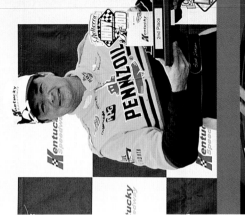

Below far right: **Bobby Labonte was the dominant force in the Joe Gibbs Pontiac.**
Robert Laberge/Allsport USA

Bottom right: **The once-dominant Jeff Gordon found victories hard to find.**
Jon Ferrey/Allsport USA

Bottom centre right: **Veteran Ricky Rudd successfully teamed up with Robert Yates Racing to race the Ford Taurus.**
Robert Laberge/Allsport USA

Bottom far right: **Jeff Burton was consistently competitive in Jack Roush's five-car Ford Team.**
Jamie Squire/Allsport USA

Right: **Scott Goodyear, Buddy Lazier and Sarah Fisher on the podium at Sparta, Kentucky.**
Jon Ferrey/Allsport USA

Far right: **Goodyear leads Lazier at Pike's Peak Raceway. The veteran was edged out by Lazier in the final IRL standings.**
Craig Jones/Allsport USA

Below right: **Al Unser Jr. was the IRL'S big-name attraction, but was only able to garner a single victory.**
Darrell Ingham/Allsport USA

---

and Servia. Da Matta was very competitive in many races and scored his first champ car victory at Chicago, beating Michael Andretti. Wells's team has quit CART for NASCAR and da Matta jumps to Newman-Haas next year in place of Andretti.

CART's manufacturers' championship was won by Ford/Cosworth for the first time since 1995, beating Honda 335 points to 313. Toyota was another 38 points back in third. Honda won eight races, Ford/Cosworth seven and Toyota five. Mercedes-Benz had a dismal final year in CART; its engines were uncompetitive and often spectacularly unreliable, scratching out just one podium finish all year, a second place by Mauricio Gugelmin at Nazareth in May.

CART's constructors' title was won for the sixth straight year by Reynard, supplier to 11 of the 17 champ car teams. Reynards won 13 races in 2000, Lolas took the other seven. Lola rebounded this year with Newman-Haas switching back its loyalty after three years using Swifts, while Ganassi also joined the Lola camp. Swift's fortunes plummeted, running a lone car for Tarso Marques with Dale Coyne's team.

The 2001 season? De Ferran, Castroneves and Penske will be very strong as everybody else copes with some type of change in drivers, chassis, engines or personnel. No question, Penske is back.

Dixon and Rice are young champions

CART has owned and operated both the Indy Lights and Toyota/Atlantic series for the last two years as the champ car owners have made a deliberate attempt to properly promote and market the two series. This year's Lights champion was 20-year-old Kiwi Scott Dixon who beat American up-and-comers Townsend Bell and Casey Mears to the title. The Atlantic series was won by Buddy Rice who defeated promising young Brit Daniel Wheldon.

Dixon won six of 12 Lights races and showed tremendous speed and aggression. Born in Australia and raised in New Zealand, Dixon won the Formula Holden championship in 1998 before moving to the States to race Indy Lights in '99, taking over the luckless Mark Blundell's seat.

Rice, 23, wrapped up the Toyota/Atlantic championship with one race remaining after winning five of the year's 12 rounds. Wheldon won two races as did Canadian Andrew Bordin who finished third in the championship. Rice is likely to race in F3000 in 2001, driving for David Sears's Super Nova team, while Wheldon moves up to Indy Lights.

Lazier is IRL champion

Buddy Lazier won the nine-race IRL championship. Lazier, 33, is the IRL's most experienced driver, having started all but one IRL race since the series' inception in 1995. He has driven for Ron Hemelgarn's team during this time, winning the '96 Indy 500 and three other races, one in 1997 and two this year. Before moving to the IRL Lazier ran 50 CART races between 1990–'95, his best result being seventh in the '92 Michigan 500.

Nevertheless, Buddy has become one of the IRL's top drivers, and carried the organisation's flag better than anyone else at Indianapolis where Juan Montoya and Chip Ganassi's team invaded mightily, blowing the IRL regulars into the weeds.

Lazier was the only IRL man able to give chase to Montoya in the closing laps of the once-great 500, but there was nothing he could do as Juan hustled his way through some lapped cars much more quickly and decisively. Lazier complained after the race that the slower IRL drivers had done nothing to help him or delay Montoya, suggesting he could have caught and challenged the CART champion had he enjoyed an open track unencumbered by lapped cars.

In the IRL championship, Lazier outpointed three other former CART drivers – Scott Goodyear, Eddie Cheever and Eliseo Salazar. The championship went down to the last race where Lazier finished fourth behind Goodyear, Cheever and Billy Boat. Lazier won two races, the only man to win more than once. Others to win IRL races were Montoya, Goodyear, Cheever, Al Unser Jr., '99 champion Greg Ray, Robbie Buhl and Scott Sharp.

1999 champion Ray had a miserable year, losing his ride at the end of the year with John Menard's team, the largest and wealthiest in the IRL. Ray beat Montoya to pole at Indianapolis and led the opening laps, but Montoya destroyed him in the pits and in traffic, and Ray crashed twice trying to keep up.

After six years with Penske and 17 years in CART, Al Unser Jr. found work in the IRL with Rick Galles's team. Unser drove for Galles for eight years back in his CART heyday and was able to win one IRL race with Galles and finish ninth in the championship.

An impressive IRL rookie was 19-year-old Sara Fisher, the fastest woman to appear in many years. Fisher graduated to the IRL with Derrick Walker's team from USAC sprint cars and ran the whole season. Her best finish was third in Kentucky in September where she led nine laps. Fisher continues with Walker's IRL team in 2001.

Labonte's first NASCAR title

Bobby Labonte won NASCAR's Winston Cup title in a doddle, leading the championship for most of the year and pulling steadily away from the rest in the second half of the year. At 36, in his eighth year in the Winston Cup, Labonte took his first title and the first also for retired NFL coach Joe Gibbs's team. Labonte joined Gibbs in 1995 and started winning races right away, steadily moving up the points standings each year. He finished second to Dale Jarrett in the '99 championship, winning five races, and took command of the 2000 points battle fairly early in the year.

Labonte may not have been the most dominant Winston Cup driver of the year, but he was certainly the most consistent, which is what NASCAR's championship is all about. With three races still to go at the AUTOCOURSE deadline, Labonte had won four of the 31 races, finishing in the top five in another 11 and in the top ten in five more. He had also finished every race, completing no less than 99.9 per cent of the year's total laps by the end of the 31st race – not bad in a series that comprises a grand total of 10,158 laps!

Joe Gibbs's team was definitely the most successful of the year with Labonte's team-mate Tony Stewart winning a series-high five of the first 31 races. Labonte and Stewart drove Pontiacs, the champion's turned out in the green and black of Interstate Batteries, while Stewart's was in the orange and white of Home Depot. Former IRL champion Stewart was nothing like as consistent or reliable as his team-mate and was sixth in the points as we closed for press.

Nor is Stewart anything like as popular with the fans as new champion Labonte. In fact, Stewart has become NASCAR's newest bad boy as he earned the fans' wrath on more than a few occasions with petulant, spoiled-boy behaviour – not the way to gain fans among the good ol' boys and gals. Stewart is also a Mid-Westerner from USAC's sprint and midget ranks

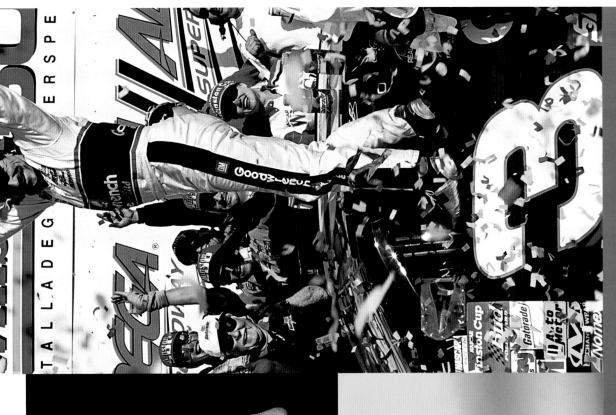

Right: Nearly 50 but still a winner. Dale Earnhardt celebrates at Talladega.

Below: Dale Jarrett fought hard but in vain to retain his NASCAR crown.

Bottom: A big future looks assured for rookie Matt Kenseth.

All photographs: Jon Ferrey/Allsport USA

and has cast himself, whether he likes it or not, as NASCAR's latest unwelcome outsider.

Labonte, on the other hand, is the younger brother of 1984 and '96 champion Terry, one of the most down-home, fan-friendly drivers in the business. The Labontes are from the Gulf coast of Texas and are a laid-back, taciturn lot who know how to deliver on the race track.

The last man standing in the championship battle against Labonte was no less a character than Dale Earnhardt, Chevrolet's biggest star. The 49-year-old seven-times champion won his last title in 1994 and has had a tough time in recent years, surviving a couple of big crashes, some broken bones, and orthopaedic surgery at the end of 1999. Earnhardt rebounded in 2000, hanging in the points race all year and winning two races. Both his wins in the past year and his three victories in 1999 were in 'restrictor plate' events on the super-speedways at Daytona and Tal-

ladega, where horsepower is drastically reduced and it's all about slipstreaming and manoeuvring sharply in close packs of cars. Nevertheless, it was pretty impressive for Earnhardt to finish second in the championship in his 21st full Winston Cup season.

One of the most consistently competitive NASCAR drivers in 2000 was Jeff Burton who dogged Earnhardt's tracks in the championship and won three races. Burton is part of Jack Roush's massive five-car Ford team which included Mark Martin, another regular front runner who was eighth in the points after 31 races.

Champion in 1999 with Robert Yates's Ford team, Dale Jarrett was unable to repeat his achievement, although he did win the season-opening Daytona 500. Jarrett was fourth in the 2000 championship and new team-mate Ricky Rudd, who joined Yates for his own cars, was in fifth at the time of writing.

Fastest man of the year was Rusty Wallace who led many more laps than anyone else and took eight poles with Penske Racing South's Ford, but all too often ran into trouble. Wallace won four races, but never featured in the championship battle. Team-mate Jeremy Mayfield was equally fast, but even less lucky, and also found himself at the centre of an illegal fuel controversy which resulted in the resignation from the team of Penske's partner Michael Kranefuss.

Then there was triple champion Jeff Gordon who has gone off the boil in recent years. After winning no fewer than 33 races between 1990 and '98, Gordon won seven races in '99 and only three in 2000. He was sixth in the '99 championship and in eighth after 31 races. Many critics say the reason for his fading form was the departure of crew chief Ray Evernham at the end of '99 for Dodge's new NASCAR programme which debuts in 2001.

NASCAR's rookie of the year was

Matt Kenseth, a 28-year-old from Wisconsin who scored his first Winston Cup victory at Charlotte in May and beat the highly touted Dale Earnhardt Jr. for the rookie trophy. Kenseth had finished third in the 1999 Busch Grand National championship, NASCAR's second-level series, and moved up to the top league with Jack Roush's Ford team. Earnhardt Jr. won the '99 BGN title and made his move into the Winston Cup in a Chevrolet run by his father's burgeoning team.

Finally, coming to the end of a remarkable career in 2000 was 53-year-old Darrell Waltrip who retired at the end of the season, his 28th in the Winston Cup. Waltrip won three championships in 1982, '83 and '84 and a total of 84 races during his career. He scored his last win in 1992 and hung in there in recent years, filling out the field as he struggled with the question of retirement. Affable and extremely popular, Waltrip looks likely to take up a second career as a T.V. broadcaster.

TEAM KOOL GREEN
FIGHTS THE HARD FIGHT

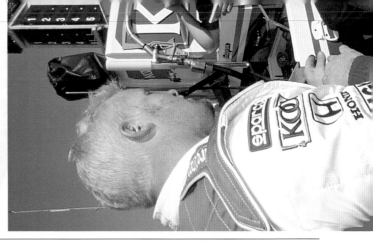

I is the mark of true champions to persevere in the face of adversity. Every effort must overcome obstacles en route to the ultimate goal, but only the very best do so with the same determination and focus put forth during the best of times. And then come away stronger for the effort. Everyone at Team KOOL Green would agree they faced some adversity during the 2000 season.

Following a stellar 1999 season that saw Dario Franchitti and Paul Tracy combine for five wins, including three dominating 1-2 victories, and finishes of second and third respectively in the championship standings, the TKG driving duo were poised to make another serious run at the drivers' title.

While a lot of teams made driver, chassis and/or engine changes, TKG was set to run the same drivers with the same engine/chassis package (Honda-Reynard) for a third-consecutive year. And it bolstered its already strong technical package with a comprehensive wind-tunnel program overseen by Tino Belli, the team's talented aerodynamicist. The work in the wind tunnel was combined with an extensive track-testing program headed-up by team managers Tony Cotman (Tracy) and Kyle Moyer (Franchitti), and conducted by a top-flight staff of engineers led by Scott Graves.

Franchitti had taken some much-needed time off following the 1999 season, while Tracy handled the bulk of the initial off-season testing and development of the team's new 2000 Honda-Reynards. The plan was for Tracy to do the majority of the track testing leading up to

CART's Spring Training test days in early February, then have Franchitti take over the brunt of the task leading up to the season opener in March.

However, on February 10th, in the closing moments of the two-day Spring Training test, Franchitti's car suffered a mechanical failure in the right rear suspension and he hit the Homestead Speedway wall, causing several injuries including a broken pelvis.

As a result, when the team returned to Homestead for the season opener on March 26 — Tracy was just six weeks later — Tracy was in high gear while Dario was just happy to be starting the race. Franchitti, who had embarked on a rigorous rehabilitation program, overcame the obvious pain for a respectable 11th-place finish.

Tracy put on one of his now legendary charges through the field to move from 17th on the grid to the lead, eventually finishing third. Tracy's dramatic run earned the Budweiser Hard Charger Award for making the biggest improvement from start to finish. "We had the chance to win this thing," Tracy said afterward. "But I'm really happy to get third when we had a 10th-place car."

Franchitti said he didn't suffer any substantial pain but admitted "It was a pretty long day out there. I felt fine, except for a small bump when they dropped the car off the airjacks and it bottomed out pretty hard. I leaned heavily on the area of my injury and I felt it."

In front of more than 100,000 people in Long Beach, Tracy continued what became his trademark for the 2000 season, as he tenaciously fought his way from another 17th-place starting

position to win the 16th race of his career and take the lead in the championship. It was the first time since going into the Molson Indy Toronto in 1997 that Tracy had led the drivers' standings.

Tracy went on to score his third-consecutive podium with a third-place finish in Brazil, and with a sixth-place finish in Japan two weeks later, he built himself a 14-point lead in the championship.

Franchitti was still feeling the effects of his injury and lack of off-season seat testing time. Following a DNF at Long Beach and an 11th in Brazil, he appeared poised to turn his season around in Japan. Taking a page from team-mate Tracy, he qualified 17th then proceeded to work his way through the field for a solid second-place finish, his first podium of the year.

After a string of races that saw Tracy score only 11 points in six events, he returned to form with another brilliant drive through the field, this time in front of his hometown fans at the Molson Indy Toronto. Starting 12th, Tracy carved his way through the field for a rewarding third-place finish. He followed it up a week later with the pole — and a new track record — at Michigan Speedway, then a run to seventh in the 500-mile race.

Franchitti also had a good run at Michigan, as he started fourth and finished third — his best qualifying and race result ever on a superspeedway.

Road America looked promising for Franchitti when he scored his first pole of the year, but a mechanical failure ended his day and it was Tracy who claimed the win with another brilliant come-from-the-back charge

"When I was coming up the hill

SEASON 2000 WITH TEAM KOOL GREEN

Paul Tracy (*right*) took three victories, and remained a title contender right to the last round of the gruelling 20-race series.

Dario Franchitti (*bottom*) overcame a serious injury in pre-season testing to bounce back to his best form by mid-season. The Scottish driver will be looking forward to better luck in 2001.

to take the green flag, the car just died," recalls Paul. "I radioed the team and they told me to reset the electronics and that did the trick. After that I just put my head down, got into the 'zone' and drove."

Two weeks later it was all TKG on the streets of Vancouver, as Franchitti earned his second-consecutive pole, with team-mate Tracy starting alongside. Franchitti led easily for much of the race, before Tracy's pit crew got him out ahead of Dario on the final stop. Tracy went on to lead the TKG duo home to their fourth 1-2 finish in the last two seasons and become the first back-to-back winner of the season in CART.

Franchitti's second-place finish in Vancouver, combined with his third-place result the next week at Laguna Seca, moved him up to eighth place in the standings with four races to go.

The results were hard to come by for Tracy towards the end of the season, but 11th at Laguna Seca and a strong fourth-place finish in Houston kept him in the championship hunt.

Though his title hopes remained alive until the season finale at California Speedway, a mechanical failure early in the 500-mile race ended Tracy's day and championship dreams. He finished the season with three wins (tied for most in series), one pole and fifth place in the driver standings.

Franchitti also suffered an early mechanical problem in the season finale, capping what he termed a "character-building" season. Franchitti's 2000 season, highlighted by two poles and four podiums, netted him 13th place in the drivers' championship.

TIME OUT

ONE might be inclined to assume that after the rigors and intensity of a day of competition on the race track, professional race drivers would be looking for more sedate ways to spend their spare time.

Not a chance. When Paul Tracy isn't driving the Team KOOL Green Champ car, you're apt to find him on the open road, at the controls of one of his custom-built Harley-Davidson motorcycles that are his pride and joy or working on and racing one of his Paul Tracy Karts. Or, depending on the season, he might be making waves in his powerboat, taming the moguls on a ski slope, or joining friends in tackling mountain-bike trails.

Among Paul's custom-built motorcycles is a recent addition from the famed technicians at Ron Simms Bay Area Custom Cycles in Oakland, California. The bike has been described as "one man-sized hunk of American iron," with a massive frame and huge 131 ci engine that give the bike a commanding presence on the roadway. When Paul isn't 'cruisin' with his magnificent machines, he might be found at motorcycle events such as Bike Week at Daytona Beach or the annual Harley rally in Sturgis, South Dakota, indulging in his passion.

"When you drive race cars for a living you tend to look at street vehicles for their visual appeal," Tracy said. His current "head turner" is one of the new Honda S2000 sports cars. "It's a little two-seat convertible that I can run around town in doing errands and still have some fun. It's a new model so there aren't a lot of them on the road and people are always trying to figure out what it is. They're quite impressed when they realize it's a Honda. It's not your typical Honda."

Tracy can't drive his Team KOOL Green Honda-Reynard on the highways, and he's limited to the amount of people and packages he can carry in his Honda S2000 convertible, so even he has a practical car. "When I need a bigger car for taking friends out to dinner or whatever, I've got an Acura RL. It's a nice four-door sedan that can carry up to six people in comfort."

When Tracy needs to carry an even bigger load he takes his Chevrolet Crew Cab Dually out of the garage. "I own and sponsor a kart racing team and I use the Dually to tow a trailer with karts and equipment to the track. I also use it to tow my boat to the lake."

Franchitti's life away from racing is more sedate — but not much. His personal vehicles include a Ferrari F40, Acura RL and Ducati 916 Senna motorcycle.

Of course, team-mate Tracy shares his optimism.

"We had a very good season, but we just fell a little short of our goal of winning the championship in both 1999 and 2000," Tracy said. "Everyone at Team KOOL Green knows we're capable of taking it all, so we've set that as our goal again for 2001 — and this time we don't intend to be denied. Our strategy is simple: work hard in the off-season, take the season one race at a time, try to score maximum points at each event, and don't let up until the championship is ours."

With such a strong team pulling together in a bid to achieve that elusive championship, there's little doubt that at the end of the 2001 season the green and white Team KOOL Green cars will continue to be among the leaders in the ultra-competitive FedEx CART Championship Series.

"As much as I enjoy racing, I try to keep a balance in my life by having some interests away from the track," Franchitti said. "Of course, I spend a lot of time training in the gym, but I also like to mix in some fun stuff like soccer and water skiing."

Besides his intense physical regimen, Franchitti's time away from the track also includes working on his golf game, riding his mountain bike and hanging out with friends.

But it's racing that is his passion and his profession, and he intends to be on form in 2001.

"This is the second year in a row that Team KOOL Green went to the last race at Fontana with a chance to win the championship, and I think that's a credit to the entire organization," Franchitti said.

"From a personal standpoint, the 2000 season was a big contrast to last year, when we were in the hunt right to the end. It's been frustrating, but I've also learned a lot about myself. I have no doubt that I'm going to come back strong next season."

12 SECONDS OF TEAMWORK CAN WIN

It's been called the "the most dangerous 12 seconds in sports". It has become consistently the most frenetic "break" in motorsports action.

Four wheels must be changed, a tank must be filled with 35 gallons of fuel and wings may need adjustments. More and more, as cars are designed and manufactured with equal skill and the drivers are among the finest tuned athletes existing, time in the pit can determine the eventual race winner.

Here are some things you need to know about pit stops:

- Stops are scheduled on the minimum consumption rate of 1.85 mile per gallon from a 35-gallon tank

- A 200-mile race will require two, sometimes three stops

- A 500-mile race will require at least 5 stops

- Only six crew members can go "over the wall"

- Two crewmen re-fuel the car... The fueler attaches the three-inch diameter main fuel hose so the 35-gallon on-board fuel cell can be filled by gravity flow, taking 10 seconds. The vent man connects both the fuel vent hose and the air jack hose, which raises the car off the ground.

- Four members then change the tires (which weigh about 35 lbs each) in about 6 seconds and then make any wing changes requested by the driver

- The entire stop for a full load of methanol can be done in 10 to 12 seconds

TIME LINE DURING A FULL FUEL LOAD

Minus one lap: Signal to driver for next pit stop and crew moves into position

Driver enters pit lane : Maximum Speed of 50 mph

PIT BOX

-30 seconds:	Six crewmen are over the wall and are ready
0.0 seconds:	Car stops in pit box
0.5 seconds:	Fuel and vent hoses are connected and the car is raised
1.0 seconds:	Air guns are in place on all four wheel nuts
2.0 seconds:	Wheels are off the car
3.5 seconds:	Driver resets his fuel meter
5.0 seconds:	New tires are on
6.0 seconds:	Car drops
6.5 seconds:	Crewmen on the front tires may do a wing adjustment
10.0-12.0 seconds:	The car is fully serviced and driver takes off

Illustrations & desktop editing:
© Alain Boisjoly 2000

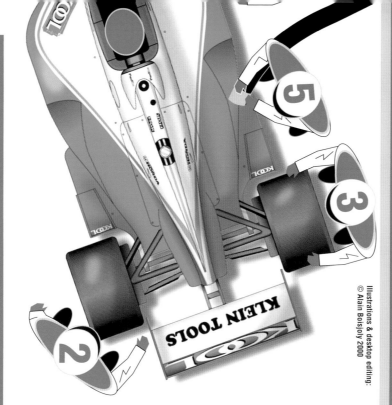

RACING INTANGIBLES

MUCH of the success of Team KOOL Green can be attributed to the quality of the individual team members, and particularly the job they do on pit stops during the races.

For the second year in a row, the crew of Paul Tracy's #26 Team KOOL Green Honda-Reynard, led by crew chief Tony Cotman, won the prestigious $50,000 Craftsman Pit Crew Challenge. The team kept their unbeaten streak alive by defeating four other crews that had earned the right to compete in a final pit stop competition at the last race of the season.

"Pit stops are a huge element of race strategy and I know that the guys on this team take great pride in being able to help Paul in a race. And I think the drivers respect us and appreciate what we do for the team," said Cotman.

"We sure do," Tracy agrees. "The difference between a great pit stop and an average one might be just a second or less but that can translate into several spots on the track.

"On the other hand, poor pit stops can prevent a driver from winning a race. Dario and I, as drivers, have to have complete trust and confidence in our pit crews. It's like football or baseball, you can have the greatest quarterback or pitcher in the game, but if you don't have the team members to catch the ball or hit it, you won't win consistently."

Franchitti concurs. "Pit stops are so critical to our overall success that we have a special pit stop pad set up in the race shop where the guys can practice. They take it very seriously and it shows."

But even the best team in the business is only part of the mix for success.

Tracy and Franchitti know it's crucial to follow a personalized fitness routine to be competitive in the CART FedEx Championship Series, and physicians will back them up. Studies show that race drivers regularly sustain heart rates of about 175 beats per minute during a race. This kind of stamina and strength places them in the high-performance athlete category, along with marathon runners.

"Driving a race car is the toughest thing I can think of," Franchitti said. "I've biked in the mountains for four to five hours and it doesn't even come close to the physical exertion from driving."

Considering drivers face more G-force loads in one lap than astronauts do during the launch of the space shuttle, it's little wonder they need to be in top physical condition. Add in cockpit temperatures that can soar over 130°F during a two-hour race, and drivers must deal with mental fatigue as well as physical, so it's little wonder that Franchitti has sometimes lost almost 10 pounds during a race.

Tracy and Franchitti don't slow down when they get out of the car. While both drivers spend time in the gym doing both cardiovascular and strength training, they prefer to get their exercise by faster means. Tracy snowboards, plays volleyball, and bikes (dirt and mountain) in the hills surrounding his Las Vegas home. Franchitti goes running, skiing, mountain biking and gets in the odd game of soccer with pals like Max Papis at the track.

#26 Paul Tracy's pit crew

1 – Outside Front: Tony Cotman
2 – Outside Rear: Chuck Miller
3 – Inside Rear: Steve Price
4 – Inside Front: Leonard Gauci
5 – Fueler: Eric Haverson
6 – Vent/Jack: Jeff Stafford

Pit Strategy: Barry Green
Engineer: Tony Cicale
Pit-to-car Radio: Barry Green

#27 Dario Franchitti's pit crew

1 – Outside Front: Kyle Moyer
2 – Outside Rear: John Cummiskey
3 – Inside Rear: Kris Badger
4 – Inside Front: Alex Herring
5 – Fueler: Keith Badger
6 – Vent/Jack: Jack Christiansen

Pit Strategy: Scott Graves
Engineer: Tino Belli / Steve Challis
Pit-to-car Radio: Kim Green

WHAT'S YOUR PLEASURE?...

Specifics

	2000 Civic Coupe Si	2000 Team KOOL Green Honda/Reynard
Sticker Price	$17,545.00 (msrp)	$600,000.00 (approx.)
Engine	DOHC, 16-Valve, In-Line 4, VTECTM, Aluminum-Alloy	Turbocharged, Aluminum Alloy Block V-8
0 – 60 mph in....	7.4 seconds	2.2 seconds
Horsepower @ rpm	160 @ 7600	800 @ 14,000
Gas Mileage	31 miles per gallon	1.85 miles per gallon
Fuel Capacity (gal.)	11.9	35
Standard Transmission	Manual	6 Speed Sequential
Curb Weight (Manual, lbs.)	2612	1550
Length (in.)	175.1	199
Width (in.)	67.1	78.5
Height (in.)	54.1	36
Alloy Wheels	15" Alloy Wheels	15" BBS Forged Magnesium
Tires	All Season 195/55R15	Firestone Firehawk slicks
Warranty	36 mos. / 36000 miles	You break it, you buy it!!!
5-Year Maintenance/ Repair Costs	$3,239	Unlimited....
Trunk Space (Manufacturer, cu. ft.)	11.9	Trunk? That's where the engine goes!
Seating	5	1...at a time

Special Features

	2000 Civic Coupe Si	2000 Team KOOL Green Honda/Reynard
Airbags	Standard	Nope. Cushioned padding does the trick.
Air Conditioning	Standard	Driver flips their visor up to cool down
Tachometer	Standard	Standard
Power Windows	Standard	No roof, no windows.
Power Locks	Standard	Just try to steal it!
Tilt Steering	Standard	Removable steering wheel
Front Bucket Seat(s)	Standard	Contoured to driver's body
AM/FM / CD Player	AM/FM Stereo with CD Player and 6 speakers and clock	Two-way radio
Beverage Holder	Standard	On-board water bottle
Pit Stop	3 - 4 hours	Less than 15 seconds

2000 Civic Coupe Si: A scorching 160-horsepower, all-aluminum dual overhead camshaft and 1.6 liter VTEC™ engine.
Five-speed transmission, 4-wheel double wishbone suspension, HV shock absorbers, front and rear stabilizer bars,
P195/55/R15 tires on 15-in alloy wheel and 4-wheel disc brakes.

TEAM KOOL GREEN

OTHER MAJOR RESULTS

Compiled by David Hayhoe

International Formula 3000 Championship

All cars are Lola B99/50-Zytek V8.

FIA INTERNATIONAL FORMULA 3000 CHAMPIONSHIP, Autodromo Enzo e Dino Ferrari, Imola, Italy, 8 April. Round 1. 42 laps of the 3.065-mile/ 4.933-km circuit, 128.592 miles/206.949 km.
1 Nicolas Minassian, F, 1h 11m 06.160s, 108.513 mph/ 174.634 km/h.
2 Bruno Junqueira, BR, 1h 11m 08.404s; **3** Mark Webber, AUS, 1h 11m 08.838s; **4** Jaime Melo Jr., BR, 1h 11m 11.038s; **5** Tomas Enge, CZ, 1h 11m 12.004s; **6** Fabrizio Gollin, I, 1h 11m 22.271s; **7** Stéphane Sarrazin, F, 1h 11m 23.031s; **8** Justin Wilson, GB, 1h 11m 25.388s; **9** Fernando Alonso, E, 1h 11m 30.212s; **10** Mario Haberfeld, BR, 1h 11m 40.624s; **11** Kristian Kolby, DK, 1h 11m 43.039s; **12** Darren Manning, GB, 1h 11m 46.426s; **13** Jeffrey van Hooydonk, B, 1h 11m 50.220s; **14** Soheil Ayari, F, 1h 11m 53.910; **15** Kevin McGarrity, GB, 1h 12m 01.341s; **16** Bas Leinders, B, 1h 12m 11.004s; **17** André Couto, P, 29 laps (DNF - accident); **18** Andrea Piccini, I, 28 (DNF - oil pressure); **19** Christijan Albers, NL, 24 (DNF - accident); **20** Sébastien Bourdais, F, 22 (DNF - accident); **21** David Saelens, B, 23 (DNF - accident); **22** Ananda Mikola, RI, 15 (DNF - accident); **23** Ricardo Mauricio, BR, 7 (DNF - accident); **24** Fabrice Walfisch, F, 5 (DNF - accident); **25** Enrique Bernoldi, I, 3 (DNF - gearbox); **26** Franck Montagny, F, 0 (DNF - gearbox).
Fastest race lap: Sarrazin, 1m 40.429s, 109.877 mph/ 176.829 km/h.
Fastest qualifying lap: Junqueira, 1m 38.038s, 112.556 mph/181.142 km/h.
Did not qualify: Hidetoshi Mitsusada, J; Yves Olivier, B; Viktor Maslov, RUS; Andreas Scheld, D.
Championship points: 1 Minassian, 10; **2** Junqueira, 6; **3** Webber, 4; **4** Melo Jr., 3; **5** Enge, 2; **6** Gollin, 1.

AUTOSPORT INTERNATIONAL TROPHY, Silverstone Grand Prix Circuit, Towcester, Northamptonshire, Great Britain, 22 April. Round 2. 40 laps of the 3.194-mile/5.141-km circuit, 127.714 miles/205.536 km.
1 Mark Webber, AUS, 1h 22m 24.239s, 92.991 mph/149.654 km/h.
2 Darren Manning, GB, 1h 22m 25.187s; **3** Justin Wilson, GB, 1h 22m 29.219s; **4** Enrique Bernoldi, I, 1h 22m 36.090s; **5** Bruno Junqueira, BR, 1h 22m 40.736s; **6** Soheil Ayari, F, 1h 22, 54.966s; **7** Franck Montagny, F, 1h 22m 59.199s; **8** David Saelens, B, 1h 23m 02.119s; **9** Jeffrey van Hooydonk, B, 1h 23m 06.619s; **10** Sébastien Bourdais, F, 1h 23m 07.648s; **11** Nicolas Minassian,F, 1h 23m 17.353s; **12** Kristian Kolby, DK, 1h 23m 24.810s; **13** Tomas Enge, CZ, 1h 23m 53.022s; **14** André Couto, P, 1h 24m 06.783s; **15** Ananda Mikola, RI, 1h 24m 07.218s; **16** Jaime Melo Jr., BR, 1h 24m 09.591s; **17** Mario Haberfeld, BR, 1h 24m 16.631s; **18** Kevin McGarrity, GB, 39 laps (DNF - battery); **19** Stéphane Sarrazin, F, 39; **20** Yves Olivier, B, 39; **21** Ricardo Mauricio, BR, 35 (DNF - accident); **22** Bas Leinders, B, 34 (DNF - accident); **23** Andreas Scheld, D, 33 (DNF - accident); **24** Christijan Albers, NL, 22 (DNF - accident); **25** Viktor Maslov, RUS, 20 (DNF - accident); **26** Fabrice Walfisch, F, 1 (DNF - accident).
Fastest race lap: Sarrazin, 1m 54.304s, 100.610 mph/ 161.916 km/h.
Fastest qualifying lap: Manning, 1m 56.776s, 98.480 mph/ 158.488 km/h.
Did not qualify: Fabrizio Gollin, I; Hidetoshi Mitsusada, J; Andrea Piccini, I.
Excluded: Fernando Alonso, E (engine bolt studs outside permitted measurement)
Championship points: 1 Webber, 14; **2** Minassian, 10; **3** Junqueira, 8; **4** Manning, 6; **5** Wilson, 4; **6=** Bernoldi, 3; **6=** Melo Jr., 3.

FIA INTERNATIONAL FORMULA 3000 CHAMPIONSHIP, Circuit de Catalunya, Montmeló, Barcelona, Spain, 6 May. Round 3. 44 laps of the 2.939-mile/4.730-km circuit, 129.241 miles/207.993 km.
1 Bruno Junqueira, BR, 1h 11m 52.068s, 107.899 mph/ 173.646 km/h.
2 Nicolas Minassian,F, 1h 11m 55.632s; **3** David Saelens, B, 1h 12m 02.847s; **4** Jeffrey van Hooydonk, B, 1h 12m 04.400s; **5** Justin Wilson, GB, 1h 12m 05.920s; **6** Franck Montagny, F, 1h 12m 07.756s; **7** Darren Manning, GB, 1h 12m 10.359s; **8** Sébastien Bourdais, F, 1h 12m 11.305s; **9** Stéphane Sarrazin, F, 1h 12m 11.995s; **10** André Couto, P, 1h 12m 24.623s; **11** Andrea Piccini, I, 1h 12m 29.332s; **12** Christijan Albers, NL, 1h 12m 29.809s; **13** Bas Leinders, B, 1h 12m 30.149s; **14** Jaime Melo Jr., BR, 1h 12m 30.885s; **15** Fernando Alonso, E, 1h 12m 36.436s; **16** Yves Olivier, B, 1h 13m 03.339s; **17** Fabrizio Gollin, I, 1h 13m 04.022s; **18** Viktor Maslov, RUS, 1h 13m 06.214s; **19** Ananda Mikola, RI, 43 laps; **20** Mark Webber, AUS, 39 (DNF - fuel pressure); **21** Ricardo Mauricio, BR, 33 (DNF - accident damage); **22** Enrique Bernoldi, I, 33 (DNF - accident damage); **23** Tomas Enge, CZ, 22 (DNF - spin); **24** Kristian Kolby, DK, 10 (DNF - accident damage); **25** Soheil Ayari, F, 2 (DNF - accident); **26** Kevin McGarrity, GB, 2 (DNF - accident damage).
Fastest race lap: Webber, 1m 36.740s, 109.373 mph/ 176.018 km/h.
Fastest qualifying lap: Bernoldi, 1m 33.280s, 113.430 mph/ 182.547 km/h.
Did not start: Mario Haberfeld, BR (accident in qualifying).
Did not qualify: Andreas Scheld, D; Hidetoshi Mitsusada, J; Fabrice Walfisch, F.
Championship points: 1 Junqueira, 18; **2** Minassian, 16; **3** Webber, 14; **4** Manning, 6; **5** Wilson, 6; **6** Saelens, 4.

FIA INTERNATIONAL FORMULA 3000 CHAMPIONSHIP, Nürburgring, Nürburg/Eifel, Germany, 20 May. Round 4. 45 laps of the 2.831-mile/4.556-km circuit, 127.383 miles/ 205.003 km.
1 Bruno Junqueira, BR, 1h 24m 07.832s, 90.847 mph/ 146.204 km/h.
2 Fabrizio Gollin, I, 1h 24m 18.714s; **3** André Couto, P, 1h 25m 06.370s; **4** Sébastien Bourdais, F, 1h 25m 06.952s; **5** Stéphane Sarrazin, F, 1h 25m 36.257s; **6** Jaime Melo Jr., BR, 44 laps; **7** Yves Olivier, B, 44; **8** Jamie Davies, GB, 44; **9** Andrea Piccini, I, 40; **10** Christijan Albers, NL, 29 (DNF - spin); **11** Tomas Enge, CZ, 22 (DNF - accident); **12** Fabrice Walfisch, F, 22 (DNF - accident); **13** Darren Manning, GB, 22 (DNF - spin); **14** Justin Wilson, GB, 17 (DNF - accident); **15** Franck Montagny, F, 17 (SNF - accident); **16** Enrique Bernoldi, I, 13 (DNF - suspension/accident); **17** Bas Leinders, B, 9 (DNF - spin); **18** Nicolas Minassian, F, 9 (DNF - spin); **19** David Saelens, B, 0 (DNF - accident); **20** Soheil Ayari, F, 0 (DNF - accident); **21** Kevin McGarrity, GB, 0 (DNF - accident); **22** Ricardo Mauricio, BR, 0 (DNF - accident); **23** Mark Webber, AUS, 0 (DNF - accident); **24** Fernando Alonso, E, 0 (DNF - accident); **25** Jeffrey van Hooydonk, B, 0 (DNF - accident).
Andreas Scheld, D, finished 2nd in 1h 24m 12.629s, but was disqualified due to an illegal front wing.
Fastest race lap: Junqueira, 1m 32.151s, 110.595 mph/ 177.986 km/h.
Fastest qualifying lap: Saelens, 1m 30.043s, 113.185 mph/ 182.153 km/h.
Did not qualify: Kristian Kolby, DK; Ananda Mikola, RI; Marc Hynes, GB; Viktor Maslov, RUS.
Championship points: 1 Junqueira, 28; **2** Minassian, 16; **3** Webber, 14; **4** Gollin, 7; **5=** Manning, 6; **5=** Wilson, 6.

FIA INTERNATIONAL FORMULA 3000 CHAMPIONSHIP, Monte Carlo Street Circuit, Monaco, 3 June. Round 5. 50 laps of the 2.094-mile/3.370-km circuit, 104.701 miles/ 168.500 km.
1 Bruno Junqueira, BR, 1h 19m 08.755s, 79.373 mph/ 127.739 km/h.
2 Jamie Davies, GB, 1h 19m 10.353s; **3** David Saelens, B, 1h 19m 16.480s; **4** Kevin McGarrity, GB, 1h 19m 17.010s; **5** Nicolas Minassian, F, 1h 19m 19.910s; **6** Franck Montagny, F, 1h 19m 20.514s; **7** Justin Wilson, GB, 1h 19m 21.177s; **8** Fernando Alonso, E, 1h 19m 22.039s; **9** Jeffrey van Hooydonk, B, 1h 19m 23.466s; **10** Fabrizio Gollin, I, 1h 20m 08.309s; **11** Andreas Scheld, D, 48 laps; **12** Mark Webber, AUS, 47 (DNF - accident); **13** Christijan Albers, NL, 35 (DNF - accident); **14** Enrique Bernoldi, I, 31 (DNF - accident); **15** Darren Manning, GB, 30 (DNF - accident); **16** Marc Hynes, GB, 30 (DNF - accident); **17** Andrea Piccini, I, 17 (DNF - accident); **18** Soheil Ayari, F, 17 (DNF - accident); **19** Ananda Mikola, RI, 9 (DNF - spin); **20** André Couto, P, 8 (DNF - engine); **21** Bas Leinders, B, 7 (DNF - spin); **22** Stéphane Sarrazin, F, 4 (DNF - fuel pressure/accident); **23** Ricardo Mauricio, BR, 4 (DNF - accident); **24** Sébastien Bourdais, F, 0 (DNF - accident); **25** Fabrice Walfisch, F, 0 (DNF - gearbox); **26** Viktor Maslov, RUS, 0 (DNF - accident damage).
Fastest race lap: Alonso, 1m 30.539s, 83.262 mph/133.998 km/h.
Fastest qualifying lap: Saelens, 1m 29.178s, 84.533 mph/ 136.043 km/h.
Did not qualify: Kristian Kolby, DK; Tomas Enge, CZ; Jaime Melo Jr., BR; Yves Olivier, B.
Championship points: 1 Junqueira, 38; **2** Minassian, 18; **3** Webber, 14; **4** Saelens, 8; **5** Gollin, 7; **6=** Manning, 6; **6=** Wilson, 6; **6=** Davies, 6.

FIA INTERNATIONAL FORMULA 3000 CHAMPIONSHIP, Circuit de Nevers, Magny-Cours, France, 1 July. Round 6. 49 laps of the 2.641-mile/4.251-km circuit, 129.315 miles/ 208.113 km.
1 Nicolas Minassian, F, 1h 15m 44.627s, 102.436 mph/ 164.856 km/h.
2 Sébastien Bourdais, F, 1h 15m 48.186s; **3** David Saelens, B, 1h 15m 52.563s; **4** Franck Montagny, F, 1h 15m 59.057s; **5** Tomas Enge, CZ, 1h 16m 00.360s; **6** Stéphane Sarrazin, F, 1h 16m 07.858s; **7** Christijan Albers, NL, 1h 16m 12.647s; **8** Darren Manning, GB, 1h 16m 21.396s; **9** Justin Wilson, GB, 1h 16m 23.199s; **10** Bas Leinders, B, 1h 16m 43.956s; **11** Mario Haberfeld, BR, 1h 16m 48.923s; **12** Andrea Piccini, I, 1h 16m 51.473s; **13** Bruno Junqueira, BR, 1h 16m 52.268s; **14** Fabrizio Gollin, I, 1h 16m 53.011s; **15** Kevin McGarrity, GB, 1h 16m 53.535s; **16** Mark Webber, AUS, 1h 16m 54.322s; **17** Jaime Melo Jr., BR, 1h 16m 59.234s; **18** Fabrice Walfisch, F, 1h 17m 04.088s; **19** Jeffrey van Hooydonk, B, 1h 17m 09.355s; **20** Ananda Mikola, RI, 1h 17m 18.159s; **21** André Couto, P, 48 laps; **22** Soheil Ayari, F, 48; **23** Enrique Bernoldi, I, 48; **24** Fernando Alonso, E, 15 (DNF - electrics); **25** Ricardo Mauricio, BR, 1 (DNF - accident); **26** Marc Hynes, GB, 1 (DNF - accident).
Fastest race lap: Webber, 1m 30.105s, 105.535 mph/ 169.842 km/h.
Fastest qualifying lap: Bourdais, 1m 27.071s, 109.212 mph/ 175.760 km/h.
Did not qualify: Kristian Kolby, DK; Yves Olivier, B; Viktor Maslov, RUS; Andreas Scheld, D.
Championship points: 1 Junqueira, 38; **2** Minassian, 28; **3** Webber, 14; **4** Saelens, 12; **5** Bourdais, 9; **6** Gollin, 7.

FIA INTERNATIONAL FORMULA 3000 CHAMPIONSHIP, A1-Ring, Spielberg, Austria, 15 July. Round 7. 48 laps of the 2.688-mile/4.326-km circuit, 129.026 miles/207.648 km.
1 Nicolas Minassian, F, 1h 10m 42.354s, 109.490 mph/ 176.207 km/h.
2 Justin Wilson, GB, 1h 10m 43.768s; **3** Darren Manning, GB, 1h 10m 48.263s; **4** Mark Webber, AUS, 1h 10m 48.490s; **5** Jaime Melo Jr., BR, 1h 10m 49.304s; **6** Fernando Alonso, E, 1h 10m 49.575s; **7** Bruno Junqueira, BR, 1h 10m 50.897s; **8** Mario Haberfeld, BR, 1h 10m 51.280s; **9** Sébastien Bourdais, F, 1h 10m 51.673s; **10** Marc Goossens, B, 1h 10m 52.522s; **11** Bas Leinders, B, 1h 10m 53.936s; **12** Jeffrey van Hooydonk, B, 1h 10m 54.593s; **13** Yves Olivier, B, 1h 10m 58.727s; **14** Enrique Bernoldi, I, 1h 11m 00.012s; **15** Ananda Mikola, RI, 1h 11m 12.771s; **16** Tomas Enge, CZ, 47 laps; **17** Franck Montagny, F, 46; **18** Tomas Scheckter, ZA, 40; **19** Soheil Ayari, F, 39 (DNF - accident); **20** Andrea Piccini, I, 39 (DNF - accident); **21** David Saelens, B, 35 (DNF - spin); **22** Christijan Albers, NL, 12 (DNF - spin); **23** Ricardo Mauricio, BR, 12; **24** André Couto, P, 11 (DNF - spin); **25** Andreas Scheld, D, 4 (DNF - accident); **26** Viktor Maslov, RUS, 3 (DNF - accident).
Fastest race lap: Enge, 1m 23.461s, 115.946 mph/186.597 km/h.
Fastest qualifying lap: van Hooydonk, 1m 33.336s, 103.679 mph/166.855 km/h.
Did not qualify: Fabrizio Gollin, I; Kristian Kolby, DK; Kevin McGarrity, GB; Dino Morelli, GB.
Championship points: 1= Junqueira, 38; **1=** Minassian, 38; **3** Webber, 17; **4=** Saelens, 12; **4=** Wilson, 12; **6** Manning, 10.

FIA INTERNATIONAL FORMULA 3000 CHAMPIONSHIP, Hockenheimring Grand Prix Circuit, Heidelberg, Germany, 29 July. Round 8. 31 laps of the 4.241-mile/6.825-km circuit, 131.467 miles/211.575 km.
1 Tomas Enge, CZ, 1h 14m 50.567s, 105.394 mph/169.616 km/h.
2 Tomas Scheckter, ZA, 1h 14m 56.883s; **3** Mark Webber, AUS, 1h 15m 06.890s; **4** Andrea Piccini, I, 1h 15m 08.811s; **5** Kristian Kolby, DK, 1h 15m 10.896s; **6** Enrique Bernoldi, I, 1h 15m 20.002s; **7** Nicolas Minassian, F, 1h 15m 20.021s; **8** Jaime Melo Jr., BR, 1h 15m 23.584s; **9** Mario Haberfeld, BR, 1h 15m 25.622s; **10** Marc Goossens, B, 1h 15m 32.031s; **11** Kevin McGarrity, GB, 1h 15m 57.680s; **12** Andreas Scheld, D, 1h 16m 00.891s; **13** Darren Manning, GB, 1h 16m 00.973s; **14** Ricardo Mauricio, BR, 1h 16m 04.429s; **15** Viktor Maslov, RUS, 1h 16m 12.540s; **16** Yves Olivier, B, 1h 16m 28.127s; **17** André Couto, P, 30 laps; **18** David Saelens, B, 30; **19** Franck Montagny, F, 20 (DNF - loose wheel); **20** Jeffrey van Hooydonk, B, 12 (DNF - accident); **21** Dino Morelli, GB, 10 (DNF - fuel leak); **22** Bruno Junqueira, BR, 9 (DNF - gearbox); **23** Fernando Alonso, E, 6 (DNF - spin); **24** Justin Wilson, GB, 5 (DNF - spin); **25** Fabrizio Gollin, I, 4 (DNF - spin).
Fastest race lap: Manning, 2m 04.173s, 122.950 mph/ 197.869 km/h.
Fastest qualifying lap: Enge, 2m 11.990s, 115.669 mph/ 186.150 km/h.
Did not start: Sébastien Bourdais, F (accident during warm-up).
Did not qualify: Christijan Albers, NL; Bas Leinders, B; Ananda Mikola, RI.
Championship points: 1= Junqueira, 38; **1=** Minassian, 38; **3** Webber, 21; **4** Enge, 14; **5=** Wilson, 12; **5=** Saelens, 12.

FIA INTERNATIONAL FORMULA 3000 CHAMPIONSHIP, Hungaroring, Mogyorod, Budapest, Hungary, 12 August. Round 9. 52 laps of the 2.470-mile/3.975-km circuit, 128.437 miles/206.700 km.
1 Bruno Junqueira, BR, 1h 21m 30.052s, 94.554 mph/ 152.170 km/h.
2 Fernando Alonso, E, 1h 21m 30.647s; **3** Ricardo Mauricio, BR, 1h 21m 35.865s; **4** Nicolas Minassian, F, 1h 21m 41.193s; **5** Justin Wilson, GB, 1h 21m 42.557s; **6** Enrique Bernoldi, I, 1h 21m 48.154s; **7** Bas Leinders, B, 1h 21m 56.485s; **8** Darren Manning, GB, 1h 21m 58.420s; **9** Mark Webber, AUS, 1h 22m 00.053s; **10** Fabrice Walfisch, F, 1h 22m 05.444s; **11** David Saelens, B, 1h 22m 10.228s; **12** Franck Montagny, F, 1h 22m 10.550s; **13** Soheil Ayari, F, 1h 22m 10.978s; **14** Sébastien Bourdais, F, 1h 22m 14.773s; **15** Mario Haberfeld, BR, 1h 22m 21.265s; **16** Andrea Piccini, I, 1h 22m 25.120s; **17** Tomas Enge, CZ, 1h 22m 25.434s; **18** Fabrizio Gollin, I, 1h 22m 27.680s; **19** Marc Goossens, B, 51 laps; **20** Kristian Kolby, DK, 51; **21** Tomas Scheckter, ZA, 50; **22** Christijan Albers, NL, 22 (DNF - suspension); **23** Jeffrey van Hooydonk, B, 21 (DNF - spin); **24** André Couto, P, 17 (DNF - spin); **25** Kevin McGarrity, GB, 1 (DNF - suspension); **26** Ananda Mikola, RI, 1 (DNF - fuel pump).
Fastest race lap: Goossens, 1m 30.320s, 98.45 mph/ 158.436 km/h.
Fastest qualifying lap: Junqueira, 1m 27.531s, 101.585 mph/163.485 km/h.
Did not qualify: Yves Olivier, B; Viktor Maslov, RUS; Andreas Scheld, D; Jaime Melo Jr., BR.
Championship points: 1 Junqueira, 48; **2** Minassian, 41; **3** Webber, 21; **4=** Enge, 14; **4=** Wilson, 14; **6** Saelens, 12.

FIA INTERNATIONAL FORMULA 3000 CHAMPIONSHIP, Circuit de Spa-Francorchamps, Stavelot, Belgium, 26 August. Round 10. 30 laps of the 4.330-mile/6.968-km circuit, 129.891 miles/209.040 km.
1 Fernando Alonso, E, 1h 08m 04.964s, 114.471 mph/ 184.223 km/h.
2 Marc Goossens, B, 1h 08m 19.565s; **3** Nicolas Minassian, F, 1h 08m 20.300s; **4** David Saelens, B, 1h 08m 27.135s; **5** Justin Wilson, GB, 1h 08m 32.932s; **6** Tomas Enge, CZ, 1h 08m 43.418s; **7** Ricardo Mauricio, BR, 1h 08m 43.714s; **8** Christijan Albers, NL, 1h 08m 49.512s; **9** Bruno Junqueira, BR, 1h 08m 52.906s; **10** Enrique Bernoldi, I, 1h 08m 54.761s; **11** André Couto, P, 1h 09m 00.502s; **12** Jamie Davies, GB, 1h 09m 01.667s; **13** Andrea Piccini, I, 1h 09m 2.568s; **14** Soheil Ayari, F, 1h 09m 06.617s; **15** Kristian Kolby, DK, 1h 09m 24.917s; **16** Mark Webber, AUS, 1h 09m 28.465s; **17** Yves Olivier, B, 29 laps; **18** Jaime Melo Jr., BR, 29; **19** Bas Leinders, B, 23 (DNF - accident); **20** Fabrizio Gollin, I, 20 (DNF - handling); **21** Jeffrey van Hooydonk, B, 9 (DNF - accident); **22** Sébastien Bourdais, F, 9 (DNF - accident); **23** Franck Montagny, F, 8 (DNF - accident); **24** Darren Manning, GB, 1 (DNF - accident); **25** Mario Haberfeld, BR, 0 (DNF - accident).
Fastest race lap: Alonso, 2m 10.096s, 119.811 mph/192.818 km/h.
Fastest qualifying lap: Alonso, 2m 07.184s, 122.555 mph/ 197.232 km/h.
Did not start: Tomas Scheckter, ZA (accident during warm-up).
Did not qualify: Kevin McGarrity, GB; Fabrice Walfisch, F; Ananda Mikola, RI; Viktor Maslov, RUS,

Final championship points
1 Bruno Junqueira, BR, 48; **2** Nicolas Minassian, F, 45; **3** Mark Webber, AUS, 21; **4** Fernando Alonso, E, 17; **5** Justin Wilson, GB, 16; **6=** Tomas Enge, CZ, 15; **6=** David Saelens, B, 15; **8** Darren Manning, GB, 10; **9** Sébastien Bourdais, F, 9; **10** Fabrizio Gollin, I, 7; **11=** Jaime Melo Jr., BR, 6; **11=** Jamie Davies, GB, 6; **11=** Marc Goossens, B, 6; **11=** Toby Scheckter, ZA, 6; **15=** Franck Montagny, F, 5; **15=** Enrique Bernoldi, BR, 5; **17=** André Couto, P, 4; **17=** Ricardo Mauricio, BR, 4; **19=** Stéphane Sarrazin, F, 3; **19=** Jeffrey van Hooydonk, B, 3; **19=** Kevin McGarrity, GB, 3; **19=** Andrea Piccini, I, 3; **23** Kristian Kolby, DK, 2; **24** Soheil Ayari, F, 1.

Formula 3000 Italia

All cars are Lola-Zytek V8.

FORMULA 3000 ITALIA, Autodromo di Vallelunga, Campagnano di Roma, Italy, 2 April. Round 1. 32 laps of the 2.001-mile/3.220-km circuit, 64.026 miles/103.040 km.
1 Gabriele Lancieri, I, 38m 37.468s, 99.459 mph/160.064 km/h.
2 Rodrigo Sperafico, BR, 38m 40.568s; **3** Warren Hughes, GB, 38m 40.822s; **4** Thomas Biagi, I, 38m 44.352s; **5** Marcelo Battistuzzi, BR, 38m 48.093s; **6** Manuel Giao, P, 38m 48.522s; **7** Viktor Maslov, RUS, 38m 49.515s; **8** Yann Goudy, F, 38m 49.946s; **9** Sascha Bert, D, 38m 50.346s; **10** Gabriele Gardel, CH, 38m 51.115s.
Fastest race lap: Lancieri, 1m 06.444s, 108.406 mph/ 174.463 km/h.

FORMULA 3000 ITALIA, Autodromo Internazionale del Mugello, Scarperia, Firenze (Florence), Italy, 16 April. Round 2. 20 laps of the 3.259-mile/5.245-km circuit, 65.182 miles/104.900 km.
1 Ricardo Sperafico, BR, 38m 34.389s, 101.389 mph/63.170 km/h.
2 Thomas Biagi, I, 38m 37.244s; **3** 'Babalus', 38m 50.238s; **4** Gabriele Lancieri, I, 38m 51.399s; **5** Giovanni Montanari, I, 38m 52.036s; **6** Rodrigo Sperafico, BR, 38m 56.987s; **7** Sascha Bert, D, 39m 01.016s; **8** Warren Hughes, GB, 39m 01.462s; **9** Marcelo Battistuzzi, BR, 39m 03.964s; **10** Gianluca Calcagni, I, 39m 04.896s.
Fastest race lap: Sperafico (Ricardo), 1m 41.223s, 115.910 mph/186.539 km/h.

FORMULA 3000 ITALIA, Autodromo Enzo e Dino Ferrari, Imola, Italy, 14 May. Round 3. 21 laps of the 3.065-mile/4.933-km circuit, 64.370 miles/103.593 km.
1 Warren Hughes, GB, 35m 43.155s, 108.126 mph/174.012 km/h.
2 Gabriele Lancieri, I, 35m 53.588s; **3** Rodrigo Sperafico, BR, 35m 53.947s; **4** Ricardo Sperafico, BR, 36m 02.518s; **5** Manuel Giao, P, 36m 20.841s; **6** Gianluca Calcagni, I, 36m 26.564s; **7** Danilo Rossi, I, 36m 31.942s; **8** Derek Hill, USA, 36m 32.660s; **9** Leonardo Nienkotter, BR, 36m 37.022s; **10** Paolo Ruberti, I, 36m 38.247s.
Fastest race lap: Hughes, 1m 41.605s, 108.605 mph/ 174.783 km/h.

FORMULA 3000 ITALIA, Autodromo Nazionale di Monza, Milan, Italy, 25 June. Round 4. 18 laps of the 3.585-mile/ 5.770-km circuit, 64.536 miles/103.860 km.
1 Warren Hughes, GB, 30m 12.705s, 64.536 mph/103.860 km/h.
2 Tomas Scheckter, ZA, 30m 15.205s; **3** Rodrigo Sperafico, BR, 30m 17.581s; **4** Gianluca Calcagni, I, 30m 22.118s; **5** Gabriele Lancieri, I, 30m 22.663s; **6** Manuel Giao, P, 30m 23.356s; **7** Leonardo Nienkotter, BR, 30m 35.559s; **8** Michele Spoldi, I, 30m 38.633s; **9** Danilo Rossi, I, 30m 40.360s; **10** Angel Burgueno, E, 30m 42.214s.
Fastest race lap: Hughes, 1m 39.465s, 129.765 mph/ 208.837 km/h.

FORMULA 3000 ITALIA, Autodromo di Vallelunga, Campagnano di Roma, Italy, 23 July. Round 5. 32 laps of the 2.001-mile/3.220-km circuit, 64.026 miles/103.040 km.
1 Ricardo Sperafico, BR, 35m 19.101s, 108.770 mph/175.048 km/h.
2 Gabriele Lancieri, I, 35m 27.168s; **3** 'Babalus', 35m

27.507s; **4** Gabriele Varano, CH, 35m 28.925s; **5** Gianluca Calcagni, I, 35m 41.585s; **6** Rodrigo Sperafico, BR, 35m 42.146s; **7** Leonardo Nienkotter, BR, 35m 43.038s; **8** Andrej Pavicevic, AUS, 35m 50.455s; **9** Sascha Bert, D, 35m 51.047s; **10** Michele Spoldi, I, 35m 51.428s.
Fastest race lap: Thomas Biagi, I, 1m 05.162s, 110.539 mph/177.895 km/h.

FORMULA 3000 ITALIA, Donington Park Grand Prix Circuit, Derbyshire, Great Britain, 6 August. Round 6. 24 laps of the 2.500-mile/4.023-km circuit, 60.000 miles/ 96.561 km.
1 Ricardo Sperafico, BR, 37m 16.669s, 96.572 mph/155.418 km/h.
2 Warren Hughes, GB, 37m 18.709s; **3** Manuel Giao, P, 37m 19.445s; **4** Rodrigo Sperafico, BR, 37m 21.799s; **5** Thomas Biagi, I, 37m 23.521s; **6** Gabriele Lancieri, I, 37m 27.580s; **7** Sascha Bert, D, 37m 36.690s; **8** Derek Hill, USA, 37m 40.562s; **9** Mark Shaw, GB, 37m 41.002s; **10** Michele Spoldi, I, 37m 46.108s.
Fastest race lap: Sperafico (Ricardo), 1m 26.334s, 104.246 mph/167.768 km/h.

FORMULA 3000 ITALIA, Ente Autodromo di Pergusa, Enna-Pergusa, Sicily, 3 September. Round 7. 21 laps of the 3.076-mile/4.950-km circuit, 64.592 miles/103.950 km.
1 Darren Manning, GB, 33m 18.404s, 116.358 mph/187.259 km/h.
2 Gianluca Calcagni, I, 33m 26.338s; **3** Thomas Biagi, I, 33m 27.835s; **4** Ricardo Sperafico, BR, 33m 31.436s; **5** Manuel Giao, P, 33m 35.590s; **6** Warren Hughes, GB, 33m 37.084s; **7** Salvatore Tavano, I; **8** Rodrigo Sperafico, BR; **9** Gabriele Gardel, CH; **10** Sascha Bert, D.
Fastest race lap: Manning, 1m 33.816s, 118.027 mph/ 189.946 km/h.

FORMULA 3000 ITALIA, Autodromo Santamonica, Misano Adriatico, Rimini, Italy, 22 October. Round 8. 24 laps of the 2.523-mile/4.060-km circuit, 60.546 miles/97.440 km.
1 Ricardo Sperafico, BR, 33m 48.550s, 107.450 mph/172.924 km/h.
2 Warren Hughes, GB, 33m 51.779s; **3** Darren Manning, GB, 33m 53.843s; **4** Rodrigo Sperafico, BR, 33m 54.298s; **5** Soheil Ayari, F, 34m 00.934s; **6** Michele Spoldi, I, 34m 12.704s; **7** Gianluca Calcagni, I, 34m 13.415s; **8** 'Babalus', 34m 15.146s; **9** Leonardo Nienkotter, BR, 34m 25.749s; **10** Thomas Biagi, I, 34m 26.255s.

Final championship points
1 Ricardo Sperafico, BR, 46; **2** Warren Hughes, GB, 37; **3** Gabriele Lancieri, I, 28; **4** Rodrigo Sperafico, BR, 22; **5** Thomas Biagi, I, 15; **6** Darren Manning, GB, 14; **7** Gianluca Calcagni, I, 12; **8** Manuel Giao, P, 10; **9** 'Babalus', 8; **10** Tomas Scheckter, ZA, 6; **11** Gabriele Varano, CH, 3; **12=** Soheil Ayari, F, 2; **12=** Marcelo Battistuzzi, BR, 2; **12=** Giovanni Montanari, I, 2; **15** Michele Spoldi, I, 1.

Formula 3000 Italia Non-Championship Race

F3000 ITALIA NON-CHAMPIONSHIP RACE, Assen, Netherlands, 20 August, 26 laps of the 2.389-mile/3.845-km circuit, 62.118 miles/99.970 km.
1 Thomas Biagi, I, 32m 49.409s, 113.550 mph/182.741 km/h.
2 Gabriele Lancieri, I, 32m 50.833s; **3** Jacky van der Ende, NL, 33m 06.961s; **4** Andrej Pavicevic, AUS, 33m 09.977s; **5** Ricardo Sperafico, BR, 33m 34.516s; **6** Gabriele Gardel, CH, 33m 36.224s.
Fastest race lap: Biagi, 1m 14.906s, 114.824 mph/184.792 km/h.

Green Flag British Formula 3 Championship

GREEN FLAG BRITISH FORMULA 3 CHAMPIONSHIP, Thruxton Circuit, Andover, Hampshire, Great Britain, 26 March. Round 1. 23 laps of the 2.356-mile/3.792-km circuit, 54.188 miles/87.207 km.
1 Antonio Pizzonia, BR (Dallara F300-Mugen Honda), 30m 52.035s, 105.331 mph/169.514 km/h.
2 Tomas Scheckter, ZA (Dallara F300-Mugen Honda), 30m 53.225s; **3** Narain Karthikeyan, IND (Dallara F300-Mugen Honda), 30m 56.419s; **4** Matt Davies, GB (Dallara F300-Renault), 31m 10.507s; **5** Andy Priaulx, GB (Dallara F300-Renault), 31m 14.112s; **6** Milos Pavlovic, YU (Dallara F300-Opel), 31m 21.857s; **7** Gianmaria Bruni, I (Dallara F300-Mugen Honda), 31m 25.499s; **8** Nicolas Kiesa, DK (Dallara F300-Opel), 31m 26.664s; **9** Gary Paffett, GB (Dallara F398-Renault), 31m 29.845s (1st Scholarship class); **10** Westley Barber, GB (Dallara F300-Mugen Honda), 31m 37.743s.
Fastest race lap: Scheckter, 1m 12.242s, 117.405 mph/ 188.946 km/h.
Fastest qualifying lap: Scheckter, 1m 12.421s, 117.115 mph/188.479 km/h.
Championship points: 1 Pizzonia, 20; **2** Scheckter, 16; **3** Karthikeyan, 12; **4** Davies, 10; **5** Priaulx, 8; **6** Pavlovic, 6.
Scholarship Class: 1 Paffett, 21; **2** Christian Colombo, I, 15; **3** Atsushi Katsumata, J, 12.

GREEN FLAG BRITISH FORMULA 3 CHAMPIONSHIP, Croft Circuit, Croft-on-Tees, North Yorkshire, Great Britain, 9 April. Round 2. 24 laps of the 2.127-mile/3.423-km circuit, 51.048 miles/82.154 km.
1 Antonio Pizzonia, BR (Dallara F300-Mugen Honda), 30m 02.796s, 101.938 mph/164.053 km/h.
2 Tomas Scheckter, ZA (Dallara F300-Mugen Honda), 30m 07.406s; **3** Michael Bentwood, GB (Dallara F300-Mugen Honda), 30m 17.955s; **4** Gianmaria Bruni, I (Dallara F300-Mugen Honda), 30m 20.276s; **5** Takuma Sato, J (Dallara F300-Mugen Honda), 30m 27.856s; **6** Milos Pavlovic, YU (Dallara F300-Opel), 30m 29.952s; **7** Westley Barber, GB (Dallara F300-Mugen Honda), 30m 30.310s; **8** Ben Collins, GB (Dallara F300-Mugen Honda), 30m 30.526s; **9** Andy Priaulx, GB (Dallara F300-Renault), 30m 30.670s; **10** Juan Manuel Lopez, RA (Dallara F300-Mugen Honda), 30m 37.020s.
Fastest race lap: Scheckter, 1m 14.313s, 103.040 mph/ 165.827 km/h.
Fastest qualifying lap: Nicolas Kiesa, DK (Dallara F300-Opel), 1m 13.953s, 103.541 mph/166.634 km/h.
Scholarship class winner: Gary Paffett, GB (Dallara F398-Renault), 30m 49.701s (11th).
Championship points: 1 Pizzonia, 40; **2** Scheckter, 32; **3** Bruni, 14; **4=** Karthikeyan, 12; **4=** Bentwood, 12; **4=** Pavlovic, 12. **Scholarship class:** 1 Paffett, 42; **2** Katsumata, 27; **3** Philip Hopkins, GB, 20.

GREEN FLAG BRITISH FORMULA 3 CHAMPIONSHIP, Oulton Park International Circuit, Tarporley, Cheshire, Great Britain, 1 May. Round 3. 18 laps of the 2.775-mile/ 4.466-km circuit, 49.950 miles/80.387 km.
1 Tomas Scheckter, ZA (Dallara F300-Mugen Honda), 31m 18.772s, 95.711 mph/154.033 km/h.
2 Antonio Pizzonia, BR (Dallara F300-Mugen Honda), 31m 19.257s; **3** Andy Priaulx, GB (Dallara F300-Renault), 31m 20.998s; **4** Matt Davies, GB (Dallara F300-Renault), 31m 21.906s; **5** Narain Karthikeyan, IND (Dallara F300-Mugen Honda), 31m 22.498s; **6** Gianmaria Bruni, I (Dallara F300-Mugen Honda), 31m 26.926s; **7** Michael Bentwood, GB (Dallara F300-Mugen Honda), 31m 28.007s; **8** Martin O'Connell, GB (Dallara F300-Mugen Honda), 31m 28.661s; **9** Milos Pavlovic, YU (Dallara F300-Opel), 31m 33.162s; **10** Juan Manuel Lopez, RA (Dallara F300-Mugen Honda), 31m 35.983s.
Fastest race lap: Pizzonia, 1m 30.478s, 110.414 mph/ 177.693 km/h.
Fastest qualifying lap: Pizzonia, 1m 30.185s, 110.772 mph/ 178.271 km/h.
Scholarship class winner: Gary Paffett, GB (Dallara F398-Renault), 31m 45.773s (11th).
Championship points: 1 Pizzonia, 56; **2** Scheckter, 52; **3** Priaulx, 22; **4=** Karthikeyan, 20; **4=** Bruni, 20; **4=** Davies, 20.
Scholarship class: 1 Paffett, 63; **2** Katsumata, 27; **3=** Colombo, 21; **3=** Marcel Romanio, BR, 21.

GREEN FLAG BRITISH FORMULA 3 CHAMPIONSHIP, Donington National Circuit, Derbyshire, Great Britain, 6/7 May. 28 and 26 laps of the 1.957-mile/3.150-km circuit.
Round 4a (54.805 miles/88.200 km)
1 Ben Collins, GB (Dallara F300-Mugen Honda), 30m 54.264s, 106.402 mph/171.238 km/h.
2 Narain Karthikeyan, IND (Dallara F300-Mugen Honda), 30m 55.011s; **3** Michael Bentwood, GB (Dallara F300-Mugen Honda), 30m 57.047s; **4** Gary Paffett, GB (Dallara F398-Renault), 31m 04.440s (1st Scholarship class); **5** Nicolas Kiesa, DK (Dallara F300-Opel), 31m 05.177s; **6** Martin O'Connell, GB (Dallara F300-Mugen Honda), 31m 06.642s; **7** Gianmaria Bruni, I (Dallara F300-Mugen Honda), 31m 11.505s; **8** Andrew Kirkcaldy, GB (Dallara F300-Opel), 31m 13.825s; **9** Andy Priaulx, GB (Dallara F300-Renault), 31m 18.524s; **10** Westley Barber, GB (Dallara F300-Mugen Honda), 31m 23.307s.
Fastest race lap: Antonio Pizzonia, BR (Dallara F300-Mugen Honda), 1m 04.810s, 108.723 mph/174.973 km/h.
Fastest qualifying lap: Takuma Sato, J (Dallara F300-Mugen Honda), 1m 04.116s, 109.900 mph/176.867 km/h.

Round 4b (50.890 miles/81.900 km)
1 Tomas Scheckter, ZA (Dallara F300-Mugen Honda), 30m 06.205s, 101.431 mph/163.237 km/h.
2 Antonio Pizzonia, BR (Dallara F300-Mugen Honda), 30m 06.396s; **3** Andy Priaulx, GB (Dallara F300-Renault), 30m 21.846s; **4** Matt Davies, GB (Dallara F300-Renault), 30m 26.338s; **5** Michael Bentwood, GB (Dallara F300-Mugen Honda), 30m 32.828s; **6** Martin O'Connell, GB (Dallara F300-Mugen Honda), 30m 33.370s; **7** Nicolas Kiesa, DK (Dallara F300-Opel), 30m 33.724s; **8** Narain Karthikeyan, IND (Dallara F300-Mugen Honda), 30m 34.010s; **9** Takuma Sato, J (Dallara F300-Mugen Honda), 30m 36.230s; **10** Gary Paffett, GB (Dallara F398-Renault), 30m 46.711s (1st Scholarship class).
Fastest race lap: Pizzonia, 1m 04.772s, 108.787 mph/ 175.076 km/h.
Fastest qualifying lap: Scheckter, 1m 04.516s, 109.219 mph/175.770 km/h (Sato was stripped of his pole position due to an illegal air restrictor).
Championship points: 1 Pizzonia, 74; **2** Scheckter, 72; **3** Karthikeyan, 38; **4** Priaulx, 37; **5** Bentwood, 36; **6** Davies, 30.
Scholarship class: 1 Paffett, 105; **2** Romanio, 48; **3** Hopkins, 42.

GREEN FLAG BRITISH FORMULA 3 CHAMPIONSHIP, Silverstone International Circuit, Towcester, Northamptonshire, Great Britain, 21 May. Round 5. 20 laps of the 2.249-mile/3.619-km circuit, 44.980 miles/72.388 km.
1 Takuma Sato, J (Dallara F300-Mugen Honda), 25m 46.228s, 104.725 mph/168.538 km/h.
2 Antonio Pizzonia, BR (Dallara F300-Mugen Honda), 25m 47.111s; **3** Nicolas Kiesa, DK (Dallara F300-Opel), 25m 54.694s; **4** Tomas Scheckter, ZA (Dallara F300-Mugen Honda), 25m 56.198s; **5** Gianmaria Bruni, I (Dallara F300-Mugen Honda), 25m 58.672s; **6** Narain Karthikeyan, IND (Dallara F300-Mugen Honda), 26m 03.326s; **7** Juan Manuel Lopez, RA (Dallara F300-Mugen Honda), 26m 10.381s; **8** Ben Collins, GB (Dallara F300-Mugen Honda), 26m 11.723s; **9** Martin O'Connell, GB (Dallara F300-Mugen Honda), 26m 13.780s; **10** Gary Paffett, GB (Dallara F398-Renault), 26m 24.307s (1st Scholarship class).
Fastest race lap: Pizzonia, 1m 16.606s, 105.689 mph/ 170.090 km/h.
Fastest qualifying lap: Sato, 1m 15.573s, 107.134 mph/ 172.415 km/h.
Championship points: 1 Pizzonia, 90; **2** Scheckter, 82; **3** Karthikeyan, 44; **4** Priaulx, 37; **5** Bentwood, 36; **6** Bruni, 34.
Scholarship class: 1 Paffett, 126; **2** Romanio, 58; **3** Colombo, 50.

GREEN FLAG BRITISH FORMULA 3 CHAMPIONSHIP, Brands Hatch Grand Prix Circuit, Dartford, Kent, Great Britain, 4 June. Round 6. 23 laps of the 2.6228-mile/4.221-km circuit, 60.324 miles/97.083 km.
1 Antonio Pizzonia, BR (Dallara F300-Mugen Honda), 30m 43.445s, 117.805 mph/189.588 km/h.
2 Takuma Sato, J (Dallara F300-Mugen Honda), 30m 54.910s; **3** Narain Karthikeyan, IND (Dallara F300-Mugen Honda), 30m 55.402s; **4** Tomas Scheckter, ZA (Dallara F300-Mugen Honda), 31m 02.031s; **5** Michael Bentwood, GB (Dallara F300-Mugen Honda), 31m 06.506s; **6** Milos Pavlovic, YU (Dallara F300-Opel), 31m 13.490s; **7** Martin O'Connell, GB (Dallara F300-Mugen Honda), 31m 16.455s; **8** Gianmaria Bruni, I (Dallara F300-Mugen Honda), 31m 16.938s; **9** Matt Davies, GB (Dallara F300-Renault), 31m 17.627s; **10** Gary Paffett, GB (Dallara F398-Renault), 31m 18.675s.
Fastest race lap: Pizzonia, 1m 18.822s, 119.790 mph/ 192.783 km/h.
Fastest qualifying lap: Ben Collins, GB (Dallara F300-Mugen Honda), 1m 18.891s, 119.685 mph/192.615 km/h.
Championship points: 1 Pizzonia, 111; **2** Scheckter, 92; **3** Karthikeyan, 56; **4** Sato, 45; **5** Bentwood, 44; **6=** Priaulx, 37; **6=** Bruni, 37. **Scholarship class:** 1 Paffett, 147; **2=** Romanio, 58; **2=** Walker, 58.

GREEN FLAG BRITISH FORMULA 3 CHAMPIONSHIP, Donington Grand Prix Circuit, Derbyshire, Great Britain, 1/2 July. 2 x 20 laps of the 2.500-mile/4.023-km circuit.
Round 7a (50.000 miles/80.467 km)
1 Antonio Pizzonia, BR (Dallara F300-Mugen Honda), 30m 05.545s, 99.693 mph/160.440 km/h.
2 Gianmaria Bruni, I (Dallara F300-Mugen Honda), 30m 10.864s; **3** Takuma Sato, J (Dallara F300-Mugen Honda), 30m 12.640s; **4** Narain Karthikeyan, IND (Dallara F300-Mugen Honda), 30m 19.648s; **5** Milos Pavlovic, YU (Dallara F300-Opel), 30m 22.262s; **6** Nicolas Kiesa, DK (Dallara F300-Opel), 30m 23.105s; **7** Michael Bentwood, GB (Dallara F300-Mugen Honda), 30m 23.565s; **8** Ben Collins, GB (Dallara F300-Mugen Honda), 30m 24.280s; **9** Andy Priaulx, GB (Dallara F300-Renault), 30m 29.235s; **10** Martin O'Connell, GB (Dallara F300-Mugen Honda), 30m 33.731s.
Fastest race lap: Bruni, 1m 29.091s, 101.020 mph/162.576 km/h.
Fastest qualifying lap: Pizzonia, 1m 28.698s, 101.468 mph/ 163.297 km/h.
Scholarship class winner: Gary Paffett, GB (Dallara F398-Renault), 30m 37.155s (12th).

Round 7b (50.000 miles/80.467 km)
1 Nicolas Kiesa, DK (Dallara F300-Opel), 30m 14.449s, 99.204 mph/159.653 km/h.
2 Andrew Kirkcaldy, GB (Dallara F300-Opel), 30m 19.291s; **3** Antonio Pizzonia, BR (Dallara F300-Mugen Honda), 30m 20.360s; **4** Gianmaria Bruni, I (Dallara F300-Mugen Honda), 30m 25.228s; **5** Milos Pavlovic, YU (Dallara F300-Opel), 30m 27.568s; **6** Tomas Scheckter, ZA (Dallara F300-Mugen Honda), 30m 28.802s; **7** Michael Bentwood, GB (Dallara F300-Mugen Honda), 30m 30.963s; **8** Andy Priaulx, GB (Dallara F300-Renault), 30m 33.011s; **9** Takuma Sato, J (Dallara F300-Mugen Honda), 30m 38.134s; **10** Narain Karthikeyan, IND (Dallara F300-Mugen Honda), 30m 39.744s.
Fastest race lap: Kiesa, 1m 29.945s, 100.061 mph/161.033 km/h.
Fastest qualifying lap: Kiesa, 1m 28.544s, 101.644 mph/ 163.581 km/h.
Scholarship class winner: Paffett, 30m 42.819s (11th).
Championship points: 1 Pizzonia, 143; **2** Scheckter, 98; **3** Karthikeyan, 67; **4** Bruni, 63; **5** Sato, 59; **6** Kiesa, 56. **Scholarship class:** 1 Paffett, 189; **2** Colombo, 86; **3** Walker, 80.

GREEN FLAG BRITISH FORMULA 3 CHAMPIONSHIP, Croft Circuit, Croft-on-Tees, North Yorkshire, Great Britain, 23 July. Round 8. 25 laps of the 2.127-mile/3.423-km circuit, 53.175 miles/85.577 km.
1 Takuma Sato, J (Dallara F300-Mugen Honda), 31m 13.030s, 102.203 mph/164.480 km/h.
2 Tomas Scheckter, ZA (Dallara F300-Mugen Honda), 31m 21.114s; **3** Nicolas Kiesa, DK (Dallara F300-Opel), 31m 24.635s; **4** Ben Collins, GB (Dallara F300-Mugen Honda), 31m 27.769s; **5** Marcos Ambrose, AUS (Dallara F300-Mugen Honda), 31m 37.861s; **6** Andrew Kirkcaldy, GB (Dallara F300-Opel), 31m 42.521s; **7** Milos Pavlovic, YU (Dallara F300-Opel), 31m 43.687s; **8** Gary Paffett, GB (Dallara F398-Renault), 31m 47.827s (1st Scholarship class); **9** Michael Bentwood, GB (Dallara F300-Mugen Honda), 31m 50.236s; **10** Narain Karthikeyan, IND (Dallara F300-Mugen Honda), 31m 50.855s.
Fastest race lap: Sato, 1m 14.292s, 103.069 mph/165.873 km/h.
Fastest qualifying lap: Sato, 1m 13.773s, 103.794 mph/ 167.040 km/h.
Championship points: 1 Pizzonia, 143; **2** Scheckter, 113; **3** Sato, 80, 4 Karthikeyan, 69; **5** Kiesa, 68; **6** Bruni, 63. **Scholarship class:** 1 Paffett, 210; **2** Colombo, 101; **3** Walker, 92.

GREEN FLAG BRITISH FORMULA 3 CHAMPIONSHIP, Silverstone International Circuit, Towcester, Northamptonshire, Great Britain, 20 August. Round 9. 24 laps of the 2.249-mile/3.619-km circuit, 53.976 miles/86.866 km.
1 Takuma Sato, J (Dallara F300-Mugen Honda), 30m 59.030s, 104.524 mph/168.215 km/h.
2 Antonio Pizzonia, BR (Dallara F300-Mugen Honda), 31m 00.684s; **3** Gianmaria Bruni, I (Dallara F300-Mugen Honda), 31m 14.070s; **4** Tomas Scheckter, ZA (Dallara F300-Mugen Honda), 31m 14.755s; **5** Narain Karthikeyan, IND (Dallara F300-Mugen Honda), 31m 21.165s; **6** Ben Collins, GB (Dallara F300-Mugen Honda), 31m 22.137s; **7** Matt Davies, GB (Dallara F300-Renault), 31m 23.000s; **8** Martin O'Connell, GB (Dallara F300-Mugen Honda), 31m 27.245s; **9** Marcos Ambrose, AUS (Dallara F300-Mugen Honda), 31m 27.309s; **10** Nicolas Kiesa, DK (Dallara F300-Opel), 31m 35.266s.
Fastest race lap: Sato, 1m 16.453s, 105.900 mph/170.430 km/h.
Fastest qualifying lap: Sato, 1m 15.827s, 106.775 mph/ 171.837 km/h.
Scholarship class winner: Gary Paffett, GB (Dallara F398-Renault), 31m 48.644s (14th).
Championship points: 1 Pizzonia, 158; **2** Scheckter, 123; **3** Sato, 101; **4** Karthikeyan, 77; **5** Bruni, 75; **6** Kiesa, 60. **Scholarship class:** 1 Paffett, 231; **2** Colombo, 101; **3** Walker, 92.

GREEN FLAG BRITISH FORMULA 3 CHAMPIONSHIP, Snetterton Circuit, Norfolk, Great Britain, 3 September. Round 10. 29 laps of the 1.952-mile/3.141-km circuit, 56.608 miles/91.102 km.
1 Antonio Pizzonia, BR (Dallara F300-Mugen Honda), 30m 03.594s, 112.990 mph/181.840 km/h.
2 Tomas Scheckter, ZA (Dallara F300-Mugen Honda), 30m 04.851s; **3** Ben Collins, GB (Dallara F300-Mugen Honda), 30m 19.478s; **4** Michael Bentwood, GB (Dallara F300-Mugen Honda), 30m 20.294s; **5** Narain Karthikeyan, IND (Dallara F300-Mugen Honda), 30m 20.862s; **6** Takuma Sato, J (Dallara F300-Mugen Honda), 30m 22.416s; **7** Matt Davies, GB (Dallara F300-Renault), 30m 22.937s; **8** Andy Priaulx, GB (Dallara F300-Renault), 30m 27.791s; **9** Marcos Ambrose, AUS (Dallara F300-Mugen Honda), 30m 31.370s; **10** Westley Barber, GB (Dallara F300-Mugen Honda), 30m 38.954s.
Fastest race lap: Scheckter, 1m 01.706s, 113.882 mph/ 183.275 km/h.
Fastest qualifying lap: Pizzonia, 1m 01.809s, 113.692 mph/ 182.970 km/h.
Scholarship class winner: Atsushi Katsumata, J (Dallara F398-Toyota), 30m 58.929s (13th).
Championship points: 1 Pizzonia, 178; **2** Scheckter, 139; **3** Sato, 107; **4** Karthikeyan, 85; **5** Bruni, 75; **6** Kiesa, 69. **Scholarship class:** 1 Paffett, 247; **2** Colombo, 113; **3** Walker, 102.

ELF F3 MASTERS featuring GREEN FLAG BRITISH F3 CHAMPIONSHIP, Circuit de Spa-Francorchamps, Stavelot, Belgium, 24 September. Round 11. 13 laps of the 4.317-mile/6.948-km circuit, 56.125 miles/90.324 km.
1 Tiago Monteiro, P (Dallara F300-Renault), 30m 04.938s, 111.942 mph/180.154 km/h.
2 Antonio Pizzonia, BR (Dallara F300-Mugen Honda), 30m 06.508s; **3** Narain Karthikeyan, IND (Dallara F300-Mugen Honda), 30m 07.045s; **4** Gianmaria Bruni, I (Dallara F300-Mugen Honda), 30m 08.027s; **5** Tomas Scheckter, ZA (Dallara F300-Mugen Honda), 30m 09.439s; **6** Nicolas Kiesa, DK (Dallara F300-Opel), 30m 15.056s; **7** Matt Davies, GB (Dallara F300-Renault), 30m 19.275s; **8** Andy Priaulx, GB (Dallara F300-Renault), 30m 19.867s; **9** Andrew Kirkcaldy, GB (Dallara F300-Opel), 30m 25.894s; **10** Martin O'Connell, GB (Dallara F300-Mugen Honda), 30m 26.901s.
Fastest race lap: Takuma Sato, J (Dallara F300-Mugen Honda), 2m 17.589s, 112.961 mph/181.794 km/h.
Fastest qualifying lap: Sato, 2m 15.019s, 115.111 mph/ 185.254 km/h.
Scholarship class winner: Atsushi Katsumata, J (Dallara F398-Toyota), 2m 18.932s (13th).
Championship points: 1 Pizzonia, 198; **2** Scheckter, 149; **3** Sato, 108; **4** Karthikeyan, 100; **5** Bruni, 87; **6** Kiesa, 77.
Scholarship class: 1 Paffett, 247; **2** Colombo, 113; **3** Walker, 112.

AUTUMN GOLD CUP, Silverstone Grand Prix Circuit, Towcester, Northamptonshire, Great Britain, 8 October. Round 12. 18 laps of the 3.194-mile/5.140-km circuit, 57.492 miles/92.524 km.
1 Takuma Sato, J (Dallara F300-Mugen Honda), 31m 11.567s, 110.587 mph/177.973 km/h.
2 Andy Priaulx, GB (Dallara F300-Renault), 31m 22.345s; **3** Tomas Scheckter, ZA (Dallara F300-Mugen Honda), 31m 22.771s; **4** Ben Collins, GB (Dallara F300-Mugen Honda), 31m 31.744s; **5** Gianmaria Bruni, I (Dallara F300-Mugen Honda), 31m 32.757s; **6** Westley Barber, GB (Dallara F300-Mugen Honda), 31m 40.017s; **7** Michael Bentwood, GB (Dallara F300-Mugen Honda), 31m 40.616s; **8** Martin O'Connell, GB (Dallara F300-Mugen Honda), 31m 42.717s; **9** Antonio Pizzonia, BR (Dallara F300-Mugen Honda), 31m 43.300s; **10** Marcos Ambrose, AUS (Dallara F300-Mugen Honda), 31m 46.800s.
Fastest race lap: Sato, 1m 43.012s, 111.622 mph/179.638 km/h.
Fastest qualifying lap: Priaulx, 2m 00.804s, 95.182 mph/ 153.181 km/h.
Scholarship class winner: Gary Paffett, GB (Dallara F398-Renault), 32m 04.326s (12th).

Final championship points
1 Antonio Pizzonia, BR, 200; **2** Tomas Scheckter, ZA, 161; **3** Takuma Sato, J, 129; **4** Narain Karthikeyan, IND, 100; **5** Gianmaria Bruni, I, 95; **6** Nicolas Kiesa, DK, 77; **7** Michael Bentwood, GB, 69; **8** Ben Collins, GB, 67; **9** Andy Priaulx, GB, 64; **10** Matt Davies, GB, 47; **11** Milos Pavlovic, YU, 41; **12** Martin O'Connell, GB, 32; **13** Andrew Kirkcaldy, GB, 28; **14** Westley Barber, GB, 17; **15** Marcos Ambrose, AUS, 13; **16** Juan Manuel Lopez, RA, 6; **17** Tor Sriachavanon, T, 2.

Scholarship Class
1 Gary Paffett, GB, 268; **2** Christian Colombo, I, 128; **3** Ryan Walker, USA, 122; **4** Atsushi Katsumata, J, 108; **5** Mark Mayall, GB, 88; **6** Philip Hopkins, GB, 76; **7** Craig Fleming, GB, 73; **8** Marcel Romanio, BR, 58; **9** Peter Nilsson, S, 30; **10** Enzo Buscaglia, GB, 22; **11** Julian Westwood, GB, 20; **12** Matthew Gilmore, GB, 3.

French Formula 3 Championship

COUPES DE PAQUES DE NOGARO, Circuit Automobile Paul Armagnac, Nogaro, France, 23/24 April. Round 1. 2 x 20 laps of the 2.259-mile/3.636-km circuit.
Race 1 (45.186 miles/72.720 km)
1 Romain Dumas, F (Martini MK79-Opel), 32m 29.435s, 83.445 mph/134.291 km/h.
2 Ryo Fukuda, J (Dallara F399-Renault), 32m 29.769s; **3** Lucas Lasserre, F (Dallara F399-Renault), 32m 37.551s; **4** James Andanson Jr., F (Martini MK79-Opel), 32m 50.942s; **5** Ying Kin Lee, RC (Martini MK79-Opel), 33m 32.993s; **6** Adam Jones, GB (Martini MK73-Opel), 33m 38.985s; **7** Julien Piguet, F (Dallara F396-Opel), 33m 48.184s; **8** Frédéric Makowiecki, F (Dallara F396-Fiat), 34m 06.531s; **9** Tristan Gommendy, F (Dallara F399-Renault), 19 laps; **10** David Moretti, F (Dallara F396-Fiat), 19.
Fastest race lap: Julien Beltoise, F (Dallara F399-Renault), 1m 24.246s, 96.545 mph/155.374 km/h.
Fastest qualifying lap: Beltoise, 1m 23.523s, 97.380 mph/ 156.719 km/h.

Race 2 (45.186 miles/72.720 km)
1 Jonathan Cochet, F (Dallara F399-Renault), 28m 09.329s, 96.293 mph/154.968 km/h.
2 Julien Beltoise, F (Dallara F399-Renault), 28m 12.952s; **3** Ryo Fukuda, J (Dallara F399-Renault), 28m 16.205s; **4** Mathieu Zangarelli, F (Dallara F399-Renault), 28m 16.857s; **5** Tiago Monteiro, P (Dallara F399-Renault), 28m 19.755s; **6** Romain Dumas, F (Martini MK79-Opel), 28m 30.996s; **7** Yannick Schroeder, F (Dallara F399-Renault), 28m 31.920s; **8** James Andanson Jr., F (Martini MK79-Opel), 28m 32.190s; **9** Marcos Ambrose, AUS (Martini MK79-Renault), 28m 39.478s; **10** Tristan Gommendy, F (Dallara F399-Renault), 28m 40.685s.
Fastest race lap: Cochet, 1m 23.733s, 97.136 mph/156.325 km/h.
Fastest qualifying lap: Cochet, 1m 21.937s, 99.265 mph/ 159.752 km/h.

TROPHÉE MOBIL 1 DE PRINTEMPS, Circuit de Nevers, Magny-Cours, France, 7/8 May. Round 2. 22 and 18 laps of the 2.641-mile/4.250-km circuit.
Race 1 (58.098 miles/93.500 km)
1 Jonathan Cochet, F (Dallara F399-Renault), 34m 10.796s, 101.987 mph/164.131 km/h.
2 Ryo Fukuda, J (Dallara F399-Renault), 34m 11.839s; **3** Julien Beltoise, F (Dallara F399-Renault), 34m 17.173s; **4** Lucas Lasserre, F (Dallara F399-Renault), 34m 30.698s; **5** Yannick Schroeder, F (Dallara F399-Renault), 34m 35.702s; **6** Mathieu Zangarelli, F (Dallara F399-Renault), 34m 36.175s; **7** Marcos Ambrose, AUS (Martini MK79-Renault), 34m 40.133s; **8** Romain Dumas, F (Martini MK79-Opel), 34m 44.515s; **9** Adam Jones, GB (Martini MK73-Opel), 34m 51.043s; **10** Julien Piguet, F (Dallara F396-Opel), 34m 53.476s.
Fastest race lap: Fukuda, 1m 32.607s, 102.659 mph/165.214 km/h.
Fastest qualifying lap: Cochet, 1m 31.880s, 103.472 mph/166.522 km/h.

Race 2 (47.535 miles/76.500 km)
1 Ryo Fukuda, J (Dallara F399-Renault), 28m 03.876s, 101.626 mph/163.551 km/h.
2 Jonathan Cochet, F (Dallara F399-Renault), 28m 11.257s; **3** Mathieu Zangarelli, F (Dallara F399-Renault), 28m 12.685s; **4** Lucas Lasserre, F (Dallara F399-Renault), 28m 13.822s; **5** Romain Dumas, F (Martini MK79-Opel), 28m 23.433s; **6** James Andanson Jr., F (Martini MK79-Opel), 28m 24.229s; **7** Julien Beltoise, F (Dallara F399-Renault), 28m 25.719s; **8** Yannick Schroeder, F (Dallara F399-Renault), 28m 26.766s; **9** Marcos Ambrose, AUS (Martini MK79-Renault), 28m 27.364s; **10** Tiago Monteiro, P (Dallara F399-Renault), 28m 29.392s.
Fastest race lap: Fukuda, 1m 32.682s, 102.576 mph/165.081 km/h.
Fastest qualifying lap: Fukuda, 1m 31.538s, 103.858 mph/167.144 km/h.

60th GRAND AUTOBILE DE PAU, FIA FORMULA 3 EUROPEAN CUP, Circuit de Pau Ville, France, Round 3. 12 June. 36 laps of the 1.715-mile/2.760-km circuit, 61.739 miles/99.360 km.
1 Jonathan Cochet, F (Dallara F399-Renault), 43m 40.066s, 84.831 mph/136.522 km/h.
2 Tiago Monteiro, P (Dallara F399-Renault), 43m 43.072s; **3** Patrick Freisacher, A (Dallara F300-Opel), 43m 43.500s; **4** Ryo Fukuda, J (Dallara F399-Renault), 43m 49.093s; **5** Nicolas Kiesa, DK (Dallara F300-Opel), 43m 51.544s; **6** Mathieu Zangarelli, F (Dallara F399-Renault), 44m 02.330s; **7** Milos Pavlovic, YU (Dallara F300-Opel), 44m 04.846s; **8** André Lotterer, D. (Dallara F300-Opel), 44m 06.252s; **9** Paolo Montin, I (Dallara F399-Opel), 44m 17.346s; **10** Juan Manuel Lopez, RA (Dallara F300-Mugen Honda), 44m 21.877s.
Fastest race lap: Cochet, 1m 11.939s, 85.822 mph/138.117 km/h.
Fastest qualifying lap: Cochet, 1m 11.096s, 86.840 mph/139.755 km/h.

9th COUPE DU VAL DE VIENNE, Circuit du Val de Vienne, Le Vigeant, France, 24/25 June. Round 4. 2 x 18 laps of the 2.334-mile/3.757-km circuit.
Race 1 (42.021 miles/67.626 km)
1 Ryo Fukuda, J (Dallara F399-Renault), 28m 26.471s, 88.648 mph/142.665 km/h.
2 Mathieu Zangarelli, F (Dallara F399-Renault), 28m 35.840s; **3** James Andanson Jr., F (Martini MK79-Opel), 28m 38.813s; **4** Tiago Monteiro, P (Dallara F399-Renault), 28m 39.648s; **5** Lucas Lasserre, F (Dallara F399-Renault), 28m 40.211s; **6** Jonathan Cochet, F (Dallara F399-Renault), 28m 40.904s; **7** Yannick Schroeder, F (Dallara F399-Renault), 28m 42.626s; **8** Marcos Ambrose, AUS (Martini MK79-Renault), 28m 45.634s; **9** Adam Jones, GB (Martini MK73-Opel), 28m 51.049s; **10** Philip Giebler, USA (Martini MK73-Opel), 28m 51.635s.
Fastest race lap: Fukuda, 1m 33.922s, 89.480 mph/144.005 km/h.
Fastest qualifying lap: Cochet, 1m 32.446s, 90.909 mph/146.304 mph.

Race 2 (42.021 miles/67.626 km)
1 Jonathan Cochet, F (Dallara F399-Renault), 34m 35.182s, 72.897 mph/117.317 km/h.
2 Tiago Monteiro, P (Dallara F399-Renault), 34m 36.063s; **3** Julien Beltoise, F (Dallara F399-Renault), 34m 51.982s; **4** Lucas Lasserre, F (Dallara F399-Renault), 34m 54.357s; **5** Ryo Fukuda, J (Dallara F399-Renault), 34m 55.187s; **6** Romain Dumas, F (Martini MK79-Opel), 35m 07.541s; **7** Ying Kin Lee, RC (Martini MK79-Opel), 35m 13.962s; **8** Philip Giebler, USA (Martini MK73-Opel), 35m 23.801s; **9** Marcos Ambrose, AUS (Martini MK79-Renault), 35m 28.693s; **10** Mathieu Zangarelli, F (Dallara F399-Renault), 35m 31.548s.
Fastest race lap: Fukuda, 1m 54.149s, 73.625 mph/118.487 km/h.
Fastest qualifying lap: Cochet, 1m 32.083s, 91.267 mph/146.881 km/h.

FRENCH FORMULA 3 CHAMPIONSHIP, Circuit de Spa-Francorchamps, Stavelot, Belgium, 8/9 July. Round 5. 10 and 3 laps of the 4.330-mile/6.968-km circuit.
Race 1 (43.297 miles/69.680 km)
1 Takuma Sato, J (Dallara F300-Mugen Honda), 22m 45.106s, 114.181 mph/183.757 km/h.
2 Martin O'Connell, GB (Dallara F300-Mugen Honda), 27m 50.457s; **3** Jonathan Cochet, F (Dallara F399-Renault), 27m 56.850s; **4** Julien Beltoise, F (Dallara F399-Renault), 27m 57.230s; **5** Adam Jones, GB (Martini MK73-Opel), 28m 07.711s; **6** Romain Dumas, F (Martini MK79-Opel), 28m 09.196s; **7** James Andanson Jr., F (Martini MK79-Opel), 28m 10.814s; **8** Ryo Fukuda, J (Dallara F399-Renault), 28m 11.579s; **9** Tristan Gommendy, F (Dallara F399-Renault), 28m 12.026s; **10** Lucas Lasserre, F (Dallara F399-Renault), 28m 13.523s.
Fastest race lap: Sato, 2m 15.424s, 115.098 mph/185.232 km/h.
Fastest qualifying lap: Tiago Monteiro, P (Dallara F399-Renault), 2m 14.403s, 115.972 mph/186.639 km/h.

Race 2 (12.989 miles/20.904 km)
1 Narain Karthikeyan, IND (Dallara F300-Mugen Honda), 8m 12.313s, 94.982 mph/152.859 km/h.
2 Jonathan Cochet, F (Dallara F399-Renault), 8m 20.020s; **3** Mathieu Zangarelli, F (Dallara F399-Renault), 8m 26.915s; **4** Martin O'Connell, GB (Dallara F300-Mugen Honda), 8m 30.562s; **5** Andy Priaulx, GB (Dallara F399-Renault), 8m 31.722s; **6** Tomas Scheckter, ZA (Dallara F300-Mugen Honda), 8m 32.075s; **7** Matt Davies, GB (Dallara F399-Renault), 8m 36.252s; **8** Tiago Monteiro, P (Dallara F399-Renault), 8m 49.311s; **9** Ryo Fukuda, J (Dallara F399-Renault), 8m 50.334s; **10** Tristan Gommendy, F (Dallara F399-Renault), 8m 53.875s.
Fastest race lap: Sato, 2m 37.107s, 99.212 mph/159.667 km/h.
Fastest qualifying lap: Cochet, 2m 14.258s, 116.097 mph/186.840 km/h.

58th GRAND PRIX D'ALBI, Circuit d'Albi, France, 3 September. Round 6. 26 laps of the 2.206-mile/3.551-km circuit, 57.369 miles/92.326 km
1 Tiago Monteiro, P (Dallara F399-Renault), 31m 44.768s, 108.427 mph/174.496 km/h.
2 Julien Beltoise, F (Dallara F399-Renault), 31m 45.412s; **3** Mathieu Zangarelli, F (Dallara F399-Renault), 31m 49.266s; **4** Lucas Lasserre, F (Dallara F399-Renault), 31m 51.380s; **5** Tristan Gommendy, F (Dallara F399-Renault), 31m 54.333s; **6** Jonathan Cochet, F (Dallara F399-Renault), 31m 59.289s; **7** Ying Kin Lee, RC (Martini MK79-Opel), 32m 10.023s; **8** Philip Giebler, USA (Martini MK79-Opel), 32m 13.604s; **9** Frédéric Makowiecki, F (Dallara F396-Fiat), 32m 20.576s; **10** Nassim Sidi Said, DZ (Dallara F398-Opel), 32m 42.648s.
Fastest race lap: Monteiro, 1m 09.087s, 114.976 mph/185.036 km/h.
Fastest qualifying lap: Monteiro, 1m 08.413s, 116.109 mph/186.859 km/h.

COUPES D'AUTOMNE, Circuit Le Mans-Bugatti, France, 17 September. Round 7. 20 laps of the 2.675-mile/4.305-km circuit, 53.500 miles/86.100 km
1 Tiago Monteiro, P (Dallara F399-Renault), 32m 55.084s, 97.515 mph/156.935 km/h.
2 Mathieu Zangarelli, F (Dallara F399-Renault), 32m 58.823s; **3** Jonathan Cochet, F (Dallara F399-Renault), 32m 59.458s; **4** Julien Beltoise, F (Dallara F399-Renault), 33m 04.363s; **5** Romain Dumas, F (Dallara F399-Renault), 33m 04.667s; **6** Yannick Schroeder, F (Dallara F399-Renault), 33m 07.490s; **7** Philip Giebler, USA (Martini MK73-Opel), 33m 10.234s; **8** Ying Kin Lee, RC (Martini MK79-Opel), 33m 12.565s; **9** James Andanson Jr., F (Martini MK79-Opel), 33m 19.125s; **10** Adam Jones, GB (Martini MK73-Opel), 33m 20.013s.
Fastest race lap: Cochet, 1m 37.927s, 98.339 mph/158.261 km/h.
Fastest qualifying lap: Fukuda, 1m 36.046s, 100.265 mph/161.360 km/h.

COUPES D'AUTOMNE 2000, Circuit de Lédenon, Remoulins, Nimes, France, 8 October. Round 8. 28 laps of the 1.957-mile/3.150-km circuit, 54.796 miles/88.200 km.
1 Tiago Monteiro, P (Dallara F399-Renault), 37m 41.912s, 87.226 mph/140.377 km/h.
2 Romain Dumas, F (Martini MK79-Opel), 37m 42.131s; **3** James Andanson Jr., F (Martini MK79-Opel), 37m 46.747s; **4** Mathieu Zangarelli, F (Dallara F399-Renault), 37m 46.878s; **5** Jonathan Cochet, F (Dallara F399-Renault), 37m 51.994s; **6** Yannick Schroeder, F (Dallara F399-Renault), 37m 56.277s; **7** Lucas Lasserre, F (Dallara F399-Renault), 38m 12.332s; **8** Ying Kin Lee, RC (Martini MK79-Opel), 38m 14.761s; **9** Julien Piguet, F (Dallara F396-Opel), 38m 37.492s; **10** Philip Giebler, USA (Martini MK73-Opel), 38m 37.606s.
Fastest race lap: Monteiro, 1m 19.879s, 88.213 mph/141.965 km/h.
Fastest qualifying lap: Cochet, 1m 18.085s, 90.239 mph/145.226 km/h.

Final championship points

Class A
1 Jonathan Cochet, F, 162.5; **2** Tiago Monteiro, P, 133; **3** Ryo Fukuda, J, 130; **4** Mathieu Zangarelli, F, 121; **5** Lucas Lasserre, F, 104; **6** Julien Beltoise, F, 102; **7** Romain Dumas, F, 97; **8** James Andanson Jr., F, 88; **9** Yannick Schroeder, F, 67.5; **10** Ying Kin Lee, RC, 55; **11** Tristan Gommendy, F, 54; **12** Marcos Ambrose, AUS, 49; **13** Kevin Nadin, MC, 6.

'Championnat de France Promotion' (Class B)
1 Adam Jones, GB, 186; **2** Philip Giebler, USA, 181; **3** Julien Piguet, F, 140; **4** Frédéric Makowiecki, F, 124; **5** David Moretti, F, 69.

German Formula 3 Championship

All cars are Dallara F300-Opel unless stated.

NEW RACE FESTIVAL, Omloop van Zolder, Hasselt, Belgium, 15/16 April. 21 and 19 laps of the 2.609-mile/4.198-km circuit.
Round 1 (54.779 miles/88.158 km)
1 Giorgio Pantano, I, 32m 37.053s, 100.766 mph/162.167 km/h.
2 Stefan Mücke, D, 32m 37.628s; **3** André Lotterer, D (Dallara F399-Opel), 32m 44.676s; **4** Jeroen Bleekemolen, NL (Dallara F399-Opel), 32m 52.396s; **5** Tom van Bavel, B (Dallara F399-Opel), 32m 52.656s; **6** Alexander Müller, D (Dallara F300-Mugen), 32m 52.821s; **7** Zsolt Baumgartner, H (Dallara F399-Opel), 32m 52.638s; **8** Patrick Freisacher, A, 32m 53.917s; **9** Nicolas Stelandre, B (Dallara F399-Opel), 33m 02.014s; **10** Frank Diefenbacher, D, 33m 03.572s.
Fastest race lap: Pierre Kaffer, D, 1m 31.327s, 102.825 mph/165.480 km/h.
Fastest qualifying lap: Bleekemolen, 1m 43.456s, 90.770 mph/146.079 km/h.

Round 2 (49.562 miles/79.762 km)
1 Alexander Müller, D (Dallara F300-Mugen), 29m 13.924s, 101.728 mph/163.715 km/h.
2 Giorgio Pantano, I, 29m 16.209s; **3** Elran Nijenhuis, NL (Dallara F300-Mugen Honda), 29m 20.985s; **4** Björn Wirdheim, S (Dallara F300-Mugen Honda), 29m 23.879s; **5** Zsolt Baumgartner, H (Dallara F399-Opel), 29m 30.018s; **6** Kari Mäenpää, FIN (Dallara F399-Renault), 29m 30.571s; **7** Stefan Mücke, D, 29m 31.079s; **8** Pierre Kaffer, D, 29m 31.458s; **9** Toshihiro Kaneishi, J, 29m 31.665s; **10** Tony Schmidt, D (Dallara F399-Opel), 29m 33.988s.
Fastest race lap: Pantano, 1m 31.107s, 103.073 mph/165.880 km/h.
Fastest qualifying lap: Müller, 1m 42.316s, 91.781 mph/147.707 km/h.

INT. AvD/MAC RENNSPORTFESTIVAL, Hockenheimring short circuit, Heidelberg, Germany, 27/28 May. 31 and 30 laps of the 1.639-mile/2.638-km circuit.
Round 3 (50.814 miles/81.778 km)
1 André Lotterer, D (Dallara F399-Opel), 30m 58.652s, 98.422 mph/158.395 km/h.
2 Pierre Kaffer, D (Dallara F399-Opel), 30m 59.224s; **3** Patrick Freisacher, A, 31m 01.124s; **4** Zsolt Baumgartner, H (Dallara F399-Opel), 31m 01.784s; **5** Alexander Müller, D (Dallara F300-Mugen), 31m 20.903s; **6** Toshihiro Kaneishi, J, 31m 21.308s; **7** Enrico Toccacelo, I, 31m 23.344s; **8** Kari Mäenpää, FIN (Dallara F399-Renault), 31m 24.279s; **9** Martin Tomcyzk, D, 31m 24.821s; **10** Giorgio Pantano, I, 31m 25.273s.
Fastest race lap: Lotterer, 58.564s, 100.762 mph/162.161 km/h.
Fastest qualifying lap: Frank Diefenbacher, D, 1m 08.665s, 85.940 mph/138.306 km/h.

Round 4 (49.175 miles/79.140 km)
1 André Lotterer, D (Dallara F399-Opel), 30m 33.191s, 96.570 mph/155.414 km/h.
2 Giorgio Pantano, I, 30m 46.192s; **3** Nicolas Stelandre, B (Dallara F399-Opel), 30m 52.904s; **4** Björn Wirdheim, S (Dallara F300-Mugen), 30m 59.286s; **5** Tom van Bavel, B (Dallara F399-Opel), 31m 03.408s; **6** Toshihiro Kaneishi, J, 31m 04.909s; **7** Alexander Müller, D (Dallara F300-Mugen), 31m 05.252s; **8** Jeroen Bleekemolen, NL (Dallara F399-Opel), 31m 08.579s; **9** Kari Mäenpää, FIN (Dallara F399-Renault), 31m 08.927s; **10** Pierre Kaffer, D (Dallara F399-Opel), 31m 09.287s.
Fastest race lap: Pantano, 58.946s, 100.109 mph/161.110 km/h.
Fastest qualifying lap: Pantano, 1m 07.640s, 87.242 mph/140.402 km/h.

INT. ADAC-PREIS DER TOURENWAGEN VON SACHSEN-ANHALT, Oschersleben Motopark, Germany, 17/18 June. 2 x 22 laps of the 2.279-mile/3.667-km circuit.
Round 5 (50.128 miles/80.674 km)
1 André Lotterer, D (Dallara F399-Opel), 30m 08.441s, 99.789 mph/160.595 km/h.
2 Frank Diefenbacher, D, 30m 13.042s; **3** Nicolas Stelandre, B (Dallara F399-Opel), 30m 17.791s; **4** Giorgio Pantano, I, 30m 17.978s; **5** Alexander Müller, D (Dallara F300-Mugen), 30m 26.935s; **6** Stefan Mücke, D, 30m 28.052s; **7** Kari Mäenpää, FIN (Dallara F399-Renault), 30m 28.737s; **8** Patrick Freisacher, A, 30m 29.006s; **9** Thomas Mutsch, D (Martini MK80-Opel), 30m 46.992s; **10** Hannu Wiinikainen, FIN (Dallara F399-Renault), 30m 47.471s.
Fastest race lap: Diefenbacher, 1m 21.252s, 100.956 mph/162.472 km/h.
Fastest qualifying lap: Lotterer, 1m 19.918s, 102.641 mph/165.184 km/h.

Round 6 (50.128 miles/80.674 km)
1 Giorgio Pantano, I, 30m 03.593s, 100.057 mph/161.027 km/h.
2 Enrico Toccacelo, I, 30m 09.667s; **3** Pierre Kaffer, D (Dallara F399-Opel), 30m 16.016s; **4** André Lotterer, D (Dallara F399-Opel), 30m 21.598s; **5** Frank Diefenbacher, D, 30m 27.353s; **6** Armin Pörnbacher, I (Dallara F399-Opel), 30m 28.104s; **7** Stefan Mücke, D, 30m 28.764s; **8** Zsolt Baumgartner, H (Dallara F399-Opel), 30m 29.047s; **9** Philip Cloostermans, B, 30m 29.375s; **10** Nicolas Stelandre, B (Dallara F399-Opel), 30m 30.585s.
Fastest race lap: Pantano, 1m 20.907s, 101.386 mph/163.165 km/h.
Fastest qualifying lap: Freisacher, 1m 20.351s, 102.088 mph/164.294 km/h.

INT. ADAC NORISRING SPEEDWEEKEND, Norisring, Nürnberg, Germany, 8/9 July. 2 x 35 laps of the 1.429-mile/2.300-km circuit.
Round 7 (50.020 miles/80.500 km)
1 Pierre Kaffer, D (Dallara F399-Opel), 30m 09.649s, 99.507 mph/160.142 km/h.
2 Giorgio Pantano, I, 30m 12.153s; **3** Stefan Mücke, D, 30m 25.945s; **4** Sven Heidfeld, D (Dallara F399-Opel), 30m 26.687s; **5** Alexander Müller, D (Dallara F300-Mugen), 30m 28.796s; **6** Tony Schmidt, D (Dallara F399-Opel), 30m 32.159s; **7** Toshihiro Kaneishi, J, 30m 33.341s; **8** Enrico Toccacelo, I, 30m 35.569s; **9** Zsolt Baumgartner, H (Dallara F399-Opel), 30m 41.265s; **10** Thomas Mutsch, D (Martini MK80-Opel), 30m 41.861s.
Fastest race lap: Kaffer, 50.776s, 101.326 mph/163.069 km/h.
Fastest qualifying lap: Heidfeld, 59.736s, 86.128 mph/138.610 km/h.

Round 8 (50.020 miles/80.500 km)
1 Pierre Kaffer, D (Dallara F399-Opel), 29m 57.247s, 100.194 mph/161.247 km/h.
2 Sven Heidfeld, D (Dallara F399-Opel), 29m 59.781s; **4** Zsolt Baumgartner, H (Dallara F399-Opel), 30m 08.176s; **5** Jeroen Bleekemolen, NL (Dallara F399-Opel), 30m 09.007s; **6** Toshihiro Kaneishi, J, 30m 09.837s; **7** Thomas Mutsch, D (Martini MK80-Opel), 30m 20.271s; **8** Val Hillebrand, B (Dallara F399-Opel), 30m 20.965s; **9** Alexander Müller, D (Dallara F300-Mugen), 30m 22.478s; **10** Nicolas Stelandre, B (Dallara F399-Opel), 30m 24.829s.
Björn Wirdheim, S (Dallara F300-Mugen), finished 3rd in 30m 01.318s, but was disqualified.
Fastest race lap: André Lotterer, D (Dallara F399-Opel), 50.447s, 101.987 mph/164.133 km/h.
Fastest qualifying lap: Mücke, 59.556s, 86.388 mph/139.029 km/h.

INT. ADAC SPARKASSENPREIS, Sachsenring, Germany, 5/6 August. 2 x 24 laps of the 2.104-mile/3.386-km circuit.
Round 9 (50.495 miles/81.264 km)
1 Patrick Freisacher, A, 30m 02.448s, 100.853 mph/162.307 km/h.
2 Alexander Müller, D (Dallara F300-Mugen), 30m 02.710s; **3** Enrico Toccacelo, I, 30m 04.424s; **4** Stefan Mücke, D, 30m 04.813s; **5** Pierre Kaffer, D (Dallara F399-Opel), 30m 09.727s; **6** André Lotterer, D (Dallara F399-Opel), 30m 10.910s; **7** Giorgio Pantano, I, 30m 12.065s; **8** Frank Diefenbacher, D, 30m 21.131s; **9** Thomas Mutsch, D (Martini MK80-Opel), 30m 21.686s; **10** Ken Grandon, IRL (Dallara F300-Fiat), 30m 49.47s.
Fastest race lap: Müller, 1m 14.394s, 101.813 mph/163.852 km/h.
Fastest qualifying lap: Freisacher, 1m 14.611s, 101.517 mph/163.375 km/h.

Round 10 (50.495 miles/81.264 km)
1 Alexander Müller, D (Dallara F300-Mugen), 30m 17.259s, 100.031 mph/160.984 km/h.
2 Giorgio Pantano, I, 30m 20.105s; **3** Sven Heidfeld, D (Dallara F399-Opel), 30m 23.266s; **4** Pierre Kaffer, D (Dallara F399-Opel), 30m 23.746s; **5** Martin Tomcyzk, D, 30m 24.202s; **6** Björn Wirdheim, S (Dallara F300-Mugen), 30m 25.536s; **7** André Lotterer, D (Dallara F399-Opel), 30m 26.161s; **8** Stefan Mücke, D, 30m 26m 701s; **9** Enrico Toccacelo, I, 30m 28.173s; **10** Patrick Freisacher, A, 30m 28.541s.
Fastest race lap: Müller, 1m 14.693s, 101.405 mph/163.196 km/h.
Fastest qualifying lap: Freisacher, 1m 14.408s, 101.794 mph/163.821 km/h.

INT. ADAC GROSSER PREIS DER TOURENWAGEN, Nürburgring Grand Prix circuit, Nürburg/Eifel, Germany, 19/20 August. 2 x 18 laps of the 2.831-mile/4.556-km circuit.
Round 11 (50.957 miles/82.008 km)
1 Stefan Mücke, D, 29m 10.146s, 104.818 mph/168.688 km/h.
2 Enrico Toccacelo, I, 29m 17.039s; **3** Tom van Bavel, B (Dallara F399-Opel), 29m 19.452s; **4** Alexander Müller, D (Dallara F300-Mugen), 29m 23.288s; **5** André Lotterer, D (Dallara F399-Opel), 29m 23.787s; **6** Tony Schmidt, D (Dallara F399-Opel), 29m 29.497s; **7** Zsolt Baumgartner, H (Dallara F399-Opel), 29m 30.409s; **8** Patrick Freisacher, A, 29m 35.807s; **9** Armin Pörnbacher, I (Dallara F399-Opel), 29m 40.654s; **10** Giorgio Mecattaf, CH (Dallara F399-Opel), 29m 40.816s.
Fastest race lap: Giorgio Pantano, I, 1m 36.398s, 105.723 mph/170.145 km/h.
Fastest qualifying lap: Mücke, 1m 47.801s, 94.540 mph/152.147 km/h.

Round 12 (50.957 miles/82.008 km)
1 Toshihiro Kaneishi, J, 29m 16.963s, 104.411 mph/168.034 km/h.
2 André Lotterer, D (Dallara F399-Opel), 29m 19.757s; **3** Tom van Bavel, B (Dallara F399-Opel), 29m 20.142s; **4** Enrico Toccacelo, I, 29m 21.174s; **5** Patrick Freisacher, A, 29m 25.783s; **6** Björn Wirdheim, S (Dallara F300-Mugen), 29m 27.837s; **7** Pierre Kaffer, D (Dallara F399-Opel), 29m 28.433s; **8** Martin Tomczyk, D, 29m 29.042s; **9** Philip Cloostermans, B, 29m 29.621s; **10** Giorgio Pantano, I, 29m 29.994s.
Fastest race lap: Freisacher, 1m 36.374s, 105.749 mph/170.187 km/h.
Fastest qualifying lap: Müller, 1m 36.701s, 105.392 mph/169.611 km/h.

INT. ADAC RUNDSTRECKENRENNEN, EuroSpeedway Lausitz, 2/3 September. 18 and 17 laps of the 2.817-mile/4.534-km circuit.
Round 13 (50.711 miles/81.612 km)
1 Pierre Kaffer, D (Dallara F399-Opel), 29m 48.158s, 102.094 mph/164.305 km/h.
2 Enrico Toccacelo, I, 29m 50.605s; **3** Giorgio Pantano, I, 29m 51.020s; **4** Sven Heidfeld, D (Dallara F399-Opel), 29m 55.294s; **5** Patrick Freisacher, A, 29m 55.769s; **6** Martin Tomcyzk, D, 30m 01.979s; **7** Stefan Mücke, D, 30m 05.370s; **8** Alexander Müller, D (Dallara F300-Mugen), 30m 06.060s; **9** Frank Diefenbacher, D, 30m 06.439s; **10** Björn Wirdheim, S (Dallara F300-Mugen), 30m 08.759s.
Fastest race lap: Kaffer, 1m 37.235s, 104.307 mph/167.865 km/h.
Fastest qualifying lap: Toccacelo, 1m 38.969s, 102.479 mph/164.924 km/h.

Round 14 (47.894 miles/77.078 km)
1 Alexander Müller, D (Dallara F300-Mugen), 30m 20.044s, 94.733 mph/152.458 km/h.
2 André Lotterer, D (Dallara F399-Opel), 30m 23.763s; **3** Enrico Toccacelo, I, 30m 29.776s; **4** Sven Heidfeld, D (Dallara F399-Opel), 30m 30.982s; **5** Giorgio Pantano, I, 30m 32.086s; **6** Frank Diefenbacher, D, 30m 32.772s; **7** Jeroen Bleekemolen, NL (Dallara F399-Opel), 30m 40.212s; **8** Tom van Bavel, B (Dallara F399-Opel), 30m 40.914s; **9** Stefan Mücke, D, 30m 41.447s; **10** Philip Cloostermans, B, 30m 42.440s.
Fastest race lap: Diefenbacher, 1m 39.287s, 102.151 mph/164.396 km/h.
Fastest qualifying lap: Toccacelo, 1m 37.749s, 103.758 mph/166.983 km/h.

INT. ADAC-PREIS VON NIEDERSACHSEN, Oschersleben Motopark, Germany, 23/24 September. 22 and 20 laps of the 2.279-mile/3.667-km circuit.
Round 15 (50.128 miles/80.674 km)
1 Giorgio Pantano, I, 29m 47.782s, 100.942 mph/162.451 km/h.
2 Stefan Mücke, D, 29m 49.459s; **3** Pierre Kaffer, D (Dallara F399-Opel), 29m 58.967s; **4** Patrick Freisacher, A, 30m 05.086s; **5** Alexander Müller, D (Dallara F300-Mugen), 30m 05.587s; **6** André Lotterer, D (Dallara F399-Opel), 30m 10.328s; **7** Tom van Bavel, B (Dallara F399-Opel), 30m 11.791s; **8** Martin Tomcyzk, D, 30m 15.375s; **9** Toshihiro Kaneishi, J, 30m 15.831s; **10** Peter Sundberg, S (Dallara F300-Mugen), 30m 16.245s.
Fastest race lap: Pantano, 1m 20.426s, 101.992 mph/164.141 km/h.
Fastest qualifying lap: Pantano, 1m 19.985s, 102.555 mph/165.046 km/h.

Round 16 (45.571 miles/73.340 km)
1 Patrick Freisacher, A, 30m 53.070s, 88.532 mph/142.479 km/h.
2 Giorgio Pantano, I, 30m 53.571s; **3** Pierre Kaffer, D (Dallara F399-Opel), 30m 54.195s; **4** Martin Tomcyzk, D, 30m 55.786s; **5** Stefan Mücke, D, 30m 57.023s; **6** Alexander Müller, D (Dallara F300-Mugen), 30m 59.112s; **7** Sven Heidfeld, D (Dallara F399-Opel), 31m 05.549s; **8** Toshihiro Kaneishi, J, 31m 05.660s; **9** Enrico Toccacelo, I, 31m 06.412s; **10** Frank Diefenbacher, D, 31m 10.218s.
Fastest race lap: Kaffer, 1m 21.102s, 101.142 mph/162.773 km/h.
Fastest qualifying lap: Pantano, 1m 19.878s, 102.692 mph/165.267 km/h.

INT. ADAC EIFELRENNEN, Nürburgring Grand Prix circuit, Nürburg/Eifel, Germany, 7/8 October. 2 x 18 laps of the 2.828-mile/4.551-km circuit.
Round 17 (50.901 miles/81.918 km)
1 Pierre Kaffer, D (Dallara F399-Opel), 28m 24.462s, 107.509 mph/173.019 km/h.
2 Frank Diefenbacher, D, 28m 31.566s; **3** André Lotterer, D

(Dallara F399-Opel), 28m 32.380s; **4** Toshihiro Kaneishi, J, 28m 32.664s; **5** Patrick Freisacher, A, 28m 41.301s; **6** Enrico Toccacelo, I, 28m 41.856s; **7** Stefan Mücke, D, 28m 42.390s; **8** Giorgio Pantano, I, 28m 44.204s; **9** Alexander Müller, D (Dallara F300-Mugen), 28m 44.737s; **10** Martin Tomczyk, D, 28m 45.154s.
Fastest race lap: Kaffer, 1m 33.760s, 108.578 mph/174.740 km/h.
Fastest qualifying lap: Kaffer, 1m 33.529s, 108.846 mph/175.171 km/h.

Round 18 (50.901 miles/81.918 km)
1 Enrico Toccacelo, I, 31m 03.659s, 98.326 mph/158.240 km/h.
2 Toshihiro Kaneishi, J, 31m 04.350s; **3** Val Hillebrand, B (Dallara F399-Opel), 31m 08.640s; **4** Tony Schmidt, D (Dallara F399-Opel), 31m 08.867s; **5** Armin Pörnbacher, I (Dallara F399-Opel), 31m 17.967s; **6** Martin Tomczyk, D, 31m 20.906s; **7** Tom van Bavel, B (Dallara F399-Opel), 31m 21.873s; **8** Peter Sundberg, S (Dallara F300-Mugen), 31m 22.444s; **9** Björn Wirdheim, S (Dallara F300-Mugen), 31m 23.178s; **10** Giorgio Mecattaf, CH (Dallara F399-Opel), 31m 23.626s.
Fastest race lap: Kaneishi, 1m 34.308s, 107.947 mph/173.724 km/h.
Fastest qualifying lap: Toccacelo, 1m 33.378s, 109.022 mph/175.455 km/h.

INT. ADAC PREIS, Hockenheimring Grand Prix circuit, Heidelberg, Germany, 28/29 October. 2 x 12 laps of the 4.240-mile/6.823-km circuit.
Round 19 (50.875 miles/81.876 km)
1 Stefan Mücke, D, 25m 42.529s, 118.734 mph/191.085 km/h.
2 Alexander Müller, D (Dallara F300-Mugen), 25m 46.026s; **3** Tony Schmidt, D (Dallara F399-Opel), 25m 49.821s; **4** Giorgio Pantano, I, 25m 51.761s; **5** Toshihiro Kaneishi, J, 25m 52.401s; **6** Patrick Freisacher, A, 25m 53.630s; **7** Pierre Kaffer, D (Dallara F399-Opel), 25m 54.452s; **8** Björn Wirdheim, S (Dallara F300-Mugen), 26m 01.569s; **9** Philip Cloostermans, B, 26m 02.164s; **10** Tom van Bavel, B (Dallara F399-Opel), 26m 03.168s.
Fastest race lap: Mücke, 2m 07.425s, 119.777 mph/192.763 km/h.
Fastest qualifying lap: Mücke, 2m 16.510s, 111.806 mph/179.934 km/h.

Round 20 (50.875 miles/81.876 km)
1 Alexander Müller, D (Dallara F300-Mugen), 31m 57.608s, 95.510 mph/153.709 km/h.
2 Patrick Freisacher, A, 31m 57.945s; **3** Giorgio Pantano, I, 32m 09.491s; **4** Martin Tomczyk, D, 32m 32.364s; **5** Jeroen Bleekemolen, NL (Dallara F399-Opel), 32m 35.221s; **6** Elran Nijenhuis, NL (Dallara F300-Mugen), 32m 51.756s; **7** Andreas Feichtner, D (Dallara F300-Mugen), 32m 52.458s; **8** Marc Caldonazzi, D (Dallara F399-Opel), 32m 55.999s; **9** Tony Schmidt, D (Dallara F399-Opel), 32m 56.045s; **10** Nicolas Stelandre, B (Dallara F399-Opel), 33m 04.549s.
Fastest race lap: Freisacher, 2m 09.137s, 118.189 mph/190.207 km/h.
Fastest qualifying lap: Frank Diefenbacher, D, 2m 07.817s, 119.410 mph/192.172 km/h.

Final championship points
1 Giorgio Pantano, I, 205; **2** Alexander Müller, D, 181; **3** Pierre Kaffer, D, 164; **4** André Lotterer, D, 151; **5** Stefan Mücke, D, 136; **6** Patrick Freisacher, A, 126; **7** Enrico Toccacelo, I, 125; **8** Toshihiro Kaneishi, J, 82; **9** Sven Heidfeld, D, 64; **10** Frank Diefenbacher, D, 57; **11** Tom van Bavel, B, 52; **12** Martin Tomczyk, D, 49; **13** Zsolt Baumgartner, H, 41; **14** Björn Wirdheim, S, 38; **15** Tony Schmidt, D, 37; **16** Jeroen Bleekemolen, NL, 36; **17** Nicolas Stelandre, B, 29; **18** Elran Nijenhuis, NL, 18; **19** Armin Pörnbacher, I, 16; 20= Val Hillebrand, B, 15; 20= Kari Mäenpää, FIN, 15; **22** Thomas Mutsch, D, 9; **23** Philip Cloostermans, B, 7; **24=** Andreas Feichtner, D, 4; **24=** Peter Sundberg, S, 4; **26** Marc Caldonazzi, I, 3; **27** Giorgio Mecattaf, CH, 2; **28=** Ken Grandon, IRL, 1; **28=** Hannu Wiinikainen, FIN, 1.

Junior (Rookie) Championship
1 André Lotterer, D, 228; **2** Frank Diefenbacher, D, 141; **3** Tom van Bavel, B, 127.

Italian Formula 3 Championship

GRAN PREMIO CAMPAGNANO - TROFEO IGNAZIO GIUNTI, Autodromo di Vallelunga, Campagnano di Roma, Italy, 2 April. Round 1. 2 x 23 laps of the 2.001-mile/3.220-km circuit.
Race 1 (46.019 miles/74.060 km)
1 Valerio Scassellati, I (Dallara F300-Opel), 26m 57.078s, 102.449 mph/164.875 km/h.
2 Davide Uboldi, I (Dallara F399-Fiat), 26m 57.756s; **3** Ivan Bellarosa, I (Dallara F398-Fiat), 27m 05.557s; **4** Sergio Ghiotto, I (Dallara F399-Opel), 27m 10.253s; **5** Franco Ghiotto, I (Dallara F399-Opel), 27m 24.288s; **6** Lorenzo del Gallo, I (Dallara F399-Fiat), 27m 37.288s.
Fastest race lap: Uboldi, 1m 09.379s, 103.820 mph/167.082 km/h.
Fastest qualifying lap: Bellarosa, 1m 09.644s, 103.425 mph/166.446 km/h.

Race 2 (46.019 miles/74.060 km)
1 Davide Uboldi, I (Dallara F399-Fiat), 27m 09.124s, 101.691 mph/163.656 km/h.
2 Ivan Bellarosa, I (Dallara F398-Fiat), 27m 09.618s; **3** Sergio Ghiotto, I (Dallara F399-Opel), 27m 13.052s; **4** Franco Ghiotto, I (Dallara F399-Opel), 27m 21.477s; **5** Lorenzo del Gallo, I (Dallara F399-Fiat), 27m 22.481s; **6** 'Linos', BR (Dallara F399-Fiat), 5 laps.
Fastest race lap: Bellarosa, 1m 09.607s, 103.480 mph/166.535 km/h.
Fastest qualifying lap: del Gallo, 1m 09.411s, 103.772 mph/167.005 km/h.

ITALIAN FORMULA 3 CHAMPIONSHIP, Autodromo Internazionale del Mugello, Scarperia, Firenze (Florence), Italy, 16 April. Round 2. 21 laps of the 3.259-mile/5.245-km circuit, 68.441 miles/110.145 km.
1 'Linos', BR (Dallara F399-Fiat), 37m 52.172s, 108.437 mph/174.512 km/h.
2 Davide Uboldi, I (Dallara F399-Fiat), 37m 52.770s; **3** Ivan Bellarosa, I (Dallara F398-Fiat), 38m 02.755s; **4** Sergio Ghiotto, I (Dallara F399-Opel), 38m 02.801s; **5** Franco Ghiotto, I (Dallara F399-Fiat), 38m 18.042s; **6** Lorenzo del Gallo, I (Dallara F399-Fiat), 38m 21.045s.
Fastest race lap: Ghiotto (Sergio), 1m 46.827s, 109.829 mph/176.753 km/h.
Fastest qualifying lap: Bellarosa, 1m 47.095s, 109.554 mph/176.311 km/h.

ITALIAN FORMULA 3 CHAMPIONSHIP, Autodromo Enzo e Dino Ferrari, Imola, Italy, 14 May. Round 3. 20 laps of the 3.065-mile/4.933-km circuit, 61.304 miles/98.660 km.
1 Ivan Bellarosa, I (Dallara F398-Fiat), 36m 07.074s, 101.841 mph/163.897 km/h.
2 Valerio Scassellati, I (Dallara F300-Opel), 36m 07.511s; **3** Davide Uboldi, I (Dallara F399-Fiat), 36m 14.462s; **4** Lorenzo del Gallo, I (Dallara F300-Fiat), 36m 36.793s; **5** Silvio Alberti, I (Dallara F398-Fiat), 37m 09.336s; **6** Massimo Carli, I (Dallara F398-Fiat), 19 laps.
Fastest race lap: Scassellati, 1m 47.137s, 102.997 mph/165.758 km/h.
Fastest qualifying lap: Bellarosa.

ITALIAN FORMULA 3 CHAMPIONSHIP, Autodromo di Magione, Perugia, Italy, 28 May. Round 4. 32 laps of the 1.616-mile/2.600-km circuit, 51.698 miles/83.200 km.
1 Davide Uboldi, I (Dallara F399-Fiat), 36m 09.628s, 85.781 mph/138.051 km/h.
2 Ivan Bellarosa, I (Dallara F398-Fiat), 36m 29.466s; **3** Lorenzo del Gallo, I (Dallara F300-Fiat), 36m 29.838s; **4** Valerio Scassellati, I (Dallara F300-Opel), 36m 30.032s; **5** Franco Ghiotto, I (Dallara F399-Opel), 37m 03.020s; **6** Massimo Carli, I (Dallara F398-Fiat), 37m 03.200s.
Fastest race lap: Uboldi, 1m 07.264s, 86.466 mph/139.153 km/h.
Fastest qualifying lap: Uboldi, 1m 06.496s, 87.464 mph/140.760 km/h.

39th TROFEO AUTOMOBILE CLUB PARMA, Autodromo Riccardo Paletti, Varano, Parma, Italy, 18 June. Round 5. 45 laps of the 1.118-mile/1.800-km circuit, 50.331 miles/81.000 km.
1 Ivan Bellarosa, I (Dallara F398-Fiat), 34m 01.202s, 88.767 mph/142.857 km/h.
2 Davide Uboldi, I (Dallara F399-Fiat), 34m 04.779s; **3** Franco Ghiotto, I (Dallara F399-Opel), 44 laps; **4** Massimo Carli, I (Dallara F398-Fiat), 44; **5** Valerio Scassellati, I (Dallara F300-Opel), 44; **6** Lorenzo del Gallo, I (Dallara F300-Fiat), 30.
Fastest race lap: Bellarosa, 44.888s, 89.701 mph/144.359 km/h.
Fastest qualifying lap: Uboldi, 44.440s, 90.605 mph/145.815 km/h.

41st GRAN PREMIO LOTTERIA DI MONZA, Autodromo Nazionale di Monza, Milan, Italy, 25 June. Round 6. 16 laps of the 3.585-mile/5.770-km circuit, 57.364 miles/92.320 km.
1 Valerio Scassellati, I (Dallara F300-Opel), 29m 09.708s, 118.028 mph/189.947 km/h.
2 Ivan Bellarosa, I (Dallara F398-Fiat), 29m 14.957s; **3** Sergio Ghiotto, I (Dallara F399-Opel), 29m 32.531s; **4** Lorenzo del Gallo, I (Dallara F300-Fiat), 29m 33.398s; **5** Angelo Valentino, I (Dallara F399-Fiat), 29m 40.495s; **6** Franco Ghiotto, I (Dallara F399-Opel), 15 laps.
Fastest race lap: Scassellati, 1m 48.333s, 119.143 mph/191.742 km/h.
Fastest qualifying lap: Scassellati, 1m 46.505s, 121.188 mph/195.033 km/h.

GRAN PREMIO ROMA, Autodromo di Vallelunga, Campagnano di Roma, Italy, 23 July. Round 7. 30 laps of the 2.002-mile/3.222-km circuit, 60.062 miles/96.660 km.
1 Davide Uboldi, I (Dallara F399-Fiat), 35m 10.372s, 102.457 mph/164.888 km/h.
2 Michele Gasparini, I (Dallara F398-Fiat), 35m 15.103s; **3** Valerio Scassellati, I (Dallara F399-Opel), 35m 18.589s; **4** Ivan Bellarosa, I (Dallara F398-Fiat), 35m 39.780s; **5** Sergio Ghiotto, I (Dallara F399-Opel), 35m 40.985s; **6** Massimo Carli, I (Dallara F398-Fiat), 35m 57.541s.
Fastest race lap: Uboldi, 1m 09.691s, 103.420 mph/166.438 km/h.
Fastest qualifying lap: Uboldi, 1m 08.675s, 104.950 mph/168.900 km/h.

44th PREMIO PERGUSA, Ente Autodromo di Pergusa, Enna-Pergusa, Sicily, 3 September. Round 8. 20 laps of the 3.076-mile/4.950-km circuit, 61.516 miles/99.000 km.
1 Davide Uboldi, I (Dallara F399-Fiat), 33m 44.139s, 109.408 mph/176.075 km/h.
2 Michele Gasparini, I (Dallara F398-Fiat), 33m 44.323s; **3** Valerio Scassellati, I (Dallara F300-Opel), 33m 45.465s; **4** Massimo Carli, I (Dallara F398-Fiat), 34m 35.444s; **5** 'Linos', BR (Dallara F399-Fiat), 34m 45.346s; **6** Ivan Bellarosa, I (Dallara F398-Fiat), 19 laps.
Fastest race lap: Gasparini, 1m 39.826s, 110.921 mph/178.511 km/h.
Fastest qualifying lap: Uboldi, 1m 39.586s, 111.189 mph/178.941 km/h.

11th GRAN PREMIO DEL LEVANTE, Autodromo del Levante, Binetto, Italy, 24 September, Round 9. 53 laps of the 0.980-mile/1.577-km circuit, 51.935 miles/83.581 km.
1 Ivan Bellarosa, I (Dallara F398-Fiat), 39m 31.396s, 78.842 mph/126.884 km/h.
2 Davide Uboldi, I (Dallara F398-Fiat), 39m 46.397s; **3** Michele Gasparini, I (Dallara F398-Fiat), 39m 54.359s; **4** Massimo Carli, I (Dallara F398-Fiat), 40m 14.699s; **5** Gabriele de Bono, I (Dallara F399-Fiat), 51 laps; **6** Valerio Scassellati, I (Dallara F300-Opel), 51.
Fastest race lap: Bellarosa, 43.893s, 80.369 mph/129.342 km/h.
Fastest qualifying lap: Bellarosa, 43.588s, 80.932 mph/130.247 km/h.

ITALIAN FORMULA 3 CHAMPIONSHIP, Autodromo Santamonica, Misano Adriatico, Rimini, Italy, 22 October. Round 10. 24 laps of the 2.523-mile/4.060-km circuit, 60.546 miles/97.440 km.
1 Alessandro Manetti, I (Dallara F399-Opel), 35m 24.621s, 102.591 mph/165.104 km/h. **2** Armin Pörnbacher, I (Dallara F398-Opel), 35m 25.448s; **3** Ivan Bellarosa, I (Dallara F398-Fiat), 35m 45.500s; **4** Davide Uboldi, I (Dallara F399-Fiat), 36m 14.032s; **5** Michele Gasparini, I (Dallara F398-Fiat), 36m 14.523s; **6** Massimo Carli, I (Dallara F398-Fiat), 36m 15.567s.
Fastest race lap: Manetti, 1m 27.874s, 103.352 mph/166.329 km/h.
Fastest qualifying lap: Pörnbacher, 1m 27.676s, 103.585 mph/166.705 km/h.

Final championship points
1 Davide Uboldi, I, 173; **2** Ivan Bellarosa, I, 164; **3** Valerio Scassellati, I, 106; **4** Massimo Carli, I, 59; **5** Sergio Ghiotto, I, 55; **6** Franco Ghiotto, I, 54; **7** Lorenzo del Gallo, I, 53; **8** Michele Gasparini, I, 51; **9** 'Linos', BR, 40; **10** Alesandro Manetti, I, 21; **11** Armin Pörnbacher, I, 16; **12** Angelo Valentino, I, 14; **13=** Silvio Alberti, I, 8; **13=** Gabriele de Bono, I, 8.

Formula 3 Junior
1 Ivan Bellarosa, 113.5; **2** Massimo Carli, I, 58.5; **3** Michele Gasparini, I, 35.

Major Non-Championship Formula 3 Results

1999 Results

The Macau and Korea Formula 3 races were run after AUTOCOURSE 1999-2000 went to press.

FIA F3 WORLD CUP, 46th MACAU GP, Circuito Da Guia, Macau, 21 November. 2 x 15 laps of the 3.803-mile/6.120-km circuit, 114.084 miles/183.600 km.
Aggregated results from two races.
1 Darren Manning, GB (Dallara F399-TOM'S Toyota), 1h 07m 56.279s, 100.754 mph/162.148 km/h.
2 Jenson Button, GB (Dallara F399-Renault), 1h 08m 20.869s; **3** Daisuke Itoh, J (Dallara F399-Mugen Honda), 1h 09m 02.880s; **4** Tsugio Matsuda, J (Dallara F399-Mugen Honda), 1h 09m 17.267s; **5** Yves Olivier, B (Dallara F399-Opel), 1h 09m 47.258s; **6** Michele Spoldi, I (Dallara F399-Opel), 1h 09m 58.259s; **7** Alex Yoong, MAL (Dallara F399-Mugen Honda), 1h 10m 04.203s; **8** Ryo Fukuda, J (Martini MK79-Opel), 29 laps; **9** Toby Scheckter, ZA (Dallara F399-Mugen Honda), 29; **10** Michael Ho, MAC (Dallara F399-Opel), 29.
Fastest race lap: Manning, 2m 14.264s, 101.964 mph/164.095 km/h.
Fastest qualifying lap: Manning, 2m 14.143s, 102.056 mph/164.243 km/h.

FORMULA 3 KOREAN GRAND PRIX, Changwong circuit, South Korea, 28 November. 21 and 25 laps of the 1.892-mile/3.045-km circuit, 87.035 miles/140.070 km.
Aggregated results from two races.
1 Darren Manning, GB (Dallara F399-TOM'S Toyota), 1h 04m 41.805s, 80.717 mph/129.901 km/h.
2 Jenson Button, GB (Dallara F399-Renault), 1h 04m 42.882s; **3** Benoit Tréluyer, F (Dallara F399-Renault), 1h 05m 17.104s; **4** Jonathan Cochet, F (Dallara F399-Renault), 1h 05m 20.736s; **5** Toshihiro Kaneishi, J (Dallara F399-Opel), 1h 05m 24.296s; **6** Tiago Monteiro, P (Dallara F399-Renault), 1h 05m 30.573s; **7** Marc Hynes, GB (Dallara F399-Mugen Honda), 1h 05m 31.238s; **8** Yves Olivier, B (Dallara F399-Opel), 1h 05m 44.576s; **9** Toby Scheckter, ZA (Dallara F399-Mugen Honda), 1h 05m 49.229s; **10** Michele Spoldi, I (Dallara F399-Opel), 1h 05m 55.010s.
Fastest race lap: Manning, 1m 13.466s, 92.716 mph/149.212 km/h.
Fastest qualifying lap: Manning, 1m 12.861s, 93.486 mph/150.451 km/h.

2000 Result

10th MARLBORO MASTERS OF FORMULA 3, Circuit Park Zandvoort (Grand Prix Circuit), Holland, 6 August. 19 laps of the 2.672-mile/4.300-km circuit, 50.766 miles/81.700 km.
1 Jonathan Cochet, F (Dallara F399-Renault), 33m 09.939s, 91.841 mph/147.804 km/h.
2 Ben Collins, GB (Dallara F300-Mugen Honda), 33m 13.368s; **3** Tomas Scheckter, ZA (Dallara F300-Mugen Honda), 33m 13.740s; **4** Benoit Tréluyer, F (Dallara F399-Renault), 33m 17.916s; **5** Toshihiro Kaneishi, J (Dallara F399-Opel), 33m 18.455s; **6** Tom van Bavel, B (Dallara F399-Opel), 33m 19.134s; **7** Jeroen Bleekemolen, NL (Dallara F399-Opel), 33m 20.454s; **8** Andrew Kirkcaldy, GB (Dallara F399-Opel), 33m 21.186s; **9** Nicolas Kiesa, DK (Dallara F300-Opel), 33m 22.539s; **10** Matteo Grassotto, I (Dallara F300-Opel), 33m 24.391s.
Fastest race lap: Cochet, 1m 35.553s, 100.665 mph/162.004 km/h.
Fastest qualifying lap: Cochet, 1m 33.192s, 103.215 mph/166.109 km/h.

Results of the Macau and Changwong Formula 3 races will be given in AUTOCOURSE 2001-2002.

FIA GT Championship

1999 Result

The Zhuhai race was run after AUTOCOURSE 1999-2000 went to press.

FIA GT CHAMPIONSHIP, Zhuhai International Circuit, Nanshan, Zhuhai, Guangdong Province, China, 28 November. Round 11. 105 laps of the 2.684-mile/4.320-km circuit, 281.854 miles/453.600 km.
1 Karl Wendlinger/Olivier Beretta, A/MC (Chrysler Viper GTS-R), 3h 00m 52.807s, 93.494 mph/150.464 km.
2 Christian Vann/Christian Gläsel, GB/D (Chrysler Viper GTS-R), 3h 01m 10.495s; **3** Dominique Dupuy/Jean-Philippe Belloc, F/F (Chrysler Viper GTS-R), 104 laps; **4** Wolfgang Kaufmann/Bob Wollek, D/F (Porsche 911 GT-R), 103 laps; **5** Vincent Vosse/Jean-Phillipe Belloc, B/F (Chrysler Viper GTS-R), 102; **6** Yukihiro Hane/Manfred Jurasz, J/A (Porsche 911 GT2), 101; **7** Andrea Garbagnati/Mauro Casadei, I/I (Porsche 911 GT2), 101; **8** Gerold Ried/Christian Ried, D/D (Porsche 911 GT2), 100; **9** Adam Topping/Ugo Colombo/Rob Schirle, USA/USA/USA (Porsche 911 GT2), 97; **10** Michael Eschmann/Patrick Spadacini/Paul Hulverschied, D/I/D (Porsche 911 MR-GT), 96.
Fastest race lap: Sascha Maassen, D (Porsche 911 GT2), 1m 33.761s, 103.066 mph/165.869 km/h.

Final championship points

Drivers
1= Karl Wendlinger, A, 78; **1=** Olivier Beretta, MC, 78; **3** Jean-Philippe Belloc, F, 53; **4** David Donohue, USA, 25; **5** Dominique Dupuy, F, 24; **6=** Christian Gläsel, D, 21; **6=** Christian Vann, GB, 21; **6=** Wolfgang Kaufmann, D, 21; **9** Paul Belmondo, F, 19; **10=** Bob Wollek, F, 16; **10=** Vincent Vosse, B, 16; **12=** Ni Amorim, P, 14; **12=** Toni Seiler, CH, 14; **12=** Michel Ligonnet, F, 14; **15** Franz Konrad, D, 13; **16** Justin Bell, GB, 12; **17** Emmanuel Clérico, F, 11; **18=** Ron Atapattu, USA, 10; **18=** Marc Duez, B, 10; **20=** Julian Bailey, GB, 9; **20=** Didier Defourny, B, 9; **22** Luca Drudi, I, 8; **23** Hans Hugenholtz, NL, 7; **24=** William Hewland, GB, 6; **24=** Andy Wallace, GB, 6; **24=** Sascha Maassen, D, 6; **27** Xavier Pompidou, F, 5; **28=** David Hart, NL, 4; **28=** Mike Hezemans, NL, 4; **28=** Claude-Yves Gosselin, F, 4.

Teams
1 Chrysler Viper Team ORECA, 137; **2** Chamberlain Motorsport, 40; **3** Freisinger Motorsport, 23; **4** Paul Belmondo Racing, 20; **5=** Lister Storm Racing, 13; **5=** Konrad Motorsport, 13; **7** GL PK Racing, 9; **8** Roock Racing, 3; **9** Roock Sportsystem 2.

2000 Results

FIA GT CHAMPIONSHIP, Circuit de a Comunitat Valenciana Ricardo Tormo, Valencia, Spain, 26 March. Round 1. 109 laps of the 2.489-mile/4.005-km circuit, 271.256 miles/436.545 km.
1 Julian Bailey/Jamie Campbell-Walter, GB/GB (Lister Storm GT2), 3h 00m 11.626s, 90.322 mph/145.359 km/h (1st GT class).
2 Paul Belmondo/Vincent Vosse, F/F (Chrysler Viper GTS-R), 108 laps; **3** Claude-Yves Gosselin/Boris Derichebourg, F/F (Chrysler Viper GTS-R), 108; **4** Mike Hezemans/David Hart, NL/NL (Chrysler Viper GTS-R), 108; **5** Yukihiro Hane/Ernst Palmberger, J/D (Porsche 911 GT2), 106; **6** Toni Seiler/Walter Brun, CH/CH (Chrysler Viper GTS-R), 105; **7** Guy Martinolle/Jean-Claude Lagniez, F/F (Chrysler Viper GTS-R), 105 (1st N-GT class); **8** Christophe Bouchut/Patrice Goueslard, F/F (Porsche 911 GT3-R), 105; **9** Franz Konrad/Jurgen von Gartzen, A/A (Porsche 911 GT2), 105; **10** Magnus Wallinder/Robert Nearn, S/GB (Porsche 911 GT3-R), 104.
Fastest race lap: Bailey, 1m 33.951s, 95.357 mph/153.463 km/h.
Fastest qualifying lap: Bailey/Campbell-Walter, 1m 33.635s, 95.679 mph/153.981 km/h.

FIA GT CHAMPIONSHIP, Autódromo do Estoril, Alcabideche, Portugal, 2 April. Round 2. 23 laps of the 2.599-mile/4.182-km circuit, 59.767 miles/96.186 km.
Race shortened due to heavy rain.
1 Julian Bailey/Jamie Campbell-Walter, GB/GB (Lister Storm GT2), 54m 26.717s, 65.865 mph/105.999 km/h (1st GT class).
2 Paul Belmondo/Vincent Vosse, F/F (Chrysler Viper GTS-R), 54m 29.595s; **3** Claude-Yves Gosselin/Boris Derichebourg, F/F (Chrysler Viper GTS-R), 54m 30.824s; **4** Mike Hezemans/David Hart, NL/NL (Chrysler Viper GTS-R), 54m 32.765s; **5** Ni Amoim/Stephen Watson, P/ZA (Chrysler Viper GTS-R), 54m 36.042s; **6** Cor Euser/Christian Vann, NL/GB (Marcos Mantara LM600), 54m 38.676s; **7** Wolfgang Kaufmann/Stephane Ortelli, D/F (Porsche 911 GT2), 54m 41.245s; **8** Christophe Bouchut/Patrice Goueslard, F/F (Porsche 911 GT3-R), 54m 42.958s (1st N-GT class); **9** Peter Hardman/Nicolaus Springer/Philippe Favre, GB/D/CH (Lister Storm GT2), 54m 44.385s; **10** Luca Riccitelli/Hans-Jorg Höfer/Hans Willems, I/A/B (Porsche 911 GT3-R), 54m 45.392s.
Fastest race lap: Belmondo/Vosse, 1m 51.370s, 83.998 mph/135.182 km/h.
Fastest qualifying lap: Bailey/Campbell-Walter, 1m 38.427s, 95.044 mph/152.958 km/h.

500 KM DI MONZA, Autodromo Nazionale di Monza, Milan, Italy, 16 April. Round 3. 87 laps of the 3.585-mile/5.770-km circuit, 311.922 miles/501.990 km.
1 Mike Hezemans/David Hart, NL/NL (Chrysler Viper GTS-R), 2h 43m 26.373s, 114.509 mph/184.285 km/h (1st GT class).
2 Wolfgang Kaufmann/Bob Wollek, D/F (Porsche 911 GT2), 2h 44m 25.136s; **3** Julian Bailey/Jamie Campbell-Walter, GB/GB (Lister Storm GT2), 86 laps; **4** Toni Seiler/Walter Brun, CH/CH (Chrysler Viper GTS-R), 86; **5** Jean-Pierre Jarier/François Lafon, F/F (Chrysler Viper GTS-R), 85; **6** Guy Martinolle/Jean-Claude Lagniez, F/F (Chrysler Viper GTS-R), 85; **7** Gabriele Sabatini/Marco Spinelli/Fabio Villa, I/I/I (Porsche 911 GT2), 84; **8** Michel Neugarten/Nigel Smith, B/GB (Porsche 911 GT3-R), 84 (1st N-GT class); **9** Tim Sugden/Steve O'Rourke, GB/GB (Porsche 911 GT3-R), 83; **10** Christophe Bouchut/Patrice Goueslard, F/F (Porsche 911 GT3-R), 83.
Fastest race lap: Campbell-Walter, 1m 46.665s, 121.006 mph/194.741 km/h.
Fastest qualifying lap: Hezemans/Hart, 1m 58.250s, 109.151 mph/175.662 km/h.

SILVERSTONE 500, Silverstone Grand Prix Circuit, Towcester, Northamptonshire, Great Britain, 14 May. Round 4. 94 laps of the 3.194-mile/5.140-km circuit, 300.236 miles/483.183 km.
1 Julian Bailey/Jamie Campbell-Walter, GB/GB (Lister Storm GT2), 3h 01m 26.689s, 99.282 mph/159.778 km/h (1st GT class).
2 Mike Hezemans/David Hart, NL/NL (Chrysler Viper GTS-R), 3h 02m 27.025s; **3** Paul Belmondo/Claude-Yves Gosselin, F/F (Chrysler Viper GTS-R), 93 laps; **4** Stephen Watson/Didier Defourny, ZA/B (Chrysler Viper GTS-R), 93; **5** Guy Martinolle/Jean-Claude Lagniez, F/F (Chrysler Viper GTS-R), 93; **6** Franz Konrad/Jurgen von Gartzen, A/A (Porsche 911 GT2), 92; **7** Toni Seiler/Walter Brun, CH/CH (Chrysler Viper GTS-R), 92; **8** Philippe Favre/Nicolaus Springer, CH/D (Lister Storm GT2), 92; **9** Jean-Pierre Jarier/François Lafon, F/F (Chrysler Viper GTS-R), 91; **10** Horst Felbermayr/Horst Felbermayr Jr., A/A (Chrysler Viper GTS-R), 91.
Fastest race lap: Bailey/Campbell-Walter, 1m 50.233s, 104.310 mph/167.871 km/h.

Fastest qualifying lap: Bailey/Campbell-Walter, 1m 48.653s, 105.827 mph/170.312 km/h.
Winner N-GT class: Christophe Bouchut/Patrice Goueslard, F/F (Porsche 911 GT3-R), 91 laps (11th).

BUDAPEST 500KM, Hungaroring, Mogyorod, Budapest, Hungary, 2 July. Round 5. 104 laps of the 2.467-mile/3.971-km circuit, 256.616 miles/412.984 km.
1 Boris Derichebourg/Vincent Vosse, F/B (Chrysler Viper GTS-R), 3h 01m 47.041s, 84.699 mph/136.310 km/h (1st GT class).
2 Philippe Favre/Nicolaus Springer, CH/D (Lister Storm GT2), 3h 02m 10.053s; **3** Stephen Watson/Tamas Illes, ZA/H (Chrysler Viper GTS-R), 102 laps; **4** Ernst Palmberger/Yukihiro Hane, D/J (Porsche 911 GT2), 101; **5** Franz Konrad/Jurgen von Gartzen, A/A (Porsche 911 GT2), 101; **6** Mike Hezemans/David Hart, NL/NL (Chrysler Viper GTS-R), 101; **7** Wolfgang Kaufmann/Bob Wollek, D/F (Porsche 911 GT2), 100; **8** Christophe Bouchut/Patrice Goueslard, F/F (Porsche 911 GT3-R), 100 (1st N-GT class); **9** Robert Nearn/Michel Neugarten, GB/B (Porsche 911 GT3-R), 100; **10** Magnus Wallinder/Nigel Smith, S/GB (Porsche 911 GT3-R), 100.
Fastest race lap: Springer/Favre, 1m 39.708s, 89.089 mph/143.375 km/h.
Fastest qualifying lap: Springer/Favre, 1m 38.138s, 90.514 mph/145.668 km/h.

ZOLDER 500KM, Omloop van Zolder, Hasselt, Belgium, 23 July. Round 6. 108 laps of the 2.600-mile/4.184-km circuit, 280.780 miles/451.872 km.
1 Julian Bailey/Jamie Campbell-Walter, GB/GB (Lister Storm GT2), 3h 01m 19.425s, 92.910 mph/149.524 km/h (1st GT class).
2 Vincent Vosse/Boris Derichebourg, B/F (Chrysler Viper GTS-R), 3h 03m 01.161s; **3** Marc Duez/Paul Belmondo, B/F (Chrysler Viper GTS-R), 107 laps; **4** Wolfgang Kaufmann/Bert Longin, D/B (Porsche 911 GT2), 106; **5** Cor Euser/Harald Becker, NL/D (Marcos Mantara LM600), 105; **6** Yukihiro Hane/Ernst Palmberger, J/D (Porsche 911 GT2), 104; **7** Luca Cappellari/Gabriele Matteuzzi/Rafiee Sangiuolo, I/I/I (Chrysler Viper GTS-R), 104; **8** Luca Riccitelli/Hans Willems, I/B (Porsche 911 GT3-R), 104 (1st N-GT class); **9** Christophe Bouchut/Patrice Goueslard, F/F (Porsche 911 GT3-R), 104; **10** Michel Neugarten/Robert Nearn, B/GB (Porsche 911 GT3-R), 102.
Fastest race lap: Mike Hezemans/David Hart, NL/NL (Chrysler Viper GTS-R), 1m 36.032s, 97.461 mph/156.848 km/h.
Fastest qualifying lap: Bailey/Campbell-Walwer, 1m 34.527s, 99.012 mph/159.345 km/h.

FIA GT CHAMPIONSHIP, A1-Ring, Spielberg, Austria, 6 August. Round 7. 113 laps of the 2.688-mile/4.326-km circuit, 303.750 miles/488.838 km.
1 Mike Hezemans/Tom Coronel, NL/NL (Chrysler Viper GTS-R), 3h 00m 01.811s, 101.233 mph/162.919 km/h (1st GT class).
2 Emmanuel Clérico/Boris Derichebourg, F/F (Chrysler Viper GTS-R), 3h 00m 40.141s; **3** Wolfgang Kaufmann/Gottfried Grasser, D/A (Porsche 911 GT2), 112 laps; **4** Paul Belmondo/Claude-Yves Gosselin, F/F (Chrysler Viper GTS-R), 112; **5** Franz Konrad/Jurgen von Gartzen, A/A (Porsche 911 GT2), 112; **6** Franz Wieth/Niko Wieth, D/D (Porsche 911 T2), 109; **7** Horst Felbermayr/Horst Felbermayr Jr., A/A (Chrysler Viper GTS-R), 109; **8** Giovanni Colloni/Fabio Mancini, I/I (Porsche 911 GT3-R), 107 (1st N-GT class); **9** Tim Sugden/Steve O'Rourke, GB/GB (Porsche 911 GT3-R), 107; **10** Gabriele Sabatini/Marco Spinelli/Manfred Jurasz, I/I/A (Porsche 911 GT2), 106.
Fastest race lap: Hezemans/Coronel, 1m 31.586s, 105.660 mph/170.043 km/h.
Fastest qualifying lap: Hezemans/Coronel, 1m 42.707s, 94.219 mph/151.631 km/h.

FIA GT CHAMPIONSHIP, EuroSpeedway Lausitz, Germany, 2 September. Round 8. 79 laps of the 2.817-mile/4.534-km circuit, 222.566 miles/358.186 km.
1 Wolfgang Kaufmann/Hubert Haupt, D/D (Porsche 911 GT2), 3h 01m 10.734s, 73.706 mph/118.618 km/h (1st GT class).
2 Vincent Vosse/Boris Derichebourg, B/F (Chrysler Viper GTS-R), 3h 03m 00.046s; **3** Luca Riccitelli/Dieter Quester, I/A (Porsche 911 GT3-R), 3h 03m 05.961s (1st N-GT class); **4** Christophe Bouchut/Patrice Goueslard, F/F (Porsche 911 GT3-R), 78 laps; **5** Julian Bailey/Jamie Campbell-Walter, GB/GB (Lister Storm GT2), 78; **6** Magnus Wallinder/Nigel Smith, S/GB (Porsche 911 GT3-R), 78; **7** Tim Sugden/Steve O'Rourke, GB/GB (Porsche 911 GT3-R), 77; **8** Hans-Jorg Höfer/Patrick Huisman, A/NL (Porsche 911 GT3-R), 76; **9** Mike Hezemans/David Hart, NL/NL (Chrysler Viper GTS-R), 76; **10** Ferdinand de Lesseps/André Ahrle, F/D (Porsche 911 GT3-R), 76.
Fastest race lap: Bailey/Campbell-Walter, 1m 43.830s, 97.681 mph/157.203 km/h.
Fastest qualifying lap: Hezemans/Hart, 1m 43.854s, 97.659 mph/157.167 km/h.

FIA GT CHAMPIONSHIP, Automotodrom Brno, Brno, Czech Republic, 17 September. Round 9. 73 laps of the 3.357-mile/5.403-km circuit, 245.081 miles/394.419 km.
1 Mike Hezemans/David Hart, NL/NL (Chrysler Viper GTS-R), 2h 57m 36.698s, 82.792 mph/133.241 km/h (1st GT class).
2 Julian Bailey/Jamie Campbell-Walter, GB/GB (Lister Storm GT2), 2h 57m 57.584s; **3** Philippe Favre/Nicolaus Springer, CH/D (Lister Storm GT2), 2h 58m 36.133s; **4** Vincent Vosse/Boris Derichebourg, B/F (Chrysler Viper GTS-R), 2h 59m 09.168s; **5** Wolfgang Kaufmann/Hubert Haupt, D/D (Porsche 911 GT2), 72 laps; **6** Paul Belmondo/Claude-Yves Gosselin, F/F (Chrysler Viper GTS-R), 72; **7** Christophe Bouchut/Patrice Goueslard, F/F (Porsche 911 GT3-R), 71 (1st N-GT class); **8** Luca Riccitelli/Dieter Quester, I/A (Porsche 911 GT3-R), 71; **9** Ferdinand de Lesseps/André Ahrle, F/D (Porsche 911 GT3-R), 70; **10** Ernst Palmberger/Cyril Chateau, D/F (Porsche 911 GT2), 70.
Fastest race lap: Bailey/Campbell-Walter, 2m 14.128s, 90.109 mph/145.017 km/h.
Fastest qualifying lap: Bailey/Campbell-Walter, 2m 00.157s, 100.586 mph/161.878 km/h.

FIA GT CHAMPIONSHIP, Circuit de Nevers, Magny-Cours, France, 22 October. Round 10. 106 laps of the 2.641-mile/4.250-km circuit, 279.928 miles/450.500 km.
1 Julian Bailey/Jamie Campbell-Walter, GB/GB (Lister Storm GT2), 3h 00m 24.290s, 93.100 mph/149.830 km/h (1st GT class).
2 Mike Hezemans/Tom Coronel, NL/NL (Chrysler Viper GTS-R), 3h 00m 38.382s; **3** Marc Duez/Paul Belmondo, B/F (Chrysler Viper GTS-R), 3h 01m 14.839s; **4** Anthony Kumpen/Claude-Yves Gosselin, B/F (Chrysler Viper GTS-R), 105 laps; **5** Nicolaus Springer/Philippe Favre, D/CH (Lister Storm GT2), 104; **6** Wolfgang Kaufmann/Michael Trunk, D/D (Porsche 911 GT2), 102; **7** Franz Wieth/Niko Wieth, D/D (Porsche 911 T2), 102; **8** Christophe Bouchut/Patrice Goueslard, F/F (Porsche 911 GT3-R), 102 (1st N-GT class); **9** Luca Riccitelli/Dieter Quester, I/A (Porsche 911 GT3-R), 102; **10** Magnus Wallinder/Nigel Smith, S/GB (Porsche 911 GT3-R), 101.
Fastest race lap: Springer/Favre, 1m 37.249s, 97.759 mph/157.328 km/h.
Fastest qualifying lap: Springer/Favre, 1m 36.215s, 98.810 mph/159.019 km/h.

Final championship points

GT Class
Drivers
1= Julian Bailey, GB, 59; 1= Jamie Campbell-Walter, GB, 59; 3 Mike Hezemans, NL, 50.5; 4 Boris Derichebourg, F, 37; 5 David Hart, NL, 34.5; 6 Vincent Vosse, B, 34; 7 Wolfgang Kaufmann, D, 26; 8 Paul Belmondo, F, 25; 9 Yves-Caude Gosselin, F, 17; 10 Tom Coronel, NL, 16; 11= Nicolaus Springer, D, 13; 11= Philippe Favre, CH, 13; 13 Hubert Haupt, D, 12; 14= Stephen Watson, ZA, 8; 14= Marc Duez, B, 8; 16= Jurgen von Gartzen, D, 7; 16= Franz Konrad, A, 7; 18= Emmanuel Clérico, F, 6; 18= Bob Wollek, F, 6; 18= Yukihiro Hane, J, 6; 18= Ernst Palmberger, D, 6; 22= Gottfried Grasser, A, 4; 22= Toni Seiler, CH, 4; 22= Walter Brun, CH, 4; 22= Tamas Illes, H, 4; 26= Anthony Kumpen, B, 3; 26= Bert Longin, B, 3; 26= Didier Defourny, B, 3; 26= Guy Martinolle, F, 3; 26= Jean-Claude Lagniez, F, 3.

Teams
1 Lister Storm Racing, 72; 2 Paul Belmondo Racing, 62; 3 Carsport Holland, 50.5; 4 Freisinger Motorsport, 32; 5 Chamberlain Motorsport, 12; 6 Konrad Motorsport, 7; 7 Paul Belmondo Compétition, 6; 8 Marcos Racing Int., 2.5; 9 MMI, 2; 10 Wieth Racing, 1.

N-GT Class
Drivers
1= Christophe Bouchut, F, 72; 1= Patrice Goueslard, F, 72; 3 Luca Riccitelli, I, 43; 4 Michel Neugarten, B, 33; 5 Nigel Smith, GB, 31; 6= Hans Willems, B, 25 6= Magnus Wallinder, S, 25; 6= Dieter Qester, A, 25; 9= Tim Sugden, GB, 22.5; 9= Steve O'Rourke, GB, 22.5.

Teams
1 Larbre Compétition, 89; 2 RWS /Red Bull Racing, 57; 3 Pennzoil Quaker State G-Force, 51; 4 EMKA /GTC, 22.5; 5 ART Engineering, 15.

Other Sports Car Race

68th 24 HEURES DU MANS, Circuit International Du Mans, Les Raineries, Le Mans, France, 17-18 June. 368 laps of the 8.454-mile/13.605-km circuit, 3110.982 miles/5006.640 km.
1 Frank Biela/Tom Kristensen/Emanuele Pirro, D/DK/I (Audi R8) (1st LMP900 class), 129.624 mph/208.610 km/h.
2 Laurent Aiello/Allan McNish/Stephane Ortelli, F/GB/F (Audi R8), 367 laps; **3** Christian Abt/Michele Alboreto/Rinaldo Capello, D/I/I (Audi R8), 365; **4** Olivier Grouillard/Sébastien Bourdais/Emmanuel Clérico, F/F/F (Courage C52-Peugeot), 344; **5** Johnny O'Connell/Hiroki Katoh/Pierre-Henri Raphanel, USA/J/F (Panos LMP Roadster S), 342; **6** Toshio Suzuki/Masami Kageyama/Masahiko Kageyama, J/J/J (Panos LMP Roadster S), 340; **7** Dominique Dupuy/Olivier Beretta/Karl Wendlinger, F/MC/A (Chrysler Viper GTS-R), 333 (1st GTS class); **8** Keiichi Tsuchiya/Akira Iida/Masahiko Kondo, J/J/J (Panoz LMP Roadster S), 330; **9** David Donohue/Ni Amorim/Anthony Beltoise, USA/P/F (Chrysler Viper GTS-R), 328; **10** Franck Fréon/Andy Pilgrim/Kelly Collins, F/USA/USA (Chevrolet Corvette C5R), 327; **11** Ron Fellows/Chris Kneifel/Justin Bell, CDN/USA/GB (Chevrolet Corvette C5R), 326; **12** Tommy Archer/Marc Duez/Patrick Huisman, USA/B/NL (Chrysler Viper GTS-R), 324; **13** Dirk Müller/Lucas Luhr/Bob Wollek, D/D/F (Porsche 911 GT3-R), 319 (1st GT class); **14** Mike Hezemans/David Hart/John Hugenholtz, NL/NL/NL (Chrysler Viper GTS-R), 317; **15** Charlie Slater/Tom Kendall/Jurgen von Gartzen, USA/USA/A (Porsche 911 GT2), 317; **16** David Brabham/Jan Magnussen/Mario Andretti, AUS/DK/USA (Panoz LMP Roadster S), 315; **17** Hideo Fukuyama/Atsushi Yogo/Bruno Lambert, J/J/B (Porsche 911 GT3-R), 310; **18** Johnny Mowlem/David Murry/Sascha Maassen, GB/USA/D (Porsche 911 GT3-R), 304; **19** Max Cohen-Olivar/Michel Neugarten/Tony Burgess, MA/B/CDN (Porsche 911 GT3-R), 302; **20** Emmanuel Collard/Eric Bernard/Franck Montagny, F/F/F (Cadillac Northstar LMP), 300; **21** Didier Theys/Jeffrey van Hooydonk/Didier Andre, B/B/F (Reynard 2KQ-LM-Mopar), 292; **22** Butch Leitzinger/Franck Lagorce/Andy Wallace, USA/F/GB (Cadillac Northstar LMP), 291; **23** Max Angelelli/Wayne Taylor/Eric van de Poele, I/ZA/B (Cadillac Nrthstar LMP), 287; **24** Thierry Perrier/Jean-Louis Ricci/Romano Ricci, F/F/F (Porsche 911 GT3-R), 286; **25** Kent Dujardyn/Philip Verellen/Rudi Penders, B/B/B (Porsche 911 GT3-R), 285; **26** Scott Maxwell/John Graham/Greg Wilkins, CDN/CDN/CDN (Lola B2k/40-Nissan), 274 (1st LMP675 class); **27** Richard Balandras/Sylvain Boulay/Yojiro Terada, F/F/J (WR LMP-Peugeot), 266; **28** Michael Lauer/Michael Brockman/Gunnar Jeannette, USA/USA/USA (Porsche 911 GT3-R), 261; **29** John Nielsen/Mauro Baldi/Klaus Graf, DK/I/D (Panoz LMP Roadster S), 205; **30** Wolfgang Kaufmann/Yukihiro Hane/Katsunori Iketani, D/J/J (Porsche 911 GT2), 313 (DNF - suspension); **31** Gabrio Rosa/Michel Ligonnet/Franco Babini, I/F/I (Porsche 911 GT3-R), 310 (DNF - accident); **32** Philippe Gache/Gary Formato/ Didier Cottaz, F/ZA/F (Courage C60-Judd), 219 (DNF - engine); **33** Toni Seiler/Walter Brun/Christian Gläsel, CH/CH/D (Chrysler Viper GTS-R), 210 (DNF - accident); **34** Boris Derichebourg/Jean-Claude Lagniez/Guy Martinolle, F/F/F (Chrysler Viper Gts-R), 180 (DNF - engine); **35** Thomas Bscher/Geoff Lees/Jean-Marc Gounon, D/GB/F (BMW LM98 V12), 180 (DNF - accident damage); **36** Xavier Pompidou/ Jean-Bernard Bouvet/Stephane Daoudi, F/F/F (WR LMP-Peugeot), 169 (DNF - fire); **37** Domenico 'Mimmo' Schiattarella/Didier de Radigues/Emanuele Naspetti, I/B/I (Lola B2k/10-Judd), 154 (DNF - engine); **38** Stefan Johansson/Guy Smith/Jim Matthews, S/GB/USA (Reynard 2KQ-Judd), 133 (DNF - engine); **39** Tomas Saldana/Jesus Diez Villaroel/Giovanni Lavaggi, E/E/I (Porsche 911 GT3-R), 78 (DNF - engine); **40** Jean-Christophe Boullion/Jordi Gené/Jérôme Policand, F/E/F (Reynard 2KQ-LM-Volkswagen), 72 (DNF - engine); **41** Ralf Kelleners/David Terrien/Jean-Denis Deletraz, D/F/CH (Reynard 2KQ-LM-Volkswagen), 44 (DNF - engine); **42** Jan Lammers/Tom Coronel/Peter Kox, NL/NL/NL (Lola B2k/10-Ford Cosworth), 38 (DNF - lost wheel); **43** Christophe Bouchut/Jean-Luc Chereau/Patrice Goueslard, F/F/F (Porsche 911 GT3-R), 34 (DNF - accident); **44** Jean-Luc Maury-Laribiere/Bernard Chauvin/Angelo Zarda, F/F/I (Porsche 911 GT3-R), 32 (DNF - accident); **45** Patrick Lemarié/Jean-François Yvon/Yann Goudy, F/F/F (Debora LMP-BMW), 24 (DNF - engine); **46** Shane Lewis/Bob Mazzuoccola/Cort Wagner, USA/USA/USA (Porsche 911 GT3-R), 22 (DNF - accident); **47** Marc Goossens/Christophe Tinseau/Kristian Kolby, B/F/DK (Cadillac Northstar LMP), 4 (DNF - fire); **48** Yannick Dalmas/Nicolas Minassian/Jean-Philippe Belloc, F/F/F (Reynard 2KQ-LM-Mopar), 1 (DNF - oil pressure).
Fastest race lap: McNish, 3m 37.359s, 140.015 mph/225.332 km/h.
Fastest qualifying lap: Aiello, 3m 36.124s, 140.815 mph/226.620 km/h.

FedEx CART Championship Series

MARLBORO GRAND PRIX OF MIAMI PRESENTED BY TOYOTA, Homestead-Miami Speedway, Homestead, Florida, USA, 26 March. Round 1. 150 laps of the 1.502-mile/2.417-km circuit, 225.300 miles/362.585 km.
1 Massimiliano 'Max' Papis, I (Reynard 2KI-Ford Cosworth XF), 1h 22m 01.975s, 164.788 mph/265.200 km/h.
2 Roberto Moreno, BR (Reynard 2KI-Ford Cosworth XF), 1h 22m 02.595s; **3** Paul Tracy, CDN (Reynard 2KI-Honda), 1h 22m 05.810s; **4** Jimmy Vasser, USA (Lola B2k/00-Toyota), 1h 22m 06.429s; **5** Patrick Carpentier, CDN (Reynard 2KI-Ford Cosworth XF), 1h 22m 06.806s; **6** Gil de Ferran, BR (Reynard 2KI-Honda), 1h 22m 14.394s; **7** Christian Fittipaldi, BR (Lola B2k/00-Ford Cosworth XF), 1h 22m 16.261s; **8** Shinji Nakano, J (Reynard 2KI-Honda), 1h 22m 16.831s; **9** Alex Tagliani, CDN (Reynard 2KI-Ford Cosworth XF), 1h 22m 27.445s; **10** Tony Kanaan, BR (Reynard 2KI-Mercedes Benz), 149 laps.
Most laps led: de Ferran, 41.
Fastest qualifying lap: de Ferran, 25.942s, 208.434 mph/335.442 km/h.
Championship points: 1 Papis, 20; 2 Moreno, 16; 3 Tracy, 14; 4 Vasser, 12; 5= Carpentier, 10; 5= de Ferran, 10.

TOYOTA GRAND PRIX OF LONG BEACH, Long Beach Street Circuit, California, USA, 16 April. Round 2. 82 laps of the 1.968-mile/3.167-km circuit, 161.376 miles/259.709 km.
1 Paul Tracy, CDN (Reynard 2KI-Honda), 1h 57m 11.132s, 82.626 mph/132.973 km/h.
2 Helio Castro-Neves, BR (Reynard 2KI-Honda), 1h 57m 14.323s; **3** Jimmy Vasser, USA (Lola B2k/00-Toyota), 1h 57m 14.430s; **4** Alex Tagliani, CDN (Reynard 2KI-Ford Cosworth XF), 1h 57m 14.916s; **5** Bryan Herta, USA (Reynard 2KI-Honda), 1h 57m 15.340s; **6** Oriol Servia, E (Reynard 2KI-Toyota), 1h 57m 16.272s; **7** Gil de Ferran, BR (Reynard 2KI-Honda), 1h 57m 16.681s; **8** Mark Blundell, GB (Reynard 2KI-Mercedes Benz), 1h 57m 18.869s; **9** Roberto Moreno, BR (Reynard 2KI-Ford Cosworth XF), 1h 57m 21.057s; **10** Mauricio Gugelmin, BR (Reynard 2KI-Mercedes Benz), 81 laps.
Most laps led: Tracy, 21.
Fastest qualifying lap: de Ferran, 1m 07.494s, 104.969 mph/168.932 km/h.
Championship points: 1 Tracy, 34; 2 Vasser, 26; 3= Moreno, 20; 3= Papis, 20; 5 de Ferran, 18; 6= Castro-Neves, 16; 6= Tagliani, 16.

RIO 200, Emerson Fittipaldi Speedway at Nelson Piquet International Raceway, Jacarepagua, Rio de Janeiro, Brazil, 30 April. Round 3. 108 laps of the 1.864-mile/3.000-km circuit, 201.312 miles/323.980 km.
1 Adrian Fernandez, MEX (Reynard 2KI-Ford Cosworth XF), 1h 37m 12.490s, 124.256 mph/199.971 km/h.
2 Jimmy Vasser, USA (Lola B2k/00-Toyota), 1h 37m 13.421s; **3** Paul Tracy, CDN (Reynard 2KI-Honda), 1h 37m 13.828s; **4** Cristiano da Matta, BR (Reynard 2KI-Toyota), 1h 37m 14.071s; **5** Christian Fittipaldi, BR (Lola B2k/00-Ford Cosworth XF), 1h 37m 14.846s; **6** Roberto Moreno, BR (Reynard 2KI-Ford Cosworth XF), 1h 37m 16.177s; **7** Mark Blundell, GB (Reynard 2KI-Mercedes Benz), 1h 37m 17.569s; **8** Memo Gidley, USA (Reynard 2KI-Ford Cosworth XF), 1h 37m 18.994s; **9** Michael Andretti, USA (Lola B2k/00-Ford Cosworth XF), 107 laps; **10** Kenny Bräck, S (Reynard 2KI-Ford Cosworth XF), 107.
Most laps led: Alex Tagliani, CDN (Reynard 2KI-Ford Cosworth XF), 76.
Fastest qualifying lap: Tagliani, 38m.587s, 173.903 mph/279.870 km/h.
Championship points: 1 Tracy, 48; 2 Vasser, 42; 3 Moreno, 28; 4= Papis, 20; 4= Fernandez, 20; 6= de Ferran, 18; 6= Tagliani, 18.

FIRESTONE FIREHAWK 500, Twin Ring Motegi, Haga gun, Japan, 14 May. Round 4. 201 laps of the 1.549-mile/2.493-km circuit, 311.349 miles/501.068 km.
Rain delayed the race by a day.
1 Michael Andretti, USA (Lola B2k/00-Ford Cosworth XF), 1h 58m 52.201s, 157.154 mph/252.915 km/h.
2 Dario Franchitti, GB (Reynard 2KI-Honda), 1h 58m 52.747s; **3** Roberto Moreno, BR (Reynard 2KI-Ford Cosworth XF), 1h 58m 55.026s; **4** Cristiano da Matta, BR (Reynard 2KI-Toyota), 1h 58m 55.743s; **5** Kenny Bräck, S (Reynard 2KI-Ford Cosworth XF), 1h 58m 56.126s; **6** Paul Tracy, CDN (Reynard 2KI-Honda), 1h 58m 56.460s; **7** Juan Pablo Montoya, CO (Lola B2k/00-Toyota), 1h 58m 57.053s; **8** Massimiliano 'Max' Papis, I (Reynard 2KI-Ford Cosworth XF), 200 laps; **9** Gil de Ferran, BR (Reynard 2KI-Honda), 200; **10** Adrian Fernandez, MEX (Reynard 2KI-Ford Cosworth XF), 200.
Most laps led: Montoya, 172.
Fastest qualifying lap: Montoya, 26.237s, 212.540 mph/342.049 km/h.
Championship points: 1 Tracy, 56; 2= Vasser, 42; 2= Moreno, 42; 4= Papis, 25; 4= da Matta, 25; 6 Fernandez, 23.

BOSCH SPARK PLUG GRAND PRIX PRESENTED BY TOYOTA, Nazareth Speedway, Pennsylvania, USA, 27 May. Round 5. 225 laps of the 0.946-mile/1.522-km circuit, 212.850 miles/342.549 km.
Race postponed from 9 April, due to bad weather.
1 Gil de Ferran, BR (Reynard 2KI-Honda), 2h 06m 10.334s, 101.219 mph/162.896 km/h.
2 Mauricio Gugelmin, BR (Reynard 2KI-Mercedes Benz), 2h 06m 11.149s; **3** Kenny Bräck, S (Reynard 2KI-Ford Cosworth XF), 2h 06m 12.214s; **4** Juan Pablo Montoya, CO (Lola B2k/00-Toyota), 2h 06m 12.442s; **5** Adrian Fernandez, MEX (Reynard 2KI-Ford Cosworth XF), 2h 06m 15.050s; **6** Michael Andretti, USA (Lola B2k/00-Ford Cosworth XF), 2h 06m 16.011s; **7** Jimmy Vasser, USA (Lola B2k/00-Toyota), 2h 06m 17.322s; **8** Tony Kanaan, BR (Reynard 2KI-Mercedes Benz), 2h 06m 18.923s; **9** Oriol Servia, E (Reynard 2KI-Toyota), 224 laps; **10** Paul Tracy, CDN (Reynard 2KI-Honda), 224.
Most laps led: Montoya, 110.
Fastest qualifying lap: Montoya, 19.255s, 176.868 mph/284.642 km/h.
Championship points: 1 Tracy, 59; 2 Vasser, 48; 3= Moreno, 42; 3= de Ferran, 42; 5 Fernandez, 33; 6 Andretti, 28.

MILLER LITE 225, The Milwaukee Mile, Wisconsin State Fair Park, West Allis, Milwaukee, Wisconsin, USA, 4 June. Round 6. 225 laps of the 1.032-mile/1.661-km circuit, 232.200 miles/373.690 km.
1 Juan Pablo Montoya, CO (Lola B2k/00-Toyota), 1h 37m 38.526s, 142.684 mph/229.628 km/h.
2 Michael Andretti, USA (Lola B2k/00-Ford Cosworth XF), 1h 37m 39.541s; **3** Patrick Carpentier, CDN (Reynard 2KI-Ford Cosworth XF), 1h 37m 46.983s; **4** Kenny Bräck, S (Reynard 2KI-Ford Cosworth XF), 1h 37m 53.128s; **5** Roberto Moreno, BR (Reynard 2KI-Ford Cosworth XF), 1h 37m 53.685s; **6** Dario Franchitti, GB (Reynard 2KI-Honda), 1h 37m 54.159s; **7** Massimiliano 'Max' Papis, I (Reynard 2KI-Ford Cosworth XF), 1h 37m 55.726s; **8** Adrian Fernandez, MEX (Reynard 2KI-Ford Cosworth XF), 1h 37m 56.425s; **9** Christian Fittipaldi, BR (Lola B2k/00-Ford Cosworth XF), 1h 37m 57.378s; **10** Tony Kanaan, BR (Reynard 2KI-Mercedes Benz), 1h 38m 01.296s.
Most laps led: Montoya, 179.
Fastest qualifying lap: Montoya, 20.899s, 177.769 mph/286.092 km/h.
Championship points: 1 Tracy, 59; 2 Moreno, 52; 3 Vasser, 48; 4= Andretti, 44; 4= Montoya, 44; 6 de Ferran, 43.

TENNECO AUTOMOTIVE GRAND PRIX OF DETROIT, The Raceway on Belle Isle, Detroit, Michigan, USA, 18 June. Round 7. 84 laps of the 2.346-mile/3.776-km circuit, 197.064 miles/317.144 km.
1 Helio Castro-Neves, BR (Reynard 2KI-Honda), 2h 01m 23.607s, 97.401 mph/156.752 km/h.
2 'Max' Papis, I (Reynard 2KI-Ford Cosworth XF), 2h 01m 28.022s; **3** Oriol Servia, E (Reynard 2KI-Toyota), 2h 01m 34.072s; **4** Dario Franchitti, GB (Reynard 2KI-Honda), 2h 01m 37.244s; **5** Patrick Carpentier, CDN (Reynard 2KI-Ford Cosworth XF), 2h 01m 48.920s; **6** Alex Tagliani, CDN (Reynard 2KI-Ford Cosworth XF), 2h 01m 50.009s; **7** Jimmy Vasser, USA (Lola B2k/00-Toyota), 2h 02m 14.863s; **8** Michel Jourdain Jr., MEX (Lola B2k/00-Mercedes Benz), 2h 02m 31.647s; **9** Gil de Ferran, BR (Reynard 2KI-Honda), 83 laps; **10** Tarso Marques, BR (Swift 2KI-Ford Cosworth XF), 82.
Most laps led: Juan Pablo Montoya, CO (Lola B2k/00-Toyota), 59.
Fastest qualifying lap: Montoya, 1m 13.056s, 115.604 mph/186.047 km/h.
Championship points: 1 Tracy, 59; 2 Vasser, 54; 2 Moreno, 52; 4= de Ferran, 47; 4= Papis, 47; 6 Montoya, 46.

FREIGHTLINER G.I.JOE'S 200 PRESENTED BY TEXACO, Portland International Raceway, Oregon, USA, 25 June. Round 8. 98 laps of the 1.969-mile/3.169-km circuit, 220.528 miles/354.905 km.
1 Gil de Ferran, BR (Reynard 2KI-Honda), 2h 00m 46.002s, 109.564 mph/176.326 km/h.
2 Roberto Moreno, BR (Reynard 2KI-Ford Cosworth XF), 2h 00m 48.627s; **3** Christian Fittipaldi, BR (Lola B2k/00-Ford Cosworth XF), 2h 00m 54.984s; **4** Michael Andretti, USA (Lola B2k/00-Ford Cosworth XF), 2h 01m 15.733s; **5** Cristiano da Matta, BR (Reynard 2KI-Toyota), 2h 01m 16.072s; **6** Kenny Bräck, S (Reynard 2KI-Ford Cosworth XF), 2h 01m 16.592s; **7** Helio Castro-Neves, BR (Reynard 2KI-Honda), 2h 01m 19.712s; **8** Oriol Servia, E (Reynard 2KI-Toyota), 2h 01m 40.471s; **9** Dario Franchitti, GB (Reynard 2KI-Honda), 2h 01m 48.486s; **10** Patrick Carpentier, CDN (Reynard 2KI-Ford Cosworth XF), 111 laps.
Most laps led: Castro-Neves, 85.
Fastest qualifying lap: Castro-Neves, 57.738s, 122.768 mph/197.577 km/h.
Championship points: 1 Moreno, 68; 2 de Ferran, 67; 3 Tracy, 59; 4 Andretti, 56; 5 Vasser, 54; 6= Papis, 47; 6= Bräck, 47.

MARCONI GRAND PRIX OF CLEVELAND PRESENTED BY FIRSTAR, Burke Lakefront Airport Circuit, Cleveland, Ohio, USA, 2 July. Round 9. 100 laps of the 2.106-mile/3.389-km circuit, 210.600 miles/338.928 km.
1 Roberto Moreno, BR (Reynard 2KI-Ford Cosworth XF), 1h 52m 12.092s, 112.619 mph/181.242 km/h.
2 Kenny Bräck, S (Reynard 2KI-Ford Cosworth XF), 1h 52m 12.918s; **3** Cristiano da Matta, BR (Reynard 2KI-Toyota), 1h 52m 14.069s; **4** Michael Andretti, USA (Lola B2k/00-Ford Cosworth XF), 1h 52m 19.654s; **5** Patrick Carpentier, CDN (Reynard 2KI-Ford Cosworth XF), 1h 52m 20.445s; **6** Juan Pablo Montoya, CO (Lola B2k/00-Toyota), 1h 52m 22.365s; **7** Adrian Fernandez, MEX (Reynard 2KI-Ford Cosworth XF), 1h 52m 31.458s; **8** Jimmy Vasser, USA (Lola B2k/00-Toyota), 1h 52m 31.843s; **9** Bryan Herta, USA (Reynard 2KI-Mercedes Benz), 1h 52m 33.293s; **10** Mauricio Gugelmin, BR (Reynard 2KI-Mercedes Benz), 1h 53m 14.599s.
Most laps led: Moreno, 91.
Fastest qualifying lap: Moreno, 57.436s, 132.001 mph/212.435 km/h.
Championship points: 1 Moreno, 90; 2 Andretti, 68; 3 de Ferran, 67; 4 Bräck, 63; 5= Tracy, 59; 5= Vasser, 59.

MOLSON INDY, Canada National Exhibition Place Circuit, Toronto, Ontario, Canada, 16 July. Round 10. 112 laps of the 1.755-mile/2.824-km circuit, 196.560 miles/316.333 km.
1 Michael Andretti, USA (Lola B2k/00-Ford Cosworth XF), 2h 00m 02.313s, 98.248 mph/158.116 km/h.
2 Adrian Fernandez, MEX (Reynard 2KI-Ford Cosworth XF),

2h 00m 08.840s; **3** Paul Tracy, CDN (Reynard 2KI-Honda), 2h 00m 11.431s; **4** Cristiano da Matta, BR (Reynard 2KI-Toyota), 2h 00m 17.283s; **5** Alex Tagliani, CDN (Reynard 2KI-Ford Cosworth XF), 2h 00m 23.935s; **6** Gil de Ferran, BR (Reynard 2KI-Honda), 2h 00m 26.663s; **7** Patrick Carpentier, CDN (Reynard 2KI-Ford Cosworth XF), 2h 00m 29.480s; **8** Massimiliano 'Max' Papis, I (Reynard 2KI-Ford Cosworth XF), 2h 00m 31.353s; **9** Jimmy Vasser, USA (Lola B2k/00-Toyota), 2h 00m 41.051s; **10** Kenny Bräck, S (Reynard 2KI-Ford Cosworth XF), 2h 00m 49.242s.
Most laps led: da Matta, 73.
Fastest qualifying lap: Helio Castro-Neves, BR (Reynard 2KI-Honda), 57.200s, 110.455 mph/177.759 km/h.
Championship points: **1** Moreno, 90; **2** Andretti, 88; **3** de Ferran, 75; **4** Tracy, 73; **5** Bräck, 66; **6** Vasser, 63.

MICHIGAN 500 PRESENTED BY TOYOTA, Michigan International Speedway, Brooklyn, Michigan, USA, 23 July. Round 11. 250 laps of the 2.000-mile/3.219-km circuit, 500.000 miles/804.672 km.
1 Juan Pablo Montoya, CO (Lola B2k/00-Toyota), 2h 48m 49.790s, 177.694 mph/285.970 km/h.
2 Michael Andretti, USA (Lola B2k/00-Ford Cosworth XF), 2h 48m 49.830s; **3** Dario Franchitti, GB (Reynard 2KI-Honda), 2h 48m 51.411s; **4** Patrick Carpentier, CDN (Reynard 2KI-Ford Cosworth XF), 2h 48m 51.895s; **5** Helio Castro-Neves, BR (Reynard 2KI-Honda), 2h 48m 52.920s; **6** Adrian Fernandez, MEX (Reynard 2KI-Ford Cosworth XF), 2h 48m 53.633s; **7** Paul Tracy, CDN (Reynard 2KI-Honda), 2h 48m 56.676s; **8** Oriol Servia, E (Reynard 2KI-Toyota), 249 laps; **9** Massimiliano 'Max' Papis, I (Reynard 2KI-Ford Cosworth XF), 247; **10** Memo Gidley, USA (Reynard 2KI-Toyota), 247.
Most laps led: Castro-Neves, 85.
Fastest qualifying lap: Tracy, 30.645s, 234.949 mph/378.113 km/h.
Championship points: **1** Andretti, 104; **2** Moreno, 90; **3** Tracy, 80; **4** de Ferran, 75; **5** Montoya, 74; **6** Fernandez, 69.

TARGET GRAND PRIX AT CHICAGO MOTOR SPEEDWAY, Chicago Motor Speedway, Cicero, Illinois, USA, 30 July. Round 12. 225 laps of the 1.029-miles/1.656-km circuit, 231.525 miles/372.603 km.
1 Cristiano da Matta, BR (Reynard 2KI-Toyota), 2h 01m 23.727s, 114.432 mph/184.160 km/h.
2 Michael Andretti, USA (Lola B2k/00-Ford Cosworth XF), 2h 01m 25.417s; **3** Gil de Ferran, BR (Reynard 2KI-Honda), 2h 01m 26.246s; **4** Kenny Bräck, S (Reynard 2KI-Ford Cosworth XF), 2h 01m 26.511s; **5** Adrian Fernandez, MEX (Reynard 2KI-Ford Cosworth XF), 2h 01m 38.413s; **6** Roberto Moreno, BR (Reynard 2KI-Ford Cosworth XF), 2h 01m 39.276s; **7** Mauricio Gugelmin, BR (Reynard 2KI-Mercedes Benz), 224 laps; **8** Jimmy Vasser, USA (Lola B2k/00-Toyota), 224; **9** Alex Tagliani, CDN (Reynard 2KI-Ford Cosworth XF), 223; **10** Memo Gidley, USA (Reynard 2KI-Toyota), 223.
Most laps led: Juan Pablo Montoya, CO (Lola B2k/00-Toyota), 111.
Fastest qualifying lap: Montoya, 22.107s, 167.567 mph/269.673 km/h.
Championship points: **1** Andretti, 120; **2** Moreno, 98; **3** de Ferran, 89; **4** da Matta, 82; **5** Tracy, 80; **6** Fernandez, 79.

MILLER LITE 200, Mid-Ohio Sports Car Course, Lexington, Ohio, USA, 13 August. Round 13. 83 laps of the 2.258-mile/3.634-km circuit, 186.448 miles/300.059 km.
1 Helio Castro-Neves, BR (Reynard 2KI-Honda), 1h 44m 59.029s, 106.558 mph/171.488 km/h.
2 Gil de Ferran, BR (Reynard 2KI-Honda), 1h 45m 03.454s; **3** Christian Fittipaldi, BR (Lola B2k/00-Ford Cosworth XF), 1h 45m 04.941s; **4** Massimiliano 'Max' Papis, I (Reynard 2KI-Ford Cosworth XF), 1h 45m 07.116s; **5** Kenny Bräck, S (Reynard 2KI-Ford Cosworth XF), 1h 45m 07.890s; **6** Adrian Fernandez, MEX (Reynard 2KI-Ford Cosworth XF), 1h 45m 08.623s; **7** Patrick Carpentier, CDN (Reynard 2KI-Ford Cosworth XF), 1h 45m 09.075s; **8** Michael Andretti, USA (Lola B2k/00-Ford Cosworth XF), 1h 45m 09.835s; **9** Alex Tagliani, CDN (Reynard 2KI-Ford Cosworth XF), 1h 45m 10.358s; **10** Oriol Servia, E (Reynard 2KI-Toyota), 82 laps.
Most laps led: Castro-Neves, 55.
Fastest qualifying lap: de Ferran, 1m 05.347s, 124.394 mph/200.193 km/h.
Championship points: **1** Andretti, 125; **2** de Ferran, 106; **3** Moreno, 100; **4** Bräck, 88; **5** Fernandez, 87; **6** da Matta, 82.

MOTOROLA 220, Road America Circuit, Elkhart Lake, Wisconsin, USA, 20 August. Round 14. 55 laps of the 4.048-mile/6.515-km circuit, 222.640 miles/358.304 km.
1 Paul Tracy, CDN (Reynard 2KI-Honda), 1h 37m 53.681s, 136.457 mph/219.606 km/h.
2 Adrian Fernandez, MEX (Reynard 2KI-Ford Cosworth XF), 1h 38m 01.131s; **3** Kenny Bräck, S (Reynard 2KI-Ford Cosworth XF), 1h 38m 02.517s; **4** Roberto Moreno, BR (Reynard 2KI-Ford Cosworth XF), 1h 38m 17.260s; **5** Jimmy Vasser, USA (Lola B2k/00-Toyota), 1h 38m 27.630s; **6** Memo Gidley, USA (Reynard 2KI-Toyota), 1h 39m 28.245s; **7** Massimiliano 'Max' Papis, I (Reynard 2KI-Ford Cosworth XF), 1h 39m 33.819s; **8** Tony Kanaan, BR (Reynard 2KI-Mercedes Benz), 54 laps; **9** Helio Castro-Neves, BR (Reynard 2KI-Honda), 54; **10** Oriol Servia, E (Reynard 2KI-Toyota), 54.
Most laps led: Alex Tagliani, CDN (Reynard 2KI-Ford Cosworth XF), 23.
Fastest qualifying lap: Dario Franchitti, GB (Reynard 2KI-Honda), 1m 39.866s, 145.924 mph/234.841 km/h.
Championship points: **1** Andretti, 125; **2** Moreno, 112; **3** de Ferran, 106; **4** Fernandez, 103; **5** Bräck, 102; **6** Tracy, 100.

MOLSON INDY VANCOUVER, Vancouver Street Circuit, Concord Pacific Place, Vancouver, British Columbia, Canada, 3 September. Round 15. 90 laps of the 1.781 mile/2.866-km circuit, 160.290 miles/257.962 km.
1 Paul Tracy, CDN (Reynard 2KI-Honda), 1h 53m 06.024s, 85.034 mph/136.849 km/h.
2 Dario Franchitti, GB (Reynard 2KI-Honda), 1h 53m 06.408s; **3** Adrian Fernandez, MEX (Reynard 2KI-Ford Cosworth XF), 1h 53m 25.055s; **4** Christian Fittipaldi, BR (Lola B2k/00-Ford Cosworth XF), 1h 53m 25.638s; **5** Gil de Ferran, BR (Reynard 2KI-Honda), 1h 53m 26.137s; **6** Jimmy Vasser, USA (Lola B2k/00-Toyota), 1h 53m 26.583s; **7** Cristiano da Matta, BR (Reynard 2KI-Toyota), 1h 53m 37.972s; **8** Massimiliano 'Max' Papis, I (Reynard 2KI-Ford Cosworth XF), 1h 53m 51.466s; **9** Kenny Bräck, S (Reynard 2KI-Ford Cosworth XF), 1h 53m 51.856s; **10** Roberto Moreno, BR (Reynard 2KI-Ford Cosworth XF), 89 laps.
Most laps led: Franchitti, 50.

Fastest qualifying lap: Franchitti, 1m 00.405s, 106.144 mph/170.821 km/h.
Championship points: **1** Andretti, 126; **2** Tracy, 120; **3** Fernandez, 117; **4** de Ferran, 116; **5** Moreno, 115; **6** Bräck, 106.

HONDA GRAND PRIX OF MONTEREY FEATURING THE SHELL 300, Laguna Seca Raceway, Monterey, California, USA, 10 September. Round 16. 83 laps of the 2.238-mile/3.602-km circuit, 185.754 miles/298.942 km.
1 Helio Castro-Neves, BR (Reynard 2KI-Honda), 1h 46m 11.800s, 104.949 mph/168.899 km/h.
2 Gil de Ferran, BR (Reynard 2KI-Honda), 1h 46m 12.754s; **3** Dario Franchitti, GB (Reynard 2KI-Honda), 1h 46m 14.442s; **4** Bryan Herta, USA (Reynard 2KI-Ford Cosworth XF), 1h 46m 16.219s; **5** Kenny Bräck, S (Reynard 2KI-Ford Cosworth XF), 1h 46m 16.958s; **6** Juan Pablo Montoya, CO (Lola B2k/00-Toyota), 1h 46m 19.101s; **7** Mauricio Gugelmin, BR (Reynard 2KI-Mercedes Benz), 1h 46m 26.614s; **8** Jimmy Vasser, USA (Lola B2k/00-Toyota), 1h 46m 32.697s; **9** Patrick Carpentier, CDN (Reynard 2KI-Ford Cosworth XF), 1h 46m 33.409s; **10** Christian Fittipaldi, BR (Lola B2k/00-Ford Cosworth XF), 1h 46m 34.092s.
Most laps led: Castro-Neves, 81.
Fastest qualifying lap: Castro-Neves, 1m 07.722s, 118.969 mph/191.462 km/h.
Championship points: **1** de Ferran, 132; **2** Andretti, 126; **3** Tracy, 122; **4** Fernandez, 118; **5** Bräck, 116; **6** Moreno, 115.

MOTOROLA 300, Gateway International Raceway, Madison, Illinois, USA, 17 September. Round 17. 236 laps of the 1.270-mile/2.044-km circuit, 299.720 miles/482.353 km.
1 Juan Pablo Montoya, CO (Lola B2k/00-Toyota), 1h 55m 38.003s, 155.519 mph/250.284 km/h.
2 Patrick Carpentier, CDN (Reynard 2KI-Ford Cosworth XF), 1h 55m 49.807s; **3** Roberto Moreno, BR (Reynard 2KI-Ford Cosworth XF), 235 laps; **4** Cristiano da Matta, BR (Reynard 2KI-Toyota), 235; **5** Oriol Servia, E (Reynard 2KI-Toyota), 235; **6** Massimiliano 'Max' Papis, I (Reynard 2KI-Ford Cosworth XF), 235; **7** Jimmy Vasser, USA (Lola B2k/00-Toyota), 235; **8** Gil de Ferran, BR (Reynard 2KI-Honda), 235; **9** Helio Castro-Neves, BR (Reynard 2KI-Honda), 235; **10** Adrian Fernandez, MEX (Reynard 2KI-Ford Cosworth XF), 235.
Most laps led: Michael Andretti, USA (Lola B2k/00-Ford Cosworth XF), 121.
Fastest qualifying lap: Montoya, 25.353s, 180.334 mph/290.219 km/h.
Championship points: **1** de Ferran, 137; **2** Moreno, 129; **3** Andretti, 127; **4** Tracy, 122; **5** Fernandez, 121; **6** Bräck, 118.

TEXACO/HAVOLINE GRAND PRIX OF HOUSTON, Houston Street Circuit, Texas, USA, 1 October. Round 18. 100 laps of the 1.527-mile/2.457-km circuit, 152.026 miles/244.662 km.
1 Jimmy Vasser, USA (Lola B2k/00-Toyota), 1h 59m 02.370s, 76.626 mph/123.318 km/h.
2 Juan Pablo Montoya, CO (Lola B2k/00-Toyota), 1h 59m 04.284s; **3** Gil de Ferran, BR (Reynard 2KI-Honda), 1h 59m 04.687s; **4** Paul Tracy, CDN (Reynard 2KI-Honda), 1h 59m 05.099s; **5** Helio Castro-Neves, BR (Reynard 2KI-Honda), 1h 59m 10.709s; **6** Christian Fittipaldi, BR (Lola B2k/00-Ford Cosworth XF), 1h 59m 17.689s; **7** Adrian Fernandez, MEX (Reynard 2KI-Ford Cosworth XF), 1h 59m 19.647s; **8** Shinji Nakano, J (Reynard 2KI-Honda), 1h 59m 23.785s; **9** Oriol Servia, E (Reynard 2KI-Toyota), 1h 59m 28.197s; **10** Tony Kanaan, BR (Reynard 2KI-Mercedes Benz), 1h 59m 33.822s.
Most laps led: de Ferran, 69.
Fastest qualifying lap: de Ferran, 58.757s, 93.558 mph/150.567 km/h.
Championship points: **1** de Ferran, 153; **2** Tracy, 134; **3** Moreno, 131; **4** Andretti, 127; **5** Fernandez, 127; **6** Montoya, 122.

HONDA INDY 300, Surfers Paradise Street Circuit, Gold Coast, Queensland, Australia, 15 October. Round 19. 59 laps of the 2.795-mile/4.498-km circuit, 164.905 miles/265.389 km.
1 Adrian Fernandez, MEX (Reynard 2KI-Ford Cosworth XF), 2h 01m 14.605s, 81.607 mph/131.334 km/h.
2 Kenny Bräck, S (Reynard 2KI-Ford Cosworth XF), 2h 01m 14.929s; **3** Jimmy Vasser, USA (Lola B2k/00-Toyota), 2h 01m 18.664s; **4** Cristiano da Matta, BR (Reynard 2KI-Toyota), 2h 01m 19.418s; **5** Patrick Carpentier, CDN (Reynard 2KI-Ford Cosworth XF), 2h 01m 19.836s; **6** Helio Castro-Neves, BR (Reynard 2KI-Honda), 2h 01m 24.945s; **7** Michel Jourdain Jr., MEX (Lola B2k/00-Mercedes Benz), 2h 01m 25.614s; **8** Tony Kanaan, BR (Reynard 2KI-Mercedes Benz), 2h 01m 30.375s; **9** Oriol Servia, E (Reynard 2KI-Toyota), 2h 01m 32.786s; **10** Mauricio Gugelmin, BR (Reynard 2KI-Mercedes Benz), 2h 01m 33.186s.
Most laps led: Fernandez, 17.
Fastest qualifying lap: Juan Pablo Montoya, CO (Lola B2k/00-Toyota), 1m 31.722s, 109.701 mph/176.547 km/h.
Championship points: **1** de Ferran, 153; **2** Fernandez, 148; **3=** Tracy, 134; **3=** Brack, 134; **5=** Moreno, 131; **5=** Vasser, 131.

MARLBORO 500 PRESENTED BY TOYOTA, California Speedway, Fontana, California, USA, 30 October. Round 20. 250 laps of the 2.029-mile/3.265-km circuit, 507.250 miles/816.340 km.
The race on 29 October was stopped after 34 laps due to heavy rain. Continued the following day.
1 Christian Fittipaldi, BR (Lola B2k/00-Ford Cosworth XF), 3h 10m 46.608s, 159.532 mph/256.742 km/h. **2** Roberto Moreno, BR (Reynard 2KI-Ford Cosworth XF), 3h 10m 46.802s; **3** Gil de Ferran, BR (Reynard 2KI-Honda), 3h 10m 47.134s; **4** Casey Mears, USA (Reynard 2KI-Ford Cosworth XF), 3h 10m 47.329s; **5** Adrian Fernandez, MEX (Reynard 2KI-Ford Cosworth XF), 3h 10m 47.753s; **6** Alex Tagliani, CDN (Reynard 2KI-Ford Cosworth XF), 248 laps; **7** Tarso Marques, BR (Swift 2KI-Ford Cosworth XF), 247; **8** Alex Barron, USA (Lola B2k/00-Ford Cosworth XF), 239; **9** Helio Castro-Neves, BR (Reynard 2KI-Honda), 226; **10** Juan Pablo Montoya, CO (Lola B2k/00-Toyota), 219.
Most laps led: Kenny Bräck, S (Reynard 2KI-Ford Cosworth XF), 47
Fastest qualifying lap: de Ferran, 30.255s, 241.428 mph/388.540 km/h.

Final championship points
1 Gil de Ferran, BR, 168; **2** Adrian Fernandez, MEX, 158; **3** Roberto Moreno, BR, 147; **4=** Paul Tracy, CDN, 134; **4=** Kenny Bräck, S, 134; **6** Jimmy Vasser, USA, 131; **7** Helio Castro-Neves, BR, 129; **8** Michael Andretti, USA, 127; **9** Juan Pablo Montoya, CO, 126; **10** Cristiano da Matta, BR, 112; **11** Patrick Carpentier, CDN, 101; **12** Christian Fittipaldi, BR, 97; **13** Dario Franchitti, GB, 92; **14** Massimiliano 'Max' Papis, I, 88; **15** Oriol Servia, E, 60; **16** Alex Tagliani, CDN, 53; **17** Mauricio Gugelmin, BR, 39; **18** Bryan Herta, USA, 26; **19** Tony Kanaan, BR, 24; **20** Memo Gidley, USA, 20; **21=** Mark Blundell, GB, 18; **21=** Michel Jourdain Jr., MEX, 18; **23=** Casey Mears, USA, 12; **23=** Shinji Nakano, J, 12; **25** Tarso Marques, BR, 11; **26=** Alex Barron, USA, 6; **26=** Luiz Garcia Jr., BR, 6; **28** Norberto Fontana, RA, 2; **29** Takuya Kurosawa, J, 1.

Nations' Cup
1 Brazil, 332; **2** United States, 256; **3** Canada, 226; **4** Mexico, 165; **5** Sweden, 135; **6** Colombia, 126; **7** Scotland, 92; **8** Italy, 88; **9** Spain, 60; **10** England, 18; **11** Japan, 13; **12** Argentina, 2.

Manufacturers' Championship (engines)
1 Ford Cosworth, 335; **2** Honda, 313; **3** Toyota, 275; **4** Mercedes Benz, 74.

Constructors' Championship
1 Reynard, 394; **2** Lola, 312; **3** Swift, 11.

Rookie of the Year
1 Kenny Bräck, S, 135; **2** Oriol Servia, E, 60; **3** Alex Tagliani, CDN, 53; **4=** Casey Mears, USA, 12; **4=** Shinji Nakano, J, 12; **6** Norberto Fontana, RA, 2; **7** Takuya Kurosawa, J, 1.

Marlboro Pole Award
1 Juan Pablo Montoya, CO, 7; **2** Gil de Ferran, BR, 5; **3** Helio Castro-Neves, BR, 3

Indy Car Race

84th INDIANAPOLIS 500, Indianapolis Motor Speedway, Speedway, Indiana, USA, 28 May. 200 laps of the 2.500-mile/4.023-km circuit, 500.000 miles/804.672 km.
1 Juan Pablo Montoya, CO (G-Force-Aurora), 2h 58m 59.431s, 167.607 mph/269.737 km/h.
2 Buddy Lazier, USA (Dallara-Aurora), 2h 59m 06.615s; **3** Eliseo Salazar, RCH (G-Force-Aurora), 2h 59m 15.133s; **4** Jeff Ward, USA (G-Force-Aurora), 2h 59m 17.844s; **5** Eddie Cheever, Jr., USA (Dallara-Infiniti), 2h 59m 18.157s; **6** Robby Gordon, USA (Dallara-Aurora), 2h 59m 18.505s; **7** Jimmy Vasser, USA (G-Force-Aurora), 199 laps; **8** Stéphan Grégoire, F (G-Force-Aurora), 199; **9** Scott Goodyear, CDN (Dallara-Aurora), 199; **10** Scott Sharp, USA (Dallara-Aurora), 198; **11** Mark Dismore, USA (Dallara-Aurora), 198; **12** Donnie Beechler, USA (Dallara-Aurora), 198; **13** Jacques Lazier, USA (G-Force-Aurora), 198; **14** Jeret Schroeder, USA (Dallara-Aurora), 198; **15** Billy Boat, USA (G-Force-Aurora), 198; **16** Raul Boesel, BR (G-Force-Aurora), 197; **17** Jason Leffler, USA (G-Force-Aurora), 197; **18** Buzz Calkins, USA (Dallara-Aurora), 194; **19** Steve Knapp, USA (G-Force-Infiniti), 193; **20** Davey Hamilton, USA (G-Force-Aurora), 188; **21** Robby McGehee, USA (G-Force-Aurora), 187; **22** Johnny Unser, USA (G-Force-Aurora), 186; **23** Stan Wattles, USA (Dallara-Aurora), 172 (DNF - engine); **24** Sam Hornish Jr., USA (Dallara-Aurora), 153 (DNF - accident); **25** Airton Dare, BR (G-Force-Aurora), 126 (DNF - engine); **26** Robbie Buhl, USA (G-Force-Aurora), 99 (DNF - engine); **27** Richie Hearn, USA (Dallara-Aurora), 97 (DNF - electrics); **28** Andy Hillenburg, USA (Dallara-Aurora), 91 (DNF - wheel bearing); **29** Al Unser Jr., USA (G-Force-Aurora), 89 (DNF - engine overheating); **30** Jimmy Kite, USA (G-Force-Aurora), 74 (DNF - engine); **31** Sarah Fisher, USA (Dallara-Aurora), 71 (DNF - accident); **32** Lyn St. James, USA (G-Force-Aurora), 69 (DNF - accident); **33** Greg Ray, USA (Dallara-Aurora), 67 (DNF - accident).
(Engines: Aurora = Oldsmobile; Infiniti = Nissan)
Most laps led: Montoya, 167.
Fastest race lap: Lazier, 41.191s, 218.494 mph/351.633 km/h.
Fastest leading lap: Montoya, 41.343s, 217.691 mph/350.340 km/h.
Pole position/Fastest qualifying lap: Ray, 2m 41.095s, 223.472 mph/359.643 km/h (over four laps).

NASCAR Winston Cup

1999 Results

The following races were run after AUTOCOURSE 1999-2000 went to press.

PENNZOIL 400 PRESENTED BY KMART, Miami-Dade Homestead Motorsports Complex, Florida, USA, 14 November. Round 33. 267 laps of the 1.500-mile/2.414-km circuit, 400.500 miles/644.542 km.
1 Tony Stewart, USA (Pontiac Grand Prix), 2h 51m 14s, 140.335 mph/225.847 km/h.
2 Bobby Labonte, USA (Pontiac Grand Prix), 2h 51m 19.289s; **3** Jeff Burton, USA (Ford Taurus), 267 laps; **4** Mark Martin, USA (Ford Taurus), 267; **5** Dale Jarrett, USA (Ford Taurus), 267; **6** Mike Skinner, USA (Chevrolet Monte Carlo), 267; **7** Kyle Petty, USA (Pontiac Grand Prix), 267; **8** Dale Earnhardt, USA (Chevrolet Monte Carlo), 266; **9** Wally Dallenbach, USA (Chevrolet Monte Carlo), 266; **10** Jeff Gordon, USA (Chevrolet Monte Carlo), 266.
Fastest qualifying lap: David Green, USA (Pontiac Grand Prix), 34.669s, 155.759 mph/250.669 km/h.
Championship points: **1** Jarrett, 5087; **2** Labonte (Bobby), 4876; **3** Martin, 4778; **4** Stewart, 4651; **5** Burton (Jeff), 4573; **6** Gordon, 4571.

NAPA 500, Atlanta Motor Speedway, Hampton, Georgia, USA, 21 November. Round 34. 325 laps of the 1.540-mile/2.478-km circuit, 500.500 miles/805.477 km.
1 Bobby Labonte, USA (Pontiac Grand Prix), 3h 37m 43s, 137.932 mph/221.979 km/h.
2 Dale Jarrett, USA (Ford Taurus), 3h 37m 45.428s; **3** Jeremy Mayfield, USA (Ford Taurus), 325 laps; **4** Mark Martin, USA (Ford Taurus), 325; **5** Jeff Burton, USA (Ford Taurus), 325; **6** Chad Little, USA (Ford Taurus), 325; **7** Ricky Rudd, USA (Ford Taurus), 325; **8** Mike Skinner, USA (Chevrolet Monte Carlo), 325; **9** Dale Earnhardt, USA (Chevrolet Monte Carlo), 325; **10** Bobby Hamilton, USA (Chevrolet Monte Carlo), 325.
Fastest qualifying lap: Kevin Lepage, USA (Ford Taurus), 28.617s, 193.731 mph/311.780 km/h.

Final championship points

Drivers
1 Dale Jarrett, USA, 5262; **2** Bobby Labonte, USA, 5061; **3** Mark Martin, USA, 4943; **4** Tony Stewart, USA, 4774; **5** Jeff Burton, USA, 4733; **6** Jeff Gordon, USA, 4620; **7** Dale Earnhardt, USA, 4492; **8** Rusty Wallace, USA, 4155; **9** Ward Burton, USA, 4062; **10** Mike Skinner, USA, 4003; **11** Jeremy Mayfield, USA, 3743; **12** Terry Labonte, USA, 3580; **13** Bobby Hamilton, USA, 3564; **14** Steve Park, USA, 3481; **15** Ken Schrader, USA, 3479; **16** Sterling Marlin, USA, 3397; **17** John Andretti, USA, 3394; **18** Wally Dallenbach, USA, 3367; **19** Kenny Irwin Jr., USA, 3338; **20** Jimmy Spencer, USA, 3312; **21** Bill Elliott, USA, 3246; **22** Kenny Wallace, USA, 3210; **23** Chad Little, USA, 3193; **24** Elliott Sadler, USA, 3191; **25** Kevin Lepage, USA, 3185; **26** Kyle Petty, USA, 3103; **27** Geoff Bodine, USA, 3053; **28** Johnny Benson Jr., USA, 3012; **29** Michael Waltrip, USA, 2974; **30** Joe Nemechek, USA, 2956.

Raybestos Rookie of The Year: Tony Stewart.
Bud Pole Award Winner: Jeff Gordon.
Most Popular Driver: Bill Elliott.
MCI Worldcom Fast Pace Award (fastest lap): Bobby Labonte.

2000 Results

DAYTONA 500, Daytona International Speedway, Daytona Beach, Florida, USA, 20 February. Round 1. 200 laps of the 2.500-mile/4.023-km circuit, 500.000 miles/804.672 km.
1 Dale Jarrett, USA (Ford Taurus), 3h 12m 43s, 155.669 mph/250.525 km/h.
2 Jeff Burton, USA (Ford Taurus), 200 laps (under caution); **3** Bill Elliott, USA (Ford Taurus), 200; **4** Rusty Wallace, USA (Ford Taurus), 200; **5** Mark Martin, USA (Ford Taurus), 200; **6** Bobby Labonte, USA (Pontiac Grand Prix), 200; **7** Terry Labonte, USA (Chevrolet Monte Carlo), 200; **8** Ward Burton, USA (Pontiac Grand Prix), 200; **9** Ken Schrader, USA (Pontiac Grand Prix), 200; **10** Matt Kenseth, USA (Ford Taurus), 200.
Fastest qualifying lap: Jarrett, 47.098s, 191.091 mph/307.531 km/h.
Drivers' Championship points: **1** Jarrett, 185; **2=** Burton (Jeff), 170; **2=** Elliott, 170; **4=** Wallace (Rusty), 160; **4=** Martin, 160; **6** Labonte (Bobby), 150.

DURA LUBE/KMART 400, North Carolina Motor Speedway, Rockingham, North Carolina, USA, 27 February. Round 2. 393 laps of the 1.017-mile/1.637-km circuit, 399.681 miles/643.224 km.
1 Bobby Labonte, USA (Pontiac Grand Prix), 3h 07m 32s, 127.875 mph/205.795 km/h.
2 Dale Earnhardt, USA (Chevrolet Monte Carlo), 3h 07m 33.068s; **3** Ward Burton, USA (Pontiac Grand Prix), 393 laps; **4** Tony Stewart, USA (Pontiac Grand Prix), 393; **5** Dale Jarrett, USA (Ford Taurus), 392; **6** Ricky Rudd, USA (Ford Taurus), 392; **7** Jeremy Mayfield, USA (Ford Taurus), 392; **8** Mark Martin, USA (Ford Taurus), 392; **9** Steve Park, USA (Chevrolet Monte Carlo), 392; **10** Jeff Gordon, USA (Chevrolet Monte Carlo), 392.
Fastest qualifying lap: Rusty Wallace, USA (Ford Taurus), 23.167s, 158.035 mph/254.333 km/h.
Drivers' Championship points: **1** Jarrett, 340; **2** Labonte (Bobby), 335; **3** Burton (Ward), 312; **4** Martin, 307; **5** Wallace (Rusty), 295; **6** Mayfield, 276.

CARSDIRECT.COM 400, Las Vegas Motor Speedway, Nevada, USA, 5 March. Round 3. 148 laps of the 1.500-mile/2.414-km circuit, 222.000 miles/357.274 km.
Race shortened due to heavy rain.
1 Jeff Burton, USA (Ford Taurus), 1h 51m 01s, 119.982 mph/193.092 km/h.
2 Tony Stewart, USA (Pontiac Grand Prix), 148 laps (under caution); **3** Mark Martin, USA (Ford Taurus), 148; **4** Bill Elliott, USA (Ford Taurus), 148; **5** Bobby Labonte, USA (Pontiac Grand Prix), 148; **6** Johnny Benson, USA (Pontiac Grand Prix), 148; **7** Dale Jarrett, USA (Ford Taurus), 148; **8** Dale Earnhardt, USA (Chevrolet Monte Carlo), 148; **9** Joe Nemechek, USA (Chevrolet Monte Carlo), 148; **10** Dale Earnhardt Jr., USA (Chevrolet Monte Carlo), 148.
Fastest qualifying lap: Ricky Rudd, USA (Ford Taurus), 31.293s, 172.563 mph/277.713 km/h.
Drivers' Championship points: **1** Labonte (Bobby), 490; **2** Jarrett, 486; **3** Martin, 477; **4** Stewart, 442; **5** Burton (Jeff), 427; **6** Elliott, 418.

CRACKER BARREL OLD COUNTRY STORE 500, Atlanta Motor Speedway, Hampton, Georgia, USA, 12 March. Round 4. 325 laps of the 1.540-mile/2.478-km circuit, 500.500 miles/805.477 km.
1 Dale Earnhardt, USA (Chevrolet Monte Carlo), 3h 47m 55s, 131.759 mph/212.045 km/h.
2 Bobby Labonte, USA (Pontiac Grand Prix), 3h 47m 55.010s; **3** Mark Martin, USA (Ford Taurus), 325 laps; **4** Steve Park, USA (Chevrolet Monte Carlo), 325; **5** Joe Nemechek, USA (Chevrolet Monte Carlo), 325; **6** Chad Little, USA (Ford Taurus), 325; **7** Todd Bodine, USA (Chevrolet Monte Carlo), 325; **8** Ward Burton, USA (Pontiac Grand Prix), 324; **9** Jeff Gordon, USA (Chevrolet Monte Carlo), 324; **10** Bill Elliott, USA (Ford Taurus), 324.
Fastest qualifying lap: Dale Jarrett, USA (Ford Taurus), 28.789s, 192.574 mph/309.917 km/h.
Drivers' Championship points: **1** Labonte (Bobby), 666; **2** Martin, 647; **3** Earnhardt, 597; **4** Elliott, 557; **5** Burton (Ward), 548; **6** Jarrett (Dale), 546.

MALL.COM 400, Darlington Raceway, South Carolina, USA, 19 March. Round 5. 293 laps of the 1.366-mile/2.198-km circuit, 400.238 miles/644.121 km.
1 Ward Burton, USA (Pontiac Grand Prix), 3h 07m 30s, 128.076 mph/206.119 km/h.
2 Dale Jarrett, USA (Ford Taurus), 3h 07m 31.420s; **3** Dale Earnhardt, USA (Chevrolet Monte Carlo), 293 laps; **4** Tony Stewart, USA (Pontiac Grand Prix), 293; **5** Jeff Burton, USA (Ford Taurus), 293; **6** Matt Kenseth, USA (Ford Taurus), 293; **7** Bobby Hamilton, USA (Chevrolet Monte Carlo), 293; **8** Jeff Gordon, USA (Chevrolet Monte Carlo), 293; **9** Mark Martin, USA (Ford Taurus), 293; **10** Kevin Lepage, USA (Ford Taurus), 293.
Fastest qualifying lap: Gordon, 28.481s, 172.662 mph/277.873 km/h.
Drivers' Championship points: **1** Labonte (Bobby), 794; **2** Martin, 785; **3** Earnhardt, 762; **4** Burton (Ward), 733; **5** Jarrett, 721; **6** Stewart, 663.

FOOD CITY 500, Bristol Motor Speedway, Tennessee, USA, 26 March. Round 6. 500 laps of the 0.533-mile/0.858-km circuit, 266.500 miles/428.890 km.
1 Rusty Wallace, USA (Ford Taurus), 3h 01m 40s, 88.018 mph/141.652 km/h.
2 Johnny Benson, USA (Pontiac Grand Prix), 3h 01m 42.622s; 3 Ward Burton, USA (Pontiac Grand Prix), 500 laps; 4 Jeremy Mayfield, USA (Ford Taurus), 500; 5 Terry Labonte, USA (Chevrolet Monte Carlo), 500; 6 Bobby Labonte, USA (Pontiac Grand Prix), 500; 7 Steve Park, USA (Chevrolet Monte Carlo), 500; 8 Jeff Gordon, USA (Chevrolet Monte Carlo), 500; 9 Jeff Burton, USA (Ford Taurus), 500; 10 Sterling Marlin, USA (Chevrolet Monte Carlo), 500.
Fastest qualifying lap: Park, 15.184s, 126.370 mph/203.373 km/h.
Drivers' Championship points: 1 Labonte (Bobby), 944; **2** Burton (Ward), 903; **3** Martin, 900; **4** Jarrett, 826; **5** Earnhardt, 813; **6** Wallace (Rusty), 775.

DIRECTV 500, Texas Motor Speedway, Fort Worth, Texas, USA, 2 April. Round 7. 334 laps of the 1.500-mile/2.414-km circuit, 501.000 miles/806.281 km.
1 Dale Earnhardt Jr., USA (Chevrolet Monte Carlo), 3h 49m 12s, 131.152 mph/211.068 km/h.
2 Jeff Burton, USA (Ford Taurus), 3h 49m 17.920s; 3 Bobby Labonte, USA (Pontiac Grand Prix), 334 laps; 4 Rusty Wallace, USA (Ford Taurus), 334; 5 Kevin Lepage, USA (Ford Taurus), 334; 6 Jeremy Mayfield, USA (Ford Taurus), 334; 7 Dale Earnhardt, USA (Chevrolet Monte Carlo 334; 8 Terry Labonte, USA (Chevrolet Monte Carlo), 334; 9 Tony Stewart, USA (Pontiac Grand Prix), 334; 10 Ricky Rudd, USA (Ford Taurus), 334.
Fastest qualifying lap: Labonte (Terry), 28.105s, 192.137/309.214 km/h.
Drivers' Championship points: 1 Labonte (Bobby), 1114; **2** Martin, 1030; **3** Burton (Ward), 1024; **4** Earnhardt, 959; **5** Wallace (Rusty), 940; **6** Burton (Jeff), 934.

GOODY'S BODY PAIN 500, Martinsville Speedway, Virginia, USA, 9 April. Round 8. 500 laps of the 0.526-mile/0.847-km circuit, 263.000 miles/423.257 km.
1 Mark Martin, USA (Ford Taurus), 3h 41m 45s, 71.161 mph/114.523 km/h.
2 Jeff Burton, USA (Ford Taurus), 3h 41m 46.505s; 3 Michael Waltrip, USA (Chevrolet Monte Carlo), 500 laps; 4 Jeff Gordon, USA (Chevrolet Monte Carlo), 500; 5 Dale Jarrett, USA (Ford Taurus), 500; 6 Tony Stewart, USA (Pontiac Grand Prix), 500; 7 Jeremy Mayfield, USA (Ford Taurus), 500; 8 Bill Elliott, USA (Ford Taurus), 500; 9 Dale Earnhardt, USA (Chevrolet Monte Carlo), 500; 10 Rusty Wallace, USA (Ford Taurus), 500.
Fastest qualifying lap: Wallace (Rusty), 19.969s, 94.827 mph/152.609 km/h.
Drivers' Championship points: 1 Labonte (Bobby), 1246; **2** Martin, 1210; **3** Burton (Ward), 1159; **4** Burton (Jeff), 1104; **5** Earnhardt, 1102; **6** Wallace (Rusty), 1084.

DIEHARD 500, Talladega Superspeedway, Alabama, USA, 16 April. Round 9. 188 laps of the 2.660-mile/4.281-km circuit, 500.080 miles/804.801 km.
1 Jeff Gordon, USA (Chevrolet Monte Carlo), 3h 06m 11s, 161.157 mph/259.358 km/h.
2 Mike Skinner, USA (Chevrolet Monte Carlo), 3h 06m 11.189s; 3 Dale Earnhardt, USA (Chevrolet Monte Carlo), 188 laps; 4 Kenny Irwin Jr., USA (Chevrolet Monte Carlo), 188; 5 Jimmy Spencer, USA (Ford Taurus), 188; 6 Mark Martin, USA (Ford Taurus), 188; 7 Terry Labonte, USA (Chevrolet Monte Carlo), 188; 8 Sterling Marlin, USA (Chevrolet Monte Carlo), 188; 9 Kyle Petty, USA (Pontiac Grand Prix), 188; 10 Ward Burton, USA (Pontiac Grand Prix), 188.
Fastest qualifying lap: Jeremy Mayfield, USA (Ford Taurus), 51.217s, 186.969 mph/300.898 km/h.
Drivers' Championship points: 1 Martin, 1370; **2** Labonte (Bobby), 1346; **3** Burton (Ward), 1293; **4** Earnhardt, 1272; **5** Burton (Jeff), 1236; **6** Jarrett, 1167.

NAPA AUTO PARTS 500, California Speedway, Fontana, California, USA, 30 April. Round 10. 250 laps of the 2.000-mile/3.219-km circuit, 500.000 miles/804.672 km.
1 Jeremy Mayfield, USA (Ford Taurus), 3h 20m 50s, 149.378 mph/240.400 km/h.
2 Bobby Labonte, USA (Pontiac Grand Prix), 3h 20m 50.300s; 3 Matt Kenseth, USA (Ford Taurus), 250 laps; 4 Ricky Rudd, USA (Ford Taurus), 250; 5 Jeff Burton, USA (Ford Taurus), 250; 6 Ward Burton, USA (Pontiac Grand Prix), 250; 7 Mike Skinner, USA (Chevrolet Monte Carlo), 250; 8 Rusty Wallace, USA (Ford Taurus), 250; 9 Dale Jarrett, USA (Ford Taurus), 250; 10 Tony Stewart, USA (Pontiac Grand Prix), 250.
Fastest qualifying lap: Skinner, 38.697s, 186.061 mph/299.436 km/h.
Drivers' Championship points: 1 Labonte (Bobby), 1516; **2** Martin, 1496; **3** Burton (Ward), 1443; **4** Burton (Jeff), 1396; **5** Earnhardt, 1384; **6** Jarrett, 1305.

PONTIAC EXCITEMENT 400, Richmond International Raceway, Virginia, USA, 6 May. Round 11. 400 laps of the 0.750-mile/1.207-km circuit, 300.000 miles/482.803 km.
1 Dale Earnhardt Jr., USA (Chevrolet Monte Carlo), 3h 01m 08s, 99.374 mph/159.927 km/h.
2 Terry Labonte, USA (Chevrolet Monte Carlo), 3h 01m 08.159s; 3 Dale Jarrett, USA (Ford Taurus), 400 laps; 4 Ricky Rudd, USA (Ford Taurus), 400; 5 Rusty Wallace, USA (Ford Taurus), 400; 6 Ward Burton, USA (Pontiac Grand Prix), 400; 7 Jeff Burton, USA (Ford Taurus), 400; 8 Tony Stewart, USA (Pontiac Grand Prix), 400; 9 Bill Elliott, USA (Ford Taurus), 400; 10 Dale Earnhardt, USA (Chevrolet Monte Carlo), 400.
Fastest qualifying lap: Wallace (Rusty), 21.645s, 124.740 mph/200.750 km/h.
Drivers' Championship points: 1 Labonte (Bobby), 1601; **2** Burton (Ward), 1598; **3** Martin, 1568; **4** Burton (Jeff), 1542; **5** Earnhardt, 1523; **6** Jarrett, 1470.

COCA-COLA 600, Lowe's Motor Speedway, Concord, North Carolina, USA, 28 May. Round 12. 400 laps of the 1.500-mile/2.414-km circuit, 600.000 miles/965.606 km.
1 Matt Kenseth, USA (Ford Taurus), 4h 12m 23s, 142.640 mph/229.557 km/h.
2 Bobby Labonte, USA (Pontiac Grand Prix), 4h 12m 23.573s; 3 Dale Earnhardt, USA (Chevrolet Monte Carlo), 400 laps; 4 Dale Earnhardt Jr., USA (Chevrolet Monte Carlo), 400; 5 Dale Jarrett, USA (Ford Taurus), 400; 6 Jeremy Mayfield, USA (Ford Taurus), 400; 7 Mike Skinner, USA (Chevrolet Monte Carlo), 400; 8 Rusty Wallace, USA (Ford Taurus), 400; 9 Steve Park, USA (Chevrolet Monte Carlo), 400; 10 Jeff Gordon, USA (Chevrolet Monte Carlo), 400.
Fastest qualifying lap: Earnhardt Jr., 29.027s, 186.034 mph/299.392 km/h.
Drivers' Championship points: 1 Labonte (Bobby), 1776; **2** Burton (Ward), 1722; **3** Martin, 1695; **4** Earnhardt, 1693; **5** Burton (Jeff), 1672; **6** Jarrett, 1630.

MBNA PLATINUM 400, Dover Downs International Speedway, Dover, Delaware, USA, 4 June. Round 13. 400 laps of the 1.000-mile/1.609-km circuit, 400.000 miles/643.738 km.
1 Tony Stewart, USA (Pontiac Grand Prix), 3h 39m 09s, 109.514 mph/176.246 km/h.
2 Matt Kenseth, USA (Ford Taurus), 3h 39m 10.215s; 3 Bobby Labonte, USA (Pontiac Grand Prix), 400 laps; 4 Dale Jarrett, USA (Ford Taurus), 400; 5 Ricky Rudd, USA (Ford Taurus), 400; 6 Dale Earnhardt, USA (Chevrolet Monte Carlo), 399; 7 Joe Nemechek, USA (Chevrolet Monte Carlo), 398; 8 Ward Burton, USA (Pontiac Grand Prix), 398; 9 Mike Skinner, USA (Chevrolet Monte Carlo), 398; 10 Dale Earnhardt Jr., USA (Chevrolet Monte Carlo), 398.
Fastest qualifying lap: Rusty Wallace, USA (Ford Taurus), 22.870s, 157.411 mph/253.329 km/h.
Drivers' Championship points: 1 Labonte (Bobby), 1946; **2** Burton (Ward), 1864; **3** Earnhardt, 1848; **4** Jarrett, 1790; **5** Martin, 1755; **6** Burton (Jeff), 1733.

KMART 400, Michigan International Speedway, Brooklyn, Michigan, USA, 11 June. Round 14. 194 laps of the 2.000-mile/3.219-km circuit, 388.000 miles/624.425 km.
Scheduled for 200 laps but stopped early due to rain.
1 Tony Stewart, USA (Pontiac Grand Prix), 2h 41m 45s, 143.926 mph/231.626 km/h.
2 Dale Earnhardt, USA (Chevrolet Monte Carlo), 194 laps (under caution); 3 Bobby Labonte, USA (Pontiac Grand Prix), 194; 4 Dale Jarrett, USA (Ford Taurus), 194; 5 Robert Pressley, USA (Ford Taurus), 194; 6 Ward Burton, USA (Pontiac Grand Prix), 194; 7 Rusty Wallace, USA (Ford Taurus), 194; 8 Bill Elliott, USA (Ford Taurus), 194; 9 John Andretti, USA (Pontiac Grand Prix), 194; 10 Sterling Marlin, USA (Chevrolet Monte Carlo), 194.
Fastest qualifying lap: Labonte (Bobby), 37.918s, 189.883 mph/305.588 km/h.
Drivers' Championship points: 1 Labonte (Bobby), 2116; **2** Earnhardt, 2018; **3** Burton (Ward), 2014; **4** Jarrett, 1955; **5** Burton (Jeff), 1868; **6** Wallace (Rusty), 1855.

POCONO 500, Pocono Raceway, Long Pond, Pennsylvania, USA, 18 June. Round 15. 200 laps of the 2.500-mile/4.023-km circuit, 500.000 miles/804.672 km.
1 Jeremy Mayfield, USA (Ford Taurus), 3h 34m 41s, 139.741 mph/224.891 km/h.
2 Dale Jarrett, USA (Ford Taurus), 3h 34m 41.581s; 3 Ricky Rudd, USA (Ford Taurus), 200 laps; 4 Dale Earnhardt, USA (Chevrolet Monte Carlo), 200; 5 Mark Martin, USA (Ford Taurus), 200; 6 Tony Stewart, USA (Pontiac Grand Prix), 200; 7 Jeff Burton, USA (Ford Taurus), 200; 8 Jeff Gordon, USA (Chevrolet Monte Carlo), 200; 9 Mike Skinner, USA (Chevrolet Monte Carlo) 200; 10 Rusty Wallace, USA (Ford Taurus), 200.
Fastest qualifying lap: Wallace (Rusty), 52.440s, 171.625 mph/276.203 km/h.
Drivers' Championship points: 1 Labonte (Bobby), 2240; **2** Earnhardt, 2183; **3** Jarrett, 2125; **4** Burton (Ward), 2096; **5** Burton (Jeff), 2019; **6** Wallace (Rusty), 1999.

SAVE MART/KRAGEN 350, Sears Point Raceway, Sonoma, California, USA, 25 June. Round 16. 112 laps of the 1.949-mile/3.137-km circuit, 218.288 miles/351.300 km.
1 Jeff Gordon, USA (Chevrolet Monte Carlo), 2h 46m 14s, 78.789 mph/126.798 km/h.
2 Sterling Marlin, USA (Chevrolet Monte Carlo), 2h 46m 18.101s; 3 Mark Martin, USA (Ford Taurus), 112 laps; 4 Bobby Labonte, USA (Pontiac Grand Prix), 112; 5 Ricky Rudd, USA (Ford Taurus), 112; 6 Dale Earnhardt Jr., USA (Chevrolet Monte Carlo), 112; 7 Dale Jarrett, USA (Ford Taurus), 112; 8 Jerry Nadeau, USA (Chevrolet Monte Carlo), 112; 9 Robby Gordon, USA (Ford Taurus), 112; 10 Tony Stewart/ John Andretti, USA/USA (Pontiac Grand Prix), 112.
Fastest qualifying lap: Rusty Wallace, USA (Ford Taurus), 1m 10.652s, 99.309 mph/159.823 km/h.
Drivers' Championship points: 1 Labonte (Bobby), 2400; **2** Earnhardt, 2333; **3** Jarrett, 2271; **4** Burton (Ward), 2196; **5** Burton (Jeff), 2134; **6** Rudd, 2130.

PEPSI 400, Daytona International Speedway, Daytona Beach, Florida, USA, 1 July. Round 17. 160 laps of the 2.500-mile/4.023-km circuit, 400.000 miles/643.738 km.
1 Jeff Burton, USA (Ford Taurus), 2h 41m 32s, 148.576 mph/239.110 km/h.
2 Dale Jarrett, USA (Ford Taurus), 2h 41m 32.149s; 3 Rusty Wallace, USA (Ford Taurus), 160 laps; 4 Mark Martin, USA (Ford Taurus), 160; 5 Ricky Rudd, USA (Ford Taurus), 160; 6 Tony Stewart, USA (Pontiac Grand Prix), 160; 7 Ward Burton, USA (Pontiac Grand Prix), 160; 8 Dale Earnhardt, USA (Chevrolet Monte Carlo), 160; 9 Mike Skinner, USA (Chevrolet Monte Carlo); 160; 10 Jeff Gordon, USA (Chevrolet Monte Carlo), 160.
Fastest qualifying lap: Jarrett, 47.988s, 187.547 mph/301.827 km/h.
Drivers' Championship points: 1 Labonte (Bobby), 2527; **2** Earnhardt, 2475; **3** Jarrett, 2451; **4** Burton (Ward), 2347; **5** Burton (Jeff), 2314; **6** Rudd, 2285.

THATLOOK.COM 300, New Hampshire International Speedway, Loudon, New Hampshire, USA, 9 July. Round 18. 273 laps of the 1.058-mile/1.703-km circuit, 288.834 miles/464.833 km.
Race scheduled for 300 laps, but shortened due to rain.
1 Tony Stewart, USA (Pontiac Grand Prix), 2h 48m 01s, 103.145 mph/165.995 km/h.
2 Joe Nemechek, USA (Chevrolet Monte Carlo), 273 laps (under caution); 3 Mark Martin, USA (Ford Taurus), 273; 4 Jerry Nadeau, USA (Chevrolet Monte Carlo), 273; 5 Jeff Gordon, USA (Chevrolet Monte Carlo), 273; 6 Dale Earnhardt, USA (Chevrolet Monte Carlo), 273; 7 Dale Jarrett, USA (Ford Taurus), 273; 8 Jeremy Mayfield, USA (Ford Taurus), 273; 9 Bobby Labonte, USA (Pontiac Grand Prix), 273; 10 Ricky Rudd, USA (Ford Taurus), 273.
Fastest qualifying lap: Rusty Wallace, USA (Ford Taurus), 28.835s, 132.089 mph/212.577 km/h.
Drivers' Championship points: 1 Labonte (Bobby), 2670; **2** Earnhardt, 2625; **3** Jarrett, 2602; **4** Burton (Ward), 2456; **5** Stewart, 2455; **6** Martin, 2453.

PENNSYLVANIA 500, Pocono Raceway, Long Pond, Pennsylvania, USA, 23 July. Round 19. 200 laps of the 2.500-mile/4.023-km circuit, 500.000 miles/804.672 km.
1 Rusty Wallace, USA (Ford Taurus), 3h 49m 36s, 130.662 mph/210.280 km/h.
2 Jeff Burton, USA (Ford Taurus), 3h 49m 36.126s; 3 Jeff Gordon, USA (Chevrolet Monte Carlo), 200 laps; 4 Dale Jarrett, USA (Ford Taurus), 200; 5 Matt Kenseth, USA (Ford Taurus), 200; 6 Bobby Labonte, USA (Pontiac Grand Prix), 200; 7 Mike Skinner, USA (Chevrolet Monte Carlo), 200; 8 Rick Mast, USA (Pontiac Grand Prix), 200; 9 Jimmy Spencer, USA (Ford Taurus), 200; 10 Jeremy Mayfield, USA (Ford Taurus), 200.
Fastest qualifying lap: Tony Stewart, USA (Pontiac Grand Prix), 52.207s, 172.391 mph/277.436 km/h.
Drivers' Championship points: 1 Labonte (Bobby), 2825; **2** Jarrett, 2772; **3** Earnhardt, 2718; **4** Burton (Jeff), 2624; **5** Wallace (Rusty), 2557; **6** Stewart, 2540.

BRICKYARD 400, Indianapolis Motor Speedway, Speedway, Indiana, USA, 5 August. Round 20. 160 laps of the 2.500-mile/4.023-km circuit, 400.000 miles/643.738 km.
1 Bobby Labonte, USA (Pontiac Grand Prix), 2h 33m 56s, 155.912 mph/250.915 km/h.
2 Rusty Wallace, USA (Ford Taurus), 2h 34m 0.229s; 3 Bill Elliott, USA (Ford Taurus), 160 laps; 4 Jerry Nadeau, USA (Chevrolet Monte Carlo), 160; 5 Tony Stewart, USA (Pontiac Grand Prix), 160; 6 Jeff Burton, USA (Ford Taurus), 160; 7 Dale Jarrett, USA (Ford Taurus), 160; 8 Dale Earnhardt, USA (Chevrolet Monte Carlo), 160; 9 Mike Skinner, USA (Chevrolet Monte Carlo); 160; 10 Scott Pruett, USA (Ford Taurus), 160.
Fastest qualifying lap: Ricky Rudd, USA (Ford Taurus), 49.705s, 181.068 mph/291.401 km/h.
Drivers' Championship points: 1 Labonte (Bobby), 3005; **2** Jarrett, 2918; **3** Earnhardt, 2860; **4** Burton (Jeff), 2774; **5** Wallace (Rusty), 2737; **6** Stewart, 2695.

GLOBAL CROSSING ; THE GLEN, Watkins Glen International, New York, USA, 13 August. Round 21. 90 laps of the 2.450-mile/3.943-km circuit, 220.500 miles/354.860 km.
1 Steve Park, USA (Chevrolet Monte Carlo), 2h 24m 51s, 91.336 mph/146.991 km/h.
2 Mark Martin, USA (Ford Taurus), 2h 24m 51.384s; 3 Jeff Burton, USA (Ford Taurus), 90 laps; 4 Robby Gordon, USA (Ford Taurus), 90; 5 Bobby Labonte, USA (Pontiac Grand Prix), 90; 6 Tony Stewart, USA (Pontiac Grand Prix), 90; 7 Dale Jarrett, USA (Ford Taurus), 90; 8 Joe Nemechek, USA (Chevrolet Monte Carlo), 90; 9 Wally Dallenbach, USA (Ford Taurus), 90; 10 Matt Kenseth, USA (Ford Taurus), 90.
Fastest qualifying lap: qualifying rained out.
Drivers' Championship points: 1 Labonte (Bobby), 3165; **2** Jarrett, 3064; **3** Earnhardt, 2948; **4** Burton (Jeff), 2944; **5** Stewart, 2845; **6** Wallace (Rusty), 2798.

PEPSI 400 PRESENTED BY MEIJER, Michigan International Speedway, Brooklyn, Michigan, USA, 20 August. Round 22. 200 laps of the 2.000-mile/3.219-km circuit, 400.000 miles/643.738 km.
1 Rusty Wallace, USA (Ford Taurus), 3h 01m 00s, 132.597 mph/213.394 km/h.
2 Ricky Rudd, USA (Ford Taurus), 3h 01m 02.971s; 3 Bobby Labonte, USA (Pontiac Grand Prix), 200 laps; 4 Dale Jarrett, USA (Ford Taurus), 200; 5 Johnny Benson, USA (Pontiac Grand Prix), 200; 6 Dale Earnhardt, USA (Chevrolet Monte Carlo), 200; 7 Jimmy Spencer, USA (Ford Taurus), 200; 8 Matt Kenseth, USA (Ford Taurus), 200; 9 Ward Burton, USA (Pontiac Grand Prix), 200; 10 Jeff Burton, USA (Ford Taurus), 200.
Fastest qualifying lap: Dale Earnhardt Jr., USA (Chevrolet Monte Carlo), 37.667s, 191.149 mph/307.624 km/h.
Drivers' Championship points: 1 Labonte (Bobby), 3335; **2** Jarrett, 3224; **3** Earnhardt, 3098; **4** Burton (Jeff), 3083; **5** Wallace (Rusty), 2983; **6** Stewart, 2885.

GORACING.COM 500, Bristol Motor Speedway, Tennessee, USA, 26 August. Round 23. 500 laps of the 0.533-mile/0.858-km circuit, 266.500 miles/428.890 km.
1 Rusty Wallace, USA (Ford Taurus), 3h 07m 15s, 85.394 mph/137.428 km/h.
2 Tony Stewart, USA (Pontiac Grand Prix), 3h 07m 15.501s; 3 Mark Martin, USA (Ford Taurus), 500 laps; 4 Dale Earnhardt, USA (Chevrolet Monte Carlo), 500; 5 Steve Park, USA (Chevrolet Monte Carlo), 500; 6 Jeff Burton, USA (Ford Taurus), 500; 7 Elliott Sadler, USA (Ford Taurus), 500; 8 Sterling Marlin, USA (Chevrolet Monte Carlo), 500; 9 Dale Jarrett, USA (Ford Taurus), 500; 10 Ricky Rudd, USA (Ford Taurus), 500.
Fastest qualifying lap: Wallace (Rusty), 15.292s, 125.477 mph/201.936 km/h.
Drivers' Championship points: 1 Labonte (Bobby), 3335; **2** Jarrett, 3224; **3** Earnhardt, 3098; **4** Burton (Jeff), 3083; **5** Wallace (Rusty), 2983; **6** Stewart, 2885.

PEPSI SOUTHERN 500, Darlington Raceway, South Carolina, USA, 3 September. Round 24. 328 laps of the 1.366-mile/2.198-km circuit, 448.048 miles/721.063 km.
1 Bobby Labonte, USA (Pontiac Grand Prix), 4h 08m 20s, 108.253 mph/174.217 km/h.
2 Jeff Burton, USA (Ford Taurus), 328 laps (under caution); 3 Dale Earnhardt, USA (Chevrolet Monte Carlo), 328; 4 Jeff Gordon, USA (Chevrolet Monte Carlo), 328; 5 Dale Jarrett, USA (Ford Taurus), 328; 6 Ward Burton, USA (Pontiac Grand Prix), 328; 7 Kevin Lepage, USA (Ford Taurus), 328; 8 Ricky Rudd, USA (Ford Taurus), 328; 9 Tony Stewart, USA (Pontiac Grand Prix), 328; 10 Steve Park, USA (Chevrolet Monte Carlo), 328.
Fastest qualifying lap: Jeremy Mayfield, USA (Ford Taurus), 29.022s, 169.444 mph/272.693 km/h.
Drivers' Championship points: 1 Labonte (Bobby), 3638; **2** Jarrett, 3527; **3** Earnhardt, 3433; **4** Burton (Jeff), 3413; **5** Wallace (Rusty), 3238; **6** Stewart, 3198.

CHEVROLET MONTE CARLO 400, Richmond International Raceway, Virginia, USA, 9 September. Round 25. 400 laps of the 0.750-mile/1.207-km circuit, 300.000 miles/482.803 km.
1 Jeff Gordon, USA (Chevrolet Monte Carlo), 3h 00m 14s, 99.871 mph/160.726 km/h.
2 Dale Earnhardt, USA (Chevrolet Monte Carlo), 3h 00m 14.744s; 3 Mark Martin, USA (Ford Taurus), 400 laps; 4 Steve Park, USA (Chevrolet Monte Carlo), 400; 5 Jeff Burton, USA (Ford Taurus), 400; 6 Tony Stewart, USA (Pontiac Grand Prix), 400; 7 Johnny Benson, USA (Pontiac Grand Prix), 400; 8 Ward Burton, USA (Pontiac Grand Prix), 400; 9 Ricky Rudd, USA (Ford Taurus), 400; 10 Jerry Nadeau, USA (Chevrolet Monte Carlo), 400.
Fastest qualifying lap: Burton (Jeff), 21.466s, 125.780 mph/202.424 km/h.
Drivers' Championship points: 1 Labonte (Bobby), 3751; **2** Earnhardt, 3603; **3** Jarrett, 3597; **4** Burton (Jeff), 3578; **5** Stewart, 3353; **6** Wallace (Rusty), 3307.

DURA-LUBE 300 SPONSORED BY KMART, New Hampshire International Speedway, Loudon, New Hampshire, USA, 17 September. Round 26. 300 laps of the 1.058-mile/1.703-km circuit, 317.400 miles/510.806 km.
1 Jeff Burton, USA (Ford Taurus), 3h 06m 42s, 102.003 mph/164.158 km/h.
2 Bobby Labonte, USA (Pontiac Grand Prix), 300 laps (under caution); 3 Ricky Rudd, USA (Ford Taurus), 300; 4 Dale Jarrett, USA (Ford Taurus), 300; 5 Rusty Wallace, USA (Ford Taurus), 300; 6 Jeff Gordon, USA (Chevrolet Monte Carlo), 300; 7 John Andretti, USA (Pontiac Grand Prix), 300; 8 Mark Martin, USA (Ford Taurus), 300; 9 Joe Nemechek, USA (Chevrolet Monte Carlo), 300; 10 Ken Schrader, USA (Pontiac Grand Prix), 300.
Fastest qualifying lap: Labonte (Bobby), 29.842s, 127.632 mph/205.404 km/h.
Drivers' Championship points: 1 Labonte (Bobby), 3931; **2** Burton (Jeff), 3763; **4** Jarrett, 3757; **4** Earnhardt, 3730; **5=** Wallace (Rusty), 3462; **5=** Rudd, 3462.

MBNA.COM 400, Dover Downs International Speedway, Dover, Delaware, USA, 24 September. Round 27. 400 laps of the 1.000-mile/1.609-km circuit, 400.000 miles/643.738 km.
1 Tony Stewart, USA (Pontiac Grand Prix), 3h 28m 21s, 115.191 mph/185.382 km/h.
2 Johnny Benson, USA (Pontiac Grand Prix), 3h 28m 27.752s; 3 Ricky Rudd, USA (Ford Taurus), 400 laps; 4 Steve Park, USA (Chevrolet Monte Carlo), 400; 5 Bobby Labonte, USA (Pontiac Grand Prix), 400; 6 Mark Martin, USA (Ford Taurus), 400; 7 Joe Nemechek, USA (Chevrolet Monte Carlo), 400; 8 Rusty Wallace, USA (Ford Taurus), 400; 9 Jeff Gordon, USA (Chevrolet Monte Carlo), 400; 10 Rick Mast, USA (Pontiac Grand Prix), 399.
Fastest qualifying lap: Jeremy Mayfield, USA (Ford Taurus, 22.518s, 159.872 mph/257.289 km/h.
Drivers' Championship points: 1 Labonte (Bobby), 4091; **2** Earnhardt, 3842; **3** Jarrett, 3824; **4** Burton (Jeff), 3823; **5=** Stewart, 3632; **5=** Rudd, 3632.

NAPA AUTOCARE 500, Martinsville Speedway, Virginia, USA, 1 October. Round 28. 500 laps of the 0.526-mile/0.847-km circuit, 263.000 miles/423.257 km.
1 Tony Stewart, USA (Pontiac Grand Prix), 3h 33m 39s, 73.859 mph/118.865 km/h.
2 Dale Earnhardt Jr., USA (Chevrolet Monte Carlo), 3h 33m 39.672s; 3 Jeff Burton, USA (Ford Taurus), 500 laps; 4 Ricky Rudd, USA (Ford Taurus), 500; 5 Jeff Gordon, USA (Chevrolet Monte Carlo), 500; 6 Dale Jarrett, USA (Ford Taurus), 500; 7 Jimmy Spencer, USA (Ford Taurus), 500; 8 Mike Skinner, USA (Chevrolet Monte Carlo), 500; 9 Sterling Marlin, USA (Chevrolet Monte Carlo), 500; 10 Bobby Labonte, USA (Pontiac Grand Prix), 500.
Fastest qualifying lap: Stewart, 19.855s, 95.371 mph/153.485 km/h.
Drivers' Championship points: 1 Labonte (Bobby), 4225; **2** Earnhardt, 4012; **3** Burton (Jeff), 3998; **4** Jarrett, 3974; **5** Stewart, 3812; **6** Rudd, 3797.

UAW-GM QUALITY 500, Lowe's Motor Speedway, Concord, North Carolina, USA, 8 October. Round 29. 334 laps of the 1.500-mile/2.414-km circuit, 501.000 miles/806.281 km.
1 Bobby Labonte, USA (Pontiac Grand Prix), 3h 44m 57s, 133.630 mph/215.056 km/h.
2 Jeremy Mayfield, USA (Ford Taurus), 3h 44m 58.166s; 3 Ricky Rudd, USA (Ford Taurus), 334 laps; 4 Tony Stewart, USA (Pontiac Grand Prix), 334; 5 Mark Martin, USA (Ford Taurus), 334; 6 Jeff Burton, USA (Ford Taurus), 334; 7 Steve Park, USA (Chevrolet Monte Carlo), 334; 8 Johnny Benson, USA (Pontiac Grand Prix), 334; 9 Matt Kenseth, USA (Ford Taurus), 334; 10 Ward Burton, USA (Pontiac Grand Prix), 334.
Fastest qualifying lap: Jeff Gordon, USA (Chevrolet Monte Carlo), 29.101s, 185.561 mph/298.631 km/h.
Drivers' Championship points: 1 Labonte (Bobby), 4405; **2** Burton (Jeff), 4153; **3** Earnhardt, 4147; **4** Jarrett, 4017; **5** Stewart, 3977; **6** Rudd, 3972.

WINSTON 500, Talladega Superspeedway, Alabama, USA, 15 October. Round 30. 188 laps of the 2.660-mile/4.281-km circuit, 500.080 miles/804.801 km.
1 Dale Earnhardt, USA (Chevrolet Monte Carlo), 3h 01m 06s, 165.681 mph/266.637 km/h.
2 Kenny Wallace, USA (Chevrolet Monte Carlo), 3h 01m 06.119s; 3 Joe Nemechek, USA (Chevrolet Monte Carlo), 188 laps; 4 Jeff Gordon, USA (Chevrolet Monte Carlo), 188; 5 Terry Labonte, USA (Chevrolet Monte Carlo), 188; 6 Mike Skinner, USA (Chevrolet Monte Carlo), 188; 7 Mark Martin, USA (Ford Taurus), 188; 8 Rusty Wallace, USA (Ford Taurus), 188; 9 Mike Bliss, USA (Pontiac Grand Prix), 188; 10 Matt Kenseth, USA (Ford Taurus), 188.
Fastest qualifying lap: Nemechek, 50.326s, 190.279 mph/306.225 km/h.
Drivers' Championship points: 1 Labonte (Bobby), 4537; **2** Earnhardt, 4327; **3** Burton (Jeff), 4229; **4** Jarrett, 4135; **5** Rudd, 4102; **6** Stewart, 4064.

POP SECRET MICROWAVE POPCORN 400, North Carolina Motor Speedway, Rockingham, North Carolina, USA, 22 October. Round 31. 393 laps of the 1.017-mile/1.637-km circuit, 399.681 miles/643.224 km.
1 Dale Jarrett, USA (Ford Taurus), 3h 37m 11s, 110.418 mph/177.700 km/h.
2 Jeff Gordon, USA (Chevrolet Monte Carlo), 3h 37m 13.197s; 3 Ricky Rudd, USA (Ford Taurus), 393 laps; 4 Jeff Burton, USA (Ford Taurus), 393; 5 Rusty Wallace, USA (Ford Taurus), 393; 6 Steve Park, USA (Chevrolet Monte Carlo), 393; 7 Tony Stewart, USA (Pontiac Grand Prix), 393; 8 Ward Burton, USA (Pontiac Grand Prix), 393; 9 Bobby Hamilton, USA (Chevrolet Monte Carlo), 393; 10 Joe Nemechek, USA (Chevrolet Monte Carlo), 393.
Fastest qualifying lap: Jeremy Mayfield, USA (Ford Taurus), 23.269s, 157.342 mph/253.218 km/h.
Drivers' Championship points: 1 Labonte (Bobby), 4645; **2** Earnhardt, 4444; **3** Burton (Jeff), 4394; **4** Jarrett, 4315; **5** Rudd, 4272; **6** Stewart, 4210.

CHECKER AUTO PARTS/DURA LUBE 500, Phoenix International Raceway, Arizona, USA, 5 November. Round 32. 312 laps of the 1.000-mile/1.609-km circuit, 312.000 miles/502.115 km.
1 Jeff Burton, USA (Ford Taurus), 2h 58m 13s, 105.041 mph/169.047 km/h.
2 Jeremy Mayfield, USA (Ford Taurus), 312; 3 Steve Park, USA (Chevrolet Monte Carlo), 312; 4 Rusty Wallace, USA (Ford Taurus), 312; 5 Bobby Labonte, USA (Pontiac Grand Prix), 312; 6 Mark Martin, USA (Ford Taurus), 312; 7 Jeff Gordon, USA (Chevrolet Monte Carlo), 312; 8 Dave Blaney, USA (Pontiac Grand Prix), 312; 9 Dale Earnhardt, USA (Chevrolet Monte Carlo), 312; 10 Dale Jarrett, USA (Ford Taurus), 312.
Fastest qualifying lap: Rusty Wallace, USA (Ford Taurus), 26.830s, 134.178 mph/215.939 km/h.

Provisional championship points

Drivers
1 Bobby Labonte, USA, 4805; 2 Dale Earnhardt, USA, 4587; 3 Jeff Burton, USA, 4579; 4 Dale Jarrett, USA, 4449; 5 Tony Stewart, USA, 4336; 6 Ricky Rudd, USA, 4329; 7 Rusty Wallace, USA, 4280; 8 Mark Martin, USA, 4197; 9 Jeff Gordon, USA, 4050; 10 Ward Burton, USA, 3936; 11 Steve Park, USA, 3682; 12 Mike Skinner, USA, 3649; 13 Johnny Benson Jr., USA, 3337; 16 Dale Earnhardt Jr., USA, 3289; 17 Ken Schrader, USA, 3246; 18 Terry Labonte, USA, 3233; 19 Sterling Martin, USA, 3136; 20 Bill Elliott, USA, 3040; 21 John Andretti, USA, 3011; 22 Jimmy Spencer, USA, 2964; 23 Jerry Nadeau, USA, 2961; 24 Jeremy Mayfield, USA, 2936; 25 Robert Pressley, USA, 2811; 26 Kevin Lepage, USA, 2713; 27 Michael Waltrip, USA, 2690; 28 Kenny Wallace, USA, 2684; 29 Elliott Sadler, USA, 2641; 30 Chad Little, USA, 2634.

Raybestos Rookie of the Year: Matt Kenseth.
Bud Pole Award Winner: Rusty Wallace.

Manufacturers
1 Ford, 224; 2 Pontiac, 198; 3 Chevrolet, 186.

Results of the Homestead and Atlanta races will be given in AUTOCOURSE 2001-2002.

Other NASCAR Races

THE BUD SHOOTOUT AT DAYTONA, Daytona International Speedway, Daytona Beach, Florida, USA, 13 February, 25 laps of the 2.500-mile/4.023-km circuit, 62.500 miles/100.584 km.
1 Dale Jarrett, USA (Ford Taurus), 20m 34s, 182.334 mph/293.438 km/h.
2 Jeff Gordon, USA (Chevrolet Monte Carlo), 20m 34.261s; 3 Sterling Martin, USA (Chevrolet Monte Carlo), 25 laps; 4 Tony Stewart, USA (Pontiac Grand Prix), 25; 5 Kevin Lepage, USA (Ford Taurus), 25; 6 Ken Schrader, USA (Pontiac Grand Prix), 25; 7 Rusty Wallace, USA (Ford Taurus), 25; 8 Joe Nemechek, USA (Chevrolet Monte Carlo), 25; 9 Kenny Irwin Jr., USA (Chevrolet Monte Carlo), 25; 10 Ward Burton, USA (Pontiac Grand Prix), 25.
Pole Position: Wallace (Rusty).

THE WINSTON, Lowe's Motor Speedway, Concord, North Carolina, USA, 20 May. 70 laps of the 1.500-mile/2.414-km circuit, 105.000 miles/168.981 km.
Run over three segments (30, 30 and 10 laps). Aggregate results given.
1 Dale Earnhardt Jr., USA (Chevrolet Monte Carlo), 37m 43s, 167.035 mph/268.817 km/h.

2 Dale Jarrett, USA (Ford Taurus), 37m 44.295s; 3 Dale Earnhardt, USA (Chevrolet Monte Carlo), 70 laps; 4 Jerry Nadeau, USA (Chevrolet Monte Carlo), 70; 5 Jeff Burton, USA (Ford Taurus), 70; 6 Terry Labonte, USA (Chevrolet Monte Carlo), 70; 7 Rusty Wallace, USA (Ford Taurus), 70; 8 Bill Elliott, USA (Ford Taurus), 70; 9 Bobby Labonte, USA (Pontiac Grand Prix), 70; 10 Ward Burton, USA (Pontiac Grand Prix), 70.
Fastest qualifying lap: Elliott.

Dayton Indy Lights Championship

All cars are Lola T97/20-Dayton.

LONG BEACH INDY LIGHTS RACE, Long Beach Street Circuit, California, USA, 16 April. Round 1. 38 laps of the 1.968-mile/3.167-km circuit, 74.784 miles/120.353 km.
1 Townsend Bell, USA, 57m 37.375s, 78.004 mph/125.536 km/h.
2 Jason Bright, AUS, 57m 35.128s; 3 Felipe Giaffone, BR, 57m 36.300s; 4 Jeff Simmons, USA, 57m 36.761s; 5 Casey Mears, USA, 57m 37.591s; 6 Jonny Kane, GB, 57m 38.077s; 7 Rodolfo Lavin Jr., MEX, 57m 41.292s; 8 Geoff Boss, USA, 57m 41.977s; 9 Tony Renna, USA, 57m 45.314s; 10 Mario Dominguez, MEX, 58m 39.294s.
Most laps led: Kane, 34.
Fastest qualifying lap: Kane, 1m 34.269s, 75.155 mph/120.950 km/h.

MILWAUKEE INDY LIGHTS RACE, The Milwaukee Mile, Wisconsin State Fair Park, West Allis, Milwaukee, Wisconsin, USA, 5 June. Round 2. 97 laps of the 1.032-mile/1.661-km circuit, 100.104 miles/161.102 km.
Scheduled for 4 June, but delayed until next day because of rain.
1 Scott Dixon, NZ, 53m 21.168s, 112.576 mph/181.173 km/h.
2 Jason Bright, AUS, 53m 28.216s; 3 Mario Dominguez, MEX, 53m 31.684s; 4 Chris Menninga, USA, 53m 32.542s; 5 Casey Mears, USA, 99 laps; 6 Townsend Bell, USA, 98; 7 Jeff Simmons, USA, 98; 8 Rodolfo Lavin Jr., MEX, 98; 9 Rudy Junco Jr., MEX, 98; 10 Luis Diaz, MEX, 98.
Most laps led: Dixon, 66.
Fastest qualifying lap: Dixon, 23.975s, 154.961 mph/249.386 km/h.

Diaz, MEX, 18 laps; 9 Geoff Boss, USA, 18; 10 Rudy Junco Jr., MEX, 17.
Most laps led: Bright, 37.
Fastest qualifying lap: Bell, 1m 05.275s, 108.593 mph/174.763 km/h.

THE DETROIT NEWS 100, Michigan International Speedway, Brooklyn, Michigan, USA, 22 July. Round 5. 50 laps of the 2.000-mile/3.219-km circuit, 100.000 miles/160.934 km.
1 Felipe Giaffone, BR, 40m 51.222s, 146.866 mph/236.357 km/h.
2 Casey Mears, USA, 40m 51.743s; 3 Tony Renna, USA, 40m 52.169s; 4 Townsend Bell, USA, 40m 52.532s; 5 Todd Snyder, USA, 40m 53.067s; 6 Geoff Boss, USA, 40m 53.813s; 7 Mario Dominguez, MEX, 40m 54.478s; 8 Rolando Quintanilla, MEX, 40m 55.579s; 9 Jason Bright, AUS, 40m 57.313s; 10 Andy Boss USA, 40m 57.454s.
Fastest qualifying lap: Giaffone, 39.287s, 183.267 mph/264.939 km/h.

THE MI-JACK 100 OF CHICAGO, Chicago Motor Speedway, Cicero, Illinois, USA, 30 July. Round 6. 97 laps of the 1.029-mile/1.656-km circuit, 99.813 miles/160.633 km.
1 Scott Dixon, NZ, 49m 20.619s, 121.369 mph/195.324 km/h.
2 Townsend Bell, USA, 49m 24.170s; 3 Tony Renna, USA, 49m 26.130s; 4 Felipe Giaffone, BR, 96 laps; 5 Rodolfo Lavin, 96; 6 Luis Diaz, MEX, 96; 7 Jeff Simmons, USA, 96; 8 Rudy Junco Jr., MEX, 96; 9 Chris Menninga, USA, 94; 10 Casey Mears, USA, 94.
Most laps led: Dixon, 71.
Fastest qualifying lap: Menninga, 25.980s, 142.587 mph/229.471 km/h.

MID-OHIO INDY LIGHTS RACE, Mid-Ohio Sports Car Course, Lexington, Ohio. 13 August. Round 7. 34 laps of the 2.258-mile/3.634-km circuit, 75.805 miles/121.996 km.
1 Townsend Bell, USA, 51m 38.571s, 88.072 mph/141.738 km/h.
2 Scott Dixon, NZ, 51m 38.952s; 3 Jason Bright, AUS, 51m 39.423s; 4 Tony Renna, USA, 51m 44.101s; 5 Casey Mears, USA, 51m 44.531s; 6 Jeff Simmons, USA, 51m 45.234s; 7 Derek Higgins, GB, 51m 47.398s; 8 Geoff Boss, USA, 51m 47.785s; 9 Andy Boss USA, 51m 47.990s; 10 Jonny Kane, GB, 51m 49.399s.
Most laps led: Bell, 34.
Fastest qualifying lap: Bright, 1m 14.513s, 109.092 mph/175.567 km/h.

VANCOUVER INDY LIGHTS RACE, Vancouver Street Circuit, Concord Pacific Place, Vancouver, British Colombia, Canada. 3 September. Round 8. 42 laps of the 1.781-mile/2.866-km circuit, 74.802 miles/120.382 km.
1 Jonny Kane, GB, 51m 11.355s, 87.993 mph/141.612 km/h.
2 Felipe Giaffone, BR, 51m 14.257s; 3 Casey Mears, USA, 51m 15.090s; 4 Scott Dixon, NZ, 51m 15.375s; 5 Mario Dominguez, MEX, 51m 17.410s; 6 Chris Menninga, USA, 51m 18.720s; 7 Townsend Bell, USA, 51m 19.579s; 8 Todd Snyder, USA, 51m 20.730s; 9 Jeff Simmons, USA, 51m 21.139s; 10 Andy Boss USA, 51m 23.663s.
Fastest qualifying lap: Kane, 1m 21.840s, 103.196 mph/166.079 km/h.

PORTLAND INDY LIGHTS RACE, Portland International Raceway, Oregon, USA, 25 June. Round 4. 38 laps of the 1.969-mile/3.169-km circuit, 74.822 miles/120.414 km.
1 Jonny Kane, GB, 43m 54.942s, 102.226 mph/164.517 km/h.
2 Townsend Bell, USA, 43m 55.296s; 3 Jeff Simmons, USA, 43m 55.649s; 4 Tony Renna, USA, 43m 59.937s; 5 Chris Menninga, USA, 44m 05.278s; 6 Mario Dominguez, MEX, 44m 09.154s; 8 Luis

Kane, GB, 51m 21.437s; 6 Felipe Giaffone, BR, 51m 23.087s; 7 Luis Diaz, MEX, 51m 23.735s; 8 Jason Bright, AUS, 51m 25.339s; 9 Andy Boss, USA, 51m 31.574s; 10 Mario Dominguez, MEX, 51m 31.939s.
Most laps led: Dixon, 32.
Fastest qualifying lap: Mears, 1m 15.891s, 106.163 mph/170.852 km/h.

GATEWAY INDY LIGHTS RACE, Gateway International Raceway, Madison, Illinois, 17 September. Round 10. 79 laps of the 1.270-mile/2.044-km circuit, 100.330 miles/161.465 km.
1 Townsend Bell, USA, 47m 57.839s, 125.507 mph/201.983 km/h.
2 Casey Mears, USA, 48m 04.596s; 3 Jason Bright, AUS, 48m 09.278s; 4 Tony Renna, USA, 48m 10.381s; 5 Chris Menninga, USA, 48m 14.870s; 6 Mario Dominguez, MEX, 48m 16.410s; 7 Felipe Giaffone, BR, 48m 25.692s; 8 Rodolfo Lavin Jr., MEX, 78 laps; 9 Jonny Kane, GB, 78; 10 Rolando Quintanilla, MEX, 78.
Most laps led: Bell, 79.
Fastest qualifying lap: Bell, 28.625s, 159.721 mph/257.045 km/h.

HOUSTON INDY LIGHTS RACE, Houston Street Circuit, Texas, USA, 1 October. Round 11. 45 laps of the 1.527-mile/2.457-km circuit, 68.715 miles/110.586 km.
1 Casey Mears, USA, 1h 00m 01.256s, 68.691 mph/110.548 km/h.
2 Townsend Bell, USA, 1h 00m 02.497s; 3 Felipe Giaffone, BR, 1h 00m 03.038s; 4 Geoff Boss, USA, 1h 00m 03.622s; 5 Chris Menninga, USA, 1h 00m 11.864s; 6 Rodolfo Lavin Jr., MEX, 1h 00m 13.026s; 7 Luis Diaz, MEX, 1h 00m 13.999s; 8 Rolando Quintanilla, MEX, 41 laps; 9 Andy Boss, USA, 40; 10 Tony Renna, USA, 40.
Most laps led: Mears, 45.
Fastest qualifying lap: Mears, 1m 04.722s, 84.936 mph/136.691 km/h.

INDY LIGHTS 100 PRESENTED BY THE LOS ANGELES TIMES, California Speedway, Fontana, California, USA, 29 October. Round 12. 50 laps of the 2.029-mile/3.265-km circuit, 101.450 miles/163.268 km.
1 Scott Dixon, NZ, 33m 08.441s, 183.672 mph/295.591 km/h.
2 Townsend Bell, USA, 33m 08.457s; 3 Tony Renna, USA, 33m 08.573s; 4 Casey Mears, USA, 33m 09.126s; 6 Jeff Simmons, USA, 33m 09.477s; 8 Mario Dominguez, MEX, 33m 09.108s; 5 Rodolfo Lavin Jr., MEX, 48; 12 Geoff Boss, USA, 33m 09.590s; 10 Jonny Kane, GB, 33m 09.749s.
Most laps led: Dixon, 48.
Fastest qualifying lap: Giaffone, 39.478s, 185.025 mph/297.768 km/h.

YAHOO! SPORTS MONTEREY CHALLENGE, Laguna Seca Raceway, Monterey, California, USA, 10 September. Round 9. 34 laps of the 2.238-mile/3.602-km circuit, 76.092 miles/122.458 km.
1 Scott Dixon, NZ, 51m 11.041s, 89.198 mph/143.551 km/h.
2 Casey Mears, USA, 51m 13.926s; 3 Jeff Simmons, USA, 51m 18.407s; 4 Tony Renna, USA, 51m 21.039s; 5 Jonny

Final championship points
Drivers
1 Scott Dixon, NZ, 155; 2 Townsend Bell, USA, 146; 3 Casey Mears, USA, 141; 4 Felipe Giaffone, BR, 118; 5 Tony Renna, USA, 105; 6 Jason Bright, AUS, 91; 7 Jeff Simmons, USA, 88; 8 Mario Dominguez, MEX, 67; 9 Chris Menninga, USA, 61; 10 Jonny Kane, GB, 52; 11 Rodolfo Lavin Jr., MEX, 48; 12 Geoff Boss, USA, 43; 13 Luis Diaz, MEX, 31; 14 Rudy Junco Jr., MEX, 26; 15 Andy Boss USA, 18; 16 Rolando Quintanilla, MEX, 16; 17 Todd Snyder, USA, 15; 18 Derek Higgins, GB, 12; 19 Cory Witherill, USA, 2.

Nations' Cup
1 United States, 200; 2 New Zealand, 155; 3 Brazil, 118; 4 Mexico, 98; 5 Australia, 91; 6 Ireland, 61.

Rookie of the year
1 Townsend Bell; 2 Jason Bright; 3 Jeff Simmons.